THE PAPERS OF ALEXANDER HAMILTON

Alexander Hamilton, *circa* 1799. Oil painting by P. T. Weaver
The painting represents Hamilton in the uniform of
inspector general of the United States Army

THE PAPERS OF
Alexander Hamilton

VOLUME XXII
JULY 1798–MARCH 1799

HAROLD C. SYRETT, EDITOR

Associate Editors

BARBARA A. CHERNOW

JOSEPH G. HENRICH   PATRICIA SYRETT

COLUMBIA UNIVERSITY PRESS

NEW YORK AND LONDON, 1975

FROM THE PUBLISHER

The preparation of this edition of the papers of Alexander Hamilton has been made possible by the support received for the work of the editorial and research staff from the generous grants of the Rockefeller Foundation, Time Inc., and the Ford Foundation, and by the far-sighted cooperation of the National Historical Publications and Records Commission, which administered the Ford Foundation grant during its ten years of existence, has continued its support of research and editing, and, in addition, has provided funds toward the cost of publication of this volume.

To these organizations, the publisher expresses gratitude on behalf of all who are concerned about making available the record of the founding of the United States.

ACKNOWLEDGMENTS

SINCE THE PUBLICATION in 1974 of Volumes XX and XXI of *The Papers of Alexander Hamilton* the editors have incurred new obligations which they wish to take this opportunity to acknowledge. Of the many individuals who generously shared their specialized information or provided assistance, the editors are especially indebted to

Mr. Henry F. Bedford, Librarian, The Phillips Exeter Academy, Exeter, New Hampshire

Miss Ruth M. Blair, Manuscript Cataloguer, Connecticut Historical Society, Hartford

Miss Doris E. Cook, Manuscript Cataloguer, Connecticut Historical Society, Hartford

Mr. Thomas Dunnings, New-York Historical Society, New York City

Miss Joyce L. Eakin, Assistant Director, Libraries, United States Army Military History Research Collection, Carlisle Barracks, Pennsylvania

Dr. Louis Jones, Cooperstown, New York

Dr. Mary-Jo Kline, Associate Editor, The Adams Papers, Boston, Massachusetts

Mr. John Knowlton, Washington, D.C.

Professor Richard Kohn, Rutgers University, The State University of New Jersey

Mr. James Ward Willson Loose, President and Editor, Lancaster County Historical Society, Lancaster, Pennsylvania

Miss Anne McCabe, Columbia University Libraries

Dr. Edward C. Papenfuse, Assistant Archivist, Hall of Records, Annapolis, Maryland

Miss Martha L. Simonetti, Associate Archivist, Division of Archives and Manuscripts, Pennsylvania Historical and Museum Commission, Harrisburg, Pennsylvania

Professor David Syrett, Queens College, City University of New York

Miss Betty Thomas, Associate Editor, The Law Practice of Alexander Hamilton

PREFACE

THIS EDITION of Alexander Hamilton's papers contains letters and other documents written by Hamilton, letters to Hamilton, and some documents (commissions, certificates, etc.) that directly concern Hamilton but were written neither by him nor to him. All letters and other documents have been printed in chronological order. Two volumes of Hamilton's legal papers, entitled *The Law Practice of Alexander Hamilton*, have been published by the Columbia University Press under the editorial direction of the late Julius Goebel, Jr. The third and last volume of this distinguished work is being completed by Professor Joseph H. Smith, George Welwood Murray Professor of Legal History of the School of Law, Columbia University.

Many letters and documents have been calendared. Such calendared items include routine letters and documents by Hamilton, routine letters to Hamilton, some of the letters or documents written by Hamilton for someone else, letters or documents which have not been found but which are known to have existed, letters or documents which have been erroneously attributed to Hamilton, and letters to or by Hamilton that deal exclusively with his legal practice.

Hamilton's significant legal opinions appear in *The Law Practice of Alexander Hamilton*, and they have accordingly been omitted from these volumes.

Because a large part of Hamilton's correspondence from July, 1798, to July, 1800, concerns routine—and even petty and trivial—Army matters, such letters have been neither printed nor calendared. Instead they are listed chronologically in an appendix with a key indicating the nature of the contents of each letter. Army returns, warrants, and bonds are neither printed nor listed in the appendix.

The notes in these volumes are designed to provide information concerning the nature and location of each document, to identify

Hamilton's correspondents and the individuals mentioned in the text, to explain events or ideas referred to in the text, and to point out textual variations or mistakes. Occasional departures from these standards can be attributed to a variety of reasons. In many cases the desired information has been supplied in an earlier note and can be found through the use of the index. Notes have not been added when in the opinion of the editors the material in the text was either self-explanatory or common knowledge. The editors, moreover, have not thought it desirable or necessary to provide full annotation for Hamilton's legal correspondence. Finally, the editors on some occasions have been unable to find the desired information, and on other occasions the editors have been remiss.

GUIDE TO EDITORIAL APPARATUS

I. SYMBOLS USED TO DESCRIBE MANUSCRIPTS

AD	Autograph Document
ADS	Autograph Document Signed
ADf	Autograph Draft
ADfS	Autograph Draft Signed
AL	Autograph Letter
ALS	Autograph Letter Signed
D	Document
DS	Document Signed
Df	Draft
DfS	Draft Signed
LS	Letter Signed
LC	Letter Book Copy
[S]	[S] is used with other symbols (AD[S], ADf[S], AL[S], D[S], Df[S], L[S]) to indicate that the signature on the document has been cropped or clipped.

II. SHORT TITLES AND ABBREVIATIONS

Adams, *Works of John Adams*
Charles Francis Adams *The Works of John Adams* (Boston, 1850–1856).

Annals of Congress
The Debates and Proceedings in the Congress of the United States; with an Appendix, Containing Important State Papers

and Public Documents, and All the Laws of a Public Nature (Washington, 1834–1849).

Archivo, Miranda, XV — *Archivo del General Miranda: Negociaciones 1770–1810* (Caracas, 1938), XV.

ASP — *American State Papers, Documents, Legislative and Executive, of the Congress of the United States* (Washington, 1832–1861).

Carter, *Territorial Papers* — Clarence E. Carter, ed., *The Territorial Papers of the United States* (Washington, 1934–1952).

Duvergier, *Lois* — J. B. Duvergier, *Collection Complète des Lois, Décrets, Ordonnances, Réglemens, et Avis du Conseil-d'Etat, Publiée sur les Editions Officielles du Louvre; de L'Imprimerie Nationale, Par Baudouin; et Du Bulletin des Lois* (Paris, 1824–1825).

Executive Journal, I — *Journal of the Executive Proceedings of the Senate* (Washington, 1828), I.

Godfrey, "Provisional Army" — Charles E. Godfrey, "Organization of the Provisional Army of the United States in the Anticipated War with France, 1798–1800," *The Pennsylvania Magazine of History and Biography,* XXXVIII (1914: Reprinted, New York, 1965). Godfrey confuses the Provisional Army with the Additional Army.

Goebel, *Law Practice* — Julius Goebel, Jr., ed., *The Law Practice of Alexander Hamilton: Documents and Commentary* (New York and London, 1964–).

Hamilton, *Intimate Life* — Allan McLane Hamilton, *The Intimate Life of Alexander Hamilton* (New York, 1910).

HCLW — Henry Cabot Lodge, ed., *The Works of Alexander Hamilton* (New York, 1904).

Heitman, *United States Army* — Francis B. Heitman, *Historical Register and Dictionary of the United States Army, From Its Organization, September 29, 1789, to March 2, 1903* (Washington, 1903).

JCC — *Journals of the Continental Congress, 1774–1789* (Washington, 1904–1937).

JCHW — John C. Hamilton, ed., *The Works of Alexander Hamilton* (New York, 1851–1856).

Journal of the Assembly of the State of New-York. 22nd Sess., 1st Meeting — *Journal of the Assembly of the State of New-York. At Their Twenty-Second Session, Began and Held at the City of Albany, the Ninth Day of August, 1798* (Albany, n.d.).

Journal of the Assembly of the State of New-York. 22nd Sess., 2nd Meeting — *Journal of the Assembly of the State of New-York; At Their Twenty-Second Session, Second Meeting, Began and Held at the City of Albany, the Second Day of January, 1799* (Albany, n.d.).

Journal of the House, I, II, III, IV — *Journal of the House of Representatives of the United States* (Washington, 1826), I, II, III, IV.

Journal of the House of Delegates of Virginia, 1798 — *Journal of the House of Delegates of the Commonwealth of Virginia: Begun and Held at the Capitol, in the City of Richmond, on Monday, the Third Day of December, One Thousand Seven Hundred and Ninety-Eight* (Richmond, 1798).

Journal of the Senate of the State of New-York. 22nd Sess., 2nd Meeting — *Journal of the Senate of the State of New-York; At Their Twenty-Second Session, Second Meeting, Began and Held at the City of Albany, the Second Day of January, 1799* (Albany, n.d.).

King, *The Life and Correspondence of Rufus King* — Charles R. King, ed., *The Life and Correspondence of Rufus King* (New York, 1894–1900).

Minutes of the Common Council

Minutes of the Common Council of the City of New York, 1784–1831 (New York, 1917).

Monroe, *A View of the Conduct of the Executive*

James Monroe, *A View of the Conduct of the Executive, in the Foreign Affairs of the United States, Connected with the Mission to the French Republic, During the Years 1794, 5 & 6* (Philadelphia: Printed by and for Benjamin Franklin Bache, 1797).

Naval Documents, Quasi-War, February, 1797–October, 1798

Naval Documents Related to the Quasi-War Between the United States and France: Naval Operations from February 1797 to October 1798 (Washington, 1935).

Naval Documents, Quasi-War November, 1798–March, 1799

Naval Documents Related to the Quasi-War Between the United States and France: Naval Operations from November 1798 to March 1799 (Washington, 1935).

PRO: F.O. (Great Britain)

Public Record Office of Great Britain.

Réimpression, Moniteur

Réimpression de L'Ancien Moniteur Seule Histoire Authentique et Intaltérée de la Révolution Française Depuis la Réunion des Etats Géneraux Jusqu'au Consulat (Mai 1798–Novembre 1799) Avec des Notes Explicatives (Paris, 1847).

Révolution Française, Moniteur

Révolution Française, ou Analyse Complette et Impartiale du Moniteur: Suivie d'une Table Alphabétique des Personnes et des Choses (Paris, 1801).

1 *Stat.;* 2*Stat*

The Public Statutes at Large of the United States of America, I (Boston, 1845); II (Boston, 1850).

Steiner, *James McHenry*

Bernard C. Steiner, *The Life and Correspondence of James McHenry* (Cleveland, 1907).

III. INDECIPHERABLE WORDS

Words or parts of words which could not be deciphered because of the illegibility of the writing or the mutilation of the manuscript have been indicated as follows:

1. ⟨– – – – –⟩ indicates illegible words with the number of dashes indicating the estimated number of illegible words.
2. Words or letters in broken brackets indicate a guess as to what the words or letters in question may be. If the source of the words or letters within the broken brackets is known, it has been given a note.

IV. CROSSED-OUT MATERIAL IN MANUSCRIPTS

Words or sentences crossed out by a writer in a manuscript have been handled in one of the three following ways:

1. They have been ignored, and the document or letter has been printed in its final version.
2. Crossed-out words and insertions for the crossed-out words have been described in the notes.
3. When the significance of a manuscript seems to warrant it, the crossed-out words have been retained, and the document has been printed as it was written.

V. TEXTUAL CHANGES AND INSERTIONS

The following changes or insertions have been made in the letters and documents printed in these volumes:

1. Words or letters written above the line of print (for example, 9th) have been made even with the line of print (9th).
2. Punctuation and capitalization have been changed in those instances where it seemed necessary to make clear the sense of the writer. A special effort has been made to eliminate the dash, which was such a popular eighteenth-century device.

3. When the place or date, or both, of a letter or document does not appear at the head of that letter or document, it has been inserted in the text in brackets. If either the place or date at the head of a letter or document is incomplete, the necessary additional material has been added in the text in brackets. For all but the best known localities or places, the name of the colony, state, or territory has been added in brackets at the head of a document or letter.

4. In calendared documents, place and date have been uniformly written out in full without the use of brackets. Thus "N. York, Octr. 8, '99" becomes "New York, October 8, 1799." If, however, substantive material is added to the place or date in a calendared document, such material is placed in brackets. Thus "Oxford, Jan. 6" becomes "Oxford [Massachusetts] January 6 [1788]."

5. When a writer made an unintentional slip comparable to a typographical error, one of the four following devices has been used:

a. It has been allowed to stand as written.

b. It has been corrected by inserting either one or more letters in brackets.

c. It has been corrected without indicating the change.

d. It has been explained in a note.

6. Because the symbol for the thorn was archaic even in Hamilton's day, the editors have used the letter "y" to represent it. In doing this they are conforming to eighteenth-century manuscript usage.

1798

From Rufus King [1]

London July 14. 1798

Private

Dear sir

I send you inclosed an interesting little piece addressed to Gallatin by a former Citizen of Geneva—if translated and published it may do good.[2] We have no news from the mediterranean since the

ALS, Hamilton Papers, Library of Congress.

1. King was United States Minister Plenipotentiary to Great Britain.

2. When this letter was written, Albert Gallatin was a member of the House of Representatives from Pennsylvania.

On September 19, 1798, the following item appeared in the [New York] *Commercial Advertiser:* "We have lately received from England a Pamphlet, entitled, 'The conduct of the French Government towards the Republic of Geneva,' addressed to Mr. Gallatin, member of the House of Representatives of the United States, by D. Chauvet. The pamphlet contains a brief history of the conduct of France towards Geneva, from the first invasion of that little republic by Gen. [François de] Montesquiou[-Fezensac], about the year 1792, to its final subjugation and annexation to France, in the present year. It is too lengthy for a newspaper, and besides the general facts it contains, are fresh in the memories of most intelligent Americans.

"But the introductory address to Mr. Gallatin, is of too much importance not to merit insertion. It unfolds to that steady friend of France, the errors which he indulges in regard to the views of France, and assures him, that France is pushing towards universal dominion."

David Chauvet's letter to Gallatin, dated June 22, 1798, reads in part: "To whom could I, with more propriety, present the picture of the crimes of the French Directory towards the Republic of Geneva, than to one of my compatriots, to a Citizen of Geneva, who is at present, placed in a distinguished situation among the Representatives of the United States of America. Your success in your adopted country, doubtless, has not extinguished your affection for that which gave you birth, and in which your talents, received, in a liberal education, that development, to which you owe your elevation. The name of Geneva, awakens in you sentiments of gratitude and love, and the shameful persecutions which it hath suffered, cannot fail to excite your indignation. . . .

"I am so ignorant of the true causes of the differences between the parties in America, that I shall be cautious of pronouncing a hasty judgment on them. But if you have supposed, that you see in the French the true friends of liberty; if you have taken the declarations of the Directory, for the principles of their conduct; if you imagine that they are the protectors of weakness, and the defenders of the interests of mankind; if you judge them by your own

Capture of Malta,[3] nor can we do more than conjecture the future
destination of Buonaparte. Turin with its arsenals is possessed by a
french army, so that Sardignia is at the feet of the Directory. The
Emperor continues to recruit his armies and is now laying up Magazines in the Tyrol. His expences are said to be equal to those of an
open war, and his Resources unequal to his present Expenditures.
Prussia manifests no inclination to enter into a new coalition agt.
france, and there are who suspect a more intimate connection between these Powers—in short the fate of Europe is as uncertain and
difficult to understand as at any period of the war.

It is at least ten days since the spirited measures pursued in America, must have been known at Paris; we are therefore anxious to
learn the Effect they have produced.[4] They will be intirely disappointed and my conjecture is that contrary to their wishes, their

---

wishes, and if you measure your hopes by their promises, read the following
pamphlet—See how they have dissolved a small State, whose independence
they were bound by most solemn treaties to respect. Following them into the
complication of their infamous intrigues. This is not a great and dazzling point
of political interest—It is no Cromwell who usurps a throne—it is a forger,
who compels a feeble man, with a knife at his throat, to sign away to him all
his estate, and afterwards boast of the legitimacy of his title. I know not Sir,
what direct consequence you will draw in relation to the politics between
France and America; but you will see at least, that you must, in regard to
France, count for nothing, justice, generosity, and the most sacred engagements, and that in the employment of means, she is most audacious, the most
perfectly indifferent to morality, the most oblique and deceptious of all that
ever disgraced the most scandalous and iniquitous reign of royalty,—Yes out
of the political range of the French Directory, Machiavel himself appears
a prodigy of virtue, and the cabinet of Philip 2d the sanctuary of good
faith. . . ." ([New York] *Commercial Advertiser*, September 19, 1798.)

On October 27, 1798, Secretary of State Timothy Pickering wrote to John
Adams: "The original French of Chauvets letter to Galatin, exhibiting the
perfidy and violence of France in subverting the Swiss Republic, I rec'd from
Mr. King. It appeared to me so important a detail of facts at the present
moment, I put it into the hand of a son [Robert Hunt] of Mr. Abraham Hunt,
whom I found at leisure, to translate. It has been faithfully done. I encouraged
the printer here to give it to the public in a pamphlet. To-day I recd. some
copies, & have the honor to inclose a couple" (ALS, Adams Family Papers, deposited in the Massachusetts Historical Society, Boston). The pamphlet is entitled *The Conduct of the Government of France Towards the Republic of
Geneva. Translated from the French. By a Citizen of Trenton* (Trenton:
Printed by G. Craft, October, 1798).

3. See King to H, June 6, 1798, note 1.

4. In a postscript dated July 15, 1798, to a letter dated July 12, 1798, Charles
Maurice de Talleyrand-Périgord wrote to Elbridge Gerry: "A circumstance,
sir, of infinite importance, has delayed the despatching of this letter. I do not
know how it happens that at every step towards a reconciliation a cause of
irritation intervenes, and that the United States always give rise to it. Some
days since different advices were successively received by the Executive Direc-

Pride will drive them to declare war agt. us. On the 13 of June Gl. Pinckney was still at Lyons, his Daughter was much better and he flattered himself with the Expectation of being able to reach Bourdeaux and to embark by the middle of this month.[5] On the 26 of June Mr. Gerry was at Paris, waiting say Letters from americans who are about him for the Ultimatum of the Directory.[6] Letters are sent in every Direction by the americans at Paris, which say that the Directory hold a conciliatory language and that Mr. Gerry is in Hopes to procure terms which will be honorable & satisfactory to his Country. I thought it impossible that any future step of Mr. G. could exceed in ——— & ——— what had passed when he decided to separate from his Colleagues & remain at Paris—but I was mistaken—his answer to Talleyrand's demands of the names of X. Y. and Z. place him in a more degraded light than I ever believed it possible that he or any other american could be exhibited.[7]

---

tory. It seems that, hurried beyond every limit, your Government no longer preserves appearances. A law of the 7th of last month authorizes it to cause every French vessel of war to be attacked, which may have stopped or *intended* to stop American vessels. A resolution of the House of Representatives suspends, from the 13th of this month, all commercial relations with the French republic and its possessions. Several plans of a law have been proposed for banishing the French and sequestrating French property" (*ASP, Foreign Relations*, II, 220).

Talleyrand's reference to the "law of the 7th of last month" is mistaken concerning the date. He was referring to "An Act more effectually to protect the Commerce and Coasts of the United States" (1 *Stat.* 561 [May 28, 1798]).

The reference to the "resolution of the House of Representatives" concerns House action on what eventually became "An Act to suspend the commercial intercourse between the United States and France, and the dependencies thereof" (1 *Stat.* 565–66 [June 13, 1798]). The date on which this bill was to go into effect was July 1, 1798, rather than July 13, as stated by Talleyrand. For the House action on this bill, see *Annals of Congress*, VIII, 1854–55, 1859–66. For an explanation of the contents of Talleyrand's final sentence, see H to Pickering, June 7, 1798, note 6.

5. Following the XYZ affair, Charles Cotesworth Pinckney and John Marshall demanded and received their passports. Marshall embarked for the United States, but Pinckney, because of the illness of his daughter, had to remain in France. On July 18, 1798, he left Paris for the south of France (King to Pickering, May 11, 1798 [copy, RG 59, Despatches from United States Ministers to Great Britain, 1791–1906, Vol. 7, January 9–December 22, 1798, National Archives]). See also Gerry to Talleyrand, April 4, 20, 1798 (*ASP, Foreign Relations*, II, 209).

6. For Gerry's correspondence with Talleyrand after the departure of Marshall and Pinckney from Paris, see *ASP, Foreign Relations*, II, 208–22. See also Gerry to Pickering, October 1, 1798 (*ASP, Foreign Relations*, II, 204–08).

7. On May 30, 1798, Talleyrand wrote to Gerry and requested the names of the agents designated as "W.X.Y.Z." in the printed editions of the dispatches of

I send you Bellamy's address [8]—it, as well as all that has been published serves to confirm the public detestation agt. the Directory. The american Dispatches [9] have been circulated throughout Europe, and have every where done much good, and increased the Reputation of our Government.

Yrs &c   R K

---

the United States envoys to France. On the following day Gerry refused to name the agents. Talleyrand, however, persisted in his request, and on June 3, Gerry agreed to supply the names (*ASP, Foreign Relations,* II, 210–11). For the identities of "W.X.Y.Z.," see "The Stand No. V," April 16, 1798, note 28.

8. See "The Stand No. V," April 16, 1798, note 28.

9. For the publication of the XYZ dispatches, see Pickering to H, April 9, 1798, note 1.

From George Washington

[Mount Vernon, July 14, 1798]

Introductory Note

This letter contains the first mention in Hamilton's extant correspondence of the question of who was to serve directly under Washington in his capacity as "Commander in Chief of all the armies raised, or to be raised, in the United States." [1] When Washington wrote this letter, he assumed that Congress would pass "An Act to augment the Army of the United States, and for other purposes," which authorized the President "to raise, in addition to the present military establishment, twelve regiments of infantry, and six troops of light dragoons" and provided "that there shall be two major-generals, with aids-de-camp each; one inspector-general, with the rank, pay and emoluments of a major-general, and two aids-de-camp." [2] The ranking of the three major generals was obviously a question of some importance, for the one ranked first would be second in command to Washington. In the letter printed below Washington ranked Hamilton first, named him inspector general, and placed Charles

ALS, Hamilton Papers, Library of Congress; ALS, letterpress copy, George Washington Papers, Library of Congress; copy, George Washington Papers, Library of Congress; copy, in James McHenry's handwriting, James McHenry Papers, Library of Congress.

1. See H to Washington, July 8, 1798, note 1.

2. 1 *Stat.* 604–05 (July 16, 1798). This act should not be confused with either "An Act authorizing the President of the United States to raise a Provisional Army" (1 *Stat.* 558–61 [May 28, 1798]) or "An Act supplementary to, and to amend the act, intituled 'An act authorizing the President of the United States to raise a provisional army'" (1 *Stat.* 569–70 [June, 22, 1798]).

H's activities as inspector general concerned the first four regiments of in-

Cotesworth Pinckney [3] second and Henry Knox [4] third. In addition, Secretary of War James McHenry, who at the request of President Adams [5] had visited Washington at Mount Vernon, returned to Philadelphia on July 17, 1798, with Washington's list ranking Hamilton ahead of Pinckney and Knox.[6] Washington's preference for Hamilton, however, placed him in direct conflict with Adams, who favored Knox and Pinckney. The result was an unseemly squabble which lasted three months and which in one way or another damaged the reputations of most of those who were directly involved.

What can charitably be termed a messy situation was made both more complicated and more tedious by the distances separating most of the principals. Following the adjournment of Congress on July 19, 1798, Adams left Philadelphia for Quincy, Massachusetts, where he stayed throughout the dispute, while the members of the cabinet remained at the seat of the Government. Washington was in Mount Vernon; Hamilton was in New York; Knox divided his time between Boston and his lands in Maine; and Pinckney had not yet returned from his mission to France. On one occasion, a letter mailed by Washington on September 25 did not reach Adams until October 8.[7] But this was not all, for Adams's absence permitted his far from loyal cabinet members to plot and connive in a fashion and to a degree that presumably would not have been possible if he had not left Philadelphia.

Throughout the controversy McHenry and Secretary of State Timothy Pickering left no doubt that their allegiance was to Hamilton rather than to the President they were putatively serving. On more than one occasion they schemed, dissimulated, procrastinated, and withheld information in their efforts to achieve their objective. Hamilton, who supported them at every step in their campaign, was undoubtedly motivated by his ambition and quest for military fame, but it has also been sug-

---

fantry (often referred to as "the old regiments"), the Corps of Artillerists and Engineers, and the twelve additional regiments provided for in the statute of July 16, 1798, and not the Provisional Army provided for in the earlier statutes. The twelve additional regiments and the cavalry regiment are incorrectly listed as constituting the Provisional Army in Godfrey, "Provisional Army," 129–82.

3. During the American Revolution, Pinckney served as an aide to Washington and a commander of troops in the campaigns against the British in the South. At the end of the war he was brevetted a brigadier general. When this letter was written, he had not yet returned to the United States from his unsuccessful mission with Elbridge Gerry and John Marshall to France.

4. Knox had been a major general during the American Revolution, and from 1785 through 1794 he had been Secretary of War.

5. Adams to McHenry, July 6, 1798 (LC, Adams Family Papers, deposited in the Massachusetts Historical Society, Boston; copy, George Washington Papers, Library of Congress). See also McHenry to Washington, July 6, 1798 (ALS, George Washington Papers, Library of Congress).

6. See Timothy Pickering to H, July 18, 1798. For Washington's list, see note 27.

7. See Adams to Washington, October 9, 1798 (ALS, George Washington Papers, Library of Congress).

gested that he and his allies in the cabinet were hoping to have him appointed the *de facto* head of an army that could be used to support Francisco de Miranda's plans for the liberation of Spain's American colonies.[8] On August 22, 1798, when the question of the relative rank of Hamilton, Pinckney, and Knox had not been settled, Hamilton wrote to Miranda that he approved of Miranda's project, but he "could personaley have no participation in it unless patronised by the Government of this Country." Hamilton, however, then added: "We are raising an army of about Twelve Thousand men. Genl. Washington has resumed his station at the head of our armies. I am appointed second in command." On the other hand, a few months earlier Hamilton had written that he considered Miranda "an intriguing adventurer." [9]

On July 18, 1798, Adams sent his nominations for general officers for the Army to the Senate. Hamilton was nominated inspector general, and his name was first on the list of major generals, followed by the names of Pinckney and Knox.[10] On the following day the Senate approved the three appointments in the order in which the President had submitted them.[11] On July 25 McHenry wrote to Hamilton: "I am directed to inform you that the President of the United States, by, and with the advice and consent of the Senate, has appointed you Inspector General, with the rank of Major General; and to transmit you your commission made out accordingly." On July 28 Hamilton wrote to McHenry accepting the appointment.

The difficulty with the list approved by the Senate arose from the fact that at the conclusion of the American Revolution Pinckney outranked Hamilton and Knox outranked both Pinckney and Hamilton. When Washington wrote the letter printed below, he was more concerned with the implications of placing Pinckney second than with having Knox third. As early as July 6, 1798, Pickering wrote to Washington: "There is one man who will gladly be *Your Second.* . . . You too well know Colo. Hamilton's distinguished ability, energy and fidelity, to apply my remark to any other man." [12] On July 11 Washington replied that he was well aware of Hamilton's ability, but that there were also reasons for placing Pinckney first.[13] Pickering immediately relayed this information to Hamilton,[14] who answered: "I had contemplated the possibility that *Knox* might come into service & was content to be second to him, if *thought indispensable.* Pinckney, if placed over me puts me a grade lower. I don't believe it to be necessary." [15] Hamilton also wrote to

8. Adams, *Works of John Adams,* VIII, 590, note 15. For Miranda's plans, see Miranda to H, April 1, 1797; February 7, April 6–June 7, August 17, 1798.
9. Miranda to H, February 7, 1798, note 9.
10. *Executive Journal,* I, 292.
11. *Executive Journal,* I, 293.
12. ALS, George Washington Papers, Library of Congress; ADfS, Essex Institute, Salem, Massachusetts; copy, Hamilton Papers, Library of Congress.
13. ALS, Massachusetts Historical Society, Boston; ALS, letterpress copy, George Washington Papers, Library of Congress.
14. Pickering to H, July 16, 1798.
15. H to Pickering, July 17, 1798.

Washington: ". . . I must conclude that General Pinckney, on a fair estimate of circumstances ought to be well satisfied with the [present] arrangement." [16] Pinckney, who had not yet returned from France, was unable to speak for himself. But it made little difference, for it was Knox, not Pinckney, who insisted on outranking Hamilton.

Although Washington originally was more concerned about putting Pinckney second than placing Knox third, he nevertheless took the trouble to write to Knox on July 16 concerning his decision.[17] On July 29 Knox replied in a long and bitter letter in which he implied that he would refuse the appointment "unless the relative rank of the late War, should govern according to the established and invariable usuage of the former War." [18] Washington, in turn, sent copies of both letters to Hamilton,[19] and on August 9 he again wrote Knox an explanatory letter concerning the relative rankings.[20] In the meantime, Knox had written to the Secretary of War a letter dated August 5 in which he all but said that he would not accept the appointment if the "names as specified in the last, is intended to establish the priority of rank." [21]

Adams, who alone had the authority to settle the dispute, soon made clear his preference. On August 14, 1798, in reply to a letter from Mc-Henry asking for permission "to call effectually to my aid, the Inspector General, and likewise General Knox; and to charge them with the management of particular branches of the service," [22] Adams wrote: "Calling any . . . general officers [other than Washington] into service at present will be attended with difficulty, unless the rank were settled. In my opinion, as the matter now stands, General Knox is legally entitled to rank next to General Washington, and no other arrangement will give satisfaction. If General Washington is of this opinion, and will consent to it, you may call him into actual service as soon as you please. The consequence of this will be that Pinckney must rank before Hamilton. If it shall be consented, that the rank shall be Knox, Pinckney & Hamilton, you may call the latter too into immediate service when you please. Any other plan will occasion long delay and much confusion. You may depend upon it, the five New England States will not patiently submit to the humiliation that has been meditated for them." [23]

16. H to Washington, July 29–August 1, 1798.

17. ALS, Massachusetts Historical Society, Boston; ALS, letterpress copy, George Washington Papers, Library of Congress; copy, Hamilton Papers, Library of Congress.

18. ALS, George Washington Papers, Library of Congress; copy, Hamilton Papers, Library of Congress.

19. Washington to H, August 9, 1798.

20. ALS, letterpress copy, George Washington Papers, Library of Congress.

21. ALS, Adams Family Papers, deposited in the Massachusetts Historical Society, Boston; ALS (photostat), James McHenry Papers, Library of Congress; copy, James McHenry Papers, Library of Congress.

22. McHenry to Adams, August 4, 1798 (ALS, Adams Family Papers, deposited in the Massachusetts Historical Society, Boston).

23. Copy, Hamilton Papers, Library of Congress. Adams's reference to the dissatisfaction in New England may have been inspired by Knox, who, on July 29, 1798, had written to Washington: "New England which must furnish

Before receiving Adams's letter, McHenry sent Hamilton a copy of
Knox's letter of August 5 and asked: "What is to be said to General
Knox?" [24] Hamilton, as always, was only too willing to help, and on
August 19 he wrote two letters to McHenry—one official and the other
private—and enclosed a draft of a reply to Knox's August 5 letter.[25] On
August 20 McHenry forwarded to Adams the drafts of two letters—
one private and the other official—addressed to Knox.[26] If anything, Mc-
Henry's proposals served to strengthen the President's resolve. On Au-
gust 29 he wrote from Quincy to the Secretary of War: "I have received your letter of August 20th, I believe, though the o is obscure.

"General Knox is gone to the Eastward as I understand, to return in
ten or fifteen days. But if he were in Boston, I could not send him
either your official or private letter, as neither contains sentiments that
I can approve. My opinion is and has always been clear, that as the law
now stands, the order of nomination or of recording has no weight or
effect, but that officers appointed on the same day, in whatever order,
had a right to rank according to antecedent services. I made the nomination according to the list presented to me, by you, from General
Washington,[27] in hopes that rank might be settled among them by agreement or acquiescence, believing at the same time, and expressing to you
that belief, that the nomination and appointment would give Hamilton
no command at all, nor any rank before any Major-General. This is my
opinion still.

"I am willing to settle all decisively at present (and have no fear of
the consequences) by dating the commissions Knox, on the first day,
Pinckney on the 2nd. Hamilton on the third. If this course is not taken
& the commissions are all made out on the same day, I tell you my

---

the Majority of the Army if one shall be raised, will be without a Major
General or have the junior One. Whether they will possess such a sense of in-
feriority as to bear such a state of things patiently, or whether their zeal and
confidence will thereby be excited Time will discover" (ALS, George Washington Papers, Library of Congress).

24. McHenry to H, August 11, 13, 1798.

25. The draft is enclosed in H's private letter.

26. ALS, Adams Family Papers, deposited in the Massachusetts Historical
Society, Boston. The drafts of the two letters which McHenry enclosed have
not been found.

27. The list in Washington's handwriting, dated July 14, 1798 (ADS, Adams
Family Papers, deposited in the Massachusetts Historical Society, Boston; ADS,
letterpress copy, George Washington Papers, Library of Congress), was ap-
pended to Washington's answers, also dated July 14, to questions submitted to
him by McHenry (ADS, Adams Family Papers, deposited in the Massachusetts
Historical Society, Boston; copy, in McHenry's handwriting, George Washington Papers, Library of Congress; copy, in Tobias Lear's handwriting, MS
Division, New York Public Library). McHenry's queries, in his own handwriting, are in the Adams Family Papers, deposited in the Massachusetts Historical Society, Boston. A copy of these queries, also in McHenry's handwriting, is in the George Washington Papers, Library of Congress, and a
second copy, in Lear's handwriting, is in the MS Division, New York Public
Library.

opinion is clear that Hamilton will legally rank after Hand [28] and I fear even after Lee.[29]

"You speak to me of the expediency of attempting an alteration in the rank of the gentlemen in question. You know, Sir, that no rank has ever been settled by me. You know my opinion has always been as it is now, that the order of names in the nomination and record was of no consequence.

"General Washington has through the whole, conducted with perfect honor and consistency. I said and I say now, if I could resign to him the office of President, I would do it immediately and with the highest pleasure, but I never said I would hold the office & be responsible for its exercise, while he should execute it. He has always said in all his letters that these points must ultimately depend upon the President.

"The power & authority is in the President. I am willing to exert this authority at this moment and to be responsible for the exercise of it. All difficulties will in this way be avoided. But, if it is to be referred to General Washington or to mutual & amicable accomodation among the gentlemen themselves, I foresee it will come to me at last, after much altercation & exasperation of passions & I shall then determine it exactly as I should now—Knox, Pinckney & Hamilton.

"There has been too much intrigue in this business both with General Washington & me. If I shall ultimately be the dupe of it, I am much mistaken in myself." [30]

McHenry broke the news to Hamilton on September 6 in a letter enclosing Adams's letter of August 29. McHenry held out no hope to Hamilton, for he concluded: "I hope you will acquiesce in the necessity which seems to govern, and save us from the confusion which may result from a different conduct." On the same day he wrote to Adams: ". . . I shall follow the order you prescribe, and date Genl. Knox's on the first day, General Pinckney's on the second, and General Hamilton's on the third." [31] On September 8 Hamilton replied to McHenry: "I shall certainly not hold the commission on the plan proposed, and only wait an official communication to say so."

Pickering, like McHenry, had apparently done all within his power

28. Dr. Edward Hand had been a brigadier general during the American Revolution and adjutant general of the Continental Army from 1781 to 1783. At the end of the war he was brevetted a major general. After the war he resumed his medical practice in Lancaster, Pennsylvania, and entered local and state politics. From 1791 to 1801 he was inspector of the revenue for Survey No. 3 in Pennsylvania. On July 19, 1798, he was appointed a major general of the Provisional Army (*Executive Journal*, I, 292, 293).

29. At the end of the Revolution, Henry Lee held the rank of lieutenant colonel, the same rank that H held. After the war Lee served in the Continental Congress and as governor of Virginia. On July 19, 1798, he was appointed a major general in the Provisional Army (*Executive Journal*, I, 292, 293).

30. Copy, Hamilton Papers, Library of Congress.

31. ALS, Adams Family Papers, deposited in the Massachusetts Historical Society, Boston; copy, Hamilton Papers, Library of Congress.

to support Hamilton and defeat Knox. He had been the first to suggest Hamilton's name to Washington; [32] he had gone out of his way to keep Hamilton informed on Washington's views on how the major generals should be ranked; [33] and early in August he had sought to force Adams's hand by urging the President to call Hamilton and Knox into service.[34] In addition, when Hamilton wrote to him on July 17 indicating his "willingness to serve under Knox," Pickering had "concealed" the letter "in order that the arrangement of nominations of Major Generals, . . . as formed by General Washington . . . might leave . . . [Hamilton] in the first place." [35] Pickering's efforts, however, had had no effect on Adams, and by the end of August the Secretary of State had run out of suggestions and had little advice to offer Hamilton beyond urging him to stand firm.[36]

By the end of the first week in September, Pickering and McHenry had every reason to be discouraged, for Adams's letter of August 29 to McHenry had apparently deprived them of any further opportunities for machination. They did not, however, give up easily. For a time they considered a letter to the President to be signed by Pickering, Secretary of the Treasury Oliver Wolcott, Jr., and Secretary of the Navy Benjamin Stoddert.[37] But, "after . . . a good deal of deliberation, the idea of a joint address was relinquished for a representation from Mr. Wolcott alone, who did not appear to be implicated in his [Adams's] suspicions of intrigue." [38] Accordingly, on September 17, Wolcott wrote Adams a long, detailed brief on behalf of Hamilton.[39] In the course of this letter, Wolcott attempted to refute Knox's contentions that the order of rank at the end of the Revolution should prevail and Adams's insistence that Knox was popular in New England; but most important of all, he subtly—but insistently—emphasized the importance of not offending Washington by denying him his choice for the second in command. "The circumstances of the case in respect to Genl Washington," Wolcott wrote, "appear therefore to be, first, that he was nominated to command the armies without any previous consultation or notice; second, that his 'advice in the formation of a List of Officers' was requested, accompanied with an intimation that 'his opinion on all subjects would have great weight;' third, that General Washington formed a List of Officers, and after *mature deliberation* settled the rank, which *in his judgement,* the Officers in question ought to enjoy in the proposed

32. Pickering to Washington, July 6, 1798 (ALS, George Washington Papers, Library of Congress; ADfS, Essex Institute, Salem, Massachusetts; copy, Hamilton Papers, Library of Congress).

33. Pickering to H, July 17, 1798.

34. Pickering to Adams, August 8, 1798 (ALS, Adams Family Papers, deposited in the Massachusetts Historical Society, Boston).

35. Pickering to H, August 21–22, 1798.

36. Pickering to H, August 21–22, 23, 1798.

37. McHenry to H, September 10, 1798.

38. McHenry to Washington, September 19, 1798 (ALS, George Washington Papers, Library of Congress).

39. ALS, Adams Family Papers, deposited in the Massachusetts Historical Society, Boston; ADfS, Connecticut Historical Society, Hartford.

Army; fourth, that in the nominations exhibited by the President to the Senate, the order proposed by General Washington respecting those Gentlemen was preserved.

"The 'advice' of General Washington was therefore that Alexander Hamilton should be appointed Inspector General, with the rank of *first* Major General, Charles Cotesworth Pinckney, *second* Major General, and Henry Knox, *third* Major General—whatever may have been the opinion of the President respecting the effect of the order of appointment, the opinion of General Washington and the expectation of the public is, that General Hamilton will be confirmed in a rank second only to the Commander in Chief.

"I am persuaded that no personal considerations distinct from the public Interest have influenced General Washington, and it is impossible that the public should be governed by any but views of the general Welfare, in awarding the second rank to General Hamilton; there does not exist a more sincere friend to General Knox than the Commander in Chief; the preference has been founded solely on public considerations; on a peculiar fitness of character, and on the utility of vesting a high command in the Office of Inspector General.

"Contrary to expectation, General Knox claims the first rank, and in support of his pretensions refers to a rule adopted in the revolutionary War, by which according to his statement, among Officers appointed to the same grade, on the same day, their relative rank in the new grade, was to be determined by their respective ranks, prior to such new appointments.

"No general and unqualified rule of the kind alluded to by General Knox, is to be found by me in the resolutions of Congress; it is however presumed that the regulations prescribed on the 24th. of November 1778,[40] are those to which he refers. A due attention to these regulations will evince, that they are wholly inapplicable to the present state of things, and that they contain many exceptions with reference to the Army for which they were formed.

"The first of the rules established on the 24th. of November 1778, is the only one, which can in any degree support General Knox's pretensions; this merely determines the rank of Commissions in the eighty eight battalions ordered to be raised during the war, by the resolution of Congress of the 16th. of September 1776.[41] Prior to this time the force of the United States consisted of Troops engaged for limited periods; some under the authority of Congress, others under the authority of the respective States. After the permanent Army was raised, new Commissions were issued to the Officers; the powers of appointment except of General Officers, being vested in the States, it could not but happen, that the dates would be filled up very erroneously; the true effect of the rule above referred to, was merely to correct these errors; —the rank of the Officers in the sixteen additional Battalions, of the new Levies, of the flying Camp and Militia, of Officers who had been or were prisoners with the Enemy and cases where different rules had

40. *JCC*, XII, 1154–56.
41. *JCC*, V, 762.

been established in the respective States, were expressly excepted from
the regulation; it was moreover provided that a *resignation* should preclude any claim or benefit from former rank, under a new appointment.

"Giving therefore the utmost latitude to the rule presumed to be
refered to, by General Knox, it only proves, that in cases of *continued*
service, under a Commission from *Congress*, and in respect to appointments made under the *same Act*, and where the rank has *not been
settled;* and where *no different rule* was established by the *particular
State*, the rank under a former Commission should govern. There is
clearly nothing in this rule, which is highly equitable and perfectly
well adapted to the difficulty which it was intended to redress, that
can settle the grade of rank, between distinct Offices namely between
the Office of *Inspector General* and that of *Major General*.

"But if it is contended that the Office of Inspector General and Major
General are of the same dignity or if the former draws after it no
precise rank and if recourse must be had to the obsolete resolutions of
Congress, to settle the relative rank of the Gentlemen in question, the
most apposite rule which I can discover will be found in the resolution
of Congress passed on the 4th. day of January 1776. viz.

" 'Resolved that in all elections of Officers by Congress, where more
than one are elected on the same day, to commands of the same rank,
they shall take rank of each other according to their election and the
entry of their names on the minutes; and their Commissions shall be
numbered to shew their priority.' [42] The principle of this resolution
pointedly applies to the present case; having been adopted to settle the
rank of *newly appointed* Officers, for a *new Army*.

"My opinion however is, that the resolutions of Congress afford no
rule for deciding the question, except as they are reconciliable with the
present Constitution of the United States, the actual state of the Country,
and as being founded in reason they may hereafter be adopted for the
government of an Army when *actually formed*.

"The President is *now about to form an Army;* and it is an uncontro-
vertible fact, that before their recent appointments, Alexander Hamilton
and Henry Knox possessed *no rank whatever;* they were *private Citizens;*
their just pretensions to appointments were founded solely on their
merits; and their *new stations*, were consequently to be determined by
their *comparative qualifications*.

"It would have been as becoming in the Candidates and certainly less
embarrassing to the President if all had submitted in silence to the Presidents determination after consultation with General Washington; super-
lative disinterestedness is however rare; what has happened in this case,
will eternally happen; there is not one man of real merit and virtue
among a thousand whose estimate of himself does not exceed that of his
acquaintance; if General Hamilton thinks the second rank his due, so
does General Knox in respect to himself; General Hamiltons pretensions
are however seconded by the wishes of General Washington and by the
opinion of a vast majority of the wisest and most efficient supporters
of the Government in every part of the United States; the political en-

42. *JCC*, IV, 29.

emies of both Gentlemen are the same, but while they respect and confide in the great talents of the former, they estimate the abilities of the latter by a different scale.

"The opinion of General Washington being in favour of General Hamilton; the public voice having awarded the second rank to him, in consequence of his merits and the supposed effect of the act of the President himself; it being certain to my mind that General Knox will not accept an appointment with rank inferiour to Generals Hamilton and Pinckney; and it being equally certain, that General Hamilton will not renounce the station in which he supposes himself properly placed, but rather decline the service, the interesting question arises, What is to be done? Taking it for granted that General Knox or General Hamilton will decline service, it is necessary to consider maturely the consequences of a decision against either of these Gentlemen.

"The question of rank so far as it is a *personal question* ought to be entirely out of view, for surely the public Interest ought not to yield to the ambition or vanity of either of these Gentlemen: their relative *rank* is important only in relation to the *duties of their Offices*, and as it may affect the *continuance of one of them in service;* the Office of General Hamilton as that of *Inspector General* as well as Major General; that of General Knox only *Major General.*

"I am no Soldier, and no judge of military questions except so far as they are capable of being tested by the principles of Common sense; there are I presume some *special duties,* annexed to the Office of *Inspector General,* distinct from that of a *Major General* and also presume that it is important that the former should have an elevated rank to secure the full effect of his arrangements; The Law only determines that the Inspector General, shall enjoy the rank of Major General; the *official grade* being the same, *personal rank,* must therefore depend on the pleasure or determination of the President, on a full consideration of all the circumstances, which must influence his decision.

"General Washington has clearly expressed his opinion or rather 'advice' on this point, and by a Letter of his to General Hamilton, which I learn from the Secretary of War, was by him submitted to the Presidents perusal, but which doubtless has escaped his recollection, I find that General Washington *relies,* upon the efficient aid of General Hamilton. By the same Letter it appears further, that the only difficulty in his mind arose, (and that very much from local considerations) on the relative rank of Generals Hamilton and Pinckney, and that with a knowledge of all the Gentlemen and with the most intimate acquaintance with Generals Hamilton & Knox, General Washington deliberately and explicitly arranged the last below the other two; These are his words; 'with respect to my friend General Knox, whom I love and esteem, I have ranked him below you both.'

"Considering all the circumstances of General Washingtons services and retirement, it was certainly a serious question for him to determine, whether he should again encounter the perils of public life—having consented, it will be expected by all dispassienate men, that his reasonable wishes should be gratified—and what is the present question? Merely,

whether General Hamilton shall or shall not precede General Knox in
command. If the question is important to one of the Gentlemen, it is
equally so to the other. If the services of both cannot be retained,
ought not General Washingtons deliberate advice, seeing it has been
asked, to influence the final decision?"

Hamilton's supporters in the cabinet also turned to Washington in
their efforts to reverse the decision of their President. McHenry relayed
the news to Washington that Adams was determined to place Knox first
and Hamilton third,[43] and on September 13 Pickering wrote to Washington: ". . . The Secretary of War has received from the President a
Letter *deciding* the ranks of the three first General Officers in question
—that they shall stand, Knox—Pinckney—Hamilton. . . . It is a decision
which ought not to stand: I hope in God the President may be prevailed to reverse it: we have taken it upon ourselves to delay its execution. . . ."[44] This letter was followed on September 19 by a detailed
account of the situation by McHenry, in which he wrote that the President "agreed to follow your arrangement upon my admitting, that any
of the parties, if dissatisfied with the order of arrangement might have
their claims discussed and settled by a board of officers or the commander in chief."[45]

Washington then attempted to do for Hamilton, Pickering, and Mc-
Henry what they had been unable to do for themselves. He indicated
to McHenry the possibility that he would resign if Adams changed the
ranking of the three major generals, and on September 25, in a polite,
but firm, letter to Adams, he made clear his preference for Hamilton.[46]
He wrote the letter, he said, "With all the respect which is due to your
public station, and with the regard I entertain for your private character," and he stated that "To encrease the Powers of the Commander in
Chief—or to lessen those of the President of the United States . . . was
most foreign from my heart." But he wrote: "In the arrangement made
by me, with the Secretary of War, the three Major Generals stood—
Hamilton, Pinckney, Knox; and in this order I expected their Commissions would have been dated. This, I conceive, must have been the
understanding of the Senate. And certainly, was the expectation of all
those with whom I have conversed. But you have been pleased to order
the last to be first, and the first to be last. . . .

"But if no regard was intended to be had to the *order* of my arrangement, why was it not altered before it was submitted to the Senate?
This would have placed matters upon simple ground. It would then have
been understood as it is at present—namely—that the Gentlemen would

43. McHenry to Washington, September 7, 10, 1798 (both ALS, George
Washington Papers, Library of Congress; copies, Hamilton Papers, Library of
Congress).

44. ALS, George Washington Papers, Library of Congress; copy, Hamilton
Papers, Library of Congress.

45. ALS, George Washington Papers, Library of Congress.

46. ALS, Adams Family Papers, deposited in the Massachusetts Historical
Society, Boston; ALS, letterpress copy, George Washington Papers, Library
of Congress; Washington to McHenry, September 16, October 1, 1798 (ALS,
letterpress copies, George Washington Papers, Library of Congress).

rank in the order they were named: but the change will contravene this, and excite much conversation, & unpleasant circumstances. . . .

"It is an invidious task, at all times to draw comparisons; and I shall avoid it as much as possible; but I have no hesitation in declaring, that if the Public is to be deprived of the Services of Coll. Hamilton in the Military line, that the Post he was destined to fill will not be easily supplied; and that this is the sentiment of the Public, I think I can venture to pronounce. . . .

"I have addressed you, Sir, with openess and candour—and I hope with respect, requesting to be informed whether your determination to reverse the order of the three Major Generals is final. . . ."

On October 9 Adams replied to Washington: "I received, yesterday, the Letter you did the Honor to write to me on the 25th. of September.

"You request to be informed, whether my determination to preserve the order of the three Major Generals is final. . . . I presume that before this Day you have received Information, from the Secretary at War, that I some time ago Signed the three Commissions and dated them on the Same day, in hopes Similar to yours that an amicable Adjustment or Acquiescence might take place among the Gentlemen themselves. But, if these hopes should be disappointed, and Controversies should arise, they will of course be submitted to you as Commander in Chief, and if after all any one should be so obstinate as to appeal to me from the Judgment of the Commander in Chief, I was determined to confirm that Judgment. Because, whatever Construction may be put upon the Resolutions of the ancient Congress which have been applied to this Case, and whether they are at all applicable to it or not, there is no doubt to be made that by the present Constitution of the United States, the President has Authority to determine the Rank of Officers." [47]

Most historians have suggested that Washington's letter forced Adams's hand and made him change his mind.[48] Such a conclusion is at best only partially correct, for it appears that long before Adams had received the letter in question he had decided to refer the matter back to the principals in the dispute. In the first place, Adams signed the commissions of the three men on the same day and sent them to McHenry on September 30 (or eight days before he had received Washington's letter).[49] Secondly, the members of the cabinet proceeded on the assumption that the fact that Adams had signed the commissions on the same day meant that the order in which the names had been approved by the Senate now prevailed and that Hamilton was second in command

47. ALS, George Washington Papers, Library of Congress.

48. See, for example, John Alexander Carroll and Mary Wells Ashworth, *George Washington* (New York, 1957), VII, 533–34; Broadus Mitchell, *Alexander Hamilton: The National Adventure 1788–1804* (New York, 1962), 431; Page Smith, *John Adams* (Garden City, New York, 1962), II, 983; Bernhard Knollenberg, "John Adams, Knox, and Washington," *Proceedings of the American Antiquarian Society*, new ser., Vol. 56, Part 2 (October, 1946), 233–38.

49. Adams to McHenry, September 30, 1798 (ALS, James McHenry Papers, Library of Congress).

to Washington.[50] Finally, and most important, there is evidence that Adams had made up his mind more than two weeks before he had received Washington's letter. In a draft of a letter to Wolcott, which is dated September 24 and which was never sent, Adams replied in detail to Wolcott's letter of September 17.[51] In Adams's letter, which he said was "written in deep Affection" for Wolcott, he discussed all the reasons why he did not think Hamilton should be ranked first among the major generals; but he also stated: "I have given so much Attention to your Representations that I have dated the Commissions to Knox Pinckney and Hamilton all on the same Day, in hopes that under the Auspices of General Washington the Gentlemen may come to some amicable settlement of the dispute. . . ."

Adams's letter to McHenry of September 30 consists of a single sentence reading: "Inclosed are the commissions for the three generals signed and all dated on the same day." [52] McHenry immediately relayed this news to Hamilton in a letter which concluded: "I shall, I expect, soon call upon you. Burn this letter," [53] and on October 10 Wolcott wrote to Hamilton that Adams's letter to McHenry, "covering the Commissions of the Major Generals, dated on *one day*," had settled the question of rank and "that you are established in the rank of first Major General." But McHenry was still not sure. Instead of asking Adams what should be done, on October 12 he sent his fellow cabinet members most of the relevant documents and asked them the following four questions: "1st. Whether from the tenor of the letters, collectively, and particularly, from the President's last letter (No. 13) including the commissions for the Major Generals of the army of the United States, all dated on the same day, it ought to be concluded, that the President acquiesces, in the settlement of the relative rank of the Major Generals, upon the principle of, and agreeably to, the order of their nomination and approbation by the Senate. If answered in the affirmative, then,

"2d. Whether the Secretary of war should immediately transmit their commissions to the Major Generals, and inform them respectively, that their relative rank is considered as definitively settled by the order of nomination, and approbation aforesaid, or

"3d. Whether the transmission of the commissions, and the communications aforesaid, ought not to be previously transmitted to the President.

"4th. Whether, if the Secretaries shall collectively agree in their answers to the above questions, it will not be proper for the Secretary of war to communicate to the President a copy of the questions now proposed and the answers thereto, as inducing to the opinion he entertains of the President's will, and the conduct he has pursued." [54]

50. See McHenry to H, October 5, 1798; Wolcott to H, October 10, 1798.

51. Copy, with interlineations in Adams's handwriting, and copy (incomplete), Adams Family Papers, deposited in the Massachusetts Historical Society, Boston.

52. ALS, James McHenry Papers, Library of Congress.

53. McHenry to H, October 5, 1798.

54. McHenry to Pickering, Wolcott, and Stoddert, October 12, 1798 (ALS, Connecticut Historical Society, Hartford; copy, Hamilton Papers, Library of

On October 13, Pickering, Wolcott, and Stoddert replied to McHenry: "The only inference we can draw from the facts . . . is, that the President consents to the arrangement of rank as proposed by General Washington and pursued in the order of nomination and appointment by the President and Senate.

"This being the conclusion which we make, it is our opinion, that the Secretary of war, ought to transmit the Commissions and inform the Generals that in his opinion the rank is definitively settled according to the original arrangement.

"We are of opinion that it will not be respectful to the President to address him again on a subject, which appears to have been attended with difficulties in his mind, and the discussion of which can produce no public advantage; we also think that no communication of our sentiments will be necessary, unless the Secretary of War shall discover hereafter, that we have mistaken the Presidents intentions, in which case it will be proper, that we should share in the censure." [55]

On October 15 McHenry sent Hamilton his commission and stated: "With respect to the relative rank between you, Generals Pinckney and Knox, I deem it necessary or observe, that the order of nomination and approval by the Senate is considered definitive." Hamilton acknowledged the receipt of his commission on October 19, but Knox, stating that "no Officer can consent to his own degradation," declined his appointment.[56] Pinckney, who had had the good fortune to be out of the country throughout most of the dispute, returned to the United States in mid-October. Following his arrival he wrote to McHenry accepting his appointment and stating that he had no objections to being outranked by Hamilton.[57]

Mount Vernon 14th. July 1798

My dear Sir,   (Private & confidential)

Your letter of the 8th. instant, was presented to me by the Secretary of War on the 11th.,[58] and I have consented to embark once

---

Congress). This letter is misdated October 13, 1798, in George Gibbs, *Memoirs of the Administrations of Washington and John Adams: Edited from the Papers of Oliver Wolcott, Secretary of the Treasury* (New York, 1846), II, 101.

55. Two copies, Connecticut Historical Society, Hartford.

56. Knox to McHenry, October 23, 1798 (copy, George Washington Papers, Library of Congress; copy, Adams Family Papers, deposited in the Massachusetts Historical Society, Boston).

57. Pinckney to McHenry, October 31, 1798 (copy, George Washington Papers, Library of Congress; copy, Adams Family Papers, deposited in the Massachusetts Historical Society, Boston). See also H to McHenry, October 19, 1798.

58. On July 6, 1798, Adams asked McHenry to "embrace the first opportunity to sett out on your Journey to Mount Vernon, and wait on general Washington with the Commission of Lt. General and Commander in Chief of the armies of the United States. . . . His advice in the formation of a List of Officers would be extremely desirable to me . . ." (LC, Adams Family Papers,

more on a boundless field of responsibility & trouble, with two reservations—first, that the principal Officers in the line, and of the Staff, shall be such as I can place confidence in; and, that I shall not be called into the field until the Army is in a situation to require my presence, or it becomes indispensible by the urgency of circumstances. Contributing in the meanwhile, every thing in my power to its efficient Organization, but nothing to the public expence until I am in a situation to incur expence myself.

It will be needless after giving you this information, and having indelibly engraved on my mind, the assurance contained in your letter of the 2d. of June, to add, that I rely upon you as a Coadjutor, and assistant in the turmoils I have consented to encounter.

I have communicated very fully with the Secretary of War on the several matters contained in the Powers vested in him by the President; [59] who, as far as it appears by them, is well disposed to accomodate; But I must confess that, besides nominating me to the Command of the Armies without any previous consultation or notice,[60] the whole of that business seems to me to stand upon such ground, as may render the Secretarys journey, & our consultation, of no avail.

Congress, it is said, would rise this week. What then *has* been done, or *can* the President do, with respect to appointments under that Bill, if it has been enacted? [61] Be his inclinations what they may, unless a Law *could*, and *has* Passed, enabling him, in the recess of the Senate, to make appointments, conformably thereto, the nominations must have been made; & the business *done here*, with the Secretary is rendered nugatory.

By the pending Bill, if it passes to a Law, two Major Generals, and an Inspector Genl. with the Rank of Majr General and three Brigadiers are to be appointed. Presuming on its passing, I have given the following as my sentiments respecting the characters fit, & proper to be employed; in which the Secretary concurs.

---

deposited in the Massachusetts Historical Society, Boston). McHenry reached Mount Vernon on July 11, where he remained until July 13, and on July 17 he arrived in Philadelphia. See H to Washington, July 8, 1798, note 1.

59. This is a reference to a series of questions which McHenry asked and Washington answered. See note 27.

60. See H to Washington, July 8, 1798, note 1.

61. "An Act to augment the Army of the United States, and for other purposes" (1 *Stat.* 604–05) authorized the President during the recess of the

Alexr. Hamilton. Inspector ⎤
Chas. C. Pinckney   ⎟
Henry Knox—or if either of ⎬   Majr. Genls.
  the last mend. refuses   ⎟
Henry Lee of Virginia   ⎦

Henry Lee (if not Majr. Genl.) ⎤
John Brooks [62]—Massachusetts ⎟
Willm. S. Smith [63]—N: York—or ⎬ Brigadiers
John E. Howard [64]—Maryld.   ⎦

Either Edward Hand—Pennsa.   ⎤
Jonathan Dayton Jr.[65] N. Jer ⎟
          or   ⎬   Adjt. Genl.
Willm. S. Smith to be   ⎦

Edwd. Carrington [66]   Qr. Mr. Genl.
James Craik [67]   Directr. Hosl

Senate "to appoint all regimental officers . . . and . . . to make appointments to fill any vacancies in the army. . . ."

62. Dr. John Brooks held the rank of lieutenant colonel at the end of the American Revolution. He served from 1792 to 1796 in the United States Army as a brigadier general.

63. Smith, John Adams's son-in-law, held the rank of lieutenant colonel at the end of the Revolution. After a brief tour of Europe with Francisco de Miranda, he returned to America and successively held the offices of United States marshal for New York and supervisor of the revenue for the District of New York. For his land speculations and financial difficulties, see Benjamin Walker to H, October 4, 1796, note 1. Although Adams nominated Smith as adjutant general with the rank of brigadier general on July 18, 1798, the Senate rejected the nomination. On January 8, 1799, he was appointed a lieutenant colonel of the Twelfth Regiment of Infantry (*Executive Journal*, I, 292, 293, 299, 303).

64. At the close of the American Revolution, Howard held the rank of lieutenant colonel. Following the Revolution he held various offices. He was a delegate to the Continental Congress from 1784 to 1788, governor of Maryland from 1788 to 1791, member of the Maryland Senate from 1791 to 1795, and United States Senator from 1796 to 1803.

65. Dayton was a captain at the close of the Revolution. After the war he studied law and entered politics. He served in the Ratifying Convention, in the New Jersey Assembly in 1786, 1787, and 1790, and was a Federalist member of the House of Representatives from 1791 to 1799. He was speaker of the House from March 4, 1795, to March 3, 1799. On July 19, 1798, the Senate confirmed his appointment as brigadier general (*Executive Journal*, I, 292, 293). Dayton, however, declined the appointment (Godfrey, "Provisional Army," 133–34).

66. At the close of the Revolution, Carrington held the rank of lieutenant colonel. During the Washington Administration, Carrington held the offices of United States marshal and supervisor of the revenue in Virginia. Washington asked Carrington to serve as quartermaster general (Washington to Carrington, July 15, August 5, 1798 [ALS, letterpress copies, George Washington Papers,

And I have enumerated the most prominent characters that have occurred to my mind, from whom to select field Officers for the Regiments of Infantry, & that of Cavalry, which are proposed to be raised.[68]

And now, my dear Sir, with that candour which you always have, and I trust ever will experience from me, I shall express to you a difficulty which has arisen in my mind, relative to seniority between you & Genl. Pinckney; for with respect to my friend General Knox, whom I love & esteem, I have ranked him below you both. That you may know from whence this difficulty proceeds, it is proper I should observe, & give it as my decided opinion, that if the French should be so mad as to Invade this Country in expectation of making a serious impression, that their operations will commence in the States South of Maryland: 1. because they are the weakest; 2. because they will expect, from the tenor of the debates in Congress to find more friends there; 3. because there can be no doubt of their arming the Negros against us; and 4. because they would be more contiguous to their Islands, & to Louisiana & the Floridas, if they can obtain possession of them; & that this will be the case, if they are able to accomplish it, is, to my mind, a matter that admits of no doubt.

If these premises are just, the inference is obvious, that the services and influence of General Pinckney in the Southern States would be of the highest, and most interesting importance. Will he serve then, under one whom he will consider a Junr. Officer? and what would be the consequence if he should refuse, and his numerous, & powerful connections & acquaintances in those parts, get disgusted? You have no doubt heard that his Military reputation stands high in the Southern States; that he is viewed as a brave, intelligent and enterprising Officer; and, if report be true, that no Officer in the late American Army made Tactics, & the art of War so much his Study. To this account of him, may be added, that his character has received much celebrity by his conduct as Minister & Envoy at Paris.

Under this view of the subject, my wish to put you first, and my

Library of Congress]). Carrington declined the appointment unless Washington assumed active command in the field (Carrington to Washington, August 14, 1798 [ALS, George Washington Papers, Library of Congress]).

67. Craik had been chief physician and surgeon of the Continental Army. Following the war he remained as Washington's personal physician. On July 19, 1798, Craik was appointed physician general of the Provisional Army.

68. ALS, letterpress copy, George Washington Papers, Library of Congress.

fear of loosing him, is not a little embarrassing. But why? for after all it rests with the President to use his pleasure. I shall only add therefore, that as the welfare of the country is the object, I persuade myself, we all have in view, I shall sanguinely hope that smaller matters will yield to measures which have a tendency to promote it. I wish devoutly that either of you, or any other fit character had been nominated in my place; for no one *can* make a greater sacrafice —at least of inclination, than will

Your ever Affectionate   Go: Washington [69]

Alexander Hamilton Esqr.

69. At the end of the copy of this letter in the James McHenry Papers, McHenry wrote: "The General gave me the letter of which this is a copy open, at my instance, that I might take a copy of it. James McHenry."

From Marquis de La Tour du Pin

London, July 15, 1798. "j'ai eu l'honneur de vous écrire, Monsieur, vers le mois de mars dernier. . . .[1] ma lettre en renfermoit une pour Mss. le Roy, Bayard, et mc Evers,[2] et une pour m nicholas olive[3] negotian a newyork. je n'ai recu ni d'eux, ni de vous, monsieur, aucune Reponse, ce qui fait que je viens vous importuner encore une fois. L'objet de la lettre ci jointe a messieurs le Roy &c. est de les prier de vendre ma petite ferme d'albany, et d'en placer le prix dans les fonds americains qui paroitront les plus avantageux, mais avant tout les plus Surs. j'osois vous prier, monsieur, de vouloir bien donner votre avis pour cette petite affaire, devenue d'une très grande importance, pour moi, et ma famille, puisque nous Sommes une fois encore emigrés. . . . c'est donc encore une fois chez vous que nous meditons de chercher azile. . . ."

ALS, Hamilton Papers, Library of Congress.
   1. La Tour du Pin to H, February 21, 1798.
   2. William Bayard, Herman LeRoy, and James McEvers were New York City merchants.
   3. Olive was a New York City merchant who had emigrated from France to the United States in 1793, where he became involved in the Castorland project to establish a French colony on land formerly owned by Alexander Macomb on the Black River in northern New York.

From Daniel C. Brent [1]

Woodstock [*Virginia*] *July 16, 1798.* "In a letter which I had the
Honor of receiving from you, dated the 26th of Decemr 1793
. . . [2] you did me the favor to assure me that . . . I might at all times
consider myself as entitled to your good Offices, whenever they
could be useful to me . . . and as I am desirous of obtaining an
appointment under the Government at this time, you will give me
leave therefore to ask the favor of you to furnish me with letters of
recommendation to such of the Executive officers at Phila, including
the President, as you shall think proper, to be made use of by myself. . . ."

Copy, in Brent's handwriting, Hamilton Papers, Library of Congress.
  1. This copy was enclosed in Brent to H, February 2, 1799.
  Brent had been a clerk in the Treasury Department until his resignation on
January 5, 1794. See Brent to H, December 27, 1793; January 27, 1794. In 1796,
Brent, who was pledged to Thomas Jefferson, ran against Charles Simms of
Alexandria for the position of elector of the President and Vice President. On
October 17, 1796, Brent published an address defending Jefferson from renewed
Federalist attacks on his conduct as governor of Virginia during the American
Revolution ([Richmond] *Virginia Gazette & General Advertiser*, November 9,
1796). On November 16, 1796, the *Virginia Gazette & General Advertiser* an-
nounced Brent's election as elector "for District of Stafford &c."
  2. Letter not found.

From Timothy Pickering [1]

Philadelphia July 16. 1798.

D Sir,

  I have just received from Genl. Washington an answer [2] to my
letter [3] which I showed you.

  The General appears to have contemplated attentively the nature
of the impending war with France, and that the southern states (if
any part of the Union) will be invaded. Admitting this idea to be
correct, the General says, "the inference I am going to draw from
placing Colo. Hamilton over General Pinckney, is natural and ob-

vious. The latter is an officer of high military reputation, fond of the profession, spirited, active, & judicious; and much advanced in the estimation of the public by his late conduct as minister and envoy at Paris. With these pretensions, and being senior to Colo. Hamilton, he would not, I am morally certain, accept a junior appointment; and its influence * would spread where most to be deprecated, as his connections are numerous, powerful, and more influential than any other in the three southern states. Under this view of the subject, it would be impolitic, and might be dangerous to sow the seeds of discontent, at so important a crisis. To this may be added, that impediments to the return of Genl. Pinckney, and causes unforseen, might place Colo. Hamilton in the situation you wish to see him. You will readily perceive, that the difficulty in my mind arises from thorough conviction that if an invasion is attempted, it will commence south of Maryland; and from the importance of so influential a character as Pinckney (if among us) being heartily engaged in repelling it." The general concludes, from this reasoning with hoping, that the office of Inspector General, with a command in the line, will prove satisfactory to you. I ought to have first quoted the General's preliminary observation: "Of the abilities and fitness of the Gentleman you have named for a high command in the provisional army, I think as you do; and that his services ought to be secured at *almost* any price."

These communications from the General to me are "in confidence," and as such you will receive them. I presume there is some understanding between you on the subject. At all events, I trust that the same genuine patriotism which determined you and some others to encounter the perils of the American revolution, and by your talents and active labours to swell anothers glory, will prompt you again to come forth in a situation, if not at the height of my wishes and of those of your friends, certainly in a situation in which you can render invaluable services, and as certainly obtain a large share of honor and military fame.

With great sincerity I am   ever yours   T. Pickering

Alexander Hamilton Esqr

* I suppose of Genl. Pinckney's *non* acceptance.

ALS, Hamilton Papers, Library of Congress; ALS, letterpress copy, Massachusetts Historical Society, Boston; copy, Hamilton Papers, Library of Congress.

1. For an explanation of the contents of this letter, see the introductory note to George Washington to H, July 14, 1798.
2. Washington to Pickering, July 11, 1798 (ALS, letterpress copy, George Washington Papers, Library of Congress; copy, Hamilton Papers, Library of Congress).
3. Pickering to Washington, July 6, 1798. See Washington to H, July 14, 1798, note 12.

To Timothy Pickering [1]

[New York, July 17, 1798]

My Dear Sir

I thank you for your friendly letter by the Post.[2] I had contemplated the possibility that *Knox* might come into service & was content to be second to him, if *thought indispensable*. *Pinckney*, if placed over me puts me a grade lower. I dont believe it to be necessary. I am far from certain that he will not be content to serve under me—but I am willing that the affair should be so managed as that the relative ranks may remain open to future settlement, to ascertain the effect of the arrangement which has been contemplated. I am not however ready to say that I shall be satisfied with the appointment of Inspector General with the rank & command of Major General on the principle that every officer of higher rank in the late army who may be appointed is to be above me. I am frank to own that this will not accord with my opinion of my own pretensions & I have every reason to believe that it will fall far short of public opinion. Few have made so many sacrifices as myself—to few would a change of situation for a military appointment be so injurious as to myself—if with this sacrifice, I am to be degraded below my just claim in public opinion—ought I to acquiesce?

Yrs. Affecly   A Hamilton

July 17

Timothy Pickering Esq

ALS, Massachusetts Historical Society, Boston; copy, Hamilton Papers, Library of Congress.
1. For an explanation of the contents of this letter, see the introductory note to George Washington to H, July 14, 1798.
2. Pickering to H, July 16, 1798.

From Timothy Pickering [1]

(Confidential) Philadelphia July 18. 98

Dr Sir,

I have before me yours of yesterday. In the morning of yesterday Mc.Henry returned with Genl. Washington's acceptance of the command of the armies, and a list, in the General's own hand writing,[2] in which the names of the Inspector General and Major Generals stand thus

Inspector General,	Alexander Hamilton.
Major General,	Charles C. Pinckney
ditto	Henry Knox
ditto	Henry Lee ⎱ for the provi-
ditto	Edwd. Hand ⎰ sional army

Then follow the names of old officers from whom to select brigadiers &c. and unfortunately, among those for brigadiers, was that of William S. Smith, the President's son-in-law. It was concluded yesterday to nominate Mr. Dayton (the Speaker of the House) Adjutant General, with the rank of Brigadier Genl. But I believe the President has changed his mind, and will appoint Dayton 3d brigadier, & Smith 4th with the office of Adjutant Genl. Your nomination stands first, as above—thus—A. Hamilton of New York, Inspector Genl. with the rank of Major General.[3] I deprecate the appointment of Smith,[4] which will injure the President in two ways 1st. because he is the President's son-in-law—for this will be contrasted with Genl. Washington's caution to steer clear of his relations. 2d. because Smith is a bankrupt,[5] and if I am rightly informed, *with a ruined reputation.*

I have not time now to add but that I am as ever Sincerely yours T. P.

P.S. I wish the Senate, after passing on the Inspector General & Major General, may postpone all the Brigadiers, till next session, in autumn. Then perhaps a better arrangement may be made. Pardon me for repudiating exceedingly the idea of your being made subordinate to Knox.[6] Nobody ever thought of such a thing.

Coll. Hamilton

ALS, Hamilton Papers, Library of Congress.

1. For an explanation of the contents of this letter, see the introductory note to George Washington to H, July 14, 1798.

2. See Washington to H, July 14, 1798, note 27.

3. On July 18, 1798, John Adams submitted to the Senate his nominations for general officers for the Army. With only a few exceptions the President's nominations followed Washington's recommendations. See Washington to H, July 14, 1798; *Executive Journal*, I, 292.

4. Washington had included the name of William S. Smith, John Adams's son-in-law, in two places on his list of proposed general officers—among the brigadier generals and again with Edward Hand and Jonathan Dayton as a possible choice for adjutant general. See Washington to H, July 14, 1798. When Adams presented his list to the Senate on July 18, 1798, he designated Smith as adjutant general with the rank of brigadier general. The Senate rejected Smith's appointment (*Executive Journal*, I, 292, 293).

On May 25, 1800, after John Adams had dismissed him from the cabinet, Pickering wrote to Charles Cotesworth Pinckney and assigned as one of the reasons for his dismissal his opposition in 1798 to Smith's appointment. Pickering wrote: "Finding that Colo. Smith was to be nominated to the offices of briga-dier & adjutant general; I went immediately to the Senate, called out some members of my acquaintance, told them of this intended nomination, expressed my opinion of Colo. Smith's capacity and character . . . and urged them to put their negative upon him, if they regarded the public interest, or the public safety. When the nomination was sent to the Senate, the members manifested their disapprobation. The President's true & honest friends wished to save him from the mortification of a negative; and three of them ([Uriah] Tracey, [Benjamin] Goodhue and [James] Hillhouse) waited upon him in the evening, and mentioned the objections to Colo. Smith—that he was not only a bankrupt—but a bankrupt with dishonour . . ." (LS, Massachusetts Historical Society, Boston). See also Pickering to Timothy Williams, May 19, 1800 (ALS, Massachusetts Historical Society, Boston); Pickering to Timothy Pickering, Jr., June 27, 1800 (copy, Massachusetts Historical Society, Boston).

5. See Benjamin Walker to H, October 4, 1796, note 1.

6. See H to Pickering, July 17, 1798.

From James McHenry

Philad. 20 July 1798.

My dear Hamilton.

I retained the inclosed letter [1] which was put into my hands with permission to take a copy of it. I hope every thing has been arranged to your satisfaction, or if not wholly, yet nearly so.

I shall transmit you very soon the rules & regulations for the formation & movements of his Britannic Majestys forces,[2] and manual exercise for the same, in order that you may consider and report whether the whole or what parts of them are suitable to be introduced into our service. If a proper system is formed, and becomes a Presidential act it will save you an infinity of trouble and perplexity. I wish you therefore to pay the earliest attention to the subject.

Yours sincerely   James McHenry

Alexr. Hamilton.

ALS, Hamilton Papers, Library of Congress; ADf, James McHenry Papers, Library of Congress.
    1. See George Washington to H, July 14, 1798, note 69.
    2. This is a reference to David Dundas, *Principles of military movements, chiefly applied to infantry. Illustrated by manoeuvres of the Prussian troops, and by an outline of the British campaigns in Germany, during the war of 1757* (London: T. Cadell, 1788).

From Rufus King

[*London, July 21, 1798.* Kings notation [1] of this letter reads: "Hamilton. Duplicates of address Gallatin." [2] *Letter not found.*]

    1. Letter listed in Rufus King's "Memorandum of Private Letters, &c., dates & persons, from 1796 to Augt 1802," owned by Mr. James G. King, New York City.
    2. See King to H, July 14, 1798.

From Ambrose Spencer [1]

Hudson [*New York*] *July 21, 1798.* "It is undoubtedly time, that the affair of Avery & others with Proctor, be brought to a close. . . ."

ALS, Hamilton Papers, Library of Congress.
    1. For an explanation of the contents of this letter, see Spencer to H, October 30, 1797.

To James McHenry [1]

(private)   New York July 22d ⟨1798⟩

My Dear Sir

    Your letter of the 20th. instant, inclosing one from General Washington came to hand this day.

    The object you suggest in it is one, which no doubt deserves a primary attention; and it will be paid to it. But it will be useful, that I should shortly confer with you fully on a variety of subjects, and after receiving an official communication of my appointment, I shall without delay, repair to Philadelphia.

I count always upon your confidence as well in my personal friendship for you as in my zeal for the public service; and having no inclination to spare myself it only remains for us to trace together the plan in which I can best second your operations and promote the service.

Yrs. with true attachment   A Hamilton
New York July 22. 1798

PS In some instances we have missed it in our Brigadiers. It [is] very essential there should be no mistake about the field office. *Festina lente* in your choice of Officers.

J McHenry Esqr &c

ALS, James McHenry Papers, Library of Congress; copy, Hamilton Papers, Library of Congress.

1. For an explanation of the contents of this letter, see the introductory note to George Washington to H, July 14, 1798.

To Louis Le Bègue Du Portail [1]

[New York, July 23, 1798]

My dear General

Though it is a great while since I have heard from you, I have not ceased to enquire after you, and I shall never cease to interest myself in your welfare.

You have seen the progress of things between this Country and France and you must have made reflections on your own situation. I am aware that the idea of your entering in any way into the Military service of this Country on such an occasion is one of Great delicacy & opposed by many motives. But knowing your opinion as to the Revolution and Revolutionary leaders of your Country, I have thought it not wholly impossible that such an idea would not be intirely disagreeable to you—and I am desirous of ascertaining in the most scrupulous confidence the state of your mind on this point. The Subject may divide itself into employment *in the Field* and employment *out of the Field*.

When I take the liberty to sound you on this head, I ought to assure you as is truly the case, that the Step is wholly from the suggestion of my own mind, and that I am altogether at a loss to conjecture, whether those who must decide the matter would be at all disposed to avail themselves of your services.

I pray you nevertheless to open to me freely your heart on this point in the fullest reliance upon my prudence honor & delicacy. If it were not to intrude too much upon you, I would request you to favor me with a digested plan of an establishment for a military School. This is an object I have extremely at heart.

Yrs. with true esteem & regard   A Hamilton

New York July 23d. 1798

General du Portail

Copy, Hamilton Papers, Library of Congress.
1. Du Portail, a native of France, had been chief of engineers with the rank of major general at the close of the American Revolution. When this letter was written, he owned and lived on a farm in Swedesburg, Montgomery County, Pennsylvania.

From Timothy Donovan [1]

New York, July 24, 1798. "Permit me to Congratulate you most Respectfully on your promotion. . . . I make one of the number, who can make you no other recompence but my Fervent prayers to the allmighty God, for your Long life and Prosperity."

ALS, Hamilton Papers, Library of Congress.
1. Donovan owned and operated a tobacco shop in New York City.
H endorsed this letter: "Timothy Donavan aged sixty Gruff Manner."

From James McHenry [1]

War Department
25th July 1798 [2]

Sir,

I am directed to inform you that the President of the United States, by, and with the advice and consent of the Senate, has ap-

LS, Hamilton Papers, Library of Congress; LS, letterpress copy, James Mc-Henry Papers, Library of Congress.
1. For an explanation of the contents of this letter, see the introductory note to George Washington to H, July 14, 1798.

pointed you Inspector General, with the rank of Major General; and to transmit you your commission made out accordingly.

It may be proper to mention that the nominations to the Senate for the General Officers of the established, and provisional army were presented on the same day, [3] and in the order, in which they appear in the annexed list, and that in registering them in this Department, the same order will be observed.

Permit me to add to this information, that, as no command can be immediately given to the general officers, the President conceives they will consider it proper, that the pay and emoluments of their respective commissions ought not to commence previous to their being called into active service; and to flatter myself that all considerations of a private nature will yield to the crisis, and afford me the pleasure of communicating your acceptance to the President.

I am, Sir, with great respect your obdt. Hb Set   James McHenry

Genl. A. Hamilton

[ENCLOSURE]

Commission as Major General [4]

[Philadelphia, July 19, 1798]

John Adams,
President of the United States of America.
To all who shall see these Presents Greeting:

2. In the letter which H received, the date was originally July 27, but "5" was written over the "7" to make the date July 25. On the letterpress copy the date is July 27. H thought that the date was July 25, for he endorsed this letter: "From the Secy of War July 25. 1798." In addition, when he replied to this letter on July 28, he wrote: "I last evening had the honor of receiving your letter of the 25 instant."

3. This is a reference to the fact that H's commission is dated July 19, 1798, the same day on which the Senate acted on the nomination of officers to serve under Washington (*Executive Journal*, I, 293).

4. DS, Hamilton Papers, Library of Congress. There are two commissions for H in the Hamilton Papers, Library of Congress. They are identical except for the fact that the one printed above is headed "John Adams" and is endorsed as being registered in the War Department by the chief clerk, John Caldwell. One of these commissions was enclosed in this letter; the other was enclosed in McHenry to H, October 15, 1798.

Know Ye, That reposing special Trust and Confidence in the Patriotism, Valour, Fidelity and Abilities of Alexander Hamilton I have nominated and by and with the Advice and Consent of the Senate do appoint him Inspector General of the Army with the rank of Major General in the Service of the United States:

He is therefore carefully and diligently to discharge the Duty of Inspector and Major General by doing and performing all Manner of Things thereunto belonging And I do strictly charge and require all Officers and Soldiers under his Command, to be obedient to his Orders as Inspector and Major General And he is to observe and follow such Orders and Directions from time to time, as he shall receive from me, or the future President of the United States of America, or the General or other superior Officers set over him, according to the Rules and Discipline of War. This Commission to continue in Force during the Pleasure of the President of the United States for the Time being.

By Command of the President of the United-States of America.
James McHenry
Secy of War

Given under my Hand, at Philadelphia this Nineteenth day of July in the Year of our Lord One Thousand Seven Hundred and Ninety eight and in the twenty third Year of the Independence of the United States.

John Adams.

Registered
John Caldwell
Ch. Clk. War Deptmt.

[ENCLOSURE] [5]

Appointments by authority

Alexander Hamilton, of New York, to be Inspector General of the Army with the rank of Major General.

Charles Cotesworth Pinckney of South Carolina to be a Major General

Henry Knox of Massachusetts to be a Major General

5. Copy, Hamilton Papers, Library of Congress.

Henry Lee of Virginia to be a Major General of the provisional
army.

Edward Hand of Pennsylvania to be a Major General in the provisional army.

John Brooks of Massachusetts to be a Brigadier general

William Washington [6] of South Carolina to be a Brigadier general

Jonathan Dayton of New Jersey to be a Brigadier general

William North [7] of New York to be Adjutant General of the army
with the rank of Brigadier general

Ebenezer Huntington [8] of Connecticut to be a Brigadier of the provisional army.

Anthony Walton White [9] to be a Brigadier General of the provisional army.

William Richison Davie [10] of North Carolina to be a Brigadier general of the provisional army.

6. William Washington held the rank of lieutenant colonel at the close of
the American Revolution.

7. At the end of the American Revolution, North, who had been an aide-de-
camp to Baron von Steuben, was inspector of the army with the rank of major.
He had served in the New York Assembly in 1792, 1794, 1795, and 1796, and
was speaker in 1795 and 1796. From May 5, 1798, to August 17, 1798, he was
United States Senator, filling the vacancy which had been created by the resignation of John Sloss Hobart. On July 19, 1798, North was appointed adjutant
general with the rank of brigadier general (*Executive Journal*, I, 293).

8. Huntington served throughout the American Revolution and at the end of
the war was a lieutenant colonel.

9. Anthony Walton White of New Jersey held the rank of colonel at the
close of the American Revolution. On March 3, 1797, he was appointed surveyor for the port and inspector of the revenue for New Brunswick, New
Jersey (*Executive Journal*, I, 232). On September 9, 1798, Washington wrote
to Timothy Pickering concerning this appointment: "What in the name of
Military Prudence could induce the appointments of White & Severe as Brigadiers? The latter never was celebrated for anything . . . except the murder of
Indians—and the former for nothing but frivolity and empty shew and something worse . . ." (ALS, letterpress copy, George Washington Papers, Library
of Congress). On September 14, 1798, Washington wrote to McHenry: "Of
all the characters in the Revolutionary Army, I believe one more obnoxious to
the Officers who composed it could not have been hit upon for a Genl. Officer
than White—especially among those to the Southward where he was best
known, and celebrated for nothing but frivolity—dress—empty shew & something worse—in short, for being a notorious L—r. This appointment will, I am
told exclude many valuable Officers who will not serve as his juniors" (ALS,
letterpress copy, George Washington Papers, Library of Congress).

10. William Richardson (not Richison) Davie served as colonel of the North
Carolina cavalry during the American Revolution. After the war he pursued
his legal career and was a member of the North Carolina legislature almost
continuously from 1786 to 1798. In 1798 he was elected governor of North
Carolina.

John Sevier[11] of Tennessee to be a Brigadier general of the provisional army.

James Craik of Virginia to be Physician general of the Army.

11. Sevier had been a colonel of the North Carolina militia during the
American Revolution. Following the war he became governor of the abortive
state of Franklin. He was also an Indian fighter, land speculator, and a member
of the House of Representatives in the First Congress from that section of
North Carolina which was to become Tennessee. He was elected the first governor of Tennessee and held the post from 1796 until 1801 and again from 1803
to 1809. Francis B. Heitman states that Sevier was "not employed" as a brigadier general (*United States Army*, I, 21). See also note 9.

From Lewis Murarius

New York, July 25, 1798. ". . . When I had the honor to wait
upon you some time ago, I neglected to present you the Testimonies
of my Military Conduct, which by your Leave I hereby ref. to
your perusal.[1] I take the Liberty to recommend myself to your
favor. . . ."

ALS, Hamilton Papers, Library of Congress.
1. The enclosure, which is dated March 27, 1784, and is entitled "Dismission
for Captain Murarius with the rank of Major . . . ," is a statement by Frederic,
Landgrave of Hesse, that Murarius had been "Nineteen Years in our Military
Service" and had resigned with the rank of major (copy, Hamilton Papers,
Library of Congress).

From Jonathan Dayton

[*Elizabethtown, New Jersey, July 27, 1798.* On August 6, 1798,
Hamilton wrote to Dayton: "I received at Philadelphia your letter
of the 27th of July." *Letter not found.*]

From John Jay

Albany 28 July 1798

Dr Sir

Since I left N York I have had the Satisfaction of seeing your
late appointment announced in the Papers; but I have seen nothing

that decides your Rank in Relation to other Majr. Generals.¹ Doubts
on such a point ought not to remain.

Many will doubtless apply for Commands in the army, & it is to
be wished that a judicious Selection may be made.

There is a Gentleman (who for your Information I will mention)
who I am told would accept a Company, and of whose military
Qualifications I have imbibed a very good opinion. I mean Warren
De Lancey.² I think he was a Lt. in the british Service and sold out.

Yours sincerely   John Jay

Majr. Genl. Hamilton

ALS, Hamilton Papers, Library of Congress.
   1. See James McHenry to H, July 25, 1798.
   2. During the American Revolution, De Lancey was a New York Loyalist
who in 1780 had been "commissioned a cornet of dragoons" (Lorenzo Sabine,
*The American Loyalists; or, Biographical Sketches of adherents to the British
crown in the war of the revolution; alphabetically arranged; with a preliminary
historical essay* [Boston: C. C. Little and J. Brown, 1847], 255).

To James McHenry ¹

Philadelphia July 28. 1798

Sir

I last Evening had the honor of receiving your letter of the 25
instant, announcing to me my appointment as Inspector and Major
General.

At a crisis like the present I esteem it my duty to obey the call of
the Government. Feeling too, as I ought, the value of the high confidence which is reposed in me, I beg you to convey to The President
my most cordial acknowlegements and the assurance of my best
endeavours to merit it.

With great respect and esteem   I am Sir   Yr. Obed servant

The Secy at War

ADf, Hamilton Papers, Library of Congress.
   1. For an explanation of the contents of this letter, see the introductory
note to George Washington to H, July 14, 1798.

To James McHenry

Philadelphia
July 28. 1798

Dear Sir

I send you a number of applications for Military appointments with br[i]ef notes of my opinion.

Allow me to remind you in writing of my nephew Philip Church [1] whom I warmly recommend for a Captaincy in the Infantry. He is the eldest son of his father, has had a good education is a young man of sense of genuine spirit and worth—of considerable expectation in point of fortune. I shall esteem his appointment to this grade a personal favour, while I believe that it will consist with every rule of propriety.

There are two other young Gentlemen whom I must also recommend to your attention. They are Volckert Peter Van Rensselaer and Jeremiah H. Van Rensselaer nephews of Mrs. Schuyler.[2] They are of honest and brave blood and of fair character—I recommend one as a first the other as a second Lieutenant.[3]

Yrs with great regard   A H

ADfS, Hamilton Papers, Library of Congress.

1. Church, the son of John B. and Angelica Church, was Elizabeth Hamilton's nephew. He attended Eton for six years and studied law at the Middle Temple in London. After the Church family returned to the United States in 1797, Philip Church entered the law office of Nathaniel Pendleton. On January 8, 1799, he was commissioned a captain in the Twelfth Regiment of Infantry (*Executive Journal*, I, 299, 303), and on January 12, 1799, he became an aide-de-camp to H (H to Church, January 12, 1799). In 1800, at a sale ordered by Chancellor Robert R. Livingston, he purchased for his father the Genesee tract that Robert Morris had mortgaged to John B. Church as security for a debt. He agreed to manage the land for his father and named the first town in the tract Angelica for his mother (see Morris to H, June 7, 1795). In 1807 Philip Church became a judge of the Court of General Sessions for Allegany County.

2. Catherine Van Rensselaer Schuyler was H's mother-in-law. Volkert and Jeremiah H. Van Rensselaer were the sons of her brother, Henry John Van Rensselaer.

3. In the margin opposite this paragraph H wrote: "I ought not to have left for the Margin a young Gentleman whose success extremely interests me Richard Willing son of The President of the Bank who applies for a Captaincy

in the horse. He has strong pretensions & all things considered will I doubt not be a judicious appointment."

On January 8, 1799, Willing, who was the son of Thomas Willing, president of the Bank of the United States, was appointed a captain in the cavalry (*Executive Journal*, I, 298, 303).

To George Washington [1]

[*Philadelphia, July 28, 1798. Letter not found.*]

1. "List of Letters from General Hamilton to General Washington," Columbia University Libraries.

To George Washington [1]

Philadelphia [and New York] July 29 [–August 1] 1798

My Dear Sir

Your letter of the 14th instant did not reach me 'till after the appointments mentioned in it were made. I see clearly in what has been done a new mark of your confidence, which I value as I ought to do.

With regard to the delicate subject of the relative rank of the Major Generals, it is very natural for me to be partial judge, and it is not very easy for me to speak upon it. If I know myself however, this at least I may say, that were I convinced of injustice being done to oth⟨ers⟩ in my favour, I should not hesitate even to volun⟨teer⟩ a correction of it, as far as my consent could avai⟨l.⟩ But in a case like this, am I not to take the opinion of others as my guide? If I am, the conclusion is that the Gentlemen concerned ought to acquiesce. It is a fact, of which there is a flood of evidence that a great majority of leading fœderal men were of opinion, that in the event of your declining the command of the army, it ought to devolve upon me, and that in case of your acceptance, which every body ardently desired, the place of second in command ought to be

ALS, George Washington Papers, Library of Congress; ADfS, Hamilton Papers, Library of Congress.

1. For an explanation of the contents of this letter, see the introductory note to Washington to H, July 14, 1798.

mine. It is not for me to examine the justness of this opinion. The illusions of self-love might be expected too easily to give it credit with me. But finding it to exist, am I at liberty to seek to postpone myself to others, in whose hands, according to that opinion, the public interests would be less well considered? Such are the reflections which would have determined me to let the business take its course.

My own opinion, at the same time, is that of the two Gentlemen postponed to me, the cause of complaint, if any, applies emphatically to General Knox. His rank in the army was much higher than that either of Pinckney or myself. Pinckney's pretensions on the score of real service are not extensive—those of Knox are far greater. Pinckney has no doubt studied tactics with great care and assiduity. But it is not presumeable that he is as well versed in the tactics of a General as *Knox*.[2] Pinckney's rank at the close of the War was only nominally greater than mine. It was indeed of more antient date. But when in the year 1777 the Regiments of Artillery were multiplied, I had good reason to expect that the command of one of them would have fallen to me had I not changed my situation;[3] and this in all probability would have led further. I am aware at the same time that there were accidental impediments to Pinckney's progress in preferment, but an accurate comparison would I imagine shew that on the score of rank merely the claim of superiority on his part is not strongly marked. As to military *service* I venture to believe that the general understanding of the late army would allow a considerable ballance to me. As to civil services since the war, I am extremely mistaken, if in the minds of Fœderal men there is any comparison between us. The circumstances of the moment, it is true, give him a certain *eclat*, but judicious men reduce the merit to the two points of prudent *forbearance* and the *firmness* not to sacrifice his country by base compliances. In all this, it is very far from my inclination to detract from General Pinckney. I have a sincere regard for him and hold him in high estimation. At the same time,

2. At this point in the draft H wrote and then crossed out: "(and from you Sir I ought not to conceal that General Greene once told me that Pinckney was more of a *martinette* than an efficient officer)."

3. H became Washington's aide-de-camp on March 1, 1777. See "General Orders, Appointing Alexander Hamilton Aide-de-Camp to General Washington," March 1, 1777.

endeavouring to view the matter with all the impartiality which my situation permits, I must conclude that General Pinckney, on a fair estimate of circumstances ought to be well satisfied with the arrangement.

After saying this much, I ⟨will⟩ add that regard to the public interest is ever predominant with me—that if the Gentlemen concerned are dissatisfied & the service likely to suffer by the preference given to me—I stand ready to submit our relative pretensions to an impartial decision and to wave the preference. It shall never be said, with any color of truth, that my ambition or interest has stood in the way of the public good.[4]

Thus, Sir, have I opened my heart to you with as little reserve, as if to myself; willing rather that its weaknesses should appear than that I should be deficient in frankness. I will only add that I do not think it necessary to make public beforehand the ultimate intention I have now disclosed. It is possible the difficulties anticipated may not arise.

But, My Dear Sir, There is a matter of far greater moment than all this which I must do violence to my friendship by stating to you; but of which it is essential you should be apprised. It is that my friend, McHenry,[5] is wholly insufficient for his place, with the additional misfortune of not having himself the least suspicion of the fact! This generally will not surprise you, when you take into view the large scale upon which he is now to act. But you perhaps may not be aware of the whole extent of the insufficiency. It is so great as to leave no probability that the business of the War Department [6] can make any tolerable progress in his hands.[7] This has been long observed; and has been more than once mentioned to the President by members of Congress.[8] He is not insensible, I believe, that the

4. At this point in the draft H wrote and then crossed out: "It is however to be understood as far as my acquiescence may go, that if relative rank is to govern that of Knox as well as that of Pinckney is to be attended to."

5. In the letter in the George Washington Papers, Library of Congress, McHenry's name has been inked out. It has been taken from the draft in the Hamilton Papers, Library of Congress.

6. The words "War Department" have been inked out in the letter in the George Washington Papers, Library of Congress. They have been taken from the draft in the Hamilton Papers, Library of Congress.

7. In the draft at this point H wrote and then crossed out: "That a speedy change is absolutely indispensable."

8. For example, see Robert G. Harper to H, April 27, 1798.

execution of the department does not produce the expected results; but the case is of course delicate and embarrassing.[9]

My real friendship for McHenry [10] concurring with my zeal for the service predisposed me to aid him in all that he could properly throw upon me. And I thought that he would have been glad in the organisation of the army and in the conduct of the recruiting service, to make me useful to him. With this view I came to this City & I previously opened the way, as far as I could with the least decency. But the idea has been thus far very partially embraced and tomorrow or the next day I shall return to New York without much fruit of my journey.[11] I mention this purely to apprise you of the course of things and the probable results. It is to be regretted that the supposition of cooperation between the Secretary at War [12] and the principal military officers will unavoidably throw upon the latter a part of the blame which the ill success of the operations of the war department may be expected to produce. Thus you perceive, Sir, your perplexities are begun.

Most respectfully & affectionately I have the honor to remain Dr Sir   Yr. very obed serv   A Hamilton

P.S. Since writing the above I concluded to write a letter of which the inclosed is a copy.[13] This effort to save a man I value & promote the service has under the circumstances cost something to my delicacy.

Mr. Harpur [14] of the house of Representatives is desirous of being in your family. He is a man of *very considerable* talents & has the temper of a soldier. The shade to his useful qualities is *Vanity*. But I think the good much outweighs the ill. Pardon this liberty in a point so delicate.

9. This sentence was substituted for two sentences in the draft which read: "In my situation I could not if so disposed make any communication to him. The idea that I favoured the choice rather of Pinckney than of himself in the late Election has hitherto been an obstacle to free communication."

10. See note 5.

11. This sentence was substituted for a sentence in the draft which reads: "But there seems to be not the least disposition to embrace the idea—and tomorrow or next day I shall return to New York with no other fruit of the journey than the mere loss of so much time."

12. The words "Secretary at War" have been inked out in the copy of this letter in the George Washington Papers, Library of Congress. The words have been taken from the copy in the Hamilton Papers, Library of Congress.

13. H to McHenry, July 30, 1798.

14. Robert G. Harper of South Carolina.

New York Aug. 1. The above was written at Philadelphia—But a very pressing call to this place added to occupations there prevented my being able to copy & forward it 'till now.

Give me leave to suggest the expediency of your asking of McHenry a statement of all the *Military Supplies* (Cannon Arms &c &c) which are already provided and of the means & measures provided and in execution for augmenting the quantity. This will give you necessary information & prompt to exertion.

The writer of the inclosed letter [15] is a man of respectability. But I could recommend his primary object.

15. Lewis Murarius to H, July 25, 1798. See also Murarius to Washington, July 16, 1798 (ALS, George Washington Papers, Library of Congress); Washington to Murarius, August 9, 1798 (ALS, letterpress copy, George Washington Papers, Library of Congress).

From James McHenry [1]

War Department
30th July 1798

Sir,

You must be fully aware how liable the Executive is to be misled in forming a just estimate of the character of candidates for military appointments, when it must, so often, depend upon recommendations that may have been obtained by the importunity of applicants, from a desire to oblige some friend, or to avoid creating an enemy or, perhaps given in the hope that the army may serve to suppress habits, or eradicate vices, which had resisted all other modes of correction.

You must also be sensible of the great importance of a proper choice of men to command the troops directed to be raised; [2] especially when you consider that they may have to contend with the most successful and enterprising army of the present age.

These reflections have induced me to submit to your remarks and observations the annexed list of Gentlemen, candidates for military promotion, belonging to the States of New York, New Hampshire, Vermont, New Jersey and Pennsylvania.

I entreat you to examine this list with attention, to gain information where you have no personal knowledge of characters and affix, opposite to each candidate's name his pretensions to military promotion, and the rank to which they may intitle him; assured that whatever you may say will be received in confidence.

Should any other Gentlemen occur to you, possessing talents for military service you will please to add them to the list, and transmit the whole to me as soon as possible.

I beg you to excuse me for taking this liberty, and ascribe it to the conviction I have of the inextinguishable love you bear your country, and the desire which must be natural to all good men, attached to our Government to see public officers, whether civil or military, filled with characters the best qualified to discharge their respective duties.

I am, Sir with very great respect your most Ob H Servt

James McHenry

Genl A. Hamilton

ALS, Hamilton Papers, Library of Congress.
1. McHenry sent the letter printed above, with minor variations, to George Washington, Henry Knox, John Brooks, and Jonathan Dayton. See McHenry to Washington, August 25, 1798 (ALS, George Washington Papers, Library of Congress). For other copies of the letter printed above, see McHenry to Brooks, July 31, 1798 (AL, Adams Family Papers, deposited in the Massachusetts Historical Society, Boston); McHenry to Washington, 1798 (copy, George Washington Papers, Library of Congress).
2. This is a reference to "An Act to augment the Army of the United States, and for other purposes" (1 Stat. 604–05 [July 16, 1798]).

To James McHenry [1]

Philad July 30. 1798

My Dear McHenry

Scruples of delicacy have occasionned me to hesitate about offering to you certain ideas which it appears to me on mature reflection cannot be witheld consistently either with friendship to you or regard to the service. They are these—

I observe you plunged in a vast mass of details. I know from experience that it is impossible for any man whatever be his talents or diligence to wade through such a mass without neglecting the most material things and attaching to his operations a feebleness and sloth of execution. It is essential to the success of the Minister of a great Department that he subdivide the objects of his care, distribute them among competent assistants and content himself with a general but vigilant superintendence. This course is particularly necessary when an unforeseen emergency has suddenly accumulated a number of new objects to be provided for and executed.

Hence you will give me leave in all the frankness of friendship to express to you an opinion, that you will do well to call effectually to your aid the Inspector General, and likewise Major General Knox, and to charge them with the management of particular branches of the service. You already contemplate & very properly that the Inspector General shall occupy himself in preparing a system of *tactics* and discipline.[2] But will it not be expedient & natural to charge him also with superintending the Recruiting service? and may he not be made auxiliary in other ways to the business of the Department? General Knox if he can be drawn to the seat of Governt may be rendered extensively useful especially in whatever relates to the Artillery branch.

But you will perceive that ideas of this sort presuppose an abandonment of the plan of suspending the emoluments of these Officers.[3] They cannot afford to give their time and attention without compensation. As to myself, I must be free to confess that this is utterly impossible. I have the less embarrassment in making the declaration because it must be obvious that the plan is against my pecuniary interest. Serious occupation in my military office must involve the relinquishment substantially of my profession and the exchange of from three to four thousand pounds a year, from the law, for the compensation of Inspector General is evidently but a sorry bargain.[4]

Yrs. truly   A H

J McHenry Esq.

ALS, marked "Copy" in H's handwriting, Connecticut Historical Society, Hartford; ALS, marked "Copy" in H's handwriting, Hamilton Papers, Library of Congress; ADfS, Hamilton Papers, Library of Congress; copy, Hamilton Papers, Library of Congress.

1. A copy of this letter in H's handwriting was enclosed in H to George

Washington, July 29–August 1, 1798, and another copy in H's handwriting was enclosed in H to Oliver Wolcott, Jr., August 6, 1798.

There are minor word variations in the two copies in H's handwriting and the draft.

2. See McHenry to H, July 20, 1798.

3. See McHenry to H, July 25, 1798.

4. Section 4 of "An Act to augment the Army of the United States, and for other purposes" provided: "That the major-generals respectively shall be entitled to one hundred and sixty-six dollars monthly pay, with twenty dollars allowance for forage monthly, and for daily subsistence fifteen rations, or money in lieu thereof at the contract price . . ." (1 *Stat.* 604 [July 16, 1798]).

From Uriah Tracy [1]

Litchfield [Connecticut] 30th July 1798

Sir

I meant to have called upon you on my way home from Philada —but was prevented by finding an uncommonly good & speedy passage. I have now troubled you, to call yr. attention to a subject, with which I was not then as well acquainted as I am now. I find Col. Tallmadge [2] will accept of an appointmt in the Army of which I was doubtful untill I saw him. He will draw after him, in this State, more of the Old & worthy Officers than any other man. It is with reluctance Tallmadge consents that I may mention his name, but so much am I convinced, he will be very serviceable in the Army, that I hope you will pardon Me for this importunity. It is well understood that Mr North [3] does not accept his appointment of Adjutant Genl. If you believe Tallmadge qualified for that Office, will you mention him to the Secy at War? I do not hesitate to say he is better qualified for that business than any man I know. I could not ask him to accept an appointment under the rank of a Brigadr. If Tallmadge can have this birth; most of the Valuable Officers who served the last War, will come forward & join the army.

I am Sir with great respect   Yr. Obedt. servt   Uriah Tracy

Genl. Hamilton.

ALS, Hamilton Papers, Library of Congress.

1. Tracy was United States Senator from Connecticut.

2. Benjamin Tallmadge, who was brevetted a lieutenant colonel at the close of the American Revolution, was a merchant and deputy postmaster in Litchfield, Connecticut, and treasurer of the Ohio Company. From 1778 to 1783 he

had engaged in secret service and carried on a confidential correspondence with George Washington.

3. William North.

From Rufus King

[London, July 31, 1798] [1]

Dear Sir

You will believe that I have been much gratified with the late intelligence from home. France has calculated all her plans on our decisions, and the expectation that her friends if not more numerous, would be more active, and possess greater energy, than the friends of our Government—or rather she has believed that our Government like that of every country, that she has succeeded to overturn and enslave, would act with such timidity, and in so qualified a manner, that the Affections and support of the People would be easily withdrawn from, and even turned against, it. If the Govt. continues to speak and act with Decision, the People will become more and more united, and still better inclined to execute its purposes. This opinion should be taken in connection with an observation (the importance of wh. appears to me the greater the oftener I consider it) that I have suggested in more than one of my late letters.[2] The composition of addresses,[3] and the forming of volunteer associations,[4] who will have nothing to do, are for the present well; but they will cease to be novelties, and soon become tiresome, and to be secure you must have some sufficient Object that will interest and employ the Passions of the Nation. The mere defensive system of the enemies of france has been a principal cause of her Success; and if we adopt the Error, we shall be exposed to greater Risques, than by a bold and active System, which exclusive of being the most certain means of Safety, would promise the acquisition of great and lasting Advantages.

The destiny of the new world, and I have a full and firm Persuasion that it will be both happy and glorious, is, in our Hands: we have a Right, and it is our Duty to deliberate, and to act not as secondaries, but as Principals. The object and the occasion are such as we ought not in respect to ourselves or others to suffer to pass unimproved.[5]

I have nothing to observe in reference to the Subject of regret
and complaint, mentioned in your last letters.[6] You will not doubt
that all the means in my Power have been employed to correct the
mischief—they have served only to convince me that it is incor-
rigible—it is an evil too deeply rooted, and too powerfully protected to be cured; and it is something gained to know that it is so—
if we are wise we shall hasten the event that will place the Remedy
in our own Hands.

A frigate returning from malta to Toulon with Despatches and a
general Officer has been captured by an Eng. frigate, and we are
told that Buonaparte had sailed on his Expedition two Days before
the Eng. fleet that pursues him arrived there [7]—if so the french fleet
is in great Danger. Many Persons think that great events depend on
the success, or failure, of Buonaparte's Expedition—all the late accounts from Paris say a new Storm is at hand, but none express a
hope that the changes it may effect will make the condition of
france or of others better. Gerry still hangs about the Directory!! [8]
At Rastadt the Congress continues,[9] and the jealousies between
Austria & Prussia artfully kept alive by the common Enemy, prevents that hearty union without which no successful cooperation
will take place agt. france.

In Ireland the Rebellion is suppressed,[10] and our Government will
I hope have the power and the inclination to exclude those disaffected Characters who will be suffered to seek an asylum among
us.[11] England is more than ever united, and resolves with confidence
in the superiority of her Resources to prosecute the war. There is
no talk of Peace—nor is there any appearances wh wd. lead to an
opinion that new overtures for the Purpose are likely soon to be
made.

On the other hand france is undoubtedly extremely embarrassed
any longer to find the money necessary to maintain her Army, and
carry on the war.

Be so kind as to present my affectionate respects and congratulations to the Governor.[12] I ought to write to him, but I consider a
Letter to him or you as nearly the same.

With great truth and attachment I am   My Dear Sir   yrs &c

31. July. 1798

P.S. We have just heard that Gerry has recd. his Passport, at the close of Talleyrands Letter sending it, he says, tho the Directory as a measure of Precaution has laid an Embargo on all american vessels, "telle est la repugnance du directoire à considerer les Etats unis comme Ennemis, que malgré leurs demonstrations hostiles, il veut attendre qu'il y soit irresistablement forcé par des Hostilités reelles." [13]

ALS, Hamilton Papers, Library of Congress; LC, New-York Historical Society, New York City; copy, New-York Historical Society, New York City.

1. In *JCHW*, VI, 411, this letter is dated July 31, 1799.

2. See, for example, King to H, May 12, June 6, July 7, 1798.

3. For these addresses supporting President John Adams's policy toward France, see William Austin, ed., *A Selection of the Patriotic Addresses, to the President of the United States. Together with the President's Answers. Presented in the Year One Thousand Seven Hundred and Ninety-Eight, and the Twenty-Second of the Independence of America* (Boston: Printed by John Folsom, 1798). See also George Washington to H, May 27, 1798.

4. King is referring to the Corps of Volunteers which was authorized on May 28, 1798, by Section 3 of "An Act authorizing the President of the United States to raise a Provisional Army" (1 *Stat.* 558–61).

5. This is apparently a reference to Francisco de Miranda's plan for British and American cooperation in the liberation of Spain's American possessions. See Miranda to H, April 1, 1797; February 7, April 6–June 7, 1798.

6. See H to King, May 1, June 6, 1798.

7. See King to H, June 6, 1798, notes 1 and 2.

8. See King to H, July 14, 1798, note 5.

9. See King to H, July 7, 1798, note 4.

10. See King to H, June 6, 1798, note 3.

11. King wrote to Timothy Pickering on July 28, 1798: ". . . In Ireland the Rebellion is at an end, a general amnesty, with a few exceptions, will soon be proclaimed; many of the inferior chiefs will be permitted to go into Exile; I have before intimated the Probability of such a measure, and hope the President will have Power to exclude from our Country all such foreigners whose Residence among us would be dangerous" (LS, RG 59, Despatches from United States Ministers to Great Britain, 1791–1906, Vol. 7, January 9–December 22, 1798, National Archives).

12. John Jay had been re-elected governor of New York. See King to H, July 7, 1798, note 8.

13. On July 12, 1798, Elbridge Gerry received his passport from Talleyrand, the French Foreign Minister. In a postscript, dated July 15, to the letter dated July 12, 1798, which enclosed the passport, Talleyrand informed Gerry that the Executive Directory "In the present crisis . . . confines itself to a measure of security and self-preservation, by laying a temporary embargo on American vessels, with a reserve of indemnities if there be occasion for them . . ." (*ASP, Foreign Relations*, II, 220).

From Rufus King

[*London, August 1, 1798.*[1] *Letter not found.*]

1. Letter listed in Rufus King's "Memorandum of Private Letters, &c., dates & persons, from 1796 to Augt 1802," owned by Mr. James G. King, New York City.

To James McHenry [1]

[New York, August 1–2, 1798]

Sir

Inclosed are sundry recommendations for appointments with notes of mine concerning them.[2] I do not recollect whether I have heretofore mentioned to you Mr William Armstrong.[3] This gentleman was a British Officer and served in the British army in America last War. But for a number of years he has been a citizen of this State—having also married in America and being the father of a Family. He would accept a Commission as Major, and I have no doubt would be a real acquisition to our service in this capacity. Whether former circumstances form an objection will depend on the general system which may in this respect be adopted. I am myself of opinion that sooner or later, if hostilities progress, it will be expedient to avail ourselves of men of merit of this description.

Christopher Hutton,[4] formerly an Ajutant of a New York Regiment a very respectable Citizen, would it is believed make a very good Major. Means have been taken indirectly to sound him. He may be provisionally brought into the view of the President.

With respect &c   I have the honor to be &c   Yr. Obedt Sert

The Secy at War

Df, in the handwriting of William LeConte, Hamilton Papers, Library of Congress.
1. William LeConte, who wrote this draft for H, was one of H's law clerks. On April 24, 1801, the New York Supreme Court read "the Certificate of

Alexander Hamilton . . . whereby it appears that William Le Conte has served
a regular Clerkship in his Office, and that he is of good Moral Character," and
on May 2, 1801, LeConte was admitted to practice as an attorney in that court
(MS Minutes of the New York Supreme Court, 1801–1805 [Hall of Records,
New York City]).
  2. This enclosure has not been found.
  3. Armstrong was a New York City merchant.
  4. Hutton was a resident of Rensselaerwyck.

To ——————[1]

[New York, August 3, 1798]

My Dr Sir
  You will oblige me much by letting me know by a brief note in
the margin of each name what you think of the persons in the inclosed list who are known to you (say the list at foot). Yrs. truly
                                                         A Hamilton
                                                         Aug 3. 1798

[E N C L O S U R E] [2]

Robert Heaton Junr.	Captain	
George W. Kirkland	Col. or Major	a good of ⟨ficer⟩
Jno Keating	Colonel	Bad
Francis Drake		Bad
William Scudder	Captain	unknown
Walter B. Vrooman		Bad
Thos U Williams	Adjutant	unknown
Benjamin C. Curtis	Captain	Do
William Cocks	ditto	*good Lieuten⟨ant⟩*
A A. Rutgers	Capt Cavalry	unknow⟨n⟩
Hermanus P. Sch⟨uyler⟩	⟨Captain⟩	⟨good⟩

ALS, Museum of the City of New York.
  1. For background to this letter, see James McHenry to H, July 30, 1798.
  2. D, in the handwriting of William LeConte, Museum of the City of New
York. The comments written after each name are in two unidentified hand-
writings.
  This list is incomplete, for the page is torn at the bottom and part of the
MS is missing.

From John Jay

[*Albany, August 3, 1798.*[1] *Letter not found.*]

1. "List of Letters from Mr. Jay . . ." to H, Columbia University Libraries.

From Theodore Sedgwick [1]

[*Stockbridge, Massachusetts, August 3, 1798.* On August 29, 1798, Hamilton wrote to Sedgwick: "Your letter of the 3. instant came seasonably to hand." *Letter not found.*]

1. Sedgwick, a leading Massachusetts Federalist, was a member of the Massachusetts Assembly in 1780, 1782, 1783, 1787, and 1788 and of the state Senate in 1784 and 1785. From 1785 to 1788 he was a delegate to the Continental Congress. He served in the House of Representatives from 1789 to 1796, when he was elected to the United States Senate to fill the vacancy caused by the resignation of Caleb Strong. He served in that capacity until 1801.

To Uriah Tracy

New York August 3rd 1798

Dear Sir

I received yesterday your letter of the 30th of July.

Had my opinion of Col. Talmage actuated others, he would be now a Brigadier. I estimate highly his military merit. But an appointment to that grade in the first instance will now be difficult if not impracticable. North has not resigned and the probability in my mind is that he will not.

Cannot Col. Talmage be prevailed on to accept a Regiment? I exceedingly wish that he may. He ought to contemplate that hereafter a Regiment will be commanded by a full Colonel and consist of a thousand rank and file. At present the organisation is absurd. It ought to be and no doubt will be changed on the ground as well of œconomy as of military Efficiency.

With great esteem and regard   I remain Dear Sir   Your obedt Servt

U Tracy Esqr

Copy, Hamilton Papers, Library of Congress.

From James McHenry

[*Philadelphia, August 5, 1798.* On this date McHenry wrote to Hamilton "asking for a list of officers from the southern states and stating that Wolcott holds back the order for clothing." [1] *Letter not found.*]

1. Steiner, *James McHenry*, 321.

To Jonathan Dayton

New York August 6th. 1798

My dear Sir.

I received at Philadelphia your letter of the 27th of July [1] the answer to which has been delayed by excessive occupation. You know, I trust, sufficiently my sentiments of you, not to need being told how much pleasure your appointment [2] gave me, and how highly I value the confidence you express in me.

It will probably be unexpected to you to be told that I am not yet in the exercise of the functions of my Military office [3] and that my participation in the preliminary arrangements is only occasional and very limited. Such however is the course of the Plan which has been adopted by the Executive.

But I have notwithstanding had conversations with the Secretary

Copy, in the handwriting of Philip Church, Hamilton Papers, Library of Congress.
1. Letter not found.
2. See George Washington to H, July 14, 1798, note 65.
3. See the introductory note to Washington to H, July 14, 1798.

at War on the points you mention, and to the extent of my opportunity have endeavored to promote a right direction. You no doubt
have before this received a letter from the Secretary on the Subject
of proper Characters for Officers.[4] It seemed to be determined in
his mind to appoint Coll. Aaron Ogden to the command of a Regiment.[5] Every body must consider him as a great acquisition in this
Station. The part of your letter which respects him, announcing
the certainty of his acceptance, was particularly grateful to me. Inclosed you will receive the Instructions for the Recruiting Service [6]

4. See James McHenry to H, July 30, 1798, note 1.
5. Ogden, a native of New Jersey, served throughout the American Revolution, and at the close of the war he held the rank of captain. He studied law
after the war and became a prominent attorney in Elizabethtown, New Jersey.
On January 8, 1799, Ogden was appointed lieutenant colonel of the Eleventh
Regiment of Infantry (*Executive Journal*, I, 299, 303).
6. Although this enclosure has not been found, it was a copy of the War
Department pamphlet entitled *Rules and Regulations Respecting the Recruiting
Service*. Originally prepared by James McHenry for use in recruiting for the
Regular Army (see McHenry to H, March 13, 1799), which had been autho-
rized by "An Act to ascertain and fix the Military Establishment of the United
States" (1 *Stat.* 483–86 [March 30, 1796]), the pamphlet had been printed sometime before July 28, 1798, the date on which H prepared his enclosure to
the letter printed above. On February 4, 1799, McHenry ordered H to submit
any revisions or additions to this pamphlet which H believed were necessary.
On March 10 and 15, 1799, H sent his criticisms to McHenry, and on March
18, 1799, McHenry informed H that, where possible, his revisions had been
incorporated in the new edition then being printed. On March 21, 1799, Mc-
Henry wrote to H that he was sending him ninety copies of the new edition.
Five copies of the printed *Rules and Regulations Respecting the Recruiting
Service* have been found. Four of these copies (in the Boston Athenæum; New
York Public Library; Hamilton Papers, Library of Congress; and the Philip
Lightfoot Papers, Swem Library, College of William and Mary) each contain
thirty-seven articles and are identical in their printed texts, differing only in
how the blanks in Articles II, V, and XXVIII are, or are not, filled in. These
four copies are all signed "James McHenry Secy. of War." The fifth copy is
in the George Washington Papers, Library of Congress. This copy contains
only thirty-five articles, and its printed text is markedly different from that of
the other four copies. In addition, it is not signed by McHenry. In the letter
printed above H is referring to the copy in the George Washington Papers.
Although none of the five copies indicates when each was printed, there is
ample evidence that the copy in the George Washington Papers was issued in
1798 and that the other four copies were issued in March, 1799. On September 12, 1798, McHenry ordered Major Daniel Jackson to take charge of the
recruiting parties in Massachusetts. He enclosed a copy of the *Rules and Regulations Respecting the Recruiting Service* and stated: "As the fifteenth and sixteenth articles of the regulations are intended to have application only upon an
extensive scale of recruiting—they are to be considered in the present state of
things as inapplicable and not intitling the Commandant &c to any extra
allowance other than the actual expence they are at for stationery and postage
of letters to be certified as required" (copy, enclosed in McHenry to John

which were previously prepared by the Secretary at War. I made such remarks upon them as hastily occurred. Examine them carefully and Suggest to me whatever amendments or additions may present themselves to you. You will oblige me by free communication at all times.

Yours truly I remain   Your friend & obedt Servant   A Hamilton

Brigadier General Dayton
E Town

[ENCLOSURE]

Remarks upon the proposed Regulations for the Recruiting Service [7]

[New York, July 28, 1798]

Article III   The penalty on the officer in this article appears

---

Adams September 15, 1798 [ALS, Adams Family Papers, deposited in the Massachusetts Historical Society, Boston]). McHenry's statement obviously refers to a version of the *Rules and Regulations Respecting the Recruiting Service* in which neither Article 15 nor Article 16 deals solely with stationery and postage. This applies only to the copy in the George Washington Papers. In a letter to H on May 9, 1799, McHenry described the physical appearance of the two editions: "The old [1798] are printed in a large type, and without my signature." A comparison of the size of the type in the various copies and the fact that only the copy in the George Washington Papers lacks McHenry's signature reinforces the conclusion that the copy in the George Washington Papers is the 1798 edition and that the other copies are the March, 1799, edition. Finally, H's "Remarks" enclosed in the letter printed above make it clear that he was referring to the copy in the George Washington Papers.

In addition to the printed versions of this document, there is a manuscript in the National Archives which is a partial revision of the 1798 edition. This document, which is dated August 27, 1798, differs from the 1798 edition in the George Washington Papers in that it contains some minor changes in wording and provides for an inspector general who would be in charge of the recruiting service (D, enclosed in McHenry to William Simmons, September 19, 1798 [LS, RG 94, Adjutant General's Office, Miscellaneous Letters Received and Sent by the Secretary of War, 1798–1799, National Archives]).

Charles Evans, ed., *American Bibliography: A Chronological Dictionary of All Books, Pamphlets and Periodical Publications in the United States From the Genesis of Printing in 1739 Down to and Including the Year 1820* (Chicago, 1931), XII, 224, mistakenly lists two different 1798 editions of the printed pamphlet as being located in the Boston Athenæum. Actually only one copy of *Rules and Regulations Respecting the Recruiting Service* is in the Boston Athenæum (Evans No. 34894), and it is a copy of the March, 1799, edition. In addition, Appleton P. C. Griffin, *A Catalogue of the Washington Collection in the Boston Athenaeum* (Boston: The Boston Athenæum, 1897), 211, incorrectly lists the 1799 edition as being the 1798 edition.

7. ADS, Hamilton Papers, Library of Congress.

to be of questionable expediency. It may hurt the service more by discouraging exertion than benefit it by the œconomy which it may promote. It is believed the general responsibility of the Officer ought to be relied upon.[8]

Article IV   The utility of this restriction is doubtful. There are men above the common class in qualification, very desireable as non commissioned officers, who might be willing to engage as such and useful in inducing others to engage, but who would not enter into the service as privates.[9]

Article V   Perhaps it may be well to allow a limited small portion of this bounty to be advanced immediately as earnest money to bind the individual in his own opinion. In raw recruits there are apt to be sudden fluct[u]ations of mind which render it desireable to fix at once their condition—otherwise many a good soldier may be lost. It is easy on this subject to refine too much.[10]

Article VII   It is not recollected what these injunctions are. If they are of a nature to alarm the mind of the recruit concerning the rigour of his future lot the article had better be omitted.[11]

Article XIII   It is not recollected whether the articles of War allow of such Courts Martial. It is taken for

8. The relevant sentence in Article III reads: ". . . Any recruiting officer enlisting a transient person who shall desert before marching from the place of rendezvous shall reimburse out of his pay the loss sustained by such desertion."

9. Article IV reads: "No recruit is to be enlisted or attested in any other capacity than as a private soldier."

10. The portion of Article V to which H is referring reads: ". . . no part of the bounty to which a recruit is entitled, before joining his company or corps, is to be advanced until he shall have been sworn before a magistrate according to the form herein prescribed."

11. Article VII reads: "The injunctions of section 3, article 1, of the articles of War, are to be observed towards each recruit."

The articles of war were originally adopted by the Continental Congress on September 20, 1776 (JCC, V, 788–807). Although they were amended on several occasions, they were continued in force after the adoption of the Constitution under the provisions of "An Act for regulating the Military Establishment of the United States" (1 Stat. 119–21 [April 30, 1790]). In 1794 the articles of war which were then in effect were published as Rules and Articles for the Better Government of the Troops, Raised, or to be raised, and kept in pay, by and at the expence of the United States of America (Philadelphia: Printed granted they do—but it is a point on which there should be no misconception.[12]

Article XXI The utility of this is not obvious. While the sale at an under price may prove a loss to the soldier —he is deprived of cloathing which may be useful when off duty. The French have a practice of allowing particular cloathing for the intervals of duty. Why should his shirts be sold? [13]

Article XXII Will suspicion thus openly & formally manifested be useful? [14]

---

by Steiner and Kammerer, 1794). In this edition, Article 14, which had been amended on May 31, 1786 (*JCC*, XXX, 316-22), was called "Administration of Justice" and was printed as an appendix to the articles of war.

In the articles of war adopted by the Continental Congress on September 20, 1776, Section III, Article 1, reads: "Every non-commissioned officer and soldier, who shall inlist himself in the service of the United States, shall at the time of his so inlisting, or within six days afterwards, have the articles for the government of the forces of the United States read to him, and shall, by the officer who inlisted him, or by the commanding officer of the troop or company into which he was inlisted, be taken before the next justice of the peace, or chief magistrate of any city or town-corporate, not being an officer of the army, or, where recourse cannot be had to the civil magistrate, before the judge-advocate, and, in his presence, shall take the following oath, or affirmation, if conscientiously scrupulous about taking an oath:

"*I swear, or affirm, (as the case may be,) to be true to the United States of America, and to serve them honestly and faithfully against all their enemies or opposers whatsoever; and to observe and obey the orders of the Continental Congress, and the orders of the generals and officers set over me by them.*

"Which justice or magistrate is to give the officer a certificate, signifying that the man inlisted, did take the said oath or affirmation." (*JCC*, V, 790.)

12. Article XIII reads: "Courts Martial to consist of three commissioned officers, may be ordered at the discretion of the officer commanding a regimental circle or a district, for the trial of such offences as shall be committed by the non-commissioned officers and soldiers of the recruiting parties under his command, and which would be cognizable by a regimental court-martial, the said officer to decide upon the sentences of such court-martial and direct the punishments awarded, to be executed, or remitted as he shall think expedient." For the revelant sections on courts-martial, see Articles 3 and 4 of the articles of war as revised by the Continental Congress on May 31, 1786 (*JCC*, XXX, 317).

13. Article XXI reads: "No recruit is to be permitted to keep in his possession, after being sworn, any clothing except that which he may receive from the public. The officer is therefore, to oblige him to dispose of all his private clothing immediately, or to take the keeping of it upon himself, 'til an opportunity offers to sell it for account of the recruit."

14. Article XXII reads: "No recruit is to be allowed to absent himself from his quarters 'till such time as he has proved himself faithful, without a corporal or trusty private to attend him."

Article XXVII   See the Remark on article the IVth.[15]

Article XXIX   There is perhaps too much detail here. It may be
                 sufficient to direct that recruits should be in-
                 structed immediately after being inlisted. The
                 recruiting officers will not be the proper persons
                 to instruct. Officers *stationed* at the different ren-
                 dezvouses must perform this duty.[16]

Article XXX   Quare whether this postponement of the bounty
                 after the soldier joins his corps will not be a dis-
                 couragement to the recruiting service? [17]

Article XXXIII   last clause. Will it not be useful that deserters in
                 one district with descriptions of their persons

15. Article XXVII reads: "No recruiting officer is to promise a recruit that
he shall be a non-commissioned officer; but he is permitted to empower any
recruit to act as a non-commissioned officer to a squad or to the first or second
class herein after mentioned until the recruits shall join the companies or regiments to which they are destined, for the purpose of giving such recruit an
opportunity to shew by his conduct, whether he is qualified for promotion
when it can take place in the course of service."

16. Article XXIX reads: "Every recruiting officer will cause his recruits to
be separated into two classes, and will begin to instruct them immediately after
their being sworn.

"The first class to consist of those recruits who have learned the step and
management of their arms.

"The new recruits to form the second class and be instructed in their positions to march and in the manual exercise at least once every day (Sundays
excepted) by a skilful sergeant, corporal or soldier. Instructions may be given
to the recruits of the second class in quarters, on parade, or under cover in
bad weather, first one by one, then two by two, and lastly in parties. But they
are not to be taught the management of their arms 'till after they have been
habituated to the different positions and steps, commencing by the simplest
and progressively advancing to the most complex.

"When the officer shall judge a recruit qualified to pass to the first class he
will give orders accordingly.

"The exercise of the first class will be directed and superintended by the recruiting officer, and be the same as is usual for the perfecting of a company
for actual service."

17. Article XXX reads: "Each recruiting officer shall transmit monthly to the
officer of the district a duplicate receipt, signed by each recruit, for the bounty
he shall have received within that period. This regulation is to be strictly observed 'till the recruits have joined their respective corps, after which it is
not allowable for the officer to make them any payment on account of their
bounty. It is to be understood also, that no credit will be allowed to a recruiting officer in the settlement of his accounts, which is not substantiated by such
receipts thus transmitted, and that whatever part of the bounty remains due to
a recruit on his union with his corps, or company, shall not be paid by the recruiting officer, but be stated in the first pay-roll after his arrival, and paid to
him at the same time as his pay."

should be reported to the superintending officers in all the other districts, to the end that they also may endeavour to apprehend & secure them? [18]

July 28th.

The foregoing remarks comprise all the ideas which occurred on a cursory perusal of the Regulations. Several of them may not be well founded. Those least relied upon are upon Articles the V & XXI. A H

18. The last paragraph of Article XXXIII reads: "On the desertion of a recruit, besides the usual exertions and means to be employed on such occasions, the recruiting officer will transmit, as soon as possible, a description of the deserter to the field officer of the district, and will cause all descriptions of deserters that may be sent to him, to be entered in a book kept for that purpose, and will use his endeavors to discover and apprehend all deserters."

From James McHenry

[*Philadelphia, August 6, 1798.* On this date McHenry wrote to Hamilton "stating that he is indisposed and feverish, and told of the rejection of the nomination of W. S. Smith as adjutant general,[1] and of the need that the appointments should be hastened." [2] *Letter not found.*]

1. *Executive Journal*, I, 292, 293.
2. Steiner, *James McHenry*, 321.

From Philip Schuyler

Albany August 6th 1798

I am not surprized My Dear Sir that you found much had not been done in the execution of the important Objects, for I have some time since perceived that Mr McHenry had not a mind sufficiently extensive & energetic to embrace & execute all the Objects incident to the war department, and I foresee that you will be under the necessity to direct the principle operations of that department, to avoid those embarrassments which must otherwise inevitably result from incompetency in the Officer, indeed I see no alternative, for I doubt much If a man of adequate abilities can be found properly to discharge the duties of an Office, on which so much depends, even should the present incumbent resign.

Who is to be quarter master General? and who commissary General? If these are not men of business, If they cannot form a system by which to conduct their departments, we shall experience all that confusion and waste which distressed and disgraced us in the revolutionary war. The President's Ideas of the importance of these offices, is probably inadequate and with the best intentions he may be led to improper appointments, unless advice is interposed by those who are capable of affording it, and to whose recommendation he ought to yield.

The principles and spirit from which have emanated the addresses to the president,[1] and that attention which has been paid him would not fail of affording him solid Satisfaction and yet not without some alloy perswaded as I was that every disaster which might befall the first executive would be deeply Injurious to my country in the present critical Juncture. I dreaded lest the injected Gaz should become so highly inflamable as to injure the upper works of the machine, but It is not surprizing that the Old Cock should be elated and Crow audibly for

"The Young disease which must prevail at length

"has grown with his growth, Strengthened with his strength.[2]

A report Via Boston prevails, which advises that Tallerain is dismissed,[3] and that we shall have no war. I hope the latter is unfounded for I feel that war with all its calamities, would be less Injurious to my country, than a peace which might be followed, and probably would be with the reintroduction of the pernicious and destructive principles which prevail in france.

Harmanus P. Schuyler[4] a distant relation of mine, believes he could raise a company of foot, if he was honored with a commission. He has been long and is now a captain of Militia in the Albany regiment—is about thirty five years old, discreet and Sober, he has been a protegé and a pupil of mine in surveying. If ⟨a co⟩mmission can be Obtained for him, It would be pleasing to me. His politics are ⟨-⟩.

God bless you My Dear Sir, take care of your health for without It you cannot sustain the labours you decided to endure. Let my Children share with you in that tender affection which I feel with so much force. Ever Yours &ca.   P Schuyler

Hon: Genl Hamilton

ALS, Hamilton Papers, Library of Congress.
1. See Rufus King to H, July 31, 1798, note 3.
2. Alexander Pope, *Essay on Man*, Epistle II, lines 135 and 136. In the first line of this quotation the word "prevail" should be "subdue."
3. The "report Via Boston" was incorrect, for Talleyrand did not resign as Minister of Foreign Affairs until June 20, 1799.
4. Harmanus P. Schuyler was the great-grandson of Peter Schuyler, who was the brother of Philip Schuyler's grandfather.
On December 31, 1798, John Adams nominated Harmanus P. Schuyler to be a captain of infantry, but on January 14, 1799, Schuyler's name was withdrawn (*Executive Journal*, I, 299, 305). See also the enclosure to H to ———, August 3, 1798.

To Oliver Wolcott, Junior

[New York, August 6, 1798]

My Dear Sir

You are probably apprised that in announcing to the General Officers their appointments, they are told that the emoluments are to be suspended until called into actual service and that as a consequence of this plan they are to remain inactive.[1]

The project suits admirably my private arrangements, by leaving me to pursue in full extent my profession. But I believe it accords neither with the intention of the Individuals who framed the laws nor with the good of the service. It is impossible for McHenry to get through all that is now upon his hands in a manner honorable to himself—satisfactory to the public—or proportioned to the energy of the conjuncture. You will see by the inclosed[2] that I have sacrificed my delicacy to my friendship & public zeal. I have heared nothing in reply. I thought it expedient that You and Colonel Pickering should understand in confidence the situation of things. Without a change of plan they will not go well and the Government and all concerned will be discredited.

Yrs. truly
A Hamilton
Aug 6th. 1798

Shew this to *Pickering*

O Wolcott Esq

ALS, Connecticut Historical Society, Hartford; copy, Hamilton Papers, Library of Congress.
1. See James McHenry to H, July 25, 1798.
2. The enclosure is a copy of H to McHenry, July 30, 1798.

From Joseph Mangin [1]

New York, August 7, 1798. "L'orsque vous m'avez demandé les plans des Batteries de Newyork, J'ai pensé que c'etait pour les remettre au Colonnel Burr; c'est pourquoi Vous avez vu une Lettre à Son adresse, dans Laquelle Je donne quelques explications. J'ai prié un Monsieur que J'ai trouvé dans votre bureau, de Vous engager à ouvrir cette Lettre; ce matin J'ai eu L'honneur de passer Chez vous et comme Je l'ai trouvé cachettée, J'ai pensé qu'il etait de mon devoir de vous en donner L'extrait qui Suit. 'J'ai L'honneur de vous remettre cyJoint les plans des 4 batteries qui S'executent dans ce moment à Newyork, elles Sont Situés Sur la planeire dans Leur raport respectifs et telles qu'elles Sont Sur le terrein; vous remarquerez egalement les plan, coupe et elevations d'un morceau de parapet qui donneront une Idée Juste de la Construction. . . .' "

ALS, Hamilton Papers, Library of Congress.
1. Mangin was an engineer born in France, who in 1795 succeeded his superior, Charles Vincent, as engineer-in-chief of the fortifications of the port and harbor of New York. On May 9, 1796, Mangin was "admitted & sworn a Free Man of . . . [New York] City" and on May 18, 1796, was appointed "a Surveyor of this City" (*Minutes of the Common Council*, II, 236, 238). For Mangin's citizenship, see also the MS Minutes of the New York Supreme Court, January 19–November 5, 1796, under the date of May 7, 1796 (Hall of Records, New York City). On June 18, 1798, Ebenezer Stevens appointed Mangin to work with John Hills and George Flemming to draw up plans for fortifying the harbor of New York. These plans were completed on August 10, and on September 11, 1798, Stevens placed Mangin in charge of completing

the fortification of Fort Jay on Governors Island (Stevens to H, February 28, April 4, 1799). Mangin was also the architect of several important buildings erected in New York City in the late seventeen-nineties and with John Mc-Comb, Jr., won a competition in 1802 for the plans for New York City Hall.

For background to this letter, see Mangin to the Military Committee of New York City, June 18, 1798. See also the introductory note to H to James Mc-Henry, June 1, 1798.

From Loomis and Tillinghast [1]

New York, August 8, 1798. "We have recd. a Letter from the party interested in the Policy of the ship Elizabeth. . . . We have seen Mr. Murray [2] on the . . . subject & he refers us to you & says that if the present evidence be insufficient he will procure what may be wanted if you will Obtain a Commission from the Court for the purpose."

LS, Hamilton Papers, Library of Congress.
1. Libeus Loomis and Stephen Tillinghast were New York City merchants and partners in a countinghouse.
2. This is a reference to the case of *Robert Murray, James V. Murray, George W. Murray, and John R. Wheaton* v *Richard Alsop and George W. Pomeroy.* For information about this case, see Goebel, *Law Practice,* II, 550–51.

To Benjamin Stoddert [1]

[New York, August 8, 1798]

Dear Sir

Capt. *Robert Hamilton,* a first cousin of mine,[2] is desirous of entering into our naval service. He is regularly bred to the sea which he has followed since he was fourteen years old. His opportunities have been of the best, among others that of voyages to the East Indies. I feel myself warranted in recommending him as an able well informed seaman—who adds to this qualification the sentiments of a Gentleman and a good moral character, intelligence and prudence. I verily believe he will be an acquisition to our navy and as I feel myself extremely interested in his success I shall esteem his appointment a personal favour to myself. He is now about Thirty years of age.

Were it not that he is a foreigner, I should think myself warranted to solicit for him the Commission of Captain, but under this disadvantage I ask for him that of first lieutenant. It is his intention to settle in the Country & become naturalized as soon as our laws permit.[3] Being on the point of departing on a journy [4] I can add no more than the repetition of a strong wish that he may be able to obtain this appointment.[5]

With great respect & esteem   I have the honor to be   D Sr   Your Obed ser   A Hamilton

N York Aug 8. 1798

The Secretary of the Marine

ALS, RG 45, Naval Records Collection of the Office of Naval Records and Library, Subject File: Personnel (NN), National Archives; DfS, dated August 7, 1798, Hamilton Papers, Library of Congress.

1. For the draft, which is substantially the same as the letter printed above, see *JCHW*, VI, 336, and *HCLW*, X, 306.

For background to this letter, see H to William Hamilton, May 2, 1797, note 5; Alexander Hamilton to H, August 4, 1797.

2. Robert W. Hamilton was the son of William Hamilton of Scotland, who was the brother of James Hamilton, H's father.

3. See "An Act supplementary to and to amend the act, intituled 'An act to establish an uniform rule of naturalization; and to repeal the act heretofore passed on that subject' " (1 *Stat.* 566–69 [June 18, 1798]).

4. H was about to leave on a trip to Albany, New York, and Salisbury, Connecticut. See Philip Schuyler to H, August 17, 1798.

5. On February 5, 1799, the Senate confirmed the appointment of Robert W. Hamilton as a lieutenant in the Navy, and he was assigned to the frigate *Constitution* (*Executive Journal*, I, 308, 310).

To Elizabeth Hamilton

[*Poughkeepsie, New York, August 9, 1798*. On August 9, 1798, Hamilton wrote to his wife: "I have just written you by the Post." *Letter not found.*]

To Elizabeth Hamilton

Poughkepsie [New York] Aug 9. 1798

My beloved Eliza

I have just written you by the Post.[1] This will be brought by Robert, who from the heat of the sun has become sick & is to be left here to return by the first Vessel. Fearing the same effect upon me (for the heat is excessive) I have resolved to moderate my movements, which will unavoidably occasion delay. But my Betsey will prefer my staying somewhat longer to my seriously risking my health. The vessel passed West Point in the night—so that I shall have to make that visit on my return. Have patience my Angel & love me always as you have done.

God bless you prays always Yr. Affect   A.H

ALS, Hamilton Papers, Library of Congress.
1. Letter not found.

From George Washington [1]

Private   Mount Vernon 9th. Augt. 1798.

My dear Sir,

By the same Post which brought me your favour,[2] began in Philadelphia and ended in New York the 1st. instant, I received a letter from General Knox dated the 29th. Ulto, in answer to one I had written him on the 16th. of that month. In confidence, and as a proof of my frankness & friendship, I send both of them to you, together with my reply of this date; which, after reading be so good as to return to me.[3]

Giving you the perusal of this correspondence, supercedes the necessity of my going into further details on the subject of relative rank; except, if the Commissions are yet to issue, and it be practicable at this time, and consistent also, I should not be indisposed (so far as my agency in the business extends, if that would satisfy General Knox) to make him the Senior of General Pinckney. But as the President is absent [4]—and it might have been the understanding of the Senate that the latter should be first—the propriety of the change, unless it could be effected with the consent of Genl. Pinckney, might at least be questioned. Though, upon more mature reflection I do not see upon what principle he could object. I have a high opinion of General Pinckneys qualifications as an Officer, and his integrity as a Man, but under the impression I am that the Southern Hemisphere will be the grand theatre of action, I shall honestly confess that my primary object in gratifying him, is, that he may come forward with all his force.

Your opinion respecting the unfitness of a certain Gentleman for the Office he holds,[5] accords with mine, and it is to be regretted, *sorely*, at this time, that these opinions are so well founded. I early discovered, after he entered upon the Duties of his Office, that his talents were unequal to great exertions, or deep resources. In truth they were not expected; for the fact is, it was a Hobson's choice. But such is the case, and what is to be done?

I am held in the most profound ignorance of every step that has been taken since he left this place; [6] and but for other letters which I have been obliged to have ready for this days Post, I should have written very seriously to him on several matters highly interesting to me, if I am to be called to the field; and that which you have mentioned among the rest. I am not, at this moment, made acquainted with a single step that is taken to appoint an Officer, or Recruit a man, or where the rendezvouses are. Numberless applications have been made to me, to be recommended for Commissions, and such as appeared to have merit I forwarded, but know nothing of the Result.

Let me hope that you will be able to devote a good deal of your time to the business of recruiting *good* men—and the choice of *good* Officers. It is all important. I will endeavour to impress him with the propriety of requiring your assistance in these matters; and of the necessity of making you the full allowance of Pay &ca. for these Services. By bringing you thus in contact, a thousand other matters will fall in of course. Delicacy—if matters become serious—must yield to expediency. The stake we play for, is too great to be trifled with.

Mr: Harper has been presented to my consideration before, as an Aid de Camp, but as I shall have no use for my Military family until matters are more matured, I am unwilling to be embarrassed by engagements. My Aids, as you well know, *must* be men of business; and *ought* to be Officers of experience. Many, very many *young* Gentlemen of the first families in the Country have offered their services; and all have received one answer, to the above effect. Indeed in the choice of my Aids a variety of considerations must combine—political, geographical &ca. as well as experience.

What is become of Walker? [7] Colo. Heth [8] has offered, and stands well in my estimation. No Foreigner [9] wil be admitted as a member of my family, while I retain my present ideas; nor do I think they ought to be in any situation where they can come at secrets, & betray a trust.

Write me as often as you can, conveniently; believe me to be what I really am

Your sincere & Affecte friend   Go: Washington

Genl. Hamilton

ALS, Hamilton Papers, Library of Congress; ALS, letterpress copy, George Washington Papers, Library of Congress.

1. For an explanation of the contents of this letter, see the introductory note to Washington to H, July 14, 1798.

2. H to Washington, July 29–August 1, 1798.

3. For the correspondence between Washington and Henry Knox, see Washington to H, July 14, 1798, notes 17, 18, and 20.

4. Adams was at his house in Quincy, Massachusetts.

5. James McHenry. See H to Washington, July 29–August 1, 1798.

6. For McHenry's visit to Mount Vernon, see H to Washington, July 8, 1798, note 1; Washington to H, July 14, 1798, note 58; Timothy Pickering to H, July 18, 1798.

7. Benjamin Walker, a native of London, had immigrated to America before the American Revolution and settled in New York City. During the war he served as an aide-de-camp to Baron von Steuben. In 1788 he was appointed commissioner to settle the accounts of the hospital, marine, and clothing departments. He was a director of the Society for Establishing Useful Manufactures, and from 1791 to 1798 he served as naval officer for New York. In May, 1795, Walker became a representative of the Pulteney Associates, which speculated in lands in the Genesee country in western New York. See Walker to H, September 15, 1793. In 1797 he moved to Utica, and in 1801 he was elected to the House of Representatives as a Republican.

8. William Heth, a Richmond Federalist, held the rank of colonel at the close of the American Revolution. He was collector of customs at Bermuda Hundred, Virginia. On July 18, 1798, Washington wrote to Heth: "Your favour of the 13th. Instant, with its enclosures, came duly to hand . . . I thank you . . . for the offer of becoming one of my Aides. . . . and altho' I shall keep you constantly in mind, I do not care to be under any promises . . ." (ALS, letterpress copy, George Washington Papers, Library of Congress).

9. This is a reference to Lewis Murarius who wrote to Washington on July 16, 1798, and asked to join his staff (ALS, George Washington Papers, Library of Congress). See also Murarius to H, July 25, 1798; H to Washington, July 29–August 1, 1798, note 14.

From Oliver Wolcott, Junior

(Private)   Phila. Aug 9. 1798

Dear Sir

Before I recd. your favour of the 6th. instant I had a plain conversation with Mr. McHenry and represented the necessity of having you called into service. It is unnecessary to repeat arguments—you must know their nature. The Presidents permission has been applied for by Mr. McHenry as I presumed [1]—since his illness Colo. Pickering has reinforced the request.[2]

You must my friend come on with the expectation of being *Secy of War in fact*. Mr. McH's good sense, industry & virtues, are of no avail, without a certain address & skill in business which he has not & cannot acquire.

But before you begin inlisting men, let me I pray you request your attention to the state of the public Supplies, & to some plan for conducting the Department. Depend on it, that you can take nothing for granted in respect to the Military Department, and you with the rest of us will be disgraced if measures productive of much expence are adopted, without a previous system & some considerable reforms.

A division has taken place in the Comn for settling the claims of British Creditors under the Treaty from which I apprehend trouble, this is a subject upon which I shall wish to consult you.[3]

I am Dr. Sir   yrs.   Oliv Wolcott.

A Hamilton Esqr

The progress of sickness renders it probable that all the Offices, will be removed to Trenton.[4]

ALS, Hamilton Papers, Library of Congress.
    1. On August 4, 1798, McHenry wrote to John Adams: "I hope, Sir, after considering this summary view, of a part of my business, that you will give me leave to call effectually to my aid the Inspector General, and likewise General Knox; and to charge them with the management of particular branches of the service . . ." (ALS, Adams Family Papers, deposited in the Massachusetts Historical Society, Boston).
    2. Timothy Pickering to Adams, August 8, 1798 (ALS, Adams Family Papers, deposited in the Massachusetts Historical Society, Boston).
    3. Wolcott is referring to the mixed commission authorized by Article 6 of the Jay Treaty. This commission, consisting of five members, was charged with the responsibility of examining the claims of British subjects for pre-Revolutionary debts owed to them by Americans. Two of the commissioners were to be named by the British government, two by the United States, and the fifth was to be mutually agreed upon or chosen by lot. The American nominees were Thomas FitzSimons of Pennsylvania and James Innes of Virginia; their British counterparts were Thomas Macdonald and Henry Pye Rich. The first meeting of the four commissioners was held on May 29, 1797. Because the two sides could not agree on a fifth member, John Guillemard, a British merchant then visiting the United States, was chosen by lot. The substantive work of the commission had to await the filing of complaints and applications, and it was

not until January, 1798, that the commission began to meet regularly and continuously. By the summer of 1798, however, the work of the commission was hampered by dissension between the British and American commissioners over such issues as what constituted "lawful impediments" to the collection of debts and upon whom the burden of proof of solvency or insolvency of the debtor should be placed.

In the Hamilton Papers, Library of Congress, is an undated document in the handwriting of FitzSimons with additions in H's handwriting. This document reads: "What shall be Considered as *Legal Impediments* within the Meaning of the Article.

"[The meaning of the word debts as it respects interest.]

"In Cases where Judgements have been rendered in the Competent Courts.

"Can the Cr. Claim before the Commrs. for injustice (as he may alledge) done to him by the Jury.

"For instance if he Can make it Appear that Interest during the War was disallowed and that the Comrs. decree Interest during the War ought it be allowed upon debts due to British subjects—will the decision of A Jury in such Case take it out of the Power of the Commrs.

"In Cases Where debts have been paid in paper Money to British Crs. or their Agents in States Where paper Money was by Law Made Legal tender & penaltys annexed to the refusal of it—Can the depreciation be now Claimed before the Commrs. notwithstanding the Evidence of the debt was deliverd up or discharges given & Where no other proof of Compulsion is pretended than Merely the Existance of a tender Law [that *law requiring* the surrender of the evidences under penalties.

"What description of persons shall be considered as British subjects:

"On whom does the proof of insolvency &c lie?

"Bond for book debt—can the question of depreciation retrospect?

"Are they obliged to recur to the Courts first where relief can be had?]"

The material within brackets in the document printed above is in H's handwriting.

4. This is a reference to the yellow fever epidemic in Philadelphia. It lasted from early August until late October, 1798. On August 16, 1798, Robert Troup wrote to Rufus King: "Almost all the public offices are moved to Trenton" (King, *The Life and Correspondence of Rufus King*, II, 391).

From James McHenry

War Department
10th Augst 1798

Sir,

I have written to the President [1] lately, mentioning that the more I contemplated the detail of organizing the twelve regiments of Infantry to be raised,[2] the more I perceived the difficulty of effecting it with a dispatch proportioned to the emergency, and the public expectation. That if the course is to be to concenter information in this department from all quarters of the United States then to digest an arrangement, to communicate it to him for his determination, to receive back that determination, and then to transmit the result to the parties, a great, an incalculable portion of time must be consumed. These reflections led me to submit to him the following propositions, (viz) That the arrangement for the four eastern states and vermont be made under his immediate direction commanding the aid, if necessary, of Major General Knox and Brigadier general Brooks [3] who reside within those states. That the arrangements for New York, Pennsylvania, New Jersey Deleware and Maryland be prepared by myself with the aid of the general officers within those states, for his final determination; and that Genl. Washington be requested to take charge of preparing the arrangements including the cavalry, for the states further south with the like aid of the general officers in that quarter subject also to the Presidents eventual determination.

That the distribution of the twelve regiments, for his purpose be four to be raised in the states of New Hampshire, Massachusetts, connecticut, Rhode Island and Vermont, four within the states of New York, New Jersey, Pennsylvania, Deleware, and Maryland and four within the states of Virginia Kentucky, North Carolina, Tennessee, South Carolina and Georgia.

That should difficulties occur in completing the organisation collectively, it may be adviseable to permit it by regiments successively so as to enable me, to put into motion the recruiting service, as fast as possible.[4]

After giving a summary view of the vast mass of details pressing upon my department and the impossibility of getting through them without competent assistance I also proposed to, and requested of the President to give me leave to call effectually to my aid the Inspector General and likewise General Knox, and to charge them with the management of particular branches of the service—stating that I had already taken the liberty to request the Inspector General to occupy himself in preparing, from materials furnished him, a system of Tactics and discipline. That it would be proper also, as incident to the office of Inspector General to charge him with superintending the recruiting service, and make him auxiliary in other ways to the business of this Department.

That Major General Knox, if I were permitted to call him to the seat of government would be extensively useful, especially in whatever relates to the Ordnance.

That this proposition involved an abandonment of the plan for suspending the emoluments of these officers—that they could not afford to give their time and attention to the public without compensation, neither ought it to be expected or required; that if this proposition was assented to it would make me extremely happy, not merely because the aid of these gentlemen would serve to lighten my burdens, or divide my responsibility but because, I am convinced, the subdivisions of the great objects intrusted to me, among such competent assistants, is necessary to facilitate their prompt execution; and cannot but, promote the public service.

As I persuade myself, Sir, the President will accede to the last proposition and afford me the aid of your abilities; allow me to request you will hold yourself in readiness to take your station at Trenton, to which place the public offices will be removed on account of the prevailing epidemic at the seat of Government.

I have been confined for sometime by a bilious complaint but am now recovering, and expect in a few days to return to business as heretofore.

I am, Sir, with great respect   Your most Obd Hb Sevt

James McHenry

Alexr. Hamilton Esqr
Inspector General of the
armies of the United States

LS, Hamilton Papers, Library of Congress.
   1. McHenry to John Adams, August 4, 1798 (ALS, Adams Family Papers, deposited in the Massachusetts Historical Society, Boston).
   2. See "An Act to augment the Army of the United States, and for other purposes" (1 *Stat.* 604–05 [July 16, 1798]).
   3. Henry Knox and John Brooks declined their appointments (Godfrey, "Provisional Army," 133).
   4. For an explanation of the contents of the remainder of this letter, see H to McHenry, July 30, 1798.

From James McHenry [1]

War Department 11th. August 1798.

Sir,

I have just recieved a letter (of which the enclosed is a Copy) dated the 5th. instant from General Knox.

I request you will attentively consider, the subject of it; and favour me with your opinion thereon.

I am Sir, with great respect your obedt. hble servant

James McHenry

Genl. Alexander Hamilton

[ENCLOSURE]

Henry Knox to James McHenry [2]

Boston Augt. 5th. 1798

Sir,

I have recieved your letter dated on the 25th. ultimo,[3] informing me that the President of the United States, by and with the advice and consent of the Senate, had been pleased to appoint me a Major General in the Army.

Impressed as I am with the conviction, that our Country, is about to enter into a Contest in which its existence as an independent nation will be involved, I should promptly have accepted the appointment however inconvenient to my private affairs, had not the following paragraph of your letter peculiarly attracted my notice.

"It may be proper to mention, that the nominations to the Senate for General officers of the established and provisional army were presented on the same day, and in the order, in which they appear in the annexed list, and that in registering them in this department the same order will be observed."

The names placed before mine, on the list are those of Generals Hamilton and Pinckney.

It is to be presumed you are not uninformed of the military precedence I sustained in the late war relatively to those Gentlemen.

General Hamilton was a Captain in the year 1776 in the Corps of Artillery which I commanded; and in the latter part of the same year, I had the rank of Brigadier General.

In 1777 he was appointed an aid de Camp to the Commander in Chief with the incidental rank of Lt Colonel, which was his highest grade. I was established a Major General from November 1781.

The precise state of General Pinckney's rank, is not at present recollected. He was Colonel the greater part of the war, and obtained the rank of Brigadier General, either by actual appointment, or by virtue of the General resolve respecting brevet rank in the year 1783.[4]

It is therefore important previously to my answering affirmatively or negatively, as to an acceptance, that you inform me on these points.

Whether the order of names, as specified in the list, is intended to establish, the priority of rank? Or whether the former relative rank is intended to govern, according to the heretofore established principles, and invariable practice? Those principles determine explicitly That all appointments, made *in the same grade and on the same day*, are to be governed by the former relative rank.

It is far from my intention, to deny the perfect right of the Supreme Executive to direct the precedence of all officers in the same grade in the manner he shall please. In such a case however, it would be essential, that the priority should be decidedly specified. For if such specifications should be wanting, no military tribunal would consider the order of names a sufficient cause, to destroy, or reverse the former relative situations.

If the rules for deciding rank, founded upon resolves, or laws of Congress, under the Confederation[5] and which have since continued to operate, as a part of the Military Code, have been repealed or annulled, it would be acceptable to me, to be informed by you, when, and by what authority the repeal was effected.

If these rules should be suspended or violated in the present instance, for a special purpose, the assertion is ventured, that recourse must be had to them again as the laws, whereby to decide the ranks, between officers of the same grades, who under various circumstances of claims, may be brought into the Army, about to be raised.

Anxiously desirous, of endeavouring to serve my Country and its Government, in a cause, altogether pure and just; I shall ever regret any circumstance which may oppose insurmountable obstacles to the measure, unless upon terms, which would constantly excite sensations of public degradation.

I have the honor to be Sir, with much consideration, Your humble Servant   H Knox

The Honorable
The Secretary of War

LS, Hamilton Papers, Library of Congress.
1. For an explanation of the contents of this letter and its enclosure, see the introductory note to George Washington to H, July 14, 1798.
2. Two copies, Hamilton Papers, Library of Congress.
3. ALS, James McHenry Papers, Library of Congress. This letter is the same as McHenry to H, July 25, 1798.
4. On May 26, 1783, the Continental Congress resolved: "That all promotions hereafter made in the army of the U.S. shall, in consideration of the cessation of Hostilities, be considered only as Honorary, but not entitle those promoted to any additional pay or emoluments on account thereof" (*JCC*, XXIV, 366). See also "Continental Congress Motion on Officers Holding Brevet Commissions," May 26, 1783. On November 3, 1783, Charles Cotesworth Pinckney was promoted to the rank of brigadier by brevet (*JCC*, XXV, 800).
5. For these "rules," see Oliver Wolcott, Jr., to John Adams, September 17, 1798, which is printed in the introductory note to Washington to H, July 14, 1798.

From Marquis de Lafayette [1]

Witmold [2]-Holstein August the 12th 1798

Your Letter of the 28th April Has Safely Come to Hand, My dear Hamilton. The Intelligence Respecting Beaumarchais's affair Has

ALS, Columbia University Libraries. An incomplete version of this letter in French is printed in *Mémoires, Correspondence et Manuscrits du Général Lafayette, Publiés par sa Famille* (Paris, 1838), IV, 425–31.
1. In 1792 the Austrians arrested Lafayette and handed him over to the Prussians. In 1794 the Prussians returned Lafayette to the Austrians, who imprisoned him in the fortress of Olmütz in Moravia. See "Cabinet Meeting. Opinion on Writing to the King of Prussia Concerning the Marquis de Lafayette," January 14, 1794. For the several unsuccessful efforts to arrange Lafayette's escape, see H to William Bradford, June 13, 1795; Bradford to H, July 2, 1795; H to George Washington, January 19, 1796; Washington to H, April 13, May 8, 1796; Justus Erich Bollman to H, April 13, 1796. In October, 1795, Madame de Lafayette and her daughters arrived at Olmütz. On September 19, 1797, at the intercession of the French, Lafayette and his family were released from Olmütz, and they settled temporarily in Holstein. See Washington to H, October 8, 1797; Lafayette to H, December 8, 1797; Bollman to H, June 22, 1798.
2. Lafayette stayed at Wittmold, the country estate in Holstein of Adrienne Catherine de Noailles, comtesse de Tessé, who was the aunt of Lafayette's wife, Marie Adrienne Françoise de Noailles.

Been Communicated to dumas.[3] His Answer I Have Not Yet Received, But Can Anticipate His Hearty Thanks for your Interest in His Behalf. at the Same time that you most Affectionately Speak of the Kind Reception which awaits me in America, you Cannot, Says you, in the present Circumstances urge me to Hasten My Arrival. indeed, my dear friend it Has Already Been in Spite of my Wishes too long differed. as Soon as I Was Set at liberty I Would Have gone on Board, Had not the Health of My wife Made it impossible for Her to Embark, and for me to leave Her. I Have Been thus detained Untill she was able to Move, at Least By Land, and then it Became Necessary for Her and our Daughters to Make a journey to france where to Settle Her Affairs She must Reside for a few months. I have thought of Setting out with Georges [4] to wait for them On American Ground—But Before I dispose of Myself, and Besides the Considerations on Which your Advice is founded, I expect to Hear of the State of Her Health after Such a fatigue, and of Some Private Arrangements in Which My Opinion May be Wanted. May I Receive also the Hope of a Better Understanding Between the United States and the french Government.

You Know that altho My Love to My Native Country is Unabated, the Measures of her Actual Governors Have been Generally Repugnant to My Sentiments, nor Can You Notwithstanding My obligations to Some of them for our Release, Consider me as their personal friend. You also know that the independence, dignity, and Happiness of the United States are to No Man dearer than to Me. it ought therefore to Have Some Weight with You that I Now, as far as total and political distance Enables me to judge, think Myself Warranted to Have a Better Opinion of the disposition of the directory in this Business. in Such a Case, My dear Friend, at a time when No power On the European Continent can Resist them, I think it Consistent With the Honour and interest of the United States to Meet the french Republic Half Way—Nor Can I, ever,

3. Pierre Augustin Caron de Beaumarchais and Mathieu Dumas. This is a reference to the problem of the "lost million." See the introductory note to Oliver Wolcott, Jr., to H, March 29, 1792. See also H to Thomas Jefferson, June 10, 1793; Beaumarchais to H, October 29, 1796; Charles Maurice de Talleyrand-Périgord to H, November 12, 1796; H to Wolcott, November 20, 1797; Dumas to H, December 8, 1797; Lafayette to H, December 8, 1797; H to Lafayette, April 28, 1798.

4. George Washington Motier Lafayette, Lafayette's son.

and still less after Your declarations to me, so far Reflect on Some
of My Best friends as to Suppose that Any thing like party Spirit,
prejudice, or private pique Can at this Momentous period influence
their Conduct. Let America when ill treated Unanimously Assert
Her dignity and Her Rights. But should the Hand of a friend, who
Has no former pretension to Regret or Retrieve, Be Sincerely Held
to Her, I fondly Hope Both Parties in America Will Unite to
forward a Reconciliation With Her first ally.

As You Have Alluded to a difference in our Opinions Respecting
the Revolution of Europe I shall take it up to the time when,
According to what I Had often foretold You, I Engaged in that
Affair, down to the Events of the 10 of August [5] Wherein, not-
wi[th]standing the Offers of a Successful faction it Has Been my
duty to Stand or fall By My Constitutional oath.[6]

in the Passionate Love of Liberty which Brought me to America
there were the proper Requisites to Espouse her democratic System
of Republicanism. While I was impressed with the dangers of
British Roïalty and Aristocraty, and Aknowledged the deficiencies
in our first Experiments, I lately Came to think that the Science of
Social Representative Organisation Had Not Been fairly Explored
and to Wish it Might Have an Universal trial—its first principles,
However, were to me indubitable. This fundamental doctrine of
the Rights of Men and Citizens, Reduced to what I thought Neces-
sary and Sufficient was proclaimed on the 11th july 1789 [7] in an
Assembly Surrounded with Roïal troops, and after the National
Triumph of the 14th,[8] a Civil Militia was Organized as an Over
Match for the Standing Armies of Europe.[9]

5. On August 10, 1792, a French mob attacked the Tuilleries, massacred the
Swiss guards, suspended the authority of the King, and called for elections to a
National Convention. On August 19, after Lafayette's army had refused to
join him in a march to Paris to restore the King, Lafayette deserted to the
Austrians, who arrested him.
6. The Constitution of 1791 required French officials and the King to take a
constitutional oath (Duvergier, Lois, III, 275–91).
7. On July 11, 1789, Lafayette proposed to the National Assembly a declaration of rights (Révolution Française, Moniteur, I, 44).
8. This is a reference to the storming of the Bastille on July 14, 1789.
9. An arrêt of July 13, 1789, had called for the removal of the troops and
the establishment of bourgeois guards (Duvergier, Lois, I, 35). After the fall
of the Bastille, Lafayette was appointed colonel-general of the Paris militia
(Révolution Française, Moniteur, I, 46). He became commandant of the National Guard, which was formally created on August 10, 1789, out of the
bourgeois guards (Duvergier, Lois, I, 42–43).

Soon after Every Antic Abuses, Every Hereditary Claims were no More. Yet an Hereditary presidency of the Executive was given to the Roïal family, and So Consonant it was to the will of the people, the opinion of their Representatives, and the Circumstances of those times, that in June 1791 the Almost Unanimity of our Constituant Assembly, However displeased they were with the fugitive king, Had Rather Replace Him on the Constitutional Throne than to Complete a Republican Government.[10] But the Extent of British prerogative was deemed inadmissible, the more So on Account of our Military Situation, and should Any thing short of that Cease to Be a Monarchy, or Gradually Lead to an elective Governement, this was thought a Lesser inconvenience than if it Had Been Wound Up to an Encroachment on the Rights of National Sovereignty, or the Liberties of the Citizens.[11] On this footing, Amidst popular Storms, factions intrigues, foreign Machinations, a Constitution was freely Made, and freely adopted by the Nation. It was defective indeed, But Not inconsistent with the Natural and Social Rights of Men—it Had within itself Legal and Easy Means of Melioration.[12]

Against that Constitution the old Governements did Coalesce—to them as much as to the jacobins its overthrow was owing. Hitherto Excesses, too often Unpunished, Had Not Been Official. But When Anarchy and Assassination Had Crushed Honest patriotism the

10. On June 20, 1791, Louis XVI and the royal family fled from Paris, but they were arrested at Varennes on the following day. The National Assembly, on June 21, 1791, adopted a "Décret relatif au mode d'exécution des décrets de l'Assemblée nationale," which provided that "provisoirement et jusqu'à ce qu'autrement il soit ordonné, les décrets rendus par elle seront mis à exécution par les ministres actuels, et qu'il est enjoint au ministre de la justice d'y apposer le sceau de l'Etat, sans qu'il soit besoin de la sanction ou de l'acceptation du Roi" (Duvergier, Lois, III, 60). On September 14, 1791, the King agreed to accept the Constitution of 1791, which provided that "La royauté est indivisible, et déleguée héreditairement à la race régnante . . ." and that "Le pouvoir éxecutif suprême réside exclusivement dans la main du Roi" (Duvergier, Lois, III, 281, 286).

11. The prerogative of the British sovereign is "that special pre-eminence which the king (or queen) has over and above all other persons. . . . A term used to denote those rights and capacities which the sovereign enjoys alone . . ." (Henry Campbell Black, Black's Law Dictionary [St. Paul, Minnesota, 1951], 1345). In the French Constitution of 1791 the King was given only a suspensive veto (Duvergier, Lois, III, 285).

12. For the provisions of the Constitution of 1791 that concerned revision of the Constitution, see Duvergier, Lois, III, 291–92.

Views of the Kings were So far Answered as it damped the Spirit of imitation. their Expectations of Victory were Nevertheless disappointed—National Guards disarmed within Even on the frontiers Set upon them and With their irresistible Strength fought for National independence. there was nothing in the three first years But the Empty Name of a Republic Sullied by tyrannical Bloody Madness—to this Succeeded the Republican Constitution which Has Been on the 18th fructidor [13] Avowdly Violated, nor Do I pretend that france Now Enjoys a State of freedom. But altho' our first Constitutional act, and the one of the third Year,[14] Better in Many respects (among which a division in two Houses is a Great Improvement) are By me Reckoned as Secondary objects when Compared to the importance of the fundamental doctrine, I am persuaded that the establishment of liberty in france, and in the other Countries, Can be Better Consolidated on the Basis of Elective Governements than on that of Hereditary presidencies. this Opinion does not arise only from my Republican Inclinations—But also from the Situation of Men and things. it has Been Adopted by Many Monarchical patriots who Confess that if french Roïalty was Now Raised from the dead, there Would Be more trouble to know who is the Man, what powers He is to Ask, or ought to Have, than the thing is worth. and while they start at the Stupid Ambition of the pretension in Rank, at the distortions attending Any other Choice in Aid One of that family; at the desperate Combination it would produce Among the destroïers of the Constitutional throne, why should not I, an old friend to the American principles of Equality Gladly Aknowledge the present impolicy to Reestablish an Hereditary Magistracy which at a former period it Has Been illegal and impolitic to destroy, But for the eternity of which we Had Not By far Vouched? Why should Not I Hope that Elective Governements May, with a Variety of forms But a Similarity of principles, Be So well Combined, and the Better So When the European Revolution is Compleated, as Can Answer the

13. This is a reference to the *coup d'état* of September 4, 1797 (18 Fructidor an V), by which three Republican members of the Directory, Paul François Jean Nicolas Barras, Jean François Reubell, and Louis Marie de La Révellière Lépeaux, defeated their opponents and established a dictatorship. See Rufus King to H, September 9, 1797.

14. For the Constitution of August 22, 1795 (5 Fructidor an III), see Duvergier, *Lois*, VIII, 277–98.

purposes of Social and Virtuous Liberty? is it indispensable to Be free, to Have a King? is this necessity inherent to a large and populous country? Untill proper Experiments Have Been Made, I think it is Not—and while for the undertaking that Experiment an Enormous, useles, and Ever to be lamented price Has Been Paid in Y_2 [15] and the following Years, while Amidst the Revolutionary Excesses of Anarchy and despotism, and Amidst the personal diffidences or disgusts Arising from them, No fair and free trial as Yet, in Europe, Been Given to democratic Representative Republicanism, I firmly Believe, Besides My Own Confessed Inclinations, that the Restoration of that Liberty which Has Been Nipped in the Bud, Her Establishment throughout this Continent Ought Rather to Be Conducted on American principles than After the British fashion —the More So as an House of peers, an UnRepresentative Representation, and an English prerogative with the Additional force of a french Army would Suit No Numerous party in france—and Supposing that System to be Radically altered there would Be as Much Experimental Uncertainty in it, as in a firm well poised Republican Constitution.

But there is too much of politics, my dear Hamilton; Not that I pretend that in Such a Matter friends who Have Made Up their minds Can persuade Each other. My only wish Has Been to Mention the Motives upon Which My Conduct Has Been founded.

I most Heartily thank you for the warm and Affectionate Manner in which You Express the Kind dispositions of America in my Behalf and Your own feelings on the Occasion. I am Sensible of My obligations to that Beloved Country the welfare of which I would Ever Be ready to purchase with the last drop of My Blood. I am Happy and proud of the Sentiments which Her Virtuous and Steady Inhabitants Have uniformly produced to Me— and for My More intimate Companions, particularly for you, my dear Hamilton, I Hope you know that our former friendship Has Been in My Heart Unaltered, and that from the Early times Which

15. This is a reference to events of the year II (1794) during the reign of terror. On March 24, the leading Hébertists, Jacques René Hébert, Pierre Gaspard Chaumette, and Anacharsis Cloots, were executed. The execution of Georges Jacques Danton and his supporters occurred on April 5. The law of June 10 (22 Prairial), entitled "Décret concernant le tribunal révolutionnaire," provided for jurors who could convict people without evidence or testimony (Duvergier, Lois, VII, 232-34).

Have Linked our Brotherly Union to the last Moment of my Life
I shall Ever be

Your affectionate friend   Lafayette

My most affectionate Respects wait on Mrs Hamilton, my dear
friend Mrs Church [16] and your two families. Remember me Most
Gratefully and friendly to Mr Church. My son presents his grateful Respects to you all. My best Compliments to genl Schuyler [17]
and our other friends. My wife Had, on the day of her departure,
the pleasure to Receive a most Agreeable letter from Mrs Church.

16. Angelica Schuyler Church, wife of John B. Church.
17. Philip Schuyler, H's father-in-law.

From James McHenry

Philad. 13 Augt. 1798.

My dear Hamilton.

I have been able to go today to the office, [1] to attend to business,
and prepare to leave this City to-morrow morning with my family.[2]
We shall remain at Trenton till it is safe to return again.

What is to be said to General Knox. I sent you his letter [3] with
a few lines written by my chief clerk [4] while I was indisposed? I
believe I signed it.

My letter to the President left this the 7th instant.[5] I had fortunately prepared it before I was taken ill. I have communicated to
you its contents.

Your affectionately   James McHenry

Mjr. Gen Hamilton

ALS, Hamilton Papers, Library of Congress.
    1. See McHenry to H, August 10, 1798.
    2. See Oliver Wolcott, Jr., to H, August 9, 1798, note 4.
    3. See McHenry to H, August 11, 1798.
    4. John Caldwell.
    5. McHenry's letter to Adams is dated August 4. See McHenry to H, August
10, 1798, and the introductory note to George Washington to H, July 14, 1798.

From Rufus King

Confidential   London Augt. 15. 1798.

Dear Sir,

Tho' I have very great confidence in the integrity of my Agent Mr Low,[1] I Consider it to be a measure of prudence to be attentive to the Security of my property in his hands: I don't know that he is much connected in any of those Speculations which too many of our friends have gone into, nor have I any reason to suppose him engaged in any business of hazard. Still I have concluded to request you to keep an eye upon him and his affairs, and to consider yourself invested with the same powers that I possess for the security of my property in his possession. His Connection with me is a simple agency for the receit of annuities, and the reinvestment of any Capital Sum that may be paid to him by the choice of the Debtor or recovered in cases where the Debt had become insecure and for this Service he receives a fixed Commission.

I think I can safely ask of you this token of friendship, and I shall feel more secure in the belief that you will not be unmindful of this request.

With perfect esteem &c   RK.

Col. Hamilton

Copy, Mr. James G. King, New York City.
   1. For an account of Nicholas Low's responsibilities as King's agent and of H's activities as Low's attorney, see Goebel, *Law Practice*, II, 406, note 65.

From Francisco de Miranda [1]

à Londres ce 17—Aoust 1798.

Voi-ci mon tres cher ami, la Copie d'une Lettre [2] que j'ai eû l'honneur de vous ecrir il y-a quelque tems, et dont j'atends la reponse avec impatience. C'est l'objet le plus grand et le plus glorieux qui s'est jamais presenté dans ce monde ici. Ils nous apartient de gagner l'estime de la posteritée en faisant sont bonheur; ou sa haine en laissant echapper un evenement aussi avantageux, dans le plus favorable moment possible!

Mr. King vous dira tout le reste, et plus.

à Dieu   yours allways   Miranda.

A. Hamilton Esqe.

ALS, Hamilton Papers, Library of Congress.
  1. For background to this letter, see Miranda to H, April 1, 1797; February 7, April 6–June 7, 1798.
  2. Miranda to H, April 6–June 7, 1798.

From Philip Schuyler

Albany August 17th 1798

My Dear Sir

Since you left this, Governor Jay called on me, regretted that he had not had an opportunity of conversing with you, as he wished to have proposed to you to take the Superintendance of the fortifications at NYork should the Legislature make provision for those works. I observed that as Inspector to the Army, It would interfere with the duties of that office; and that the president or General Washington might require your attendance elsewhere; he said he would try to obtain their sanction. If you would undertake the superintendance, that It was not his intention that you should be embarrassed with Accounts, that proper persons would be appointed for that purpose and Such other agents employed to carry your orders into execution, as you should deem necessary. Your taking this business under your direction would doubtless be very beneficial to the community, but the difficulty of erecting efficient works to secure the city & port against a formidable attack from an enemy, unless more money was expended than will probably be appropriated by the Legislature, may put the character of the superintendant in risk, and faults imputed where in fact there were none. This is one point of view In which I have contemplated the Governors intention; on the other hand should the Offer be made you, and you decline, the Citizens may think hard of It. I mention this subject that you may have leisure to reflect on It, before you hear from the Governor.

Much diversity of Opinion prevails as to whom are to be the Candidates for the vacant seat of senator in Congress.[1] I believe It will lay between Mr. James Watson[2] and Mr John Tayler[3] of this city, few If any of our friends like the latter, and many of them are averse to the former, and yet they cannot agree upon another—hence I apprehend that Tayler will prevail. Mr Leonard Gansevoort wanted his brother[5] to be sent, and this has created much confusion in the feoderal part of the Legislature.

I have been less afflicted with pain since you left us than whilst you were here. I hope you did ⟨not⟩ suffer from the heavy rain which ⟨fell⟩ during your Journey to Salsbury,[6] and that you Enjoy better health than when here. We all Join in love to you My Dear Eliza, the Children and all friends.

Please to Inform Mr Church that My Angelica embarks tomorrow. I have had so much writing to do, and am Still so engaged that I cannot write him by this Mail. God bless You My Dear Sir

I am Ever yours   most affectionately   Ph: Schuyler

Honl Genl. Hamilton

ALS, Hamilton Papers, Library of Congress.
1. The vacancy occurred because of the resignation of John Sloss Hobart. For Hobart's resignation and the temporary appointment of William North, see the first letter from John Jay to H, April 19, 1798.
2. James Watson, a native of Woodbury, Connecticut, had acted as agent and subcontractor for the firm of John Carter (John B. Church) and Jeremiah Wadsworth during the American Revolution. In 1786 Watson moved to New York City, where he practiced law, engaged in business, and served as a director of the Bank of the United States and of the Society for Establishing Useful Manufacturers. He represented New York City in the state Assembly in 1791, 1794, and 1795 and served in the New York Senate from 1796 to 1798. On August 17, 1798, he was appointed to the United States Senate to replace North (*Journal of the Senate of the State of New York; At Their Twenty Second Session, Begun and Held at the City of Albany, the Ninth Day of August, 1798* [Albany, n.d.], 18). He served in the Senate until 1800.
3. Tayler, an Albany merchant, had been a member of the New York Provincial Congress in 1776 and 1777 and the New York Assembly from 1777

to 1781 and in 1786 and 1787. When this letter was written, he was a judge of Albany County.

4. Gansevoort, an Albany lawyer, had been a member of the Continental Congress, a delegate to the Annapolis Convention, a member of the New York Provincial Congress in 1775 and 1776, a member of the New York Assembly in 1778 and of the New York Senate from 1791 to 1793 and from 1796 to 1802.

5. Peter Gansevoort, who held the rank of colonel at the end of the American Revolution, was major general of the militia in the western district of New York.

6. No record concerning this trip has been found, but the evidence indicates that H went to Salisbury, Connecticut, to deal with the proposed sale of John B. Church's landholdings. See Jeremiah Wadsworth to H, May 13, 1797; Uriah Tracy to H, March 23, April 6, 1797.

From Rufus King

[*London, August 18, 1798*. King's notation [1] of this letter reads: "Hamilton & President. Letters from Miranda forwarded." [2] *Letter not found.*]

1. Letter listed in Rufus King's "Memorandum of Private Letters, &c., dates & persons, from 1796 to Augt 1802," owned by Mr. James G. King, New York City.

2. Francisco de Miranda to H, August 17, 1798. For Miranda's letter to John Adams, also dated August 17, 1798, see Miranda to H, April 6–June 7, 1798, note 3.

To James McHenry [1]

New York August 19th
1798

Sir

An absence from the City,[2] upon some urgent avocations, prevented my receiving 'till yesterday your letters of the 10th & 11th instant.

I observe the suggestion which you have made to the President, towards calling General Knox and myself into immediate service.

If he shall approve, I stand ready to execute in the best manner I shall be able, whatever business, may be confided to me. But I must earnestly hope, that it will not be attended with the necessity of an immediate change of residence. The nature of my arrangements would render this absolutely ruinous to me; and I trust that I shall not be reduced to such an alternative, unless events portending public danger shall ripen faster than according to present appearances they are likely to do. I do not object to a frequent attendance at the seat of Government, for this can be reconciled with my other engagements till they can be gradually prepared for a total relinquishment and a new position. With this, I am satisfied every desireable end can be obtained, especially when the promptness of communication between this place & the seat of Government is considered. Be assured that none but very imperious motives could induce this hesitation on my part. In accepting the appointment I did not contemplate, ⟨as pr⟩obable, a speedy dislocation of residence.

The tenor of General ⟨K⟩nox's letter transmitted by you [3] and now returne⟨d,⟩ occasions to me no small regret and embarrassment. My esteem and friendship for that Gentleman w⟨ou⟩ld lead me far; but there is a very great difficulty in waving a station, to which I am well convinced I have been called no less by the public voice of the Country than by the acts of the Commander in Chief and of the President and Senate. The intention as to the relative grades of the officers appointed is presumed to be unequivocal. It is believed that the rule to which General Knox refers can have no application to the case of the formation of a new army, at a new epoch—embracing officers not previously in actual service. It was not a permanent provision of law, but a regulation adapted to the peculiar circumstances of the late army, and governing as far as I recollect only in the cases of promotions from lower subsisting grades to higher ones. At the same time, it is very delicate for me to give an opinion in a matter in which I am so personally interested.

I send you back the list of applications which you transmitted to me [4] with remarks and with the addition of names. It has been in my power to do little as to candidates in any state but New York. I have supposed that you have had recourse to better sources of information as to others.

With great respect & esteem   I have the honor to be Sir   Your very Obedient servant   Alexander Hamilton

P.S. The list cannot be copied for this Post. It will go tomorrow.

The Secretary at War

ALS, The Huntington Library, San Marino, California; Df, in the handwriting of Frederick N. Hudson, Hamilton Papers, Library of Congress.

1. For an explanation of the contents of this letter, see the introductory note to George Washington to H, July 14, 1798.

Frederick N. Hudson, who wrote the draft of this letter, was one of H's law clerks. On October 19, 1798, the New York Supreme Court read and filed H's certificate concerning the "Character and Clerkship" of Hudson, and on October 26 he was admitted to practice as an attorney before that court (MS Minutes of the New York Supreme Court, 1797–1800 [Hall of Records, New York City]).

2. H had been in Albany and in Salisbury, Connecticut. See Philip Schuyler to H, August 17, 1798.

3. Henry Knox to McHenry, August 5, 1798, printed as an enclosure to McHenry to H, August 11, 1798.

4. McHenry to H, July 30, 1798.

To James McHenry [1]

(private)   New York August 19. 1798

My Dear Sir

I write you herewith an official letter. Your private one of the 13th is before me. I regret that you have been unwell and rejoice that you are better.

The affair of General Knox perplexes me. I wish him to serve. I am pained to occasion to him pain, for I have truly a warm side for him, and a high value for his merits. But my judgment tells me, and all I consult confirm it, that I cannot reasonably postpone myself in a case in which a preference so important to the public in its *present* and *future* consequences has been given me. In denominating the preference important, I do not intend to judge whether it be well or ill founded. In either case its tendency is important. I am willing to confer—to adjust amicably with the advice of mutual friends, but how can I abandon my pretension?

At foot, My Dear Sir, I transmit you the draft of such a reply as it seems to me proper for you to make to General Knox. It may also be well for you in a private letter to advise him to accept with a reservation of his claim *ad referendum* upon the ground of the rule he quotes [2] and with the understanding that it will not be understood to engage him to continue if the matter be not finally settled according to his claim.[3]

Adieu, My Dear Sir,   Yours very truly,   A Hamilton

[ENCLOSURE]

James McHenry to Henry Knox [4]

Sir

An answer to your letter of the 5th instant has been delayed by some degree of ill health on my part.

The general disposition it marks accords with the patriotic sentiments you have so consistently manifested. It is extremely regretted that any circumstance should induce you to hesitate about the acceptance of an appointment in which it is not to be doubted your services would be eminently useful.

The paragraph of my former letter which you quote explains to you my conception of the relative ranks of the Generals in question as resulting from the order of the nominations & appointments. This conception however cannot affect the claim of either, if there be any subsisting binding rule in our military code which will arrange the priority of Rank between Officers nominated on the same day according to their relative stations in the late army. This will naturally be the subject of some future decision in some proper mode. It is not understood that there has been any formal appeal of the rule to which you allude.

It remains then for you to determine whether you will or not accept the appointment with the reservation of a claim to the benefit of that Rule.

With great &c.

ADfS, Hamilton Papers, Library of Congress; copy, Hamilton Papers, Library of Congress.

1. For an explanation of the contents of this letter, see the introductory note to George Washington to H, July 14, 1798.

2. See Henry Knox to McHenry, August 5, 1798, printed as an enclosure to McHenry to H, August 11, 1798.

For the "rule" to which H is referring, see Oliver Wolcott, Jr., to John Adams, September 17, 1798, which is printed in the introductory note to Washington to H, July 14, 1798.

3. This paragraph is missing in the draft and has been taken from the copy in the Hamilton Papers, Library of Congress.

4. Df, in H's handwriting, Hamilton Papers, Library of Congress; two copies, Hamilton Papers, Library of Congress.

With the exception of two phrases, McHenry sent this letter as H wrote it to Knox on August 22, 1798 (ADf, James McHenry Papers, Library of Congress; copy, Hamilton Papers, Library of Congress).

From Matthew Clarkson [1]

New York, August 20, 1798. "I have reflected maturely on our conversation of yesterday. The result is, as far as I can with propriety I decline, at present, any military appointment. The duty I owe my Family seems to demand this of me, nor can I believe I give too great weight to this consideration when I consider the very small probability there is of any serious military operations taking place in this Country and the real injury I should sustain by being called from my present pursuits. . . ."

ALS, Hamilton Papers, Library of Congress.

1. At the conclusion of the American Revolution, Clarkson held the rank of major, and in 1798 he was a major general of the New York State militia. Clarkson had served as United States marshal for the District of New York in 1791 and 1792, and in February, 1795, he had been appointed commissioner of loans for New York. See H to George Washington, January 14, 1795. Clarkson had been a member of the New York Assembly in 1789 and 1790 and of the state Senate in 1794 and 1795. In 1794 the New York legislature had appointed him to a seven-man committee in charge of the fortification of New York City. On May 21, 1796, Washington nominated Clarkson as the United States commissioner under Article 21 of the treaty signed at San Lorenzo el Real (Pinckney's Treaty) on October 27, 1795, between the United States and Spain, and on May 24, 1796, the Senate confirmed the appointment (*Executive Journal*, I, 210–11).

To George Washington [1]

New York August 20. 1798 [2]

My Dear Sir

A necessary absence from this City [3] prevented the receipt of your letter of the 9th instant till yesterday. It is very grateful to me to discover in each succeeding occurrence a new mark of your friendship towards me. Time will evince that it makes the impression it ought on my mind.

The effect which the course of the late military appointments has produced on General Knox though not very unexpected is very painful to me. I have a respectful sense of his pretensions as an officer—and I have a warm personal regard for him. My embarrassment is not inconsiderable between these sentiments, and what I owe to a reasonable conduct on my own part, both in respect to myself and to the public. It is a fact that a number of the most influential men in our affairs would think that in waving the preference given to me I acted a weak part in a personal view and an unwarrantable one in a public view. And General Knox is much mistaken if he does not believe that this sentiment would emphatically prevail in that Region, to which he supposes his character most interesting. I mean New England.

Yet, My Dear Sir, I can never consent to see you seriously compromitted or embarrassed. I shall chearfully place myself in your disposal, and facilitate any arrangement you may think for the general good. It does not however seem necessary to precipitate any thing. It may be well to see first what part General Pinckney will act when he arrives.

The Secretary at War has sent me a copy of General Knox's letter to him on the subject of his appointment.[4] It does not absolutely decline, but implies the intention to do it, unless a rule of the late army giving, in cases of promotions on the same day, priority according to former relative rank is understood to govern. I have advised a reply of which a copy is inclosed.[5]

The Commissions have issued so that no alteration can be now made as between Generals Knox and Pinckney—if there were not the serious difficulties in the way which you seem to have anticipated.[6]

The Secretary at War has proposed to the President a change of the plan announced in the first instance—which may bring into immediate activity the Inspector General and General Knox.[7] In this case you may depend on the best efforts in my power with a peculiar attention to the objects you mention and you shall be carefully and fully advised of whatever it interests you to know.

Col Walker resides at present in the Western parts of the State.[8] He is occupied in some important agencies for persons abroad which render it doubtful whether he would now accept military employment. He has been written to [9] and will be proposed for the command of a Regiment. *Heth* [10] is in many respects very desireable in the capacity you mention. But you are I presume aware of the impracticability of his temper. With the most respectful & affectionate attachment I have the honor to remain

My Dear General   Yr. very obed servt   A Hamilton

General Washington

The papers sent by you are now returned.[11]

ALS, George Washington Papers, Library of Congress; copy, Hamilton Papers, Library of Congress.
  1. For an explanation of the contents of this letter, see the introductory note to Washington to H, July 14, 1798.
  2. This letter is incorrectly dated August 9, 1798, in Hamilton, *Intimate Life*, 322–23.
  3. H had been in Albany and in Salisbury, Connecticut. See Philip Schuyler to H, August 17, 1798.
  4. Henry Knox to James McHenry, August 5, 1798, printed as an enclosure to McHenry to H, August 11, 1798.
  5. This is a reference to the enclosure to H to McHenry, August 19, 1798.
  6. See Washington to H, August 9, 1798.
  7. See McHenry to H, August 10, 1798.
  8. See Washington to H, August 9, 1798, note 7.
  9. Letter not found.
  10. See Washington to H, August 9, 1798, note 8.
  11. These papers were enclosed in Washington to H, August 9, 1798.

To James McHenry

New York 21st August 1798

Sir

You will herewith receive the list mentioned in mine of yesterday.[1] The names marked with an * are those which engage my preference as last ascertained.

The list comprises the names you sent me [2] and some others

Df, in the handwriting of Frederick N. Hudson and H, Hamilton Papers, Library of Congress.
  1. H to James McHenry, August 19, 1798.
  2. McHenry to H, July 30, 1798.

which have come directly to me. Besides these there are a number of
applications with my Remarks upon them which were put up in a
packet and either transmitted to you or delivered to *Mr. Lewis*[3]
to be delivered to you when I was last at Philadelphia[4] & you will
find in a letter of mine written then some names which I believe
do not appear elsewhere; among them two of the names of *Rens-
selear* nephews of Mrs. Schuyler.[5]

Give me leave now to mention to you *Rensellaer Schuyler* son
of the General[6] who married a daughter of General Tenbroeck[7]
of Albany & who is desirous of being appointed Captain of a Troop
of Horse. This Gentleman has many things in his favour. He is intelligent active and spirited. But I ought not to conceal from you
that he has committed imprudences which have been painful to his
father; whose heart needs consolation with respect to him and
would derive it from his success in his present application. I have
the strongest hope that he would make a very good officer. If the
Captaincy of a Troop is unattainable, I shall be glad to see him
appointed a first Lieutenant in the Corps of Horse.

At foot is a list of names for field Officers. Col. Walker[8] lives
at too great a distance to admit of its being yet known whether he
would accept an appointment or not—but I would advise that
he be appointed to the Command of a Regiment upon speculation
of his acceptance. Col. Platt[9] is every moment expected from
France. Should *Walker* decline, he will be an excellent substitute.

3. William Lewis was a lawyer in Philadelphia.
4. H had been in Philadelphia from July 28 to July 30, 1798. See H to
McHenry, July 28, 30, 1798.
5. See H to McHenry, July 28, 1798.
6. Philip Schuyler was H's father-in-law.
7. Elizabeth (Eliza) Ten Broeck was Abraham Ten Broeck's daughter. Ten
Broeck, a resident of Albany County, was a veteran of the American Revolution and a Federalist. From 1781 to 1794 he was judge of the Court of Common Pleas at Albany.
8. Benjamin Walker. See George Washington to H, August 9, 1798, note 9;
H to Washington, August 20, 1798.
9. Richard Platt had been a major and an aide-de-camp to Alexander Mc-
Dougall during the American Revolution. He was active in the New York
Society of the Cincinnati, William Duer's Scioto Company, the Ohio Company,
and the Society for Establishing Useful Manufactures. As a result of the
panic of 1792, he was ruined financially. See William Lewis to H, June, 1794;
Platt to H, April 26, 1796. In January, 1797, Platt left the United States and
went to France in order to escape from his creditors and, if possible, to raise
funds (Platt to Aaron Burr, January 11, 14, 1797 [ALS New-York Historical
Society, New York City]).

With great respect & Esteem I have The Honor to be sir   your Obedt servant

secretary at War [10]

Benjamin Walker Richard Platt }	Colonels	
Jacob Morton [11]	now Col of Militia never served	
	material of a very good officer eligible as first Major	
William Wilcox [12]	Aide De Camp & Major last war	
Theodosius Fowler [13]	Capt	do
Peter Talman [14]	Capt	

These two probably to be preferred

Several other meritorious Officers have occured but they will not *now* engage.

[ENCLOSURE] [15]

Candidates for Army Appointments from New York

SUBALTERNS

1 Nathaniel Paulding   would prefer Artillery
  West Chester   *Mr. Hale* [16] refers to me speaks   A
                           hyhly

10. The remainder of the letter is in H's handwriting.
11. Morton, a New York City lawyer, served in the state Assembly in 1796 and 1797. In 1797 he became one of the judges in New York City appointed under the provisions of "An Act concerning the recovery of debts and demands to the value of ten pounds, in the city of New-York" (*New York Laws*, 20th Sess., Ch. XX [February 16, 1797]).
12. Wilcocks (Wilcox), a New York City lawyer, was an aide-de-camp to General William Alexander during the American Revolution.
13. Fowler, a veteran of the American Revolution, was a New York City merchant.
14. Talman was a New York City merchant. On February 26, 1795, he was appointed a lieutenant in the Corps of Artillerists and Engineers (*Executive Journal*, I, 173, 174).
15. AD, George Washington Papers, Library of Congress.
In this list of recommendations for Army appointments, those recommended have not been identified. Whenever possible, however, the individuals making the recommendations have been identified.
16. Mordecai Hale, a veteran of the American Revolution, was a resident of Westchester County and a member of the New York Assembly in 1796 and 1797.

	probably a good Lieutantnt AH	
2 John Treat Irving	would prefer Artillery *Mr. Hale*	B
3 Timothy Shalor Albany County	H Glen [17] ⎱ D Brooks [18] ⎰ fit for an appoint- van Allen [19] ⎱ ment Cochran [20] ⎰	Unworthy AH

J V Renss [21]—has been confidential clerk & desires employt.

J Robinson [22] knows him & from his abilities will give satisfaction

5 Cornelius C Van Allen City of NY	formerly attached to French but now renounces recommended by Delegate of NY politics not good otherwise of fair character—expedient to make him lieutenant AH	B

Cortlandt

10 Garret Hallenback ⎱ 11 *Nicholus* Hilton Albany ⎰	Judge Taylor [23] reputed to be a sober clever fellow well lookg would make a good off *Hilton of good reputation* sons of Mechanics *probably tolerable* Ensigns *AH*	Ensign

17. Henry Glen, a resident of Schenectady, New York, was a member of the New York Assembly in 1786 and 1787 and a member of the House of Representatives from 1793 to 1801.

18. David Brooks was a resident of Dutchess County and a Federalist. He served as a member of the New York Assembly in 1794, 1795, and 1796. From November 24, 1795, to June 4, 1807, he was a county judge.

19. John E. Van Allen (Alen), a resident of Rensselaer County, served as a Federalist member of the House of Representatives from 1793 to 1799.

20. James Cochran, who had been H's law clerk, was admitted to practice before the New York Supreme Court on October 20, 1790 (MS Minutes of the New York Supreme Court, 1790 [Hall of Records, New York City]). He was a member of the House of Representatives from 1797 to 1799.

21. Jeremiah Van Rensselaer, a veteran of the American Revolution, was a resident of Rensselaer County and a Republican. He served in the New York Assembly in the 1788–1789 session and was a member of the House of Representatives from 1789 to 1791. In 1798 he became president of the Bank of Albany.

22. John Robinson was an Albany merchant.

23. John Tayler, a resident of Albany County, served in the New York Assembly from 1777 to 1779, from 1780 to 1781, and in 1786 and 1787. From February 7, 1797, to January, 1803, he was a county judge for Albany County.

16 Volckert Douw Jun	*van Vechten* [24]	good Ensign AH
17 Samuel B Berry Saratoga 24 years	van Vechten	Good Ensign AH
21 William Elseworth of City of NY	H Wyncoop [25] (his uncle) recommends him	
22 Zenas Washbone probably Otsego County	Jacob Morris [26]—*useful recruiting officer*	
27 Francis Drake West Chester bred to the *law* Letter well enough	*P. Van Cortlandt* [27] recommends him probably good Ensign AH perhaps Lt AH prefers artillery	
29 Walter B Vrooman Schenectady Albany C	Tenbroeck activity make & Lush [28] appearance fit him Glen for appoin Doctor Stringer [29] handsome well built fellow	will take an Ensign
30 Thomas W William Ontario *Letter well enough*	Sedgwick [30]—has heared a good character of his Uncle which he believes	
37 Richard L Walker unworthy & a Jacobin—AH	recon by E Livingston [31] Wortman [32] good moral character	bad company

24. Abraham Van Vechten, a resident of Albany, had been assistant attorney general for the Fifth District of New York from February, 1796, to February, 1797. In 1798 he was elected to the state Senate as a Federalist.

25. Henry Wynkoop was a resident of Bucks County, Pennsylvania. He served in the Continental Congress from 1783 to 1789 and was a member of the House of Representatives from 1789 to 1791.

26. Jacob Morris, a resident of the town of Butternuts, Otsego County, and a Federalist, had served in the New York Assembly from 1792 to 1793 and from 1795 to 1796. In 1798 he was elected to the state Senate.

27. Philip Van Cortlandt was brevetted a brigadier general at the end of the American Revolution. He was a member of the New York Assembly from 1788 to 1790 and a member of the state Senate from 1791 to 1793. In 1793 he was elected as a Republican to the House of Representatives and served until 1809.

28. Stephen Lush was a member of the New York Assembly from 1792 to 1793.

29. Samuel Stringer was an Albany physician.

30. Theodore Sedgwick.

31. Edward Livingston, the youngest brother of Chancellor Robert R. Livingston, was a Republican member of the House of Representatives from 1795 to 1801.

32. Tunis Wortman was a Republican lawyer in New York City.

> J *Nicholson* [33]—deserving officer

35 John Shipboy
probably *Columbia*
Unworthy—AH

Lt of Artillery
Marines
E Gilbert [34]—well calculated for such a place
J Van Renss—worthy

36 Richard Baldwin
City of New York
Good Ensign   AH

any office
J Williams [35]
Cochran
van Allen

39 John H Carr
N York
young man

Letter good hand writing & otherwise well
A Giles [36]—good character no doubt he will make a good officer
Wm Armstrong—few men better *qualified* Lt in Cavalry

probably good Ensign AH

40 Samuel Hoffman
Columbia

E Livingston   prably good
Ensign
Ph L Hoffman [37]   AH

42 Joseph C Cooper
N York
19 years old
Study of law

Lieutenancy
Cooper [38]—Brother
W North [39] of good character & abilities active & Gentlemanlike
Cochran—

33. John Nicholson, a resident of Philadelphia, speculated heavily in lands and securities. From 1782 to 1794 he was comptroller general of Pennsylvania.

34. Ezekiel Gilbert, a resident of Columbia County and a Federalist, served as a member of the New York Assembly from 1789 to 1790. From 1795 to 1797 he was a member of the House of Representatives.

35. John Williams, a resident of Washington County, was a veteran of the American Revolution. He served in the New York Senate from 1777 to 1778 and from 1782 to 1785 and in the state Assembly in 1781 and 1782. From 1795 to 1799 he was a member of the House of Representatives. Although he was originally a Republican, he frequently voted with the Federalists in Congress.

36. Aquila Giles, a resident of Kings County, served in the New York Assembly from 1788 to 1793. From May, 1792, to March, 1801, he was United States marshal for the District of New York.

37. Philip L. Hoffman, a resident of Columbia County, was a member of the New York Assembly in 1795. From 1791 to 1800 he was surrogate of Columbia County.

38. Thomas Cooper was a New York City lawyer.

39. William North.

44 Andrew Van Woort Albany *23 years old*	*E Benson* [40] unexceptionable character J Law [41] good Ensign perhapt Lieut. *AH.*
45 Alexander McComb Junr. *N York* 17 years old good Ensign AH	letter well written J. Laurance [42] sprightly young man J *Morton* [43] few young men better qualified for Ensigncy spirited & deserving

48 Wm. B. Peters
Niagara
24 years old
Connecticut man for
  2 years past British
Lt. *resigned*
	Rivardi [44] ⎱ Letters to Secy at
	        ⎰ War not pro-
	Bruff [45] ⎰ duced
	Lieutenancy in artillery or in
	infantry or horse

56 R B Batt N York	*Prior* [46] came from Ireland sev- eral years since—honest indus- trious & worthy man Employers speak well of him
57 William Winstanly N York An Englishman 10 years resident	Lively
59 Henry W. Ludlow *N York*	good family education & char- acter good Lieut. AH

40. Egbert Benson, a Federalist from Dutchess County, became New York's first attorney general in 1777. He served in the state Assembly from 1777 to 1781 and again in 1788. He was a member of the Continental Congress from 1784 to 1788, a member of the House of Representatives from 1789 to 1793, and an associate justice of the New York Supreme Court from 1784 to 1801.

41. Joseph Law was a resident of Columbia County, New York.

42. John Laurance, a veteran of the American Revolution, was one of H's closest friends. Laurance was a delegate to the Continental Congress from 1785 to 1787 and served in the New York Senate from 1788 to 1790. He was a member of the House of Representatives from 1789 to 1793. In May, 1794, he accepted the appointment as United States judge for the District of New York, and he held this position until 1796, when he was elected to the United States Senate as the successor to Rufus King. He remained in the Senate until his resignation in August, 1800.

43. John Morton, a New York City merchant, was the publisher of *The* [New York] *Daily Advertiser* from January, 1796, to July 10, 1798.

44. John J. U. Rivardi, a native of France and a resident of Pennsylvania, was a major in the Corps of Artillerists and Engineers.

45. James Bruff, a resident of Maryland and a veteran of the American Revolution, was a captain in the Corps of Artillerists and Engineers.

46. Abner Prior, a resident of New York and a veteran of the American Revolution, was captain in the First Regiment of Infantry.

61 George T Harrison
    N York   good Lieut   AH
    young man
    probably 19

65 James Griffiths   a pretty good young man
    N York

66 Frederick N Hudson
    Columbia now N   good Lt   AH
        York
    now an *Atty at law*

68 Volckert P van Rens-   first Lt.   ⎫   good Lt
        selaer
    Jeremiah H Van   second Lt.   ⎬   good En-
        Rensselaer   ⎭   sign
                                                               AH

74 James Smith   *Capt or Lieut*
    N York   Colonel Smith [47] his brother for
    Atty at law   Capt or Lieut

79 John Knoll   Nath Ogden [48] Active smart
    Rensselaer   man in prime of life

80 Peter van Antwerp   Nath D Ogden   *young man of*
    Coyemans   *sufficient* ability *for subaltern*
    about 20 & a military   *McCarty* [49] *Bryan* [50] ⎫ pledge
        penchant   von Antwerp [51]   ⎬ them-
                              North   ⎭ selves
                                                              for him

                      LIEUTENANTS

81 Thomas Kelly   offers his service as he says on
    Otsego   disinterested ground
    service of his Country
    last war

83 *Alsop Hunt*   Richard B Morris [52]—recom-
    Troy *Rensselaer*   mends
    County   General Hughes [53] *Young*

47. William S. Smith.
48. Nathaniel Ogden, a resident of Albany County, was a member of the New York Assembly from 1796 to 1798.
49. David McCarty, a resident of Albany County, was a member of the New York Assembly in 1792.
50. Lewis Bryan was a resident of Albany County.
51. This is a reference to either Abraham or Daniel J. Van Antwerp, residents of Watervliet in Albany County.
52. Morris, a Federalist who lived in Westchester County, was a former chief justice of the New York Supreme Court. From 1778 to 1780 he was a member of the New York Senate, and from 1792 to 1793 he was supervisor of the revenue for the District of New York.
53. During the American Revolution, Hugh Hughes was assistant quartermaster general of the Army.

	Gentleman of respectable character & family *Valentine Morris* [54]	
85 *Thomas Wooster*	wishes to serve his Country once more	
87 John Terril N York writes a good hand	Lt of Artillery *J Morton—fair character talents for drawing & infantry*	deserving will accept Lty in infan- try *AH*
	Lt	
92 Barent J Goes Kinderhook Columbia	well qualified to fill with honor to the UStates his father said General Schuyler [55] ⎱ *respect-* P Silvester &c [56] ⎰ *able*	
93 Arent S De Peyster *City of New York*	*Low* [57] *recommended him*	
94 John Bentley Stephen Town Rens- selar County served three years as Corporal in a West- ern Regiment & with reputation	School Master in *Stephen Town Van Allen*	
94 William Torry		
102 John Duer N York *16 or 17*		
103 William Moneton sergeant Major last war	General Schuyler promoted him to the command of an armed Vessel afterwards, *Capt in Warners* [58] *Regt. till 1782*	

54. Richard Valentine Morris, a resident of Westchester County, was com-missioned a captain in the United States Navy on June 7, 1798 (*Executive Journal*, I, 280).

55. Philip Schuyler, H's father-in-law.

56. Peter Silvester (Sylvester), a Federalist from Columbia County, served in the New York Assembly in 1788 and in the state Senate from 1796 to 1800. From 1789 to 1793 he was a member of the House of Representatives.

57. Nicholas Low, a Federalist merchant in New York City, was a member of the state Assembly from 1788 to 1789. He had been director of the Bank of New York, the New York branch of the Bank of the United States, and the Society for Establishing Useful Manufactures.

58. During the American Revolution, Seth Warner of New Hampshire held the rank of colonel and commanded his own regiment.

105 Ehanar W Wheeler   *Samuel Cooper* [59] Young Gen-
    Dutchess   tleman of Liberal Education
    34   abilities & address
                                       Unfortunate
    S A *Barker* [60] ⎤   business but
    army   ⎰   of irre-
                             proachable
                             Charm

106 *Thomas Thompson*   *Thomas Cooper*   good family
    Orange County   unexceptionable character
    23 years   good Cornet or Ensign   *AH*
    a lawyer

107 John C Cooper   T Cooper   Young Gentleman
    Dutchess   of good Character   *distant*
    20 years   *relation*
    Student of Physic   probably good Ensign   *AH*

108 Obed Gridley   * *men of good moral character*
    Columbia   Tenbroeck   acquainted with
    soldier   Tactics

109 Jesse Mathews
    Columbia   do   do   do
    orderly sergeans

110 George Shepherd   ⎤   * Mantius & Ten Eyck probably
111 Jacob C Ten Eyck * ⎟   good Ensigns   AH
112 John Willard   ⎟
113 George McKinstry   ⎬   Recommended General for Lts
114 Jacob Mancius *   ⎟
118 Gershon North   ⎟
    New York 24   ⎦

119 Jonathan Thorn *   Witmore [61] *Clergyman* recom-
    Schenectady Albany   mends
                                      ⎤ Thorns appearance
                          Col North ⎰   in his favour
                                        Young
                          North his nephew
                          Joseph C Yates [62]   respectable
                          parentage
                          authority   Glen

59. Cooper was a resident of Fishkill, Dutchess County.
60. Samuel A. Barker of Connecticut held the rank of brigade major at the close of the American Revolution.
61. Whitmore was rector of St. George's Church, the first English church in Albany.
62. Joseph C. Yates was mayor of Schenectady.

123 Paul Stickney Herkimer	Myers [63]	highly recom- mended to him believes they are men of *Integrity* *Governor Jay* [64]— nothing
124 Daniel Stevens Herkimer	Myers	
125 Daniel Potter Herkimer	Myers	
126 Jeremiah Sherwood Herkimer	Myers	

CAPTAINS

127 Rensselaer Schuyler   Governor *Jay   fond of Cavalry*
    Saratoga   G SCHUYLER
    26 *years old*
    now *Cornet &*
        Lieutenant

131 Jeremiah Landon   probably good Capt   AH

135 Frederick A De Zeng   respectable Capt   AH
    Albany

136 Warren Delancey   probably good Capt   AH
    Cap West Chester   formerly British Lt   AH

143 Andrew White   worthy of a Captaincy   AH
    served last war

LTS

149 William Yates   Henry Glen ⎤ recommended
                           Laurance   ⎬ him strongly
                           Gilbert   ⎦ as Lt of Artil-
                                         lery

    Loudon   recomd. by J Morton
    NY

CAPT

    William Moulton 4   no personal ac-
    Rensslaer County   Glen   ⎤ quaintance but   unworthy
    Formerly subaltern   Brooks ⎬ from respectabil-   AH
        & Capt   van Allen⎰ ity of Wendell [65]
                          Cochran ⎦ doubt not his
                                    fitness
    Capt   *Col Wendell*—officer in new
                          levies

63. Michael Myers, a Federalist politician from Herkimer County, was a member of the New York Assembly from 1789 to 1793 and a member of the state Senate from 1794 to 1801.

64. John Jay was governor of New York.

65. John H. Wendell, a veteran of the American Revolution and a resident of Albany County, served in the New York Assembly from 1796 to 1798.

> *Lt Gov Rensselaer* [66]   *vaguely*
> *Moses Vail* [67]   served his
> Country well & is a deserving
> character

6 Gerret J Staats
Albany
Lt. last Revolutionary
   War

Delegation of ⎱ New York ⎰	Bore the repu- tation of a good Officer deserving of a Captaincy	unworthy AH

47 or 48   ☞
strong hale & active
Major of Militia

J V Rensselaer—resigned in *80*
now reduced to a *low ebb*
his character unimpeached—
served with reputation
Lt Gov van Rensselaer—Reputation & experience will insure him an appointment
A van Vechten—Reputation of
a good officer in C. Army

7 Ephran Hunt *Albany* in H Jacksons [68] Regt Officer in late War now *Brigade Major*	No recommendation appears North is referred to he says hes now sergeant at Arms in which Capacity he will do best	unworthy AH

9 G W Kirkland
Herkeman County

G Jay ⎱ v Horne [69] ⎰	speaks favourably but bankrupt	probably good
North & ⎱ Brees [70] ⎰	excellent parade officer faculty of conciliating	Captain AH A

M Meyer—zealous excellent disciplinarian found of Military
employ
North better for military life
than any other
J *Platt* [71]—military genius—

66. Stephen Van Rensselaer, Elizabeth Hamilton's brother-in-law, was a Federalist from Albany County. He was a member of the New York Assembly from 1789 to 1790 and a member of the state Senate from 1791 to 1795. From 1795 to 1801 he was lieutenant governor of New York.

67. Vail, a resident of Rensselaer County, served in the New York Assembly in 1792 and in the state Senate from 1796 to 1801.

68. During the American Revolution, Hunt had been an ensign in Jackson's Additional Continental Regiment commanded by Colonel Henry Jackson of Massachusetts.

69. Abraham Van Horne served in the New York Assembly from 1777 to 1781 and again in 1786. From 1781 to 1784 he was sheriff of Montgomery County.

70. Arthur Breese, a resident of Herkimer County, was a member of the New York Assembly from 1796 to 1797.

71. Jonas Platt represented Herkimer County in the New York Assembly in 1796 and was county clerk from 1791 to 1798. Oneida County was formed

	head & heart fitted for soldier B Walker—thinks he will make an active enterprising Officer	
82 John Bleeker Albany See No. 9 letter	*Lt Govr. man of property & good fellow* personally acquainted & recommend pretty well as Capt AH	B
12 Wilhelmus Rickman Lt in late War	Jacob Cuyler [72] will accept a Lieutenacy fair & honorable service Wendell—behaved as an Officer & Gentl	Unworthy AH
13 Prosper Brown his own letter *very well*	will probably accept an Ensigncy myself—of good appearance & probably would make a good Officer written under signature of C Grindeson Gordon [73] Schoonoven [74] ⎱ speak well N Chipman [75] ⎰	good Subaltern Ensign A
Christopher Backus City of NY	S Jones Jun [76] well calculated for captaincy C Backus [77] fœderal & Gentlemanlike Brother in law of	B

---

from Herkimer County in 1798, and Platt was clerk of the new county from 1798 to 1802. Although an Antifederalist in the early seventeen-nineties, he was elected to the House of Representatives as a Federalist in 1799, and he served in that position until 1801.

72. Cuyler, who had been deputy commissary general of purchases from 1777 to 1782, was an Albany merchant. He was a member of the New York Assembly in the 1777–1778 session.

73. James Gordon, a veteran of the American Revolution and a Federalist, was a resident of Albany County. He was a member of the New York Assembly from 1777 to 1781, in 1784, from 1786 to 1788, and from 1789 to 1790.

74. Peter Schoonhoven was a resident of Dutchess County.

75. Nathaniel Chipman was a member of the Vermont House of Representatives in 1784 and 1785. In 1789 he was appointed chief justice of the Vermont Supreme Court, and from 1791 to 1793 he was United States judge for the District of Vermont. In 1796 he again became chief justice of the Vermont Supreme Court. In 1797 he was elected to the United States Senate to fill the vacancy caused by the resignation of Isaac Tichenor, and he served in that capacity until 1803.

76. Samuel Jones, Jr., was a New York City lawyer and second son of Samuel Jones, the first comptroller of New York State.

77. This is presumably a reference to the Reverend Charles Backus, minister of the Congregational Church in Somers, Connecticut.

G Trumball [78]
probably good Lieutenant   AH

23 John McDougall Laurance City of N York Lawyer	son of Judge Laurance good Lieutenant *AH*	B for Capt A Lt AH
24 Robert Heaton Jun West Chester County	Judge Laurance sensible well informed Young Gentleman —thinks he will do well probably good Captain *AH*	B
28. William Scudder N York 49 Years	*General Cortlandt*—esteemed him a good Officer last War	X AH

CAPTAINS

32 William Coxe City of N York Practice of law now Captain of Mili	North ⎫ Cochran ⎬ tolerably well D McCormick [79] augurs well of his military capacity of good character & abilities J Morton good moral charac- ter & would make a good Of- ficer	Lieuten- ant A AH
33 A A Rutgers New York	prefer Cavalry Judge Lau- Wm Cochran [80] ⎫ rance thinks Livingston ⎬ he would J Laurance ⎭ make an active & useful Officer *G & Kemble* [81]—son in law of Hugh Gane Cochran E Livingston	unworthy AH

78. Jonathan Trumbull was a Federalist from Connecticut. He served in the House of Representatives from 1789 to 1795, when he was elected to the United States Senate. In 1796 he resigned from the Senate to become lieutenant governor of Connecticut, and from 1797 to 1809 he was governor.

79. Daniel McCormick, a New York City merchant, was a close friend of George Clinton. He was a director of the Bank of New York from 1784 to 1799.

80. William Cochran was a New York City resident.

81. Isaac Gouverneur and Peter Kemble were partners in a New York City mercantile firm.

34 Harmanus P Schuyler
   Albany
   28
   about 30 years
   now Capt of *a Com-*
   pany of Militia
   Webster [82]—classical
   education

G Jay—believes he will make a ⎫
   good   ⎪
Ab. Van Vechten—brother in   ⎪
   law—will acquit himself well ⎪ probably
Hale   ⎱   ⎬ good
Schuyler   ⎰   ⎪ Captain
S V Rensselaer—good morals &   ⎪ AH
   education—*will engage for*   ⎪
   him   ⎪   A
Mathematician & Draftsman   ⎪
van Ingen [83]   ⎭
Hale *correct surveyor*—faithful Clerk in the Bank

38 Fitch Hall
   Col

no office
Otis [84] &c from personal knowl-   B
   ege say he will make an ac-
   tive able & brave Officer
probably respectable Captain
   AH

41 Adrian Kissam
   N York
   35
   Atty at law

Hoffman Atty [85] good family   probably
   education & character   good
G *Clarkson* [86]—probably enter- Capt
   prising & good Officer   AH
G *Jay*—fit for the officer   A

17 John White
   Lansingburgh
   now sergeant

Captaincy in corps of Artillery   X
Keating [87]—well worthy of it   AH

49 Rowland Cotton
   probably Cherry
     Valley
   38 years
   served last war with
     reputation
   has had a Captains
     Commission

J White [88] man of handsome ⎫   B
   talents character   ⎬ AH
North says *white* is a man of ⎰ Qr
   respectability

82. This is a reference to Charles R. or George Webster, Albany printers.
83. William Van Ingen, a resident of Schenectady, New York, was Henry Glen's son-in-law.
84. Harrison Gray Otis, a Boston lawyer, was a Federalist member of the House of Representatives from 1797 to 1801.
85. Josiah Ogden Hoffman, a Federalist, was the attorney general of New York from 1795 to 1802.
86. Matthew Clarkson.
87. John Keating, Jr., a resident of Lansingburg, Rensselaer County, New York.
88. Joseph White, a resident of Cherry Valley, was a member of the New York Senate from 1796 to 1799. In 1800 he became judge of Otsego County.

51 Moses Foster
Troy Rensselaer

G Jay   Recommendations merit   B Capt
confidence   Gentlemanlike   A Lt
appearance character well
deserving of Captaincy now
Captain of Militia—ambition
Dole [89] & others
van Allen supprs

52 Abraham Livingston
Albany
Capt in Revolution-
ary War   Qr

G Jay—does not know his character
his uncle Tenbroeck speaks   X
well of him
Lt Gov Renselaer generally
E Gilbert character age & activ-   *AH*
ity—*fit*

53 Jeremiah Haxton
35 years

same—Capt of *Cavalry*

54 Isaac J van Vleck *
25 years
Kinderhook

van Allen—good family fair   C
Van Vleck   character activity
& education
Haxton   fair character

55 John W Patterson   B
His family *Columbia*
about 22
Student of law

probably good Captain   *AH*

60 Caleb Brewster
Capt of Artillery late
war

applies for Captaincy of Artillery

64 Casimer S H Goerck
City of N York

provisional army
asks for Capt of Engineers
in service of Prince of Hesse last
war as Lt of Artillery
now City of surveyor
served

68 Philip Church

recommended by AH   A

71 Micah Hart
Suffolk County
was *Capt in army*
now Cap of Militia &
Magistrate

Silas Wood [90]—merely de-   X
scribes him

72 Moses Blakely
Suffolk County
now Capt of Milia

No recommendation
refers to *J Morton*   X

89. James Dole was sheriff of Rensselaer County from 1798 to 1800.
90. Wood, a resident of Suffolk County, served in the New York Assembly from 1796 to 1798 and again in 1800.

49 Rowland Colton [Cotton] J[Whitman] of handsome talents
  probably Cherry Valley — North says while in a mess
  38 years — of respectability
  served last war with reputation
  has had a captains commission
  G Jay

51 Moses Foster — Recommendations merit confidence
  Troy Renselaer — Gentleman like appearance
    character will & energy of
    captaincy now captain of
    Militia — ambition
      Cole & others
    van Allen suppose

52 Abraham Livingston — G Jay — does not know his
  Albany — character his uncle Tenbrook
  Capt in Revolutionary — speaks well of he
  War — [Maijor] Renselaer genteel
    E Gilbert character age &
      activity — fit

53 Jeremiah [Haxton]
    35 years
54 Isaac J Van Vleck ✱ — same — capt of
    25 years — Cavalry
  Kinderhook —
    van Allen good family fair
  [Vleck] character activity & education — C
    [Haxton] fair character +

55 John W Patterson — probably good Captain
  his family Columbia — [A H]
  about 22 — B
  Student of law —

60 Caleb Brewster — applies for Captaincy of Artillery
  Capt of Artillery
  last War —

64 Casimir S H Goerck — provisional army
  City of N York — applies for Capt of Engineers
    in service of Prince of Hesse Cassel
    as [Lt] of Artillery
    now City of Surveyor
    served

68 Philip Church — recommended by [A H] A
  James [Guff]

71 Micah [Hart] — Silas Wood — merely
  Suffolk County — describes him
  was Capt in army now — X
  Capt of Militia & Magistrate

73 Justus B Smith Otsego or Ontario	Col Smith *brother* recom hardy enterprising Gent	B
75 Robert Heaton *West Chester* *Atty at law*	writes a good hand & *well* speaks of Judge Laurance Col Smith—Young Gentleman of liberal education & good character	B Lt
78 Stephen Haynes Coeyman Columbia or Rensselaer	*Nathaniel D Ogden* firm friends active smart men in prime of life	C
97 Abraham Fowler N York native of West Ches- ter County	General Hughes will do justice to *any Company appt* Col Smith—prudent sensible Gentleman who enjoys the esteem of his acquaintance will acquit himself well	C
101 Thomas Trusdale If William Moulton unworthy AH 103 William Moneton sergeant Major	General Schuyler Sergeant Ma- jor promoted him to the com- mand of an armed Vessel af- terwards Capt in Warners Regt	X
104 *Osborn Parsons* Scipio Onondaga County *served last war*	Phelps [91] Members of Richardson * [92] Assembly Payne [93] man of pro- bity & strict morality & worthy of Capts Com- mission * Gentlemanly behaviour	C
117 Gouverneur Ogden City of New York	Abijah Hammond [94] Young Gentleman of good education Lt & correct principles	A

91. Seth Phelps was judge of Onondaga County from 1794 to 1804.

92. John Richardson of Onondaga County was a member of the New York Assembly from 1798 to 1799.

93. Edward Paine of Onondaga County was a member of the New York Assembly from 1798 to 1799.

94. Hammond, a New York City merchant, had been director of the Society for Establishing Useful Manufactures.

120	William Cummings Herkimer 4 years last war as non Commissioned Officer	Michael Meyers to G Jay } man of good moral character & *respectability* perhaps Ensign		C
121	William Lapping Herkimer	Myers excellent education & friend to Government	Lt	C
122	Asa Way Herkimer	Meyers *highly recommended to him*	C Lt	

☞ ALL THAT FOLLOW LTS

129	Wm. M Thompson	Cornet or Ensign good AH	A
	Wm Neilson	very good Lieutenant AH	A
130	Robert LeRoy Livingston Manor	Lieutenant eligible AH	A
132	William W Wands	Lt good Ensign AH	A
133	Garret De Bow N York	Tolerable Ensign *AH.*	C
134	Joseph Kellogg	good Lieutenant AH	B
137	Nicholas R Kirby	good Ensign perhaps Lt *AH*	B
138	William A Giles New York	good Ensign } rather young } AH	A
140	David Jones	good Lt *AH*	A
141	Philip S. Schuyler	nephew of General Schuyler good Lieutenant *AH*	A
142	William Gilliland	good Lieutenant *AH*	A
144	Samuel Youngs Lt	probably good Lt AH	B
145	Thomas Ustick	good Lt AH	A
146	Philip Cortlandt		

CAPTAINS CONTINUED

73	Justus B Smith	Otsego	
78	Stephen Haynes	Coeyman Columbia or Rensselaer	2
	Jeremiah Landon		1 Qr
121	William Lapping	Herkimer	Meyers
1	Andrew White Lt		1

105 Elhanon W Wheeler		
34	Dutchess	1 - 2
Christopher Backus	NY	1. 2
Robert Heaton Jun	West Ches	1
Moses Foster	Troy	1
Jeremiah Haxton	Kinderhood	1
John Mc.Dougall		
Laurance	NY	1
William Coxe	NY	1 - 2
Rowland Colton	Cherry Valley	3

LT COL & MAJORS

Michael G Houdin formerly *in Hazens* [95] Regiment
Albany worthy man but too old & in-
capt in Massachusetts firm AH
 line
upwards of 60

15 Douw J Fondey will only accept *Majority*
 Saratoga County
 Lt in old army
 Major in *Militia*

Van Vechten	military quali-	
Sam B Bery [96]	fications	well in-
Sidney Bery [97]	Attachment	titled to
Governor Jay	to the	a Cap-
	Governt	taincy
Lt Gov Renselaer		*AH*
Philip Schuyler		

20 Bazaleel Howe WRITES ILL
 City of *New York*
  formerly an Officer not fit *AH*
  in the army
 was in the Western
 army

26 John Keating for a Regiment Un-
 Rensselaer County commands a Company of Artil- worthy
  lery *AH*
  would accept a Majority
  Delegation of NY

150 James Bennet Nathaniel D *Ogden* See letter
 Coyemens 78 & 79
 Lt & Adjutant in late speaks well of him
  war
 Regt. of Militia

95. During the American Revolution, Moses Hazen commanded the Second
Canadian Regiment. After the war he settled in Vermont.
96. Samuel B. Berry was a resident of Albany County.
97. Sidney Berry represented Albany County in the New York Assembly in
1791. In 1791 Saratoga County was formed out of Albany County, and Berry
represented Saratoga County in the Assembly from 1792 to 1793. From 1791
to 1794 he was surrogate of Saratoga County.

William S Smith *New York*	Candidate for a Commission in the 12 Regiments
	Officers remained *two* of Election *hours in silence*
19 Abijah Hammond NY Lt last War	
Benjamin Walker	
William Torrey City of New York Lt. in late army	*no recommendation*
99 William Shepherd Ensign & Adjutant last War now a Commission of Major under Massa	*General Shepherd* [98] (his son) honest faithful would not wish to enter under rank of *field officer*
100 Palmer Kady Lt *last War* Captain in late army now Major of Militia	*General H Livingston* [99] Good Major if one appointed out of his Brigade
115 William Armstrong	
116 Cristopher Hutton	
147 Solomon Van Rens- sealer now eldest Capt of Dragoons	General Schuler prudence so- briety integrity & patriotism Gov Jay strongly recomms
William Wilcox	
Theodosius Fowler	

APPLICANTS WHOSE NAMES WERE TRANSMITTED BY
THE SECRETARY AT WAR

Nathaniel Pauding	Probably a good Lieutenant
John Treat Irving	Unknown
Timothy Shaler	Unworthy
William Moulton	Unworthy
Cornelius C Van Allen	Politics not good otherwise of fair char- acter—expedient on the whole to make him Lieutenant

98. William Shepard (Shepherd), a resident of Westfield, Massachusetts, and a Federalist, was a veteran of the American Revolution. He was a member of the Massachusetts lower house in 1785 and 1786. In 1786 he became major general of the militia for Hampshire County, and in that capacity he successfully defended the Springfield Arsenal against Daniel Shays and Shays's supporters in 1786. From 1797 to 1803 he was a member of the House of Representatives.

99. Henry Beekman Livingston, brother of Chancellor Robert R. Livingston, was a veteran of the American Revolution.

Garret J Staats	Unworthy
Ephraim Hunt	Same
Michael G Howdin	A deserving man but too old and infirm for active military service.
Kirkland	Unknown
Gerret Hellenback ⎱ Nicholas Hilton ⎰	sons of Mechanics probably tolerable Ensigns
Wilhelmus Ryckman	Unworthy
Prosper Brown ⎱ John Cuyler (surgeon) ⎰	Unknown
Dowe J Fonda	* Ensign and Adjutant last war—well intitled to a Captaincy—looks to a Majority
Volkert Dow ⎱ Samuel B Berry ⎰	* good second Lieutenant * The same
Christopher Backus	Brother in law of Governor Trumball— probably a good first Lieutenant
Bezaleel Howe	has been a Major in the army & looks to it again—is believed to be *not fit* for it
William Elsworth ⎱ Zanus Washbone ⎰	Unknown
John M D Laurance	* son of the Senator clever Young Man good Lieutenant
Robert Heaton Junior	* probably good Captain
George W Kirkland	Same
John Keating	Unworthy
Francis Drake	probably good second Lieutenant
Anthony A Rutgers	Unworthy
Harmanus P Schuyler	* propably good Captain
John Shipboy	Unworthy
Richard Baldwin	good Ensign
Richard L Walker	very violent Jacobin and *in*eligible
Fitch Hall	probably respectable Captain
John H Carr	pretty good second Lieutenant
Samuel Hoffman	probably the same
Adrian Kissam	* of good connection & character probably *good Captain*
Joseph C Cooper	* good Ensign
Andrew Van Voort ⎱ Alexander Macombe Jun * ⎰	good Ensigns
John Starns surgeon ⎤ John White ⎟ William B Peters ⎟ Rowland Colton ⎦	Unknown

ADDITIONAL NAMES

Philip Church	* good Captain of Infantry
William Maurice Thompson	good Cornet or Ensign
William Neilson	* of good connection Education & sense good first Lieutenant

John W Patterson	* of good family character & spirit—will make a good Captain
Frederick N Hudson	* a good Lieutenant
Robert LeRoy Livingston	* good lieutenant
Jacob Mantius ⎫ Jacob C Ten Eyck ⎭	* good Ensigns
Jeremiah Landon	probably a good Captain well recommended
William W Wands	good second Lieutenant
Gerret De Bow	Tolerable Ensign
John Duer	* good Ensign
Joseph Kellogg	good Lieutenant
David Leavenworth surgeon	Pretty *Well recommended*
James De Hart	*Not recommendable*
Frederick A De Zeng	formerly in German service married & a Citizen a good Captain of Horse
Warren Delancey	Native but formerly British Lieutenant a good Captain
Jacob C Ten Eyck	good Ensign
John Bleecker	pretty well recommended as Captain
Stephen Haynes	The same
John Terrill	* desirous of Lieutenancy in Artillery & probably worthy of it—would accept Lty of Infantry
Nicholas R Kirby	good second Lieutenant
William A Giles	* good Ensign
John McKenny	good surgeons Mate
David Jones	* good first Lieutenant
Thomas Trisdale	recommended as Capt but not sufficiently known
Philip S Schuyler	* nephew of General Schuyler promising young man worthy of a Lieutenancy
William Gilliland	* good Lieutenant
Andrew White	* served last war—worthy of a Captaincy & to be placed high up
Samuel Youngs	probably good first Lieutenant
Thomas Ustick	* a good first Lieutenant
Henry W Ludlow	* The same
Philip Cortlandt	* good Lieutenant

[ENCLOSURE] [100]

Candidates for *Army* Appointments from *New Hampshire*

SUBALTERNS

1 Timothy Mount- ford Philadelphia		
5 Silvester G Whip- ple *Hampton* 23 years	Livemore [101] Education & good family *Gordon* [102] collegiate educa- tion & has read law eleven mon *Whipple* [103] *Father*—[spright- ly & active]	*respectable*
6 William S Thorne Londonderry Now Philadelphia	Livemore Foster [104] Strong [106] } Inquire of McPherson [105]	

100. D, partially in H's handwriting, George Washington Papers, Library of Congress.

In this list of recommendations for Army appointments, those recommended have not been identified. Wherever possible, however, the individuals making the recommendations have been identified.

Material within brackets in this document is in the handwriting of Charles Cotesworth Pinckney.

101. Samuel Livermore, a resident of Holderness, New Hampshire, was a member of the Continental Congress from 1780 to 1782 and again in 1785. He was chief justice of the New Hampshire Supreme Court from 1782 to 1789. He was elected to the House of Representatives, where he served from 1789 to 1793. From 1793 to 1801 he was a United States Senator.

102. William Gordon, a resident of Hillsborough County, New Hampshire, was a member of the state Senate in 1794 and 1795. From 1797 to 1800 he was a member of the House of Representatives.

103. Joseph Whipple was collector of the state impost from 1785 to 1789 and United States collector of customs at Portsmouth, New Hampshire, from 1789 to 1798.

104. Abiel Foster, a Federalist from Canterbury, New Hampshire, was a delegate to the Continental Congress from 1783 to 1785. From 1791 to 1793 he served in the New Hampshire Senate. Foster was a member of the House of Representatives from 1789 to 1791 and again from 1795 to 1803.

105. A veteran of the American Revolution, William Macpherson had been an aide-de-camp to Benjamin Lincoln and at the end of the war had attained the rank of major. He had been appointed surveyor for the port of Philadelphia on September 11, 1789, inspector of the port on March 8, 1792, and naval officer for the District of Philadelphia on December 30, 1793 (*Executive Journal*, I, 25, 111, 144).

106. Caleb Strong, a Federalist from Northampton, Massachusetts, was a member of the state House of Representatives from 1776 to 1778, the state Senate from 1780 to 1788, and the United States House of Representatives from 1789 to 1796.

8 William Fisher *Exeter* resides in Boston	Gov Gilman [107] & others } good talents & good Education	respectable
13 Daniel M Durell	Carson [108] Foster } young Gentlem good ability character & educa- tion	respectable
15 Moses Sweett Boscaven	Foster *age* talents & activity fit for Lt. or Ensg	Ensign
17 Enoch Bayley Hopkinton Hilsborough	Gordon Foster } good character	[tolerable]
4 [Jacob Weeks 24 yrs old [Greenland]	good school education—some intelligence & fair Character] *Livermore generally*	[respectable]
25 [Daniel Connor Exeter 24 yrs old	Educated in a counting House unexceptionable Character— good Constitution—respecta- ble Lieutt.]	
24 Samuel [Parker [23 yrs old] Exeter	Ingenious genteel young man] —*Gilman* Livemore generally	
26 Thomas Nesmith Londonderry	G Read [109] J McGregor [110] } will discharge with faith- fulness any trust—& do well in such offices as he may be judge capable of	Ensign per- haps
27 James Moore *Bow* 35 years	*Foster* Two selectmen have recom~ to him Ensign Bow for Lt. was good *soldier* in the army	Qr. Ensign

107. John Taylor Gilman, a Federalist from Exeter, New Hampshire, was a member of the Continental Congress in 1782 and 1783. He was elected governor of New Hampshire in 1794 and served until 1805.

108. Either John or William Carson of Hillsborough County, New Hampshire.

109. George Reid had been colonel of the Second New Hampshire Regiment in the American Revolution. In 1785 he was promoted to brigadier general of militia. In 1786 he was appointed justice of the peace for Rockingham County, and in 1791 he became sheriff of the county.

110. James McGregore was a resident of Londonderry, New Hampshire.

27 Stephen Merrill Dover	Livemore see Field Officers 29 by mistake	Qr. Ensign
33 Andrew Simpson Durham	Livemore generally	
34 Arthur Rogers Pembroke	ditto	
35 Israel Bartlet Nottingham	do	
36 Wild Noble *Portsmouth*	do Qr. Master	

CAPTAINS

2 George Turner Portsmouth	Livemore has been recom- mended to him for capt of Fort J. Sheaff [111]—bred to the sea J Pickering [112]	Not strong [Too infirm & old]
7 Toppan Webster	was appointed Lt. of Artillery but on the score of rank declined *Inquire*	[wont do ac- cording to Mr. Gilman's letters suspected of want of probity]
9 Robert Parker Litchfield	*Gordon*—officer in horse Troop good understanding & true spirit—good respectability representative in Legislature Foster—good age & character firm to Gv. &c.	strong
10 Henry Tilton Exeter 30 years	J. Smith [113] well educated likely & genteel—suffered by rapacity of French	very respect- able

111. This is a reference to either James or Jacob Sheafe of Portsmouth, New Hampshire. James Sheafe, a Federalist, was a member of the state Assembly from 1788 to 1790 and the state Senate in 1791, 1793, and 1799. Jacob Sheafe became navel agent at Portsmouth in 1794. See Henry Knox to H, third letter of July 9, 1794: Tench Coxe to H, October 13, 1794.

112. John Pickering of Portsmouth, New Hampshire, was United States judge for the District of New Hampshire.

113. Jeremiah Smith was a member of the New Hampshire Assembly from 1788 to 1791. From 1791 to 1797 he was a Federalist member of the House of Representatives. In 1797 he moved from Peterborough to Exeter, and from 1797 to 1800 he was United States attorney for the District of New Hampshire.

| Major Militia | Wingate [114]   good abilities & educatn |
| | N. Rogers [115]   promising Officer good fœderalist &c. &c. |

[Mr. Gilman will
rank next to
Thompson]

| 11 John Ripley | Cap of Artillery |
| 12 Abel Hutchins Concord | Foster—has commanded a comp of Light infantry   his talents & constitution qualify him for mil: life |

| 16 Nathaniel Green Boscavan Lawyer | A Foster good talents & appear has comd. a troop of horse Livemore generally | respectable 1 - 2 |

[19 J Dunham
Hanover

Collegiate education—good military Talents
adjutant of the Militia—Mr. Freeman [116] recommends—writes well   probably good Captain]

[20 Francis Gardner
Westmoreland

recommended by Lewis Morris [117] as a Man of education, good Character—enterprizing & active, & of sound politics   respectable]

30 Edward D Long Portsmouth	Livemore generally
31 Samuel Wentworth Dover	ditto
32 Moses Durell Dover	*ditto*

114. Paine Wingate, a resident of Stratham, New Hampshire, and a brother-in-law of Timothy Pickering, was a Federalist member of the United States Senate from 1789 to 1793 and a member of the House of Representatives from 1793 to 1795.

115. Nathaniel Rogers, a resident of Newmarket, Rockingham County, was a delegate to the New Hampshire convention which adopted the Constitution in 1788.

116. Jonathan Freeman, a resident of Hanover, New Hampshire, served in the state Assembly from 1787 to 1789 and in the state Senate from 1789 to 1794. He was elected to the House of Representatives as a Federalist and served from 1797 to 1801.

117. Lewis R. Morris, a resident of Springfield, Vermont, and a veteran of the American Revolution, was a member of the Vermont Assembly in 1795 and 1796. As a Federalist, he served in the House of Representatives from 1797 to 1803.

FIELD OFFICERS

3 Ebenezer Thompson Durham	Livemore—has been recomd. to him [fair character & good school education may do for Majr. according to Mr. Gilman]
23 *Nathaniel White* *	*James & Jacob Sheaff* qualified & character very respectable Martin [118]—staunch friend to the Govermt. [good information—great activity. Better calculated for the command of a regt. than Cilley or Adams] * Judge Pickering recommends strongly important member of Legislature *Theop. Parsons* [119] Talents on any line will not disgrace recommendation—first democratic but since determined otherwise very strong
18 Rufus Graves Hanover	[good mathematical, mechanical & military genius—Commission of the Peace & Military Inspector of the Western Division of the State—Mr. Freeman. M.C.—respectable as teacher of the Mathematics]
[21 Bradbury Cilley	Marshall of N.H. Possesses more than hereditary talents [120] for a field appointment—intrepidity of Spirit will accept a majority]
[Samuel Adams 38 years old	aid de Camp to Genl: Sullivan [121] when governor—a

118. Thomas Martin was appointed surveyor of the District and port of Portsmouth on August 3, 1789, inspector of the port of Portsmouth on March 8, 1792, and collector for the District of Portsmouth on July 2, 1798 (*Executive Journal*, I, 9, 13, 103, 111, 283).

119. Parsons, a lawyer, was a delegate to the Massachusetts Ratifying Convention in 1788. He served in the state legislature from 1787 to 1791 and again in 1802.

120. This is a reference to Joseph Cilley of New Hampshire who was an officer in the Army during the American Revolution, retiring in 1781 as colonel in the First New Hampshire Regiment.

121. After a distinguished and colorful career in the Army during the American Revolution, John Sullivan served as attorney general of New

Merchant—fair candidate for
field appointment
* Adams & Cilley in talents before Thompson
Adams not preferable to Cilley
in any thing else but in having war service]

[N Gilman

will not relinquish his civil appointment—not decisive]
Gov Gilman—his father killed
at Saratoga
was Lieutenant in the army—
well qualified for command
of a Regiment

28 Daniel Fisher
New Port
N H
55

Fisher Ames [122]—active & popular Militia officer—spirited
on different occasions—farm-
er rather better instructed
than common—very active
still

29 Stephen Merrill

Livemore of respectable family served in army last war
as a sergeant desirous of be-   *Qr. Ensign*
ing in Artillery recomd as
subaltern

[E N C L O S U R E] [123]

Candidates for Army Appointments *from* Vermont

SUBALTERNS

5 Marmaduke Wait
Windsor
☞ 25 year

Payne [124] Young Gentleman
heretofore recomd by *Morris*   *pretty good*
& himself   2

Hampshire from 1782 to 1786, speaker of the state Assembly in 1785, and governor of New Hampshire in 1786, 1787, and 1789. In 1789 he was appointed
United States judge for the District of New Hampshire, a position he held
until his death in 1795.

122. Ames, a Federalist from Dedham, Massachusetts, was a member of the
House of Representatives from 1789 to 1797.

123. AD, George Washington Papers, Library of Congress.

In this list of recommendations for Army appointments, those recommended
have not been identified. Wherever possible, however, the individuals making
the recommendations have been identified.

124. Elijah Paine, a Federalist, was a member of the Vermont Assembly
from 1787 to 1790, judge of the Vermont Supreme Court from 1791 to 1793,
and a member of the United States Senate from 1795 to 1801.

Morris [125]—education common
morals   good active enterprising

CADET

9 John H Brownson   Father Brigadier General [126]   Nothing
                         Lyon [127]

ENSIGN

14 Daniel Baker   *Tichenor* [128] Young Gentleman   well
    ☞ Arlington   of Education & fair character   enough
                                                               1

LT. OR ENSN

17 Ephran Whitney   *Morris* Young Gentleman of
    ☞ 22   good con sprightly fair   Respectable
    young man good   character & well informed
    morals   enterprise & active
    <–> in education
    Himself

19 Samuel Parmele

20 Charles Hyde   *Tichenor* late an Ensign in the   *Not Strong*
                         ar obtained an Office in the
                         army

23 Jesse Lull   Chipman little personal ac-
    Rutland   quaintance but from good in-
    28 years   formation can recommend   pretty re-
    ☞   Buck [129] discreet conduct &   spectably
                         martial deport: suitable   *2*
                         Morris good education—Con-
                         fidence in his Recommenda-
                         tions

125. Lewis R. Morris.
126. Gideon Brownson served throughout the American Revolution, first
as a captain of the Green Mountain Boys and then as a captain in Warner's
Additional Continental Regiment. He was wounded at Bennington and again
at Lake George.
127. Matthew Lyon, a resident of Fair Haven, Vermont, and a veteran of
the American Revolution, was a Republican. He served in the state Assembly
from 1783 to 1786, in 1788, from 1790 to 1791, and from 1793 to 1796. From
1797 to 1801 he was a member of the House of Representatives.
128. Isaac Tichenor, a Federalist from Bennington, Vermont, served in the
state Assembly from 1781 to 1784. In 1796 he became a United States Senator,
but he resigned from the Senate in 1797 when he was elected governor of
Vermont.
129. Daniel Buck of Norwich, Vermont, served in the Vermont Assembly
in 1793 and 1794 and was a Federalist member of the House of Representatives
from 1795 to 1797.

O Gallop [130] acquiremt. in
military discipline

S Jacob [131]—respected in his
acquaintan good English education easy circumstances

25 Alexander A Peters N Chipman slight acquain-
   Rutland   tance good education & abil- *Respectable*
   letter inflated   ities—good scholar & enter-
   35 year   prising
                      Tichenor Lt or surgeon

26 John H Palmer Ensign
   Guilford   engaged in study of law
   20 years   could raise men   *Inquire*
                  No recommendation
                  his letter very well

CAPTAINS

1 Zenas Meigs Bradley   *failed in Trade*   Not strong
  27 years old   Dd Fay [132] ⎱ respectable
                     Atty General ⎰ young Gentle.
                     modesty   ⎰ *respectable fam-* *wont do*
                                    ily
                     not his fault ⎱ well qualified
                     N Chipman   ⎰ for Capt of
                                    Marine Corps

2 James Elliot   Acknowleges himself heretofore
  Brattleborough   Antifœderal but now well
  discharged sergeant disposed was Non Com Offi- *wont do*
  25 or 30   cer in 2 Sub legion—now
                     studying law
                     Lyon support him

4 William Woodward   *Payne* heretofore recom∼ him
  Castleton Rutland as Capt of Artillery would ac- Respectable
                     cept Capt of Infantry wor-
                     thy of appointment
  Does not appear on Chipman—service whole of last
  list   orderly ser- War firm friend to his Coun-
  geant last war   try would do honor to a high-
  42 years old   er grade intelligence integ-
  good   rity
                     Morris—good education morals
                     Gentlmy deserves Consid

130. As a presidential elector from Vermont in 1796, Oliver Gallup voted
for John Adams.

131. Stephen Jacobs was United States attorney for the District of Vermont
from 1791 to 1794.

132. David Fay, a lawyer from Bennington, Vermont, was that state's attorney from 1797 to 1801.

7 John Allen Finch
25 & 30
	D Fay—Young Gentleman—
	N G character & abilities
	Lyon highly suitable to com-
	    mand of company
	    family good whigs—
	    good education
	M unsteady dissipated
	    morals & politics bad
		Wont do

8 Israel Elliot Trask *Windsor 23 years* Morris—liberal edu- cation good politics worthy	S *Jacobs* young Gentleman of brilliant talents & handsome acquirmts. could easily raise a Company Payne handsome abilities edu- cated at Cambridge bred to law—friend to Governt.	*Strong*
28 Daniel Biswell ☞ *Randolph* Sergeant in 2 Con Reg not found on army list *Badge of Merit*	wishes a comp Payne could say considerable of his merit—but omit it till he can send other testimonials appearance in his favour	respectable for Lt. Qr. En- signcey
10 Simson Lester Rutland	Chipman—well qualified for the appointment	Nothing specific
13 Samuel Walker Rutland	Chipman Young Gentleman of education & merit	Respectable
15 Alancon Ferris vergennes	*Tichenor*—not personaly acquainted—recommends good *Divers* has commanded Regt. of Militia integrity & mili- tary talents	
16 Simeon Hurd Sandgate	*Tichenor* sound last war now Capt of Militia	
18 Elihu Field Guilford 43	*Morris* *honest worthy* & *brave* Major in Militia education is he believes adequate	Tolerable only
21 Thomas Leverett *33 years*	*Morris* good *morals education* & *family*—believes quafied unfortun in Trade politics formerly suspected now *cor- rect*	pretty well Qr

22 William Switzer
Springfield *Windsor*
☞ 33 years

Chipman agrees with Morris
in recommending
him   ⎫
⎬ pretty well
Buck   active *enterprising*
Morris   *good politics*   ⎫ respectable
Morris   commanded a

14 common soldier last
war active enter-
prising decent edu-
cation & informa-
tion

Compy of Militia
Cavalry has been   ⎫
high Sheriff—   ⎬ Qr. Ensign
good enough educa-
tion   ⎭

CAPT OR FIRST LT

27 Leonard Williams
Rutland

L: Williams. Aide De Camp to
Lt Gov [133] has been in prac-
tice of law in Comp with
Chipman

Elliot [134] ⎫ his education
Jackson [135] ⎭ character &   respectable
abilities intitle
him to higher
commiss

Thl. Marshall—respectable Connections

30 George Woodward
Norwich
23

Morris liberal education mercantile industry integrity &   Strong
talents easy in circumstances
politics correct

FIELD OFFICERS

3 Cornelius Lynde
Williams town
48 years
sometime Lt last war

Payne in service part of *Revo-*   *respectable*
lutionary war educated *at*
Cambrige now a Chief Justice & Brigadier General
Morris—does not appear to possess sufft military talent & information

6 James Sawyer
Burlington 40
subaltern Grade

N Chipman   respectable firm
active & brave has been a
Lt Col of a Regt

133. Paul Brigham of Norwich, Vermont, was lieutenant governor from
1797 to 1812. He was a member of the Electoral College in 1788 and 1792 and
a member of the governor's council from 1792 to 1796.

134. James Elliot, a Federalist from Vermont, served in the United States
Army from 1793 to 1796.

135. Abraham Jackson, a resident of Rutland County, Vermont, served in the
state Assembly in 1785, 1789, 1790, 1793, 1794, and 1798.

☞ *Ensign of Regt* Lt Infantry	Tichenor—will take a Majority High Sheriff of Chittendon	*probably good Capt*
	S Hitchcock[136] Morris } industrious active enterprisg	
12 John Chipman Middlebury	*Tichenor* information & respectability do honor to service	Respectable
served to end of last Qr War—captain 48 Morris— 52 years	*N. Chipman* no man in Vermont better qualified than he *S Hitchcock* Morris—good morals was Capt in Warners Regt. active intrepid & of military turn—appointed Major of levies by *Gov Clinton*	

VERMONT

2d Majr.	John Chapmen Middlebury	*Major*	
1	James Sawyer Burlington 40	Capt	No. 1
5	William Woodward Rutland 42	ditto	No. 2
8	Israel Elliot Trask Windsor	ditto	No. 3

LIEUTENANTS

3	George Woodward Norwich	ditto	No. 1
6	William Switzer Windsor	ditto	2
8	Ephraim Witney	ditto	3

ENSIGNS

3	Jesse Lull Rutland	1
6	Marmaduke Wait	2
8	Daniel Baker	3

136. Samuel Hitchcock was United States judge for the District of Vermont.

[E N C L O S U R E] [137]

Candidates for Army Appointments from New Jersey

SUBALTERNS

6 Robert Hunt
   son of A Hunt [138]
   Trenton

Lieutenant *Qr Cavalry*
Stockton [139] ⎫ liberal education
refers to   ⎬ & unblemished
Howel [140] ⎭ character
G. Dickinson [141]—read law decided fœderalist
Pickering [142] promising abilities great modesty good understandn
Stockton general terms

Attention
very strong
perhaps
Captain

7 James Rhea
   brother of Col
   Rhea [143]

Stockton—general terms

Attention

9 Charles Reed
   Burlington

Stockton active young man of good connection fit for service
Bloomfield [144]—*Dayton* [145] Lt.
or Ensign

Attention

11 Andrew Hunter Jn.
   Dayton Ensign 2

Stockton son of Reverend
Hunter for *Ensign*
Rutherford [146] genteel man-

Respectable

137. AD, George Washington Papers, Library of Congress.
In this list of recommendations for Army appointments, those recommended have not been identified. Wherever possible, however, the individuals making the recommendations have been identified.

138. Abraham Hunt, a resident of Trenton, New Jersey, was a contractor furnishing supplies for the United States Army.

139. Richard Stockton, a Federalist from Princeton, New Jersey, was elected to the United States Senate in 1796 to fill the vacancy caused by the resignation of Frederick Frelinghuysen. He served in that position until March, 1799.

140. Richard Howell, a veteran of the American Revolution and a Federalist, was governor of New Jersey from 1793 to 1801.

141. Philemon Dickinson, a resident of Trenton, New Jersey, and a veteran of the American Revolution, was elected to the United States Senate in 1790 to fill the vacancy caused by the resignation of William Paterson. He served in that position until 1793.

142. Secretary of State Timothy Pickering.

143. During the American Revolution, David Rhea was first a major and then a lieutenant colonel in the Second New Jersey Regiment.

144. Joseph Bloomfield, a veteran of the American Revolution, was a resident of Burlington, New Jersey. From 1795 to 1800 he was mayor of Burlington.

145. Jonathan Dayton.

146. John Rutherfurd was a Federalist member of the United States Senate from 1791 to 1798.

	ners & education has been dissipated now reformed		
16 Heathcote Johnston Dayton Lt. 6	*Gov Patterson* [147]—of good family connections his recommenders good men A White [148] no doubt he will Bell [149] &c fulfil the duties of his station	not much of any thing	
17 William J Leslie New Brunswick	Gov Patterson A White Freelinghuyssen [150]	young man of fair character	Qr. Qr Ensign
21 Henry G Thomas	cornet or Ensign no recommendation		
23 Joshua J Cozens Northumberland	no recommendation		
24 James Eugene Parker Woodbrige Breadun Heard Schurerman [151] not *personally acquainted Writes ill*	Horse Gen Bloomfield—generally well mentioned for Cavalry young man of property & excellent character from private to Capt expert in cavalry exercise ☞ *likely to raise men*	Not very strong *Dayton* Lt. 3 Cavalry	
25 Henry Drake New Brunswick 22 years	Neilson [152] good character G Patterson Stockton confides in recom-	Tolerably Respectable	

147. William Paterson was a Federalist member of the United States Senate from 1789 to 1790, when he was elected governor of New Jersey. He served in that capacity from 1790 to 1793. From 1793 until his death in 1806 he was an associate justice of the Supreme Court of the United States.

148. Anthony Walton White.

149. Andrew Bell, a resident of Perth Amboy, New Jersey, was a Loyalist who served as a private secretary to Sir Henry Clinton during the American Revolution. In 1800 he became collector of the district and inspector of the revenue for the port of Perth Amboy (*Executive Journal*, I, 314).

150. Frederick Frelinghuysen, a veteran of the American Revolution, was elected as a Federalist to the United States Senate. He served from 1793 until his resignation in 1796.

151. James Schureman, a Federalist from New Brunswick, New Jersey, and a veteran of the American Revolution, was a member of the House of Representatives from 1789 to 1791 and again from 1797 to 1799, when he became a United States Senator.

152. John Neilson, a veteran of the American Revolution and a resident of New Brunswick, New Jersey, was elected to the Continental Congress in 1778, but there is evidence that he never attended (Edmund C. Burnett, ed., *Letters of Members of the Continental Congress* [Washington, D.C., 1921–1938], III, lvi; IV, lvii).

His own letter *very well*

menders
         Student of Medicine
Smith [153] ⎱ College Education
Physician ⎰ Sobriety & honor
         abilities

Bray [154] Fœderal principles
Schureman—sobriety & good
     morals

34 Thomas Tallman
     fœderalist

Young man of good character &
     appearance—good family
Howel recommends him strong-
     ly much interested for his suc-
     cess favourite of his

Respectable
Lieutenant
or
Ensign

28 Samuel C Voorhiss
     Woodbury
     Dayton Lt. 5

                  young Gen-
                  tleman of
F Davenport [155] ⎫ good abil-
E Clark [156]   ⎬ ities & good
J B Caldwell [157] ⎭ morals
                  promise of
                  merit
Gov~. Howel—respectability
     & good con~ reputation high
     among his acquaintance

Respectable
Ensign
perhaps
Lieuten-
ant

33 William Potter
     Philadelphia
     may be in N Jersey
     Writes very well

Dayton Lt 4
Howel   good connection
McPherson *young Gentlen*
     sensible & accomplished
     good person *honor Moores*
     Grenadiers
Davenport Ewing [158] evi-
     dently has ability   worthy
     son of a worthy father

very *strong*
perhaps
Captain

153. William H. Smith, a physician from Luzerne County, Pennsylvania, had been a surgeon's mate in the hospital department during the American Revolution.

154. John Bray was the Army contractor at New Brunswick, New Jersey, during the Whiskey Insurrection. See H to Abraham Hunt, August 17, 1794, note 5.

155. Franklin Davenport, a nephew of Benjamin Franklin, was a resident of Woodbury, New Jersey, and a veteran of the American Revolution. He was a member of the New Jersey Assembly from 1786 to 1789. In December, 1798, he was appointed to the United States Senate to fill the vacancy caused by John Rutherfurd's resignation, and he served until 1799.

156. Elijah Clark was a resident of Woodbury, New Jersey.

157. James B. Caldwell was a resident of Woodbury, New Jersey.

158. James Ewing was the commissioner of loans for New Jersey.

Elmer [159]   well informed
readiness in business—*Giles*

52 James Johnson	Rutherford on credit of Howel	Nothing particular
44 William Piatt	Howel—had discouraged them as too late though he thought them qualified much interested *in Piatt* son of an officer good character activity can raise men—good appearance courage	respectable
Taylor Monmouth	Howel general terms	
49 George Davis New Brunswick *Somerset* Writes good hand and otherwise *well*	Freelinghinussen of respectable family attached to now resides at Albany, fair character Bayard [160]—now resides at *Albany* attached to G— will do honor &c Jo. Neilson—general terms White has observed his attention to duty	well enough perhaps *Ensign* or *Cornet*
51 Thomas J Laurance 22 years	Rutherford eldest son of Thos. Laurance late of Philadelphia nephew of Mrs. Rutherford no character	Inquire
56 Richard Jaques New Brunswick	Patterson ⎫ respectable parent- Neilson ⎪ age Shurenan ⎬ good moral charac- ⎪ ter & political ⎪ principles ⎪ now Cornet active & ⎭ attentive to duty	Respectable
57 Thomas Reading Jun Hunterdon	*Jno Bayard* ⎫ fit and capable for & others ⎭ Lt good family & character	

159. Jonathan Elmer, a resident of Bridgeton, New Jersey, was a member of the Continental Congress from 1776 to 1778, 1781 to 1784, and 1787 to 1788. He served as a Federalist in the United States Senate from 1789 to 1791.

160. John Bayard, a resident of New Brunswick, New Jersey, was mayor of that city in 1790. Before he moved to New Jersey, he was a prominent Philadelphia merchant and a member of the Pennsylvania Assembly from 1776 to 1779 and again in 1784.

	Jo. Beatty [161] activity & information moral can raise men	*respectable*
58 Robert I Champan *Allen Town* does not write very well	Lt. or Ensign Stockton—*van Imbergh* [162] deserves confidence Imlay [163]—persuaded his claim is far van Imberg respectable parentage (cap) Militia Officer conducted himself well sober & diligent friend to his Country	*Not strong*
65 Thomas Bullman Jr Easton *Sussex* only son of his father 21 years	*Sitgreaves* [164] knows his father well credit may be given to him ever in what he says of his son handsome & Genteel	respectable for Lty
John G Macwhorter New Ark	*Cummings* [165] Lt. of Lt Infantry refers to others Boudinot [166] strong *Dayton* 6th. Capt or Lieut	respectable

CAPTAINS

1 Charles Marls *Borden Town* Burlington *Dayton 2 Capt* *Howel*	*A Hunt* sober & steady Western expedition Lt. of Lt Infantry—*qualified* R Coxe [167] young man—now Adjutant & qualified *Bloomfield* company in six months service	Capt *perhaps* *Strong,* Lieutenant

161. John Beatty, a veteran of the American Revolution, was originally a resident of Pennsylvania. He moved to New Jersey and served as a delegate to the Continental Congress in 1784 and 1785 and as a member of the House of Representatives from 1793 to 1795. In 1795 he became Secretary of State of New Jersey, and he held that position until 1805.

162. John Van Emburgh was a resident of Bordentown, New Jersey.

163. James H. Imlay, a resident of Monmouth County, New Jersey, was a member of the New Jersey Assembly from 1793 to 1796 and a member of the House of Representatives from 1797 to 1801.

164. Samuel Sitgreaves, a resident of Easton, Pennsylvania, was elected to the House of Represntatives as a Federalist and served from 1795 to 1798. On August 11, 1798, he was appointed one of the commissioners for implementing Article 6 of the Jay Treaty (John Bassett Moore, ed., *International Adjudications: Ancient and Modern, History and Documents, Together with Mediatorial Reports, Advisory Opinions, and the Decisions of Domestic Commissions, on International Claims* [New York, 1931], III, 18, and note 1).

165. John N. Cummings of New Jersey held the rank of lieutenant colonel commandant at the end of the American Revolution.

166. Elisha Boudinot was a Newark, New Jersey, lawyer.

167. Richard Coxe of New Jersey held the rank of major at the end of the American Revolution.

4 Clement Woods   *Stockton* ⎫ *generally* able &   *pretty well*
  Morris County   refers to ⎬   vigilant
  Dayton 3 Capt   How   ⎭
                     Freelinghuyssen commands a
                     Mitia Batalion & has acquitted
                     himself with respectable

5 Barnes H Smock   *Stockton* ⎫ in general terms
                     refers to ⎬ able & vigilant
                     Howel   ⎭ Officer

6 Robert Hunt   *Rutherford* S
  4 Capt Dayton   see character Subalterns
                     A White Howel—2

15 Abraham Bayley   Schureman ⎫ a good citizen   now of
                     & others ⎪ and valuable   Chester
                                ⎪ officer—Capt   Pensylva
                                ⎪ of Dragoons
                                ⎪ unblemished
                                ⎬ honor & integ-
                                ⎪ rity good
                                ⎪ fœderalist—
                                ⎪ against
                                ⎭ Insurgeans
                     would prefer Cavalry

17 Abraham Kenney   *Freelinghussen* good Officer,   respectable
   Morris County   has his confidence & esteem
   served as an officer in prefers Infantry
     Dragoons Lt last
     war

18 Robert C Thompson Rob Hoops [168] ⎫ assure from   Respectable
   Sussex County   G Howell   ⎪ personal
   Dayton Lt- 2   Rob Stockton [169] ⎬ knowl-
   Young Gentleman   J Dayton   ⎭ ege he
   good letter   has an
                                       unblem-
                                       ished
                                       character
                                       —friend
                                       to Gov-
                                       ernment
                                       has com-

168. Robert Hoops was the brother of Adam Hoops, who had surveyed the Genesee country for Robert Morris. In 1789 and 1790 Robert Hoops was a member of the New Jersey Legislative Council.

169. Robert Stockton of Somerset County was a member of the New Jersey General Assembly in 1790, 1791, 1793, and from 1795 to 1796.

	manded a troop of horse —will do honor against Western Insurgents	
22 *Aaron Van Cleeve Jun~ Dayton Lt. 3*	Pensylvania *Howel is said to be worthy*	
27 Abner Woodruff young	Howel—college education will accept Lieutenany can raise men Rutherford S	Respectable
31 Gilbert D Lowe *Somerset* now Capt of Militia	Cavalry in preference Freelinghuyssen—good family merits attention as a citizen & soldier—Exped v Insurgens *Howel* good politics—conduct dignified & respectable	pretty respect-able
John White Bridge Town	HOWELL *wishes a Troop* his father killed in our service— a married man of property intelligent mind & good per-son of integrity & honor	strong
37 Walter K Cole Lawyer	now Brigade Inspector Freelinghuyssen talents & respectability	respectable
40 Robert F Howe	Habersham [170] Clerk 2 years in his Office well Stockton good family charac-ter & abilities application *withdrawn*	respectable will take *Lieuten-ancy*
41 Robert Morrison Sussex C X	Howel & others } suitable char: for Capt of foot abilities intitle him Stockton will do honor Rutherford	nothing very specific but gen-erally *well*

170. Joseph Habersham had been a partner in the Savannah mercantile firm of Joseph Clay and Company. During the American Revolution he became a colonel in the Continental Army. After the war he was twice speaker of the Georgia General Assembly, a delegate to the Continental Congress, and a mem-ber of the Georgia Ratifying Convention. On February 24, 1795, Washington nominated him Postmaster General, and the Senate confirmed the appointment on the following day (*Executive Journal*, I, 173, 174).

42 Benjamin C Curtis   liberal education
    Pompton   firmness &
    Bergen   Inhabitants ⎱   spirit attached   well
                    of Bergen ⎰   to the Gov-   enough
                                         ernmt
                    Militia Officers
                    Mr. Goodhue [171] says he is of
                    liberal Education & a fit char-
                    acter

44 William Pratt   ⎤ *young man* of
    Hunterdon *or*   ⎮ good char-
    Sussex   ⎮ acter well
                    Charles Stew-   ⎮ attached to
                    art [172] &   ⎬ Govt. & son
                    others   ⎮ of a father   perhaps
                                         ⎮ who died in   Ensign
                                         ⎮ the service in
                                         ⎮ his Country
                                         ⎦
                    Howel recom⁓ respectable
                    McCullough [173] steady & cred-
                    itable young man
                    Js Steward   Temperate indus-
                    trious active & spirited

55 Jacob Heyer   *Cummings* speaks well in gen-
    Amboy   eral terms
    Officer last war Note of Secy at War said to be   Inquire
                    addicted to liquor

61 Denise Foreman G. Patterson   not personally
    Monmouth   acquainted but relies
                                         sober honest
                    White served ⎱   brave &
                    on Western   ⎬   worthy &   respectable
                    Expedition   ⎰   of good
                                         connections

63 Job Stockton   prefers cavalry   *strong*
    Princeton   *R Stockton   young Gentleman*
                    of liberal education moral &

171. Benjamin Goodhue of Salem, Massachusetts, was a Federalist. He was a
member of the Massachusetts General Court from 1780 to 1782 and of the
state Senate from 1785 to 1788. He was elected to the House of Representatives
and served from 1789 to 1796. In 1796 he was elected to the United States
Senate to fill the vacancy caused by George Cabot's resignation, a position
he held until 1800.

172. During the American Revolution, Stewart was a colonel of the New
Jersey militia. From 1777 to 1782 he was commissary general of issues.

173. William McCullough of Sussex County was a member of the New
Jersey General Assembly from 1793 to 1797.

very handsome letter   political principles correct
Freelinghuyssen   strong

67 Fenwick Lyall   ⎫ good moral char-
   late of Middleton   │ acter firm &
   now of N York   Freeling- │ determined
                    huyssen ⎬ well qualified
                    & others │ for command
                            │ of a Company   respectable
                            ⎭
                    R Stockton—recommenders
                    good & think well of candi-
                    date
                    Howel   good recommenders

John Gifford   *Dayton*   5th Captain
New Ark   Qr. if not *in last war*

FIELD OFFICERS

Robert Hoops   strong—as to   Now
Sussex County   moral qualities   *Major* of
                    Stockdon ⎫ talented &   Artillery
                    Dayton   ⎬ spirit estab-
                    St Greaves ⎭ lished
                                character
                                & popularity

 3 Jonathan Snowden   No recommendation
   Prince Town   *writes ill*   X
   former services

12 Jonathan F Morris   Freelinghuysen—worthy char- Col or
   Somerset   acter   *surgeon*
   Brigadier of Militia was a *subaltern of Artillery*

29 Samuel Craig   Howel   when he knew him he
   Officer of Pensyl line   was a good Officer   X
   last war

32 Almerine Brooks [174]   *Howel*   Ex against Insurgents
   Ensign   appointed by G Morgan [175]
   served last war   Morgan afterwards recom~   Respectable
                       knowlege of service
                    Dayton ⎫ can't be excelled—
                    1 Capt ⎬ would deserve a
                           ⎭ Regiment discipli-
                              narian

174. In the George Washington Papers, Library of Congress, there is a list
in the handwriting of Tobias Lear of candidates from New Jersey for Army
appointments. The first entry on this list and the only one in H's handwriting
reads: "Almerine Brooks—first *Dayton*."

175. Daniel Morgan, who held the rank of brigadier general at the end of
the American Revolution, was in command of the Virginia militia during the
Whiskey Insurrection.

Samuel Dickinson 28 years old	applies for a Regiment son of General Dickinson		X
39 Adam Hoops	Regiment offer of service in Artillery		X

43 Nathaniel Donnell
   captain
   served the whole of
     last war in Artillery
     as Capt

E Stevens [176] ⎱ served as a Capt   Not strong
Hodgsdon [177] ⎰   under his
     command
     served faith-
     fully & much
     to his honor
     & reputation

Dayton ⎱
  arrangt ⎰

17 ⎱ Abraham Kenny
47 ⎰ Morris County

See *Capt 17*

53 Aaron Ogden
   E Town

Dayton   more active intelligent
     & spirited officer
     cannot be found
Howel   better qualified to
     command a Regt
     than any person
     yet named to him

54 Benjamin Williamson
   E Town

a Major or Capt of Cavalry
Dayton superior horseman &
    excellent officer   *very strong*

59 William Shute
   Elizabeth Town
   subaltern in Jersey
     line late war
   Dayton 2 Major

Cummings is in his opinion a
   very active officer of good
   abilities disciplinarian proper-   respectable
   ty & good principles
his letter very well
Dayton—*strong* preferably to
   any other applicant

---

176. Ebenezer Stevens, formerly of Rhode Island, held the rank of lieutenant colonel of the Second Continental Artillery at the close of the American Revolution. After the war he became a merchant in New York City. In 1794 the New York legislature named him to a seven-man committee in charge of the fortification of New York City, and in the same year he was first appointed War Department agent for the fortification of New York City, a position he also held in 1798. See Henry Knox to H, March 29, 1794, note 5; Stevens to H, December 1, 1794; the introductory note to H to McHenry, June 1, 1798.

177. Samuel Hodgdon had served in the commissary department of the Continental Army during the American Revolution. From March 4, 1791, until April 12, 1792, he was quartermaster general of the United States Army, and from the fall of 1792 until June, 1794, he served as Army storekeeper at Philadelphia. In June, 1794, he was appointed superintendent of military stores. See H to Knox, June 20, 1794, note 1.

SURGEONS

8 John Howel   *Stockton*
  Doctor Aaron Foreman   Rutherford
                              Howel
  Jonathan T Morris—Surgeon Freelinghuysen as a surgeon
14 Charles Smith *Physician General*   Stockton &c
  Samuel H Philips
  Benjamin Champneys   Howel & others   Dayton arrangt
  John G Wynants   *Dayton*   Mate
  William B Lindsay   Chaplain
  Abraham Van Ness   Freelinghuyssen
50 Samuel G Roy   Surgeons Mate
64 Elijah Rosegrant *Mate*

---

1 Lt Col
1 Major
6 Capts
6 Lts
6 Ensigns

FIELD OFFICERS

Jonathan F Morris No	Somerset	Subaltern of Artillery *last war* Capt
Nathaniel Donnell	Dayton 1 Major 3	*capt of Artillery last war not on the list*
Abraham Kenny	Morris County 3	Lt of Dragoons last war
Aaron Ogden	Essex *Lt Col.* 1	Capt
X Benjamin Williamson	*Essex* Major or *Capt of Cavalry*	
William Shute	*Essex* Dayton 2d	Subaltern late War *Ensign*

Gilbert D Lowe

[Walter] [178] K Cole		No. 1
John C McWhorter	Essex	2
Robert C Thompson	Sussex	3
John Eugene Parker	Middlesex	4
William Potter	4	5
Samuel C Voorhies		6
Thomas Reading Junr	Hunterton	7

Thomas Bullman Ensign		No. 1
Charles Read Burlington		2
Heathcote Johnson		3
Henry Drake Middlesex		4
James Rhea		5
William Pratt *Hunterdon*		6

ARRANGEMENT

| Aaron Ogden | | Lt Colonel |
| William Shute | | Major |

CAPTAINS

Benjamin Williamson		Cavalry
Almerine Brooks		No. 1
Clement Woods	Morris	2
Job Stockton	Somerset	3
Charles Marles	Burlington	4
Robert Hunt	Hunderton	5
Denise Foreman	Monmouth	6

[relative rank]

LIEUTS

Walter K Cole		1
John C Macwhorter	Essex	2
Robert C Thompson	Sussex	3
John Eugene Parker	Middlesex	4 - cavalry
William Potter	[Bridge Town] [179]	5
Samuel C Voorhess	[Middlesex] [180]	6
Thomas Reading Jun	Hunterdon	7

178. This word is not in H's handwriting.
179. This word is not in H's handwriting.
180. This word in not in H's handwriting.

[ENCLOSURE] [181]

Candidates for Army Appointments from Pennsylvania

LIEUTENANTS & ENSIGNS

John S Porter	McPherson	Probably
Philadelphia	Francis Johnson [182] *Inquire*	good Ensign
of Chester	David Denny [183]	perhaps Lt.
Young & writes a		
good hand & good		
English		
Archibald D Davis	Dennis Wheelen [184]	
Lancaster	David Denny	*do*
Young		
Elija Griffiths	*Richard Thomas* [185]	*Passably*
Philadelphia for-	Proctor [186]	*Inquire*
merly of Chester	F Gurney [187]	
County		
Dy Quarter Master		
in W Expedin		
Benjamin Worrell	Judge Rush [188] & others	Quære if not
of Berks County	*Sitgreaves*	good Ensign
Samuel Welsh	Hollingsworth [189]	Quære
	Sheaf [190]	
Lazarus Stow	No recommendation	
42 years		
served in the army		
of the Revolution		
was wounded		

181. AD, George Washington Papers, Library of Congress.
In this list of recommendations for Army appointments, those recommended have not been identified. Wherever possible, however, the individuals making the recommendations have been identified.

182. Johnston was a Philadelphia resident who held the rank of colonel at the close of the American Revolution. In 1798 he was the receiver general of the Pennsylvania land office.

183. Denny was a resident of Chester County, Pennsylvania.

184. Whelen, a resident of Chester County, Pennsylvania, served in the state House of Representatives and Senate.

185. From 1795 to 1801 Thomas was a Federalist member of the House of Representatives from Pennsylvania.

186. Thomas Proctor of Philadelphia held the rank of colonel at the close of the American Revolution.

187. Francis Gurney, a veteran of the American Revolution, was a Philadelphia merchant and a member of the Pennsylvania House of Representatives.

188. Judge Jacob Rush was president of the third district of the Pennsylvania Court of Commons Pleas.

189. Either John or Levi Hollingsworth, Philadelphia merchants.

190. This is a reference to Henry, Philip, or William Sheaf, all Philadelphia merchants.

Elijah B. Jarvis Philadelphia	Wm. Nichol [191] *Latimer* [192] worthy person & *capable* of rendering service speaks of property in Philadel- phia	Inquire
Robert Laurance Huntington	J Cadwallader [193] Doctor Smith [194]	Respectably as Lieut or Ensign
Eccles P. Barclay Philadelphia	James Cochran who speaks well of him	Enquire
Henry Lewis Kean Philadelphia	McPherson Miller [195]	Probably will do for *an* *Ensign*
Thomas Swearingen Washington County	son of a man of property himself a man of property *Addison* [196] Sitgreaves Hartley &c [197]	Very *Respect-* *ably* Qr. if not a Captain or in the *Artillery*
David Duncan		*Very Respect-* *ably*
William Carson young Gentlem Dauphine County Liberal Education	*Thomas Duncan* [198] James Ross [199]	Respectably
Harman Witner Lancaster	Kitera [200] Sitgreaves Heartley	Probably *Ensign*
George Hamell	*well educated*	*Not strong*

191. Nichols was inspector of the revenue for Survey No. 1 in the District of Pennsylvania.

192. George Latimer, a Philadelphia merchant, was a member of the Pennsylvania House of Representatives from 1792 to 1799. On June 29, 1798, the Senate confirmed his appointment as collector of customs at Philadelphia (*Executive Journal*, I, 282).

193. John Cadwallader was a resident of Huntingdon County.

194. William H. Smith.

195. Henry Miller, a veteran of the American Revolution, was supervisor of the revenue for the District of Pennsylvania.

196. Alexander Addison was the presiding judge of the Court of Common Pleas for the fifth Pennsylvania district.

197. Thomas Hartley, a resident of York, Pennsylvania, and a veteran of the American Revolution, was a member of the House of Representatives from 1789 to 1800.

198. Duncan was a lawyer from Cumberland County, Pennsylvania.

199. Ross, a veteran of the American Revolution, was a resident of Pittsburgh in 1798. From 1794 to 1803 he was a Federalist member of the United States Senate.

200. John Wilkes Kittera, a lawyer from Lancaster County, Pennsylvania, was a Federalist. From 1791 to 1801 he served in the House of Representatives.

Chambersburgh	*Bird* * 201 ⎫	*Qr. if*
Franklin County	Cromwell ⎪ not personally	*Ensign*
	Chambers 202 ⎬ known	
* strongly	W Elliot 203 ⎭	
John Montgomery	Militia Officers	Tolerable
Harrisburgh	*Hannah Genl* 204	perhaps
Dauphine	Sitgreaves believes application	Ensign
	merits attention	
	Kittera	
Ephraim Blaine Junr		⎧ probably
Cumberland		⎨ Ensign
		⎩ *Qr. Age*
Samuel Dickinson ⎫		
Cadwallader ⎬	Inquire Secy of State	
Meredith ⎭		
James Potts	sober honest young man	probably good
Philadelphia	McPherson & others	Lieutenant
Samuel B Magaw	*Samuel McGaw* 205	Probably
Mercersburgh	*Wm. McGaw* 206	good sub-
25 years	said to understand Mathematics	altern
		Enquire
Elisha P. Barrows	good Scholar	*Strong as*
York County	*good morals*	*Lieutenant*
native of Connecti-	Eddie 207	
cut	Miller	
28 years	Hand 208	
Daniel Lauman ⎫	Eddie Miller	*application*
York County ⎪	& others	*firm*
⎬	*Young Men*	*provision*
John Hay Jun ⎪	ditto	Probably
York County ⎭		*good*
		Ensigns

201. Benjamin Bird of Bedford County was a veteran of the American Revolution.

202. This is a reference to James or Benjamin Chambers who resided in Franklin County, Pennsylvania. James Chambers served as a colonel in the American Revolution; he was justice of the peace of Franklin County in 1784 and county commissioner from 1793 to 1795. In 1794 and again in 1798 he was brigadier general commanding the Third Brigade of Pennsylvania militia. Benjamin Chambers, a prominent iron manufacturer, served in the American Revolution and was county auditor in 1788 and from 1793 to 1794.

203. William Elliot, a resident of Franklin County, Pennsylvania, was a veteran of the American Revolution.

204. Stephen Hannah held the rank of lieutenant at the close of the American Revolution.

205. Samuel Magaw was the rector of the St. Paul's Protestant Episcopal Church in Philadelphia from 1781 to 1804.

206. William Magaw was a surgeon in the Continental Army during the American Revolution.

207. John Edie, a veteran of the American Revolution, was the clerk of the Court of Common Pleas in York County, Pennsylvania.

208. Edward Hand.

John A Douglass York County 20 years	Eddie Miller & others *Respectable connections*	Probably *Ensign*
William Irvine Cumberland	good young man of re- spectable connec- tions	Quære *prin-* *ciples*

Davidson [209]
&
Montgomery [210] } good young man of respectable connections — Quære *principles*

William C Rogers Philadelphia	clever young man Rush [211]	*Inquire*
William Beatty Jun Franklin County *22 years old*	*mild* but *resolute* asks for *Lieut* or Cornet in Cavalry Robert Johnson [212]	*cornet or* *Ensign*
	of spirit & respectable Connec- tions *Wm. Henderson* [213]	
John Milroy Mifflin County	Young man capable of duties of Lt.	Tolerably as Lieutenant
	good standing & respectable connections *George Lati- mer*	Inquire
	young man of good education & friend to the Governt—by *Will Brown* [214] supported by B Rush	

Alexander McNair	Pittsburgh 22 yrs. 1	
Edward Nicholas	do. 23 2 } James Ross {	*Strong enough* *as Subalterns*
Thomas Lee of	*Erie* 25 3	
Hugh Scot	Pittsburgh *surgeons* Mate do	
Andrew Irvin ⌉ Huntington ⎟ Robert McCab ⎟ do ⌋	Principal Inhabitants of the County John Cadwallader *manly* *young men* nothing specific	Quære Ensigns
Robert Chambers	Integrity Industry Courage &	Tolerably

209. Robert Davidson, a Presbyterian minister, was a professor of history, geography, chronology, rhetoric, and belles-lettres in Dickinson College, Carlisle, Pennsylvania.

210. John Montgomery of Cumberland County was a member of the Pennsylvania House of Representatives in 1781 and 1782 and a delegate to the Continental Congress from 1782 to 1784. In 1794 he became associate judge of Cumberland County.

211. Benjamin Rush was a prominent Philadelphia physician.

212. Johnson was a surgeon in the Continental Army during the American Revolution. From 1781 to the close of the war he was hospital physician and surgeon of the southern department.

213. Henderson, who held the rank of captain at the close of the American Revolution, was appointed a major of the Tenth Infantry Regiment on January 8, 1799 (*Executive Journal*, I, 299, 303). In 1798 he represented Franklin County in the Pennsylvania House of Representatives.

214. Brown, a veteran of the American Revolution, was elected to the 1796 Electoral College as a Republican from Mifflin County, Pennsylvania.

Huntington *Young man*	abilities　John Cadwallader	as *Ensign*
Hugh H Potts Philadelphia	Nichols McPherson & good appearance suitable appearance	*Well* as *Lieutenant* Qr. Ensign
John Biglan James Stewart		
John Sharp Cumberland	young man of handsome property *Heron* [215] James *Ross* &c	pretty well as *Ensign*
John Davis James Eakin Philadelphia	Will Henderson & good Connections & principles *Latimer Gurney*	not strong Respectably as Lieutenant
Henry *Betz* *German*	respectable *German* family *C Reed* [218] *Danl Clymer* [219] ⎱ Bingham [216] John Biddle [217] *Young Gentleman* honest active & sober	pretty well as Lieut. Inquire
Henry Lancaster	Bingham *strong* sundry inhabitants	
John Smith *qr. if not Northumber*		Tolerably as Ensign
William Davis		perhaps
Thomas Lee—misfortunes of family— good orderly Sergeant		Ensign
Doct Robert Johnson Surgeon General *offers himself*		
William Monroe *Philadelphia*	recommended by his brother & Mr. Stoddert [220]　Harwood [221]	pretty well as Lieutenant

215. In 1798 James G. Heron represented Allegheny County in the Pennsylvania House of Representatives.

216. William Bingham, a Federalist from Philadelphia, was a member of the Continental Congress in 1787 and 1788 and a member of the Pennsylvania House of Representatives in 1790 and 1791. He served in the Pennsylvania Senate in 1794 and 1795, and from 1795 to 1801 he was a member of the United States Senate.

217. John Biddle was a Philadelphia druggist.

218. Collinson Read, a resident of Reading, was commissioner of valuations for the fourth Pennsylvania division.

219. Clymer was a lawyer from Reading and a Federalist politician.

220. Benjamin Stoddert was Secretary of the Navy.

221. This is a reference to either Thomas Harwood, a veteran of the American Revolution, who was commissioner of loans in Maryland from 1790 to

Marylander by birth   Callahan [222]   all Annanpolis   or Ensign
                             respectable family
                             Marbury [223]   *Key* [224]
                             unblemished reputation

SURGEONS

John E Buchanan	by Henderson
Samuel Lyons Mate	*Rush & Shippen* [225]
John Henderson	by Js. Biddle [226] & others
John McClellan	by Doct R Johnson
Doctor Dart	by Irvin [227] *Navy*
James Irvin Mate	McCosky [228] & Wm Irvine
Roger Wales	Citizens of York County
James Ramsay	Doct Patterson [229] (*Reversed*)
Robert Ross	by his sister *Anna Thorp*
John Rippy	Hartley
Francis J Smith	Sitgreaves & others reputation
	last War
John McDowel	by Francis Johnson
James Forbes	by George Baer [230]

SUBALTERNS

James Caldwell	Sam Hughes [231]—recommends	Not strong
Wheeler Ohio	in general terms	
28 years		

1792, or Benjamin Harwood, who had been treasurer of Maryland and became commissioner of loans in Maryland in 1792.

222. John Callahan of Annapolis had been register of the Land Office for the Eastern Shore of Maryland.

223. William Marbury, a resident of Annapolis, was one of the principals in the case of *Marbury* v *Madison.*

224. This is a reference to either Philip Key, a resident of St. Marys County, Maryland, who was a member of the House of Representatives from 1791 to 1793, or Philip B. Key, an Annapolis lawyer and a member of the Maryland House of Delegates.

225. This is a reference to either William Shippen, a prominent Philadelphia physician, or Edward Shippen, an associate justice of the Pennsylvania Supreme Court.

226. Biddle was the presiding judge of the fourth district of the Pennsylvania Court of Common Pleas.

227. William Irvine, who held the rank of brigadier general at the close of the American Revolution, was a member of the House of Representatives from 1793 to 1795.

228. Samuel A. McCoskry, who had been a surgeon's mate during the American Revolution, was a Carlisle, Pennsylvania, physician.

229. Robert Patterson, a veteran of the American Revolution, was a professor of mathematics at the University of Pennsylvania.

230. Baer, a merchant from Frederick, Maryland, was a Federalist member of the House of Representatives from 1797 to 1801.

231. Hughes operated the Cecil Iron Company at Havre de Grace, Maryland.

CAPTAINS

SOME LIEUTENANTS

Samuel Llewellen served as Non Commissioned officer	*Wm Jones* [232] *Richard Thomas*	Quaere if not an *Ensign* *Probably Not.*
X Thomas Bartow	Goodhue	Respectably
X Philadelphia	H Latimer [233] S. *Smith* [234]	
Stephen Kingston		*No recommendation*
X James Blaine Cumberland	McPherson & others	Respectably
Bernard Hubly Junr Sunbury	*Capt last War*	
X Henry Lancaster	strongly recom by *Bingham*	
X Isaac Duncan Philadelphia	applies for Capt of Cavalry McPherson & Latimer strongly recommended	
X Robert Conolly Lt in Revolutionary army Bucks County	McPherson & others writes *badly.* probably not *excellent*	
Charles De Krafft Foreigner Philadelphia *dated*	alleges himself to be an old soldier Capt of Engineers No *Recommendation*	*Inquire*
Robert Taylor	William Bingham	*Qr*
Joseph Long LANCASTER	Coleman [235] ⎫ Smith ⎪ Hand ⎬ *Wheelen* ⎪ *Denny* ⎭	Respectably (not clear). Signs a letter written by *another*
James P Nelson	Gregg [236]	Likely to raise

232. Jones, a resident of Philadelphia, served in the Continental Navy during the American Revolution.

233. Henry Latimer, who practiced medicine in Wilmington, Delaware, had served as a surgeon during the American Revolution. He was a member of the House of Representatives from 1794 to 1795, when he resigned because of his election to the United States Senate. He remained in the Senate until 1801.

234. Samuel Smith, a veteran of the American Revolution, was a Baltimore merchant. He was a member of the House of Representatives from 1793 to 1803. Originally a Federalist, he changed his allegiance to the Republicans in 1796.

235. In 1796, Robert Coleman of Lancaster County, Pennsylvania, was elected to the Electoral College as a Federalist.

236. Andrew Gregg was a member of the House of Representatives from Pennsylvania from 1791 to 1807.

Mifflin County ☞	Edmiston [237] *Gurney* Wm. *Brown* Jno. *Clarke* [238] supported by *Latimer* *General Irvine*	a Company sober *young* man *surveyor* *respectably* *for a Lieu-* *tenancy* *strong*
Samuel Irvin Northampton	property & connections good *politics* good *qualities* *Sitgreaves*	strongly *rec-* *ommended* For Captain but will accept a Lieutenancy
Robert Hunter Philadelphia	Not Strong Duncan Lieper [239]	
James Ashman Huntington Major of Militia	Govr. *Howard* [240] satisfied he is a young Gentle- man of great merit	*Respectably*
Robert Provines of Huntington	Not strong	*Capt. or Lieu-* *tency*
Samuel Bowman *Luzerne* said that he was in the Revolutionary Army Letter Aug 8.[241]	Sitgreaves who is strong— advises that he be permitted to nominate his own Lieuten- ants	Provisional *Army*
William Graham *Bedford*	well recommed by James Ross *Senator*	
Joseph Gray Huntington	*vigour of Youth* Not strong	will be *Ensign*
Thomas Dewes	*Not strong.* will go into *Marine* if he cannot do better	
Thomas Anderson Mifflin County	has lost two brothers in Amer- ican service	No recom- mendation *Qr*
Jesse Smith Bucks County	Qr if not an Ensign	

237. Samuel or Joseph Edmiston of Mifflin County, Pennsylvania.

238. Clark, a resident of York, Pennsylvania, had been an aide-de-camp to Nathanael Greene during the American Revolution. On February 23, 1793, he was promoted to lieutenant colonel commandant in the Fourth Sub Legion (*Executive Journal*, I, 133, 134). He resigned from the Army on July 1, 1794 (Heitman, *United States Army*, I, 304).

239. Thomas Leiper, a resident of Philadelphia, was a Republican and a close friend of Thomas Jefferson.

240. John E. Howard.

241. Letter not found.

Robert McKee Dauphin	Nothing *strong*	
Henry G Slough Lancaster *24* years	Hand Coleman Kittera good subaltn McP.	respectably as *Lieutenant*
George Brown faithful Citizen Bucks	*Not strong*	
X John E Buchanan Jun *Franklin County*	John Cadwaller &c recommends	Respectably *Inquire*
Daniel Eddy Lucerne	Perfect Lt McP.	Not strong *Inquire* Qr. if not good Ensign
William Bell Philadelphia acquainted with Dauphin	*Hand* on credit of others	Qr
James Ralston *Easton* *Young* Gentleman	Sitgreaves J Beatty Gov Howel	Respectably
John T O Neal	undaunted *Courage* Skyren [242] *Wm* Wister [243]	
Richard Willing	very good pretensions	
Benjamin Wallace *Dauphin County*	Watts [244] Alexander [245] Duncan	Respectably as Subaltern
Hugh Brady *Sunbury* in North- umberland	Lieutenant in Western Army *Daniel Smith* [246] *Thomas Grant* [247] }	Father & brother lost in Revo- lution

242. John Skyren was a Philadelphia merchant.

243. Wister was a Philadelphia merchant.

244. David Watts was a lawyer in Carlisle, Pennsylvania.

245. William Alexander of Pennsylvania held the rank of captain at the close of the American Revolution.

246. Daniel Smith was a resident of Milton in Northumberland County, Pennsylvania.

247. In July, 1798, Grant, a resident of Northumberland County, Pennsylvania, was appointed commissioner of valuations for the seventh division of Pennsylvania (*Executive Journal*, I, 288, 289).

	McPherson Miles[248] Rawle[249] } *good Captain*	
Robert Gray *same place* came from Ireland very *Young*	*Daniel Smith* ☞ Gentleman & man of spirit Young Hall[250] *J Ewing*[251]	Now Captain of a Volunteer company *Respectably* will accept Lieutenancy
Francis Ingraham Bucks County	Refers to J Laurence & General Moylan[252]	*Property* Inquire
Samuel Fulton *Merchant Philadelphia*	McPherson Baynton[253] Fox[254] Latimer B *Rush* Rawle	Respectably capt or Lieutenancy of Artillery
Wm C. Rogers Philadelphia	very respectably recomd for Capt. of Dragoon McPherson	
Andrew Boggs Mifflin County	Gregg *reputable* for Lieutenancy Hartley speaks of his *connections good* *no impropriety*	Qr.
Benjamin Gibbs Philadelphia	Rawle McPherson Sitgreaves	Respectably recommended ☞
Charles Wm Porter Stephen S Gibbs	Rawle	Respectably

248. Samuel Miles, who held the rank of brigadier general of the Pennsylvania state troops at the close of the American Revolution, had been the mayor of Philadelphia. In 1796 he was elected to the Electoral College as a Republican.

249. William Rawle was United State attorney for the District of Pennsylvania from 1791 to 1800.

250. Charles Hall was a lawyer in Sunbury, Pennsylvania.

251. Jasper Ewing was a resident of Northumberland County, Pennsylvania.

252. In the George Washington Papers, Library of Congress, there is a list which is in an unknown handwriting and is entitled "Pennsylvania Lieutenants continued." At the bottom of this list He wrote:

"Samuel Craig
Francis Ingraham } Inquire Moylan."

Stephen Moylan, who was brevetted a brigadier general at the close of the American Revolution, was commissioner of loans for Pennsylvania.

253. Peter Baynton was a Philadelphia merchant. In 1798 he was treasurer of the Commonwealth of Pennsylvania.

254. Either George Fox, a lawyer in Philadelphia, or Edward Fox, a Philadelphia auctioneer.

Philadelphia	Rundle [255]	☞
	Bainton	
	Morgan	
Cromwel Pierce	Quaere	now Capt of
Chester	Richard Thomas	Militia
	Jno Hannum.[256]	
Andrew Johnson	*Hartly* & *Robinson* [257]	Qr
	Clarke & Eddy [258]	
	officer late War	
Frederick Evans	Hartly	Not *very*
Middle Creek	Kitera	strong Qr
Northumberland	Sitgreaves	
Richard Parker	William Alexander	Qr
Carlisle	Storekeeper	
James Reid	Russel [259]	now Adjutant
York County	Eddie	probably a
company	Miller	good Lieu-
		tenant?

CAPTAINS

Josiah McElwane 4	*Anthony* [260] *Latimer Gur-*	☞
Philadelphia	*ney* Philadelphia	
Henry *Westcot*	*Anthony Rundle Latimer*	☞
do		
Gibbs	Anthony	
Thomas W Britton	McPherson Morgan *Hare* [261]	
Matthew Henry!!	Hy. Miller—*Sitgreaves—Kittera* ⎱	☞
Lancaster Law	Hand Coleman ⎰	*Strong*
William Wallace	*Kittera*	Qr.
(law)		
Joseph Knox	*John Shippen* [262] G *Chambers*	
Young Merchant	—Hartly Kittera	
Shippensburgh	Wm Alexander	
25 years	He will take a Lieutenancy	
	well ☞	
Nelson Wade	Not Strong Benj Ritten-	
Montgomery	house [263]	
County	Quaere? ask for Ltcy.	

255. Richard Rundle was a Philadelphia merchant.

256. James Hannum represented Chester County in the 1798 Pennsylvania House of Representatives.

257. William or James Robinson, both Philadelphia merchants.

258. George Eddy was a Philadelphia merchant.

259. Alexander Russell, a veteran of the American Revolution, was the brigade inspector of York County, Pennsylvania.

260. Joseph Anthony was a Philadelphia merchant.

261. Robert Hare was speaker of the Pennsylvania Senate from 1796 to 1800.

262. In 1800 Shippen was clerk to the commissioners appointed to adjust the title to land in the Wyoming Valley.

263. Rittenhouse, the brother of David Rittenhouse, made instruments for

Edward Pearce
  Chester County
  Lieutenant
	Richard Thomas Quaere	

Jacob Ashmeade	*Capt late War*	*Inquire*
Peter Faulkener *Easton*	officer in late army Fœderal Dayton *Sitgreaves*	*Strong* ☞
John Johnston *Lewistown*	Potter [264] Edmeston	*Strong* ☞ Quaere?

George Kerr *46*
  Yk County—
    Merchant
	Hand
	Miller
	Hartly
		pretty good
		  recommen-
		  dation

Daniel Broadhead
  Junr
  Philadelphia 49
	Kittera	*property*
		Qr

James Simmons 50
  Philad
	North
	Brooks [265]
		Qr. his
		  political
		  principles?

James House 51
  Philadelphia
  Painter from *New*
  England
	Hopkinson [266]
	Harpur [267]
		Respectable
		Qr. Lieuten-
		  ant

George Armstrong Mifflin Town	*Gregg* *Otis* Wm. *Sterrit* [268] *Proctor* *James Armstrong* [269]	Subaltern *Respectably*
Alexander Jackson Mifflin Town 53	Wm. *Sterrit* Proctor	Subaltern *Qr*
James Stewart Cumberland	Col Anderson [270] supported by Latimer Nichol &c	Deserving young *man*

mathematical calculations. In 1791 Governor Thomas Mifflin of Pennsylvania commissioned him a judge of the Court of Common Pleas for Montgomery County, Pennsylvania.

264. Richard or James Potter, both Philadelphia merchants.

265. Bowyer Brooks was a Philadelphia boatbuilder.

266. Joseph Hopkinson was a lawyer in Philadelphia. On May 4, 1798, the Senate confirmed his appointment as commissioner to hold a treaty with the Oneida Indians (*Executive Journal*, I, 273–74).

267. Robert Harpur of New York City was a member of the New York Assembly from 1777 to 1784. From 1778 to 1795 he was deputy secretary of state for New York. In 1795 he moved to Broome County.

268. In 1798 William Sterrit represented Mifflin County in the Pennsylvania House of Representatives.

269. Armstrong, a physician from Mifflin County, was elected to the House of Representatives as a Federalist and served from 1793 to 1795.

270. William Anderson was a veteran of the American Revolution.

Qr. if not a
tolerable
Lieutenant

Edward Scott   56

LT COLONELS & MAJORS

1 William Richardson Atlee   Major recomd by F Johnson
   C   G Latimer
                                            McPherson & others

14 Andrew Ralston   do   recom *Irvin* & others. *P Qr*
17 Jacob Slough   do   *Kittera* & *Sitgreaves*
    C   Indifferently spoken of by the Officers of the West-
                        ern army as *to Courage*
                        well recommended by *Coleman*

Samuel Craig *41* [271]   ⎤ Moore [272]   Kittera   ⎤
   C   Well recommended ⎥ Johnson   St Greaves ⎥
                Capt in Arm   ⎬   ⎬
James Smith 61   ⎥ St Greaves   Hand   ⎥
   C   Brevet Captain   ⎦ Peters [273] Bingham   ⎦
                Gurney
                Laurance
Philip Strubing 82   Cavalry
Joseph McKinney *88—129* John Montgomery Hartley   Well worth
                          E Blaine [274]   Kittera   confidence
                          Js. Armstrong   J Shippen General Irvin
                          William Alexander   *A Grade
                                                     lower*
Andrew Johnson 38 & *96* officer in late War Clarke ⎫ Prothos ⎫ Qr if not
                                              J Eddy ⎭   ⎭ for
                                                                 Cap-
                                                                 tain
George Taylor 154   *Inquire of McPherson*
Edd. Butler   155   Recommended by George Walton [275]
                          at present Capt in the army
Benajmin R Morgan—*Qr*
James Blaine   Miller & others   Majority *too much*
   Cumberland
John Walbach   foreign Major of Cavalry
   Lancaster

271. See note 252.
272. John Moore was a prominent Philadelphia merchant and member of the
city council.
273. Richard Peters, a lawyer in Philadelphia, was a delegate to the Continental Congress in 1782 and 1783. He served in the Pennsylvania House of
Representatives from 1787 to 1790 and in the state Senate from 1791 to 1792.
In 1792 he became United States judge for the District of Pennsylvania.
274. Ephraim Blaine, who had been commissary general of purchases during
the American Revolution, was a resident of Carlisle, Pennsylvania.
275. Walton, a signer of the Declaration of Independence and of the Articles
of Confederation, was a veteran of the American Revolution. He was governor

LT COL

Alexander Patterson	No. 25	Recommended by Sitgreaves & Hand the latter knew him as quarter Master
George Stevenson	157	James Ross　　　　as Major
William *Henderson*	70	Capt in Army　*Hand* & *Irvin*
Thomas Moore	79	*Wm. Bingham*
William Alexander		
James Ross	16	well recommended *but wont do*
Lancaster		

Francis Nichols　*formerly a Major* or　　　　　Inquire particularly
　　　　Lieutenant Colonel

Thomas *Buchanan*　　　　*Captain*
Cumberland　　　　says hes as brave as Ceaser
Brigadier of Pensylvania　　*universally beloved*　　　Respectably
　　　　　　General Irvin recommends
　　　　　　him for his *intelligence*

Uriah Springer
　Fayette County　　　　T. Lewis [276]
　formerly a Captain in
　　Revol. Army　　　　　　　　　　*Inquire*
　served in Western army
　　Adlum　　　　strong by Peters
General John Gibson

PENSYLVANIA

2	Joseph McKinny	Capt	Cumberland
10	John Sharp	Lt	do
7	George Hamell	Ensign	do.
3	James Blaine	Capt	Cumberland
6	Samuel B Magaw.	Lt. Chamb.	Franklin
8	Archibald Davis	Ensign	Lancaster
[Lding Lt.] [277]	Andrew Johnston	Capt.	York
3	Elisha P Barrows	Lt	do
6	John A Douglass	Ensign	do.
6	Matthew Henry	Capt	Lancaster
7	Henry G Slough	Lt.	do
10	Thomas Witner	Ensign	do
4	George Taylor	Capt	Philadelph
1	Samuel Fulton	Lt	Philadel
2	Hugh H Potts	Ensign	do

of Georgia from 1779 to 1780 and again from 1789 to 1790. In 1795 he was elected to the United States Senate to fill the vacancy caused by the resignation of James Jackson, and he served in that position until February, 1796.

276. Francis Lewis was a resident of Northumberland County.

277. This and the following material within brackets are not in H's handwriting.

[side note:] Lt Colonels & Majors

5	William R Atlee	Capt	Philadelph
5	Josiah McElwane	Lt.	Philadelph
3	John S Porter	Chester	do
7	Hugh Brady	Capt	Sunbury Northumberland
2	James P Nelson	Lt.	Mifflin
9	John Smith	Ensign	Northumberland
8	William Graham	Capt	Bedford
8	Robert Laurance	Lt	Huntington
5	Robert Chambers	Ensign	Do.
10	David Duncan	Cap	Alleghany
4	Edward Nicholas	Lt.	do.
1	Alexander McNair	Ens	do.
9	Thomas Swearingen	Capt	Washington
9	Benjamin Wallace	Lt.	Dauphine
4	Thomas Lee	Ensign	Erie

[annexed to the New Jersey Regiment]	3	Samuel Bowman	Capt.	Lucerne
	1	Samuel Irvine	Lt.	Northampton
	6	John Milroy	Ensign	Mifflin
	2	Peter Faulkener	Cap.	Easton Northampton
	3	Henry Betz	Lt.	Read Berks
	5	Benjamin Worrall	Ensn.	do.
[annexed to the Jersey Regiment]	10	James Ralston	Capt	Easton Northampton
	10	William Carson	Lt.	Dauphine
	10	John Montgomery	Ensign	do

[PENNSYLVANIA FIELD OFFICERS]

[Thomas L Moore	Philadelphia	Lieut. Colonel
Wm: Henderson	Franklin	1st. Major
George Stephenson	Allegany	2d. Major]

From Timothy Pickering

[*Trenton, August 21, 1798.* On August 21, 1798, Pickering wrote to Hamilton: "Not to miss the mail, I wrote you one line today." *Letter not found.*]

From Timothy Pickering [1]

(Confidential)   Trenton August 21. [-22] 1798.

Dear Sir,

Not to miss the mail, I wrote you one line today,[2] and inclosed a letter from I suppose General Miranda.[3] If its contents give rise to any questions which it will be prudent for you to ask and for me to answer by the mail, it may be done, otherwise the information may be suspended till we meet.

Just before I left Philadelphia,[4] I received a letter from General Knox, in answer to one I had written at the request of Captain Mitchel of the artillery, who wished to be one of his aids de camp.[5] Mitchel, you will have observed is since dead.[6] But my object in noticing this matter is to inform you, that General Knox manifests, pretty strongly, his dissatisfaction in your being appointed in a manner to precede him in the military line; I conclude he will not serve. Altho' I should have been well pleased with his accepting his commission, I do not by any means deem his loss irreparable. Altho' by the delay of the nominations one day, I received your

ALS, Hamilton Papers, Library of Congress; ALS, letterpress copy, Massachusetts Historical Society, Boston; copy, Hamilton Papers, Library of Congress. The letterpress copy does not include the postscript.

1. For an explanation of the contents of this letter, see the introductory note to George Washington to H, July 14, 1798.

2. Letter not found.

3. Francisco de Miranda to H, April 6–June 7, 1798. See also Miranda to H, April 1, 1797; February 7, 1798.

4. The offices of the United States Government had been moved to Trenton because of the yellow fever epidemic in Philadelphia. See Oliver Wolcott, Jr., to H, August 9, 1798, note 4.

5. On August 1, 1798, Pickering wrote to Henry Knox: "About a week or ten days since, Captain Donald G. Mitchell of Connecticut (son of Mr. [Stephen Mix] Mitchell who was a senator from that state and now a judge of its superior court) of the corps of artillerists and engineers, . . . expressed to me his wishes to join some general officer, as his aide-de-camp, and particularly mentioned you . . ." (copy, Hamilton Papers, Library of Congress). On August 8, 1798, Knox replied that if he were ". . . to be in a situation of requiring an aide de camp, I should certainly place at your request Capt. Mitchell on the list of other applicants. . . . But in the present aspect of the arrangement of Genl. Officers I am apprehensive that I shall be excluded from the service" (copy, Hamilton Papers, Library of Congress).

6. Mitchell died on August 6, 1798.

letter [7] expressing your willingness to serve under Knox, yet I concealed it, in order that the arrangement of nominations of Major Generals, which I had seen, as formed by General Washington, & which I saw would govern, might leave you, where you ought to be, in the first place. In Genl. Washington's answer to my letter, of which I sent you some extracts,[8] there is not, as I recollect, the most distant idea of General Knox's making any difficulty in acting subordinately to you; his apprehensions arise wholly on General Pinckney's account. I think it right to add, That from the first moment that a commander in Chief was thought of, no name was mentioned but yours: for until the nomination was actually made, I had no suspicion that Genl. Washington would ever again enter the field of war. I know also that not only all your friends, but your political enemies have the highest respect for your abilities: while the latter, the political enemies also of General Knox, estimate his talents by a very moderate scale: and some persons have in my hearing called him a *weak* man. I think him neither *weak* nor *great:* but with pretty good abilities, possessing an imposing manner that impresses an idea of mental faculties beyond what really exist. I am certain that if he had been second to Genl. W. and of course likely to command in chief, great dissatisfaction would have been excited. I much doubt even whether the nomination would have been confirmed by the Senate.

I write this letter in the confidence of friendship, for the public good, which I conceive to be involved in your holding your present superior station. I have always supposed you & Genl. Knox to be cordial friends. I wish you to continue such: I persuade myself he is too good a patriot to suffer the present disappointment to actuate him to any improper conduct; and that he will at least passively acquiesce. I think he will *gain* no honor, by declining to serve under you: I rather believe his refusal will detract from the reputation he now possesses.

Mr. Wolcot showed me (as you requested) your letter to him [9] suggesting the expediency of calling you & General Knox into immediate service—to aid the arrangements and operations of the

7. H to Pickering, July 17, 1798.
8. Washington to Pickering, July 11, 1798; Pickering to Washington, July 6, 1798. For this correspondence, see Pickering to H, July 16, 1798, notes 2 and 3.
9. H to Oliver Wolcott, Jr., August 6, 1798.

department of war. I was so well pleased with the idea, and thought it so important, or rather so essential, to the formation of an army in time to afford some security to our country, that I told Mr. Wolcot I would write to the President, and urge the measure.[10] Mr. W. approved. I have yet no answer. The Secy. of War was at the time indisposed: but enquiring of his chief clerk, I found that he also had written for the same purpose.[11] It is since this that I received Genl. Knox's letter before mentioned; and that gave rise to a new thought—that as he manifestly intended to decline accepting his commission, and the President would be on the spot to converse with him, the taking charge of the War Department again, might be proposed to him: for the President, I have seen, has been informed of a very general dissatisfaction in its present direction.

After the appointments of General Officers were made, but before they were known beyond Philadelphia I recd. a letter from Mr. Jay,[12] expressing the same opinion respecting you which I had done to General Washington, & the same reasons (the nature of the war in which we were to be engaged) why superior talents should be sought for, without regard to rank in a former war. I therefore made Mr. Jay acquainted with my conduct in the business.[13]

I am, dear sir, with great respect & esteem   yr. obt. servt.

T. Pickering.

General A. Hamilton.

Augt. 22. Since writing the inclosed I have turned to Mr. Jay's letter. His words are—"I cannot conceal from you my solicitude that the late Secy. of the Treasury may be brought forward in a manner corresponding with his talents and services. It appears to me that his former military station & character, taken in connection

10. On August 8, 1798, in a letter to John Adams, Pickering proposed that "the Inspector General, and major General Knox, be called into immediate service, to aid the Secretary of War in the essential arrangements for the army to be raised" (ALS, Adams Family Papers, deposited in the Massachusetts Historical Society, Boston).

11. John Caldwell. See James McHenry to H, August 10, 1798.

12. A copy of John Jay's letter, dated July 18, 1798, is in the Hamilton Papers, Library of Congress.

13. Pickering to Jay, July 28, 1798 (copy, Hamilton Papers, Library of Congress).

with his late important place in the administration, would justify measuring his rank by his merit & value." The reason of Mr. Jay's solicitude is thus expressed—"We shall probably have very different Generals to contend with from those which Britain sent here last war; and we should have very different ones to oppose them from several of those who then led our troops." This, you may recollect, is the same sentiment which I expressed in my letter to General Washington which I showed you.[14] In a subsequent letter Mr. Jay joined me in regretting that the terms of the nomination and appointment left any room to question your right of preceedence.[15] I mentioned the point to you: but you answered, that it had been settled in the case of Baron Steuben.[16] No doubt you have seen some paragraphs in the Columbian Centinel (B. Russell's fulsome paper) [17] in which it is said that Genl. Knox is next in command to Genl. Washington. And a letter from the President to the Secy. of War (in answer, I suppose, to his calling you & Knox into service) expresses that to be his opinion, and consequently "that Pinckney must rank before Hamilton": [18] but that is not the only

14. See note 7.
15. On July 26, 1798, Jay wrote to Pickering: "Hamilton's Rank is I fear still liable to question—your Remarks on that Head certainly have weight. Such Doubts should not be left to be brought forward or not, at some future Day, according to Circumstances. To me it appears important, that the relative Rank of officers, and especially of General officers, should be *decidedly* ascertained known and acknowledged" (ALS, Massachusetts Historical Society, Boston).
16. This is apparently a reference to the fact that although in 1778 Baron von Steuben was appointed an inspector general with the rank of major general in the Continental Army, his highest previous rank had been that of captain in the Prussian Army.
17. Benjamin Russell was editor and publisher of the [Boston] *Columbian Centinel*, a Federalist paper and a strong supporter of John Adams.
The following item appeared in the *Columbian Centinel* on August 11, 1798, under the heading "Vermont Brattleboro' July 31": "The President, with the consent of the Senate, has appointed Generals Knox, Hamilton, Lee and Morgan, Major-Generals in the army of the United States.
"The appointment of these officers reflects high honor upon the President's discernment. They were the spirit of the army, in the war which established our *Independence*—who then so proper to defend it? An army of the Americans, headed by Washington, and seconded by Knox and his gallant associates, must be irresistable." On August 18, 1798, the *Columbian Centinel* wrote: "Major General Knox, as we before mentioned, is the first Major General, in the permanent army of the United States."
18. Adams to McHenry, August 14, 1798 (copy, Hamilton Papers, Library of Congress). See the introductory note to Washington to H, July 14, 1798.

consequence. *Lee* & *Hand* were on the *same day* named and approved as Major Generals; [19] and if Knox & Pinckney precede you, so will the other two; for I cannot see that their being named for the provisional army can make any difference, when that army shall be raised, and are you prepared for a station so much in the rear? God forbid that such an arrangement should be adopted. But the matter will rest on "General Washington's opinion and consent:" [20] and it is for this reason, principally, that I have added this postscript, that you may take such steps with the General as you may think proper to fix you in the station which the essential interests of our country require—the station in which I conceive the General meant to place you, according to the list which he sent by McHenry to the president, and in conformity with which, you, Pinckney & Knox were named.[21] I have just read the Genl's answer [22] to my letter about you; he does not hint an idea of any competition *save with Pinckney*. I inclose it for your perusal—& to be returned. If North [23] declines, the President is "prepared to appoint another and a better." [24] Is this Harry Jackson,[25] or Cobb? [26] Colo. Wm. Heth of

19. Henry Lee and Edward Hand. See Washington to H, July 14, 1798; McHenry to H, July 25, 1798.

20. On July 4, 1798, Washington wrote to McHenry: ". . . the General Staff . . . may be considered as so many parts of the Commander in Chief. Viewing them then in this light it will readily be seen how essential it is that they should be agreeable to him" (ALS, letterpress copy, George Washington Papers, Library of Congress). On July 5, 1798, Washington again wrote to McHenry: ". . . The appointment of these [general officers] are *important;* but those of the General Staff, are *all important:* insomuch that if I am looked to as Commander in Chief, I must be allowed to chuse such as will be agreeable to me" (ALS, letterpress copy, George Washington Papers, Library of Congress). On August 14, 1798, Adams wrote to McHenry: "In my opinion, as the matter now stands, General Knox is legally entitled to rank next to General Washington, and no other arrangement will give satisfaction. If General Washington is of this opinion, and will consent to it, you may call him [Knox] into actual service as soon as you please. . ." (copy, Hamilton Papers, Library of Congress).

21. See Washington to H, July 14, 1798.

22. Washington to Pickering, July 11, 1798. See Pickering to H, July 16, 1798, notes 2 and 3.

23. William North. See McHenry to H, July 25, 1798.

24. This quotation is from the last sentence of Adams to McHenry, August 14, 1798 (copy, Hamilton Papers, Library of Congress).

25. Henry Jackson, a native of Massachusetts, was a colonel during the American Revolution.

26. David Cobb of Massachusetts served as aide-de-camp to Washington from June 15, 1781, to January 7, 1783.

Virginia would joyfully take that office. But the appointment of
A. W. White [27] has grievously offended him.

Sincerely adieu!   T.P.

27. Anthony Walton White. See McHenry to H, July 25, 1798, note 9.

To Benjamin Stoddert

[New York, August 21, 1798]

Dear Sir

I, about a fortnight since, wrote to you [1] on the subject of a relation of mine desirous of entering into our Navy and recommending
him as a first Lieutenant; to which letter not having received an
answer, I am apprehensive it may have miscarried. You will oblige
me by your opinion as speedily as convenient how far there is a
prospect for him. I anticipate that there may be scruples from his
character of foreigner; but on full reflection I am satisfied it is
possible to carry this objection too far. The young man I recommend is every way worthy—I really believe he will be an acquisition. It has occurred to me that Capt Talbot [2] lately arrived who is
to take the command of the frigate building here, though an excellent man, is not a thorough bred seaman. Such a man as Capt
Hamilton would be an excellent second.

The Secry. of the ⟨Marine⟩

AL[S], RG 45, Naval Records Collection of the Office of Naval Records and
Library, Subject File: Personnel (NN), National Archives.
    1. H to Stoddert, August 8, 1798.
    2. Silas Talbot, a native of Massachusetts, had served during the American
Revolution, first as a lieutenant colonel in the Army and then as a captain
in the Navy. After the war he settled in upstate New York. He was a member of the New York Assembly in 1792 and 1793 and a member of the House
of Representatives from 1793 to 1795. On June 4, 1794, he was appointed one
of the six "Captains of the ships to be procured in pursuance of the act to
provide 'a naval armament'" (1 *Stat.* 350–51 [March 27, 1794]) with the
understanding that he would assist in "the building of the said ships" (*Executive Journal,* I, 160, 161). He was then placed in charge of the vessel that
was to be built at New York. When work on the frigate at New York was
discontinued in 1796 by "An Act supplementary to an act entitled 'An act
to provide a Naval Armament'" (1 *Stat.* 453–54 [April 20, 1796]), Talbot
either lost his commission or was placed on the inactive list. On May 31, 1796,

he was appointed agent "for the purpose of obtaining the release of impressed American citizens" in the West Indies (*Executive Journal*, I, 231), a position provided for by "An Act for the relief and protection of American Seamen" (1 *Stat.* 477–78 [May 28, 1796]). On May 11, 1798, he was reappointed a captain in the Navy (*Executive Journal*, I, 274, 275) and, as H notes, was reassigned to the frigate under construction in New York.

To Oliver Wolcott, Junior

New York August 21. 1798

My Dear Sir

Your two letters of the 9th.[1] reached this place during an absence on necessary business which only terminated on Saturday.[2]

Our friend McHenry has adopted the ideas suggested to him.[3] And you may rely on my effectual cooperation. At the same time, as a total dislocation of residence, to fulfil in all its extent the idea you intimate, would be unqualified ruin to me, I must endeavor to avoid it. Frequent visits and constant communication and the immediate charge of certain branches of the service will I doubt not substantially suffice.

The objects you indicate as deserving primary attention will engage it.

In respect to Mr. Wharton, I shall with pleasure promote whatever may suit him & the service. But I do not know that there is in the establishment any provision for a clerk or Secretary to a General officer. It is usual except in the case of the Commander in Chief for Aides-De Camp to perform the duties of such characters. In reference to *Aides*, my situation is this—I have already yielded to the strong wishes of Mr. & Mrs. Church the promise to appoint their eldest son[4] as one—for the other I must endeavor to find an experienced officer. If Mr Wharton desires an appointment in some regiment to take his chance for a place in the family of some general officer, I will assist the wish. Let me, if you please, understand this matter with precision.

Yrs. Affecty   A Hamilton

Oliver Wolcott Esqr

ALS, Connecticut Historical Society, Hartford; copy, Hamilton Papers, Library of Congress.

1. One of the two letters from Wolcott to H on August 9, 1798, is listed in the appendix to this volume. In this letter Wolcott recommended Fishburne Wharton of Philadelphia for "the situation of a Clerk or Secy to a General Officer."

2. H had been in Albany and in Salisbury, Connecticut. See Philip Schuyler to H, August 17, 1798.

3. See H to James McHenry, July 30, 1798; McHenry to H, August 10, 1798.

4. Philip Church, son of John B. and Angelica Church. See H to McHenry, July 28, 1798.

To Rufus King

New York Aug 22. 1798

My Dear Sir

Your several letters of May 12th, June the 6th and 8th have regularly come to hand.

You will be no doubt fully instructed of the measures which have taken place on the part of our government and you will have seen in the numerous addresses to the President[1] a confirmation of the opinion I gave you respecting the disposition of this Country.[2] From both you will have derived satisfaction though you should not think we are *yet* where we ought now to be. But console yourself with the assurance that we are progressive in good. The indications are to my mind conclusive that we are approaching fast to as great unanimity as any country ever experienced and that our energies will be displayed in proportion to whatever exigencies shall arise.

I have received several letters from General Miranda.[3] I have written an answer[4] to some of them, which I send you to deliver or not according to your estimate of what is passing in the scene where you are. Should you deem it expedient to suppress my letter, you may do it & say as much as you think fit on my part in the nature of a communication through you.

With regard to the enterprise in question[5] I wish it much to be undertaken but I should be glad that the principal agency was in the UStates—they to furnish the whole land force necessary. The command in this case would very naturally fall upon me—and I hope I should disappoint no favourable anticipation. The independency of the separated territory under a *moderate* government, with the joint guarantee of the cooperating powers, stipulating equal privileges in commerce would be the sum of the results to be accomplished.

Are we yet mature for this undertaking? Not quite—But we ripen fast, and it may (I think) be rapidly brought to maturity, if an efficient negotiation for the purpose is at once set on foot upon this ground. Great Britain cannot alone ensure the accomplishment of the object. I have some time since advised certain preliminary steps to prepare the way consistently with national character and justice. I was told they would be pursued, but I am not informed whether they have been or not.

Yrs. Affecly   A H

R King Esq

ALS, New-York Historical Society, New York City; copy, in the handwriting of John Church Hamilton, Hamilton Papers, Library of Congress.
1. For these addresses supporting John Adams's foreign policy toward France, see King to H, July 31, 1798, note 1.
2. H to King, June 6, 1798.
3. Francisco de Miranda to H, April 1, 1797; February 7, April 6–June 7, 1798.
4. H to Miranda, August 22, 1798.
5. For the "enterprise in question," see Miranda to H, April 6–June 7, 1798.

To Francisco de Miranda [1]

New york Aug 22. 1798

Sir

I have lately received by duplicates your letter of the 6th of April with a postscript of the 9th. of June.[2] The Gentleman you mention [3] in it has not made his appearance to me nor do I know of his arrival in this Country; so that I can only divine the object from the hints in your letter.

The sentiments I entertain with regard to that object have been long since in your knowlege. But I could personaley have no participation in it unless patronised by the Government of this Country. It was my wish that matters had been ripened for a cooperation in the course of this fall on the part of this Country.

But this can now scarcely be the case. The Winter however may mature the project and an effectual cooperation by the Ustates may take place. In this case I shall be happy in my official station to be an instrument of so good a work.

The plan in my opinion ought to be, a fleet of Great Britain, an armmy of the ustates, a Government for the liberated territorey agreable to both the Cooperators, about which there will be probably no difficulty. To arrange the plan a competent authority from Great-Britain to some person here is the best expedient. Your presence here will in this case be extremely essential.

We are raising an army of about Twelve Thousand men. Genl. Washington has resumed his station at the head of our armies. I am appointed second in command.[4]

With esteem and regard I remain   Dr Sir

Copy, in John Church Hamilton's handwriting and with corrections in H's handwriting, Hamilton Papers, Library of Congress; copy, New-York Historical Society, New York City; copy, Academia Nacional de la Historia, Caracas, Venezuela.

1. This leter was enclosed in H to Rufus King, August 22, 1798. For background to this letter, see Miranda to H, April 1, 1797; February 7, April 6–June 7, August 17, 1798.

2. H was mistaken. The postscript is dated June 7.

3. Pedro José Caro. See Miranda to H, April 6–June 7, 1798.

4. For George Washington's appointment as commander in chief, see H to Washington, July 8, 1798, note 1. For H's appointment as inspector general, see the introductory note to Washington to H, July 14, 1798.

John Church Hamilton endorsed the copy of this letter which is in the Hamilton Papers, Library of Congress, as follows: "This and the following letter were copied by me on my birth day when I was six years old—the object being to preserve secrecy until circumstances shd warrant publicity." For "the following letter," see H to King, August 22, 1798.

From Timothy Pickering [1]

[Trenton] August 22. 1798.

Dr. Sir

In writing freely as I have done yesterday and to-day in the inclosed letter to you,[2] disclosing what is contemplated respecting your military station, far from being apprehensive of justly incurring blame I consider myself as performing a hazardous duty: but I am not conscious that the risque of incurring the displeasure of any man ever deterred me from doing what I conceived to be my duty. My anxiety to see you fixed second in command, has arisen from the opinion which for twenty years I have entertained of your superior genius and talents combined with integrity. The integrity of your competitors I trust is also unimpeachable. General Pinckney's character I believe to be eminently pure: and were their other qualifications equal, my solicitude would cease: nay, there would be an evident propriety in their preceeding you. My interference has not proceeded from any claims you have on my friendship: for tho' we were never to my knowledge for one moment at enmity, our acquaintance was never so intimate as in the proper, strict sense of the word to make us friends. My respect, esteem & attachment have been founded on the qualities of your head and heart, as above suggested: and all the return I expected was, the regard due simply to an *honest man*. Viewing me as entitled to this character, you will not, nor would any one who knew as well as you my frank, downright disposition, ascribe to flattery the sentiments I have expressed of you in our correspondence: it was impossible to reason on the subject without expressing them.

Thus much I have thought proper to add in justification and as an apology for the inclosed, and for any similar sentiments in former letters.

Adieu! T. Pickering

P.S. I postpone sending Genl. Washington's letter.[3] I may want it in conversing with my colleagues, before the question of rank shall be referred to the General.

Alexander Hamilton Esqr.

ALS, Hamilton Papers, Library of Congress; ALS, letterpress copy, Massachusetts Historical Society, Boston; copy, Hamilton Papers, Library of Congress.
    1. For an explanation of the contents of his letter, see the introductory note to George Washington to H, July 14, 1798.
    2. Pickering to H, August 21–22, 1798.
    3. Washington to Pickering, July 11, 1798 (ALS, letterpress copy, George

Washington Papers, Library of Congress; copy, Hamilton Papers, Library of Congress). See also Pickering to H, July 16, August 21–22, 1798.

To Oliver Wolcott, Junior

New York August 22. 1798

My Dear Sir

No one knows better than yourself how difficult and oppressive is the collection even of taxes very moderate in their amount if there be a defective circulation. According to all the phœnomena which fall under my notice this is our case in the interior parts of the Country.

Again Individual Capitals & consequently the faculty of direct loans is not very extensive in the U States. The Banks can only go a certain length and must not be forced. Yet Government will stand in need of large anticipations.

For these and other reasons, which I have thought well of—I have come to a conclusion that our Treasury ought to raise up a circulation of its own. I mean by the issuing of Treasury notes payable some on demand, others at different periods from very short to pretty considerable—at first having but little time to run.

This appears to me an expedient equally necessary to keep the circulation full & to facilitate the anticipations which Government will certainly need. By beginning early the public eye will be familiarized—and as emergencies press it will be easy to enlarge without hazard to Credit.

Think well of this suggestion and do not discard it without perceiving well a better substitute.

Adieu Yrs   A Hamilton

O Wolcott Esq

ALS, Connecticut Historical Society, Hartford; ADf, Hamilton Papers, Library of Congress; copy, in the handwriting of William LeConte, Hamilton Papers, Library of Congress.

From Timothy Pickering [1]

(private & confidential)   Trenton Augt. 23. 1798

Dr. Sir,

Mr Mc.Henry has just handed to Mr. Wolcott & me his letter to the President on the subject of calling you and Genl. Knox into immediate service,[2] together with General Knox's letter to him [3] in answer to the one inclosing his commission. Genl. Knox's letter claiming the first rank, I see has been transmitted to you,[4] and I was glad to see you, in your answer to the Secy. of War,[5] tenacious of the station in which the Commander in Chief, the President & Senate, and the public voice have placed you. I did not know till now that Genl. Washington had so explicitly written you respecting your taking rank of Genl. Knox, *whom he loved;* [6] altho' I had formed the same conclusion from his *silence* concerning him in his letter to me—which I now inclose,[7] and which Mr. Wolcott only of my colleagues has seen. The original letter from Genl. W. to you, Mc.-Henry now informs us, was by him shown to the President: notwithstanding which you have seen where you would have been placed. Mc.Henry said also, that Genl. W. made your appointment the *sine qua non* of his accepting the chief command. The weight of these facts seems to have escaped the President's recollection, or he would not desire that Genl. Knox should take rank of you. It is plain that Genl. K. has conversed with him—referred to the rule of the former war, to determine the relative rank of officers of the same grade appointed on the same day; and the President has thence concluded that Genl. K. is "legally" entitled to the precedence.[8] But, as I yesterday informed you, the change proposed to gratify Genl. Knox and the President, is by the latter put on General Washington's "opinion and consent;" and such consent surely can never be given, after the General's letter to you in which, as Mc.Henry says, he explicitly told you that he passed by Knox whom he loved, to give you the priority of rank. Upon the principle mentioned by Genl. Knox, *Hand* must clearly precede you, as well as Knox &

Pinckney: Lee I presume must follow you, as he was only a captain of horse when you, as aid to the Commander in chief, had the rank of lieut. colonel. I see in your letter to Mc.Henry [9] you refer to the *public voice* in your favour and justly, as I yesterday mentioned: yet the President imagines that the "*five* New England States" would be offended at your preceeding Knox! [10] He is most egregiously mistaken: it was among New England members of Congress that I heard you, and you only, mentioned as the Commander in Chief— until Genl. Washington was nominated: and I dare to say, that if among the New England delegates a vote were taken, nine in ten, if not the whole, would place you before Knox.

Mc.Henry is to write you to-day on the subject. He is utterly uninformed of my correspondence with General Washington and you concerning it. The reference of the matter to General W. is suspended: you will consider whether it should not be made; for he must decide in your favour. Mc.Henry had thought of not so referring it; but of taking the course which he said he would state to you to-day—that is, to propose to General Knox to accept, with a reservation of his claim under the old rule appealed to by him: [11] at the same time Mc.Henry says that rule is not now in force, nor ought to govern. Why then urge Genl. Knox's acceptance on that ground? It would be a delusive proposition to Genl. Knox; and if it did not eventually prove so to him, you would be in a predicament to excite the extreme regret of the great body of your fellow citizens, who would the more deeply deplore the arrangement from the very possible fall or other inevitable loss of the present commander in chief.

Very truly yours   T. Pickering.

A. Hamilton Esq

ALS, Hamilton Papers, Library of Congress; ALS, letterpress copy, Massachusetts Historical Society, Boston.

1. For an explanation of the contents of this letter, see the introductory note to George Washington to H, July 14, 1795.
2. James McHenry to John Adams, August 4, 1798 (ALS, Adams Family Papers, deposited in the Massachusetts Historical Society, Boston).
3. Henry Knox to McHenry, August 5, 1798, printed as an enclosure to McHenry to H, August 11, 1798.
4. See McHenry to H, August 11, 1798.
5. H to McHenry, first letter of August 19, 1798.
6. Washington to H, July 14, 1798.

7. See Pickering to H, July 16, 1798, notes 2 and 3.

8. This is a reference to a statement in Adams to McHenry, August 14, 1798, quoted in the introductory note to Washington to H, July 14, 1795.

9. H to McHenry, first letter of August 19, 1798.

10. This is a reference to a statement in Adams to McHenry, August 14, 1798, quoted in the introductory note to Washington to H, July 14, 1798.

11. For this proposal, see H to McHenry, first letter of August 19, 1798. For the "rule," see Oliver Wolcott, Jr., to Adams, September 17, 1798, quoted in the introductory note to Washington to H, July 14 1798.

To John Adams

New York August 24th. 1798

Sir

I have recommended to the Secretary at War, Mr Philip Church, my nephew, for the appointment of a Captain of Infantry.[1] This young Gentleman is personally known to you; but your knowlege of him is too slight to render it useless to speak of his qualifications. To the advantages of a good education he adds a very discreet judicious mind and an excellent heart—duly animated by that laudable pride and emulation which are the sure foundation of military worth. He is the eldest son of his father and extremely interesting to his parents and friends. I have myself so favourable an opinion of him that it is my intention to take him into my family as an *Aide De Camp*.

Under these circumstances, very contrary to the general rules by which I govern myself, I take the liberty to request his appointment as a personal favour to myself—and I venture to undertake for him that he will not discredit it. The appointment will also lay himself and all his friends under a particular obligation.

Let me at the same time beg you to be persuaded, Sir, that I shall never on any other occasion place a recommendation to office on a similar footing.

With perfect respect & esteem   I have the honor to be Sir   Your very Obed servt.   A Hamilton

The President of The UStates

ALS, Adams Family Papers, deposited in the Massachusetts Historical Society, Boston.

1. H to James McHenry, July 28, 1798.

From Benjamin Stoddert

Trenton 24 Aug 1798.

Dr. sir

I should have replied to your letter of the 8 Inst, before this time, had it not mentioned your intention of setting out on a Journey.[1] I am since honored with yours of the 21st.

I have no motive but truth, in saying that there is no man known to me by Character only, to whose wishes I would pay so much respect as yours—that I think you have such claims on this Country & this Govt.—that to insure the appointment of a Gentn. to be a Lieutt. in our navy, it should be sufficient to know it would oblige you. Anticipating that objections might be made at New York to Capt Hamilton, on the score of his being a Foreigner, I had turned my attention to the southward for an appointment for him—& I lamented that a Lieutt had already been mentioned to the Prest. for the Montezuma, of 20 guns, at Baltimore. Two more Vessels are preparing there, of 18..9 Pounders & one of larger size at Charleston —to one of these I supposed there would be no difficulty in appointing him first Lieut. To the South there are but few qualified men for the Navy—of course less competition. The middle & Eastern States, are able—at least it seems to be thought so—to furnish officers for our navy. If however, you prefer that Capt Hamilton should be mentioned to the Prest. for the Frigate at New York, I will with the utmost pleasure exert my influence for his appointment. In this case, presuming you know Capt Talbot, it might obviate objections, if he also would desire it.

I have the honor to be with real respect & esteem Dr Sir Yr most Obed Servt   Ben Stoddert.

ALS, Hamilton Papers, Library of Congress.
  1. H had been in Albany and in Salisbury, Connecticut. See Philip Schuyler to H, August 17, 1798.

To James McHenry [1]

New York Aug 25. 1798

Dr. Sir

I perceive it would be agreeable to the Commander in Chief to receive frequent communications from you and particularly to understand the state of public supplies, that is the quantities on hand & the measures in execution to procure others. I give you this hint as a guide & would advise to have a full statement made out with notes of what is further doing & send it to him.

Yrs. truly   A H

ADfS, Hamilton Papers, Library of Congress.
1. For background to this letter, see George Washington to H, August 9, 1798.

To John Jay [1]

New York Aug 27. 1798

Dear Sir

I was very sorry when at Albany not to have seen you.[2] I called the day after my arrival but you were then indisposed or abroad & the rest of my stay I was very unwell.

An apprehension is excited here that in consequence of the Petitions of the Militia Officers the persons named to the new Companies will not be appointed.[3] I take it for granted that this must be a groundless apprehension as far as may depend on the Executive. For certainly the ordinary Militia Officers can on no military principles have any pretensions in relation to *new* and *extraordinary* Corps which grow up—or are created. And as to expediency, nothing can be clearer. The utility of these new corps in various aspects needs no comment. Their existence depends on their being officered in the manner they themselves desire. To attempt to place them under the present Militia officers is to annihilate them.

Ten to *One* the Opposition on the part of these Officers originated in an Antifœderal scheme. Let them by their disappointment be disgusted & resign. What then? They will have acted presumptuously or ignorantly. Many bad men will be gotten rid of, & the best can easily be replaced with as good or better. Tis then a plain case. There is really not a difficulty worth the least attention.

Mr. Gracie[4] has solicited my interposition with you for the pardon of *Janus* Ross lately convicted of forging a Check on the Bank. His argument is that the culprit is of respectable connections in South Carolina—quite a lad (say from 16 to 18) a very simple lad—& led to this act by the embarrassment of not being able to account for the *prudent* expenditure of a sum of money advanced him by a friend of his fathers for his own use. I confide in what Mr Gracie says, & really believe it is as favourable a case for a pardon as can easily occur.

I remain with respect & true attachment Dr Sir   Yr Obed serv

A Hamilton

Governor Jay

ALS, Columbia University Libraries.

1. For background to this letter, see the introductory note to H to James McHenry, June 1, 1798.

2. H had been in Albany in early August. See Philip Schuyler to H, August 17, 1798.

3. This sentence and those that follow concern a dispute over who was to command the volunteer companies being raised under authority of Sections 3 and 4 of "An Act authorizing the President of the United States to raise a Provisional Army" (1 *Stat.* 558 [May 28, 1798]). Several volunteer companies had been organized in New York City with such names as the Washington Dragoons, Federal Guard, New York Rangers, and Independent Volunteers ([New York] *Argus. Greenleaf's New Daily Advertiser*, June 9, July 17, 28, 1798). The members of these companies then proceeded to select their own officers, and this in turn brought them into conflict with the militia brigade of the City and County of New York. The militia brigade's orders for July 23, 1798, stated: "The Council of Appointment will meet . . . next month. . . . It is understood that a number of volunteer companies are about forming in this city, with a view to be organized at the ensuing session of the Council, and annexed to this brigade. It is, therefore proper that Brigadier Gen. [James M.] Hughes should have some information of the . . . names of the gentlemen who it is contemplated should respectively command them; but it must be understood, that the actual choice of officers is in the power of the Council solely . . ." ([New York] *Argus. Greenleaf's New Daily Advertiser*, July 31, 1798). The attitude of militia members toward the officers selected by the volunteer companies was summarized in the following public letter from "A Subaltern" to the Council of Appointment: "The military ardor prevailing

at this moment, will doubtless induce many persons to present themselves to you, as candidates for offices in the militia of this city and county. . . .

"In some of the late associations in this city, the men have selected their officers, not from the brigade, but out of their own members. If they should receive your sanction and take rank of any officer of the brigade, the dissatisfaction occasioned by a measure of much injustice, would doubtless occasion a very general resignation. . . . Regular promotion is the only means by which these gentlemen can, or ought to expect to rise into eminence." ([New York] *Argus. Greenleaf's New Daily Advertiser*, August 8, 1798.)

4. Archibald Gracie, a native of Scotland, immigrated to Virginia and then moved to New York City, where he was a prominent merchant and banker. He was president of the New-York Insurance Company and a director of the Bank of New York.

To James McHenry

New York Aug 27. 1798

Sir

You will have observed in the list transmitted you [1] the name of Mr. Jacob Morton as for a Majority. I understood him that he would accept it. But he now tells me he will take nothing less than a Regiment. This seems too much to begin with, if a competent person who has served can be found.

Mr. Abijah Hammond who was in one of the N Eng Regiments during the War though not soliciting it would accept a Regiment. I do not know his character as an Officer. But from his present condition in Society, being a man of large fortune & fair character, from his being a man of good understanding & of exertion, I conclude that he would make a respectable Commander of a Regiment & would be satisfactory. Walker is to be preferred if he will accept. But the Presidents sanction may be obtained in the alternative, for *Walker* if he will accept, for *Hammond* if Walker declines.

In the Event of Walker's declining, the place of first Major may be proposed to Hammond, which however I fear he would not accept. In this event T. Fowler must be thought of.

Mr. John Morton offers as a candidate for a Company. This Gentleman has had a liberal education has been in the Militia (a Major I am told) & is of good principles & character. His pretensions are respectable.

Inclosed is an application from a good & decent citizen; but it is necessary to tell you he was only a drummer in the late army & would not be an acceptable colleague to those in the list of Entrants &ca

ALS, Hamilton Papers, Library of Congress.
1. See H to McHenry, August 21, 1798.

From James McHenry

Trenton 28 Augt. 1798.

My dear Sir.

I received your note of the 25 inst. yesterday. I had written on saturday to the Lieutenant General as per copy annexed.[1] You will return this paper, with your opinion respecting the proposed arrangements, and say nothing to anyone about its contents (I mean a part of its contents) [2] either now or hereafter.

Yours   J McHenry

Majr Gen. Alex. Hamilton.

ALS, Hamilton Papers, Library of Congress; ADf, James McHenry Papers, Library of Congress.
1. McHenry to George Washington, August 25, 1798 (ALS, George Washington Papers, Library of Congress; ALS, letterpress copy, Hamilton Papers, Library of Congress). Except for the third paragraph, this letter concerns McHenry's proposals for recruiting, organizing, and supplying the army. The third paragraph concerns the dispute over the relative ranks of H and Henry Knox in the army. See the introductory note to Washington to H, July 14, 1798.
2. This is a reference to the third paragraph of McHenry's letter to Washington. It reads: "I have received no satisfactory answer from the President on any of these several points, except what respected the assistants necessary to yourself, and fear, that there is reason to apprehend embarrassment and delay from a disposition on his part to have the relative grade of three of the Major Generals so altered, as that Knox shall be first and Hamilton last. I have reminded him of the grounds which induced him to offer their names in a different order to the Senate; suggested the consequences that might flow from an attempt at an alteration, at this time, in the relative grade; and reasoned, that their relative grade, in the revolutionary army (on which General Knox relies for preference) cannot legally avail him, or be considered as giving him a legal claim to preeminence in the formation of the proposed army. What effect this may produce I cannot tell."

To Timothy Pickering [1]

New York Aug. 29. 1798

My Dear Sir

Your friendly letters of the 21. 22 & 23 of August have been duly received. I feel myself at once much flattered and truly indebted for the very favourable opinion of me which you manifest. The good estimation of men of sense and virtue is an ample consolation for the censure & malice of those of a different character. While the expression of your sentiments has all the value which a well known sincerity & integrity of disposition can give. Be assured that I shall be happy to be ranked by you in the number of your friends.

The course of the thing in a particular quarter does not surprise. Besides the direct influence which would be exerted, I am aware that the circumstances of the late election for President have made some unfortunate impressions. The Commander in Chief, I am authorised by his own communications to me to believe, will not easily relinquish the spirit of the primitive arrangement.[2] But in the last resort I shall be inclined to have much deference for his wishes. It is important he should well understand what I verily believe to be an undoubted fact—that New England would rather see high command in my hands than in those of G——— Knox.

With very cordial regard & esteem　I remain Dr. Sir　Yr. Obedient servt　　　　　　　　　　　　　　　　　　　　　　A Hamilton

T Pickering Esq

ALS, Massachusetts Historical Society, Boston; copy, Hamilton Papers, Library of Congress.

1. For an explanation of the contents of this letter, see the introductory note to George Washington to H, July 14, 1798.

2. See Washington to H, July 14, August 9, 1798.

To Theodore Sedgwick

New York Aug 29. 1798

My Dear Sir

Your letter of the 3. instant [1] came seasonably to hand. Business & absence from this place [2] have delayed the acknowlegement.

The persons you mention have been correspondently placed before the Secretary at War.

As to Military Affairs, they lag not a little. No appointments of Regimental Officers yet made. McHenry as you know is loaded beyond his strength. It was an obvious idea to derive aid from among the General Officers. But instead of embracing this resource they have all been told that the President hoped they would think it proper to wave the emoluments of their Offices till called into actual service.[3]

Steps have been taken towards the correction of this obvious mistake, the success of which now depends on the President—and on that success the alternative of *some* or *no energy*.

    Adieu My Dr Sir   A Hamilton

T Sedgwick Esq

ALS, Hamilton Papers, Library of Congress.
  1. Letter not found.
  2. H had been in Albany and in Salisbury, Connecticut. See Philip Schuyler to H, August 17, 1798.
  3. See McHenry to H, July 25, 1798.

To Benjamin Stoddert

New York Aug 29. 1798

Dear Sir

Your obliging letter of the 24 instant duly came to hand. The very polite ground on which you give me to expect your cooperation in procuring an appointment for Capt Hamilton has a very strong claim to my acknowlegement.

In consequence of the information in your letter, I have seen

Capt Talbot. He seems to expect an official notification from your department to ascertain and fix his own situation; considering the events subsequent to his original appointment as a kind of super-sidias.[1] The want of this makes him diffident about taking any part on the presumption of his command of the frigate here.[2] This impediment removed, I am in hope he will incline to favour my wish for an appointment of Capt H to that frigate, if it can be done with perfect convenience & propriety; otherwise we shall be completely satisfied with the alternative which you suggest.

Accept my cordial thanks & the assurances of the sincere esteem & regard with which I have the honor to be Dear Sir

Yr Obd. servant

B Stoddert Esq

AL[S], RG 45, Naval Records Collection of the Office of Naval Records and Library, Subject File: Personnel (NN), National Archives.

1. See H to Stoddert, August 21, 1798, note 2.
2. See Stoddert to John Adams, July 21, September 1, 1798 (*Naval Documents, Quasi-War, February, 1797–October, 1798*, 262–63, 367–68).

From John Jay [1]

Albany 30th Augt. 1798

Dear Sir

I was this morning favd. with yours of the 27 Inst: I regret the circumstances which prevented our seeing each other when you was here. There are several Topics on which I wish to converse with you, & particularly respecting military arrangements at N York. The Riffle Corps & a few of the new Light Infantry Companies are established—there were Reasons, which I shall mention when we meet, which induced me to suspend a Decision relative to the others for the *present*. The Objections stated in the petitions are not in my Judgmt. conclusive—so soon as the Commissions advised by the Council are dispatched, I purpose to set out for New York. The Defence of the Port &ca. in my opinion should be under your Direction.[2] The measures will be concerted between us. The Council will meet again *before* the Session, and all such new Corps as ought to be established will then without Difficulty be organized ultimately. I think with you on the subject of Resignations.

It is with me a question whether any Person convicted of *Forgery* ought to be pardoned at *present*, when offences of that kind abound. As yet I have not pardoned any convicts of that Description, except in cases where the convictions turned on a Ballance of Evidence, and where Guilt was probable but not certain. Mr. Murray [3] has just been with me on this Subject. I shall take it into further Consideration, but fear the objections will prove insuperable. The young man's father & Family are to be pitied; but the Power to pardon is a *Trust*, to be exercised on Principles of sound discretion, combining Policy Justice and Humanity. We will talk this matter over. I have an Idea of putting the Light Corps into a Regt. and making our friend Troup [4] Col. of it.

I am Dr Sir   Yours sincerely   John Jay

Majr. Genl. Hamilton

ALS, Hamilton Papers, Library of Congress.
    1. For background to this letter, see the introductory note to H to James McHenry, June 1, 1798.
    2. See Philip Schuyler to H, August 17, 1798.
    3. John Murray, one of New York's richest merchants, served as a director of the Bank of New York from 1789 to 1794. In 1798 he was a director of the New York Office of Discount and Deposit and president of the New York City Chamber of Commerce. He owned property on Murray Hill in New York City.
    4. Robert Troup, a New York City and Albany lawyer, had been a close friend of H since the time when they had been students at King's College. A veteran of the American Revolution, Troup served as secretary of the Board of War in 1778 and 1779 and secretary of the Board of Treasury in 1779 and 1780. In 1786 he was a member of the New York Assembly. Troup was involved in land speculation in western New York and was associated with Charles Williamson in the development of the Pulteney purchase in the Genesee country.

To James McHenry [1]

private   N Y Aug 30. 1798

My Dear Sir
    Col Stevens tells me he has exhausted the money you sent him in preliminary purchases of Timber &c. & is in debt with embarrassment to pay & likely to be compelled to dismiss workmen &c.

Such a state of things is hurtful to the public service, discredits the Administration & increases expence. It ought to be avoided if possible.

Stevens says pains have been taken to excite doubts about him & he fears they may have had some effect. In justice to him I think it proper to say that I have the most intire confidence in his political fidelity to the Government & that as far as my opportunity of being acquainted with his character as a man of business goes there is good ground of Confidence in his *pecuniary* fidelity also.

But the plain alternative is to *displace* or to *trust.* The ⟨ne⟩cessary operations must not stagnate on account of uncertainty about the Agent.

Yrs. truly   A H

J McHenry Esq

ALS, Montague Collection, MS Division, New York Public Library; ALS (photostat), James McHenry Papers, Library of Congress.

1. For an explanation of the contents of this letter, see the introductory note to H to James McHenry, June 1, 1798.

To Silas Talbot [1]

[New York, August 30, 1798]

Dr. Sir

I called this morning with my relation Capt Hamilton to introduce him to you. But not finding you at home I have concluded to do it by this Note of which he is the bearer.

Yrs. truly   A H

Aug 30th. 1798

ALS, Manuscript Collection, G. W. Blunt White Library, Mystic Seaport, Inc.

1. For background to this letter, see H to Benjamin Stoddert, August 8, 21, 29, 1798; Stoddert to H, August 24, 1798.

From John Adams

Quincy [Massachusetts, September 3] [1] 1798

Sir

I have received the Letter you did me the Honor to write me on the 24. of August: but not till the first of September: otherwise it would have been answered sooner. Mr Phillip Church, your Nephew whom you recommend to be a Captain of Infantry I have had the Pleasure to See, both in New York and Philadelphia, and have been so well Satisfied with all I know of him as to be very willing to appoint him and shall write to the Secretary at War accordingly.

With great Esteem I have the Honor to be Sir your most obedient and humble servant   John Adams

General Hamilton
at New York

LS, Hamilton Papers, Library of Congress; LC, Adams Family Papers, deposited in the Massachusetts Historical Society, Boston.

1. Adams incorrectly dated this letter "August 24." The correct date appears on the letter book copy.

To Timothy Pickering

[New York, September 3, 1798]

Dr. Sir

As I imagine you are acquainted with the Inhabitants of *Wilkesburgh* or *Wilksborough* in Pensylvania & the neighbouring Country,[1] I take the liberty to request information of some trusty, intelligent, active young lawyer in that quarter to be entrusted with the management of some land concerns of importance in which my Brother in law Mr Church is interested.[2] You will of course suppose that in suits which may occur, able Counsel in Philadelphia will be added. But it is desireable to have near the scene a clever fellow to be entrusted with the formal parts, with the detection of intrusions, with negotiations &c. Your answer as early as convenient will oblige

Yrs. truly   A Hamilton

Sepr. 3. 1798

T Pickering Esqr.

ALS, Wyoming Historical and Geological Society, Wilkes-Barre, Pennsylvania.
  1. In 1787 Pickering had been appointed the agent of the state of Pennsylvania to organize the new county of Luzerne located in the Wyoming Valley, and to settle disputes between Connecticut settlers in the Wyoming Valley and the state of Pennsylvania. On August 12, 1791, he was appointed Postmaster General of the United States and moved to Philadelphia.
  2. For these lands and John B. Church's interest in them, see the introductory note to Tench Coxe to H, February 13, 1795.

To Benjamin Stoddert [1]

New York September 3. 1798

Dear Sir

Considering the great length of time before the Frigate here will be ready for sea—I have concluded that it may be expedient, if it can be effected, to have Capt. Hamilton appointed & assigned to some Southern Vessel which will sooner be ready. I imagine Cap Talbot will be glad hereafter to have him as an associate. If this can be conveniently managed in the proper time, it will give me pleasure.

Accept the assurances of my esteem & regard   A Hamilton

Sept 3. 1798

B Stoddert Esq

ALS, RG 45, Naval Records Collection of the Office of Naval Records and Library, Subject File: Personnel (NN), National Archives.
  1. For background to this letter, see H to Stoddert, August 8, 21, 29, 1798; Stoddert to H, August 24, 30, 1798.

To Stephen Van Rensselaer

[New York, September 3, 1798. Letter listed in dealer's catalogue. Letter not found.]

ALS, sold by Anderson Galleries, May 9, 1912, Lot 71.

From Timothy Pickering

Trenton Sept. 4. 1798.

D. Sir,

I have recd. yours of yesterday. One or two new lawyers have settled in Luzerne County, Pennsylvania, since I left it in 1791. I am not perfectly clear in recommending any of the old ones. I have it in my power to make enquiry which I believe may be satisfactory, and will inform you of the result. The town you refer to is not Wilkesburg or Wilkesborough, but Wilkesbarré—from Jno. Wilkes and Colo. Barre.[1]

I have this moment recollected a former inhabitant of Wilkesbarre now here, on whose knowledge and opinion I can rely. He thinks *Putnam Catlin*[2] Esqr. the most eligible lawyer for such an agent as is called for. Such was my opinion also, having known him there for four or five years: but as the trust was of magnitude I wished not to rely on my own knowledge which was less intimate than that of the person of whom I have now made the enquiry. This person thinks Mr. Catlin not only the most eligible, but that his integrity may entirely be relied on & I was disposed to entertain the same opinion. I remember he always engaged with the most earnest zeal in the cause of his clients: and all his actions manifested a frankness of heart: nor has anything ever occurred, to my recollection to excite even an unfavourable suspicion of the rectitude of his character.

I am with great truth   Your respectful & obt. servt.   T. Pickering

There is a weekly mail between Philadelphia and Wilkesbarré, closing at Philaa. every Tuesday evening at sunset.

Alexander Hamilton Esqr.

☞ Reading again your letter, in which you mention the prosecution of *intruders,* by this agent of Mr. Church it becomes proper that I should inform you that Mr. Catlin was embarked in *opinion* and *feelings* with the Connecticut Susquehannah Company: and that he would reluctantly commence suits against the Connecticut settlers *before this time*, whom the Pennsylvanians call *intruders*.[3] But my informer tells me that he believes all the lawyers in the county now set their faces against *new instrusions*.   T. P.

If Mr. Church wants an agent in Northumberland County in Pennsylvania, I would recommend Charles Hall Esqr. a lawyer at Sunbury, who has a good and increasing reputation.

ALS, Hamilton Papers, Library of Congress; copy, Massachusetts Historical Society, Boston.

1. John Durkee, a settler in the Wyoming Valley in Pennsylvania, is credited with naming Wilkes-Barre for John Wilkes, the English agitator and reformer, and for Colonel Isaac Barré. Both men had defended the American colonies in the British Parliament.

2. Putnam Catlin, a native of Litchfield, Connecticut, settled in Wilkes-Barre in 1787 and was admitted to practice before the Luzerne County courts. Catlin was not in Wilkes-Barre when Pickering wrote this letter. In 1797 he had moved to Broome County, New York, where he remained for eleven years. Putnam Catlin was the father of George Catlin, the artist who painted pictures of Indians.

3. In 1753 citizens of Connecticut formed an association called the Susquehanna Company for the purpose of settling the Wyoming Valley, which was claimed by Connecticut under her colonial charter. At the end of the French and Indian war, Connecticut settlers began moving into this area. In 1768 John Penn purchased the Wyoming Valley from the Six Nations, and for several years there was open warfare between the Connecticut settlers and the proprietary government of Pennsylvania. On December 30, 1782, a commission appointed by the Continental Congress decided against the claims of Connecticut (*JCC*, XXIV, 31), but quarrels over land titles kept the dispute between the Connecticut settlers and the officials of Pennsylvania alive throughout the seventeen-eighties and seventeen-nineties.

From Benjamin Judah [1]

London, September 5, 1798. "I find by private & public Intelligence that my Country . . . is determined to defend her claims against an insidious Foe. . . . I have been in Europe about two years . . . ; from the connections I have both here, and on the Continent, I trust that I could procure on the lowest terms, any quantity of Arms &c. that our Government may want. . . ." [2]

ALS, marked "Duplicate," Hamilton Papers, Library of Congress.

1. Judah was a New York City merchant.

2. H noted on the envelope: "Answer—Letter received & transmitted to

Secy at War whose province it is to decide." H's answer to Judah's letter has not been found.

From James McHenry [1]

Trenton 6 [September] [2] 1798

My dear Hamilton.

The inclosures will explain to you, infinitely better than the longest letter I could write, the objects to which they refer. Do not I pray you, in writing or otherwise betray the confidence which has induced me to deal thus with you or make extracts or copies.

I hope you will acquiesce in the necessity which seems to govern, and save us from the confusion which may result from a different conduct.

Return the papers immediately.

Yours   James McHenry

ALS, Hamilton Papers, Library of Congress; ADfS, James McHenry Papers, Library of Congress.

  1. For an explanation of the contents of this letter, see the introductory note to George Washington to H, July 14, 1798.
  2. McHenry incorrectly dated this letter "6 Augt."

To John Jay

New York Sep. 8. 1798

Dear Sir

I beg your pardon for having omitted to attend earlier to the suggestion in your letter of the 30th. of August respecting the defence of our ports.

I am sincere in saying that a charge of this kind would on various accounts be unpleasant to me among the rest as likely to involve ill natured & foolish criticism. But I shall not decline the trust if you think proper to repose it provided the manutension of the money is no part of it, equally disposed to be useful to the public and to second you in the objects of your administration.

The idea of organising the volunteer companies in one corps is a good one & if Troupe * will act his appointment to the command will be eligible & satisfactory.

With true esteem & regard I have the honor to remain Dr Sr

Yr Obed S   A Hamilton

G Jay

* Pendleton [1] would also be a good appointment

ALS, Columbia University Libraries.
    1. Nathaniel Pendleton, who was born in Virginia, held the rank of lieutenant at the end of the American Revolution. He studied law in South Carolina and then moved to Georgia, where he was elected, but did not serve, as a delegate to the Constitutional Convention. He was appointed chief justice of Georgia on January 23, 1789, and on September 26, 1789, the Senate confirmed his appointment as United States judge for the District of Georgia. In 1796 Pendleton moved to New York and practiced law. Pendleton was one of H's seconds in the duel with Aaron Burr and was one of the executors of H's estate.

To James McHenry [1]

New York Sepr. 8th. 1798

My Dear Sir

Yours dated by mistake Augt. 6th. I received yesterday. I postponed a reply 'till to day because I wished first to reflect maturely. My mind is unalterably made up. I shall certainly not hold the commission on the plan proposed, and only wait an official communication to say so.

I return you the inclosures in your letter. You may depend on my fidelity to your friendly confidence. I shall regret whatever of inconvenience may attend you. You doubtless will take care that you retain in your own power all the evidences of this transaction.

Adieu   A Hamilton

J McHenry Esqr

ADfS, Hamilton Papers, Library of Congress.
    1. For an explanation of the contents of this letter, see the introductory note to George Washington to H, July 14, 1798.

To James McHenry

New York, Sept. 9, 1798.

My Dear Sir,

I think I heretofore mentioned to you that to avoid the chance of difficulty with the President, I had written or would write to him urging the appointment of Mr. Philip Church to a Captaincy. I have just received a very obliging letter from him,[1] and in which he assures me of his willingness to appoint him to that grade, and that he would write to you accordingly. Thus is all difficulty on this point removed. In proportion as I look to the event of my laying down my military character,[2] is my solicitude that this young gentleman shall be eligibly placed.

Yours affectionately, A. Hamilton

J. McHenry, Esq.

The Historical Magazine, and Notes and Queries, Concerning the Antiquities, History and Biography of America, 2nd ser., II (Morrisania, New York, 1867), 364.
1. John Adams to H, September 3, 1798.
2. See the introductory note to George Washington to H, July 14, 1798.

To Benjamin Walker, William Inman, and William Cooper [1]

New York, September 9, 1798. Requests "Mr. Inman and Mr. Cooper to agree upon another gentleman who jointly with me as arbitrators may pronounce upon" the account between Inman and Robert Morris.

ALS, anonymous donor.
1. Inman was an agent of Patrick Colquhoun, the English speculator who negotiated the Pulteney Associates' purchase of New York lands from Robert Morris. Cooper, who founded Cooperstown in Otsego County, New York, was a land speculator and a prominent Federalist politician.
Inman, Cooper, and Thomas H. Brantingham, an alien enabled to hold lands

in New York ("An Act to enable certain person therein named, to purchase and hold real estate within this State" [*New York Laws,* 15th Sess., Ch. LIV (April 9, 1792)]), were involved in a series of disputes concerning their conflicting claims to seventy-four thousand acres of land along the Black River in northern New York.

In the letter printed above, H is serving in his capacity as arbitrator between Walker, to whom Inman had assigned his claim, and Cooper, the assignee of Robert Morris. On February 3, 1798, the two speculators agreed to submit their claims to H and to accept as binding his division of the tract in dispute between them. H's decision, dated February 16, 1799, awarded 37,793½ acres to Walker and 36,606½ acres to Cooper (DS, Hamilton Papers, Library of Congress).

For a discussion of H's role in the Inman-Brantingham-Cooper suits and the texts of relevant documents, see the forthcoming Goebel, *Law Practice,* III.

From James McHenry [1]

Trenton 10th Septr. 1798

My dear Hamilton.

I received your letter of the 8th this morning. Mine to you to which it is an answer ought to have been dated the 6th instant.

I do not, I cannot blame you for your determination. Mr Pickering Mr Wolcott & Mr Stoddert have agreed to make a respectful representation on the subject to the President. You will not of course hear from me, relative to the commands of the President, 'till the result is known to me.

Yours affectionately   James McHenry

Majr. Gen. Alex Hamilton

ALS, Hamilton Papers, Library of Congress; ADf, James McHenry Papers, Library of Congress.

1. For an explanation of the contents of this letter, see the introductory note to George Washington to H, July 14, 1798.

From James McHenry [1]

Trenton 12 [–27] Sepr. 1798

My dear Hamilton.

I inclosed you in a note of the 28th of Augt. ulto, a copy of a letter to General Washington dated the 25 of the same month. You have forgotten to return me this copy or notice this letter. The letter to the President mentioned in my last [2] is still under deliberation.

Yours affectionately & truly   James McHenry

27 Sepr. 1798.

This letter has been at Watertown near Bosten by mistake from which place it returned this morning. The representation aluded to was sent about ten days ago, signed by Mr Wolcott only.[3] I hope and expect from it a good effect.[4]

Majr Gen Alex. Hamilton.

ALS, Hamilton Papers, Library of Congress; ADf, James McHenry Papers, Library of Congress.
  1. For an explanation of the contents of this letter, see the introductory note to George Washington to H, July 14, 1798.
  2. McHenry to H, September 10, 1798.
  3. This is a reference to Oliver Wolcott, Jr., to John Adams, September 17, 1798, which is quoted in the introductory note to Washington to H, July 14, 1798.
  4. The draft does not contain the postscript.

From Rufus King

[*Margate, England, September 13, 1798.*[1] *Letter not found.*]

  1. Letter listed in Rufus King's "Memorandum of Private Letters, &c., dates & persons, from 1796 to Augt 1802," owned by Mr. James G. King, New York City.

From James McHenry

Trenton 13 Septr 1798

My dear Hamilton.

I recd. yours of the 9th this morning. Why is it necessary you should repeat to me your request, or require any new evidence, that I will not take the same care of Philip Church as I would of my own son. Let Mrs. Church be assured I will.

Yours affecy.   James McHenry

Majr Gen. Alex. Hamilton

ALS, Hamilton Papers, Library of Congress.

From George Washington

[*Mount Vernon, September 14, 1798.*[1] *Letter not found.*]

1. "List of Letters from G—— Washington to General Hamilton," Columbia University Libraries.

To John Jay

New York Sepr. 17. 1798

Dear Sir

The death of Mr. Remsen [1] presents a vacancy of Notary which will be sought. Two applications are made to me—one by *James Inglis* Junr.[2] who has just finished a Clerkship with me & taken a license as Atty in the Supreme Court—the other *William Coleman* [3] lately connected in law business with Col Burr.

Inglis is a young man of handsome abilities, of application & of irreproacheable conduct. He is a native of this City, his father [4] has lately failed in business advanced in life & on the son must very much depend the support of the family. Worth & situation both conspire to recommend him strongly.

Coleman is a man of conspicuous talents and as far as I have learned of real worth. Notwithstanding his connection,[5] his political principles are zealously good. It is in my knowlege that he has written several valuable speculations on the public occurrences of the period. You may have seen a little attack on Judge Lewis [6] neatly executed—Of this Coleman was the author. He too is in a situation to excite sympathy. With little advantage from his present employment, he has now a wife & children of his brother (who lately died of the prevailing fever) to maintain. I mistake it, if he be not a man well worth cultivating.[7] Adieu My Dr Sir,

Respect & Affe   A H

                                                                                Sep 17

G Jay

ALS, Columbia University Libraries.
    1. John H. Remsen was a New York City lawyer and one of seventeen notaries public in New York City.
    2. For Inglis's admission to practice before the New York Supreme Court, see H to James McHenry, February 20, 1798, note 3.
    3. A native of Boston, Coleman had been a lawyer in Greenfield Massachusetts, a member of the militia in Shays's Rebellion, and a member of the Massachusetts House of Representatives in 1795 and 1796. Because of major financial losses he sustained from his speculations in Yazoo lands, Coleman moved to New York City and practiced law. In early 1800 H was instrumental in securing Coleman's appointment as clerk of the circuit of the New York Supreme Court (H to Jay, March 4, 1800; Jay to H, March 13, 1800). In 1801 Coleman became editor of the *New-York Evening Post*, which H helped to found.
    4. James Inglis owned a china and glass store at 115 Fly Market in New York City (David Longworth, *Longworth's American Almanack, New-York Register, and City Directory* . . . (New York, 1798).
    5. This is a reference to the fact that Coleman and Aaron Burr were law partners.
    6. Morgan Lewis was a judge of the New York Supreme Court.
    7. Jay endorsed this letter: "Genl Hamilton
                                                                        17⎱
                                                                 ansd. 20⎰   Sep. 1798
candidates for the place of *notary*." Jay's letter to H of September 20, 1798, has not been found.

From Rufus King

                                                                London Sep. 17. 98

    I am charmed with the military appointments;[1] in the main they are quite what they should be—such chiefs ought to give Glory as well as Security to their Country, and they will do both, if the occasions offer. You see that I relapse into my former strain. I know not what you and others whose Sentiments I respect may think, but I must unsettle all that is best settled in my opinions of the character of the present extraordinary crisis, or I cannot agree that an impassioned phlegmatic, cautious, inactive, and merely defensive war, even under the highest toned, and most vigorous form of Government, is capable of affording a tolerable chance of Security against such an adversary as France.

I do not intirely comprehend the views and proceedings of Congress, who appear to have done too much, or not enough, but I have been too long acquainted with the temper and composition of that Body, not to be able to conjecture the Difficulties that arise from the vanities of some, and the obstinacy of others, and which have given the appearance of Inconsistency to their measures.

Congress have adjourned, and it is of the highest importance that we should form a correct opinion of the course that France is likely to pursue. It is plain that discovering our union and firmness, france instantly decided upon the relinquishment of her Demands of apologies and Loans, and resolved to recede as far as shd. be necessary to regain her standing, and if possible her Influence, among our People. But she has had no intention of doing us Justice for the Past, nor of performing what she might be induced to promise in respect to the future. The Correspondence between Talleyrand & Gerry, inclusive of other cotemporaneous, and subsequent measures of the Same character, should convince us of the Justice of this Opinion.[2] Logan [3] who as we hear was provided with Letters from Jefferson, and others has been presented to *Merlin* as the Envoy of the patriotic party in America, he has been closeted with Talleyrand, and speaks openly of the probability of his success with the french Government. Since his arrival at Paris, the american seamen have been released, who in the laying of the Embargo were conducted to Prison, and the Directory have ordered the Embargo to be raised; the preamble of this arreté merits attention.[4]

"29 *Thermidor* Le Directoire executif, considerant que malgré *la manifestation hostile du Gouvernment des E. U.*, qui avait déterminé un Embargo momentané sur leurs Batimens, il doit croire qu'à moins d'etre livré aux Passions du cabinet britaniques, ce Gouvernment fidele aux interests *de la Nation americaine*, prendra des mesures analogues aux dispositions pacifiques de la republique francaise, dès qu'il en recevra la confirmation, et voulant suivre les habitudes amicales et fraternelles de la france, envers un Peuple, dont elle a defendu la liberté, arrete ce qui suit &c &c." [5] These proceedings should be compared with the Treatment and language received by our Envoys and we shall from hence be able perhaps to fathom the views, and to discover the means, of france. It is analogous to what has been done in other countries; difficulties and embarassments, complained of by the proper agents of such Countries have been aggravated and increased; and in order to divide the People from their Govt—Promises of Redress and satisfaction have been given to the Popular agents of such Countries, which had been refused to the Envoys of their Governments.

But we know nothing certain of the views of France since it has been known at Paris that our treaties are dissolved.[6] The measures above referred to were of antecedent Date. I still think they will not declare war, but endeavour to attain their Object by humiliation and intrigue.

The war is on the eve of recommencing between France and Austria. Prussia will remain neuter. Germany will suffer herself to be incorporated with france in preference to being again at war with her. Naples will be engaged & Russia according to appearances will also become active.   K.

ALS, Hamilton Papers, Library of Congress.

1. King was unaware of the struggle over the relative ranking of H, Henry Knox, and Charles Cotesworth Pinckney. See the introductory note to George Washington to H, July 14, 1798.

2. See King to H, July 14, 1798.

3. George Logan, a Pennsylvania physician, a friend of Thomas Jefferson, and a Jeffersonian Republican, had been a close friend of Edmond Charles Genet. In 1798 he sailed for Hamburg, where with the aid of the Marquis de Lafayette he obtained papers permitting him to enter France. Logan carried with him two certificates of citizenship and character. One, signed by Jefferson, is dated June 4, 1798, and the second, signed by Thomas McKean, chief justice of Pennsylvania, is dated June 11, 1798 (Frances A. Logan, *Memoir of Dr. George Logan of Stenton* [Philadelphia, 1899], 56–57). Logan also had letters from Joseph Philippe Létombe, French consul general and consul for Philadelphia, to Philippe Antoine Merlin of Douai, the head of the French Directory, and to Charles Maurice de Talleyrand-Périgord, French Minister of Foreign Affairs (Logan, *Logan*, 57). Logan arrived in Paris as a self-styled envoy on August 7 (after Elbridge Gerry had left) and was warmly received by Talleyrand and Merlin of Douai. A brief account of his trip may be found in an interview Logan had with George Washington on November 13, 1798, upon his return to the United States (AD, George Washington Papers, Library of Congress).

It was as a result of Logan's unauthorized interference in France that the

"Logan Act" ("An Act for the punishment of certain Crimes therein specified" [1 *Stat.* 613]) was passed on January 30, 1799.

4. Timothy Pickering described these actions by the French Directory as follows: "Mr. [Fulwar] Skipwith's [consul general of the United States in France] letter of the 22d of August covers another letter from Mr. Talleyrand, dated the 20th of August, in which he encloses copies of two letters from the Minister of Marine, respecting American seamen who had been imprisoned. When in July last an embargo was laid on the American merchant vessels in the ports of France, the agents of the marine took out their crews, and threw them into prison; thus hazarding the loss of the vessels, and injuring the men by confinement, and the bad provisions of their gaols. These seamen were ordered to be released. The other letter from the Minister of Marine required that no injury should be done to the safety and liberty of the officers and crews of American vessels found to be in order, nor to passengers and other citizens of the United States having passports and protections.

"The same letter from Mr. Skipwith enclosed the copy of a degree of the Directory, passed the 16th of August, for taking off the embargo, laid a month before on American vessels." (*ASP, Foreign Relations*, II, 236–37.)

5. For a discussion of United States objections to this preamble, see *ASP, Foreign Relations*, II, 237.

6. "An Act to declare the treaties heretofore concluded with France, no longer obligatory on the United States" (1 *Stat.* 578 [July 7, 1798]).

To Oliver Wolcott, Junior

[*New York, September 18, 1798.* On September 19, 1798, Wolcott wrote to Hamilton and referred to "your Letter of yesterday." *Letter not found.*]

From Oliver Wolcott, Junior

Trenton Sept. 19. 1798

Dr. sir   (Private)

I shall send by this Post a Letter to Keeper of Debtors apartment in New York granting the priviledge recommended in your Letter of yesterday.[1] As there are probably many persons ⟨liable⟩ to be held in close confinement, ought not the Governor, State Judges, and District Judges to direct the removal of the Prisoners to some Gaol in the Country?

I am acquainted with the state of a delicate question in which you personally, but the Govt. & Country are more interested.[2] Measures have been taken to bring all right, if the thing be at all practicable.

The present embarrassment might I am persuaded have been entirely avoided—and I do not despair of having it corrected. As a friend to your fame, & the Interests of the Country I request you to *say nothing* and *do nothing* untill you hear from me, which will be ten days or a fortnight hence.

Your advice respecting the use of Credit has been & will continue to be regarded.[3] The Finances will not fail before the other Departments—but the Government, will loose all confidence and will deserve none—if things are not managed with some portion of good sense. There is now no object, system or design—all is hurry, passion & imbecillity.

Yrs   Oliv Wolcott

[ENCLOSURE][4]

Oliver Wolcott, Junior, to Thomas Hazard

Trenton, September 19, 1798

Sir

It having been represented to me that the contagious fever which afflicts the City of New York has lately appeared within the prison or debtors apartment, and believing that neither justice or humanity will justify the close confinement of Prisoners, in a situation which must unavoidably expose their lives to the greatest danger, I have concluded it to be my duty to authorize you to permit Jose Joaquim Da Costa & William Duer[5] who are confined under your Custody, for debts due to the United States, *to reside at any place within the liberties of the Prison, during the continuance of the present contagious disease.*

The condition upon which this permission may be granted shall be that the Parties respectively do sign a written agreement, that they will not depart beyond the limits of the Priviledges of the Prison, and that they will return to confinement when required when the present contagious fever shall have ceased.

It must however be well understood, that this permission is to be considered as only removing any obstacles arising from Suits commenced against Mr. Da Costa, or Mr. Duer for debts due to the United States, and by no means to render the United States responsible for *any debts or Suits commenced by individuals.*

The situation of Mr. Da Costa is much regretted as a petition is depending for his enlargement, the hearing of which has been delayed by the Collector for the District of New York,[6] solely on account of the danger arising from the present malady.[7]

I enclose a Warrant for discharging George Merrill & Henry A. Williams, pursuant to the Act of Congress of June 6th. 1798.[8]

I am

Keeper of
the Debtors appartment
in the City of New York

ALS, Hamilton Papers, Library of Congress.
   1. Letter not found.
   2. For an explanation of this sentence and of the remainder of this paragraph, see the introductory note to George Washington to H, July 14, 1798.
   3. See H to Wolcott, August 22, 1798.
   4. ADf, Connecticut Historical Society, Hartford.
   5. An undated calendar of a letter listed in "Calendar Summary of Philip Church and Alexander Hamilton Papers," Personal Miscellaneous, Box 6, Schuyler, MS Division, New York Public Library, reads: "Duer's engagement to stay within 'jail liberties' (copy of document sent to Wolcott)."
   6. Joshua Sands.
   7. On October 25, 1798, Da Costa was "discharged from Custody" in the case of *José Francisco Esmeraldo, José Joaquim da Costa, and Joao José da Silva* v *Amos Hare* (MS Minutes of the New York Supreme Court, 1797–1800 [Hall of Records, New York City]).
   8. "An Act providing for the relief of persons imprisoned for Debts due the United States" (1 *Stat.* 561–62). See Henry A. Williams to H, March 31, 1798. Merrill had owned a distillery and soap manufactory.

From John Jay

[*Albany, September 20, 1798.* On the back of a letter that Hamilton wrote to Jay on September 17, 1798, Jay wrote: "ansd. 20 Sep. 1798." *Letter not found.*]

From Rufus King

London Sep. 23d. 98

You will have no war! France will propose to renew the negotiation upon the Basis laid down in the Presidents Instructions to the Envoys [1]—at least so I conjecture.[2]

If the negotiation is recommenced the most obvious precaution suggests the expediency of confiding it to hands above all suspicion.

We see that we have nothing to fear from the arms of France; all her skill, and energy, & Resentment, will nevertheless be employed to attain her Ends.

A Treaty liberal in Terms & Stipulations, tho' neither shd. be performed nor observed would gain time, and go a great way to restore her injured credit.

The Election of President would return before the Efficacy and sincerity of the new Stipulations and Engagements could be experimentally ascertained! To give them any chance of Success they must be liberal to the utmost bounds of our Expectations.

Buona parte reached G. Cairo on the 22 July, but we are quite ignorant whether he was opposed by the Beys. It does not yet appear whether he will remain some time in Egypt in order to consolidate his Conquest & Authority over that Country, or proceed immediately by the Red Sea for India. We are without Details, or confirmation, of the victory which the french Papers of the 15. & 16 instant state to have been gained over the french fleet by Nelson.[3] The news is on the whole highly probable, and the victory has according to these Reports been very decisive & glorious.

The war is about to recommence.

Yours &c

Col. Hamilton

AL, Hamilton Papers, Library of Congress.

1. See Secretary of State Timothy Pickering's "Instructions to Charles Coteswirth Pinckney, John Marshall, and Elbridge Gerry, Esquires, Envoys Extraordinary and Ministers Plenipotentiary from the United States of America to the French republic," July 15, 1797 (*ASP, Foreign Relations*, II, 153–57).

2. On September 21, 1798, King wrote to Pickering: "I this morning received the Paris Papers to the 16th instant. 'L'ami des lois' of the 15. fructidor (Sep. 1st) announces the arrival of a flag of truce at Bourdeaux in 24 days from Philadelphia, and [François Martin] Poultier, the editor asserts that she brings Dispatches of the most satisfactory nature to the friends of Peace. 'Le parti anglais (dit il) loin d'avoir prís décidément le dessus dans les E. U. est au contraire déjoué dans ses projects sanguinnaires, et la majorité du congrès vaincue par les procédés généreuses du gouvernment de la grande nation, a rejété tous les plans hostiles qui lui avaient été présentés par M. Adams: elle a repoussé toutes mesures qui tendraient à troubler, la bonne harmonie qui doit exister entre deux peuples amis, et après avoir manifesté très clairment ses intentions à ce sujet, le congrès s'est séparé au milieu des Bénédictions d'un peuple, qui sent tout le prix de son alliance avec la republique fran-

caise, et qui avait déjà donné en plusiers occasions des preuves non équivoques de son éloignement pour les actes de rupture projettés par un fonctionaire infidèle que l'opinion publique accuse d'etre vendu au plus infâme de Gouvernemens. En apprenant l'heureuse nouvelle que nous transmittons à nos lecteurs, nous n'avons pu nous défendre d'un Sentiment d'admiration pour la conduite politique tenue dernièrement par la directoire envers les E: T. conduite qui a opéré des changemens si avantageux dans notre position vis-à-vis cette puissance, et qui doit nous concilier l'estime de tous les peuples.'

"It is probably known to you that Poultiers journal, tho' not strictly official, is one that furnishes the means of conjecturing the Politicks of the Luxembourg. Paragraphs of the same tenor appear in the French papers of a later date. . . ." (ALS, RG 59, Despatches from United States Ministers to Great Britain, 1791–1906, Vol. 7, January 9–December 22, 1798, National Archives.)

3. This is a reference to the Battle of the Nile, August 1, 1798.

From George Washington [1]

Mount Vernon 24th Sep. 1798.

My dear Sir,

I have seen the correspondence between the President of the United States & Secretary of War, on the subject of the relative Rank of the three Major Generals first appointed.[2] But as it was given in confidence, unaccompanied with an Official letter, I had no ground on which I could proceed, without betraying that confidence. I have therefore written for an official account of the President's determination, as the foundation of the representation I propose to offer him, on this occasion.

Until the result of this is known, I hope you will suspend a final decision, and let matters remain in Statu quo till you hear again from

Your Affectionate   Go: Washington

Genl Hamilton

ALS, Hamilton Papers, Library of Congress; ALS, letterpress copy, George Washington Papers, Library of Congress.

1. For an explanation of the contents of this letter, see the introductory note to Washington to H, July 14, 1798.

2. James McHenry sent this correspondence to Washington on September 10, 1798 (ALS, George Washington Papers, Library of Congress).

From Rufus King

[London, September 25, 1798.[1] Letter not found.]

1. Letter listed in Rufus King's "Memorandum of Private Letters, &c., dates & persons, from 1796 to Augt 1802," owned by Mr. James G. King, New York City.

From John Jay [1]

Albany 26. Sept. 1798

Dr. Sir

I take the Liberty of communicating to you a letter which I have this day written to the Presidt. of the U States.[2] and in which I have enclosed a Copy of the Act[3] lately passed for the further defence of this State. If you understand the act as I do, and concur in the measure submitted by that Letter to the Presidents consideration be pleased to seal and to send it to the Post Office. But if material objections should occur to you which have escaped me be so good as to return it with your remarks.

I am Dr. Sir

Majr. Genl. Hamilton

LC, Governor's Letter Books, from the original in the New York State Library, Albany.

1. For background to this letter, see the introductory note to H to James McHenry, June 1, 1798.

2. Jay wrote to John Adams: "During the late special Session of the Legislature of this State, an act was passed for the further Defence of this State of which a Copy is herewith enclosed. The first section of this Act appropriated a Sum not exceeding 150.000 Dollars towards the defence of the City and port of New York, and provides that the said sum shall be expended under the direction of the President of the United States. . . .

"It appears to be the intention of the Legislature that this money shall be laid out only in the manner which the National Government will recognize as useful and advisable. I therefore take the liberty of submitting to your Consideration whether as Majr. Genl. Hamilton is a national Officer in whom great confidence may be reposed, it would not be expedient to authorize him to concert with me the plan of laying out this money to the best advantage and to appoint him to superintend the execution of it. I think it would be best that I should leave the money in the Bank of New York, and appoint a proper person to audit and keep the accounts of the Expenditures directed from time to time by Genl. Hamilton relative to the works and pay them as they become due, by Checks on the Bank." (LC, Governor's Letter Books, from the original in the New York State Library, Albany; copy, Dr. Frank Monaghan, Washington, D.C.)

3. "An Act for the further defence of this State and for other purposes" (*New York Laws*, 22nd Sess., Ch. V [August 27, 1798]). For the contents of this act, see H to McHenry, June 1, 1798, note 16.

From George Washington

[*Mount Vernon, September 26, 1798.*[1] *Letter not found.*]

1. "List of Letters from G—— Washington to General Hamilton," Columbia University Libraries.

To George Washington [1]

New York September 30. 1798

My Dear Sir

Your obliging favour of the 24th instant has duly come to hand. I see in it a new proof of sentiments towards me which are truly gratifying. But permit me to add my request to the suggestion of your own prudence, that no personal considerations for me may induce more on your part than on mature reflection you may think due to public motives. It is extremely foreign to my wish to create to you the least embarrassment; especially in times like the present when it is more than ever necessary that the interest of the *whole* should be *paramountly* consulted.

I shall strictly comply with the recommendation in the close of your letter; remaining always your very respectful & affec servt

A Hamilton

General Washington

ALS, Hamilton Papers, Library of Congress; ADfS, Hamilton Papers, Library of Congress.
1. For an explanation of the contents of this letter, see the introductory note to Washington to H, July 14, 1798.

To Rufus King

N York Oct 2d. 1798

My Dear Sir

Mr. R——[1] delivered me your letter of the 31 of July. The opinion in that and other of your letters concerning a very important point has been acted upon by me from the very moment that it became unequivocal that we must have a decisive rupture with France. In some things my efforts succeeded, in others they were disappointed—in others I have had promises of conformity to lay the foundation of future proceeding the performance and effect of which promises are not certainly known to me. The effect indeed cannot yet be known.

The public mind of the Country continues to progress in the right direction. That must influence favourably the present Congress at the ensuing session. The next will be in all appearances intrinsically better.

Of the executive I need say little you know its excellent dispositions, its general character and the composition of its parts. You know also how widely different the *business* of Government is from the *speculation* of it, and the energy of the imagination, dealing in general propositions, from that of *execution* in *detail*.

There are causes from which delay and feebleness are experienced. But difficulties will be surmounted and I anticipate with you that the Country will ere long assume an attitude correspondent with its great destinies majestic efficient, and operative of great things. A noble carreer lies before it.

Why does not Gouverneur Morris come home? [2] His talents are wanted. Men like him do not superabound. Indeed I wish that you were here rather than where you are, though I think your position an important one at the existing juncture. But we want to infuse more abilities into the management of our internal affairs.

Governor Jay is well. He & all your friends continue to take a lively interest in whatever concerns you.

Adieu   Yrs. Affectly

R King Esq

AL, New-York Historical Society, New York City.

1. Henry M. Rutledge, the son of Edward Rutledge of South Carolina, had been secretary to Charles Cotesworth Pinckney when Pinckney was United States Minister Plenipotentiary to France from 1796 to 1797 and one of the three United States commissioners to France from 1797 to 1798. The two men returned from France to the United States separately. Rutledge arrived in New York on October 1, 1798, while Pinckney arrived in New York on October 12 (*Gazette of the United States, and Philadelphia Daily Advertiser,* October 1, 15, 1798).

2. After Morris had been superseded as United States Minister Plenipotentiary to France in 1794, he remained in Europe for four more years. He arrived in New York on December 23, 1798 (Anne Cary Morris, ed., *The Diary and Letters of Gouverneur Morris, Minister of the United States to France, Member of the Constitutional Convention, etc.* [New York, 1888], II, 377).

To Marquis de la Tour du Pin [1]

New York October 3. 1798

I had yesterday, My Dear Sir, the pleasure of receiving your letter of the 15 of July, accompanied by two others, one for Messrs Le Roy & Bayard, the other for Mr. Olive; which will be sent to them in the Country where they now continue, in consequence of the sickness in this city.[2] The letters which you mention to have before written have also been received.[3] To mine I replied [4] shortly after; nor can I imagine how it has happened that you have received no answer from either of the parties.

On the subject of the sale of your farm. Mr. Bayard & myself had a conference and we agreed that a sale at this time was inexpedient—as it could not be hoped that the farm would bring near its value—owing to the embarassments in pecuniary operations produced by the prospect of war. I shall however now advise that an experiment be made. The offers received, if any, will determine whether a sale can take place without an imprudent sacrifice for you; and the result can be regulated accordingly.

Be assured, My Dear Sir, that I shall be happy to be useful to you in this or any other matter. In doing so, I shall equally gratify the esteem and friendship with which you have inspired me for yourself, and that lively and affecting interest in whatever concerns Madame DeGouverne, which cannot but be felt by all who have had an opportunity to know her value.

If it shall conduce to her and your happiness to return to this Country, it will certainly add to ours; & if you will beforehand apprise me of your resolution when taken and your general plan you will find me zealous to cooperate in giving it effect.

I would invite you to return with the more confidence from the assurance in the stability of affairs in this country which is derived from the late happy course of the public mind. An extraordinary union among the people in the support of their own government, and in resistance to all foreign encroachment, leaves nothing to be feared for our future security and prosperity. The most reasonable ideas in every respect prevail.

Accept, whenever you shall come, under the roof of Mrs. Hamilton & myself, an asylum, where you may be perfectly at home, until you shall have completed your arrangements for your future establishment. She joins me in cordial remembrances to M: De Gouverne & yourself. Believe me always very truly *D Sir*

Yr Obed ser   A Hamilton

The Count Latour Du pin Gouver

ALS, Hamilton Papers, Library of Congress; copy, Mr. George T. Bowdoin, New York City.
    1. For background to this letter, see La Tour du Pin to H, February 21, July 15, 1798.
    2. This is a reference to the yellow fever epidemic in New York City during the late summer and fall of 1798.
    3. La Tour du Pin to H, February 21, 1798.
    4. Letter not found.

From James McHenry [1]

Trenton 5th Octbr. 1798

My dear Hamilton.

The sun begins to shine. I reced. this morning from the President a letter dated the 30th ulto. containing the following words.

Sir. Inclosed are the commissions for the three generals signed and all dated on the same day. I am Sir your ob sr

This is a Regal letter, and at the same time a loyal proceeding. Hasten the military regulations.[2] I shall, I expect, soon call upon you. Burn this letter.

Yours   James McHenry [3]

Alexr. Hamilton, Esq.

ALS, Hamilton Papers, Library of Congress.
    1. For an explanation of the contents of this letter, see the introductory note to George Washington to H, July 14, 1798.
    2. See McHenry to H, July 20, 1798; H to Jonathan Dayton, August 6, 1798, note 6.
    3. On the envelope of this letter McHenry wrote: "To be opened *only* by Gen. Hamilton and the contents known only to himself."

To James McHenry

New York October 9. 1798

I thank you, My Dear Sir, for the prompt communication of the intelligence contained in your letter by yesterdays Post.[1]

As to the Regulations [2] (if as I suppose you mean) those for the tactics & discipline of the army—I must answer that hitherto I have done nothing more towards it than some preliminary readings & reflection. The undetermined situation, & the necessity of a close attention to my law business (which in such a state I could neither abandon nor diminish) has prevented my doing more in respect to the matter in question. It will henceforth engage my particular attention; but it ought not to be precipitated. My plan will suppose a different organisation of the troops & some previous legislative measures to precede its execution. Besides the present sistem must be essentially the basis of another & there is no urgency for a change. The course of the Winter will fulfill every useful idea—& allow time to digest well additions or innovations. To organise & to raise the army are the immediate *desiderata*.

I shall be ready to attend your call.

Yrs. affectly.   A Hamilton

J McH Esq

P.S. Young *Rutlege*,[3] late Secy of General Pinckney, is himself desirous of going into the army but he cannot in propriety decide upon an application without the previous consent of his father whose permission he has asked. In the mean time I would suggest for your consideration the expediency of keeping open for him a Captaincy of Infantry. His connections & qualifications give him pretension to look to this. You will understand that he cannot now ask & may not perhaps be allowed to accept; so that whatever is done must be *provisory*. Adieu   AH

ALS, Columbia University Libraries; ALS (photostat), James McHenry Papers, Library of Congress.
    1. McHenry to H, October 5, 1798.
    2. See McHenry to H, July 20, 1798; H to Jonathan Dayton, August 6, 1798, note 6.
    3. Henry M. Rutledge. See H to Rufus King, October 2, 1798, note 1. On July 12, 1799, during the recess of the Senate, Rutledge was appointed a major in the Fifth Regiment of Infantry (Heitman, *United States Army*, I, 855). The Senate approved his appointment on May 14, 1800 (*Executive Journal*, I, 343, 355).

From George Washington

[*Mount Vernon, October 9, 1798.*[1] *Letter not found.*]

    1. "List of Letters from G—— Washington to General Hamilton," Columbia University Libraries.

From Oliver Wolcott, Junior[1]

Trenton Octr. 10. 1798

Dear Sir   (Private)
    At the close of the last week or on Monday of this, a Letter was recd. by the Secy of War from the President covering the Commissions of the Major Generals, dated on *one day*.[2] This circumstance taken in connexion with others which preceeded, fully justify an opinion that the rank may [be] considered as settled in the order in which the appointments were made—of course that you are established in the rank of first Major General. I supposed till yester-

day that the Commissions had been transmitted by Mr. Mc.Henry with an Official Letter settling the grade. I find however that our friend Mc.Henry still hesitates; I will however prevail on him to do this duty if I can. In the mean time permit me to say to you with confidence, that the affair which has caused so much doubt delay and perplexity, ought not in justice to be attributed entirely to the President. I will admit that he has been in my opinion greatly *mistaken*, the affair was however unfortunately managed and General Washington & the President have not been understood by each other.

The question of rank being settled, I sincerely hope that General Knox will decline service. His pencuniary affairs are I believe so embarrassed, that there is no prospect of his preserving his independence & I much fear, that the fortune of modern speculators, some loss of character, awaits him.

As a friend to your fame & the public Interest I cannot omit to request that no conversation may take place respecting the question of rank—even your personal feelings will be much alleviated by such an explanation as I will give you when we have the fortune to meet.

In the next place let me request, that as little may be done as possible relative to the organization of the Army, before there can be a *deliberate consultation* upon the state of our affairs. Depend upon it, that the arrangements of the War Department are all defective, and that nothing will succeed without a thorough reform. Besides do not countenence the plan for making appointments in the great Sections of our Country on the recommendations of individual officers. Though you may feel confidence in your own judgement, yet it will be well to remember that the same power, will be exercised by others who may not be equally well informed. If a few more mistakes are made, the service will be irretrievably ruined.

If I can do it without danger,[3] I will call on you as I go on to Connecticut at the close of this month, when I will explain &c

I am Dr Sir, your obedt servt.   Oliv. Wolcott.

Alexander Hamilton Esq.

ALS, Hamilton Papers, Library of Congress.
 1. For an explanation of the contents of this letter, see the introductory note to George Washington to H, July 14, 1798.

2. See James McHenry to H, October 5, 1798.
3. This is a reference to the yellow fever epidemic in New York City.

From James McHenry [1]

War Department
11th October 1798

Dr Sir

As it may be attended with very great inconvenience to add any new buildings this season to the Barracks on Governors Island, or to add new ones on Bedlows, or Oyster Islands, to accomodate the men at present on two of these Islands, I submit to your decision, whether it would not be best, after retaining such a number of the troops as can be comfortably wintered at Governors Island, to remove the others to the Garrison at West Point where they can be accommodated, and may be in a situation to receive instructions and from whence they can be easily drawn at any time.

We shall then have the whole of next year before us to determine respecting the necessary permanent garrisons for the Islands, and, consequently, the necessary barracks required to be erected.

I am D Sir, your most obed Hle Serv   James McHenry

Majr. Genl. A. Hamilton

ALS, Hamilton Papers, Library of Congress.
    1. For background to this letter, see the introductory note to H to McHenry, June 1, 1798.

From Charles W. Goldsborough [1]

[*Trenton, October 15, 1798.* On October 20, 1798, Hamilton wrote to Benjamin Stoddert: "I have received a letter from Mr. Goldsborough of the 15th." *Letter not found.*]

    1. Goldsborough was chief clerk of the Navy Department.

From James McHenry [1]

War Department 15 Octbr. 1798

Sir

I have the honour to inclose your Commission as Major General in the army of the United States,[2] and to request your attendance at Trenton or Philadelphia as soon as possible, and in all events by the 10th day of November next.

The object of this request is to obtain your advice and assistance in concert with General Knox, and perhaps General Washington, in forming preliminary arrangements relative to the army proposed to be raised, to be submitted to the President of the United States, and also to charge you especially with a branch of the military service.

With respect to the relative rank between you, Generals Pinckney and Knox, I deem it necessary to observe, that the order of nomination and approval by the Senate is considered as definitive.

With great respect I have the honor to be Sir   Your obt

James McHenry

Alexr Hamilton Es Major General

ALS, James McHenry Papers, Library of Congress.
    1. For an explanation of the contents of this letter, see the introductory note to George Washington to H, July 14, 1798.
    2. For H's commission, see the first enclosure to McHenry to H, July 25, 1798.

From James McHenry

(Confidential)   Trenton 16 Octbr. 1798

My dear Hamilton.

You will see by the enclosed,[1] the steps I have taken, and the information and the aid which I expect to derive from the Major Generals in case it is approved. I know not how all this is to end, and feel perfectly tired of the uncertainty in which so many important measures are kept fettered and involved.

I hope you will approve of this exposition, and the propriety of my fortifying or correcting my own opinions by those of the Generals.

Yours ever & affectionately   James McHenry

ADfS, James McHenry Papers, Library of Congress.

1. On October 16, 1798, McHenry wrote in part to John Adams: ". . . My design is, to derive from the knowledge the Generals may have, of the several characters, who have applied for military appointments, and others disposed to enter in the Army effectual and necessary aid, in the selection and application of the most suitable to the different grades; and to prepare in conjunction with them a list for your final determination: and also, to avail myself of their knowledge and experience in digesting a report, to be submitted for your approbation relative to the measures necessary to be pursued, to give efficacy and ensure success to the recruiting Service—to the distribution of the military force of the United States; the most certain, regular and economical mode of provisioning the recruits and the troops in the field —the quantity and kinds of artillery, military stores and other articles necessary to be procured in addition to what we already have in our Magazines and Arsenals and the proper places for occasional and permanent deposits for the same. I also purpose to assign to the two Major Generals Hamilton and Knox such branches of the military Service as were suggested in my letter of the 4th Aug ultimo" (copy, Hamilton Papers, Library of Congress).

From John Adams [1]

Quincy [Massachusetts] October 17. 1798

Sir

I have received, last night, a Letter from His Excellency Governor Jay, inclosing a Copy of an Act of the Legislature of New York for the further Defence of that State and for other Purposes.[2] The Governor Observes that it appears to be the intention of that Act, that the Money appropriated in it, 150,000 dollars, Shall be laid out only in the manner which the National Government will recognize as usefull and adviseable, and His Excellency proposes to my Consideration whether it would not be expedient to authorize Major General Hamilton, as a national officer in whom Great Confidence may be placed to concert with the Governor the Plan of laying out the Money to the best Advantage, and to appoint the General to superintend the Execution of it.

I have not hesitated to comply with the Governors Request, Saving all Rights of the Legislature of the United States.

Accordingly I hereby request you Sir, to concert with His Excellency the Plan and to superintend the Execution of it, at least untill some other Arrangement shall be made, if any other should hereafter be thought expedient.

With great Esteem I have the Honor to be, sir your most obedient and humble sert   John Adams

Major General Alexander Hamilton
New York

ALS, Hamilton Papers, Library of Congress; LC, Adams Family Papers, deposited in the Massachusetts Historical Society, Boston; copy, in James McHenry's handwriting, Adams Family Papers, deposited in the Massachusetts Historical Society, Boston.

1. For background to this letter, see the introductory note to H to James McHenry, June 1, 1798. For John Jay's letter to John Adams, see Jay to H, September 26, 1798, note 2.

2. On October 17, 1798, Adams wrote to Jay in reply to Jay's letter of September 26: ". . . I shall not hesitate to comply with your Excellency's Request so far as to authorize General Hamilton to concert with you, the Plan of laying out the Money in question to the best Advantage and to appoint him to superintend the Execution of it" (ALS, Columbia University Libraries; LC, Adams Family Papers, deposited in the Massachusetts Historical Society, Boston; copy, in John Jay's handwriting, Hamilton Papers, Library of Congress; copy, Dr. Frank Monaghan, Washington, D.C.).

From Rufus King

[London, October 19, 1798.[1] Letter not found.]

1. Letter listed in Rufus King's "Memorandum of Private Letters, &c., dates & persons, from 1796 to Augt 1802," owned by Mr. James G. King, New York City.

To James McHenry [1]

N York Oct 19. 1798

My Dear Sir

I received yesterday your private letter of the 16th, with its inclosures, now returned.

It was essential for you to take a decisive course & to leave the blame of further delay at some other door. There can be no doubt of the propriety of combining the aid of General Officers. But *Pinckney* being now arrived,[2] it seems to me very proper & necessary that he also should be called upon. You will learn with pleasure that he sent me a message by young Rutlege [3] purporting his intire satisfaction with the military arrangement & readiness to serve under my command.[4] Communicate this to our friends *Pickering* & *Wolcott,* as I am not well enough to write them by this post.

Yrs. Affectly   A Hamilton

J M. Henry Esq

ALS, The Sol Feinstone Collection, Library of the American Philosophical Society, Philadelphia; ALS (photostat), James McHenry Papers, Library of Congress.

1. For background to this letter, see the introductory note to George Washington to H, July 14, 1798.

2. When Charles Cotesworth Pinckney arrived in New York from France on October 12, 1798, he remained on board his ship because of the yellow fever epidemic in that city. On the following day he disembarked at Paulus Hook, New Jersey (*Gazette of the United States, and Philadelphia Daily Advertiser,* October 15, 1798).

3. Henry M. Rutledge. See H to Rufus King, October 2, 1798, note 1.

4. On October 31, 1798, Pinckney wrote to McHenry: ". . . A few hours after the Ship in which I came, had cast anchor in the North River, it was intimated to me, that it had been doubted whether I would accept an appointment, as General Hamilton, who was of inferior Rank to me, in the last war, was ranked before me, in the new arrangement. I declared then, and still declare, it was with the greatest pleasure I saw his name at the head of the list of the Major Generals, and applauded the discernment which placed him there. I knew that his talents in war were great, that he had a genius capable of forming an extensive military plan, and a spirit courageous & enterprizing, equal to the execution of it. I therefore without any hesitation immediately sent him word, by Major Rutledge, that I rejoiced at his appointment and would with pleasure serve under him" (copy, George Washington Papers, Library of Congress; copy, Adams Family Papers, deposited in the Massachusetts Historical Society, Boston).

To James McHenry [1]

New York October 19. 1798

Sir

I was yesterday honourd with your letter [2] transmitting my commission as Inspector and Major General.

Agreeably to your desire I hold myself prepared to attend you within the period you assign. But as the object appears to embrace a concert of advice and assistance with General Knox, who cannot be expected in much less than the utmost limit of the time pre-[s]cribed, I shall permit myself to defer my journey so as to reach you about the first of November; unless I am told that an anticipation of that day is deemed requisite.

I cannot but observe with satisfaction the conclusion of your letter as to the relative rank of the three Major Generals.

I received at the same time your letter of the 11th instant—having been absent from the city for five days past. I shall to-day confer with Major Hoops & Col Stevens [3] on the subject of it chiefly to ascertain the actual state of things, and by tomorrow's post will communicate my Opinion.[4]

With great respect & esteem   I have the honor to be   Sir Your Obedt Servant   Alexander Hamilton

Copy, Hamilton Papers, Library of Congress; copy, Adams Family Papers, deposited in the Massachusetts Historical Society, Boston.

1. For an explanation of the contents of this letter, see the introductory note to George Washington to H, July 14, 1798.

2. McHenry to H, October 15, 1798.

3. Adam Hoops was commandant of New York Harbor. Ebenezer Stevens was the agent for the War Department in New York City.

4. On October 30, 1798, McHenry sent a copy of H's letter to President John Adams (ALS, Adams Family Papers, deposited in the Massachusetts Historical Society, Boston).

To James McHenry [1]

New York 19th Oct. 1798.

Sir

The state of my health and of the Weather yesterday and to day must prevent my communicating the result of the consultation intended to be had with the Gentlemen I mentioned in my letter of Yesterday.[2]

I answer your inquiry [3] Thus far according to the data which I previously possessed. It cannot be expedient to keep men on such of the Islands as the winter shall find without fortifications in a state to protect them and be useful. This as to Bidlams Island is now certainly not the case—nor do I know what is intended or can be done there before the coming on of winter. If it is contemplated to have till spring that Island in the state in which it now is the sooner the Troops there are Withdrawn the better, as to Ellis's Island the case is different. The Works there may easily be in a state of defence and I think a little expence will complete the Requisite accomodations for a company.

Less than two can hardly be thought of for Governors Island—and for these with the accessories, some increase of barracks will it is imagined be necessary. Col. Stevens informed me some days since that a ⟨–⟩ barrack with six Rooms within the fort may be completed this season for 4,000 Dols. You are sure that this will not give all the accomodation which is permanently Requisite.

The conclusion is that in my opinion it will be expedient to add a building of that kind on Governors Island and to fit such as may already exist at Ellis's Island for the accomodation of one company —keeping consequently one company there and two on Governors Island.

As to Bedlams supposing as I do that it will not be put in a defensible state this season it will be inexpedient to keep Troops there and equally so to *build* or *Repair* for their accomodation.

Let me suggest that it is always desirable when practicable to keep the Troops of each Regiment together or in close vicinity so as to be under the eye of their own Commanders to oversee the care and discipline of them—That consequently it will be well to have such troops as are kept in this quarter of one and not of different Regiments.

With respect & Esteem I have the honor to be sir   yr very Obedt servt.

Copy, Hamilton Papers, Library of Congress.
  1. For background to this letter, see the introductory note to H to James McHenry, June 1, 1798.
  2. H was mistaken, for he was referring to the second letter that he wrote to McHenry on October 19, 1798, in which he mentioned Adam Hoops and Ebenezer Stevens.
  3. McHenry to H, October 11, 1798.

From Francisco de Miranda[1]

[London, October 19–November 10, 1798]

C'est avec bien du Plaisir, mon très cher Général, que j'ai reçu hier Votre Lettre du 22. aout dernier. Vos Souhaits sont déja en quelque Sorte remplis, puisque on est convenu ici que, d'un Coté, on n'employera point aux opérations terrestres des Troupes anglaises, vu que les forces auxiliares de Terre devront ètre uniquement américaines, tandis que, de l'autre, la Marine Sera purement anglaise. Tout est applani, et on attend Seulement le *fiat* de Votre illustre Président pour partir comme l'Eclair. En Effet, le moment parait des plus favorables, et les derniers Evenémens Semblent nous laisser un Champ Vaste et tranquille pour agir à notre entiére Satisfaction. Profiterons avec Sagesse de la Nature des Circonstances, et rendons à notre Pays le plus grand Service qu'un Mortel Soit capable d'offrir à ses Semblables! Sauvons l'amérique des Calamités affreuses qui, en bouleversant une grande partie du monde, menacent de la Déstruction les parties intactes encore.

Mon Compatriote D. Pedro Caro qui, effectivement, avait du être le Porteur de ma Lettre du 6. Avril dernier, n'a pas pu Se rendre alors à New-York, un Accident imprévu l'en ayant empêché; Il dirigea Sa Route en Droiture vers le Continent méridional de l'amérique, dont une partie, pressée de Secouer un Joug justement odieux, et ne voulant pas attendre plus longtems les Secours des Puissances Co-opératrices, se disposait alors à effectuer un Mouvement insurrectionnel qui, pour n'être que partiel, aurait pu nuire aux Intérèts de la Masse entière.[2] Heureusement qu'ils ont consenti à ajourner leurs Démarches. Les Renseignemens, que nous avons d'ailleurs Sur la Situation présente des Choses, Sont du plus heureux Augure. M. Caro repart dans ce moment ci pour la mème Destination par la Voie de l'Ile de la Trinité, afin que tout Soit disposé Conformément aux Plans arrêtés, lesquels j'aurai l'honneur de Vous Soumettre à tems.

Je Vous prie de remettre la Lettre ci-jointe à notre ami Commun le Général Knox,[3] dont la Nomination dans l'Armée me fait aussi le plus grand Plaisir. Continuez toujours, mon cher ami, d'ètre le Bienfacteur du Genre humain qui, jamais, n'a eu autant Besoin de tels Appuis. Réunissons nous tous bien fermement pour opérer le Salut de notre chére Patrie, et peut-ètre, qu'en l'arrachant aux Malheurs qui la menacent, nous Sauverons le Monde entier qui chancèle au Bord de l'Abîme.

à Vous bien sincerement   F. de Miranda.

Londres le 19. Octobre 1798.

P.S. Ayez la bonté d'offrir mes Respects au General Washington— dont la conduitte ferme, et Sage, attire dans ce moment les hommages de tout le monde; et doit contribuer essentiellement à Sauver notre pais.[4]

à Londres ce 10 Nove. 1798.
Alexr. Hamilton, Esq:—&c. &c. &c.

LS, Hamilton Papers, Library of Congress; copy, Academia Nacional de la Historia, Caracas, Venezuela.
    1. For background to this letter, see Miranda to H, April 1, 1797, February 7, April 6–June 7, August 17, 1798; H to Miranda, August 22, 1798; H to Rufus King, August 22, 1798.
    2. For Pedro José Caro's proposed visit to the United States and the subsequent change in his plans, see Miranda to H, April 6–June 7, 1798, note 2.
    3. Miranda to Henry Knox, October 19, 1798 (*Archivo, Miranda*, XV, 309).
    4. The postscript is in Miranda's handwriting.

To John Adams

New York October 20. 1798

Sir

The very obliging manner, in which you was pleased to assure me of the appointment of my nephew *Philip Church*,[1] and the actual appointment of my relation *Capta[i]n Hamilton* to a Lieutenancy in the Navy,[2] which I just learn from the Marine Department, are circumstances from which I derive much pleasure, which I consider as conferring upon me a personal obligation, and for which I beg you to accept my very cordial acknowlegements.

With perfect respect & esteem   I have the honor to be Sir   Your Very Obed servant   A Hamilton

The President of The UStates

ALS, Adams Family Papers, deposited in the Massachusetts Historical Society, Boston.
  1. See H to Adams, August 24, 1798; Adams to H, September 3, 1798.
  2. See H to Benjamin Stoddert, October 20, 1798.

From Rufus King

London Oct. 20. 1798

My dear sir

I have received your letter of the 22. of august with an inclosure [1] that has been delivered as directed. On that subject, things are here, as we could desire: there will be precisely such a cooperation as we wish, the moment *we are* ready.[2] The Secretary of State will shew you my communications on this Subject, tho' I have not a word from him respecting it;[3] your outline corresponds with what had been suggested by me, and approved by this Government—fortunately some months past I obtained a fac Simile of the latest map of the Country. It has been now two months in the Hands of an Engraver, who has engaged to deliver the Copies in January.[4] This Government has considerable information respecting the interior, as well as concerning the condition and Dispositions of the Inhabitants, tho' I apprehend it is not of a recent date.[5] What we know is favorable; but if we are to be betrayed by France, the glorious opportunity will be lost. I am gratified in receiving your Opinion of the good condition of our public affairs, but I do not feel confident that we are as Safe as you appear to think we are. It is fraud not force that I fear. A Paris Paper of the 8th. instant which is the latest that takes any notice of the U. S. says, "les dernieres Lettres de Bourdeaux assurent qu'il y est arrivé un courier extraordinaire, porteur d'ordres pour remettre l'embargo sur les navires américains. Voilà donc la guerre inevitable avec ce peuple; de moins toutes nos correspondances coincident avec ce bruit."

Yrs   K

P:S: As I presume from your present connection with the Government that you are acquainted with ⟨all the⟩ information possessed by it ⟨I need⟩ not say any thing to you upon ⟨these⟩ Subjects that I should otherwise ⟨think⟩ of. Another reason, we have no cy⟨pher. It⟩ may be advantageous that we should establish one. Genl. Schuyler invented a most excellent cipher, & I wish you would send it to me by the Packet or other safe conveyance, preserving the counter part.   K.

ALS, Hamilton Papers, Library of Congress.

1. The enclosure was H to Francisco de Miranda, August 22, 1798. For information on Miranda's plans to liberate the Spanish-American colonies, see Miranda to H, April 1, 1797; February 7, April 6–June 7, August 17, October 19–November 10, 1798.

2. On August 17, 1798, King wrote to Timothy Pickering and described his conference with Lord Grenville of August 16: "Our Conference here took a turn to the probability of the revolution of South America; he was fuller and more explicit than he had been on any former occasion, always understanding that my conversation on this Subject was merely personal and wholly unauthorised. This digression which treated of the practicability and the means of effecting the measure tended to shew to me that they have at times considered and combined with their views of a future connection with the United States the independence of the Spanish Continental colonies. I did not perceive nor do I believe it to be the Case that they have any recent information of the present temper disposition or plans of the Spanish Colonies more easily procured from the UStates than from Europe and which is indispensably requisite to the success of an enterprize to accomplish the revolution. We spoke of the government to be established in case of a revolution. He thought our system would naturally attract and receive their approbation and made some remarks upon the apprehensions to be Entertained on account of their genius and character which especially in Peru was said to be highly animated and full of enthusiasm and Concluded by observing that he was more and more confirmed in the opinion that none but Englishmen and their descendants knew how to make a revolution . . ." (LS [deciphered], RG 59, Despatches from United States Ministers to Great Britain, 1791–1906, Vol. 7, January 9–December 22, 1798, National Archives). In a private letter to Pickering on October 20, 1798, King wrote: ". . . You are silent concerning South America; I have again and again touched upon it; I have wished to say much more, but I have not thought it prudent. As England is ready she will furnish a fleet and military stores and we should furnish the army . . ." (King, *The Life and Correspondence of Rufus King*, II, 453–54).

3. For King's dispatches to Pickering, dated February 7, 26. April 6, 1798; see Miranda to H, February 7, 1798, note 5; April 6–June 7, 1798, note 1.

4. On August 20, 1798, King wrote to Miranda asking him "to secure . . . an early and certain publication of the Map. . . . I have recommended to the Col. [John Turnbull] to take a Receit for the Map in my name, with an engagement to Engrave it . . ." (*Archivo, Miranda*, XV, 299). Turnbull was a member with John Forbes of the London mercantile firm of Turnbull, Forbes, and Company.

On January 1, 1799, William Faden published a copy of "Mapa Geográfico de America Meridional Dispuesto y Gravado por D. Juan de la Cruz Cano y

Olmedilla, Geogfo Pensdo. de S.M. individuo de la Rl Academia de Sn Fernando y de la sociedad Bascongada de los Amigos del Pais; teniendo presentos varios Mapas y noticias originales con arreglo à Observaciones astronómicas, Ano de 1775" (PRO: F.O. [Great Britain], 925/1216).

5. See Miranda to H, April 6–June 7, 1798, note 3.

To Benjamin Stoddert [1]

New York October 20. 1798

Dear Sir

I have received a letter from Mr. Goldsborough of the 15th.[2] transmitting me one for Capt Hamilton to notify him of his appointment as a Lieutenant in our navy.

This event gives me particular pleasure and claims a renewal of my acknowlegemants to you for the obliging part you have taken in the matter.

Capt. Hamilton is now absent on a vesel to Albany. I dayly expect him back. On his return, he will be ready immediately to obey the orders of the Department—and I ever know it to be his wish, if thought adviseable, in case the Ship for which he may be destined be not ready, to go as a volunteer on board some other to have the advantage of seeing the course of management on board a Ship of War, with which he is not yet acquainted.[3]

With great respect & esteem   I have the honor to remain   Dr Sir
Yr very obed serv   A Hamilton

Benjamin Stoddert Esq

ALS, RG 45, Naval Records Collection of the Office of Naval Records and Library, Subject File: Personnel (NN), National Archives.

1. For background to this letter, see H to Stoddert, August 8, 21, 29, September 3, 1798; Stoddert to H, August 24, 1798.

2. Letter not found.

3. On November 5, 1798, Timothy Pickering wrote to Robert Hamilton: ". . . you may if you please, repair as soon as convenient to Providence in Rhode Island, where you will find the Ship of War the George Washington nearly ready for sea, and on presenting the enclosed letter to the Commander, Capt. Patrick Fletcher, you will be received on board for the present Cruise as a volunteer: The Lieutenants for that ship being already appointed . . ." (LC, RG 45, Naval Records Collection of the Office of the Naval Records and Library, Letters to Officers of Ships of War, National Archives).

From George Washington [1]

Mount Vernon 21 Octr. 1798.

My dear Sir,

The last mail to Alexandria brought me a letter from the President of the United States,[2] in which I am informed that he had signed, and given the Commissions to yourself, Generals Pinckney & Knox, the same date, in hopes that an amicable adjustment, or acquiescence might take place among you. But, if these hopes should be disappointed, and controversies should arise, they will of course be submitted to me, as Commander in Chief, and if after all, any one should be so obstinate as to appeal to him from the judgment of the Commander in chief, he was determined to confirm that judgment.

General Knox is fully acquainted with my sentiments on this subject; and I hope no fresh difficulties will arise with General Pinckney. Let me entreat you therefore to give, without delay, your *full* aid to the Secry of War. At present I will only add that I am always, & affectly yours   Go: Washington

Majr. Genl. Hamilton

ALS, Hamilton Papers, Library of Congress; ALS, letterpress copy, Hamilton Papers, Library of Congress.
   1. For an explanation of the contents of this letter, see the introductory note to Washington to H, July 14, 1798.
   2. John Adams to Washington, October 9, 1798 (ALS, George Washington Papers, Library of Congress).

From James McHenry [1]

War Department
22 October 1798

Sir

I have been favored with your letter of the 19th instant.

You will see by the enclosed copy of a letter to Colo Stevens dated 21st of august [2] the instructions which respect the fortifications on Governors, Bedlows and Ellis's Islands.

In conformity with your opinion I have directed Col Stevens to contract for the necessary additional barracks on Governors Island, and to have such buildings as already exist on Ellis's Island fitted up for the immediate accommodation of a company and the works put in a state of defence as speedily as possible agreeably to my instructions contained in the letter enclosed.

With respect and esteem   I have the honor to be Dr Genl.   Your most obd Hb St   James McHenry

Major Genl A Hamilton

ALS, Hamilton Papers, Library of Congress.
    1. For background to this letter, see the introductory note to H to James McHenry, June 1, 1798.
    2. On August 21, 1798, McHenry wrote to Ebenezer Stevens: "I have received and examined the plans and estimates for the different defences of the City and Harbour of New York. The Military committee of New York being on the spot, and composed of Gentlemen of competent judgement, I have determined to submit to their decision the choice of a plan for the parapet for the work on Governors Island. They will therefore decide between the plans offered by Mr Mangin and those of Messrs Fleming and Hill.
    "As soon as the committee have announced their preference, you will advertise for proposals to undertake the same and the other reparations and additions which may be necessary on Governors Island, Bedlows Island, Oyster Island and Paulus Hook agreeably to the plans furnished. . . ." (ALS, Hamilton Papers, Library of Congress.)

From John Jay [1]

Albany 24 Octr. 1798

Dear Sir

I subjoin for your Information a copy of a Letter of the 17 Instant which I recd. this morning from the Presidt. of the U.S. [2] in answer to mine of the 26 ult. by which he consents to authorize you to concert with me the plan of laying out the money in question to the best advantage, & to appoint you to superintend the Execution of it.

Will it not be proper immediately to form an accurate Survey of such parts of the Shores & waters of the port, as from their Situation or other Circumstances, it may be desireable to fortify? Col. Burr [3] informs me that this has already been partially done by Mr. Coles; [4] & I submit to your Consideration whether it would not be adviseable to confer with them respecting, and perhaps obtain their aid in executing the measures proper to be taken to perfect that necessary work.

That being done, I conceive the next object of Inquiry will be, the manner in which the port is capable of being the most effectually fortified. The Result I think should then be laid before the President, thro' the Secy at War, and our future operations will necessarily depend greatly on what he may direct to be communicated to us on the Subject. I wish all this may be done and ascertained before the next Session of our Legislature; [5] that my Communications to them may be full and early. The Expence incident to the orders which you may give for these purposes, will of Course be paid; for it gives me pleasure now to consider you as being perfectly authorized to superintend the Fortifications contemplated by the act.

I purpose to be in Town next month, and am with great Esteem & Regard

Dear Sir   your most obt. Servt   John Jay

Majr. Genl. Hamilton

ALS, Hamilton Papers, Library of Congress; LC, Governor's Letter Books, from the original in the New York State Library, Albany; copy, Dr. Frank Monaghan, Washington, D.C.

1. For background to this letter, see the introductory note to H to James McHenry, June 1, 1798.

2. Copy, in the handwriting of Jay, Hamilton Papers, Library of Congress. For an extract from this letter, see John Adams to H, October 17, 1798, note 1.

3. Aaron Burr and H were both members of the Military Committee of New York City. See "Call for a Meeting," June 4, 1798, note 2.

4. John B. Coles, a New York City merchant, was vice president of the New York Chamber of Commerce and alderman from the second ward. On May 28, 1798, he, Gabriel Furman, John Bogert, and Ebenezer Stevens were appointed a committee "to attend to the Measures . . . for the Defence of the City and Harbor of New York." See the introductory note to H to McHenry, June 1, 1798.

5. The legislature had adjourned on August 27, 1798, and was scheduled to convene on January 2, 1799.

From John Skey Eustace [1]

[New York, October 27, 1798]

Sir,

As I find myself obliged to make a voyage to Georgia,[2] where some important concerns demand my attention, I have a favor to ask of you—it is simply that you will permit me to depose in your care (and to offer you as a humble legacy, if I do not return) a trunk containing all my papers, as well personal as official.

Though it has so happened, that nothing like private friendship or confidence could ever exist between us (I allude to the untoward circumstance of our attachment to Chiefs who were at variance) [3] yet I am not sensible that any action of my life could justify your aversion for *I* can truly declare, not only that Colonel Hamilton has ever possessed my esteem, but my good will and good wishes—I should say very much more were I not addressing him personally—so that I auger no censure from him on the object or terms of this

ALS, Hamilton Papers, Library of Congress.

1. Eustace, who was born in Flushing, New York, was graduated from William and Mary College in 1776. During the American Revolution, he attained the rank of major and served as an aide-de-camp to Major General Charles Lee, Major General John Sullivan, and Major General Nathanael Greene. In 1781 he became adjutant general of Georgia, and three years later he was admitted to practice law in that state. In 1784 Eustace went to Europe and in 1792 he joined the French army. He servied as an aide to Marshall Nicolas Luckner and General Charles François Dumouriez and attained the rank of major general and maréchal-de-camp. Eustace was expelled from France and England in 1797 and from the Netherlands in 1798. On June 22, 1798, the House of Representatives read a memorial from Eustace "praying that he may receive the commutation of half pay due to him for military services rendered the United States, during the Revolutionary war with Great Britain . . ." (*Journal of the House*, III 347–48). On July 10, 1798, the House resolved that Eustace "have leave to withdraw his said memorial" (*Journal of the House*, III, 380). For Eustace's earlier effort to receive such compensation, see JCC, XVII, 462.

2. The purpose of Eustace's trip to Savannah was to settle his mother's business affairs (Albert Matthews, "General J. S. Eustace," *Notes and Queries for Readers and Writers, Collectors and Librarians*, CL [January, 1926], 49).

3. This is a reference to the court-martial concerning the conduct of Charles Lee at the Battle of Monmouth in 1778. As a result of H's testimony against Lee, Eustace tried unsuccessfully to draw H into a duel. See "Proceedings of a General Court-Martial for the Trial of Major-General Charles Lee," July 4, 13, 1778; Hamilton, *Intimate Life*, 280–81.

letter. When you reflect, Sir, on the boyish period of my life, 1775, when general Lee first won my esteem, neither its force or direction can excite reproach. If you consider that I was then the heir-declared of his fortune,[4] and that I formally disclaimed, four years thereafter, this proffered boon [5] (and this shall be proved to you) from motives of patriotic submission to the Commander in Chief; when you combine with these facts, the successive assaults on my family rights at home; a long residence abroad; a dangerous service in France, and an unmerited check to my fortune in the rival State; if, Sir, you take the trouble to cast a comprehensive glance over these various and coefficient causes of irritation, whatever warmth of character I may, at any time ⟨have displayed⟩ in my public and ingenious opinions of men or measures here, will deserve your commiseration, rather than provoke your censure. I may cite the late example of Mr. Jay,[6] who receivd and visited me with friendship, nay affection, under a due impression of these facts.

My present efforts being wholly destined to solace the aged and parental members of my family, you will be assured, Sir, that it is not to the influential general Hamilton, but to the private Citizen that I address myself. From the first I cannot honorably receive or patronage or favor, because I feel that I do not deserve either: On

4. On February 26, 1777, Lee wrote to George Washington: "Eustace I consider as my adopted son, considering the circumstances of his being taken out of other hands and his affection for me, I ought to look upon him in this light—in short should any accident happen to me, it has long been my resolution to leave everything I possess on this side of the water, between these two young men [Eustace and Jacob Morris]" (ALS, George Washington Papers, Library of Congress). Morris was also one of Lee's aides during the American Revolution.

5. On December 13, 1779, Eustace wrote to Lee: "I am perfectly tired of having my peace of mind disturbed by the daily alterations in your temper —I therefore am determined to withdraw myself from their influence. I've no idea faith of battling your cause, on every occasion with civil and military, adding to the number of my own Enemies, . . . To your friendship Sir, I bid adieu—of every connexion with you—I take leave with a painful kind of pleasure" (Matthews, "Eustace," 46).

6. In the "Embassy of Mr. Monroe," printed in *The New-York Gazette and General Advertiser* on August 24, 1798, Eustace wrote, over the signature of "An American Soldier,": ". . . by the candor and magnanimity of Governor [John] Jay, *in a recent instance* have I become enabled to serve my country with confidence—and to lay aside a previous determination to abandoning it forever. How far my fellow citizens may be benefitted by my publications of the Facts respecting Mr. [James] Monroe, or by my presence among their defenders, time alone can decide."

the legal talents and personal sympathy of Mr. Hamilton I consider that I have a collateral claim with my uncle, whose cause he has generously consented to advocate [7]—and under this alone shall I offer a tribute of grateful attachment. And here I am called on to relate an anecdote which cannot displease you, whilst it is a debt I owe to the candor and friendship of Mr. Brockholst Livingston.

I called on this gentleman, after your return from Philadelphia, to consult with him on the expediency of resorting to the Court of Errors in the case of my uncle. I told him that I felt less restraint in conferring with him than with Colonel Hamilton, because I had never been acquainted with him; and, under existing circumstances, might not be well received: besides, that I had a rooted aversion to appearing at the levee of any man, who had places or pensions at his disposal. His reply was exactly in these words. "It is a duty you owe to your uncle, to yourself, and above all to colonel Hamilton, to pay him a respectful and confidential visit. He is indisputably the most distinguished member of our Bar; he has generously protected general Campbells claim; he has, therefore, an undoubted right to every mark of gratitude from you—nor will he misinterpret the object of your visit. It is true, there is no man in this country who so strongly unites the power with the wish to patronize every citizen who has a just title to his friendship or humanity; yet, he must think, however disinterested his general motives, that some testimony of

7. Eustace's uncle was Colonel Donald Campbell, who had been deputy quartermaster general of the New York Department from 1775 to 1784.

H and Brockholst Livingston were Campbell's attorneys in the case of *Donald Campbell* adsm. *Joshua Sands, James Barron and Sarah Malcom.* H made the following entry in his Cash Book, 1795–1804, under the date of May 12, 1796: "Donald Campbell Dr. to . . . [Account of Costs and Fees] . . . for perusing papers & arguing cause in Chancery Adsm. Executors of Malcolm 25" (AD, Hamilton Papers, Library of Congress). On December 15, 1797, the New York Court of Chancery orderd that "the Register of this Court [Peter R. Livingston] deliver to James Hughes Esquire the Master to whom this Cause is referred the Original Bond mentioned in the Readings in this Cause to have been executed by the Defendant and one Malcolm Campbell to Cornelius Lynsen and by the said Cornelius Lynsen assigned to William Malcom the Complainants Testator bearing date the sixteenth day of November in the year of Our Lord One thousand seven hundred and sixty five and filed with the said Register as an Exhibit in this Cause. And further Ordered that upon payment by the Defendant of the principal Interest and Costs reported to be due to the Complainants the said Master deliver up the said Bond to the said Defendant to be cancelled" (MS, Minutes of the New York Court of Chancery, 1798–1801 [Hall of Records, New York City]).

this sort is due from those whom he has so essentially servd. Do me, therefore, the favor to wait on him and refer to me for a professional consultation on general Campbell's affairs."

This communication, Sir, needs no commentary and will serve to account for the *two* visits I made to you. To the governor alone have I *made* any other—and, except Mr. Livingston's, I have not had one, of consequence, *to repay!*

Thus, Sir, you are presented with a full detail of my private conduct since my return. As it is *wholly negative,* you must feel that [it] is exhibited not to secure your esteem, but to shew that I have done nothing which can prove ⟨an⟩ obstacle to the attainment; you will therefore accept the sincere assurance of my respectful and grateful attachment.   J. S. Eustace

New York 27. Oct 1798
80, Barclay Street

Will you have the goodness to tell me, how I can best dispose of the Papers relative to Mr. Monroe's imbassy? [8] and in what manner I can most properly attest their authenticity?

8. On August 9, 1798, over the signature "An American Soldier," Eustace wrote the following letter to Archibald McLean and John Lang, the editors of *The New-York Gazette and General Advertiser*: "I shall offer you, gentlemen, in the first moment of leisure, several Facts respecting the Embassy of Mr. Monroe—occasioned by the shameful silence on the outrage on our People and Government, in the Speech of Citizen Barras; and his more shameful defence of the French Directory, by his late publication. It will be shewn, that the unwarrantable censure he has aimed at Mr. Jay, belongs exclusively to himself *and to his negociators:* that the Author of this paper, when he saved him—perhaps from condign punishment in this country, did not suppose him the Agent of France, but of America; or he would then have suffered him to appear the Author of Gen. [Charles Cotesworth] Pinckney's rejection, and the Cause of the impending contest—for he will now be proved to have provoked it" (*The New-York Gazette and General Advertiser*, August 14, 1798). Eustace is referring to the speech made by Paul François Jean Nicolas Barras, the president of the Directory, to James Monroe on December 30, 1797. For this speech, which Barras delivered when Monroe presented his letters of recall, see Uriah Tracy to H, March 23–24, 1797, note 4. Monroe's book, entitled *A View of the Conduct of the Executive, in the Foreign Affairs of the United States, Connected with the Mission to the French Republic, During the Years 1794, 5, & 6* (Philadelphia: Printed by and for Benjamin Franklin Bache), was published on December 21, 1797. See the [Philadelphia] *Aurora. General Advertiser,* December 29, 1797. Eustace's articles, entitled the "Embassy of Mr. Monroe" and signed by "An American Soldier," appeared in *The New-York Gazette and General Advertiser* on August 22, 23, 24, 25, 27, 31, September 1, 4, 6, 7, 1798.

From John Adams

Quincy [Massachusetts] October 29. 1798

Sir

I have received the Letter you did me the Honor to write me on the 20th and am glad to have had the opportunity of consenting to the Appointment of Officers who will do so much Credit in their Stations to the service as I believe Captain Church [1] and Lieutenant Hamilton [2] will do in theirs.

I have recd from Hauteval [3] a Packet of Addresses, one of which is inclosed. I dont think them of consequence enough to Suppress them.

I have the Honor to be, Sir   your most obedient & humble servant

John Adams

General Alexander Hamilton

ALS, Hamilton Papers, Library of Congress; LC, Adams Family Papers, deposited in the Massachusetts Historical Society, Boston.

1. Philip Church.
2. Robert W. Hamilton.
3. Lucien Hauteval was the "Z" of the XYZ affair. See "The Stand No.V," April 16, 1798, note 28. For these addresses, see Hauteval to Adams, 9 Fructidor an 6 (August 26, 1798) (ALS, RG 59, Miscellaneous Letters, 1789–1825, National Archives), which was enclosed in Adams to Pickering, October 28, 1798 (ALS, RG 59, Miscellaneous Letters, 1789–1825, National Archives).

To John Adams

New York October 29. 1798

Sir

I shall with pleasure obey the command contained in your letter of the 17th instant and shall accordingly inform the Governor that I am ready to proceed in the execution of the measure.

With perfect respect & esteem   I have the honor to be   Sir   Yr obed servant   A Hamilton

The President of The U States

ALS, Adams Family Papers, deposited in the Massachusetts Historical Society, Boston; ADf, Hamilton Papers, Library of Congress.

From Alexander Hamilton [1]

Edinburgh 29 Oct 1798

My Dear Cousin.

I received a few days ago a letter from my brother Robert, overflowing with the warmest sensibility of the many important obligations for which he is indebted both to you & Mrs. Hamilton.[2] Since you take a pleasure in conferring happiness, it will no doubt afford you satisfaction to learn the joy which your friendly reception, & endeavors to effect my brother's appointment into the American navy have communicated to his family in this country. The result of your application for the first lieutenancy of one of the new frigates was still uncertain when he wrote; but without anticipating the event, I may truely assure you that the endeavor has impressed the most indelible gratitude on our minds; & that we view with sensations of no common kind the excellent portrait which ornaments our chimney-peice. By the way my father [3] has been informed by an American gentleman who visited Edinburgh lately, that it is a striking, tho' not a flattering likeness of the original. In addition to the pleasure I received from the fair prospect of a permanent provision for my Brother, I was not a little pleased that it removed him from the mercantile line, into one for which he is much better qualified. A perfect knowledge of seamanship & the routine of naval duty he has acquired both from long & various experience, but from the natural bent of his disposition, which early pointed to the sea. To amass a fortune by traffic requires talents of a different kind. Without affecting to undervalue these talents it may be granted that eminent success in the mercantile line frequently depends on artful schemes & devices, which certainly confer no claim to respect, however necessary to success, & with these poor Robert can boast but little acquaintance. In the navy, I consider him as in his element. Courage, attention & naval skill constitute the excellence of a seaofficer, & of these qualities (unless my partiality deceive me) he is eminently possessed. With these impressions, you must conceive of what importance his admission into the American Navy as first lieutenant appears to me. To a mind like yours the pleasure of doing good is (I am sensible) a sufficient impulse. Yet as my brother resides under your roof I am willing to hope that the unaffected simplicity, candor & urbanity of his manners will in time produce a still more cogent motive, in personal freindship. I hope you will forgive my talking in this manner of my own brother, yet I must add (even at the risque of having Mr. Shandy's oddities imputed to myself) that excepting in the want of professional pedantry, Sterne's character of Uncle Toby seems to me more applicable to my brother, than to any I have ever conversed with.

In reply to your account of my acquaintance Mr. Thomas Law,[4] I am almost tempted to exclaim in the words of a statesman to whom a manuscript plan of the famous projector Law [5] had been submitted for his consideration. Oh la! Oh la! I am seriously concerned, however, to learn the embarrassed state of his affairs, tho' what could induce a man of his fortune to embark in such extensive speculation is not easily imagined. Your letter affords us some hope, tho' but a distant one, of seeing some of our young cousins in this country. Wherever they are they will be followed by our kindest wishes for their prosperity.

I do not pretend to transmit you information on political subjects, yet they occupy at present so considerable a portion of the thoughts & conversation of the world, that they are not easily avoided. I anticipate the pleasure our late glorious victories will have communicated to the true freinds of the present american constitution. The destruction nearly total of the Toulon & Brest squadrons, the former destined for Egypt,[6] & the latter for Ireland [7] must have given the death wound to the french navy. The rebellion, too, which lately appeared so formidable in Ireland utterly extinguished,[8] & only reviving occasionally in predatory attacks on the lives & properties of individuals, will enable ministry to open the parliament with unusual eclat. The party of opposition has lately fallen into considerable discredit from their cond⟨uct⟩ at the trial of O Connor,[9] for whose principles they vouched in the ⟨most un⟩qualified manner. Yet notwithstanding these high att⟨estations⟩ O Connor proves to be a traitor actually conspiring to introduce ⟨the⟩ enemy into his native country, at the very time in which our patriots were so loud in his praises. If it be admitted that they were unacquainted with O Connor's insidious designs, the vehemence of their protestations must shew how open they are to deception, & argues little in favor of their understandings. Whether Buonaparte has reached his ultimate destination, or intends to prosecute his expedition to India must soon appear; as the change of monsoon, which happens in the month of September, will prevent his traversing the Indian ocean, unless he has previously effected his passage. There are no authentic accounts of his having left Cairo. I beg to offer my best compliments to Mrs. Hamilton, & that you will ever believe me, my dear Cousin

faithfully yours   A Hamilton

Edinburgh
29th. October 1798.

ALS, Hamilton Papers, Library of Congress.
    1. The writer of this letter was the son of William Hamilton of Scotland, a brother of H's father, James Hamilton.
    2. Through H's influence, Robert W. Hamilton had been commissioned in the United States Navy as a lieutenant on the *Constitution.* See H to Benjamin Stoddert, October 20, 1798; H to John Adams, October 20, 1798.
    3. William Hamilton.
    4. See Alexander Hamilton to H, August 4, 1797.
    5. This is a reference to John Law, a financier born in Scotland in 1671, whose attempt to straighten out French finances during the regency of the Duke of Orleans led to the speculative boom in the seventeen-twenties in France known as the Mississippi Bubble.
    6. On August 1, 1798, the French fleet which had accompanied Bonaparte's expedition to Egypt was decisively defeated by the English navy in the Battle of the Nile.
    7. "The French squadron, of one ship of the line, the Hoche, and eight frigates, with troops and ammunition on board, destined for Ireland, was, on the eleventh of October, taken or dispersed, by a British squadron, under sir John Borlase Warren. The whole French squadron, with the exception of two frigates, fell ultimately into the hands of the English" (*Annual Register, or a View of the History, Politics, and Literature, for the Year 1798. The Second Edition* [London, 1806], 165). For Warren's account of this engagement, see *The* [London] *Times*, October 22, 1798. See also *The Times*, November 3, 1798.
    8. See Rufus King to H, June 6, 1798, note 3.
    9. Arthur O'Connor was an Irish revolutionist who joined the United Irishmen in 1796 and was imprisoned in Dublin in 1797. In 1798 O'Connor went to England where he was arrested and brought to trial at Maidstone for high treason. Distinguished members of the British opposition appeared as character witnesses at his trial, and he was acquitted. He returned to Ireland, was again arrested, and remained in prison until 1802.

To John Jay

New York October 29th 1798

Sir

I received this day a letter from the President of the United States,[1] requesting me to concert with you the plan, & to superintend the execution of it, for giving effect to the Act of the Legislature of this state for the further Defence of this state and for other purposes. This I am accordingly ready to do, whenever you shall be pleased to require it.

With very great respect & esteem I have the honor to be Yr Excelys Most Obed ser A Hamilton

Governor Jay

ALS, Yale University Library; ADfS, Hamilton Papers, Library of Congress; copy, Dr. Frank Monaghan, Washington, D.C.

1. John Adams to H, October 17, 1798.

To George Washington

New York Oct 29. 1798

Dear Sir

Some ill health in my family, now at an end as I hope, interfered with an earlier acknowlegement of your favour of the 21st instant. The contents cannot but be gratifying to me.

It is my intention, if not prevented by further ill health in my family, to proceed on the first of November to Trenton.[1] My aid to the Secretary to the full extent of what he shall permit me to afford will not be withheld. But every day brings fresh room to apprehend that whatever may be the props the administration of the war department cannot prosper in the present *very well disposed* but *very unqualified* hands.

Most respectfully & affecty   I have the honor to remain Dr. Sir
Yr obliged & obet servant   A Hamilton

General Washington

PS   I had forgotten to say that General Pinckney has given proof
of a cordial satisfaction with the Military arrangement.[2]

ALS, George Washington Papers, Library of Congress; ADfS, Hamilton
Papers, Library of Congress.
    1. See H to James McHenry, second letter of October 19, 1798.
    2. See H to McHenry, first letter of October 19, 1798; Washington to H,
October 21, 1798.

To Rufus King

New York November 1. 1798

My Dear Sir
    This will be delivered to you by Mr. Bruce, son of the Widow
Bruce,[1] both of whom you will no doubt recollect and that they are
connections of our family. He goes to Europe to complete his
studies in Medecine. Doctors Bard & Hosack [2] with whom he has
pursued them here speak handsomely of his qualifications & progress.
He visits London in the first instance. Permit me to recommend him
to your kindness. I have every reason to believe he is discreet intelligent and deserving.
    I intend if I can to write you another letter by this opportunity—
but lest I should be disappointed, I take occasion to assure of a careful attention to the *private concern* mentioned in one of your latest
letters.[3] Every thing that I know tends to your security & tranquillity in this respect.
    Yrs. truly & affecy   A Hamilton

Rufus King Esq

ALS, New-York Historical Society, New York City.
    1. Archibald Bruce, son of William Bruce who was the head of the medical
department of the British army stationed in New York during the American
Revolution, was graduated from Columbia College in 1795. After five years
in Europe he returned to the United States in 1803. In 1807 he was appointed

professor of materia medica and minerology in the College of Physicians and Surgeons, New York City. Bruce's mother was Judith Bayard Van Rensselaer Bruce. Her first husband, Jeremias Van Rensselaer, was the brother of Catherine Van Rensselaer Schuyler, who was H's mother-in-law.

2. David Hosack had been a student of Samuel Bard and later became his partner. Hosack was professor of botany and materia medica at Columbia College. Bard, who had been professor of theory and practice and Dean of Faculty at Columbia College, retired in 1798.

Hosack and Bard were the Hamilton family's physicians. See H's Cash Book, 1795–1804, for entries under the dates of February 1, 1797, June 7, 1798, November 16, 1802, July 3, 1804 (AD, Hamilton Papers, Library of Congress).

3. See King to H, August 15, 1798.

From John Skey Eustace [1]

Saturday Morning [New York, November 3, 1798]

Mr Eustace presents his compliments to general Hamilton, and sends him the packet for Col. P, *which he permitted to be forwarded in this Way*.[2] The cover is left open, and the note on the first blank leaf of the book will serve as an advertisement; so that the general, in running over its contents, probably may be tempted (as he will certainly be enabled) to enforce some of the inferences, *hastily* drawn by the writer from the facts held forth—by a note or two on a separate paper, simply marked by a number indicative of the page it belongs to. This will be gratefully acknowledged; if therefore the general will peruse the *private* letter to Col. P. (sent some days ago) and join his *influence* to the writer's *entreaties* for the adoption of *the Queries* contained in the printed letter (already forwarded) [3] E. ventures to think much good may result to the Country. At any rate, if it is no more than threatened, as a future scourge of Gallicanism among us, even thus, in terrorem, no small advantage will accrue.

Mr. Eustace sincerely wishes general Hamilton a prompt apparition in the field *of inspection*—as this includes the great objects of personal and national concern and provides for that ample store of health which can alone produce this salutary effect, it is unnecessary to detail the compliments of usual salutation and validiction.

As *the wish* to serve as the extra aid-de-camp of general Hamilton was not officially conveyed, general Eustace *now makes it a request,* and would thank general Hamilton to accept his services, if they can be useful.

Major General Hamilton.

AL, Hamilton Papers, Library of Congress.
    1. For background to this letter, see Eustace to H, October 27, 1798.
    2. Timothy Pickering. A few days after Eustace wrote this letter, H left New York for Philadelphia to discuss plans for the Army with George Washington, James McHenry, and Charles Cotesworth Pinckney. See H to McHenry, November 9, 1798.
    The "packet" contained extracts from Eustace's articles in *The New-York Gazette and General Advertiser* on August 14, 22, 23, 24, 25, 27, 29, 31, September 1, 4, 6, 7, 11, 12, 1798, on the "Embassy of Mr. Monroe" and a "vindication" of Fulwar Skipwith, former United States consul general in France.
    3. On November 1, 1798, Eustace wrote to Pickering: "In compliance with the wish expressed in your favor of the 30th. October, I send you the printed Letter in a more connected and legible form than that of the news-paper. You will have the goodness, Sir, to return it when perused" (ALS, Massachusetts Historical Society, Boston).
    The letter from Eustace to Pickering, dated September 13, 1798, was printed in installments in *The New-York Gazette and General Advertiser* on October 10, 11, 12, 13, 20, 24, 25, 1798. In the second part of an article defending Skipwith, Eustace wrote: "I propose, within a very short time, to present to the Secretary of State (through the medium of your paper) a simple Plan for obtaining from every American who has visited or sojourned in France, *a detail of all the circumstances which tend to illustrate the Conduct of the French Regents, or Agents, and that of the Citizens of those States*—so far as the Peace, the Honor, and the Safety of the Union are, or have been concerned. This will open a vast field for the exercise of their talents, *in every possible line*. Each, it may be presumed, will afford to our government all the information he really possesses (*and this will enable us to ascertain the subjects and persons of which he is wholly ignorant*): we shall then exhibit to our indignant and insulted Nation, a series of woes, and wrongs, of which they have *even now* but a very faint Idea . . ." (*The New-York Gazette and General Advertiser*, September 12, 1798).

From Adam Hoops

New York, November 5, 1798. "Inclosed are two letters: one from Captain Frye [1] Stationed at Governors Island describing the Cloathing & accoutrements furnished to his men and the Other from Doctor Dwight . . .[2] stating certain particulars relative to the Troops on Bedloes Islands."

ALS, Hamilton Papers, Library of Congress.
    1. Frederick Frye of Massachusetts had been appointed a captain in the

Corps of Artillerists and Engineers on June 2, 1794 (*Executive Journal*, I, 159, 160). On November 3, 1798, Frye wrote to Hoops: "In conformity to your request respecting the uniform Clothing &c. of my Company—I beg leave to state to you the deficiencies that exist, both in respect to the bad quality of some part of the Clothing, and the improper construction of other parts. . . . Permit me, Sir, to add that a considerable part of the Garrison are, at present, incapable of doing duty for want of Clothing . . ." (ALS, Hamilton Papers, Library of Congress).

2. Nathaniel Dwight was a surgeon's mate in the Corps of Artillerists and Engineers (*Executive Journal*, I, 278, 279). On November 4, 1798, Dwight wrote to Hoops: ". . . Since my arrival here there has been, at a time, twenty men in the hospital, affected with a Dysentery which arises, in this instance, I apprehend, from the following general causes: Viz: a change in mode of living —from some carthartic quality in the *water* on this Island—& from a dificiency in *clothing*, suitable to the present, & approaching season" (ALS, Hamilton Papers, Library of Congress).

From John Jay

Albany 5 Novr. 1798

Dear Sir

On the 24 ult. I had the pleasure of writing to you on the Subject of fortifying the port of New York, and the measures preparatory to a Plan for it. Presuming that it has come to your Hands, it will only be necessary for me to inform you, that pursuant to an Intimation contained in it, I shall provide for the Expenses of perfecting the Survey, by immediately writing to Genl. Clarkson,[1] and enclosing to him an order on the Bank of New York for five hundred Dollars to be applied towards that object.

An unexpected and painful Complaint (the Piles) will render the Time of my being at New York uncertain. I had intended to have set out this week for Bedford and Rye, and to have gone on from the latter place to N York, but at present I must postpone it.

When the Survey is finished, and all such Information as you deem requisite shall be obtained, it would in my opinion be adviseable that you should consult with Genl. Clarkson Col. Burr and Col. Stevens, and such others as you may think proper, as to the Plan which ought to result.

Fortification being an art to which my attention has not been turned, I must rely less on my own Judgment than on that of those to whom the Subject is familiar—my absence therefore ought not to occasion Delay.

I am Dr. Sir with great Esteem and Regard   your most obt. Servt   John Jay

Majr. Genl. Hamilton

LS, Hamilton Papers, Library of Congress; LC, Governor's Letter Books, from the original in the New York State Library, Albany; copy, Dr. Frank Monaghan, Washington, D.C.

1. For background to this letter, see the introductory note to H to James McHenry, June 1, 1798.

On November 5, 1798, Jay wrote to Matthew Clarkson: "The Presidt. of the U.S. having authorized Genl. Hamilton to concert with me a Plan for fortifying the port of New York, an accurate Survey of such of its Shores and waters, as may have Relation to that object should be made. In a late Letter to General Hamilton I have intimated my opinion that this should be immediately done, and that the Expences incident to the Execution of his orders for it, should be paid. The General will superintend the whole Business, except the Settlement and payments of accounts. The Expences attending the proposed Survey should be immediately provided for; and therefore I take the Liberty of enclosing an order on the Bank of New York, to pay you five hundred Dollars for that purpose. I hope it will not be inconvenient to you to keep settle and pay all the accounts of the Expenditures that shall be made of the monies appropriated by the State for fortifying the port of New York, and on the Terms of which Business of that kind is usually transacted" (ALS, New York Society Library, New York City; LC, Governor's Letter Books, from the original in the New York State Library, Albany; copy, Dr. Frank Monaghan, Washington, D.C.).

From Rufus King

[London, November 5, 1798.[1] Letter not found.]

1. Letter listed in Rufus King's "Memorandum of Private Letters, &c., dates & persons, from 1796 to Augt 1802," owned by Mr. James G. King, New York City.

To John Jay [1]

New York November 8. 1798

My Dear Sir

The Attorney General [2] has shewn me, in confidence, a late letter of yours to him and has asked my good offices as far as may consist with my judgment. These I always readily yield to misfortune.

I have had a full and minute explanation with him of the money subject, and in my mind, there results a full conviction that there is no cause of reproach from that source, whatever may have been represented to you or whatever loose or unguarded expressions may have escaped through a levity not uncommon to the person. Indeed the sums received are so small and the known expenditures so large in proportion that the case does not seem in candour to admit of derogatory imputation—*without precise proof of misapplication.* Every construction should in such a case be admitted against an unfavourable conclusion, else every man must expect contamination from the very touch of public money. While real evidence of abuse should be strictly attended to, the light indulgence of suspicion cannot but have every bad effect. It is the common cause of innocence that it shall not prevail. I am persuaded from the tenor of your letter that the thing has come in a very direct and strong shape before you. But I am equally persuaded that there has been misconception or misrepresentation.

As to the general state Hoffman's affairs, he assures me & *Troupe* [3] confirms it, that there is a prospect of extrication. On this point I am a sceptic, though I presume something will have been accomplished to divert the storm. But I have fairly told Hoffman that if he cannot put things upon a footing to shield himself from affront and humiliation in time to come he ought to resign. He promises me to act on this principle.

Here also there is a medium to be observed. Tis not merely temporary embarrassment that will justify the removal of an Officer of this description. Something permanent and unequivocally irretrievable ought to appear as the basis of the procedure.

The removal of Mr. Hoffman at the present juncture would be ruinous to him. In his fall, the welfare of his children is concerned.

On the whole I think it is best not to precipitate any thing against him—But to give him a further chance. The occasion has given me an opportunity of speaking very freely to him on certain points.

Let me My Dear Sir caution you on the subject of the *Comptroller.* [4] He is *Hoffman's* enemy on personal grounds & it is easy to confide too much in his candor.

With true esteem & regard   Dr Sir   Yr. Obed serv   A Hamilton

Governor Jay

ALS, Columbia University Libraries.

1. For background to this letter, see Stephen Van Rensselaer to H, November 6, 1797, note 2.

2. Josiah Ogden Hoffman.

3. Robert Troup.

4. Samuel Jones of Oyster Bay, New York, was appointed the first comptroller of New York State on March 15, 1797. He served in that capacity until 1800. He had been a member of the Continental Congress, the New York Ratifying Convention, and the New York Assembly from 1786 to 1790. From 1791 to 1799 he was a member of the New York Senate from the Southern District.

From Ebenezer Stevens [1]

New york 8th November 1798

Dear General

Agreeable to your request, and to ease the minds of some of our Citizens with respect to the Solidity of our Batteries I have this day loaded the guns with a Service charge—that is One third the weight of the Shot, and fired them by angles, by word of Command (similar to Plattoon firing) and have the pleasure to inform you, that they have not started in the least degree. This piece of information, I wish you to mention to the secretary of war.

I think this the best method of making Water Batteries or Coastways batteries for two reasons—

First. The Works are much stronger by the Embrasures being made close

Secondly. That the men are perfectly covered, and secure, from an Enemy's Shot.

Shall I beg the favour of you to mention to the secretary of war in the course of conversation, respecting the Charge I am to make the united states for my Services, as agent, and in fact superintendant &c. I have spent all my time on those operations, and if I had only to buy, and deliver articles, a Common Commission would be sufficient—but I undertake all, Proving Cannon & Powder, making of Carriages & ammunition, mustering the Troops &c. I mention these Circumstances, because I am persuaded you are a judge of my Services, and shall be satisfied with what you and the secretary of war decide on the Subject. I want nothing but what is just—and you will oblige me by attending to this matter for me.

I have the honor to be   Dear General   Yours sincerely

Ebenr Stevens.

P.S.   Permit me to observe to you that there is at this time a great quantity of Gunpowder in this City, and some of it of an Excellent quality—as there is much used for the navy of the U.S. if they wanted, it would be a good opportunity to purchase reasonably; and I am also sure that our state will want to purchase some and you may possibly think right to recommend it at this juncture.

General Alexander Hamilton
Trenton

ALS, Hamilton Papers, Library of Congress; copy, New-York Historical Society, New York City.

1. For background to this letter, see the introductory note to H to James McHenry, June 1, 1798.

From Rufus King

London Nov. 9. 1798

Dear sir

The same uncertainty continues respecting the recommencement of the war. Both austria & Prussia are bolder than before the late naval success of this Country,[1] but the conduct of the Emperor [2] is rather calculated to shew that he may be purchased by further acquisitions in Italy. Naples will not decline a war; [3] her existence perhaps depends upon his provoking it. The Casus fœderis with austria is a defensive war; but the Emperor has said he should not be critical on that Head. The news of the Capitulation of Buonaparte and the Destruction of the transports at Alexandria is not confirmed, tho' they are events which must take place. The Expeditions agt. Ireland are annihilated—of the Nine ships that sailed from Brest seven including the Hoche are in the English Ports [4]—the two frigates that escaped from the Texel have both been taken,[5] and of three that sailed from Rochefort, & appeared off Ireland soon after the defeat of the Brest squadron, two are said to be taken.[6]

The Dutch frigates were probably bound to Demarara, tho the Soldiers were told they were to go to Ireland.

Parliament meets on the 20th. Mr. Pitt will have a good account to give of the extension of their Commerce and of the increase of the Revenue. The assessed taxes which have been shamefully evaded will be given up, and a tax upon the income of the nation substituted.[7] There will be great Difficulties in the Details, as well as strong prejudices to overcome, but I hear that the Body of Merchants in London are to support the Plan.[8] The late naval Success has excited a high degree of animation throughout the nation, and the Govt. will be generally and cordially supported in such measures as it shall adopt to prosecute the war. The funds have got up to 57. pr Ct. which is a great rise and in a short time. You will see that I have prevented the sending to you of about fifty Irish State Prisoners, who were at the head of the Rebellion in Ireland and closely connected with the Directory of Paris.[9] Probably our Patriots will think my conduct presumptuous.

In the present posture of our affairs I could have no hesitation! We have an account that the Constellation Cap Truxton has taken a french frigate on our Coast.[10]

This news is brought by Cap Cochran of the Thetis,[11] who will not be permitted to return to the amer. station.

Yrs very truly

PS. The Hamburgh mail just arrived, informs us that very great Resistance is made to the Requisition of 200.000 men in Belgium. 12.000 young men are embodied, and the spirit of Revolt extends itself every hour! The scene is too near the army of the Rhine.

AL, Hamilton Papers, Library of Congress; copy, New-York Historical Society, New York City.
    1. This is a reference to the Battle of the Nile, August 1, 1798.
    2. Francis II of Austria. On November 10, 1798, King wrote to Timothy Pickering: "The same uncertainty continues with respect to the recommencement of the war between Austria and France, and for nearly three weeks we are without any precise information from France" (LS, RG 59, Despatches from United States Ministers to Great Britain, 1791–1906, Vol. 7, January 9–December 22, 1798, National Archives).
    3. On October 15, 1798, The [London] Times reported: "A long article in

the *Redacteur,* relative to the hostile preparations of the Court of Naples, confirms the general opinion that a rupture between the French Republic and that Court will shortly take place." Four days later *The Times* stated: "Hostilities between the King of NAPLES and FRANCE appear every day more inevitable."

4. See Alexander Hamilton to H, October 29, 1798, note 7.

5. On November 6, 1798, *The* [London] *Times* printed a report from Hull dated November 3. This report reads: "The *Sirius* frigate, of 36 guns, Capt. [Richard] King, arrived in the Humber yesterday, with the *Fury,* Dutch frigate of 36 guns, in tow. Capt. King fell in with this frigate and another of 26 guns, off the Texel; the latter he took without exchanging a shot, and immediately sent her for Yarmouth Roads, and then went in pursuit of the *Fury.* After a long chace and running fight of 40 minutes, he obliged her to strike to the superior gallantry of British seamen. She had 500 men, including soldiers, on board, and a large quantity of stores, soldier's arms, baggage &c. It is reported that the *Sirius* had one man killed, and one wounded; the Dutch frigate had ten men killed and several wounded. The Officers and Men are all Frenchmen, and are intended to be landed here. . . ." Richard King's official dispatch describing the captures is printed in *The* [London] *Times,* November 7, 1798.

6. On October 20, 1798, *The* [London] *Times* reported: "The three French frigates which appeared on the 13th in *Donegal Bay,* left it, without any serious attempt to land. They are supposed to be wholly detached from the larger squadron [which had sailed from Brest], and to have sailed from *Rochefort.*" On October 23 the same paper stated: "Several private letters by the Dublin Mail . . . contain the very agreeable news, that the three frigates, which appeared off Donegal Bay on the 13th instant, had been driven into *Sligo Bay,* but whether by stress of weather, or by the squadron of Sir George Home, is not mentioned. But the . . . Government has received no official information on the subject."

7. For William Pitt's proposals to Parliament, see *The Annual Register, or a View of the History, Politics, and Literature, for the Year 1799* (London, 1813), 174–77.

8. On November 9, 1798, *The* [London] *Times* reported that "the Committee for superintending the Voluntary Contributions" resolved: "That the Committee was determined to give their most decided support to every measure of finance which could give stability to Government, and distribute the burthens equally among all classes of society; that it was, however, with concern the Committee had learnt that the ASSESSED TAXES had been in many instances most shamefully evaded, while in other cases they did not reach those who were best able to pay them;—they therefore begged leave to recommend to the MINISTER some other mode of taxation, which would oblige every man to contribute in proportion to his means."

9. On July 28, 1798, King wrote to Pickering: "In Ireland the Rebellion is at an end . . . ; many of the inferior chiefs will be permitted to go into Exile. I . . . hope the President will have Power to exclude from our Country all such foreigners whose residence among us would be dangerous . . ." (ALS, RG 59, Despatches from United States Ministers to Great Britain, 1791–1906, Vol. 7, January 9–December 22, 1798, National Archives). On September 13 King wrote to Pickering warning him of the possibility that the leaders of the Irish rebellion might end up as exiles in the United States (ALS, RG 59, Despatches from United States Ministers to Great Britain, 1791–1906, Vol. 7, January 9–December 22, 1798, National Archives). On September 13 and October 17 King wrote to William Henry Cavendish Bentinck, third duke of Portland, asking for some assurances that the rebel leaders would not be permitted

to settle in the United States (copies, RG 59, Despatches from United States Ministers to Great Britain, 1791–1906, Vol. 7, January 9–December 22, 1798, National Archives). On September 22 the Duke of Portland wrote to King: "I can assure you with the most perfect confidence that the King will never permit any of the persons in question to set his foot in the Territory of any state in amity with his Majesty, by whom there is any reason to suppose that such a visitor would be objected to" (copy, RG 59, Despatches from United States Ministers to Great Britain, 1791–1906, Vol. 7, January 9–December 22, 1798, National Archives). See also the Duke of Portland to Charles Cornwallis, Lord Lieutenant of Ireland, October 17, 1798 (copy, RG 59, Despatches from United States Ministers to Great Britain, 1791–1906, Vol. 7, January 9–December 22, 1798, National Archives).

10. On November 9, 1798, *The* [London] *Times* reported: "The American frigate *Constellation*, of 36 guns, has captured a French frigate of 44 guns, after a severe and well-fought action, off the Coast of America." This report was not correct.

11. Sir Alexander Forester Inglis Cochrane. See H to King, June 6, 1798.

On October 31, 1798, *The* [London] *Times* reported that ". . . the Thetis frigate, Capt. Cochrane, from Halifax" arrived on October 29 in Portsmouth.

To James McHenry

[*Trenton,*[1] *November 9, 1798.* In a letter to Hamilton on November 10, 1798, McHenry wrote: "I received your letter of yesterday this morning at 5 o'clock." *Letter not found.*]

1. H was on his way to Philadelphia to meet with George Washington, McHenry, and Charles Cotesworth Pinckney to discuss plans for the Army.

To Elizabeth Hamilton

Philadelphia November 10. 179[8] [1]

I wrote to you, My Eliza, from Trenton. Yesterday afternoon I arrived at this place. I have yielded to the pressing solicitations of Mr. Wolcott to take up my abode at his house, which you know is at the corner of Spruce and Fourth Streets. Mrs Wolcott is in better health than she was but is still very thin and feeble. Without much more care than the thing is worth, her stay in this terrestrial scene is not likely to be long. She desires her affectionate compliments to you.

I am quite well, but I know not what impertinent gloom hangs over my mind, which I fear will not be entirely dissipated until I rejoin my family. A letter from you telling me that you and my dear Children are well will be a consolation. I presume before this reaches you Mrs Church and Philip will have gone to Elisabeth Town. General Washington was at Chester last night.[2] He will be here about twelve to-day.

  Adieu My very precious Betsey   A. H.

Mrs Hamilton. No 26 Broadway. New York

Copy, Columbia University Libraries.
  1. The copy is incorrectly dated 1790.
  2. See John C. Fitzpatrick, ed., *The Diaries of George Washington, 1748–1799* (Boston, 1925), IV, 288.
  On November 10, 1798, the *Gazette of the United States, and Philadelphia Daily Advertiser* reported: "This day about eleven o'clock our beloved General [Washington] arrived in town. . . . Major General Alexander Hamilton and the Hon. James McHenry, Secretary of War, also arrived in town this day, and accompanied . . . Lieutenant General [Washington] to his lodgings in Eighth Street." On November 13 the same newspaper reported: "General Pinckney arrived in town this day, from Trenton."
  H remained in Philadelphia until December 15, 1798.

From John Jay

Albany 10 Novr. 1798

Dear Sir

I this moment recd. your's dated the 8 Instant. My letter to Mr. Hoffman [1] was not official. It was written to convey Information which however unpleasant was in my opinion useful to him to receive.

His pecuniary Embarrassments called for circumspection on his part, and I intimated to him the propriety of accounting for the Expenditure of the amount of a preceding warrant before he recd. a subsequent one. His Zeal in my favor rendered such punctuality adviseable also in Reference to me. The Sums he has recd. are not large; and had his circumstances been easy, the Delay to account would have made little Impression.

Carpenter [2] himself complained that his account was unsatisfied, & mentioned to me that Mr. Hoffman in *Excuse* for it, observed to him that there was no money in the Treasury; but that he would endeavour to *negociate* the warrant &c. I am not the only person to whom Carpenter mentioned the same thing.

As to the Principles on which you think a Removal should turn, I admit the Propriety of them. I really and most sincerely wish well to the Hoffman family—they have been my Father's Friends, and generally my Friends and I have no personal motives to actuate me in Relation to the Attorney General, but such as he would wish them to be—but in my official capacity these motives must not be primary ones.

The fact is, that his affairs are generally believed to be, not merely embarrassed, but utterly irretrievable. I wish this Belief may prove to be unfounded, and that it may soon appear to be so. Should he be again humiliated by a Cause, I shall certainly think it my duty to place the office in a situation where it will not be exposed to such Indignity.

Whatever may be the feelings of the *Gentleman* [3] you mention, Justice demands of me to say, that I have seen nothing to enduce me to ascribe any part of his Conduct to Hostility. I have had Conversations with him respecting Mr. H., and altho' I make it a Rule to think well of a man as long as I can, yet I think that an attempt to add pressure and poignancy to misfortune would not have escaped my observation. On the contrary no opinion or Sentiment has been expressed by him to me on the Subject in question, that indicated a want of Candor or Humanity. He undoubtedly is strict in doing what he conceives to be his official Duty; and that Disposition has probably in more than one Instance drawn his personal motives into question.

Your Letter is very much what such a Letter ought to be—free friendly and candid—and perfectly harmonizes with that Esteem and Regard with which I am

Dear Sir   Your most obt Ser   John Jay

P.S. I have recd. a letter from Mr. H. but have not time at present to consider and answer it.

ALS, Hamilton Papers, Library of Congress; ADf, Columbia University Libraries.

1. For background to this letter, see Stephen Van Rensselaer to H, November 6, 1797; H to Jay, November 8, 1798.

2. Matthew Carpenter was a member of the New York Assembly from Tioga County.

3. This is a reference to Samuel Jones. See H to Jay, November 8, 1798.

From James McHenry

War Department [November 10, 1798]

My dear Hamilton.

I received your letter of yesterday [1] this morning at 5 o'clock. mr wolcott will send instructions by the express to secure the powder provisionally for the public.[2] We do not absolutely want the article, and could go on for some time without it. I think it right however that it should not leave the country.

Yours affectionately

Alexr Hamilton

ADf, James McHenry Papers, Library of Congress.

1. Letter not found.

2. See Ebenezer Stevens to H, November 8, 1798.

From Samuel Ward [1]

New York, November 10, 1798. ". . . Will you permit me again to remind you of the conversation I had the honour to have with you in June last relative to importing a quantity of Powder—in consequence of which the owners of the ship Harvard orderd & have imported about 26 Tuns from Sweden in said Ship. Mess Mintum & Champlin [2] who were equally concerned with me in this adventure have offerd this togather with a further quantity to the secy at War. The total abt 50 tuns. If the U S should want the whole quantity it would be agreeable to me to receive in part of payment three bonds I have lately given at the customs house in Providence due 24 March—June—& september next—for nearly 19.000 dollars."

ALS, Hamilton Papers, Library of Congress.

1. Ward, the son of Samuel Ward, a colonial governor of Rhode Island, was a veteran of the American Revolution and in 1786 was elected a delegate to

the Annapolis Convention. Following the war, he moved from Rhode Island to New York, where he established the firm of Samuel Ward and Brother. His mercantile interests were world-wide, and in 1788 he was one of the first Americans to travel to the Far East.

2. William Minturn and John T. Champlin were New York City merchants.

To Elizabeth Hamilton

[Philadelphia,[1] November 11, 1798]

I have not yet received a line from you since my departure. It is a consolation which my heart needs & which I hope not to be long without. As yet it is uncertain when I shall be able to return though I dare not now hope that it will be less than a fortnight from this time. The delay will be to me irksome. I discover more and more that I am spoiled for a military man. My health and comfort both require that I should be at home—at that home where I am always sure to find a sweet asylum from care and pain in your bosom.

Adieu my excellent wife   AH

Philadelphia Sunday Nov 11

ALS, Hamilton Papers, Library of Congress.

1. H was in Philadelphia to discuss military affairs with George Washington, Charles Cotesworth Pinckney, and members of the Adams Administration.

From John Jay [1]

Albany Novr 12. 1798

Dr. Sir

I wrote by the last post an answer to yours respecting Mr. Hoffman. Inclosed is my answer to the one I recd. from him. Be so good as to *seal* and send it to him. I shall write to you in a few Days on other Subjects. Being still troubled with the *piles*, I am constrained to postpone my Journey to N York—if they should continue obstinate much longer, I shall not be with you this Season.

Yours sincerely   John Jay

Majr. General Hamilton

ALS, Hamilton Papers, Library of Congress.

1. For background to this letter, see Stephen Van Rensselaer to H, November 6, 1797, note 2. See also H to Jay, November 8, 1798; Jay to H, November 10, 1798.

From William Neilson [1]

New York, November 12, 1798. "From the conversation we had on the Subject of field Artillery I made several experiments on this metal while at Salisbury. . . .[2] I am now fully persuaded that guns can be made there . . . *even lighter* than brass. . . . I would request some discussion may be had before you leave the Seat of Government. . . ."

ALS, Hamilton Papers, Library of Congress.

1. Neilson was a New York City merchant and financier and a director of the New-York Insurance Company.

2. During the American Revolution, munitions were produced in Salisbury, Connecticut, from iron mines and forges located in the town.

From Stephen Van Rensselaer

[*Albany, November 12, 1798.* On January 27, 1799, Hamilton wrote to Van Rensselaer: "I ought to beg your pardon for not having before answered your letters of the 12th. of November and 11th instant." *Letter of November 12, 1798, not found.*]

From George Washington [1]

Philadelphia, Novr. 12th. 1798

Sir,

Herewith you will be furnished with the Copy of a letter from the Secretary of War to me, suggesting many very important matters for consideration, and to be reported on.

LS, in the handwriting of Tobias Lear, Hamilton Papers, Library of Congress; ADfS, George Washington Papers, Library of Congress.

1. Although this letter is addressed to H, the draft is endorsed in Tobias Lear's handwriting: "Major Generals Hamilton and Pinckney Nov. 12, 1798."

It is my desire, that you will bestow serious and close attention on them, and be prepared to offer your opinion on each head, when called upon.

I also propose, for your consideration and opinion, a number of queries which had been noted by me, previous to the receipt of the Secretary's letter (now enclosed). In stating these, I had endeavoured to avoid, and make them additional to, the objects which the Secretary of War, in a letter to me, dated the 16th ultimo, informed me would be subjects for my consideration.[2] I find, however, that several of them, in substance, are contained in his *last* letter. But as they were digested previous thereto, and written, I shall, to save copying, lay them before you as they are, without expunging those parts which now appear in the Secretary's Statement.

With very great esteem & regard, I am, Sir, Your most Obedt. Servt. Go: Washington

Major General Hamilton.

2. On October 16, 1798, McHenry wrote to Washington: "The President of the United States on the 30th of Sept. ulto inclosed to me commissions for the three Major Generals of the Army, signed and dated on the same day.

"When I considered the communications which may be expected from this department, at the time of presenting his commission to each of the generals, I found myself embarrassed respecting the course which he meant I should pursue on the occasion. It was my earnest wish to avoid the renewal of a subject, that had already been attended with too many unpleasant circumstances by returning the question upon him for more precise instructions. After therefore considerable deliberation, and as the most respectful course to him, I at last was induced to transmit the commissions to Generals Hamilton & Knox, and to inform them that I considered the order of nomination and approval by the Senate as determining their relative rank.

"I have also, my dear Sir, written to Generals Hamilton & Knox, calling them into service, and soliciting their presence, as soon as possible, and in all events by the 10th of November proximo. I suggested also to the President that it would be desireable I should be authorised to require your attendance, and that his own presence would be important and give facility to all measures relative to this meeting.

"My object in convening these officers is to derive from the knowledge they may have of the several characters, who have applied for military appointments, and others disposed to enter into the army, effectual and necessary aid in the selection and application of the most suitable to the different grades, and to prepare in conjunction with them, a list for the Presidents final approbation —relative—1st. To the measures necessary to be pursued to give efficacy and ensure success to the recruiting service. 2 To the distribution of the military force of the United States. 3d To the most certain, regular and œconomical mode of provisioning and recruiting and the troops in the field. 4 Use quantity and kind of artillery, military stores and other articles necessary to be

[ENCLOSURE]

James McHenry to George Washington [3]

War Department
10th Novr. 1798

Sir.

It appears by a letter from the President, dated Quincy Octr. 22. 1798,[4] that it will not be in his power to be in Philadelphia 'till near the time fixed upon for the meeting of Congress.[5] In order however to prevent any injury to the public service, as it respects officering the troops, directed to be raised by the late acts of Congress,[6] he has written to me as follows: "If you, and the generals, judge it necessary to appoint the officers of Battalions, before we can have an opportunity to nominate them to the Senate, you may fill up the Commissions with the blanks you have, or if you have not enough, send new ones by post."

I have thought it proper, in pursuance of this authority, to submit to you a list of all those persons, who have been recommended for commissions in the army, with their letters of pretensions, and also a list of all the officers of the revolutionary army,[7] and to re-

procured, in addition to what we already have in our magazines and arsenals, and the proper places for occasional or permanent deposits of the same." (ALS, George Washington Papers, Library of Congress.)

3. ALS, George Washington Papers, Library of Congress; ADfS, James McHenry Papers, Library of Congress; ALS (incomplete), letterpress copy, Massachusetts Historical Society, Boston; copy, in the handwriting of James McHenry, Connecticut Historical Society, Hartford; copy, in the handwriting of Tobias Lear, Hamilton Papers, Library of Congress.

4. ALS, Adams Family Papers, deposited in the Massachusetts Historical Society, Boston.

5. The third session of the Fifth Congress convened on December 3, 1798 (*Annals of Congress*, IX, 2418).

6. For "the late acts of Congress," see Washington to H, July 14, 1798, notes 1 and 2.

7. Although McHenry failed to enclose this list, a list of the officers of the Revolutionary Army may be found in the James McHenry Papers, Library of Congress, and a second list may be found in the George Washington Papers, Library of Congress.

McHenry did not enclose the other items mentioned in this letter. See Washington to McHenry, November 13, 1798, printed as an enclosure to H to Washington, November 13, 1798.

quest that you will, with the aid of Generals Hamilton and Pinckney, prepare from these, and any other sources of information, a list of the most deserving and suitable characters, in your estimation to fill the different grades to which the authority cited applies.

I have also, in conformity with my letter to you, dated the 16th of August ulto.[8] to request, that you would submit to Generals Hamilton and Pinckney (General Knox having declined this appointment) [9] the following questions; and that you would be pleased to take the same into your mature consideration, and report to me, the result of your deliberations.

1st. Will it be expedient and proper, to select the officers, and raise the men for the 12 Regiments of Infantry, and 6 companies of Cavalry, from the following districts, & in the folowing proportions or as nearly so, as circumstances will admit?

1. The officers and men for 4 regiments of Infantry, from within the States of New Hampshire, Massachusetts, Connecticut, Rhode Island and Vermont.

2. The officers and men, for 4 Regiments of Infantry, from within the States of New York, New Jersey, Pennsylvania, Delaware and Maryland.

3d. The officers and men, for 4 regiments of Infantry from within the States of Virginia, Kentucky, N. Carolina, Tennessee, South Carolina, and Georgia.

4th. The whole, or a principal part of the officers and men, of the 6 companies of cavalry, from within the district, where it is most likely they will have to serve.

2d. If these questions are determined in the affirmative, then, whether in making the selection of officers, the least exceptionable rule, for determining the numbers to be taken from each State, within the respective divisions aforesaid, will not be, by their relative number of Inhabitants, according to the Census, wherever the application of this Rule, will not introduce the least worthy to the exclusion of more meritorious Characters.

According to this rule, the following table will exhibit, pretty

8. McHenry is mistaken about the date of his letter to Washington. He is referring to McHenry to Washington, October 16, 1798 (ALS, George Washington Papers, Library of Congress).

9. See the introductory note to Washington to H, July 14, 1798.

nearly, the proportion of officers and men, to be drawn from the respective States, for the 12 regiments of Infantry.

INFANTRY.		LT. COLONELS.	MAJORS.	CAPTS.	LIEUTS.	ENSIGNS
New Hampshire	396	1	1	4	4	4
Massachusetts	1326	2	4	20	20	20
Rhode Island	192	"	"	3	3	3
Connecticut	663	1	2	10	10	10
Vermont	239	–	1	3	3	3
New York	719	1	2	10	10	10
New Jersey	380	1	1	6	6	6
Pennsylvania	917	1	2	13	13	13
Delaware	126	"	1	1	1	1
Maryland	676	1	2	10	10	10
Virginia	1400	2	4	20	20	20
N. Carolina	630	1	2	9	9	9
S. Carolina	420	1	1	6	6	6
Georgia	140	"	1	2	2	2
Kentucky	140	"	"	2	2	2
Tennessee	86	"	"	1	1	4

3d. Whether, in the present state of things, it is expedient and proper, to proceed *immediately* to the appointment of the officers, or to suspend their apointment, until the meeting of Congress.

4. Whether, in the present state of our foreign relations, it is expedient and proper, to proceed immediately after the appointment of the officers to recruit the whole of the 12 Regiments of Infantry and six companies of Cavalry. If inexpedient to recruit the whole, then, what part thereof will it be proper to recruit, and in which district or districts of the Union?

5. Whether, if determined that a part only ought to be forthwith recruited, it will be expedient notwithstanding to appoint the whole of the Officers, and whether it ought to be signified to them, that they are not to be intitled to pay &c. previous to being called into active service?

6. Will it be expedient and proper, to withdraw any of the troops stationed upon the Northwestern and Southern frontiers, viz. on the Lakes, between the Lakes and the Rivers Ohio & Mississippi and on the Tennessee and Georgia Frontier bound⟨ing⟩ on the Indians and the river St Mary's, with a view to reinforce the troops of the seaboard frontier.

7. The stations of the before mentioned troops, and their num-

bers, will be seen by the annexed return,[10] and letters from Brigadier General Wilkinson.[11] If expedient that any of these should be withdrawn, will it be proper to reinforce them with the two companies directed, by a late act of Congress,[12] to be added to each of the old regiments of Infantry?

8th. What distribution, under the present aspect of affairs ought to be made of the troops and recruits, *now* on our sea-board frontier; the description, places of rendezvous,[13] stations and numbers of which is exhibited in the annexed return.[14]

9. What number of the *troops to be raised* ought to be stationed in the respective divisions aforesaid, and in what places.

10. Will it be best for the service and discipline, that the recruits should be supplied by contracts at the inlisting rendezvouses, as now practiced; or to allow to each recruit, a fixed sum per diem, in lieu of his ration, previous to his joining the general rendezvous, or encampment within his division.

11. Ought the Army, when in the field, to be supplied with rations, by means of purchasing and issuing commissions, or by contracts,[15] as at present?

12. What quantity and kinds of Cannon, Field Artillery, military stores, and other Articles necessary to an operating army, such as may be raised, will it be proper to procure, in addition to what is

10. "Return of Troops at the undermentioned places" (D, George Washington Papers, Library of Congress; copy, Hamilton Papers, Library of Congress).

11. On November 14, 1798, McHenry wrote to Washington and enclosed ". . . Letters from Brigadier General Wilkinson dated 6. and 9 of April, July 14, August 10, and September 6, 1798. . . . These you will . . . be pleased to return.

". . . Copy of a letter from the Secretary of War to Brigadier General Wilkinson dated the 2. August 1798." (LS, George Washington Papers, Library of Congress.)

On October 4, 1799, McHenry sent to H a copy of his letter of August 2, 1798, to Wilkinson (listed in the appendix to the appropriate volume of this edition of H's papers).

12. "An Act to augment the Army of the United States, and for other purposes" (1 *Stat.* 604–05 [July 16, 1798]).

13. "Names of places at which recruiting rendezvous have been established" (copy, George Washington Papers, Library of Congress).

14. See note 10.

15. "List of contracts for 1798" (copy, George Washington Papers, Library of Congress).

exhibited, as on hand, agreeably to the annexed return, by the Superintendant of Military Stores,[16] and that may be expected to be procured in consequence of the annexed letter from the Secretary of
the Treasury to   dated the   .[17]

13. Our greatest deposits of artillery and military stores, are at
Springfield, Massachusetts, and Philadelphia, Pennsylvania. We are
besides forming magazines near Harpers Ferry on the Potomac,
Virginia, at Fayetteville No. Carolina. Ought there to be any other
places established, for principal magazines than these four, and the
subordinate deposits mentioned in the aforesaid return.

As it will be proper, in the course of your deliberations, to ascertain from the Secretary of the Treasury, whether he can furnish
the monies necessary for the military service, I enclose an estimate
made out some time since, shewing the monies which I thought
would be required,[18] and the periods at which it might be wanted,
for the maintanence of the old and new army; and to provide certain military articles for which appropriations have been made by
late acts of Congress, and for cloathing for the provisional army.

It may also be proper, that you should confer with the Secretary

16. "Return of Ordnance, and the most important Articles of Military
Stores belonging to the United States at the several Posts; as herein stated,"
November 15, 1798 (DS, signed by Samuel Hodgdon, George Washington
Papers, Library of Congress). This document was enclosed in McHenry to
Washington, first letter of November 16, 1798 (LS, George Washington
Papers, Library of Congress).

17. Spaces left blank in MS. In the copies of McHenry's letter to Washington printed above which are in the Massachusetts Historical and the Connecticut Historical societies the first blank space is filled in with Rufus King's name.
On July 3, 1798, Oliver Wolcott, Jr., wrote to King in London and stated
that "forty five thousand Six hundred and eighty six pounds Sterling" had been
sent to London to be used under King's direction to buy "Muskets with
Bayonets . . . iron cannon for the Naval Service [and] . . . iron cannon for
the land Service" (copy, George Washington Papers, Library of Congress).
McHenry endorsed this letter: "recd from the Treasury the 20th Sept. 1798."

18. On November 14, 1798, McHenry wrote to Wolcott: "The estimate of
the monies wanted for the military service, alluded to in the last paragraph but
one, of my letter of the 10th to General Washington, is a copy of that transmitted to you, in my letter of the 3d. September last with the exception of
some blanks, being since filled in" (LS, Connecticut Historical Society, Hartford). In his letter to Wolcott of September 3, 1798, McHenry submitted
". . . a detailed view of the expenditure that will be required in the department
of War, at certain periods within this, and the first six Months of the ensuing
Year, and the objects to which it applies" (copy, George Washington Papers,
Library of Congress).

of State, on the subject of our foreign relations, as well as the Secretary of the Treasury on the extent and reliance which may be placed on our resources and finances, to assist you to mature your opinion upon some of the points submitted. I need not add, that the Secretary of State and Secretary of the Treasury, will chearfully give you every information which you may think it necessary to request.

With the greatest Respect I have the honour to be, Sir, your most obedt. & hble St   James McHenry

His Excellency
George Washington Lieutenant General
and Commander in chief of the armies
of the United States

[ENCLOSURE]

Queries propounded by the Commander in Chief
To Majors Genl. Hamilton & Pinckney [19]

[Philadelphia, November 10, 1798]

1st. Is an Invasion of the United States, by France, to be apprehended whilst that Power continues at War with Great Britain?
2d. In case such an Invasion should take place, what part of the United States, in their opinion, is most likely to be first attacked?
3d. Is it probable that the French will, in the way of exchange or by other means, become possessed of the Floridas & Louisiana?
4th. In case of such an event, what, probably, will be the consequences, as they relate to the United States? What measures will be best to counteract them? and can those measures be carried into effect *promptly*, by the Commander in chief of the Armies? or, must they be previously submitted to the War Office? ☞ This question, it will be perceived, presupposes a force in existence.
5th. What can be done to supply our *present* deficiency of Engineers? From whence, and by what means are they to be obtained? Should a *Frenchman* be employed *at any rate?*
6th. Would not Riflemen, in place of Light Infantry, be eligable as

19. ADS, Hamilton Papers, Library of Congress; ADfS, George Washington Papers, Library of Congress.

a component part of each Regiment? and in that case, would Fergusons Rifles [20] claim a preference?

7th. Under the idea that each grand division of the U: States is to furnish four Regiments of the augmented forces; and each State, according to the Census, the population, or medium between the two is to raise its proportion;—how many places in each (its extent being considered) and where, ought to be assigned as rendezvouses during the Recruiting Service? At what place ought the *general* rendezvous in each State to be fixed, during the said period? And at what place, or places in the U: States, ought the augmented force to assemble? If at more than one place, how many, where, and the number at each?

8th. Of how many pieces of Ordnance, of what sorts, and of what Calliber, ought the Park of artillery to consist, independently of what is attached to Brigades, or Regiments? And how many ought each of these to have?

9th Would it be advisable (after an adequate force is recruited) to withdraw the Troops wh. at present occupy the Posts on our Northern and Western Frontiers, & replace them with new raised corps?

10th. Of how many Ranks do the French form their line of Battle *generally?* [21] Do they make much use of Pikes? And would it be an eligible weapon, with which to arm part of our Soldiery, as that is the Nation with which we expect to contend? Genl Pinckney may, from personal observation, be enabled to solve these two questions.

Queries relative to smaller matters, but mer[i]ting consideration, as an army is now commencing more systematically than formerly; the rules, regulations, and distinctions in which, may give a tone to measures which may prevail hereafter.

1st. If the clothing of the Regiments and the fashion of that clothing; with distinctions between one Regiment and another are not already ordered by the proper authority, and in train of execution, what had they best be?

20. This is a reference to a breech-loading rifle which had been invented in 1776 by Patrick Ferguson, a British army officer. In 1780 Major Ferguson, in command of approximately one thousand soldiers from the army of Lord Cornwallis, was killed at the Battle of King's Mountain in North Carolina.

21. This is a reference to *Règlement concernant l'exercice et les manœuvres de l'infanterie. Du ler aout 1791* (Paris, 1791).

2d Would not cotton or (still more so) Flannel be advisable for shirting, and linings for the Soldiery?

3d What had best be the distinctions in dress, in the badges and other peculiarities, between the Commander in Chief and his suit, and the Majors General & their Aids? Between the latter, & the Brigadiers & theirs? and betwn these again & the Regimental Officers? Also among the Regimental officers themselves, Commissioned & non-commisioned? and whether the Staff (not in the line of the Army) of the different Departments, both Commisioned & Warrant Officers, ought not to be designated by their dress, or some appropriate mark, or badge? and in every case, & at all times, in the camp or Field be compelled to wear them, as well for the purpose of denoting the Corps to which they belong, as a means by which irregularities, rioting, and improper conduct may be discovered with more ease.

4th. As there has been many objections to, and remarks made upon, the black Cockade, (being that of Great Britain) might not something be devised by way of annexation thereto, to distinguish it from that of any other Nation? I have seen, and it appeared to have had no bad effect, a small Eagle (of Pewter, tin, & in some instances silver) fixed by way of Button in the center of a rose cockade; which was not only very distinguishable, but somewhat characteristic.

The sooner these queries are taken into consideration and opinions given on them more agreeable will it be to   Go: Washington

Philadelphia
10th. November 1798.

To George Washington

[Philadelphia, November 13, 1798]

General Hamilton presents his respects to the Commander in Chief & sends the sketch of a letter in conformity to what passed this morning.

Nov 13

[ENCLOSURE]

George Washington to James McHenry [1]

[Philadelphia, November 13, 1798]

Sir

I observe by the concluding paragraph of your letter of the 10th.[2] instant that you contemplate conferences between the Secretaries of State and of the Treasury and myself, for the purpose of obtaining auxiliary information from their departments. Several of the questions which you state seem indeed to require such information. But on reflection, it has occurred to me as most regular, that you should settle with those officers what it may be reciprocally deemed necessary and proper for them to communicate; to the end that they may themselves bring forward, either through you or directly to me as may be agreed, but without any previous application from me, such communications as the case shall be supposed to require. Whereever, too, I am to report a formal opinion, you will I daresay think with me, that the data [3] upon which it shall be given ought substantially to be deposited with me in writing. Personal conferences besides, for more full explanation, may be useful and will be very agreeable to me. Allow me to request your speedy attention to this matter.[4]

I find also, that the documents referred to in your letter of the 10. inst. did not accompany it.[5] As these will be necessary in forming an opinion on several points submitted to me in your letter aforesaid, and which I have communicated to Majr. Genls. Hamilton and Pinckney, I must beg you to furnish me with them without delay.

The documents referred to are as follows— viz—

"List of persons who have been recommended for Commissions in the Army, with their letters of pretensions."

(N.B. A list of Applicants south of the River Potomac,[6] and their letters, are in my hands. The list & letters from the other parts will be wanting)

"Returns and Letters from Brigad. Genl. Wilkinson shewing

the stations and number of the Troops on the N. Western and Southern frontier."

"Return shewing the description, places of rendezvous, stations and number of Troops, *now* on our Seaboard frontier."

Return from the Superintendent of Military Stores, shewing the quantity & kinds of Cannon, Field artillery, Military Stores, and other Articles now on hand belonging to the U.S.

(N.B. This Return shd. also exhibit the places at which these are deposited, and the quantity at each place.)

To these must be added the estimate which you had made out of the monies which you conceived wd. be required for military services, and the times at which the same might be wanted.

I have in my hands a list of the Genl. & Field Officers who served in the Revolutionary War,[7] and of the Captains and sub-alterns from the States so. of the Potomac. You will therefore be pleased to add to the documents a list of the Captains & Subalterns, from the other States, that the whole may be before me. I am Sir with very great regard & esteem

yr mo. obt Svt

Jas. McHenry Esqr.
Secretary of War

AL, George Washington Papers, Library of Congress; copy, Hamilton Papers, Library of Congress.

1. Df, in the handwriting of H and Tobias Lear, George Washington Papers, Library of Congress.

2. McHenry to Washington, November 10, 1798, printed as an enclosure to Washington to H, November 13, 1798.

3. On November 14, 1798, McHenry wrote to Oliver Wolcott, Jr., and Timothy Pickering in compliance with Washington's request (LS, Connecticut Historical Society, Hartford; LS, Massachusetts Historical Society, Boston; copy, James McHenry Papers, Library of Congress). On November 16, 1798, Wolcott sent to McHenry "a view of the public finances" "stating the perma-nent Revenue & permanent Expenditures of the United States and shewing the balance remaining for Military and Naval Operations" (copy, George Wash-ington Papers, Library of Congress; copy, Hamilton Papers, Library of Con-gress; copy, Connecticut Historical Society, Hartford). McHenry sent Wol-cott's report to Washington on November 19, 1798 (LS, Hamilton Papers, Library of Congress).

Wolcott also prepared a report entitled "Estimated Receipts & Expenditures of the United States for the Quarter ending 31st December 1798" (copy, George Washington Papers, Library of Congress). H endorsed this copy: "No-vember 25 received from the Secy of the Treasury as a guide for the last quarter of 1798. A H."

In his second letter to Washington on November 16, 1798 (LS, George

Washington Papers, Library of Congress), McHenry enclosed a document entitled "Army of the United States on the present establishment . . . shewing the component parts, number of Men and pay of the Officers composing the present Army Establishment" (copy, George Washington Papers, Library of Congress).

4. The remainder of this letter is in Lear's handwriting.

5. On November 14, 1798, McHenry wrote to Washington: "I had the honor to receive your Excellencys letter of the 13th instant last night.

"Some of the documents which were referred to in my letter of the 10th, I find cannot be completed by my Clerks, in any reasonable time. I shall therefore be obliged to submit the original books and records of the Office containing them, in their place, and request the same may be carefully returned.

"You will be furnished in consequence, as soon as the same shall be wanted with, 1. The book containing a list of all the candidates and abridgement of their recommendations. 2. The original letters of recommendation." (LS, George Washington Papers, Library of Congress.)

6. "List of applications for Commissi[o]ns in the Army from Virginia No Carolina So Carolina Georgia Kintucky & Tennessee" (D, George Washington Papers, Library of Congress).

7. See Washington to H, November 12, 1798, note 7.

From Ebenezer Stevens [1]

New York 15 November 1798.

Dear General,

The Batteries on this Island [2] being completed it is necessary a guard should be appointed to take charge of the Artillery to prevent their being spiked. I have been with the Military Committee [3] this day to view them and they think the Government of the United States ought to take care of them. But it will not do for the Troops to furnish guards, they will desert, and I am sorry to add that three have already deserted from the magazine on this Island. Captain Frye [4] picked out the best of his company and is fearful they will all go off. He wishes me to hire some of our Citizens to relieve his men, and I think it would be best to get three trusty men for that purpose.

I cannot forbear mentioning that the troops on the Island are in a manner naked and in no respect properly provided with Clothing to defend them from the Cold.[5] They ought to have watch-coats, particularly the Guards as it is very bleak there.

Every thing in my department goes on rapidly.

I have the honor to be dr General   Your obdt svt

Ebenezer Stevens

Copy, New-York Historical Society, New York City.

1. For background to this letter, see the introductory note to H to James McHenry, June 1, 1798.

2. Governors Island.

3. The Military Committee of New York consisted of Aaron Burr, H, and Stevens. See "Call for a Meeting," June 4, 1798, note 2.

4. Frederick Frye.

5. See Adam Hoops to H, November 5, 1798.

From Ebenezer Stevens [1]

New york 17th. November 1798

Sir

The fifty thousand Dollars loaned by the Corporation, for the Batteries, Cannon, Carriages, and Military Stores, are expended: and Mr Furman [2] the Treasurer wishes me to write you on the subject. I suppose that Ten thousand Dollars more, would pay what remains due, and that it would be best for Mr. F to pay the whole, and not be blending the accounts—but this, Sir, you can best judge of, as you observed to me, you would help this business through; and the persons to whom money is due, really want it.

General Clarkson [3] has received from his Excellency the Governor, a Draught on the New York Bank of Five hundred Dollars, to pay for surveying this Harbour; [4] which business was committed to Messrs Burr & Coles [5] by the military Committee, [6] and it is done. General C—— informed me that if you orderd Ten thousand Dollars to be paid, he would furnish Mr. Furman with it, and I would thank you to attend to this necessary business.

The secretary of war has commissioned me to furnish Overalls for the Troops on the Islands, and Four hundred pairs for West point. They want Blankets, and in fact, every species of Cloathing; and if they can be had here at Contract prices, it would save at any rate the expence of transportation from Philadelphia to this.

I wish you health and am with great respect   Sir   Your most obedt Servt.   Eben Stevens

Major General Hamilton

ALS, Hamilton Papers, Library of Congress; copy, New-York Historical Society, New York City.

1. For background to this letter, see the introductory note to H to James McHenry, June 1, 1798.

2. Gabriel Furman.
3. Matthew Clarkson.
4. See John Jay to H, November 5, 1798.
5. Aaron Burr and John B. Coles.
6. See Jay to H, October 24, 1798, notes 3 and 4.

To Elizabeth Hamilton

Philadelphia
Nov [19] 1798

I am always very happy My Dear Eliza when I can steal a few moments to sit down and write to you. You are my good genius; of that kind which the ancient Philosophers called a *familiar;* and you know very well that I am glad to be in every way as familiar as possible with you. I have formed a sweet project, of which I will make you my confident when I come to New York, and in which I rely that you will cooperate with me chearfully.

"You may guess and guess and guess again
Your guessing will be still in vain."
But you will not be the less pleased when you come to understand and realize the scheme.[1]

Adieu best of wives & best of mothers. Heaven ever bless you & me in you   A H

Mrs. Hamilton

ALS, Lloyd W. Smith Collection, Morristown National Historical Park, Morristown, New Jersey.
1. This may be a reference to H's plans for a house in northern Manhattan which he subsequently built and named "The Grange." In any event, a history of "The Grange" states: "This was Hamilton's first mention of his plans for the acquisition of land on which he was to build a country house" (Eric Sloane and Edward Anthony, *Mr. Daniels and the Grange* [New York, 1968], 41).

To John Jay [1]

Philada: Novr. 19th 1798

Sir.
Your letter of the 5 of November has recently reached me at this place and found me amongst avocations that scarcely leave me a

moment to spare. You will probably have learnt from General Clarkson that the survey of the Port has been completed.[2]

But I do not recollect that I have had any answer to a suggestion in one of my letters respecting the employment of Engineers to assist in forming the desired plan.[3] This appears to me an essential preliminary. It is very possible the contrary may have been said to you by persons of whose intelligence you may have a good opinion. Self-sufficiency and a contempt of the science & experience of others are too prevailing traits of Character in this Country. But as far as I am to be concerned auxiliary lights are a *sine qua non*. I do not feel myself adequate to the complicated task of an Engineer unaided by men of more technical knowledge than myself.

With the greatest respect & esteem   I have the honor to be   Sir Yr. obedt Servant   A Hamilton

Governor Jay

Copy, in the handwriting of Philip Church, Hamilton Papers, Library of Congress; copy (incomplete), Dr. Frank Monaghan, Washington, D.C.
   1. This letter was enclosed in H to Ebenezer Stevens, November 19, 1798. For background to this letter, see the introductory note to H to James Mc-Henry, June 1, 1798.
   2. See Stevens to H, November 17, 1798.
   3. Letter not found. On November 26, 1798, Jay wrote to H: "No letter from you containing such a suggestion has reached me."

To Ebenezer Stevens [1]

Philadelphia
Nov. 19. 1798

Sir

Since my arrival here I have received three letters from you [2] to the contents of which I have attended though my engagements have not before admitted a reply.

If I recollect rightly the law of the State,[3] it authorises, and in my opinion expediency requires, that the sum requisite to complete the batteries undertaken by order of the Military Committee, in addition to the 50000 Dollars provided by the Corporation,[4] be paid out of the fund appropriated by the Legislature. It seems to me that our city will stand in need of all its resources for purposes relative to the health of its inhabitants [5] and that it is not adviseable further to engage them for an object of defence which it has an absolute right to look for from other quarters. But with this opinion, I do not know that I have as yet any power to direct the application of the fund and for this reason only forbear to do it. You may shew this letter to General Clarkson to possess him of the sanction of my Opinion if his discretion shall happen to be otherwise adequate. [6]

I have not time to add more than the assurance of the esteem & regard with which I am Dr Sir

Yr obed servant   A Hamilton

P S. I put the inclosed letter for Governor Jay [7] under cover to you that you may forward it or not according to the advice which may have been received of the Governor's being on his way or about to set out for N York.

Col E Stevens

ALS, New-York Historical Society, New York City; copy, in the handwriting of Philip Church, Hamilton Papers, Library of Congress.

1. For background to this letter, see the introductory note to H to James McHenry, June 1, 1798.
2. These letters are dated November 8, 15, 17, 1798.
3. "An Act for the further defence of this State and for other purposes" (*New York Laws*, 22nd Sess., Ch. V [August 27, 1798]). For the contents of this act, see H to McHenry, June 1, 1798, note 16.
4. See Stevens to H, November 17, 1798, note 2.
5. The city was recovering from the yellow fever epidemic of the late summer and fall of 1798.
6. See Stevens to H, November 17, 1798.
7. H to Jay, November 19, 1798.

From John Skey Eustace [1]

[New York, November 20, 1798]

Dear General,

It had totally escaped my recollection that, in reading the "Embassy of Mr. Monroe", you would want to see the Dramitis Personæ

ALS, Hamilton Papers, Library of Congress.

1. For background to this letter, see Eustace to H, October 27, November 3, 1798.

unmasked. I shall annex them to the unepistolary leaf of this sheet, and now ⟨ven⟩ture to express a hope, that you will not be offended with *any part of the enclosed reply to a Philadelphia Jacobin.* The *scouted* paragraph was in these words: "By way of Postscript, let all the *plundered churches* be noted at bottom." [2]

2. Eustace is referring to the following item printed in *The Philadelphia Gazette and Universal Daily Advertiser* on November 13, 1798: "A correspondent will be glad to know, through the medium of this paper, the names of the 'Towns AND CITIES' *which were conquered by General Eustace,* to the principal squares of which he gave the name of Washington.

"By way of Postscript, let all the *plundered churches* be noted at the bottom."

In this response, dated November 17, Eustace wrote: "He will forward to Major-General Hamilton, by to-morrow's mail, a printed copy of a letter addressed by him to [Charles François] Dumouriez, his commander in chief. It is dated from Antwerp, the 14th March, 1793, *and was then published in that city.* If the most pointed attack on this General, for the robberies and disorders committed by his army, is an evidence of conscious probity; if the highest encomiums or 'the immortal WASHINGTON,' to heighten the crimes of Dumouriez; if to boast of all the civic virtues, declaring them *'common to all his countrymen,'* be a testimony of attachment to America or to her Savior-guardian; if to tell Dumouriez, in this same Letter, when surrounded by hords of lawless assassins; when the head of a French General Offices scarcely held by a single hair; if to declare, at so trying, so awful a moment, *'in all the cities where general Eustace has planted the Tree of Liberty, the street of Dumouriez leads to the square of WASHINGTON';* if the most *grateful* assurances of respect from his serene highness prince Frederick of Hesse Cassel, governor-general of Maestricht; and from Lieutenant-general the Baron of Reidesel, commanding in chief the Brunswick auxiliaries in that garrison of the Dutch frontier, be admitted as a proof of regard for the allies of the United States, when placed at the mercy of the French army he commanded; if more than an hundred Letters, Poems and Memorials, from Bishops, regular Abbots, Superiors of Convents and Seminaries, replete with tributes of gratitude and veneration, (long after the passage of his troops) be considered as a sufficient barrier against the poinard of a lurking traitor; if special authority to visit and reside in Nunneries of noble Ladies, and others of the most austere orders, by an *unsolicited* licence from their episcopal patron, be regarded as a patent of virtuous manners; if to guard, even in absence, the persons and property of the *English* carmelite Nuns of Liere, at the risk of life and honor (*after war had been proclaimed by France against their nation, and their effects declared a forfeit to their Foes*) and daringly to command, by a public proclamation, the execution of any commissary or other Agent who should attempt even the seizure or sequestration of their fortunes, can place an officer above reach of public censure, as a sacrelegious plunderer; if joined to the original, and to the *then published* documents of these facts, he shall (*and he will*) jointly remit to general Hamilton the most irrefragable proofs that, *when invested with more than dictorial powers,* he performed a conquering march through a vast extent of territory, through populous towns, and wealthy cities, without the exaction of one *livre* of tribute; and not only without incurring the slightest whisper of reproach or discontent on his personal conduct, or on that of the detached army he commanded; but, on the contrary, that the grateful benedictions of one million of captives have been bestowed on him

You will feel, my dear Sir, with me that no man in his senses would announce to a Minister of State the Conquest of towns and cities, which had not been subdued by him; nor the Dedication of their Squares, unless they had really been consecrated to *Washington*. I might therefore have pretended ignorance of any Squib in a Philadelphia paper, until it was republished in the gazette [3] which conveyed my ⟨sentiment⟩ to the Public; or I could very consistently have refered Mr. Brown's [4] readers to Colonel Pickering, to whose doubts and censures I was alone subject: but our Public is so singularly composed—so peculiarly prying and credulous in the traffic of scandal—so constitutionally potent to condeming as a mass, by the political charters of our country; and so constitutionally impotent to defend as individuals from their almost Gallic levity, that I could not withhold the refutation I have offered them. My situation and my views being alike questionable, with the very class of our citizens to which I am, and must long remain, perfectly

---

—(since he reti[r]ed from the service of France in August 1793) and that, in these evidences of attachment consists the sole recompense or profit he has ever derived from his services—*at home or abroad: if these truths obtain due credit, enough has been said—to satisfy the Public of America.*

"General Eustace will cheerfully submit to the perusal of any of his fellow-citizens, who read French, all the documents here alluded to: they were prepared as a Legacy for General Hamilton, should any accident have happened to the present proprietor in his projected voyage; and to this officer he the more confidently refers, because he had kindly consented to receive this pledge of confidence and of respect—it is only to a man of this exalted merit, that an officer who has attained to any distinction abroad, as a general, and a knight of a military order, could safely confide his fame: where envy and jealousy are excluded by valor, by genius and philanthrophy, there, only there, can the virtuous citizen sleep securely under his vine or his fig-tree?

"General Eustace having offered his services to Major General Hamilton, *as a volunteer aid-de-camp*, no additional reason need be assigned, for his non-appearance on regimental parade with his patriotic fellow citizens: and this patient and detailed narrative can leave no doubt with the public, of the very profound deference which he pays to their suffrage—a deference the more unequivocal, as they have not within their gift or power, one single thing, against which he would exchange one single moment of his domestic comforts." (*The New-York Gazette and General Advertiser*, November 17, 1798.) In the Hamilton Papers, Library of Congress, there is a newspaper clipping of this article, along with a copy of Eustace's printed letter to Dumouriez. On a blank page at the end of the printed letter H wrote: "General Eustace a very unwelcome correspondent."

3. An extract from the essay by "A Philadelphia Jacobin" was printed in *The New-York Gazette and General Advertiser*, November 17, 1798.

4. Andrew Brown, publisher of *The Philadelphia Gazette and Universal Daily Advertiser.*

unknown—I have felt more alive to inuendo than generally consists with the rank I bear, or with the conscious integrity I boast.

A stranger in my native City, the most purgatory (I might say hellish) of all positions; bereft of counsel or example to guide or guard me in my march through hostile bands of lurking Assassins— the avowed Author of a Project tending to unfold the conduct of all our travelled delinquents, so that our very widows consider it a duty, next after the panygric of their departed Lords, to restrain or ridicule my truth-searching endeavors: under these auspices, I am not to be judged with the herd of those who approach the Government, to fatten on its precious gifts; who intrude on the Public, to captivate their lucrative suffrages.

You, I well know, will judge me as you would *any other Person in the same situation;* and that you may (if you will Kindly take the trouble) empannel a *ministerial* Jury, *equally impartial,* I send you enclosed a Letter which speaks for itself. My Squiblists have not yet been taught, that in France, as in England and Holland, I regularly published my official and private correspondence [5] well knowing I sh⟨ould⟩ otherwise have been pestered with as many queries, as there were honorable facts in the Series ⟨of⟩ Events comprising my history when abroad.

May I request you, General, to do me the favor to hand the *printed Letter* to General Wash⟨ington⟩ as a small tribute of veneration for his character? If he still views me only as the Aid-de-⟨camp⟩ and friend of general Lee (though I had never officiated after their difference, and ceased even to rank, as a mem⟨ber of⟩ his Suite, prior to the rupture) let Washington at least be informed that this friend of Lee was ⟨then an⟩ Admirer of Washington; that this once *aid-de-camp* and *Heir*, resigned and abjured a proferred ⟨fortune⟩ rather than abandon, at Lee's desire, the sterile appointment of extra-aid-de-camp to governor ⟨–⟩ or the filial duties which he owed to the Father of his country, two acts, which were ⟨– –⟩ as the purchase-money of Lee's American possessions—*and thus were they finally disposed ⟨of.⟩* Of these truths, his *original*

---

5. John Skey Eustace, *Official and Private Correspondence of Major-General J. S. Eustace, Citizen of the State of New-York; Aide-de-Camp to General Lee and General Sullivan; Colonel and Adjutant-General in the Service of Georgia, During The American War: and Maréchal-De-Camp in the Armies of The Republic of France. Part I* (Paris: Printed by Adlard and Son, 1796).

(*though unknown*) *Letters,* in my possession, are the indisputable testimony That I since abandoned the military rank now held by our commander in Chief, with appointments equal to those of the second Magistrate of the union, on the vague insertion in a *French* paper of *his* Proclamation of Neutrality,[6] is no Evidence, perhaps, of a *personal attachment*—yet to obey, under such circumstances of age and ambition, has some merit, on the score of patriotism— and this must erect one barrier against censure or aversion from the then chief of this Empire—or I have yet *to analyze,* what I have so long revered *on trust.*

Pardon this long letter, and believe me very respectfully yours

Jo S Eustace

Barclay Street No. 80,
20th. November 1798.
Major-General Hamilton.

[E N C L O S U R E] [7]

☞ All these characters are not referred to in "the Embassy", but they will be made serviceable, by recurring to my journal, for the establishment of the facts alledged, if further proof be required.

A . . . . Samuel Fulton.[8]

6. For Eustace's resignation, see his letter to the National Convention, August 8, 1793 (*Réimpression de L'Ancien Moniteur. Seule Histoire Authentique et Inaltérée de la Révolution Française* . . . [Paris, 1847], August 20, 1793). For George Washington's proclamation of neutrality, April 22, 1793, see John Jay to H, April 11, 1793, note 1.

7. ADS, Hamilton Papers, Library of Congress.

8. Fulton was in the service of France as a major of cavalry under George Rogers Clark. With the support of Edmond Charles Genet, Clark planned to command an expedition against Louisiana. See "Proposed Presidential Message to Congress Concerning the Revocation of Edmond Charles Genet's Diplomatic Status," January 6–13, 1794. After the failure of this project, Clark sent Fulton to France as his agent to recover money which Clark had already advanced for this expedition. Fulton was unsuccessful in his efforts in the winter of 1794–1795 and again in late 1796. See Frederick Jackson Turner, "The Policy of France toward the Mississippi Valley in the Period of Washington and Adams," *American Historical Review,* X (1904–1905), 270–71; James Alton James, *The Life of George Rogers Clark* (Chicago, 1928), 429, 432, 436.

In the "Embassy of Mr. Monroe," Eustace wrote: "I first saw A, at Paris, on the 28th December, 1794, on my return from Holland: he then was the most intimate and *most confidential* of Mr. Monroe's associates—he was the

B. . . . Gen. Rogers Clark—Kentuckey [9]
C. . . . Comdre. A. W. Waldrhyn.[10]
D. . . . Senator Blount.[11]
E. . . . Representve. Fowler.[12]
F. . . . Jasper Moylan.[13]
G. . . . Gen. Proctor [14]

---

bearer of a claim for monies due by the French Government, to several American Citizens of the West. . . . From various reports, extremely to the prejudice of this man, after a fruitless attempt made, through me, to swindle my friend, Mr. [Jules Paul Benjamin] Delessert [a Paris banker] out of the important sum of thirty thousand Dollars, by selling his draft on V. endorsed by N, I was prepared to enforce his dismission by the Government; when, on the 9th June, K. related to me from J, the violent indignation of Mr. Monroe; and his desire 'that the Scoundrel should be sent off.' Not satisfied with this nuncupative and indirect censure of A, I. endeavoured to provoke a written reply to me, on a Note to the Minister respecting him—In this I failed; and therefore waited on him with K, the next day, when he repeated and redoubled the expression of his execrations. . . . A. embarked for America, within a few days after my interview on the 10th June 1796 [1795], with Mr. Monroe. On the 16th July 1797 ([1796], he came to my apartment, in Paris, informing me he had brought Dispatches from Mr. Adet for the Directory of France: paid me a second visit the next day, saying (to me in his own words) 'I have been to see Monroe: he received me AS IF NOTHING HAD HAPPENED.' . . . I now find, to my extreme astonishment, that HIS NAME is on the list of Subscribers to an Address offered to Mr. Monroe on the 8th of December, 1796 . . ." (The New-York Gazette and General Advertiser, August 27, 1798). For the address to Monroe, dated December 6, 1796, which Eustace also signed, see Monroe, A View of the Conduct of the Executive, 401–02.

9. From 1776 to 1783 Clark was a colonel and a brigadier general of the Virginia militia. During the American Revolution, forces under his command captured Cahokia and Vincennes.

10. In the "Embassy of Mr. Monroe," Eustace wrote the following about Waldrhyn: ". . . [He] is a decent Man, and a thorough Sailor, having been bred in the Coal Trade. He was, till lately, a resident and proprietary Citizen of Kentucky; but, at Philadelphia, entered into the Service and Pay of France. . . . C. has introductory Letters to Mr. Monroe; a commission to sell Lands, for G; and is to have a credit here, from F. . . . his Letters to Mr. Monroe are from D. and E. their joint Friends. C. suspects A's courage and probity . . ." (The New-York Gazette and General Advertiser, August 31, 1798). Waldrhyn also signed the address to Monroe of December 6, 1796 (Monroe, A View of the Conduct of the Executive, 401–02).

11. William Blount was governor of the Territory Southwest of the River Ohio from 1790 until his election to the United States Senate in 1796 from the new state of Tennessee. On July 8, 1797, the Senate expelled him for his participation in a plan to attack Spanish Florida and Louisiana in order to transfer control of these territories to Great Britain.

12. John Fowler of Kentucky was a member of the House of Representatives from 1797 to 1807.

13. Moylan was a Philadelphia attorney.

14. Colonel Thomas Proctor of Philadelphia.

(H & I.... hereafter) [15]

    J.... John M. Gelston—N. York, a sub-secretary
        to Mr. Monroe.

    K.... W. S. Dalham—Maryland.[16]

    L.... Thomas Gotier—Bergen, New Jersey.[17]

    M.... Captain Barney, of Maryland [18] } formerly—now sub-

    N.... Capt. John Cooper, of Virginia [19] } jects of France.

    O.... P. Whitesides—of Philadelphia.[26]

    P.... Thomas Paine.[21]

15. "H" and "I" are not identified, but in the "Embassy of Mr. Monroe," Eustace wrote: "On the 23d July [1796], the recommendatory Letter of Adet to the Minister of Marine, had been stolen from C, at the office of H; and as he suspected I and A of being the joint thieves, he was very ready to abandon the latter whom he despised, as soon as he found that he was not an Officer of the Republic of France, but a Spy of the Directory . . ." (*The New-York Gazette and General Advertiser*, September 1, 1798).

16. William S. Dallam was a lawyer and a major of the militia in Abingdon, Harford County, Maryland.

17. Thomas Gautier.

18. After a distinguished naval career during the American Revolution, Barney engaged in commerce, agriculture, and exploration. In 1794 he was named one of six captains to command the six new frigates authorized by Congress, but he declined the commission because he had been outranked by a man who previously had been his junior. He returned to the merchant service and commanded the ship that carried Monroe to France in 1794. From 1796 to 1802 he was a captain in the French navy.

19. For examples of Cooper's privateering activities, see Sherwin McRae and Raleigh Colston, *Calendar of Virginia State Papers and Other Manuscripts, from January 1, 1794 to May 16, 1795* (Richmond, 1888), 107, 108, 489.

20. Peter Whitesides, a Philadelphia merchant. In the "Embassy of Mr. Monroe," Eustace wrote: "Saturday, 23 July [1796] . . . It is strange he [Monroe] should talk of A. *to me;* and with Patience, having so lately declared him to be a Scoundrel! A, O, R and P, are his privy Counsellors!" (*The New-York Gazette and General Advertiser*, August 31, 1798).

21. Thomas Paine, who was born in England, arrived in the United States in 1774, and in 1776 he wrote *Common Sense*. He went to Europe in 1787 and became a defender of the French Revolution. After he received French citizenship, he was elected to the National Convention in 1792. He left the Convention after the fall of the Girondins in 1793 and was imprisoned as an Englishman under a law providing for the arrest of nationals of countries at war with France. In November, 1794, Monroe secured Paine's release by claiming him as an American citizen. In 1795 Paine returned to his seat in the Convention. He lived in Paris until 1802 when he returned to the United States.

In 1796 Paine criticized George Washington in his *Letter to George Washington, President of the United States of America. On Affairs Public and Private* (Philadelphia: Printed by Benjamin Franklin Bache, No. 112 Market Street, 1796). Eustace wrote concerning Paine's *Letter to George Washington:* "The letter was not published *at Paris*; it may therefore be urged that Mr. Paine may very well have written this, or any other Libel, without the

Q.... Gen. Elisha, or Elijah Clarke—Georgia.[22]

R.... Tate of So. Carolina, *his Agent*.[23]

S.... M. Tennason, citizen of the U. S., formerly
of Philadelphia.

T.... Lo⟨uis⟩ Marshall, Brother of the late Envoy—
of Kentuckey.[24]

U.... J. B. Prevost, Secretary to Mr. Monroe.[25]

V.... Allison, a Merchant or Speculator, of Philadelphia.[26]

W.... Stephen Thorn, of Vermont.[27]

X.... A Mr. Shaler, of New York—a friend of the Gelstons.[28]

---

knowledge of the Minister in whose house he lodged; but this objection will not obtain, since it was publicly declared by J, O, and R, and by other of his dependents, that they had severally copied this Letter, in order to preclude, as far as they were able, any chance of miscarriage on the passage" (*The New-York Gazette and General Advertiser*, September 1, 1798). Paine signed the address to Monroe dated December 6, 1796 (Monroe, *A View of the Conduct of the Executive*, 401–02).

22. Elijah Clark had been a brigadier general of the Georgia militia during the American Revolution. In 1793 he became involved in Genet's abortive schemes against Spain and entered the French service as a major general. The next year he and citizens of Georgia unsuccessfully tried to erect a new state on lands reserved for the Creek Indians. See Edmund Randolph to William Bradford, H, and Henry Knox, July 11, 1794; H to Washington, July 13, 1794; "Conference Concerning the Insurrection in Western Pennsylvania," August 2, 1794, note 16.

23. In 1793 William Tate was involved with Elijah Clark in Genet's proposed attack against Florida and became a colonel in the service of France (Deposition of John S. Dart, clerk of the House of Representatives of South Carolina, December 9, 1793 [*ASP, Foreign Relations*, I, 310]). After the failure of Genet's plan, Tate went to France and led an unsuccessful expedition against Wales. He subsequently became interested in a possible attack on the Bermudas.

24. Marshall was the brother of John Marshall. After spending a year in Philadelphia in 1793, he went to Edinburgh and Paris to study. During the French Revolution he was imprisoned, and his brothers, John and James, obtained his release. Marshall signed the December 6, 1796, address to Monroe (Monroe, *A View of the Conduct of the Executive*, 401–02).

25. John B. Prevost was the stepson of Aaron Burr.

26. David Allison, a lawyer from North Carolina, moved to Nashville in 1790 and was appointed clerk of the Superior Court for the Mero district in December of that year (Carter, *Territorial Papers*, IV, 442). In 1791 he became William Blount's agent in Philadelphia for speculation in Government securities, and he also negotiated with wholesale merchants to supply stores in the Southwest Territory with goods. From 1796 to 1798 he was involved in land speculation and sold tracts to Robert Morris and James Wilson. The failure of these purchasers led to Allison's bankruptcy and imprisonment in 1797 or 1798.

27. Thorn was a Vermont manufacturer.

28. Nathaniel Shaler was a New York City merchant. During the American Revolution, he was occasionally the business partner of Jeremiah Wadsworth

Y.... Temple Franklin.[29]

Z.... A Mr. Potter, formerly a M. P. in Great Britain.[30]

A.A..... La Chaise, a *French* Spy *here;* [31]

B B.... Dr. Bache, an *American* Pirate *in France.*[32]

---

and presumably also of John B. Church. Church, who was Elizabeth Hamilton's brother-in-law, used the pseudonym John Carter in his partnership with Wadsworth during the Revolution. See Church to H, September 25, 1784.

29. William Temple Franklin, the grandson of Benjamin Franklin and the son of the Tory ex-governor of New Jersey, was born and educated in England. He settled in the United States in 1776 and spent several years with his grandfather in Europe. In October, 1790, he sailed for England and the Continent to act as Robert Morris's representative for the sale of lands Morris owned in western New York, and he negotiated the sale of Morris's lands in the Genesse country to William Pulteney, William Hornby, and Patrick Colquhoun.

30. Christopher Potter was elected to Parliament from Colchester in 1781, but was unseated for corrupt practices. He lost his seat again in 1784 for failing to meet the property qualifications required of members of Parliament. In 1789 he moved to Paris, where he established potteries. In 1793 the French imprisoned him, but three years later he delivered messages to James Harris, Lord Malmsbury, at Paris from Paul François Jean Nicolas Barras.

31. Auguste Lachaise was Genet's agent in George Rogers Clark's proposed expedition against Florida.

32. William Bache, the grandson of Benjamin Franklin and the brother of Benjamin Franklin Bache, received an M.D. in 1794 from the University of Pennsylvania. He then traveled to France and engaged in privateering.

From Adam Hoops [1]

New York, November 20, 1798. ". . . the Barracks at West point are in such order that with a few repairs they will afford comfortable winter quarters for at least three hundred men—and that a report was made not long since to the Secretary of war on the subject of repairs specifying such as were wanted. The new Barrack on Governors Island is nearly finished. . . . There are at West point about two hundred men (perhaps not full two hundred) and at New York about the same number—at each place about one half the men are of the first Regiment and one half of the Second—pursuing the idea of having the companies of the same corps together. There must be a removal of about two hundred men, by which the companies of the 1st Regt will be assembled at New York and the companies of the 2d Regt at West point or vice versa & Some of the officers of the 1st Regiment have families which are now comfortably settled at West point where there are even accomodations for more families. This would not be the case here. . . ."

ALS, Hamilton Papers, Library of Congress.
    1. For background to this letter, see James McHenry to H, October 11, 1798; H to McHenry, October 19, 1798.

From John Murray

Halifax Nova Scotia Novr 23d 1798

Sir

The command of His Britanic Majesty's Troops in this country having devolved upon me by the departure of His Royal Highness Prince Edward for England,[1] who had before communicated his previous arrangements It was with peculiar satisfaction that I became the instrument of delivering to Captain Sever [2] of the Herald Sloop of war belonging to the United States of America 25 Cannon and 1876 Shot; and Captain Sever has actually sailed from hence with them this day for his destination and as it is to be presumed you are acquainted with the intention of carrying this measure into effect I thought it my duty to give you the earliest intelligence of its being fully executed to the end that you may do me the honor to report the same with my very best respects to His Excellency General Washington & please to inform the General that the terms of the original Bond of restitution entered into and signed by the Secretary at war on the part of the United States specified only 24 Cannon & 1800 Shot yet on the arrival of Captain Sever examining the Stores I found 25 Cannon & 1876 Shot of the same Calibre & have not hesitated to give the surplus of one Cannon & 76 Shot; conceiving by this that I only acted up to the spirit of the intention of His Royal Highness who was willing to shew the real good will of Great Britain to our Bretheren of America; and has afforded me the opportunity of assuring you that

I am Sir with great respect   Your Obedient Servant
                                                      Jno. Murray B. General
                                                      Commanding His Britanic
                                                      Majesty's Troops in Nova Scotia

Major General Hamilton

LS, Hamilton Papers, Library of Congress.

1. Prince Edward held the rank of major general. In 1798 he left Canada to return to England because of an injury he had received falling from his horse (A. Aspinall, ed., *The Later Correspondence of George III* [Cambridge, 1963], II, xxxviii).

2. On October 6, 1798, Benjamin Stoddert wrote to Captain James Sever: ". . . there is a parcel of Cannon & Shot at Halifax, which are to be transported from thence to Charleston, South Carolina, under Convoy. . . . you will proceed with these Vessels under your Command to Halifax, and take on board the Guns & Shot, and carry them to Charleston . . . where they are to be delivered to . . . [an] Agent for the War Department" (*Naval Documents, Quasi-War, February, 1797–October, 1798*, 500–01).

From Ebenezer Stevens [1]

New York 23rd. November 1798

Sir

I am honoured with yours of the 19th instant, inclosing a Letter for our Governor, which after I had spoken to General Clarkson, I forwarded by mail immediately. He thinks, I had best write his Excellency respecting money to pay the Bills off, which I will do, by the mail next monday. Inclosed is the Law passed the last sessions by our State respecting the fortifications,[2] by which you will be better able to judge how the money is to be expended. It is really necessary we should, as a military Committee, enable Mr. Furman, or some other person, to discharge the Balances that now lay over.[3]

The Barracks on Ellis's Island are finished, and I have placed Twelve of the 24 pounders belonging to the state there, properly mounted. The Barracks on Governors' Island are nearly completed, and I am sorry those garrisons Supply of wood was not earlier attended to, as we cannot always get the Islands supplied in the winter. Every article for the accommodation of the Troops ought to be supplyed before winter sets in.

I wish the secretary of war would tell me to do the needful; and I am ready agreeable to the Laws of our Government, for supplying of Troops, much time would be saved, and if I did wrong, I could be always ordered different. I mentioned the propriety of having Guard for our magazine, and Battery, to prevent ill disposed Villains from spiking up the Cannon in the latter.[4]

I have the Honor to be Sir with great respect Your most obedt. Servt. Eben. Stevens

One Company for Ellis's Island is as many as can be accommodated there. & One of the Company on Bedlows Island had better be orderd to Ellis's Island and take Charge of it.

Major General Hamilton

ALS, Hamilton Papers, Library of Congress; copy, New-York Historical Society, New York City.
1. For background to this letter, see the introductory note to H to James McHenry, June 1, 1798.
2. "An Act for the further defence of this State and for other purposes" (*New York Laws*, 22nd Sess., Ch. V [August 27, 1798]). For the contents of this act, see H to McHenry, June 1, 1798, note 16.
3. See Stevens to H, November 17, 1798, note 2.
4. See Stevens to H, November 15, 1798.

From William Cooper

[*Cooperstown, New York, November 26, 1798*]. Discusses his dispute with Benjamin Walker.[1]

ALS, Hamilton Papers, Library of Congress.
1. See H to Walker, William Inman, and Cooper, September 9, 1798.

From Thomas H. Cushing [1]

Philadelphia, November 26, 1798. "The enclosed observations [2] on Arms, accoutrements, & Clothing, are Respectfully submitted, in answer to the queries which you did me the honor to make, on these subjects."

ALS, Hamilton Papers, Library of Congress.
1. Cushing, a native of Massachusetts and a veteran of the American Revolution, had been acting adjutant and inspector of the Army from February, 1797, to May 1798. When he wrote the letter printed above, he held the rank of major in the First Regiment of Infantry (*Executive Journal*, I, 154, 156).
2. "Observations on the Public Arms, Ammunition, and Clothing, in possession of the Troops of the United-States, serving on the Western frontier," November 26, 1798 (AD, Hamilton Papers, Library of Congress).

From John Jay [1]

Albany 26 Nov. 1798

Dr Sir

I was this morning favd. with yours of the 19 Inst: in which you observe that "you do not recollect to have had any answer to a Suggestion in one of your Letters respecting the Employmt. of Engineers, to assist in forming the desired plan" for fortifying the port of N York. No letter from you containing such a suggestion has reached me. Those of the 8 Septr. and 29 Octr., being the only ones on the Subject of fortifying N York, which I have recd. from you, since the passing of the act,[2] do not contain any thing about Engineers.

The plan doubtless should be formed under all attainable advantages, and I not only agree but desire that you avail yourself of all the important aid within your Reach, and I will provide for the Expence. It is proper however to bear in mind the provision of the act, that the money appropriated by it to this object, be expended under the Direction of the President of the U.S. It is therefore proper that the plan in question should be formed as much as possible under the auspices of the national govt. and with the aid & approbation of the officers they most confide in. I presume the president will on your application readily direct any of the Engineers in the Service, to assist in it; and I shall on receiving the least hint from you, be ready to request that favor from him. If in the Course of the Business, you should think any measures on my part necessary or useful, I will thank you to mention them.

I have the honor to be with great Respect and Esteem   Dr Sir your most obt. servt   John Jay

Majr. Genl. Hamilton

ALS, Hamilton Papers, Library of Congress; LC, Governor's Letter Books, from the original in the New York State Library, Albany; copy, Dr. Frank Monaghan, Washington, D.C.

1. For background to this letter, see the introductory note to H to James McHenry, June 1, 1798.

2. Jay is referring to "An Act for the further defence of this State and for other purposes" (*New York Laws*, 22nd Sess., Ch. V [August 27, 1798]). For the contents of this act, see H to McHenry, June 1, 1798, note 16.

From Orchard Cook

[*Wiscasset, District of Maine*] *November 29, 1798.* "It is now nearly 5 Months since I left your City and since which I have written you many Letters [1]—but I receive no answer not a single Line since I left you. I Beseech of you Sir to Write me and let me know what I am to depend on when I am to have a trial send the Commission to take the Depositions immediately or the Deponents will be gone to Sea. . . ." [2]

ALS, Hamilton Papers, Library of Congress.
　1. Letters not found.
　2. In H's Law Register, 1795–1804, is the following entry: "Orchard Cook agt William Thomas: Capias in trover in McKinnon's name issued 30th June 1798 Settled" (D, partially in H's handwriting, New York Law Institute, New York City).
　Under the date of October, 1799, is the following entry in H's Cash Book, 1795–1804: "Costs & Fees Dr. to Daniel McKinnen received of Orchard Cook　20" (AD, Hamilton Papers, Library of Congress).
　McKinnen was a New York lawyer.

From Ebenezer Stevens [1]

New york 29th Novemr. 1798

Dear General

I hope you will excuse me for troubling you with my letters which I would not intrude on you, if I were not press'd by the occasion to do it. In my last,[2] I informed you, that the military Committee wanted money, to pay off the Bills contracted for our Batteries &c—and as the people employed are in want of their respective balances I wish you to make some arrangement either for mr Furman [3] or myself to discharge them, for we are called upon continually for a settlement. Mr. Mangin has never received One

Dollar for his services as Engineer for the general government,[4] and I wish much to know what is allowed by them to Engineers that I may pay him, as he is a deserving man and has a large family. I write the secretary of war on the subject this mail. Your early attention to the Contents hereof, will please me very much and be peculiarly serviceable to the Tradesmen, who want their money at this season—and particularly from the late Calamity our City experienced.[5] I am sensible you have business enough on hand to engage your attention, without these matters: but I know you wish to serve our Citizens, and it is on that account chiefly that I take the liberty to importune you on their behalf.

I have the Honor to be with sentiments of esteem   Dear General Sincerely yours   Eben Stevens

Major Genl. Hamilton

ALS, Hamilton Papers, Library of Congress; copy, New-York Historical Society, New York City.
  1. For background to this letter, see the introductory note to H to James McHenry, June 1, 1798.
  2. Stevens to H, November 23, 1798.
  3. Gabriel Furman.
  4. See Joseph F. Mangin to the Military Committee of New York City, June 18, 1798; Mangin to H, August 7, 1798.
  5. This is a reference to the yellow fever epidemic in New York City during the late summer and fall of 1798.

To James McHenry

Philadelphia November 30th 1798

Sir,

I now communicate the result of my conference with the Commander in Chief and General Pinckney, on the subject of extra allowances to Officers detached on service, so as to be obliged to incur expences, *on the Road and at places where there are no military Posts*

We are all of opinion, that in such cases an extra allowance ought to be made, and this even to Officers who receive extra compensations for peculiar duties, such as Inspectors, Quarter Masters, &c. These extra compensations are considered as relative to ideas of *greater Skill* or *greater trouble*, rather than to that of *greater expence*, in the Execution of the Offices to which they are annexed. Without extra allowances in the cases in question, it is easy to see that Officers may exhaust in extra expences their whole pay, and that great difficulty must be experienced in finding fit Characters to execute employments which may expose the persons to frequent journeys. It is useless to say, that the principle will not apply where the law shall have specifically provided for travelling expences.

But the greatest embarrassment is to settle the rule of extra allowances. Shall they be left at large, on the ground of reasonable expences according to circumstances, or shall fixed rates be attempted? The former is liable to great abuse; and the latter is not easy to be regulated so as to unite œconomy with justice. It is however our opinion that it ought to be attempted.

In adjusting a rate or rates, it is to be remembered that the Officer receives established allowances for his time service and expence. A full compensation is not therefore to be aimed at, in the extra allowance, but something proportioned to the probable excess of expence. This has governed the estimate which is now submitted—viz.

A dollar and a quarter per day for man and horse for each day that the Officer must sleep at a place not a military post, and when the Officer is of a rank to be intitled to a Servant, then the addition of three quarters of a Dollar per day for the Servant and his horse. This to apply to all but the seat of Government and the principal Town in each State. At such places the allowance to be a Dollar and a half for the Officer and his horse and a Dollar for the servant and his horse. It is understood that the established allowances to the Officer go on at the same time.

But while these rates are offered as the general rule, it is foreseen, that there may arise extraordinary cases where greater allowances may be indispensible. Such cases must be referred to the special discretion of the head of the War department to be assisted by a certificate from the commanding Officer, by whom the Officer claiming was detached on the special service, stating the reasons and circumstances.

The case of an Officer detached from one Military Post to another which he may reach the same night, but yet so far distant as to incur expences on the Road, was not provided for in the above arrangement. It is my opinion, that half a dollar a day will suffice for such cases, and this only where the distance is not less than forty miles. The Servant may in such a case without inconvenience take his provisions with him.

It may, perhaps, be expedient to regulate a days journey by a number of miles and for this the following proportions may not be improper, forty miles to a day when the whole distance does not exceed two hundred miles, thirty to a day for all above two hundred and not exceeding three hundred and fifty, twenty five to a day for all above three hundred and fifty and not exceeding six hundred, twenty to a day for all above six hundred.

It is my opinion too, on which point also I have not consulted any other, that these rates ought not to retrospect, but ought to be established for the future; and that in all past and intervening cases, applying only the general principle, reasonable expences, according to circumstances, ought to govern. The application of a new rule may produce hardship and injustice, when the service may have been performed in the expectation that practice on former occasions would prevail.

with great respect and Esteem   I have the honor to be   Sir   Your obedt. Servt.   Alexander Hamilton

The Secretary of the Department of War [1]

LS, in the handwriting of Philip Church, Mr. Alvin Witt, Minneapolis, Minnesota; Df, in the handwriting of H and Philip Church, Hamilton Papers, Library of Congress.
  1. These seven words are in H's handwriting.

Candidates for Army Appointments
from Connecticut [1]

[Philadelphia, November–December, 1798]

Connecticut

CAPTAINS

1 Austin Nichols Fairfield County *Writes ill*	*Wm. Edmond* [2] good constitution single man & in prime of life education equal to place active enterprising & on the whole qualified	

believe he will make a brave & enterprising Officer "have heretofore recommended in a *certain manner*" — Allen [3] & Smith [4] } Not very strong

Tracey [5]—broken speculation & besides Lty sufficient

7 Jesse Hopkins Waterbury New Haven	Letter very well Will: Edmond—well qualified for the office he solicits David Smith [6] Capt of Militia has discovered ambition & activity integrity can raise a Company	} Respectable *enough*

D, in the handwriting of H and Charles Cotesworth Pinckney, George Washington Papers, Library of Congress.

1. In this list of recommendations for Army appointments, those recommended have not been identified. Wherever possible, however, the individuals making the recommendations have been identified.

H, George Washington, and Pinckney prepared this list, which is undated, during their meetings in Philadelphia.

The words within brackets in this list are in Pinckney's handwriting.

2. Edmond, a veteran of the American Revolution and a lawyer in Newtown, Connecticut, was elected to the House of Representatives as a Federalist in 1797 to fill the vacancy caused by the death of James Davenport. He was a member of the House until 1801.

3. John Allen, a lawyer from Litchfield, Connecticut, was a Federalist member of the House of Representatives from 1797 to 1799.

4. Nathaniel Smith was a lawyer in Woodbury, Connecticut. From 1795 to 1799 he served in the House of Representatives as a Federalist.

5. Uriah Tracy.

6. Smith, a veteran of the American Revolution and a major general of the fourth division of the Connecticut militia, represented the town of Plymouth in the General Assembly of Connecticut in 1798.

Tracey S
Wadsworth [7] *well recom-
mended to him*
Talmage No. 4 [8]

8 Aaron Benjamin *Stratford* An Ajutant of 4th. Connecticut Regt. in last war afterwards a Captain only Lieutenant	Abr. Baldwin [9]—always appeared a good Officer Tracey *a Democrat*	}

11 David Tallman
9 *Litchfield*

Allen   Smith said quite as much
  as he deserved
Wm. Edmond not particularly
  acquainted but knows him to
  be of education abilities & enterprise

Not very
strong
Allen
Worthless

Writes not very
well
Lawyer

N Smith   enterprising spirit unfortunate in speculation believe he will make a brave &
  spirited Officer

12 David Koeler
Fairfield
26 years old
Letter very well

Col Bradley [10] can easily raise a
Company   bred a Merchant
of good character   worthy of
a higher grad if known
respect

respectable
enough

16 John Foot
Danbury
37 years
6 feet high
*his letter well
  enough*
non Com Officer
last war
now Capt of Militia

Recommended by sundry Militia officers as well qualified

not strong
Qr. Ensign

18 Jasper Meade
Ridge Field

Col Bradley speaks handsomely
of him

So So

7. Jeremiah Wadsworth of Hartford, Connecticut, was deputy commissary general and commissary general of purchases during the American Revolution. From 1789 to 1795 he served in the House of Representatives as a Federalist.

8. Benjamin Tallmadge.

9. Abraham Baldwin, who was a brigade chaplain during the American Revolution, practiced law in Fairfield, Connecticut, until 1784, when he moved to Augusta, Georgia. From 1789 to 1799 he was a Federalist member of the House of Representatives from Georgia.

10. Philip Bradley, a veteran of the American Revolution, was United States marshal for the District of Connecticut.

Fairfield
42
Sergeant last War
then
Lt & Qr Master

22 [Saml. P Williams   respectable connexions & talents
Weathersfield   Mr. Goodrich [11]
                         genteel manners, fair reputation
                         good connections—Judge
                         Elsworth [12]
                         very respectable]

24 [Daniel Tillotson   Saml. Lyman [13]—good constitu-
28 yrs of age   tion active, federal—handsome
Lawyer   E   accomplishments—well]
Lebanon]

26 [John Benjamin   Was in the revolutionary war
43 years old   Lieutt. in the Artillery—
good constitution   served with reputation—good
Stratford]   Character—Certificate favour-
        Qr.   able from Genl: Knox
                         very respectable]

27 [Joseph Mix Junr.   good Character; fond of mili-
33 years old   tary affairs—
New Haven   respectably recommended]

28 [Elihu Sandford]   *Talmage No. 6*
[Woodbridge   Handsome appearance, military
39 years old   Turn adjutant of the Militia
                         —served the whole of last War
                         —private 2 years—sergeant 5
                         years—Well as Lieutenant]
                         Wadsworth

30 [Solomon Allyn   —served part of the revolution-
Junr.   ary War as private, part as
good family   Ensign—very well recom-
                         mended by Judge Elsworth &
                         other respectable Characters]

31 [Wm: Marsh   [adjutant in Militia—personable
Hartford]   & active—has been addicted to

11. Chauncey Goodrich, a lawyer from Hartford, Connecticut, was a Federalist member of the House of Representatives from 1795 to 1801.

12. Oliver Ellsworth, a Connecticut Federalist, served in the United States
Senate from 1789 to 1796. From 1796 to 1799 he was Chief Justice of the
United States.

13. Samuel Lyman of Massachusetts was a member of the House of Representatives from 1795 to 1800.

Wadsworth
Ensign
Adjutant of Militia
& active *there*
Talmage Tracey
Ensign No. 8

scenes of dissipation hurtful in civil life—his own fortune lost by speculation. His father's fortune good—connections respectable] little vigour of body & *mind*

32 [Joseph Barrett
Hartford
26 years old

Lieutt in the governor's guard. indubitable spirit—respectable military talents—well educated—had been led into excesses, but reformed—perhaps Lieutenant]

35 [Benhoni Clark

Capt: in the Militia—attached to government]

37 [Simon Clark
Hartford
30 yrs age

served in the Militia, as Captn: of Light Infantry—His Company well disciplined—fair Character—decent property —respectable]

38 [John Hart
Windsor

Healthy & well affected—prudent & sober recommended by many]

41 [Captn: Joseph
Day]
[Hartford]

W Mosely [14] very deserving.
[served as *sergeant in the* revolutionary war—commands governor's guard]

43 James Morris
Litchfield
Capt in late war
44 years

Allen taken prisoner at G. Town reputation of brave officer—public education property fair character desires a majority

} Qr Military *talents*

44 Elisha Frost
Plymouth

Allen

private in late war, now Captain of Militia —*light Infantry* Comp *can raise men*

Tracy S
Wadsworth
Talmage

} hardy brave man No 2

45 John Boolford
Southbury

Allen
Wadsworth
Talmage

same as above
} sober brave & manly respected
No. 3

14. William Moseley of Hartford was a member of the Connecticut General Assembly in 1798.

49 Gershom Burr   *Judge Hobart* [15]   well educated
   Fairfield   & well connected
   25–30 years   Capt of
                                                  Militia
                        respectable family

55 Stephen Ranney   *Tracy*   ⎫ strongly
   Litchfield   Wadsworth   ⎬
   Amherst   Talmage   ⎭ No. 1

43 Noah A Phelps   *Tracey strongly*
   Simsbury   Wadsworth—Major of Brigade
                            farmer of good health *good
                            figure* & *good character* fit
                            for service above common run
                            of Militia Officers

56 Jonathan Root   *Wadsworth* ⎫
                        Tracey   ⎬ No. 8
                        Talmage   ⎭

57 Samuel Blake*lee*   *Wadsworth* Tracy Talmage
                        No. 7

58 Ambrose Hitch-   Talmage   No 5
      cock   Wadsworth ⎫ Respectably rec-
   Suffield   Tracey   ⎭ ommended to
   34 years old   him as a Lieu-
                                     tenant
                                     sergeant in late
                                     war & ever
                                     since
                                     respectable now
                                     as Ensign of
                                     Militia

59 John Meigs   Wadsworth Tracy & Talmage
                        No. 9

60 ⎫   *Wadsworth* ⎫
   ⎬ Reuben Champion   Tracy   ⎬ No. 10
76 ⎭   Talmage   ⎭

81 Russel Bissel   desires to be transferred to
   now Captain in   twelve
      2 Reg   See his letter 81

15. John S. Hobart, who was born in Fairfield, Connecticut, was the United
States judge for the District of New York.

Connecticut

Majority

2 Garwood H Cunningham *Woodbury* writes pretty well *36 years old* *Major in Militia*	Naniel Smith abilities & patri- otish qualified David Judson—as well qualified as any one he knows Allen & Edmond—has had a *lib- eral* education—and military *turn* brave—has never served—no doubts of his tal- ents or disposi *Tracy* S *Talmage* first of their acquaintance among those *inexperienced* Wadsworth thinks him fit upon *inquiry* but no personal *knowl*	probably good Captain Qr M

LT COL COM

4 Justus Barnum
Danbury
served as a *private*
said to be Officer
last war *Qr*
Major of Militia
45 years old
Now Member of
Assembly
	General Judson [16]—much a
	  military man vigilant &
	  active
	Cooke [17] was a sergeant
	  Major active & ambitious
	  —was afterwards an Adju-
	  tant & then a Captain &
	  then a Major of Militia
	Mygatt [18]—Adjutant & an
	  active Officer
	will accept Majority
	Edmond—engages confidence &
	  good will of his neighbours
	  is reputed to have military
	  talents.
	Tracy broken speculator may
	  do for Captain but must not
	  be Col.
		Inadequate
		pretensions
		for a
		Majority

5 Samuel Hunting- ton *Norwich*	Zep: Smith [19]—Gentleman of liberal education activity & *merit*	

16. Judson, a veteran of the American Revolution, was a justice of the peace in Litchfield County, Connecticut.

17. Josiah P. Cooke, a veteran of the American Revolution, was judge of the Probate Court of the District of Danbury.

18. Eli Mygatt was a justice of the peace in Fairfield County, Connecticut.

19. Zephaniah Smith represented Glastonbury in the Connecticut General Assembly.

now a Col of   Wadsworth   honest & well dis-
  Militia   posed but *negative*
                        Tracey   incompetent

MAJORS

13 John Ripley   J. Trumball [20] ⎫ a young
   Coventry   Wadsworth   ⎰ Gentleman
   Letter—well now   of good
     Major of Militia   connec-
   30 years old   tions—
   32   character   ⎫
                                           address   ⎬ Respectable
                        Wadsworth—no personal   ⎪
                          knowlege has no doubt he   ⎪
                          will do honor to his   ⎭
                          Country
                        General Chapman [21] educated as
                          Merchant friend to G Gov-
                          ermt.—well qualified
   Talmage   General Huntington [22] his
   secondary   recommendation founded on
                          that of General Chapman
                          whom he speaks well of
                        Tracey   ⎫ *well looking man*
                        Wadsworth ⎰

17 Jabez Huntington   *J Trumball*—liberal education
   Norwich   & good genius
   son of General   now Lt Col of Militia   Respectable
     Huntington   Thinks it fortunate that there quite enough
   30 years   is a choice of such character   said
                        Wadsworth says he is fit for
                          any thing
                        Tracey   valuable Young man
                        Captaincey *high enough*

20. Jonathan Trumbull.

21. In 1797 Elijah Chapman, Jr., became brigadier general of the first brigade of the Connecticut militia.

22. Ebenezer Huntington, a veteran of the American Revolution, was appointed a brigadier general of the Provisional Army on July 19, 1798 (*Executive Journal*, I, 292–93).

21 Burr Gilbert   hopes to have grade similar to
   Fairfield   that he holds
   now Col of Militia Sundries ⎤   fair
                       none   ⎬   character
                          respectab ⎦ served
                                       as a
                                       sergeant
                                       in last
                                       war—
                                       had the
                                       badge of
                                       Merit

Thaddeus Burr [23]

42 Augustine Taylor Allen   College education—
   Sharon   Smith   suffered by all the
   41 years old   changes in military arrange-
   Lt in late war   ment—Gentleman Scholar &
     several years   brave   has a good *Regt of*   } very strong
   will not serve   *Militia*   ardent fœderalist
     under a *Junior*   *fought bravely   good prop-*
     Officer   erty
                     Talmadge & Wads
                     Wadsworth   well recom-
                        mended to him & *he thinks*
                        fit

43 James Morris   See Captain 43 for character
   Litchfield

LT COLONEL

74 Timothy Taylor   Tracy   ⎤ strongly ⎤
   Danbury   *Talmadge* ⎦   ⎬ strong
   capt in late war Wadsworth

75 Eliza Wadsworth   *Tracy*   blacksmith by
   Litchfield   strongly   Trade now a
   Captain last *War*   man of prop-
                                 erty
                                 Major of
                                 Dragoons
                     Wadsworth   served through
                     Talmage   the War in
                                 Sheldons [24]
                                 Corps
                                 man of sense not
                                 literary vigour

23. Thaddeus Burr was a merchant in Fairfield, Connecticut.
24. During the American Revolution, Elisha Sheldon was a colonel of the
Second Continental Dragoons.

Reuben Hum- phrey [25]	*Wadsworth* now Major of Militia & will be glad of a Regt. in provisional army Farmer of good health good figure & good character fit for service above common run of Militia Officers	
82 Joseph Wilcox 2d *Killingworth* served through the Revolutionary War esteemed a brave & active Officer *Lieutenant*	General E Huntington—one in his opinion well qualified— thinks good connexions otherwise well W Col ⎫ Wyllis [26] ⎪ in their ⎬ opinion ⎪ well ⎪ qualified ⎭ Swift [27] Grovenor [28] Jo. Ingersoll [29]	

SUBALTERNS

9 Robert Hosmer	H L Hosmer [30] possesses talents & integrity a friend to the Govermt good family	probably good

LT. OF ENGINEERS

14 Dyer Manning Norwich Drum Major in Revolution War	General Huntington—abilities & ambition competent to the Office	
19 Waters Clark Darby 27 years old	Dagget [31] ⎫ would accept Lieu- Bears [32] ⎬ tenancy *Hull* [33] ⎭ of good character	Respectable

25. Humphrey was the keeper of Newgate State Prison in Simsbury and a justice of the peace in Hartford County, Connecticut.

26. Samuel Wyllys, a veteran of the American Revolution, was the secretary of the state of Connecticut.

27. Herman Swift was brevetted a brigadier general at the close of the American Revolution. In 1796 he was a Federalist member of the Electoral College from Connecticut.

28. Thomas Grosvenor, who had been a lieutenant colonel during the American Revolution, was an assistant in the General Assembly of Connecticut.

29. Jonathan Ingersoll was a justice of the Superior Court of Connecticut.

30. Hezekiah L. Hosmer, a lawyer from Hudson, New York, was a member of the House of Representatives from 1797 to 1799.

31. David Daggett served in the lower house of the Connecticut General Assembly from 1791 to 1797 and in the upper house from 1797 to 1804.

32. Nathan Beers, a paymaster during the American Revolution, was a resident of New Haven, Connecticut.

33. Samuel Hull, a resident of Derby, Connecticut, served in the General Assembly of Connecticut in 1793 and 1794.

Merchant
have no doubt he
will make a good
officer

20 William Young
Jun
Eastern
no Capt of Militia

writes well—asks Captaincy
Zephaneah Swift [34]—*ambition*
& Merit

Jewett

23 [Joseph Dewett]
Greenby]
a doctor

[Soon inlist Company—Age,
sprightliness & military spirit]
Tracey violent Democrat

29 [Thomas King]
[Windsor]
[28 years old]

[Healthy & sprightly—serves as
non Commissioned officer in
the Army *so so*]

33 [John Knox]
[Hartford]

Talmage No. 8
[In the governors guard—will
make a good officer—perhaps
Ensign]
Tracey Wadsworth Sadler [35]
well made young man & he
thinks fit for soldier will
take Lieutenancy

36 [Wm J Bellamy]
[Derby]
about 26 years

[young gentleman of character
& family—recommended by
W: Allen]
Allen
Smith

[LIEUTENANTS]

39 [Albin Hurlbert
Windsor]
37 years old

served six years last war—was
at Stoney Point—Mud fort &c
—recommended by many]
Ledyard [36]

40 [Leonard Seymour—Enquire of Mr: Wolcott [37]]

46 Asa Morgan
Litchfield

Allen   stout fine Officer like
gentlemanly brave men
Smith   of about *26* years—
Tracey S   can inlist men well

47 Reuben Heard
Washington

Wadsworth
Tracy   } No. 6
Talmage

34. Zephaniah Swift, a lawyer from Windham, Connecticut, was a Federalist member of the House of Representatives from 1793 to 1797.

35. John Sadley was a resident of Milford, Connecticut.

36. Charles Ledyard was a resident of Hartford County, Connecticut.

37. Oliver Wolcott, Jr.

ENSIGNS

51 Trueman Mosely   Allen
    Southbury   Smith   ⎫ No. 7
                      Talmage   ⎭
                      21 & 22 years—promising
                      young Gentleman
52 Trueman Hinman   *Wadsworth   preference to*
    Southboro   *Mosely*
                      Wadsworth   Tracy Talmage
                      5 Ensign

L T

64 Ebenezer Bebee   *Tracey*   ⎫ *strongly—corps*
    Litchfield   *Wadsworth*   ⎬ *of Artillery*
    24 years old   *Talmage*   ⎭ No. 3   father [38]
                                       good man &
                                       good officer

63 Lemuel Harrison   *Tracey*   ⎫ *strongly*
    Waterbury   *Wadsworth*   ⎬ No. 4
                      Talmage   ⎭

65 Bennet Bronson   *Tracy*   ⎫
    Waterbury   *Wadsworth*   ⎬ *strongly 5*
                      Talmage   ⎭

61 Phineas Cadwell   *Wadsworth Tracey Talmage*
                      No. 2

62 Samuel Waugh   Wadsworth Tracey Talmage
                      No. *1*

66 Thomas Day   *Wadsworth Tracey* Talmage
                      No. 9

67 John Bissel   Wadsworth Tracey Talmage   ⎫
                      No. 1   │
68 Salmon Clark   Wadsworth Tracey Talm: │
                      No 2   │
69 Peter N Brins-   Wadsworth Tracey *Talm* 3   │
    made   │
70 Benjamin H Judd   Wads. Tracey *Talm* 6   ⎬ Ensigns
71 Philo Gibbs   Wads. Tracy *Talm* 4   │
72 Rufus Case   Wads: Trac Talm 7   │
73 Joseph A Wells   Wads: Tracey Talm 10   │
74 Walter Smith   Wads Tracey Talm. 9   │
    Job Tabor Bolls   cadet in Corps of Artillerists │
    New London   Wadsworth   ⎭

38. Bezaleel Bebee was a captain in the American Revolution and after the war served in the Connecticut militia. In 1793 and 1795 he represented Litchfield in the Connecticut General Assembly.

SURGEONS

43 Samuel R Gaup	*Allen*
53 Sharon 32 years	real education good Character surgeons mate
54 Timothy Pearce Litchfield	Allen
	excellent & truly learned ac-complished Physician
	Tracey
	Wadsworth *by Inquiry*
	Talmage
	Mate
77 Abel Catlin	Tracey Wad. Talmage
78 Thaddeus Waugh	same

79 William Bostwick	Mate Tracey ⎫
	        Wads ⎬
	        Talmage ⎭

Tudor	by Elsworth

Candidates for Army Appointments from Delaware [1]

[Philadelphia, November–December, 1798]

MAJORS

John Vining
   commands a Com-   provisional
   pany of Light
   Infantry

AD, George Washington Papers, Library of Congress.

1. In this list of recommendations for Army appointments, those recommended have not been identified. Wherever possible, however, the individuals making the recommendations have been identified.

H, George Washington, and Charles Cotesworth Pinckney prepared this list, which is undated, during their meetings in Philadelphia.

CAPTAINS

Richard Dale	handed in by Clayton [2]	Antifœderal
1 Samuel White	prudence & propriety ⎫	
young Lawyer		
Dover	Foederal	well
	good property	supported
	G Read [3]	
	Basset [4] integrity ⎭	
education ⎫	Vyning [5]	
Talents ⎬	*Bayard* [6]	
Courage ⎭		
Richard Dale	good education ⎫	
now	& principles	
Militia Light	Clayton	
Infantry		tolerably
1-2 Benjamin Burrows	Clayton ⎫ Bayard	
Major of Militia	Basset ⎭	
	attached to the Government	
	sensible active industrious &	
	brave	
John Corse	raised by merit to Capt in *Rev-*	
45 to 50	*olutionary War*	
	Clayton Latimer [7] & Bayard	
James Battel	Clayton speaks highly of him	
Dover		
Lawyer		

SUBALTERNS

Samuel Armstrong	private soldiers
James Armstrong	*1791* promoted as *sergeant Ma-*

2. Joshua Clayton, a veteran of the American Revolution, was governor of Delaware from 1793 to 1796. In January, 1798, he was elected to the United States Senate to fill the vacancy caused by the resignation of John Vining, and Clayton served in that capacity until his death on August 11, 1798.

3. George Read, a lawyer from New Castle, Delaware, was a Federalist. He was a member of the United States Senate from 1789 to 1793, when he resigned to become chief justice of Delaware. He held that position until his death on September 21, 1798.

4. Richard Bassett was a member of the United States Senate from Delaware from 1789 to 1793 and chief justice of the Court of Common Pleas from 1793 to 1799. In 1796 he was elected as a Federalist to the Electoral College.

5. John Vining, a Delaware lawyer, served in the House of Representatives from 1789 to 1793 and in the United States Senate from 1793 to January, 1798, when he resigned.

6. James A. Bayard, a lawyer from Wilmington, Delaware, was a Federalist member of the House of Representatives from 1797 to 1803.

7. Henry Latimer.

now W Territory as Qr. Master	*jor & Qr M sergeant* & ser- geant of horse men of good Characters	

Winlock Clarke
  probably Frederica
  bred a *Tanner*
	honor integrity & Talents
	provisional army
	Basset ⎤
	Vyning ⎮ respectable
	Clayton ⎬ family
	Bayard ⎦
	Andrew Barret [8]
		⎤
		  Respectably
		⎬ as
		  Lieutenant

Arthur Mason
  Christina Bridge
  served as soldier in
    Maryland Line
	Barr [9]
	Johns [10]
	good moral character	

Thomas Huston
  Dover
	young man of prudence &
	    honor
	Mercantile
	Basset & Vining
		Qr. *Ensign*

Stephen Pleasonton	by J Clayton respectable fam-
	  ily sprightly active believes
	  moral char
	Col *James Henry* [11] Latimer
	  suppo
		Lt or Ensign

Timothy Winn
  Duck Creek
	young Gentleman from New
	    England	

Taddock Crapper
  one of McPhersons
   Blues [13]
  Kent County
John Wild
	Daniel Rogers [12] *Governor*
	Clayton qualified for soldier
	  family fortune good moral
	  character
		Respectably
		Enquire of
		  McPherson

Peter Jaquett Jun
  Ensign in the late
  war
  What age
  cornet
John Merritt
	Latimer nothing positive an-
	  tient family American prin-
	  ciples
	Bayard
	
	sober active & brave
		Respectably
		Decent
		as Lieutenant
		☞

8. From 1791 to 1797, Andrew Barratt was the supervisor of the revenue for the District of Delaware (*Executive Journal*, I, 87, 88, 247). In July, 1798, he became one of the commissioners of valuations for Delaware (*Executive Journal*, I, 288, 289).

9. Samuel Barr was a Delaware clergyman.

10. Kensey Johns was an associate justice of the Delaware Supreme Court.

11. Henry was a member of the Delaware House of Representatives in 1793.

12. Rogers was governor of Delaware from 1797 to 1798.

13. This is a reference to a Pennsylvania volunteer company of troops commanded by William Macpherson. Such troops were authorized by Section 3 of "An Act authorizing the President of the United States to raise a Provisional Army" (1 *Stat.* 558–61 [May 28, 1798]).

now Philadelphia	in opinion of Clayton will make good officer	
William Keller Junior Dover	No information	
James Clayton Jun Dover 21 years	by J Clayton in respectable Terms Rodney [14] &c	Lieutenancy *respectable*
Samuel Wethered 22 years	Young Gentleman of spirit & honor James A Bayard Jo. Sykes [15] Basset Vyning *William* Miller [16]	Lieutenancy respectable
James Caskery Milson Sussex	Daniel Rogers *Governor* *pretty well*	Ensign
Levy George Foard	respectable Connections good English Educa	Ensign
David Witherspoon	Clayton good foederalist genteel young man honor &c	Not very strong

SURGEANS

John Laws	Clayton *strongly*	
George Dell	Gov Rogers— &	Antifoederal [17]

Samuel Barr Chaplan

5	Samuel White Dover	Capt
9	Peter Jacquett Junr.	Lt
4	James Clayton Junr.	Ensign

14. Thomas Rodney, a prominent landowner in Kent County, Delaware, was elected to the Continental Congress five times.

15. James Sykes, a Delaware physician, was a presidential elector in 1792. He was elected to the state Senate in 1794 and served as president of the Senate until he succeeded to the office of governor in 1801.

16. Miller, a resident of Philadelphia, was the commissioner of the revenue of the United States (*Executive Journal*, I, 259–60).

17. H endorsed the last page of this list: "Left unexamined."

Candidates for Army Appointments from Kentucky [1]

[Philadelphia, November–December, 1798]

SUBALTERNS

3 John Jamison Frankfort William Murray [3] Isaac E Gano [4] Thomas Tunstall [5] Thomas Love [6]	Lt or Ensign *Lewis* [2] recommends in general terms constitution & firmly attached to Govern Sobriety courage & Gentlemanlike behaviour	Inquire

Thomas Todd,[7] John M Scott,[8] Willis Lee,[9] Daniel Wisiger,[10] Otho Beatty,[11] Robert Alexander [12]

4 Fleming Woodridge Paris	*Lewis* & *Fowler* [13] recomd him
6 John Gerrard	*General Scot* [14] Young fellow of merit will do honor to service

AD, George Washington Papers, Library of Congress.

1. In this list of recommendations for Army appointments, those recommended have not been identified. Wherever possible, however, the individuals making the recommendations have been identified.

H prepared this list, which is undated, with George Washington and Charles Cotesworth Pinckney during their meetings in Philadelphia.

2. Thomas Lewis of Fayette County had been a member of the Kentucky House of Representatives in 1792.

3. Murray, a lawyer, represented Franklin County in the Kentucky House of Representatives in 1798.

4. In 1795 Gano was the tax collector for Franklin County.

5. Colonel Tunstall, a native of Virginia, was a veteran of the American Revolution. After the war he moved to Frankfort, Kentucky.

6. Love was a resident of Frankfort, Kentucky.

7. Todd, a lawyer and a Republican, was clerk of the Kentucky Court of appeals from 1792 to 1801.

8. Scott was a resident of Frankfort, Kentucky.

9. In 1796 Lee was a justice of the peace in Franklin County.

10. Weisiger was one of the first settlers of Frankfort, Kentucky. In 1794 he was postmaster at Frankfort, and in 1796 he was clerk of Franklin County.

11. Beatty represented Franklin County in the Kentucky House of Representatives in 1800.

12. From 1795 to 1802 Alexander represented Woodford County in the Kentucky Senate.

13. See John Skey Eustace to H, November 20, 1798, note 12.

14. Brigadier General Charles Scott served in the American Revolution and in the expeditions against the Indians led by Josiah Harmar, Arthur St. Clair, and Anthony Wayne.

7 Charles Kilgoar   General Scot   young fellow of
                      merit   will do honor

10 James Warren   Greenup [15]   Lt   pretty strong
   Danville   general terms
                      Davis [16]   good parentage &
                         character

11 Thomas Eastland   Greenup *Ensign*   pretty
   Danville   strong general terms
                      Davis—good parentage & char-
                         acter

L T

13 Willis Morgan   H Marshall [17]—Young man of
   21 years   military ardor—promised to
                         make wishes known in con-   Attention
                         sideration of merit   pretty
                         well educated moral good
                         politics

14 John Morgan   Ensn   Attn
   19   H Marshall as above

15 Elijah Johnson   *Divers*   was sergeant Major un-
   Lexington   der Way   *Ensign*
                      Lewis &   ⎫
                      other Officers   ⎬ speak well
                      Bodley [18]   ⎭

CAPTAINS

1 William Danger-   Cap of Horse
  field   *H Marshall*—has been Lt. of a
  Lexington   troop of horse respectable
  between *20 & 30*   family   good education   fair
                         character & talents
                      Heath

2 John W Johnson   *unfit*

15. Christopher Greenup, a veteran of the American Revolution and a
lawyer, was a Kentucky member of the House of Representatives from 1792
to 1797.
   16. Thomas Davis, a lawyer, represented Mercer County in the Kentucky
House of Representatives from 1795 to 1797. In 1797 he became a member of
the United States House of Representatives, and he served in that capacity
until 1803.
   17. Humphrey Marshall, a veteran of the American Revolution and a lawyer,
represented Kentucky in the United States Senate from 1795 to 1801.
   18. Thomas Bodley was a resident of Fayette County. In 1793 he was clerk
of the Kentucky Democratic Society.

8 John Grant   Divers   ⌠youth of strict probity
  Nelson   Militia ⎰doubt not he will do   wont do
                    Officers ⌡hon
                    his letter very bad

9 William Owings   Greenup   pretty strong general
        Owens   terms
  Danville   Davis   good parentage & char-
                      acter

138 Robert Bell   *Harpur* [19]   *Inquire*
    Hartford
    his own letter
    well written

                    Capt in Provisional Army
12 Thomas Bodley   says he is a good fœderalist
   Lexington   Ensign in army under Wayne
   probably Fœder- M Ghord ⎱
      alist   T Lewis ⎰ officers strong
                    R B Lee [20]

16 Jesse Ewell   *good* fœderalist *& clever man*
   Mason   good connection   1
                    will accept Lieutenancy

Jesse Ewell   Major   ⎱
William Dangerfield Lexington   ⎰ apply for Cap-
William Owens   Danville   ⎰   taincey
Robert Bell   *Hartford*   Qr if of Kentucky ⎰
John Jameson   Frankfort
Fleming Woodbridge Paris
John Gerrard
Charles Kilgoar
James Warren   Danville
Thomas Eastland   Danville
Willis Morgan
John Morgan
Elijah Johnson   Lexington

19. Robert Goodloe Harper was a Federalist member of the House of Representatives from 1795 to 1801.
20. Richard Bland Lee represented Virginia in the House of Representatives
from 1789 to 1795.

Candidates for Army Appointments
from Maryland [1]

[Philadelphia, November–December, 1798]

LT COLONELS MARYLAND

John Carlisle	Asks for Adjutant General	
Hartford County	*vain letter*	
In Revolutionary	J C Hall [2] recommends	
Army *7 years*		
Joseph Forman	*honor* & *courage*	
see below	Howard [3]	Lt Colonels
	Hindman [4]	
	Loyed [5]	
Levin Handy	Samuel Smith says he was an ex-	
Worster County	cellent Officer	[An Indolent
Old Officer	would expect *a Majority at*	man with
Captain	*least*	no vigour
	Secy says he is *Antifœderal*	of mind.] [6]
	His own Letter expects a Bri-	
	gade	
David Hopkins	Sober man was a good Officer	
Anne Arundel	of *Cavalry*	[And would
Capt Cavalry Revo-	active	be a good

AD, George Washington Papers, Library of Congress.

1. In this list of recommendations for Army appointments, those recommended have not been identified. Wherever possible, however, the individuals making the recommendations have been identified.

H, George Washington, and Charles Cotesworth Pinckney prepared this list, which is undated, during their meetings in Philadelphia.

The material within brackets in this document is not in H's handwriting.

2. Josias Carvel Hall, a resident of Havre de Grace, Maryland, had been a colonel in the American Revolution. On December 31, 1798, he was appointed lieutenant colonel of the Ninth Regiment of Infantry (*Executive Journal*, I, 299, 303).

3. John Eager Howard.

4. William Hindman, a Federalist and a lawyer, had served in the Maryland Senate from 1777 to 1784. He was a member of the Continental Congress from 1784 to 1787 and the Governor's Council from 1789 to 1792. He was a member of the Maryland Senate in 1792, when he was elected to the United States House of Representatives, in which he served until 1799.

5. James Lloyd was a lawyer who served in the Maryland militia during the American Revolution. He was a Federalist member of the United States Senate from 1787 until his resignation in 1800.

6. The material within brackets is in the handwriting of James McHenry.

lutionary War—
between 40 & 50

John Adlum
General of Militia
officer in beginning
of Revolutionary
War

strict honor & integrity
firm mind
large property
R Peters [8]

major of
Cavalry] [7]
Respectable

William D Beale *
on Potomack
G Town
Capt in Revol Army
Stoddert speaks
strongly
calls him a *hero*.

* He was esteemed a good officer
S. Smith says he was one of the
best Officers in the Maryland
line Confirmed by Mr. Stoddert [9]
Ross [10] says he was a steady
foederalist—& respectable Officer
Circumstances *low*

It would seem
probable
that he
would take
a Majority
Respectable

CAPTAINS

2 John Thompson
Queen Anne
E Shore

Seeney [11]—is *Capt of Militia*
Matthews [12]—friend of Gov-
ermt *well deserves* the appt.
Waters [13]
Clayton— [14]
Hindman—well recommended
to him
George Findey [15]   would be
glad to see him assign

young married
man stout
and resolute
*man of
property*
respectable
as Lt which
he will
accept

3 James McKinsey

by capt *Bowen* [16] *conveyed* by
Howard

7. The material within brackets is in the handwriting of Benjamin Stoddert.
8. Richard Peters.
9. Benjamin Stoddert.
10. James Ross.
11. Joshua Seney, a lawyer, served in the Maryland House of Delegates from 1785 to 1787. He was a member of the Continental Congress from 1787 to 1788, and he was elected to the First Congress. He was reelected, but he resigned on May 1, 1792, to become chief justice of the Third Judicial District of Maryland, a position he held until 1796. Seney was an unsuccessful Republican candidate for Congress in 1798.
12. William Matthews served as a judge of the Cecil County Court in 1778, 1780, and again from 1782 to 1786. He was a member of the Maryland General Assembly from 1788 to 1789 and a presidential elector in 1789. In 1796 he was elected to the Fifth Congress.
13. James Waters was a Baltimore merchant.
14. Joshua Clayton.
15. George Finley, a resident of Queen Annes County, Maryland, was appointed a commissioner of valuations on July 16, 1798 (*Executive Journal* I, 288, 289).
16. John Bowen commanded a troop of cavalry in the Baltimore militia during the Whiskey Insurrection.

5	Ezekiel Towson [17] Baltimore County	If he procures &c captaincy or Lieutenancy By Hugh McCurdy his Partner Secy doubts his principles	
6	Nathan N Wright George Town Cross Roads Eastern Shore	Appt. in *provisional* Army Tolerable *Letter* Probably not of good politics *Matthews*	*Wont do*
7	John Nicholson	Secretary thinks he drinks Antifoederal & suspected of drinking	do
9	Hugh *Matthews* *irritable* Temper studied law lively young Man	*clayton* speaks well of him as Major or Captain of Artillery His letter is well—delicate health	Pretty respectable

Howard
Loyed ⎱ only speak of him
Hindman ⎰ as a man of hon-
or
will make a good

and active officer

Jonathan Hodgson
Chester Maryland Bayard [18] ⎱ application for a
Kent County S ⎰ Company of
30 & 40 Artillery

Clayton * [19] speaks well of him will accept a
Matthews respected & Lieutenancy
esteemed by his acquaintances *respectable*
good education & appearance * allied to G
Basset [20]—worthy of the Clayton
appointment

Merril *Loyed*—not much acquainted
[if he is of Chas. with him appears *intelligent*
County, he ought & *candid*
not to be
appointed.] [21]

Rezin Davidge *DeWall* [22] (Ant.) speaks well
Anne Arundel of him
Young man *Winchester* [23] speaks well of

---

17. Ezekial Towson was a tavern owner and builder in Baltimore County. His partner in the building firm was named Mosher.
18. James A. Bayard.
19. Presumably this is a reference to James Clayton, son of Joshua Clayton.
20. Richard Bassett.
21. This sentence is in Stoddert's handwriting.
22. Gabriel Duval, a lawyer, was elected to the House of Representatives as a Republican to fill a vacancy and served from 1794 to 1796. He resigned in 1796 to become an associate justice of the Maryland Supreme Court. He was a presidential elector in 1796 and 1800.
23. William Winchester was justice of the peace in Frederick County, Maryland, from 1778 to 1780 and again in 1783. During the American Revolution he

Young Gentleman	character who recommends him	
	Davidson [24] thinks the appt. will be well bestowed	Respectable
	R Ridgly [25] of family & reputation	
	Gassaway [26]—uprightness & attachment to Government	
[If Roger Nelson [27] of Fredk. he is a detd. Enemy to Government.] [29]	*Neilson* [28] *brave active* & alert	
John R Bryce	*respectable family*	
Anne Arundel	Letter *verbose*	Inquire
Young man	says he has studied Military Discipline	
	Matthews—thinks he may make a good subaltern	
Joseph Parrot	*Federalist, now*	
Talbot County	Howard—speaks well—intelligent	Lieutenancy perhaps
Lawyer 24 years	*Secy Handsome interesting well informed*	Captain
	Winchester⎱ indefatigable in his Hindman ⎰ pursuits	
Jacob Giles Smith	Paca [30] Gentleman of *respect-*	

served as a captain in the militia. From 1794 to 1795 he represented Baltimore in the House of Delegates. In 1798 Winchester ran as the Federalist candidate for Congress, but he was defeated by Samuel Smith.

24. John Davidson, a resident of Annapolis, served in the American Revolution and retired with the rank of major. He was appointed collector of customs at Annapolis on August 3, 1789, and inspector of the port on March 6, 1792 (*Executive Journal* I, 10, 14, 102, 104, 111). In 1794 he was appointed brigadier general of the Maryland militia for Calvert and Anne Arundel counties.

25. Robert Ridgely, a lawyer and resident of Baltimore, was elected to the Continental Congress in 1785 and 1786 but declined to serve in 1786. He was a member of the Maryland Senate from 1786 to 1791.

26. John Gassaway had attained the rank of captain during the American Revolution before he was captured at Camden, South Carolina, in 1780. He was a vestryman of St. Anne's Parish, Anne Arundel County, from 1791 to 1793. In 1798 he was a member of a committee appointed to supervise the fortification of Annapolis.

27. Roger Nelson, a lawyer, was a brigadier general in the American Revolution. In 1795 he was a member of the Maryland House of Delegates.

28. George Neilson, a resident of Annapolis who had been an indentured servant, was a close friend of Charles Carroll of Carrollton.

29. The material within brackets is in the handwriting of Stoddert.

30. William Paca, a lawyer in Queen Annes County, Maryland, served in the colonial legislature from 1768 to 1774, when he was elected to the First Continental Congress. He was a member of the Second Continental Congress from 1775 to 1779 and was a signer of the Declaration of Independence. On

Hartford County	*able* family	
young Gentleman	S Hughes [31] good family man-ly figure fair character	Inquire
	G Smith His own letter decent	
Sinclair Lancaster	Capt in Militia last war	
Boh	*Oldham* [32]—strictly *fœderal*	Super-
60 years old	Matthews	annuated
Samuel Davis	Tilghman [33] Hindman & others say he is highly intitled to Ltancy	
	Matthews retracts his former recommendation wants energy is very young would take a Lieutenancy	Inquire
Elisha Jarret	*Dorsey* [34] Young Gentleman	
Hartford	of respectable family	well as
	Qr. doubtful politics honorable principles can raise	Lieutenant
	Mathews good looking & dresses neatly	
	Secretary says he is a *Gamester*	
	Montgomery [35] (Ant) speaks favourable	
	John Coleman [36] (respectable Clergyman) from several years assures his fœderal & respectability	
William Miller	Creswell [37] Fœderalist	Qr a *Lieuten-*
Cecil County	Col Coboden enterprise &	*ant* expects
Major of Militia	exertion	a Majority

January 22, 1780, he was elected a judge of the Continental Court of Appeals (*JCC*, XVI, 79). From 1782 to 1785 Paca was governor of Maryland. In 1789, in the recess of the Senate, George Washington appointed him United States judge for the District of Maryland, and the Senate approved the appointment on February 10, 1790 (*Executive Journal*, I, 38, 40).

31. Samuel Hughes.

32. Edward Oldham, a resident of Cecil County, Maryland, was a captain in the American Revolution.

33. This is a reference to either Edward, James, or Richard Tilghman. See notes 51, 56, and 57.

34. This is a reference either to Joshua Dorsey, a resident of Frederick County, Maryland, who was elected to the state Senate in 1801, or to Walter Dorsey, a resident of Baltimore, who was a member of the House of Delegates in 1797.

35. John Montgomery, a resident of Harford County, was a member of the Maryland House of Delegates from 1796 to 1797.

36. John Coleman, a native of Virginia, served as an ensign in the American Revolution. After the war he studied in England and was ordained there as a Protestant Episcopal minister. On returning to America, he settled in Harford County, Maryland.

37. John Creswell was a resident of Cecil County, Maryland.

	P Thomas [38] uniformly fœderal & he thinks fit for military service	will accept a Captaincy
	Jno Mifflin [39] distinguished Disciplinarian good fœderal & military man	
	John Miller Military appearance can raise men	
	George Gale [40] tall man & influence at elections *very* ILLITERATE	
William Savin Cecil County 30 & 40	Matthews *stout good* man *handsome*, good understanding without liberal education uniform fœderalist	respectably as Lt perhaps Captain
Thomas Porter Cecil 20 & 30	Matthews—stout good man handsome—uniform—foederalist writes good hand has had command <->	Ensign
William Spencer Kent C *30 years*	Matthews well educated genteel manners & good character—served as *Paymaster man of property* *Howard & Lloyed*	*very Respectable Quare Major*
William S Dallam *Abington* Lawyer Major of Militia	requests a *Troop* of *Horse* Chase [41] respectable family— of a brave stock—writes *pretty well* General Carlisle [42] shining tal-	*Respectable*

38. Philip Thomas began the practice of medicine in Frederick, Maryland, in 1769. During the American Revolution he was chairman of the committee of safety for Frederick County. He was a presidential elector in 1789. He was the first president of the Medical Society of Maryland.

39. John Mifflin was a resident of West Nottingham, Cecil County, Maryland.

40. George Gale represented Somerset County in the Maryland Ratifying Convention of 1788. He was an unsuccessful candidate for the Senate in 1788, but was elected to the House of Representatives in that year. On March 4, 1791, he was appointed supervisor of the revenue for the District of Maryland (*Executive Journal*, I, 81, 82).

41. Samuel Chase had served in the Maryland Assembly from 1764 to 1784. He was elected to both the First and Second Continental Congresses, serving from 1774 to 1778, and was a signer of the Declaration of Independence. He voted against the adoption of the Constitution in the Maryland Ratifying Convention of 1788. In 1791 he was appointed chief justice of the General Court of Maryland. On January 26, 1796, President Washington appointed him an associate justice of the Supreme Court of the United States (*Executive Journal*, I, 198).

42. John Carlisle, a resident of Harford County, had been a captain in the American Revolution.

	ents good education & amiable disposition	
	C Hall—respectable connections excellent officer	
	Howard probably a fœderalist	
Henry C Neale St Mary's County	*Dent* [43]—Young Gentleman of honor & good connections is recomd by R *Barnes* [44]	Probably respectable *Inquire*
	S Smith ⎰ worthy to command a Company & likely to *raise one*	
	P: Ford [45] to Lloyed ⎱ Strict honor & integrity zealous in his Country's Cause	
Richard Earl *Talbot* *25 or 26*	Hindman well will take a subalterns *Howard recommends him fully* from information *P Benson* [46]—(Anti) *Hammond* [47] *sober* moral character & well enough	pretty well as Lieutenant will probably accept Ensigncy
Isaac Spencer Kent County *25*	*Lloyd sensible & worthy* strong M *Mathews* Young active & unblemished *Tew*—of property esteemed in his neighbourhood Ferguson—	*respectable*
James Brooks	General *Crabb* [48]	*perhaps*

43. George Dent served at the Flying Camp and in the Maryland militia during the American Revolution. He was a member of the House of Delegates from 1782 to 1790, where he was a speaker *pro tem* in 1788 and speaker from 1789 to 1790. From 1791 to 1792 he was a member of the Maryland Senate, of which he was elected president in 1792. He served as a Republican in the House of Representatives from 1793 to 1801.

44. Richard Barnes was a resident of St. Marys County, Maryland, and had large landholdings in Washington County.

45. This is a reference either to Peter Ford or to Philip Ford, Jr., both of whom were members of the militia of St. Marys County, Maryland.

46. Perry Benson, a Maryland planter, served as a captain in the American Revolution. In 1794 he was appointed a lieutenant colonel in the state militia, and by 1800 he was a brigadier general. In 1798 he was elected as a Federalist to the House of Delegates.

47. Nicholas Hammond, a native of the Isle of Jersey, had been educated as a lawyer in Philadelphia. He moved to Maryland in the seventeen-eighties and became a prominent Federalist in Talbot County.

48. Jeremiah Crabb, a resident of Montgomery County, Maryland, was a member of the House of Delegates from 1788 to 1793. In 1791 he was appointed

Edward A Howard Baltimore	Rumsey [49] ⎫ Mathew S ⎬ ⎭ young vigourus of *good family* honor probity A Hall [50] person will recommend itself	*good Ensign*
William Knight Bohemia Manor	Oldham—of good *family* & thinks he will do honor Js. Tilghman,[51] superficially acquainted quite a *young man* on *Inquiry* finds him *meritorious honor integrity & sobriety*	Probably *good Ensign*
Benjamin Burch Federal City Formerly in the service	W D Beale [52] says he is a worthy of a company Writes ill	*Not much* [a pair of Columns at the most.] [53]
Benjamin Harrison Anne Arundel *Lawyer young*	*Wilmer* [54] person education & deportt intitles him at least to Comp *Gassaway* Gentleman of family & respectability *politics not mentioned*	probably well enough as *Lieutenant* [of a Federal Family] [55]
Richard Cooke Anne Arundel	His father [56] recommends him who is a good fœderalist	probably *respectable*

---

an associate justice of the Fifth Judicial District. In 1794 he was appointed brigadier general of militia for part of Montgomery and Frederick counties. He was a member of the House of Representatives from 1795 to 1796.

49. This is presumably a reference to Benjamin Rumsey, who was a colonel in the Maryland militia during the American Revolution, a member of the Continental Congress from 1776 to 1778, and chief judge of the Maryland Court of Appeals from 1778 to 1805.

50. Andrew Hall, a resident of Queen Annes County, Maryland, was appointed postmaster of Church Hill in 1802.

51. This is a reference either to James Tilghman or to his son, James Tilghman, Jr. Both men were appointed district judges in 1791.

52. William Dent Beall, a resident of Georgetown, was a major in the American Revolution.

53. The material within brackets is in the handwriting of Stoddert.

54. Jonathan R. Wilmer, a lawyer and merchant, was a vestryman of St. Anne's Parish, Anne Arundel County, Maryland, in 1795. From 1797 to 1801 he served as a member of the Governor's Council.

55. The material within brackets is in Stoddert's handwriting.

56. This is presumably a reference to Richard Cooke of "The Hermitage," who changed his name to Richard Cooke Tilghman in order to inherit "The Hermitage" from his uncle, Richard Tilghman IV.

Davidson ⎫ Thomas [58] ⎬ Johnson [59] ⎭	E Tilghman [57]—worthy good young man of generous prin- ciples John Henry [60]—*amiable man* Wilmer—activity	*Lieutenant* Desirous of being on *horse*
James Stewart Baltimore Irish Tavern Keeper	Mc.*Eldery* [61] ⎫ recommends *Anti* ⎭ him George Brown [62] speaks of him as an excellent Citizen Gam- bler suspicion Howard S ⎫ *Col* recommends O *Donnel* [63] ⎭ him strongly	*not elegible* QR
Charles M Brotherson Baltimore County	Capt in present army, if not ob- tainable provisional army *Howard* mentions but nothing positive *Goodwin* [64] sense & consider- able information *J Hamilton* [65] speaks strongly	Tolerably *well*

57. Edward Tilghman, a native of Maryland, was educated in England and practiced law in Philadelphia.

58. John Chew Thomas, a resident of Anne Arundel County, was a Federalist member of the House of Delegates from 1796 to 1797. He was elected to the House of Representatives, where he served from 1799 to 1801.

59. Thomas Johnson served in the colonial and state legislatures from 1762 to 1776, from 1780 to 1781, and from 1786 to 1787. He was a member of the First and Second Continental Congresses from 1774 to 1777, when he became briga- dier general of the Maryland militia. From 1777 to 1779 he was governor of Maryland, and in 1790 and 1791 he was chief justice of the Maryland General Court. George Washington nominated him United States judge for the District of Maryland on September 24, 1789, and associate justice of the Supreme Court of the United States on October 31, 1791 (*Executive Journal*, I, 29, 31, 86, 88). On January 22, 1791, he was appointed one of three commissioners for the District of Columbia. Failing health caused him to resign from the Supreme Court in 1793 and as a commissioner in 1794.

60. John Henry, a lawyer educated in England, served in the Continental Congress from 1778 to 1781 and from 1784 to 1787. He was elected to the United States Senate in 1788 and was reelected in 1790 and 1796. In 1796 he received two electoral votes for Vice President. He resigned from the Senate in 1797 to become governor of Maryland. He died on December 16, 1798.

61. Thomas McEldery, a resident of Baltimore, was a mayoral elector in 1796.

62. George Brown was a Baltimore physician.

63. John O'Donnell, a resident of Baltimore, was a member of the House of Delegates from 1792 to 1793. In 1793 he was awarded a contract to clean the streets of Baltimore.

64. This is a reference either to William Goodwin, Sr., a resident of Balti- more, who was a tax commissioner in 1798 and a member of the second branch of the City Council in 1799, or to Lyde Goodwin, a Baltimore physician, who was a judge of the Criminal Court in 1788 and a judge of elections in 1796.

65. Hamilton was not related to H.

<table>
<tr><td></td><td>Coulter [66] general terms fa-
vourably
Yeiser [67]—favourably
Kilty [68]—probably active &
spirited officer good educa-
tion property in business a
young family in business</td><td></td></tr>
<tr><td>Jacob Norris
Hartford
Lt. at Close of War
now Col of Militia</td><td>Col Carlisle speaks strongly of
him
asks for Command
general</td><td>Inquire
carefully</td></tr>
<tr><td>Samuel A Harpur
Eastern shore</td><td>Levin Handy [69]—recommends
him</td><td></td></tr>
<tr><td>Thomas Skinner</td><td>Handy</td><td></td></tr>
<tr><td>Gerard Briscoe
Charles County</td><td>Dent young Gentleman of
good character respectable
qualifications could raise a
Company of Natives</td><td>Respectable
Inquire of Mr
Harrison [70]</td></tr>
<tr><td>William Ogle
Frederick County</td><td>G Johnson ⎫ Believe he would
Baylor   ⎬ make a good of-
P Thomas ⎭ ficer
[The Son of a Rich & a good
Man [71]—and a good Federal-
ist.] [72]</td><td>No detail
Not very
strong</td></tr>
<tr><td>John C Beatty
Washington County
son of C W Beatty</td><td>Baer [73] favorably—has com-
manded volunteer Compy
checked Insurgents</td><td></td></tr>
</table>

66. John Coulter, a Baltimore physician, was a member of the Maryland Ratifying Convention of 1788. In 1796 he was a special commissioner of Baltimore, and in 1797 he was a mayoral elector.

67. Englehard Yeisser, a prominent Baltimore merchant, was a mayoral elector in 1797.

68. William Kilty, a native of England, was educated in France before immigrating to Annapolis before the American Revolution. After studying medicine in Annapolis, he became a surgeon's mate and then surgeon in the Fourth Maryland Regiment. Taken prisoner at Camden, South Carolina, he was paroled to Annapolis, where he remained until the end of the war. By 1798 he had abandoned medicine and was authorized by the legislature to compile the statutes of Maryland. From 1794 to 1796 he served on the Governor's Council.

69. Levin Handy, a native of Maryland, reached the rank of captain in the American Revolution before he resigned on May 1, 1780.

70. Richard Harrison, a native of Maryland, was a merchant in Alexandria, Virginia. From 1780 to 1786 he acted as unofficial consul for the United States at Cadiz. He was officially appointed consul at Cadiz on June 4, 1790 (*Executive Journal*, I, 47, 49). On November 25, 1791, he was appointed auditor in the Treasury Department (*Executive Journal*, I, 90), and he served in that post until 1836.

71. This is presumably a reference to Thomas Ogle, who was a member of the Maryland House of Delegates from Frederick County in 1782–1783.

72. The material within brackets is in McHenry's handwriting.

73. George Baer.

Benjamin Greene Hartford 27 years old	G Gale recommends but not strong—*integrity* & fœderalist Howard recommends because he can raise a Company	
	⎱ Gentleman of merit S Hughes ⎰ & friend to ⎰ Governt	Lieutenant perhaps Captain
	J Carlisle—zealous fœderalist Matthews *appearance toler- ably good* P Thomas	
James P. Heath	*Oldham* respectable family honor & spirit	*attention*
John Evans Charles County Troop of Horse Western army Revolutionary army non Commissioned Officer Corporal in Pensy Rg	Asks for Captaincy Hartly [74] deserves Attntn Irvine [75]—favorably Craick [76]	Perhaps *Ensign*
John Miller G Town Potow- mack	respectable family nothing else appears	[There was a Man of the name of Miller who lived in Geo Town: an ignorant & a violent Jacobin—I know of no Man of the name living there now.] [77]
James Harpur	G. *Gunby* [78] thinks him quali-	

74. Thomas Hartley.
75. William Irvine.
76. William Craik, a native of Maryland and a lawyer, was appointed chief justice of the Fifth Judicial District of Maryland on January 13, 1793, and he served in that position until 1796, when he resigned. In 1796 he was elected as a Federalist to the House of Representatives to fill Jeremiah Crabb's term. He was reelected twice and served until 1801.
77. The material within brakets is in the handwriting of Stoddert.
78. A native of Maryland, John Gunby was a colonel in the American Revolution. He was blamed by Nathanael Greene for the American defeat at Hobkirk's Hill. On August 3, 1798, he was appointed collector of customs at Snow

Wooster County
last war a *private*
now *Captain of Militia*
Robert Bell
Hartford County
Joshua Lamb
Eastern Shore
Patrick Sim
Bladinsburgh
Potowmack
Col of Militia
campaign of 76 as
Captain

Nathan Levy

fied for a Captain
School Education
J Dennis [79] S

Qr. if Maryland
Lloyed fœderal
Quaker Integrity
Captaincy or Cavalry
General S Sim [80] at Close of 76
was made Lt Co but resigned
on marrying niece of Bishop
Carrol [81] good looking man
Temperate
willing to go *into Infantry Inquire* particulary of Stoddert
Walter B Coxe [82]—
  himself an old
  Officer
Benjamin Brooks [83] ⎬ They speak
  himself Antifœd
  strongly
R Sprigg [84] recommends good
  conduct & *sobriety*
U Forrest [85]—dilligence & honor

country perhaps
          Ensign

Nothing very
  positive
a Jacobin

Hill, Maryland, and on March 6, 1792, he was appointed inspector of the port at Snow Hill (*Executive Journal*, I, 10, 14, 104, 111).

79. John Dennis, a resident of Worcester County, Maryland, and a lawyer, served two terms in the Maryland House of Delegates before being elected as a Federalist to the House of Representatives in 1796, where he served until 1805. In 1798 the House of Representatives appointed him one of the managers to conduct the impeachment hearings against William Blount.

80. Smith Sims was a resident of Somerset County, Maryland.

81. John Carroll, a native of Maryland, was educated in France. He was ordained as a Jesuit priest in 1767. Returning to America before the Revolution, he was appointed by the Continental Congress to the commission to Canada in 1776. On November 14, 1789, he was named the first American Roman Catholic bishop.

82. Cox was a resident of Prince Georges County, Maryland.

83. Benjamin Brooks served as a major in the American Revolution. In the seventeen-nineties he was a brigadier general of the Maryland militia. On May 29, 1798, he was appointed a major in the Corps of Artillerists and Engineers (*Executive Journal*, I, 277, 279).

84. Richard Sprigg, Jr., served in the Maryland House of Delegates in 1792 and 1793. He was elected to the House of Representatives to fill a vacancy and served from May, 1796, to March 4, 1799.

85. Uriah Forrest, a native of Maryland, was a lieutenant colonel in the American Revolution. He served as auditor of Maryland and in both branches of the state legislature. In 1786 and 1787 he was a member of the Continental Congress, and he served as a Federalist in the House of Representatives in 1793 and 1794. In 1794 he was appointed a brigadier general of the Maryland militia

| George Town Potowm | got rid of his youthful lusts was attentive & industrious as Merchant & wound up with reputation activity & accuracy usefull in Qr. M Gen *smart lively fellow Confidence* | |

LIEUTENANTS

Jesse Knock *Kent* Father [87] a zealous partisin *Byus* Stanly Byass *Kent* probably a private in *Militia*	Boardly [86] honest Citizen *foederal active industrious* Lieutenant or Ensign *Matthews young stout & active Hindman* is inclined to believe he would make a good Officer His own letter—Coats [88] *his* Militia Captain	Qr. Qr. Ensign Qr. Qr Not MUCH
John Black 21 years	His friends not active he has not taken a } Matthews part *handsome* & sprightly } Matthews presumes he might be trusted	Qr. Qr Ensign
Samuel Robinson George Town Potowmack	*Lt of Artillery U. Forrest* speaks well	Inquire of *Stoddert* [a young man I believe of property & courage & fit for a Lt.] [89]

George Bringle
Nathan Browner 22   *Dent.* Plain education, active &

---

for Prince Georges and part of Montgomery counties. He was the business partner of Benjamin Stoddert.

86. John Beale Bordley, a Maryland lawyer, was an associate judge of the Provincial Court from 1766 to 1776 and an admiralty judge from 1767 to 1776. In 1783 he was elected a member of the American Philosophical Society. He moved to Philadelphia in 1791, and there he established the first agricultural society in the United States.

87. Daniel Knock, a resident of Queen Annes County, was a justice of the peace in 1794. In 1798 he was appointed to a joint commission composed of individuals from Kent and Queen Annes counties which had been formed to establish a market at Bridgetown, Kent County.

88. John Coats, a native of Philadelphia, served as a physician in the American Revolution. Moving to Maryland in 1780, he became the first Grand Master of Masons in that state in 1783.

89. The material within brackets is in the handwriting of Stoddert.

Charles Cty

Thomas B Clements
Charles County 45
served in Revolu-
tionary army as
☞ serjeant with
Credit

Dominick T Blake
has studied law

Jacob Fowle
Stephen H Fowle
Philemon C Blake
Queen Anne C
22 years

Samuel Lane *
George Town
Potowmack

intelligent would accept of
an Ensigncy.

Key [90]   ⎫ Gent of respect-
Smith   ⎬ able *family* &
John G ⟨–⟩ ⎭ *conn*
             general reputa-
             tion *good*

☞ asks for first *Lieutenant* of
Cavalry
Matthews   Young Gentleman
*from Ireland   good scholar—
finished scholar*   connected
with first families in the state
J E *Howard*   Samuel *Tew*
John Henry   amiable sensible
worthy
willing to devote *their lives*

R Tilghman   *Sobriety probity*
J Tilghman   *integrity honor*
             their relative
Secy   modest looking   Genteel
man
Lloyed   no doubt he will make
an excellent officer

U Forrest   has commanded a ⎫
             Militia Comp   ⎪
             recommends him ⎪
             strongly for   ⎪
             Lieutency   ⎪
J: T: Mason [92] active intelli- ⎬
gent young man   ⎪
Anti mild   ⎪
General *Crabb   Stoddert*   ⎪
(Anti)   recommends   ⎪
             as Lt. strongly ⎭
B   *Edwards* [94]—his uncle ac-
knowleges that he was
DEMOCRATIC   *good education*

Qr. Qr. Qr
Ensign

Respectably as
Lieutenant

Inquire his
politics

Respectably
for Cornet
or Ensign
Qr his politics

Inquire of *Chs.
Lee Atty G*
[His Father [91]
a man of
property &
himself a
clever
young
man] [93]

90. This is a reference to either Philip or Philip Barton Key.
91. Samuel Lane's father was Hardage Lane.
92. John Thompson Mason was a resident of Annapolis, Maryland.
93. The material within brackets is in the handwriting of Benjamin Stoddert.
94. Benjamin Edwards represented Montgomery County in the Maryland Ratifying Convention of 1788. He was appointed an associate judge of the Circuit Court for Montgomery County in 1791, and from 1797 to 1798 he served as a judge of the Montgomery County Orphans' Court.

Richard W West Prince George	P. *Thomas* cavalry in prefer- ence firm fœderalist & respectable *young Gentleman* J E Howard	respectably as Lieutenant
Jarrett Bull Baltimore	promises ability & Patriotism writes a good han *James Carroll* [95] decent Gen- teel Young Man hopes he will do well And Aitkin [96] perhaps Ant: A Jarret [97] Yeyser [98] McEildere a stupid man of property J Norris [99] } Wm. Clen [100] } Antifœderal	Passably an Ensign
Levy Hillary Frederick County	*Stoddert* Young man of merit nephew of a man of *confi- dence* & character good *scribe* from knowlege of *ac- counts.* Craick handsome genteel clever young man Baer Doct *Thomas*	respectably as Ensign perhaps Lt [very clever Fellow & fit for a Lt.] [101]
William Swan Talbot County *East*	Benson recommends but *not good* *D Kerr* [102]—integrity, he under- stands acctg. R L Nichols [103]—speaks favourably	Swan Well as *Ensign*

95. This is a reference either to James Carroll, a relative of John Carroll, who was a planter in Talbot County, or to James Carroll, a Baltimore lawyer, who was appointed an associate judge of the District Court in 1791 and served as Speaker of the Maryland House of Delegates in 1797.

96. Andrew Aitkin was a prominent Baltimore physician.

97. Abraham Jarret, a resident of Harford County, was a member of the Maryland House of Delegates from 1792 to 1798.

98. See note 67.

99. This is a reference to either James Norris, Sr., or his son, James Norris, Jr., both of whom were residents of Baltimore.

100. This is presumably a reference to William Clemm, a resident of Baltimore.

101. The material within brackets is in the handwriting of Stoddert.

102. David Kerr, a native of Scotland, had settled first in Virginia, then at Annapolis, and finally at Easton, Maryland. He was a Federalist member of the House of Delegates from 1790 to 1794 and again in 1797. In 1798 Kerr tied Perry Benson in the election to the House of Delegates, but he lost to Benson in the run-off election.

103. R. L. Nichols (Nicols), a resident of Easton, Maryland, served in the American Revolution. In 1789 he became the business partner of David Kerr.

Nicholas Vanzandt

Goldsborough [104]   active attentive young man
Perry [105]   spirited active officer
Yeates [106]   integrity & sobriety
strong Lt

Ninnian Pinckney
Anne Arundel

General Davidson ⎱ favourably ⎱   probably *good*
James Lloyed   ⎰ *great merit* ⎰   *Lieutenant*
John P Wilmer   Intrepedity ⎰   [active Fel-
                                        low] [107]

Inquire

Samuel Tyler Jun *2
Bradley Beans *
John Warren x2
Barns x3

U Forrest   They will make excellent Lieutenants
* Stoddert speaks well of him
*2 do   recommends as Lieuten-
ants

[These three
ought by
all means to
be ap-
pointed.
Beans is fit
to be a
Capt.] [109]

[Barns is no relation of Jno Barnes [108] by Blood or Politics—& is an extray clever young man. Beans is older,
Federal & sensible, as all his Family are—and Warren
is the son of a very Rich man, of decided attachment
to Government. Tyler, I fear, is not very Federal, tho
I know nothing of him—& Judge from the name [110]
only.] [111]

Samuel Thomas 64

James B Brookes
Montgomery
County
was on Western
Expedition

General Crabb   *good* family
fair *Character*
Stoddert—Young man of good
property

Nothing
pointed

---

104. This is a reference to one of the following men: Charles Goldsborough,
a lawyer, who was a Federalist member of the Maryland Senate from 1791 to
1795 and from 1799 to 1801; or Charles Goldsborough, who was a clerk in the
Navy Department; or Robert Goldsborough, chief justice of the Maryland
Supreme Court from April 2, 1796, until his death in 1799; or Richard Goldsborough, a resident of Dorchester County, Maryland, who was a member of
the House of Delegates in 1796 and 1799.

105. William Perry, a native of Maryland, was justice of the peace in Talbot
County in 1774 and from 1776 to 1779. He was a member of the Maryland
Conventions of 1775 and 1776. From 1786 to 1799 he was a Federalist member
of the state Senate, and he was president of the Senate from 1796 until 1799.

106. Donaldson Yeates was quartermaster general of Maryland during the
American Revolution. He was a member of the Maryland Ratifying Convention of 1788, and he was a presidential elector in 1792.

107. The words within brackets are in Stoddert's handwriting.

108. John Barnes, a resident of Washington County, Maryland, was a member of the Maryland House of Delegates in 1777, from 1779 to 1782, and in
1795.

109. The material within brackets is in Stoddert's handwriting.

110. This is presumably a reference to Samuel Tyler, register of wills for
Prince Georges County from 1782 to 1803.

111. The material within brackets is in Stoddert's handwriting.

Aquila Beale George Town Potomack	Craick—of good family & character worthy a Lieutenancy	Probably good Lieutenant
Thomas Orne G Town Potow- mack	Inquire of Messrs Stoddert & Lear [112]	
George Lewis Cecil County *Lt of Militia*	*Oldham Young* and *active* friend to Govt. thinks he will make a good office	
	Howard retracts his recommendation	*Wont do*
William Troth Easton Eastern Shore	*Toldwell* abilities integrity *Dorsey* acquitted himself as Gentleman	Inquire
Richard G Hardestty George Town Potowmac	U Forest active sprightly likely to make good officer	Inquire
John Kerns Baltimore	speaks of the goodness of his finances	Inquire
	Wm. Smith [113] ⎱ sober active & Antifoed ⎰ industrious	Qr.
Andrew H Voorhees Queen Annes	*Seney* good education & abilities	perhaps *Ensign*
	Matthews—reported to be a spirited young man	
Louis C Bayly G Town P	No recommendation [appointed to the Navy.] [114]	
Thomas Gordon Eastern Shore	*Coates*	
William Monroe born Anapolis now residing Philadelphia	See Penyslvania	pretty well recommended as Lt. or Ensign
Richard Tilghman *the 5th* Talbot County	*Wilmer* will give importance to his Commission Hindman—meritorious & active Wm Cooke [115] large property	very Respectable
Charles Clements Charles County sergeant under St	Dent—faby as Ensign [25—good common education —possesses considerable	Not much

112. Tobias Lear.

113. William Smith, a native of Pennsylvania, represented Maryland in the Continental Congress from 1777 to 1778. He was elected to the House of Representatives in 1788 and served until 1791. In 1796 he was a presidential elector. In 1798 he was a merchant in Baltimore. He was also an executor of Otho H. Williams's estate. Josias Carvel Hall was his son-in-law.

114. The material within brackets is in the handwriting of Stoddert.

115. This is presumably a reference to William Cooke of Annapolis, father of Richard Cooke Tilghman and brother-in-law of Richard Tilghman IV.

Clair [116]	knowledge. Deserving of at least an Ensigncy. D.] [117]	
John B Barnes Charles County [mentd. in another place—a very clever Fellow, ought to be in the Cavalry.] [120]	*prefers Cavalry* U Forest—*strong* J Campbell [118]—genteel of good connections well educated John C Jones [119] talents attached to the Govt. Dent— Fitzgerald [121]—sobriety & active zeal	Probably respectable
Daniel Hughes Cecil County 26 years	S. Hughes *good family* Courage & great firmness P Thomas Foederalism & talents G Gale general good character Carvel Hall—Young Gentleman of merit health & strength active business	Probably respectable
Samuel Miles *Baltimore*	*prefers cavalry* Striker [122] ⎤ Genteel young Antif: ⎦ man Howard—a young man of activity & well calculated for army Hoffman [123] ⎤ character fair for Anti ⎦ spirit & merit	Not strong *Inquire*
Charles Gantt	*Robert Bowie* [124] formerly	*Quaere Qr*

116. Arthur St. Clair, a general in the American Revolution, was major general commanding the United States Army from March 4, 1791, to March 5, 1792, when he resigned.

117. The material within brackets is in the handwriting of McHenry.

118. John Campbell, a resident of the Eastern Shore, was a member of the Maryland Senate in 1796.

119. John Coates Jones was appointed collector of customs at Nanjemoy, Maryland, on August 3, 1798, and inspector of the port of Cedar Point, Maryland, on March 6, 1798 (*Executive Journal*, I, 11, 14, 104, 111).

120. The material within brackets is in the handwriting of Stoddert.

121. Thomas Fitzgerald was a resident of Charles County, Maryland.

122. This is a reference either to George Stricker, a native of North Carolina, who had served in the American Revolution and who had represented Frederick in the Maryland legislature, or to John Stricker, his son, also a veteran of the American Revolution. John Stricker was a resident of Baltimore and had been second in command of the Maryland militia commanded by Samuel Smith during the Whiskey Insurrection.

123. Peter Hoffman, a native of Frederick County, Maryland, was a prominent merchant. In 1771 he moved his business to Baltimore, and in 1794 he established the wholesale dry goods firm of Hoffman and Company there.

124. Robert Bowie was a captain in the American Revolution, and from 1786 to 1790 he was a member of the Maryland House of Delegates. In 1794 he was appointed a justice of the peace and a major in the militia. In 1796 he was an elector for the state Senate.

Nottingham	Antifœderal *speaks well* Stoddert S	
Benjamin Preston Hartford Major of Militia	Christie [125] *respectable family* Whig Matthews, once Sheriff of Hartford respectable man stout & active—adviseable to appoint him	*Not strong*
Eneas Noland Montgomery County	D. *Lucket* [126] Baer—S H Carbury [127] *handsome genteel* young man	Passably an *Ensign*
Alexander Cooper Washington Coun Francis W Thomas G Town	Baer s young Gentleman of virtue & bravery *to avenge his father* No recommendation	Inquire
Benjamin McCenny Anne Arundel	*Harwood* [128] ⎱ Young man well W Rive ⎰ qualified for Company Selman [129] Young Gentleman of strict honor	No sufficient Evidence
Lance Montgomery County [must be Lane— mentioned before] [130]	*Nothing of politics* ⎫ powerful & respectable Connection property in lands Craick ⎬ western expedition as Ensign & promoted to Captain can raise men	deserves *attention*

125. Gabriel Christie, a member of the Maryland militia during the American Revolution, had served in the Maryland House of Delegates. He was a Republican member of the House of Representatives from 1793 to 1797 and from 1799 to 1801.

126. David Lucket represented Montgomery County in the Maryland House of Delegates in 1794.

127. Henry Carberry, a native of Maryland, had served as a captain in the American Revolution, and he was a captain in Major Henry Gaither's battalion in the levy of 1791. He was appointed a captain in the United States Army on March 14, 1792 (*Executive Journal*, I, 114, 116). He resigned his commission on February 10, 1794. He served as adjutant general of the Maryland militia from 1794 to 1807.

128. This is a reference to one of the following men: Richard Hall Harwood, a resident of Anne Arundel County, who was a member of the Maryland House of Delegates from 1798 to 1799; or Thomas Harwood, who was appointed commissioner of loans for Maryland on August 6, 1790 (*Executive Journal*, I, 57); or William Harwood, who was clerk of the Maryland Ratifying Convention of 1788 and of the Maryland House of Delegates in the seventeen-nineties.

129. Jonathan Sellman was a resident of Anne Arundel County, Maryland.

130. The material within brackets is in the handwriting of Stoddert.

William Nicholson Queens Anne County	*Hindman*—sensible spirited & active man fœderalist	deserves attention

LIEUTENANTS

Levi Ford	Philip Thomas—much merit & fœderalism	perhaps Ensign
Daniel C Heath Jun Kent County or Cecil respectable family *19 or 20*	cavalry Oldham Ramsay [131]—real acquisition to the army Milligan [132] spirit & honor fœderal	respectable!
Levi Alexander Baltimore County *27 years*	Ramsay—mentioned to him by respectable Gentleman as qualified for an Officer Winchester respectable Connections honor & integrity Oldham—neither has nor will be better appointm	*Respectable*
William Elliot Washington County 24 years son of *R Elliot* [134]	Williams [133] Cavalry foederal—sprightly active genteel—liberal education & abilities	*respectable*
Solomon Yerving Read ⎱ Amos Reed ⎰ Farley perhaps Kent County	*Most very honorable for* Lloyed recommends as qualified in general terms	perhaps Ensign
Thomas Dent Charles Cty	G *Dent* recommends him as Ensign	

131. Nathaniel Ramsay, a resident of Cecil County, was a member of the Maryland Convention of 1775, and he served as a lieutenant colonel in the American Revolution until he was captured at Monmouth. He was a member of the Continental Congress from 1786 to 1788. On September 24, 1789, he was appointed United States marshal for the District of Maryland and was reappointed on December 27, 1793 (*Executive Journal,* I, 29, 31, 143, 144). On December 10, 1794, he was appointed naval officer for Baltimore (*Executive Journal,* I, 165).

132. This is presumably a reference to either Robert or James Milligan of Cecil County, Maryland.

133. Elie Williams, a veteran of the American Revolution, was the brother of the late General Otho H. Williams, who had been collector of customs at Baltimore. Elie Williams was clerk of the Circuit Court for Washington County during the seventeen-nineties and was an Army contractor with Robert Elliot for the western posts. During the Whiskey Insurrection the firm of Elliot and Williams was agent for provisioning the militia army.

134. Robert Elliot was Elie Williams's partner. He was killed by the Indians in the Northwest Territory on October 6, 1794.

Samuel Casson	Wm. W Bond [135] his family respectable has behaved well in a store	perhaps Ensign
William Ashe Baltimore	*Drunkard* No recommendation a *Lawyer*	Wont do
Francis Dillet Eastern *Shore*	Recom by Hindman	
John Griffith Kent County	Horse or Navy Loyed Matthews highly recommended to him by respectable Men	
James Mathers Washington County 26 years	Res Inhabitants good moral character industry & integrity E Williams S	perhaps Ensign
Levi G Ford Cecil County	Matthews good family Oldham Manners & attached to the Government	respectably *as Ensign*
Thomas York Sprague	Enquire of the Auditor.[136]	
Samuel Davis Kent County studied law	*Matthews* genteel handsome *young man*—wavering in his politics but now seems decided S *Smith* Michael *Obrien* [137] by *no means man of property not much*	Qr. Ensign

SUBALTERNS

[Matthew Tighlman 21 years old	recommended by Genl: Lloyd — attached to the government—raised a Corps of Volunteers—perhaps Lieut. if not *Ensign*] [138]	
Lloyd Beall George Town *old officer Capt.*	Stoddert says he ought to be a Captain	
John Bush old officer		
J Gassaway old captain	Council of Maryland Fidelity & honor	Respectable
[no man of the name	DuVal who is an Antifœderal	

135. William W. Bond was a resident of Baltimore.
136. Richard Harrison.
137. This is a reference either to Michael O'Brian or to Michael O'Brine, both of whom were residents of Baltimore.
138. The material within brackets is in Stoddert's handwriting.

in Maryd. fit for a
Field officer.] [139]

J Henry

Philip Stewart
old Officer
Chas. County

Uriah Forest
property
fit for any command
Stoddert *confirms*

[Wishes to be
in the Pro-
visional
Army & fit
for a Regt.
a warm
Decided
Federalist &
active in
keeping
Jacobins in
order.] [140]

Thomas Beatty Jun
Frederick County
Capt in former War
[He ought to be a
young Capt.] [141]

asks for such Commission as his
former services *may justify*
Forest says he is brave & has
good Understandg
Stoddert—ought not to be
higher than Captain

James Hindman
John C Hall
John Bush
old Captain
Talbot County

recommended by his brother
formerly commanded Regt.

Drunkard

Joseph Foreman
Cecil County or
Kent
asks command of
a Regiment

Lloyed, a man of great honor &
courage & will make a *good
Officer*
Secretary says he is a man of
property & Intelligence—
‹–›

Respectable

LT COLONELS

[Josias] Carval Hall
William D. Beale
[David Hopkins

Hartford
Prince George
Ann Arundle

[Lt Colo.]
[1st Major]
2d Major]

MAJORS

10	John C Beatty	Alleghany
5	William Elliot	Washington
10	Alexander Cooper	Ensign
2	Thomas Beatty Jun	Frederick
9	Edward A Howard	Baltimore County
2	John Brangle	Frederick

139. The material within brackets is in Stoddert's handwriting.
140. The material within brackets is in Stoddert's handwriting.
141. The material within brackets is in Stoddert's handwriting.

1 Loyed Beall	Montgomery
4 Richard W West	Prince George
3 Enos Noland	Frederick
6 Gerard Briscoe	Charles County
3 John B Barnes	do.
4 Thomas Dent	do.
9 Rozin Davidge	Anne Arundel
2 Ninnean Pinckney	do
5 Levi Hillary	Frederick
7 Bradley Beans	Prince George
8 Levi Alexander	Baltimore
9 John Warren	
4 Isaac Spencer	Kent
7 Matthew Tilghman 5th	do.
8 Samuel Davis	do
8 William Nicholson	Queen Anne
1 [Henry C. Neale St. Mary's]	do.
1 William Swan	Talbot
5 Jacob Norris	Hartford
6 Daniel C Heath	Cecil
7 Levi G Ford	do
3 William S Dallam	Hartford
10 Aquila Beale	Montgomery
6 Daniel Hughes	Cecil

Candidates for Army Appointments from Tennessee [1]

[Philadelphia, November–December, 1798]

Tennessee

CAPTAINS

2 Arthur Crozier
Knoxville

good letter
Clayborne [2]—a young man of respectable character good talents & was a Merchant

3 Nathan B Markland
Knoxville

Clayborne. possesses qualifications for a *valuable Officer surveyor* young man of amiable Character & good talents

| 6 Charles Porter | Judge Anderson [3]—recommends him as well qualified respectable connexion & unexceptionable character | 1 |

10 William Loveley
Trenton
Capt last war

McKee [4] officer during late war proper
Beyers [5] to command a Company

12 John Evans
Knoxville

Sevier [6]—conduct fair & respectable valuable & brave officer

SUBALTERNS

1 Eli Hammond

Doct Williamson [7]—raised in the family of General Davidson [8]—passion for army & has shewn spunk in scouts against the Indians

3 Nathan B Markland
Knoxville

Clayborne will accept Lty or Ensy young—amiable good talents surveyor

4 Robert Yancey
Sullivan County
Inquire of McKee

C—— the same surveyor

5 William P Anderson
Nashville
Captain

C—— the same but lawyer was lately Atty of District
Judge Anderson well qualified for Lt good connection unexceptionable character   1

6 Hardman Stow

Judge Anderson well qualified for ensign good Con except Car   1

8 Thomas McCorry
Knoxville

Clayborne—deserving young man aimable will make a valuable officer Merchant with general confidence & esteem could recruit   2
Henly [9]—speaks well of his services to Commissioners

9 Lewis Tiner
Knoxville
Lt

John McNairy [10]—young man of cleverness
John Sevier—discreet well educated alert would make a brave & valuable Officer friend to G   1

ENSIGN

11 James Desha Mero District	J *Winchester* [11] of respectable family tolerable English ed- ucation pride & ambition to make a good Officer	Ensign
12 Edmond P Gains Knoxville Qr	G Sevier good family & con- nection friend to Govern- ment would make a useful & brave Officer	

AD, George Washington Papers, Library of Congress.

1. In this list of recommendations for Army appointments, those recommended have not been identified. Wherever possible, however, the individuals making the recommendations have been identified.

H, George Washington, and Charles Cotesworth Pinckney prepared this list, which is undated, during their meetings in Philadelphia.

2. From 1797 to 1801 William C. C. Claiborne was a Republican member of the House of Representatives from Tennessee.

3. In 1791 Joseph Anderson of Delaware became one of the United States judges of the Territory South of the River Ohio (*Executive Journal*, I, 77). In 1797 he was elected to the United States Senate from Tennessee to fill the vacancy caused by the expulsion of William Blount, and in 1798 he was elected to the Senate to fill the vacancy caused by the resignation of Andrew Jackson. He was reelected to the United States Senate from 1803 to 1815.

4. John McKee was an agent to the Cherokee Indians.

5. James Byers of Tellico, Tennessee.

6. John Sevier.

7. During the American Revolution, Hugh Williamson was the surgeon general of the North Carolina troops. He was a Federalist member of the House of Representatives from 1789 to 1793, when he moved to New York City.

8. William Lee Davidson, who held the rank of brigadier general of the North Carolina militia at the close of the American Revolution, had died in 1781.

9. Colonel David Henley was the War Department's agent for Indian affairs at Knoxville, Tennessee.

10. McNairy was the United States judge for the District of Tennessee.

11. Lieutenant Colonel James Winchester of the Sumner County militia was appointed a commissioner of valuations for Tennessee in July, 1798 (*Executive Journal*, I, 288, 289).

Candidates for Army Appointments
from Virginia [1]

[*Philadelphia, November–December, 1798*]. A list of the names of one hundred and sixty-eight men from Virginia who were candidates for Army appointments together with short biographical sketches and comments based on information supplied largely by Southerners.

1. This document has been calendared because Charles Cotesworth Pinckney wrote the major portion of it. H's contribution consists of minor additions to Pinckney's material and full entries for twenty-seven candidates based on information supplied by Edward Carrington and William Heth.

H, George Washington, and Pickney prepared this list, which is undated, during their meetings in Philadelphia.

To Elizabeth Hamilton

[Philadelphia, November, 1798]

I am vexed My Dear Betsey that the blunder of a servant prevented the inclosed [1] from going by the Post of yesterday. I am well aware how much in my absence your affectionate and anxious heart needs the consolation of frequently hearing from me; and there is no consolation which I am not very much disposed to administer to it. It deserves every thing from me. I am much more in debt to you than I can ever pay; but my future life will be more than ever devoted to your happiness. Adieu My Betsey   A H

Wednesday

Tell your Sister [2] that I was much mortified at having by accident opened a letter from her to Philip.[3] It happened by its being unexpectedly put under cover to me with others of my own by a Gentleman whom I had engaged to inquire every day at the Post Office for *my letters* and who had not been desired to take up any not mine. He with good intention took up two for Philip and taking it for granted all in the packet were mine I went on opening as a matter of course till the words "My Dear Philip" convinced me of my mistake. I hope this has not been the cause of her sending her subsequent letters under cover to General Noailles.[4]

ALS, Hamilton Papers, Library of Congress.
1. Letter not found.
2. Angelica Church.

3. Philip Church.

4. Louis Marie, Vicomte de Noailles, was a veteran of the American Revolution. After playing a prominent role in the National Assembly during the opening days of the French Revolution, he broke with the revolutionary groups and left France for England in 1792. He arrived in Philadelphia in 1793 and remained there until 1800.

To Jacob Read [1]

[Philadelphia, November, 1798]

I am mortified My Dear Sir that I cannot have the pleasure of dining with you today as I promised; but I am so extremely deranged in point of health that I am compelled to stay at home repose & muse.

Yrs. truly   A Hamilton

ALS, Columbia University Libraries.

1. Read, a South Carolina Federalist, was a member of the United States Senate from 1795 to 1801.

To Elizabeth Hamilton

[Philadelphia, December 2–3, 1798] [1]

I had hoped my very Dear Betsey that I should have had no occasion to write you again from this place—but our business unavoidably spins out the time beyond our calculation. It however now certainly draws to a close, and it is hardly possible that I should not be able to leave Philadelphia on Thursday. I ardently and anxiously wish to do it. Be assured of this, and exert your patience. Take care of your repose and health as the things in the world which interest me the most. Adieu My love   A H

Monday Decr. 2d

ALS, Hamilton Papers, Library of Congress.

1. H dated this letter "Monday Decr. 2," but in 1798 December 2 was a Sunday. For evidence that this letter should be dated 1798, see H to Elizabeth Hamilton, December 6, 1798.

To Elizabeth Hamilton

[Philadelphia, December 6, 1798]

I had strongly hoped My very Dear Betsey that our business would have ended this day & that tomorrow I should have begun my journey for New York [1] but to my infinite chagrin I am obliged to submit to a further delay. It does not appear that we can now count upon leaving this place before Monday Morning. Then we rely that there will be no remaining obstacle & I shall fly to your bosom. Forgive the frequent disappointment which has been inevitable & compose your dear heart with the expectation that such another absence is not likely to happen & that I shall return to you with a heart overflowing with affection.

Adieu My darling   A H

Thursday Decr. 6th

ALS, Hamilton Papers, Library of Congress.
  1. See H to Elizabeth Hamilton, December 2-3, 1798.

From Benjamin Goodhue

[Philadelphia] Saturday Evg Decr 8th. 98

Dear Sir

I have paid all the attention in my power the short time allowed me would admit on the subject of your letter,[1] as I was wholy unacquainted with almost the whole of the names handed me I found it necessary to call together in confidence Messrs Otis [2] Parker [3]

ALS, George Washington Papers, Library of Congress.
  1. Letter not found.
  2. Harrison Gray Otis.
  3. Isaac Parker, a Federalist and a lawyer in Castine, District of Maine, was a United States Representative from Massachusetts from 1797 to 1799. On March 5, 1799, he replaced John Hobby as United States marshal for the District of Maine (*Executive Journal*, I, 144, 258, 325, 327).

Sewal [4] and Dwight Foster.[5] The result of our consultation will be found in the list markd, in which

No 1   stands for good
   2   middling
   3   Bad
   M   would in our opinion accept of a Majority
   C   would do accept of a Captaincy
   S   for Subaltern
   E   for Ensign
   DK for dont know their character

We have made some additions from our own Knowledge; in confidence let me remark that some of us are of opinion that Hunewell [6] & *Walker* [7] have the preference of Gibbs [8] as Lieutenant Colonels and that Walker would accept a majority in case you take Elliot [9] for a Lieutenant Colonel in his room which We think would be a judicious arrangement, for Elliot tho I am not much acquainted with him I have heard him very highly spoken of by Messrs. Cabot [10] Ames [11] and a number of others of our best characters.

   I am with sincere esteem   Yr Affectionate Friend   B Goodhue

my Brethren seem very desirous to Know if Elias Parker [12] is on the list of Majors for Virginia as they esteem him a valuable Character.

Genl. Hamilton

4. Samuel Sewall was a Federalist member of the House of Representatives from Massachusetts from 1796 to 1800.
5. Foster was a Federalist member of the House of Representatives from Massachusetts from 1793 to 1800.
6. Richard Hunewell, a veteran of the American Revolution, was sheriff of Penobscot, District of Maine.
7. John Walker.
8. Caleb Gibbs.
9. Simon Elliot was a Boston merchant.
10. George Cabot, who had been a Boston merchant and a Federalist member of the United States Senate from 1791 to 1796, had retired to Brookline, Massachusetts, in 1798.
11. Fisher Ames.
12. See John Lowell, Jr., to H, December 19, 1795, note 2.

[ENCLOSURE] [13]

LIEUTENANT COLONELS

1	[1]	Caleb Gibbs	Boston
78	[1]	John Walker	Woburn
76	[1]	Richard *Honeywell*	Castine [should be, *Hunewell*]

MAJORS

4	[2]	Christopher Marshall		Boston
5	[1]	Isaac Winslow	[C]	Boston
12	[1]	William Sheppard Jun~ (son of General Shepherd) [14] [would not as his Father says accept a captaincy therefore out of the question]
39	[1]	John Rowe	[DK]	Boston
40	[1]	William Jones	[C]	Concord
47		James Brown	[DK]	[C]
55	[1]	John Lillie		Milton
17	[3]	George Ulmer		
79	[1]	Ephraim Emory	[C]	[Haverhill] will accept captaincy

LT & ADJUTANT COL

31	[3]	Jacob Welsh		Lunenberg
102	[3]	Ralph Bowles		
122	[1]	John Hobby		Portlandt
136		Benjamin Shaw	[DK]	Newbury Port
143	[1]	John Blake	[C]	[Orrington in Maine]

CAPTAINS

150	[1]	Stephen Peabody	[S]	Penobscot
26	[1]	John Burbeck		Boston
19	[3]	Samuel Treat		ditto
13	[3]	Ebenezer Kent		
16	[1]	[Samuel] Jordan		Biddeford
17	[1]	Phineas Ashmen	[S]	Blanford
21	[2]	John Pyncher		Salem
28	[1]	Eliaza Williams	[S]	Springfield
29	[2]	John Cooper		Boston
33	[1]	[Hall] *Tufts*	[S]	Medford
24	[1]	Nathaniel Thwing		Boston

13. AD, with insertions in the handwriting of Benjamin Goodhue, George Washington Papers, Library of Congress. The material in brackets in this document is in Goodhue's handwriting.

In this list, as well as in similar lists, of recommendations for Army appointments, those recommemnded have not been identified.

14. William Shepherd.

43	Samuel Greene	[DK S]	Boston	2
44	Levy Meade	[DK S]	Lexington	2
46	Jonas Bridge	[DK S]	ditto	2
48	John Radford	[DK S]	Woburn	1 - 2
56 [2]	Samuel Fowles	[S]	Watertown	1 - 2
60 [2]	Augustus Hunt	[S]	Boston Qr	1 - 2
93 [1]	David C D Forest		[of Sullivan in Maine S]	
101	John Tolman	[DK]	Needham	
104 [1]	Eramus Babbit Jun		[Sturbridge, in the County of] Worcester	
105	Ebenezer Thatcher	[DK]	Lancaster	
112 [1]	John Shepherd [an English- man naturalized ab 4 years]		Waldoboro	
114	William Henshaw	[DK]	New Bedford	
115 [1]	Robert *Duncan* Jun~	[S]		
116	James Cunningham	[DK]	Lunenberg	
120 [1]	William Williams [if a hat- ter]		Boston	
123 [1]	Isaac Rand Jun	[S]		
138 [1]	Thomas Bowman [(if of ye County of)] Lincoln [in Maine]			
139 [1]	Thomas *Chandler*		Worster	
140 [1]	Nathaniel *Balch*		Boston	
144	Eli Forbes	[DK]		
145 [1]	Thomas Philips		Castine	

SUBALTERNS

	9 [1]	James Church		*Springfield* [S]	
	14 [3]	Joseph H Dwight		Belcher Town	
	10 [1]	John Page Jun~	[E]	Salem	
	11 [1]	Charles Hunt	[E]	Watertown	
[E]	22	Jonathan Nichols	[DK]		
	30 [1]	John Wheelright		Boston	
	35	Seth Smith Junr	[DK]	Norton	2
	38	William Swan	[DK]		
[E]	40	Abijah Harrington	[DK]	Lexington	
	49 [1]	Caleb Aspinwall		Portland	
	54 [1]	William Leverett	[E]	Boston	
	57 [1]	William A Barron		Cambrige	
	72	Ward Eaton, *Haverill*	[DK]		
[E]	81	Daniel Hastings		New Town	
	83 [1]	Nathaniel Soley		Charlestown	
[E]	85	Moses M Bates		Springfield	
[*E*]	86	Thomas Durant	[DK]	New Town	
	58 [1]	James M Wheaton	[E]	Maine	
	90 [1]	Willard Tayles	[E]	Maine	
[E]	91	Jacob Ulmer	[DK]	Maine	
	92	James Austin	[DK]	Boston Qr	

[E]	95		Marshall Spring	[DK]	Weston
	96		Thomas Held	[DK]	Concord
[E]	99		Daniel Bell	[DK]	Boston Qr.
	100	[1]	Charles Cutler		do
[E]	103		Duncan Ingraham		
			Tertius	[DK]	Green Wale farm Poughkeepsie
	107		Rufus Childs	[DK]	Stockbrige
	108		Alpheus Cheny	[DK]	do
	134		Samuel P. Fay	[DK]	Concord
[E]	138		James Gardner	[DK]	Boston
	141	[3]	Thomas W Hooper		Neubury Port
	145	[1]	Nathaniel Kidder		Belfast
	146	[1]	Joseph Lee		Castine Qr
	146	[1]	Warren Hall	[E]	Castine Qr

[additions by B G and others

1   John Roulstone of Boston   E
1   Solomon Phelps of Westfield for Captain
1   William Heywood of Winslow in Maine for do.
1   Jacob Allen jn of Sturbridge in Worcester Cty. S
1   Simion Draper of Brookfield for Captain
1   Samuel Flagg jn of Worcester for a lieutency.]

From Rufus King

[London, December 8, 1798.[1] Letter not found.]

1. Letter listed in Rufus King's "Memorandum of Private Letters, &c., dates & persons, from 1796 to Augt 1802," owned by Mr. James G. King, New York City.

Candidates for Army Appointments
from Massachusetts [1]

[Philadelphia, December 9–28, 1798]

SUBALTERNS

9 James Church   Shepherd [2] ⎱ sprightly active—
  Springfield   S Lyman [3] ⎰   good stature
  24 years   good abilities &   Ensign
                                 character   1
                                        now Ensign of
                  Stubbins [4] ⎰ Militia
                  Capt   judgment & mili-
                                      tary kno
                                        respectable family
                  Sykes [5]—Col.

14 Joseph H Dwight   ⎱ General Mattoon [6]
    Belcher Town   recommends
                Shepherd ⎰ fully active
                Lyman   smart *young man*   Lt
                                    right age   1
                Sykes—has been Adjutant of
                   Milia & would do honor as
                   Captain

AD, George Washington Papers, Library of Congress.

1. This list was prepared at the December meetings of H, George Washington, and Charles Cotesworth Pinckney in Philadelphia. It was prepared after H received Benjamin Goodhue's letter of December 8, 1798, and before James McHenry submitted a list of officers to John Adams on December 29, 1798 (ADfS, James McHenry Papers, Library of Congress; LS, James McHenry Papers, Library of Congress).

In this list of recommendations for Army appointments, those recommended have not been identified. Wherever possible, however, the individuals making the recommendations have been identified.

The comments on this list should be compared with the comments on the list enclosed in Goodhue to H, December 8, 1798.

2. William Shepard.

3. Samuel Lyman.

4. Joseph Stebbins, a veteran of the American Revolution, was a resident of Springfield, Massachusetts.

5. Joseph Sykes was a resident of Belchertown, Massachusetts.

6. Ebenezer Mattoon, a resident of Amherst, Massachusetts, had been a major in the American Revolution. He was a Federalist member of the state Senate from 1795 to 1796, and in 1796 he was an Adams elector. From 1797 to 1816 he was a major general of the fourth district of the state militia.

10 John Page Junr *Salem* 24 years	Goodhue [7]—Young man of good character	*Lt* 1
	respectable family well qualified—	
Abbott [8] Cushing [9]	son of respect- able father thinks his abili-	
Inquire McPherson	ties & principles qualify him	
	Pearson [10] engaging manners Thatcher [11]—J Tredwell [12]— spirited has been on the wrong side but now appears has good zeal	

ENSIGN

11 Charles Hunt *Watertown* 19 years	Wm. Hunt [13] G Hull [14]— possesses the requisites of an officer education & habits favourable	*Ensign* 1
18 John Rudberg Portland Mayne 50 years	Fosdyck [15]—fair reputation & acquainted with duties of soldier P Wadsworth [16]—no doubt of his entire ability for Lt—has	*wont do*

7. Benjamin Goodhue.

8. Benjamin Abbot became headmaster of Phillips Exeter Academy in 1788, and he held that position for fifty years.

9. William Cushing was an associate justice of the Supreme Court of the United States.

10. Eliphalet Pearson was professor of Hebrew and Oriental languages at Harvard University.

11. George Thatcher of Biddeford, Maine, was a Federalist member of the House of Representatives from 1789 to 1801.

12. John Treadwell represented Ipswich in the Massachusetts General Court in 1785. In 1786 he moved to Salem and became a flour merchant. He was justice of the peace in Essex County from 1786 to 1799 and a Federalist member of the Massachusetts House of Representatives from 1790 to 1799.

13. Hunt was a resident of Salem, Massachusetts.

14. General William Hull, a veteran of the American Revolution, was a Republican and a lawyer in Newtown, Massachusetts, and a supporter of Thomas Jefferson.

15. Nathaniel Fosdick was collector of customs for Portland and Falmouth, District of Maine.

16. Peleg Wadsworth, a brigadier general of the Massachusetts militia at the close of the American Revolution, moved to Falmouth, District of Maine, after the war. From 1793 to 1807 he was a Federalist member of the House of Representatives.

been in German & British service   Musician

22 Jonathan Nichols native of Boston has resided lately at Newark	Boudinot [17] Cummings [18]	manly good conduct will do honor to the appt. good char- acter warmly attached & otherwise well qualified	1 - 2
30 John Wheel- wright Boston 28 years Honorable	*Knox* [19] *active* & *robust* Elliot [20]—Merchant good Cadet J C Jones [21] fair reputation H Jackson [22] good abilities & connections		1
35 Seth Smith Jun *Norton* (*40*) *yrs* asks for Majority	Lt of Artillery Leonard [23]—senator—has been Capt Lt of Artillery activity & good character		
38 William Swan 22 years	Knox health activity industry & integrity information Lincoln [24]—every thing we want information acquisition to service Young Gentleman		Lieut No 1
45 Abijah Harring- ton Lexington	*Brooks* [25] would make an ex- cellent officer writes badly		2
49 Caleb Aspinwall Rutland 34 years	P. Wadsworth—Lt. of Artillery now has been in that Corps from 20 years old likely spirited & noble person and		

17. Elisha Boudinot.
18. John N. Cummings.
19. Henry Knox, former Secretary of War.
20. Simon Elliot.
21. John C. Jones, a Boston merchant.
22. Henry Jackson of Boston held the rank of colonel at the close of the American Revolution. From 1792 to 1796 he was a major general of the Massachusetts militia.
23. George Leonard of Norton, Massachusetts, was a Federalist member of the House of Representatives from 1789 to 1791 and again from 1795 to 1797.
24. Benjamin Lincoln, who held the rank of major general at the close of the American Revolution, was collector of customs for the ports of Boston and Charlestown from 1789 to 1809.
25. In 1798 Eleazer Brooks became commissioner of valuations for the fifth division of Massachusetts (*Executive Journal*, I, 287-89).

	ability all the essentials of good subaltern	
54 William Leveritt Boston 25	*Otis* [26] Lieutenancy of Artillery would in his opinion do credit to the appointment	1 - 2
63 John G Shindle	Letter a little bombastic has studied a military life &c	
67 William A Barron Cambrige	B Waterhouse [27] recommends him strongly Mathematical & Philos know	1 INQUIRE
72 Ward Eaton Haveril	Peabody [28]—son of a respectable man who was an Officer in the army—clever young man & worthy of a Lieutenancy	Inquire
31 Daniel Hastings New Town 24 years	G Hull—strong general turn good family has had a good private education good personal & constitution	1
83 Nathaniel Soley Charlestown	G Hull Young Gent of *Talents* & *merit* well fitted for subaltern D Jackson [29]—recommends him for Captaincy Brooks—from information is satisfied he will sustain a Con with hon	1
84 Shepherd Pittston	Hallowel [30] *integrity & honor* fit naturalized Englishman	
85 Moses M Bates Springfield 22 years	Ensign *in Marines*	
	S Lyman— *D Foster* S { good education & sprightly honest & honorable & capacity competent for	1

26. Harrison Gray Otis.

27. Benjamin Waterhouse was a Boston physician.

28. Nathaniel Peabody, a physician and veteran of the American Revolution, was born in Essex County, Massachusetts. He moved to New Hampshire, where he served in the state Assembly and Senate. From 1779 to 1780 he was a delegate to the Continental Congress, and from 1793 to 1798 he was a major general of the state militia.

29. Daniel Jackson, a veteran of the American Revolution, was appointed a major in the Corps of Artillerists and Engineers on June 1, 1798 (*Executive Journal*, I, 277, 279).

30. Robert Hallowell was one of the proprietors of the Kennebec Purchase in the District of Maine.

86 Thomas Durant New town 22 years	G Hull—officer of Militia faith- ful intelligent will make a valuable officer, suitable age Brooks confirms but thinks his age most suitable to Ensign	Ensign 1 perhaps Lt
88 James D Wheaton Maine	*Knox* recommends for Lt	1
89 Willard Tales Maine	Knox Ensign	1
90 David Tales Maine	Knox Ensign	1
91 Jacob Ulmer Maine	Knox ⎫ Lt ⎭ Lt or Ensign	1
92 James Austin Boston Qr	Clarke [31] ⎫ sobriety morals & Winslow [32] ⎬ good Charac- ⎭ ter fit for Lt.	
95 Marshall Spring Weston 22 years	*Selectmen* good character rep- utable family & well esteemed would prove active & faithful Knox—from every appearance would make an *excell* Lt	1 - 2
96 Thomas Heald Concord	Wm. Jones [33] to G Brook who is silent	integrity & possesses qualifications of Officer & Gentleman liberal educa- tion & well looking
97 Jeremiah Hill Boston	his own letter was Lt. in the last War such Commission as he may merit	
99 Daniel Bell Boston	Bells letter to *Knox* who is silent	

31. Jonas Clark became collector of customs of the District of Kennebunk in 1800.

32. In 1798 Samuel Winslow was appointed surveyor and inspector of the revenue for the port of Thomaston, District of Maine.

33. William Jones was a Concord, Massachusetts, lawyer.

writes good hand

	ingenious
Thomas Dawes [34]	drafts-man &
J Pierce [35]	other-wise suitable

Greenleaf Grandfather [36]

100 Charles Cutler   his letter well
    Boston

| Simon Elliot & others | virtues talents & patriotism education &c would do honor | 1 |

103 Duncan Ingraham   Letter to G Knox who is silent
    Tertius   *Judge Dawes*—his wifes relative
    Green Vale farm   thinks him remarkably ami-
    Poughkeepsie   able & accomplished qualified   *Inquire*
    25 years   as Secretary
    his letter good   transmitted by G Knox without
                        supporting it

107 Rufus Childs   N Rice [37]   education *pretty*
    Stirbridge   *good* & he thinks a clever   1 - 2
                        man asks Captaincy but he
                        supposes would accept Lieu

108 Alpheus Cheny   Rice—has had a College educa-
    ditto   tion & would make a good
                        Lieut   1

109   Lathrop   Rice   son of Col Lathrop [38]   perhaps
    Cohasset   tolerable education & decent   Ensign
                        young man

110 John Pratt   *Rice*
    Cohasset

117   Fay   *Wm. Latham* [39] just taken his
                        degree at College

34. In July, 1798, Dawes was appointed commissioner of valuations for the fourth division of Massachusetts. He had been a Federalist member of the Electoral College in 1796. From 1792 to 1803 he was a justice of the Massachusetts Supreme Court.

35. Joseph Peirce of Boston, who had been a regimental quartermaster during the American Revolution, was a business agent of Henry Knox.

36. Bell was the son of Mary Greenleaf and Daniel Bell. His grandfather, James Greenleaf, had been a partner with James Watson of the former New York City firm of Watson and Greenleaf and a United States consul at Amsterdam. Greenleaf engaged in extensive land and securities speculations.

37. Nathan Rice was a veteran of the American Revolution.

38. Thomas Lathrop represented Cohasset in the Massachusetts General Court.

39. Latham was a resident of Essex County.

118 Ambrose Keith
    Warren

    William Higgins   Otis retracts his Recommenda-
                        tion

    Franklin Tinkham   O Wood [40] recommends
    Wiscasset   Knox barely transmits

134 Samuel P Fay   ⎫ healthy active
    Concord   │ industrious
    21½ years old   │ enterprising
                        Knox   │ good morals   I
                        Jackson   ⎬ character
                        Elliot   │ *education*
                        Pres Willar [41] │ talents
                                      │ genius &
                                      │ good
                                      ⎭ acquirements

138 James Gardner   his own letter well enoug   I
    Boston   Knox   ⎫ good character &
    26 years   Jackson ⎬ probably abilities
                        Elliot ⎭ for Lt

141 Thomas W   Jackson *Supervisor* [42] Col-
        Hooper   lege education   studied law
        Newbury Port   but went into trade—unfor-
                        tunate in Trade & marriage
                        Aide De Camp to Titcomb [43]
                        for several *years*

145 Nathaniel Kidder   Lieutenant
    Belfast   Honeywell [44] good militia Of-
                        ficer   perhaps personal   2
                        knowlege sufficient

146 Joseph Lee   Honeywell—now Lt & Adju-
    Custine perhaps   tant a young man of good
                        talents active Officer great   I
                        military genius

146 Warren Hall   Honeywell he will make a   2
    Custine perhaps   good officer

40. General Abiel Wood was a resident of Wiscasset, District of Maine.
41. Joseph Willard was president of Harvard University.
42. Jonathan Jackson of Newburyport was appointed marshal for the District
of Maine in 1789 and inspector of the revenue for Survey No. 2 in Massachusetts in March, 1792 (*Executive Journal*, I, 29, 30, 102, 111). George Washington nominated him in February, 1795, to succeed Oliver Wolcott, Jr., as
comptroller of the Treasury, but Jackson declined the appointment. In December, 1796, Jackson became supervisor of the revenue for the District of Massachusetts (*Executive Journal*, I, 173, 174, 216, 217).
43. Jonathan Titcomb was naval officer for Newburyport, Massachusetts.
44. Richard Hunewell.

CAPT

2 Benjamin Larkin now Lt in Boston Artillery
recommends himself—*badly*

26 John Burbeck Knox—ought to be Capt of Ar-
64 Boston tillery & employed in an elab-
oratory excellent Officer

19 Samuel Treat *Knox*—would be a valuable Capt
66 *Boston* of Artillery—but would ac- I -
44 - 50 cept a Capt of Infantry—in
which the public would find
its account

7 John Spooner   now Adjutant of
New Bedfork   Militia active & of
28 years E Pope military turn
    Coll [45] *integrity* firmness &
      ability

    Parson Letter will accept a I - 2
    West [46] Captaincy & raise
      a Company
     refers to L L Morris
    Naval Contractor great natu-
    ral abilities

13 Ebenezer Kent Knox—services last war, conduct since & standing in so-
ciety qualify him for a Company   I -
Jackson—served in his regiment
with first Reputation as a
Gentleman & soldier

16 Samuel Jordan Thatcher (now Major of
Biddeford Militia) well qualified as of- I - 2
Maine ficer—good stature & military
turn

17 Phineas Ashmem Writes a good hand—well
Blandford enough worded—now Aide I - 2
De Camp to Major General
Sedgwick [47] Worthy man &
well qualified to command a
Company

45. Edward Pope was collector of customs for New Bedford, Massachusetts.
46. Samuel West, who preached the Arminian doctrine, was a minister in
New Bedford and Fair Haven, Massachusetts.
47. Theodore Sedgwick.

21 John Pynchon Salem		fine natural talents & good educa- tion—	Capt or Lt
	Goodhue Sewall [48] Bartley [49]	was *Ensign* in the army 86 has been Adjutant of Militia lately unfortunate in business	1

23 John Roulstone
Boston

his own letter indifferent

Bradley [50] now Capt of
Lt Col Mil Militia & fit—
Major—confirm

2 - 3

Knox—Jackson Lincoln—as far
as they know faithful Officer
& friend to his Country
Otis   enterprise industry &
good moral C

25 Samuel Mackay
Williams town
was British Offi-
cer 33 years
has served from
Ensign to *Aide*

*Sedgwick, now in a literary sit-
uation*—sincerely *believes him
worthy*

28 Eleazar Williams
Springfield
24 years

S Lyman proper for Captain
to recruit & guard the stores
elegant figure & manners integrity capable & worthy

1 - 2

29 John Cooper
Boston
Lt last war of
Artillery
77 to 82

says his circumstances are
same—
unsteady

S Higginson [51] good & faith-
W Parsons [52] ful citizen
industrious in-
tegrity &
fidelity

1 - 2

Knox—activity & good constitution

31 Jacob Welsh
Lunenbergh

some experience in foot & Artillery

37 years
Wooster

Knox—member of Legislature
4 years officer of Artillery

48. Samuel Sewall.
49. Bailey Bartlett of Essex County was a Federalist member of the House of Representatives from Massachusetts from 1797 to 1801.
50. David Bradley was a veteran of the American Revolution.
51. Stephen Higginson, a Boston merchant, was a Federalist and a frequent correspondent of H.
52. William Parsons was a Boston merchant.

	would now accept company which he could command with reputa	I - 2
	Knox & Brooks well educated & sensible clever man Major P	
32 Thomas Seward Capt last war	Knox—advanced in years & corpulent Garrison Capt few better Officers	
33 Hall Tufts Medford	*Brooks* fine liberal education & personal qualities well qualified for captain—such characters an acquisition	I—
34 Nathanial Thwing Boston	was Lt. in army & Lt of Marines— good letter— Knox—would be an acquisition as Capt	I
	Divers good accountant	
35 Seth Smith Junr Norton	See 35 Subaltern	I - 2
36 John Meacham	Divers Lt & Adjutant last war now in prime of life with good constitution good character	wont do
	Hull—in his Regt. & discharged the duty well—was dismissed by Court Martial	
40 William Jones Concord	cavalry see Field Officers	I
42 John W Greaton Scituate	speaks of his former service & asks Lty in the Navy	turned over to Navy
43 Samuel Greene Boston *Qr* between 30 & 40 years writes a good hand & good letter	second Lieutenant & Adjutant of Militia	I - 2
	Landon good man friend to his country—will support the character	
	Knox	
44 Levy Meade Lexington	*Brooks* no doubt he will do honor to his Commission writes indifferent hand	2
46 Jonas Bridge Lexington	do	2
48 John Radford *Woburn*	*Walker* [53] B G will acquit himself well	

53. Benjamin Walker.

now Major of Militia *writes ill*	Brooks Knox S R	from the soldierly manner of his con- duct as officer of Militia has confi- dence he will comd well a company	1 - 2

50 William Gordon
New Bedford
Does not appear
on the list

comp of Artillery
was Capt of Artillery last War
has always sus-
tained the   Questionable
character of
a good
Parson West   Officer
Collector Pope   proprietor
of a good
landed
estate

53 John F Jennison
Brookfield
29 years

Dwight Forster *prefers his
wishes*
Brother [54]—college education
served in Shays insurrection
unfortunate merchant
D Jackson good figure &
strong mind
Knox transmits without
remark

56 Samuel Fowles
Watertown

now Capt of Cavalry
Gill Lt Gov [55] respectable
family & character
M military knowlege & skill   1 - 2
applies for Capt of Cavalry

58 David Hobbs

Letter from himself

59 John Whitney

Letters not his own
now Store Keeper seven years   Nothing
last War five now
Gates [56]—gave him leave of
Absence

60 Augustus Hunt
Boston Qr
good letter
Lt of Militia

General Elliot [57]—favourable in
general terms
Ben diligent officer good dis-   1 - 2
ciplinarian
served as private of Cadets

54. William Jennison, a veteran of the American Revolution, was a resident
of Brookfield, Massachusetts.
55. Moses Gill was the lieutenant governor of Massachusetts.
56. Major General Horatio Gates.
57. Samuel Elliot, a Boston merchant, was a general in the militia.

74 Ebenezer Davis   said to be recom by P. Wads-
                     worth

93 David C D Forest   ⎤ *Mills* [58]
   unfortunate in   ⎟   *born Strat-*
   business   ⎟   *ford*
                     Boyd [59]   ⎬   irreproach-
                     Amasa Davis [60]   ⎟   man of
                                           ⎟   good
                                           ⎟   character
                                           ⎦
                     Hull supports Mills character

   John Hancock D   D C D Forest
       Forest   his own letter very well
   23 years   Knox transmits most qualified
                        for Lieutenancy

101 John Tolman   *Selectmen* qualified as to abil-
    Needham   ities activity & singular good
    Lt last war &   conduct last War—zealous
    wounded in the   friend to Govermt
    service   G. Adjutant unimpeached
    43 years   character vigorous & activity
    not found on   has known him several weeks
    army list   F Ames [61] bravery at Lexing-
                        ton where wounded appears
                        well informed good principles
                      Knox recommends for a Com-
                        pany

104 Erasmus Babbit   *D: Foster* lawyer educated at
    Sturbrige   Cambrige esteemed &
    Wooster   respected
                      Eaton [62] recommends him for
                        batalion
                      Rice—of good person manners
                        education good Captain

105 Ebenezer   N Rice—liberal education stud-
       Thatcher   ied law good character quali-
    Lancaster   fied will perhaps accept
                       Lieutenancy

112 John Shepherd   S Wilde [63]—amiable & unblem-

58. Elisha Mills, of Stratford, Connecticut, was appointed a justice of the
peace for Fairfield County in 1797, 1798, and 1799.
59. Colonel John P. Boyd was a resident of Boston.
60. Davis was a Boston merchant.
61. Fisher Ames.
62. Benjamin Eaton, a veteran of the American Revolution, was a custom-
house officer in Boston.
63. Samuel Wilde was a Maine lawyer. In 1794 he moved from Waldo-
boro to Warren, District of Maine.

Waldoboro perhaps	ished confidence & esteem of his acquaintance *Dan Davis* [64]—personal & mental acquaintance intitle him to first attention *Knox* only transmits	1 - 2
114 William Henshaw *N Bedford* *Lt last war* 33 years	Claghorne [65] now commands volunteer Artillery Company Puddleford [66] did his duty well *attached* to Government Knox transmits without observation	Attention
115 Robert Duncan Jun~	Knox Jackson Elliot D sergeant [67] — good politics morals & qualified for Capt of Infantry	1
116 James Cunningham *Lunenburgh* 28	now commands volunteer Company *his own* letter good Knox transmits without remark	Attention
119 Edward Hogan		
120 William Williams *Boston*	H Jackson Knox Brooks Elliot — now Capt of Militia recommended pretty strongly for Capt	1
123 Isaac Rand Junr.	J C Jones W. Parsons — Abilities fortitude health & strength	1
125 Osgood Carleton *Boston* *Lt last war*	Knox—If he does not possess every requisite possesses as many as likely to accou morals good Boston M Society— Divers Dawes Otis &c	respectable for Mathematics teacher
[Franklin] [68] 128 Seth Tinckham	Obiel Wood political senti-	

64. Daniel Davis was a lawyer in Portland, District of Maine.
65. Colonel George Claghorn was a resident of New Bedford, Massachusetts.
66. Seth Paddleford was a Taunton, Massachusetts, lawyer.
67. Daniel Sargent was a Boston merchant.
68. The name in brackets is in the handwriting of Tobias Lear. Lear was correcting H who incorrectly listed Franklin Tinkham as "Seth Tinckham."

Wiscasset   ments good, believes will
                     make good officer can raise
                     men
                     G Knox   barely transmits

133 Thomas Bowman   W Howard [69]   ⎤ no place   If recom-
    Lincoln   ⎥   mentions   mends good
                                    ⎥   *Letter to*   No. 1
                                    ⎥   President*   for Capt or Lt.
                    R Hallowell   ⎥   mental
                                    ⎥   qualifica-
                                    ⎬   tions
                    John Sheppard [70] firm friend
                                    ⎥   to the
                                    ⎥   Govern-
                                    ⎥   ment
                    James Bridge [71] moral
                                    ⎦   character
                    President says excellent fœder-
                    alist father & son

139 Thomas Chandler   ⎤ Gentleman of
    Worcester   A Bancroft [72] ⎥   good connec-
                     Caldwell [73]   ⎥   tions & educa-   1
                     N Paine [74]   ⎬   tion *fortune*
                     D: *Foster*   ⎥ —military
                     PRESIDENT S   ⎥   turn   now
                                    ⎦   com

140 Nathaniel Balch writes *good letter*
    Jun   from knowlege of his
    Boston   Knox   ⎤   general character
                    Jackson ⎬   recomd him as
                    Eliot   ⎦   eligible to comd   1
                                     of a Company
                    Bradford [75]

---

69. William Howard of Hallowell, Lincoln County, District of Maine, was a millowner and a lumber dealer.

70. Shephard was a resident of Lincoln County, District of Maine.

71. Bridge, a graduate of Harvard, was a lawyer in Hallowell, District of Maine.

72. Aaron Bancroft, a graduate of Harvard College, served as a missionary in Nova Scotia in the early seventeen-eighties. In 1786 he was appointed pastor of the Second Congregational Church in Worcester, Massachusetts.

73. William Caldwell of Worcester County was a paymaster during the American Revolution. From 1793 to 1805 he was sheriff of Rutland, Massachusetts.

74. Nathaniel Paine became a probate judge in Worcester County in 1801.

75. In December, 1796, Samuel Bradford, a resident of Boston and a veteran of the American Revolution, became United States marshal for the District of Massachusetts.

Otis—good moral character &
do credit to service

141	Thomas W Hooper Newbury Port	Jackson Supervisor } See Lt.	1 *Inquire*
142	Samuel Henly	Capt last war conductor of Military stores since	Inquire
144	Eli Forbes	*Honeywell,* now Brigade Major fit for command of Company information & abilities now Register of Deeds	1
145	Thomas Philips Custine	Honeywell hes perfect Brigade Major & a good Officer	1

FIELD OFFICERS

	Caleb Gibbs *Boston* *Major last War*	Lincoln Knox Brooks Jackson } Lt Col certify him qualified	1
3	John Frances N Beverly	{ *Dane* [76] respectable field officer perhaps Lt Col believes he would not serve lower than Major served last War— has commanded with reputation a Militia Regt.	
4	Christopher Marshall Boston	{ Major by brevet at the end of the war— good constitution	
		Lincoln Knox N Gilman [77] H Jackson } served with reputation & his services would now be valuable as Major	1 - 2

76. Nathan Dane, a lawyer in Beverly, Massachusetts, served in the Massachusetts Assembly from 1782 to 1785. He was a delegate to the Continental Congress from 1785 to 1788, and he was elected to the state Senate in 1790 and again from 1793 to 1798.

77. Nicholas Gilman of Exeter, New Hampshire, was an assistant adjutant general during the American Revolution. He was a delegate to the Continental Congress from 1786 to 1788 and a Federalist member of the House of Representatives from 1789 to 1797.

5 Isaac Winslow
  Boston
  30 years

Major or Capt of Cavalry
Knox Aide De Camp to General Elliot [78] man of *honor* & from general character qualified   mentioned no name with more confidence than this

1

6 William Perkins
  Boston
  yet capable of
     efficient duty

Major of Artillery last war
Lincoln— good service for 23 years
Knox   some expedient before mentioned   would be desireable to employ—*brave* Capt of Artillery with brevet of Lt Col & address of 35

12 William Shep-
      herd Jun
    now of *NY*

General Shep [79] honest capable faithful man   was an Ensign & Ad last war   declines less than Majority
Knox & Brooks—select him as Major   now Cap of Militia

P

26 Arthur Lithgow
    Winslow Maine
    30 years
    Otis says he is
       Anti-foederal

North [80]—respectability of family standing & character

Davis generally well
Nothing from General Knox

37 Fitch Hall
    Boston

Brooks ⎫ served in insurrection
Knox ⎬ preeminently fit for
        ⎭   comd of Regiment
declined

No. 1
Major

39 John Rowe
    Boston
    perhaps
    39 years

          Ensign in the army
Brooks ⎫ intelligence bravery
Jackson ⎬ & fidelity *fit* him
Knox ⎭ for Majority   pref-
          erable for Major

Knox   ⎫ believe he would
Lincoln ⎬ make an *excellent*
          ⎭   *Major*

1 ☞

40 William Jones
    Concord

    preferable as
       Major

Brooks young Gentleman willing to serve in Cavalry
Knox —Lawyer with handsome prospect now commands a troop— qualified for Majority

1 for
Captaincy

78. Samuel Elliot.
79. William Shepard.
80. William North.

	but will accept captaincy	
47 James Brown	*Brooks* commanded an excellent company of Artillery—talents really military good *Major* Lincoln confirms Knox Brooks opinion always of high estimation	1 - 2
55 John Lillie Milton	applicant for command of a Corps of Marines GW[81] Cert was Capt of Artillery conducted himself with *diligence bravery* & *intelligence* Knox knowlege of Gunnery & Mathematics & fortification	
5		
77 George Ulmer Richar 40 years	Major P Knox & ⎱ able energetic character Brooks ⎰ ter would do honor to appointm	
78 John Walker Woburn 35 years	Lt Colonel 28th of August Knox & ⎱ strongly for provisional Brooks ⎰	
79 Ephrain Emory [Haverhill] [82] Capt of Militia & Brigade Major Jacob Welsh	recom for *Major* Lt & Knox ⎱ adjutant last war & Brooks ⎰ now considered as a *valuable acquisition* Lovejoy [83]—activity alertness Knox & ⎱ See Capt 31 B—— ⎰	1 will accept a captaincy
57 Samson Wood Groton	*T Bigeloe* farmer in tolerable circumstances pretensions well founded in the army all last war—brave spirited punctual has been Major of Militia T Williams [84] transmits as if he *doubted*	Weak
76 Richard Honeywell	Knox ⎱ strong for Lt. Col in Brooks ⎰ *provisional army*	

81. George Washington.
82. The word in brackets is not in H's handwriting.
83. Obadiah Lovejoy was a veteran of the American Revolution.
84. Timothy Williams, a resident of Boston, was a nephew of Timothy Pickering.

94	Jeremiah Clapp Woburn now Major of Mil & Brigade Inspector	Loaman Baldwin [85] Walker [86] }	friend to government military genius	Not strong
102	Ralph Bowles	G Knox an old Officer *desires* employment *probably* a majority		
122	John Hobby Portland Capt last War	desirous of employment on the staff—fears his own health		
136	Benjamin Shaw Newbury Port	Majority Aide De Camp to G Patterson [87] late War Divers—Major Generals & others recommend him as a good officer will perhaps accept a Captaincy		*Attention*
143	John Blake not found on army list	R: Honeywell Majority military genius good disciplinarian & old Con Officer		I
150	Stephen Peabody Penobscot	*P. Wadsworth* good education fine person manners		Major perhaps Captain

25

LT COLS.

Simon Elliot
Caleb Gibbs

MAJORS

		John Walker	E
		Isaac Winslow	E
		John Hobby	Capt last War
		John Rowe	Ensign last War
40	I	William *Jones*	Concord	
47	3	James *Brown*	Lexington	I-2
79	3	Ephram *Emory*	Haverhill	
143		John Blake	Orrington *Maine*	
26	5	John Burbeck s	Boston Ela	
16		Samuel Jordan	Bideford do	
34	4	Nathaniel *Thwing Lt*	Boston	
101		John Tolman	Needham	I-2

85. Loammi Baldwin, a resident of Woburn, Massachusetts, was a veteran of the American Revolution.

86. Benjamin Walker.

87. John Paterson was brevetted a major general at the close of the American Revolution.

104		Erasmus *Babbe*	Sturbridge Worcester
105		Ebenezer Thatcher	Lancaster will perhaps
			accept Lty
		William Heywood	Winslow M
		Solomon Phelps	Westfield
133		Thomas Bowman	Lincoln Maine
139		Thomas *Chandler*	Worcester
140		Nathaniel Blach	Boston
144		Eli Forbes	[Custine] [88]
145		Thomas Phelps	Custine *M*
33	S1	Hall Tufts	Medford
21	2	John Pynchon	Salem
		Simeon Draper	Brookfield

LIEUTENANTS

150	Stephen Peabody	Penobscot M
17	Phineas Ashmem	Blanford
28	Eleazar Williams	Springfield
S 9	[James Church	Springfield] [89]
30	[John Wheelwright	Boston]
49	[Caleb Aspinwall	Portland] M
67	[Wm. A. Barron	Cambridge]
83	[Nathaniel Soley	Charlestown]
100	[Charles Cutler	Boston]
145	Nathaniel Kidder	Belfast M
146	[Joseph Lee	Castine] M.
	Jacob Allen	Sturbridge Worcester
	Samuel Flagg Junr	ditto
	Robert DUNCAN Junr	Boston Qr
	John *Shepherd*	Waldoboro *M*
38	William Swan	
	Isaac *Rand* Junr.	[Cambridge]
108	Alpheus Cheny	Stockbrige
134	Samuel P. Fay	Concord
88	James A Weaton	Maine

[ENSIGNS]

10	[John Page Junr.	Salem]
11	[Charles Hunt	Watertown]
54	[Willm. Leverett	Boston]
90	[Willard Tayles	Maine]
146	[Warren Hall	Castine] M
	John Roulstone	Boston
22	Jonathan Nichols	Boston

88. The word in brackets is in the handwriting of Charles Cotesworth Pinckney.

89. With the exception of the last two names within brackets all the remaining material in this document within brackets is in the handwriting of Tobias Lear. The last two entries are in the handwriting of Charles Cotesworth Pinckney.

40	Abijah Harrington	Lexington
81	Daniel Hastings	New town
85	Moses M Bates	Spring field
86	Thomas *Durant*	New town
91	Jacob Ulmer	Maine
95	Marshall Spring	Weston
99	Daniel Bell	Boston
103	Duncan Ingrahan Tertius	Pougkeepsie
		Boston Qr
138	James Gardner	Boston
96	Thomas Heald	Concord
90	David Tales	Maine
109	[Lathrop	Cohasset]
	[Franklin Tinkham	Maine Wiscasset]

From Louis Le Bègue Du Portail

Sweed's ford [Pennsylvania] dec 9th 1798

Je vous envoye mon cher general, le projet que vous m'avéz demandé.[1] Je souhaite qu'il remplisse vos vües. Vous trouveréz par-cy par-la quelques negligences de Stile qui exigeroient que je le recopiâsse pour les faire disparoitre. Mais je n'ay jamais eu de patience pour copier, et d'un autre coté je ne veux pas vous envoyer une piece trop pleine de ratures. Au reste si vous avéz besoin de la Com⟨mu⟩niquer à quelques personnes, ⟨alors⟩ je ⟨serai⟩ obligé de la faire traduire. Ainsi cette ⟨collection⟩ de fautes disparoitra dans la traduction à moins que le traducteur se piquant d'une trop grande fidelité ne les y porte egalement. Ce que j'espere qu'il ne fera pas et je prends la liberté de vous recommander le revision.

Je ne compte pas aller à philadelphie avant 12 ou 15 jours, mais alors jy pass⟨erai⟩ quelques semaines, si vous avéz quelque ⟨chose⟩ a me faire scavoir ou me demander, vous ⟨voules⟩ bien vous servir de la voye Convenue. Adieu.

santé et prosperité   D P

ALS, Hamilton Papers, Library of Congress.
    1. The enclosure has not been found, but see H to Du Portail, July 23, 1798.

To Elizabeth Hamilton

Philadelphia [December 10, 1798] [1]
Monday

I expected with certainty my beloved Betsey to have left this
place to day. Our business has consumed more time than was necessary. But that is not my fault. I cannot make every body else as rapid
as myself. This you know by experience. Tis a consolation however
that we *cannot* be detained much longer. It is difficult for Sloth itself to spin it out beyond this day & I shall fly to you the moment I
can.

Adieu My Angel   AH

ALS, from the original in the New York State Library, Albany.
1. This letter has been assigned the date of December 10, 1798, because
December 10, 1798, was a Monday and the letter is postmarked December 11.
In the first sentence, H is referring to his letter to Elizabeth Hamilton of
December 6, 1798.

From Peter Goelet and Robert Morris [1]

[New York, December 12, 1798]

Sir

The trustees of the Creditors of Peter Hasenclever & Co. are met
and intend to proceed in & finish this business as soon as possible.
You will please to take notice accordingly as far as you are concerned. [2]

With respect we are Sir   your humble Servts.   Peter Goelet
                                                        Robt Morris

New York Decr. 12th 1798

Mr. Hamilton

Copy, Miscellaneous Chancery Papers, American Iron Company, Clerk of the
Court of Appeals, Albany, on deposit at Queens College, New York City.

1. For an explanation of the contents of this letter, see the introductory note to Philip Schuyler to H, August 31, 1795. See also H to Phineas Bond, September 1, 1795; H to Morris, September 1, 1795; H to Barent Bleecker, March 20, 1796, April 5, 1797; Goelet to H, June 25, 27, 1796; "Receipt from Peter Goelet," October 4, 1796; "Deed from Peter Goelet, Robert Morris, and William Popham," April 4, 1797.

2. At the bottom of this letter is a list in the handwriting of Goelet of thirteen individuals, including H, to whom this letter was sent.

George Washington to James McHenry [1]

[Philadelphia, December 13, 1798]

Sir

Since my arrival at this place [2] I have been closely engaged, with the aid of Generals Hamilton and Pinckney, in fulfilling the objects of your letter of the 10th of November. [3] The result is now submitted.

The two first questions you propose, respecting the appointment of the Officers and men of the troops to be raised in virtue of the act of Congress of the 16th. of July last [4] among districts and states will naturally be answered together.

Df, in the handwriting of H, George Washington Papers, Library of Congress.

1. H drafted three letters on December 13, 1798, for Washington to send to McHenry. Washington forwarded the letters to McHenry with the following covering letter: "I am really ashamed to offer the letters &c herewith sent, with so many erazures &c, but it was not to be avoided, unless I had remained so much longer here, as to have allowed my Secretary [Tobias Lear] time to copy the whole over again;—and my impatience to be on my return homewards, on Account of the Season—the Roads—and more especially the passage of the Susquehanna—would not admit of this. . . .

"P.S. Mr. Lear, you are sensible, was engaged with myself & the Genl. Officers;—of course could not be employed in Transcribing what you will now receive, as the result of our deliberation at the mom't. We were engaged in other matters." (Steiner, *James McHenry*, 353–54).

McHenry used this letter and the third letter that Washington wrote to him on this date as the basis for his report to John Adams on December 24, 1798 (*ASP, Military Affairs*, I, 124–29). Adams sent McHenry's report to Congress on December 31, 1798 (*Annals of Congress*, VIII, 2200).

2. Washington arrived in Philadelphia on November 10, 1798. See H to Elizabeth Hamilton, November 10, 1798, note 2.

3. This letter is printed as an enclosure to Washington to H, November 12, 1798.

4. Section 2 of "An Act to augment the Army of the United States, and for other purposes" states: "That the President of the United States be, and he hereby is authorized to raise, in addition to the present military establishment,

1   As to the apportionment of the Commissioned officers of the Infantry, no particular reason is discovered to exist at the present period for combining the states into districts; but it is conceived to be expedient to adopt as a primary rule the relative representative population of the several States. The practice of the government on other occasions, in the appointment of public officers, has had regard as far as was practicable to the same general principle; as one which by a distribution of honors and emoluments among the citizens of the different states, tends both to justice and to public satisfaction. This principle however must frequently yield to the most proper solution of character among those willing as well as qualified to serve, and sometimes to collateral considerations, which arising out of particular cases do not admit of precise specification. In the application of the rule, in this, as in other instances, qualifications of it must be admitted. The arrangement which will be now offered proceeds on this basis. You will observe that it does not deviate from the table you have presented. It is contained in the Schedule A.[5]

2   As to the non commissioned officers and privates, it is conceived to be both unnecessary and inexpedient to make any absolute apportionment among the states. It is unnecessary, because, contemplating it as desireable that the men shall be drawn in nearly equal proportions from the respective states, this object, where circumstances are favourable, will be attained by the very natural and proper arrangement of assigning to the officers who shall be appointed recruiting districts within the states of which they are. It is inexpedient, because if it shall happen that the proportion of fit men cannot easily be had in a particular state, there ought to be no obstacle [6] to obtaining them elsewhere.

3   As to the officers of the dragoons, it does not seem adviseable to confine their selection to any subdivision of the UStates. Though very strong conjectures may be formed as to the quarters in which

---

twelve regiments of infantry, and six troops of light dragoons, to be enlisted for and during the continuance of the existing differences between the United States and the French Republic, unless sooner discharged . . ." (1 *Stat.* 604–05).

5. Enclosure not found, but for McHenry's table, see the enclosure to Washington to H, November 12, 1798.

6. In MS, "obstable."

they would probably be employed, in the case of invasion, there can be nothing certain on this point, if this were even the criterion of a proper arrangement. And it may be presumed that it will conduce most to general satisfaction to exclude considerations of a local aspect. But from the small number of this corps, which is to be raised it would be found too fractional and for that among reasons inconvenient to aim at a proporti[on]al distribution among all the states. It is therefore supposed most adviseable to be governed principally by a reference to the characters who have occurred as candidates; leaving the inequality in the distribution to be remedied in the event of a future augumentation of this description of troops. The proportion at present is in various views inadequate; a circumstance which it may be presumed will of course be attended to should the progress of public danger lead to an extension of military preparation.

The materials furnished by you with the addition of those derived from other sources are insufficient for a due selection of the officers whom it is proposed to allot to the States of Connecticut North and South Carolina & Georgia. Hence the selection for these states must of necessity be deferred. It is conceived, that the best plan for procuring the requisite information and accelerating a desireable conclusion as to the three last mentioned States, will be to charge Major General Pinckney, who will avail himself of the assistance of Brigadier Generals Davy and Washington,[7] to make the arrangement of those officers provisionally, and subject to the ratification of the President. It will be in their power to ascertain who are best *qualified* among those *willing* to serve; which will at the same time assure a good choice and avoid the disappointment and embarrassment of refusals. As to connecticut, you are aware of the progress which has been made and of the misapprehension which has occasioned an

7. On July 19, 1798, the Senate consented to the nominations of William Washington of South Carolina as a brigadier general in the Additional Army and William R. Davie of North Carolina as a brigadier general of the Provisional Army (*Executive Journal*, I, 292–93). See McHenry to H, July 25, 1798, notes 6 and 9. See also Washington to Davie, December 28, 1798 (Df, in the handwriting of Tobias Lear, George Washington Papers, Library of Congress); Washington to William Washington, December 28, 1798, and Washington to Charles Cotesworth Pinckney, December 30, 1798 (ALS, letterpress copies, George Washington Papers, Library of Congress).

obstacle to a definitive arrangement.[8] You will it is presumed be speedily in possession of the further information necessary, and having it can without difficulty complete the arrangement for this state.

The 3d. 4th. & 5th. of your questions may likewise be answered to gether.

The act for augmenting the army is peremptory in its provisions. The bounds of executive discretion as to the forbearance [9] to execute such a law might perhaps involve an investigation nice in its own nature and of a kind which it is generally most prudent to avoid. But it may safely be said negatively, for reasons too plain to be doubted, that the voluntary suspension of the execution of a similar law could not be justified but by considerations of decisive urgency.

The existence of any such considerations is unknown.

Nothing has been communicated respecting our foreign relations to induce the opinion that there has been any change in the situation of the Country as to external danger which dictates an abandonment of the policy of the law in question. It need not now be examined how far it may be at any time prudent to relinquish measures of security suggested by the experience of accumulated hostility, merely because there are probable symptoms of approaching accommodation: It need not be urged that if such symptoms exist they are to be ascribed to the measures of vigour adopted by the Government; and may be frustrated by a relaxation in those measures affording an argument of weakness or irresolution: For has it not been in substance stated from the highest authority that no decisive indications have been given by France of a disposition to redress our past wrongs and do us future justice, that her decree alleged to be intended to restrain the depredations of French Cruisers on our commerce has not given and from its nature cannot give relief—that the most hostile of the acts by which she has oppressed the commerce of neutrals, that which subjects to capture and condemnation of neutral vessels and cargoes, if any part of the latter be of British production or fabric, not only has not been abrogated but has recently received an

8. In a letter to McHenry on September 15, 1799, Washington wrote that because he had never been given ". . . any document relatively to the Characters of the Officers from Connecticut," he had not been able to "fix the Rank" of the officers from that state (Df, in the handwriting of Tobias Lear, George Washington Papers, Library of Congress).

9. In MS, "forfearance."

indirect confirmation—and that hitherto nothing is discoverable in the conduct of France which ought to change or relax our measures of defence.[10]

Could it be necessary to enforce by argument so authoritative a declaration as it relates to the immediate object of consideration these among other reflections would at once present themselves.

Though it may be true that some late occurrences have rendered the prospect of invasion by France, less probable or more remote: [11] Yet duly considering the rapid vicissitudes, at all times, of political and military events; the extraordinary fluctuations which have been peculiarly characteristic of the still subsisting contest in Europe; and the more extraordinary position of most of the principal nations of that quarter of the globe; it can never be wise to vary our measures of security with the continually varying aspect of European affairs. A very obvious policy dictates to us a strenuous endeavour as far as may be practicable, to place our safety out of the reach of the casualties which may befal the contending parties and the powers more immediately within their vortex. The way to effect this is to pursue a steady system—to organise all our resources and put them in a state of preparation for prompt action. Regarding the overthrow of Europe at large as a matter not intirely chimerical—it will be our prudence to cultivate a spirit of self-dependence—and to endeavour by unremitting vigilance and exertion under the blessing of providence to hold the scales of our destiny in our own hands. Standing, as it were, in the midst of falling empires, it should be our aim to assume a station and attitude which will preserve us from being overwhelmed in their ruins.

It has been very properly the policy of our Government to cultivate peace. But in contemplating the possibility of our being driven to unqualified War, it will be wise to anticipate that frequently the most effectual way to defend is to attack. There may be imagined enterprises of very great moment to the permanent interests of this Country which would certainly require a disciplined force. To raise

10. The statements in this sentence have been taken from John Adams's second annual message to Congress, December 8, 1798 (*Annals of Congress*, IX, 2420–24).

11. On August 1–2, 1798, Admiral Horatio Nelson destroyed the French fleet at the Battle of the Nile. On August 16, 1798, the French Executive Directory raised the embargo on American vessels in French ports (*ASP, Foreign Relations*, II, 229).

and prepare such a force will always be a work of considerable time; and it ought to be ready for the conjuncture whenever it shall arrive. Not to be ready then may be to lose an opportunity which it may be difficult afterwards to retrieve.

While a comprehensive view of external circumstances is believed to recommend perseverance in the precautions which have been taken for the safety of the country—nothing has come to my knowlege in our interior situation which leads to a different conclusion. The principal inquiry in this respect concerns the finances. The exhibition of their state from the Department of the Treasury which you have transmitted,[12] as I understand it, opposes no obstacle; nor have I been apprised that any doubt is entertained by the Officer who presides in that Department of the sufficiency of our pecuniary resources. But on this point I cannot be expected to assume the responsibility of a positive opinion. It is the province of the Secretary of the Treasury to pronounce definitively whether any insuperable impediment arises from this source.

The sound conclusion, viewing the subject in every light is conceived to be that no avoidable delay ought to be incurred in appointing the whole of the Officers and raising the whole of the men provided for by the act which has been cited. If immediately entered upon and pursued with the utmost activity, it cannot be relied upon that the troops will be raised and disciplined in less than a year. What may not another year produce? Happy will it be for us if we have so much time for preparation, and ill-judged indeed if we do not make the most of it! The adequateness of the force to be raised in relation to a serious invasion is foreign to the present examination. But it is certain that even a force of this extent, well instructed and well disciplined would in such an event be of great utility and importance. Besides the direct effects of its own exertions, the Militia rallying to it would derive from its example and countenance additional courage and perseverance. It would give a consistency and stability to our first efforts of which they would otherwise be destitute; and would tend powerfully to prevent great though perhaps partial calamities.

12. The report of Oliver Wolcott, Jr., dated November 16, 1798, was sent to Washington on November 19, 1798. See H to Washington, November 13, 1798, note 3.

The senate being in session the officers to be appointed must of course be nominated to that body.

The pay of all who shall be appointed ought immediately to commence. They ought all to be employed without delay in different ways, in the recruiting service; but were it otherwise there ought to be no suspension of their pay. The law annexes it as a matter of right. The attempt to apply a restriction to executive discretion might be dissatisfactory; and justice to the public does not seem to require it, because the acceptance of an office which makes the person liable at pleasure to be called into actual service will commonly from the moment of that acceptance interfere with any previous occupation on which he may have depended. This observation cannot be applicable to myself because I have taken a peculiar and distinct ground to which it is my contention to adhere.[13]

On the subject of your sixth question the opinion is that under existing circumstances; it is not adviseable to withdraw any of the troops from the quarters of the Country, which you mention, towards the Atlantic frontier. But the disposition in those quarters probably requires careful revision. It is not impossible that it will be found to admit of alterations favourable both to œconomy and to the military objects to be attained. The local knowlege of General Wilkinson [14] would be so useful in an investigation of this sort, that it is deemed very important to direct him forthwith to repair to Philadelphia. If this be impracticable by land he may it is presumed come by way of New Orleans. It is observed that in his late communications with the Spanish Governor [15] he has taken pains to obviate jealousy of the views of the UStates. This was prudent, and he ought to be encouraged to continue the policy. It will also be

13. On July 13, 1798, Washington had written to Adams: ". . . I have finally determined to accept the Commission of Commander in Chief of the Armies of the United States, with the reserve only, that I shall not be called into the field until the Army is in a situation to require my presence, or it becomes indespensible by the urgency of circumstance. . . .

"I take the liberty also to mention, that I must decline having my acceptance considered as drawing after it any immediate charge upon the Public, or that I can receive any emoluments annexed to the appointment, before entering into a Situation to incur expence." (ALS, letterpress copy, George Washington Papers, Library of Congress.)

14. James Wilkinson had been a brigadier general in the Army since 1792 and was at this time in command of the Western Army.

15. Manuel Gayoso de Lemos.

useful to employ a judicious Engineer to survey our posts on the Lakes in order that it may be ascertained in the various relations of trade and defence, what beneficial changes. if any, can be made. In this examination *Presque-Isle* and the *South Western extremity of Lake Erie* will demand particular attention.

The reply to your seventh question is that the companies directed to be [16] added to the regiments of the old establishment ought as soon as convenient to reinforce the Western army. It is probable that in the progress of events they will be not less useful there than on the sea-board. Their destination in the first instance may be Pittsburgh.

The following disposition of the Artillery (the subject of your Eighth question) is recommended. The two Regiments by their establishment consist of 28 Companies of these nearly a batalion in point of number, forms part of the western army. A complete batalion there will suffice. Let there be assigned to the fortifications at Boston one company to those at New port two companies, to those at west point one and to those at New York two to those at Mud Island two, to those at Baltimore one to those at Norfolk two to those on Cape Fear River One to those at Charles town two to those at Savannah one to those at the mouth of St Mary one. The remaining two batalions had best be reserved for the army in the field. During the Winter they may retain the stations they now occupy. But as soon as they can conveniently go into tents it will be adviseable to assemble them at some central or nearly central point there to be put in a course of regular instruction, together with successive detachments of the Officers and non commissioned Officers of the sea board garrisons, until their services shall be actually required. The field officers will of course be distributed proportionally, assigning to each the superintendence of a certain number of companies; and, as to those in garrisoning the posts at which they are stationed.

The permanent disposition of the troops after they shall have been raised which is understood to be an object of your Ninth Question will probably be influenced by circumstances yet to be unfolded, and will best be referred to future consideration.

An arrangement for the recruiting service is the point of primary urgency. For this purpose each state should be divided into as many districts as there are companies to be raised in it, and to every

16. In MS, "the."

company a particular district should be allotted, with one place of rendezvous in it, to which the recruits should be brought as fast as they are engaged: a certain number of these company districts wherever it can be done should be placed under the supervision of a field officer. During the Winter in most of the states it would be inconvenient to assemble in larger corps than companies. Great cities are to be avoided. The collection of troops there may lead to disorders and expose more than elsewhere the morals and principles of the soldiery.

But though it might now be premature to fix a permanent disposition of the troops, it may be not unuseful to indicate certain stations where they may be assembled provisionally and may probably be suffered to continue while matters remain in their present posture. The station eligible in this view may be found for two Regiments in the vicinity of Providence River some near Uxbrige for two other Regiments in the vicinity of Brunswick in New Jersey— for two other Regiments in the vicinity of the Potomack near Harpers Ferry, for two other Regiments in the vicinity of Augusta but above the falls of the Savannah. This disposition will unite considerations relative to the discipline & health of the troops and to the œconomical supply of their wants by water. It will also have some military aspects, in the first instance towards the security of Boston & New Port; in the second towards that of New York & Philadelphia in the third and fourth towards that of Baltimore Charleston Savannah and the Southern States generally and in the third particularly towards the reinforcement of the Western army in certain events. But the military motives have only a qualified influence; since it is not doubted that in the prospect of a serious attack upon this country the disposition of the army ought to look emphatically to the Southern Region as that which is by far most likely to be the scene of action.

As to your Tenth question, the opinion is, that the Government ought itself to provide the rations. The plan of furnishing money to the recruits as a substitute for this is likely to be attended with several inconveniences. It will give them a pretence for absence injurious to discipline and facilitating marauding and desertion. Many of the soldiery will be disposed to lay out too much of their money in ardent spirits and too little in provisions, which besides occasioning them to be ill fed will lead to habits of intemperance.

The subject of your 11th question is peculiarly important. The two modes have severally their advantages and disadvantages. That of purchases by Agents of the Government is liable to much mismanagement and abuse, sometimes from want of skill but much oftener from infidelity. It is too frequently deficient in œconomy; but it is preferable, as it regards the quality of the articles to be supplied, the satisfaction of the troops, and the certainty of the supply; which last is a point of the utmost consequence to the success of every military operation. The mode by contract is sometimes found more œconomical; but as the calculations of contractors have reference primarily to their own profit, they are apt to endeavour to impose on the troops articles of inferior quality; the troops suspecting this are apt to be dissatisfied even where there is no adequate cause and where defects may admit of reasonable excuse. In the attention to cheapness of price and other savings of expence, it from time to time happens that the supplies are not laid in as early as the service requires, or not in sufficient quantity, or are not conveyed with due asperity to the points where they are wanted. Circumstances like these tend to embarrass and even to defeat the best concerted military plans; which, in this mood, depend for their execution too much upon the combinations of individual avarice. It also occasionally happens that the Public, from the failures of the contractors, is under a necessity of interposing with sudden and extraordinary efforts to obviate the mischief and disappointments of those failures, producing, in addition to other evils, an accumulation of expence which the fortunes of the delinquent contractors, are insufficient to indemnify.

The union of the two modes will probably be found safest and best. Prudence always requires that magazines shall be formed beforehand at stations relative to the probable or expected scene of action. These magazines may be laid in by contract—and the transportation of the supplies from the magazines and the issuing of them to the army may be the business of the Military Agents, who must likewise be authorised & enabled to provide for the deficiencies of the contractors and for whatever may not be comprehended in the contracts. This plan will, to a great extent, admit the competition of private interest to furnish the supplies at the cheapest rate: by narrowing the sphere of action of the public agents it will proportionably diminish the opportunities of abuse; and it will unite as far as is attainable œconomy with the efficiency of military operations.

But to obtain the full advantages of this plan, it is essential that there shall be a man attached to the army, of distinguished capacity and integrity to be charged with the superintendence of the department of supplies. To procure such a man, as military honor can form no part of his reward, ample pecuniary compensation must be given; and he must be entrusted with large authority for the appointment of subordinate agents accompanied with a correspondent responsibility. Proceeding on this ground there would be a moral certainty of immense savings to the public in the business of supplies; savings the magnitude of which will easily be understood by any man who can estimate the vast difference in the results of extensive money transactions between a management at once skilful & faithful and that which is either unskilful or unfaithful.

This suggestion contemplates as a part of the plan that the procuring of supplies of every kind which in our past experience has been divided between two departments, of Quarter Master and Commissary, shall be united under one head. This unity will tend to harmony system and vigour. It will avoid the discordant mixture of civil with military functions. The Quarter Master General in this case, instead of being a purveyor as formerly, will besides the duties purely military of his station, be confined to the province of calling for the requisite supplies and of seeing that they are duely furnished; in which he may be rendered a very useful check upon the purveyor.

The extent of your twelveth question has been matter of some doubt. But no inconvenience can ensue from the answering it with greater latitude than may have been intended. It is conceived that the strongest consideration of national policy & safety require that we should be as fast as possible provided [with] Arsenals and Magazines of Artillery small arms and the principal articles of military stores and camp equipage equal to such a force as may be deemed sufficient to resist with effect the most serious invasion of the most powerful European nation. This precaution, which prudence would at all times recommend, is peculiarly indicated by the existing crisis of Europe. The nature of the case does not furnish any absolute standard of the requisite force. It must be more or less matter of judgment. The opinion is that the calculation ought to be on the basis of fifty thousand men, forty thousand infantry of the line two thousand riflemen four thousand horse, and four thousand Artillery men. And with regard to such articles as are expended by the use not less than a full years supply ought to be ready. This will allow due time from internal and external sources to continue the supply in proportion to the exigencies which shall occur. The schedule B [17] contains an estimate of the chief of these articles. It is to be observed that the quantities there exhibitted are not additional to the present supply but the totals to be provided. As to cloathing, since we may always on a sudden emergency find a considerable supply in our markets, and the articles are more perishable, the quantity in deposit may be much less than of other articles—but it ought not under present circumstances to be less than a years supply for half the abovementioned force especially of the woolen articles.

I proceed to the last of your questions, that which respects the stations for magazines. It is conceived that three principal permanent stations will suffice and that these ought to be Springfield and Harpers Ferry which are already chosen, and the vicinity of Rocky Mount on the Wateree in South Carolina. These stations are in a great measure central to three great subdivisions of the United States; they are so interior as to be entirely safe and yet on navigable waters which empty into the Ocean and facilitate a water conveyance to every point on our sea Coast—they are also in well settled and healthy districts of the Country. That near Harper's ferry it is well known possesses extraordinary advantages for founderies and other manufactories of iron. It is expected that a canal will ere long effect a good navigation between the Wateree & the Catawba; which when-ever it shall happen will render the vicinity of the Rocky Mount extremely convenient to the supply of North Carolina by inland navigation. Pittsburgh west Point in New York, the neighbourhood of Trenton in New Jersey and Fayetteville in North Carolina may properly be selected as places of particular and occasional deposit. Large Cities are as much as possible to be avoided.

17. "Estimate of Artillery small Arms principal articles of Military stores and camp Equipage for an army of 50000 men" (Df, in H's handwriting, George Washington Papers, Library of Congress). The endorsement of this document in Tobias Lear's handwriting reads: "Copy deld. to Genl. Pinckney Decr. 28th. 1798."

The foregoing comprises it is believed a full answer to the questions you have stated. I shall in another letter offer to your consideration some further matters which have occurred and are deemed to be of importance to our military service.[18]

With respect & esteem   I have the honor to be Sir   Yr. very obed servant

18. Washington endorsed this letter: "To the Secrety. of War 13th. Decr. 1798." Under Washington's endorsement Tobias Lear wrote: "Copy delivered to General Pinckney Decr. 28th. 1798."

There is an undated outline of this letter in H's handwriting in the Hamilton Papers, Library of Congress.

George Washington to James McHenry [1]

Philadelphia, December 13, 1798

Sir

You will observe that in the arrangement of the officers allotted to New York [2] there is an alternative of Wm. S. Smith [3] or Abijah Hammond [4] for Lt Colonel Commandant. Various considerations demand that the motive of this hesitation should be explained. Had military qualifications alone been consulted the name of Colonel Smith would have stood singly and he would have been deemed a valuable acquisition to the service. Had there even been no other source of objection than the erroneous political opinions of late attributed to him, his honor and attachment to his country would have been relied upon. But as well myself as the two generals whose aid I have had in the nominations [5] have been afflicted with the information well or ill founded that he stands charged in the opinion of his fellow citizens with very serious instances of private misconduct; instances which affect directly his integrity as a man. The instances alleged are various but there is one which has come forward in a shape which did not permit us to refuse it our attention. It respects an attempt knowingly to pledge property to Major Burrows [6] by way of security, which was before conveyed or mortgaged for its full value to Mr. William Constable; [7] without giving notice of the circumstance, and with the aggravation, that Major Burrows had become the Creditor of Col Smith through friendship to an amount which has proved entirely ruinous to him. While the impossibility of disregarding this information forbade the selection of Col Smith absolutely, the possibility that it might admit of some fair explanation dissuaded from a conclusion against him. As it will be in your power to obtain further lights on the subject it has appeared adviseable to leave the matter in the undetermined form in which it is presented and to assign the reason for it. You are at perfect liberty to communicate this letter to the President. Candour is particularly due to him in such a case. It is my wish to give him every proof of frankness, respect and esteem. Lest it should be suspected that Major Burrows has officiously interfered to the prejudice of Col Smith, it is but justice to him to declare that such a suspicion would be entirely without foundation.

With great consideration & regard   I have the honor to be   Sir Your obed servt

Df, in the handwriting of H, George Washington Papers, Library of Congress.

1. For evidence that this draft was sent to McHenry, see H's draft of Washington to McHenry, first letter of December 13, 1798, note 1.

2. This is a reference to a list in an unknown handwriting entitled "Company Arrangement *New York*," which is in the George Washington Papers, Library of Congress, and is filed at the end of the year 1798. The list contains the names of thirty men with their military rank and the county in which each lived.

3. William S. Smith, John Adams's son-in-law, was at this time engaged in land speculation in western New York. In addition to accusations of personal dishonesty, Smith was accused of having interfered in the New York gubernatorial election. On September 3, 1798, McHenry wrote to Uriah Tracy, United States Senator from Connecticut, enclosing a certificate which stated that Smith had not interfered in the election (copy, Hamilton Papers, Library of Congress). On July 18, 1798, Adams nominated Smith adjutant general, but the Senate rejected the nomination (*Executive Journal*, I, 292, 293). See Timothy Pickering to H, July 18, 1798, note 4. On January 8, 1799, Smith was commissioned lieutenant colonel of the Twelfth Regiment of Infantry (*Executive Journal*, I, 299, 303).

4. Hammond, a native of Massachusetts, served throughout the American Revolution as a lieutenant of the Continental Artillery. Hammond was neither nominated nor appointed to the Army.

5. H and Charles Cotesworth Pinckney.

6. William Ward Burrows of Pennsylvania had been appointed a major of Marines on July 17, 1798 (*Executive Journal*, I, 286, 290). See also Jacob Read to H, January 18, 1798.

7. Constable was a New York City merchant and land speculator.

George Washington to James McHenry [1]

Philadelphia December 13
1798

Sir

I shall now present to your view the additional objects alluded to in my letter of this date.

A proper organisation for the troops of the UStates is a principal one. In proportion as the policy of the Country is adverse to extensive military establishments ought to be our care to render the principles of our military system as perfect as possible, and our endeavouring to turn to the best account such force as we may at any time have on foot, and to provide an eligible standard for the augmentations to which particular emergencies may compel a resort.

The organisation of our military force will it is conceived be much improved, by modelling it on the following plan:

Let a Regiment of Infantry, composed as at present of two batalions and each batalion of five Companies, consist of these Officers and men (viz) [2] one Colonel two Majors, a first and second, one Adjutant one Quarter Master and one Pay Master each of whom shall be a Lieutenant, one surgeon and one surgeon's Mate, Ten Captains, Ten first and ten second lieutenants, besides the three Lts abovementioned, Two Cadets with the pay and emoluments of serjeants, Two serjeant Majors, Two Quarter Master serjeants, Two Chief Musicians first and second, Twenty other Musicians forty serjeants forty Corporals and Nine hundred and Twenty privates.

Let a Regiment of Drago[o]ns consist of Ten Troops making five squadrons and of these Officers and men (viz)—One Colonel, two Majors a first and second, one Adjutant one Quarter Master and one Pay Master each of whom shall be a Lieutenant, one surgeon and one surgeons Mate, ten Captains, ten first and ten second Lieu-

Df, in the handwriting of H, George Washington Papers, Library of Congress.

1. For evidence that this draft was sent to McHenry, see H's draft of Washington to McHenry, first letter of December 13, 1798, note 1.

2. Opposite the beginning of this paragraph H wrote and crossed out: "submission to Legislation."

tenants, besides the three Lieutenants abovementioned, five Cadets
with the pay and emoluments of serjeants, Two serjeant Majors,
two Quarter Master serjeants Two Chief Musicians first and second,
Ten other musicians Forty serjeants forty corporals and Nine hundred and Twenty privates; the privates including to each Troop
one sadler, one blacksmith and one boot Maker.

Let a Regiment of Artillery consist of four batalions each batalion
of four Companies and of these Officers and men (viz) one Colonel,
four Majors, one Adjutant one Quarter Master and one Pay Master
each of whom shall be a Lieutenant, one surgeon and Two surgeons
Mates Sixteen Captains, sixteen first and sixteen second Lieutenants,
besides the three Lieutenants abovementioned Thirty two cadets,
with the pay & emoluments of sergeants, four serjeant Majors, four
Quarter Master serjeants sixty four serjeants sixty four Corporals
one Chief Musician & ten other Musicians Eight hundred and
Ninety six privates including to each Company Eight Artificers.

The principal reasons for this organisation will be briefly suggested.

It will be observed that the proportion of men to Officers in the
Infantry & cavalry is considerably greater than by the present
establishment.

This presents in the first place the advantage of œconomy. By
the proportional decrease of the officers, savings will result in their
pay, subsistence and the transportation of their baggage. The last
circumstance by lessening the impediments of an army, is also
favourable to the celerity of its movements.

The command of each officer will become more respectable. This
will be an inducement to respectable men to accept military appointments—and it will be an incentive to exertion among those who
shall be engaged, by upholding that justifiable pride which is a necessary ingredient in the military spirit.

A company will then admit of eligible subdivision into platoons
sections and demi-sections each of a proper front.

Each batalion will then be of the size judged proper for a
manœvering column in the field—and it is that portion of an army
which in the most approved systems of Tactics is destined to fulfil
this object. A batalion ought neither to be too unwieldy for rapid
movements nor so small as to multiply too much the subdivisions,

and render each incapable either of a vigorous impulse or resistance.

The proportion of officers to men ought not to be greater than is adequate to the due management and command of them. A careful examination of this point will satisfy every judge, that the number now proposed will be equal to both. This conclusion will be assisted by the idea that our fundamental order, in conformity with that of the nations of Europe generally, ought to place our infantry in three ranks; to oppose to an enemy who shall be in the same order an equal mass for attack or defence.

These remarks explain summarily the chief reasons for the most material of the alterations which is suggested.

But it is not the intention to recommend a present augmentation of the number of rank and file to the proposed standard. It is only wished that it may be adopted as that of the war-establishment. The Regiments which have been authorised may continue in this respect upon the footing already prescribed; leaving the actual augmentation to depend on events which may create a necessity for the increase of our force.

The other alterations recommended have relation rather to systematic propriety, than to very important military ends.

The term Lt Col in our present establishment has a relative signification without any thing in fact to which it relates. It was introduced during our revolutionary war, to facilitate exchanges of prisoners, as our then enemy united the grade of Colonel with that of General. But the permanent form of our military system ought to be regulated by principle not by the changeable and arbitrary arrangement of a particular nature. The title of Colonel, which has greater respectability, is more proper for the commander of a Regiment; because it does not, like the other, imply a relation having no existence.

The term ensign is changed into that of lieutenant as well because the latter from usage has additional respectability offering an inducement to desireable candidates, as because the former, in its origin, signified a standard bearer, & supposed that each company had a distinct standard. This in practice has ceased to be the case and for a variety of good reasons a standard of colours to each batalion of infantry is deemed sufficient. This standard is intended to be confided to a cadet in whom it may be expected to excite an emulation and exertion. The multiplication of grades, inconvenient with regard to exchanges, is thus avoided.

In the cavalry it is proper to allow a standard to each squadron consisting of two troops and hence it is proposed to have five cadets to a Regiment.

The nature of the Artillery service, constantly in detachment, renders it proper to compose a Regiment of a greater number of batalions than the other corps. This our present establishment has recognised. But there is now a disorderly want of uniformity; one regiment being composed of four batalions the other of three. The same organisation ought to be common to all. The diminution of the number of musicians, while it will save expence, is also warranted by the peculiar nature of the Artillery service. They answer in this corps few of the purposes which they fulfil in the Infantry.

The existing laws contemplate and with good reason that the aids of General Officers except of the Commander in Chief & the officers in the department of Inspection shall be taken from the Regiments. But they do not provide that when so taken their places in the Regiments shall be supplied by others. It is conceived that this ought to be the case. The principles of the establishment suppose, for example, that three officers to a company of a given number are the just and due proportion. If when an officer be taken from a company to fill one of the stations alluded to his place be not filled by another, so that the number of Officers to a company may remain the same, it must follow that the company will be deficient in officers. It is true that the number of a company is continually diminishing, but it diminishes in officers as well as men; and it is not known that the proportion is varied. Practice in every institution ought to conform to principle, or there will result more or less of disorder. An army is in many respects a machine; of which the displacement of any of the organs, if permitted to continue, injures its symetry and energy and leads to disorder and weakness. The increase of the number of rank and file, while it strengthens the reasons for replacing the officers who may be removed will more than compensate in point of œconomy for the addition of officers by the substitution. This may be reduced to the test of calculation. But though the place of an officer in his Regiment ought to be supplied upon any such removal, he ought not to lose his station in the Regiment; but ought to rank and rise as if he had continued to serve in it.

The provision that Aides de Camp and the officers of Inspection shall be drawn from the line of the army is not restricted as to grades. There ought to be such a restriction. The Aides of Major Generals ought not to be taken from a rank superior to that of Captain, nor those of the Brigadiers from a rank superior to that of first Lieutenant. The Inspectors ought in like manner to be limited, those of Brigades to the rank of Captain, those of Divisions to that of Major. This will guard against the multiplication of the superior grades by removals to fill such stations.

The judicious establishment of general rules of promotion, liable to exceptions in favour of extraordinary service or merit, is a point of the greatest consequence. It is conceived that these rules are the most convenient that can be devised; namely that all officers shall rise in the Regiments to which they respectively belong up to the rank of a Major inclusively—that afterwards they shall rise in the line of the army at large; with the limitation however that the Officers of Artillery cavalry and Infantry shall be confined to their respective corps, *until* they shall attain the rank of Colonel.

It is very material to the due course of military service, that the several classes of any army shall be distinguished from each other by certain known badges, and that there shall be uniformity in dress and equipment subject to these distinctions. The dress itself will indeed constitute a part of them. It is of inferior moment what they shall be provided they are conspicuous and not inconsistent with good appearance, which in an army is far from being a matter of indifference. The following uniforms and badges are recommended; but if any of them are supposed liable to exception they may be changed at pleasure.

The uniform of the Commander in Chief to be a blue coat with yellow buttons and gold epaulettes each having three silver stars with linings cape and cuffs of buff, in Winter buff vest and breeches, in summer a white vest, & breeches of nanken. The coat to be without lappels and embroidered on the cape cuffs and pockets. A white plume in the hat to be a further distinction. The Adjutant General the aids and secretaries of the commander in Chief to be likewise distinguished by a white plume.

The uniform of the other General officers to be a blue coat with yellow buttons gold epaulets, the lining and facings of buff—the under cloaths the same with those of the Commander in Chief. The

Major General to be distinguished by two silver stars in each epaulette and except the Inspector General by a black and white plume, the black below. The Brigadier to be distinguished by one silver star on each epaulette, and by a red and white plume, the red below. The aids of all General Officers who are taken from Regiments, and the Officers of inspection to wear the uniforms of the Regiments from which they are taken. The aids to be severally distinguished by the like plumes, which are worn by the General Officers to whom they are respectively attached.

The uniform of the aids and Secretaries of the Commander in Chief when not taken from Regiments to be a blue coat with yellow buttons and gold epaulettes buff lining and facings the same under cloaths with the Commander in Chief.

The Inspector General his aids and the officers of Inspection generally to be distinguished by a blue plume. The Quarter Master General and other military officers in his department to be distinguished by a Green Plume.

The uniform of the Infantry and Artillery to be a blue Coat with white buttons and red facings white under cloath and cocked hats: The Coats of the Infantry to be lined with white, of the artillery with red. The uniform of the Cavalry to be a Green Coat with white buttons lining & facings—white vest and breeches with helmet Caps.

Each Colonel to be distinguished by two Epaulets, each Major by one Epaulette on the right shoulder and a strap on the left. All the field Officers, except as above, and the Regimental staff to wear red plumes.

Captains to be distinguished by an Epaulette on the right shoulder—Lieutents. by one on the left shoulder—Cadets by a strap on the right shoulder. The Epaulettes and straps of the Regimental Officers to be of silver.

Serjeant Majors and Quarter Master serjeants to be distinguished by two red worsted Epaulettes—serjeants by a like Epaulette on the right shoulder—Corporals by a like Epaulette on the left shoulder. The flank companies to be distinguished by red wings on the shoulder.

The Coats of the Musicians to be of the colours of the facings of the corps to which they severally belong. The Chief Musicians to wear two white worsted Epaulettes.

All the Civil Staff of the army to wear plain blue Coats with yellow buttons & white under cloaths. No gold or silver lace except in the epaulettes and straps to be worn.

The Commissioned Officers and Cadets to wear swords.

All persons belonging to the army to wear a black cockade with a small white Eagle in the Center. The Cockades of the non Commissioned officers musicians and privates to be of leather with eagles of Tin.

The Regiments to be distinguished from each other numerically. The number of each Regiment to be expressed on the buttons.

It cannot fail to happen, that cloathing made at a distance from the army will in numerous instances be ill fitted to the persons to whom it is issued. This is an inconvenience, as it respects appearance comfort and use. It merits consideration whether it may not be remedied by making provision by law for the necessary alterations at the cost of the soldiery. As there are always to be found Taylors in an army, the alterations may be made there during seasons of inactivity; and moderate compensations may be established to be deducted out of the pay. The Taylors who when so employed being exempted from military duty will be satisfied with very small allowances; and the soldiery will probably prefer this expence to the inconveniences of wearing cloaths which do not fit them.

On this subject of cloathing, it is remarked with regret that the returns which have been received exhibit none on hand—though from verbal communications it is understood that measures are in train for obtaining a present supply. It is desireable that some more effectual plan than has hitherto been pursued should be adopted to procure regular and sufficient supplies on reasonable terms. While we depend on foreigners, will it not be adviseable to import the materials rather than take the chance of markets? And will it not even be expedient with a view to œconomy to have the cloathing made up in the countries from which it may be brought? The matter certainly deserves serious attention. Our supply in the mode hitherto practiced is not only very precarious but must doubtless be obtained at a very dear rate.

Another point no less deserving of particular attention is the composition of the ration of provisions. It was in the last session augmented beyond all former example.[3] It is not recollected that the

3. Section 6 of "An Act to augment the Army of the United States, and for

ration, which was allowed during the war with Great Britain [4] was found insufficient by troops once formed to military habits and acquainted with the best methods of managing their provisions. The present ration, estimating by price, is understood to be greater than the ration in that war by at least forty per Cent. This is evidently a very important augmentation. Various disadvantages attend it—a great increase of expence—additional difficulty in furnishing under all circumstances the stipulated allowance, consequently a multiplication of the possible causes of discontent murmur and perhaps even mutiny—the necessity of a greater number of waggons for transportation, and of course the extension of this always serious source of embarrassment to military operations.

The quantity of spirituous liquors, which is a component part of the ration, is so large as to endanger, where they might not before exist, habits of intemperance, alike fatal to the health and discipline. Experience has repeatedly shewn that many soldiers will exchange their rum for other articles; which is productive of the double mischief of subjecting those with whom the exchange is made to the loss of what is far more necessary and to all the consequences of brutal intoxication.

The step having been once taken a change is delicate; but it is believed to be indispensable, and that the temporary evils of a change can bear no proportion to the permanent and immense evils of a continuance of the error.

It may not perhaps be adviseable to bring back the ration to the standard of the late war, but to modify it in some respects differently so as not materially to affect the aggregate expence.

It may consist of Eighteen Ounces of bread or flour one pound and a quarter of fresh beef or one pound of salted beef or three quarters of a pound of salted pork; salt when fresh meat is issued at

other purposes" provided "That every non-commissioned officer, private and musician shall receive daily the following rations of provisions, to wit: one pound and a quarter of beef, or three quarters of a pound of pork, eighteen ounces of bread or flour, a gill of rum, brandy or whisky, and at the rate of two quarts of salt, four quarts of vinegar, four pounds of soap, and one pound and a half of candles to every hundred rations" (1 Stat. 605 [July 16, 1798]).

4. For the ration allowed to the Continental Army during the American Revolution, see JCC, III, 322.

the rate of one quart and candles at the rate of a pound for every hundred rations.

With regard to liquor it may be best to exclude it from being a component part of the ration; allowing a discretion to Commanding officers to cause it to be issued in quantities not exceeding half a gill per day except on extraordinary occasions.

Vinegar also ought to be furnished when to be had at the rate of two quarts and soap at the rate of two pounds per hundred rations— but this ought to depend on circumstances and ought not to make part of the established ration.

There are often difficulties in furnishing articles of this description, & the equivalent in money is frequently rather pernicious than beneficial. When there is a contract, the promise of such articles is apt to prove more beneficial to the contractor than to any other person. He commonly so manages it that the substitute is not a real equivalent.

But it need not be observed that whatever is to be done in this respect must be so conducted as not to infract the conditions on which the troops now in service were enlisted.

It is deeply to be lamented that a very precious period of leisure was not improved towards forming among ourselves Engineers and Artillerists; and that owing to this neglect we are in danger of being overtaken by war without competent characters of these descriptions. To form them suddenly is impossible. Much previous study and experiment are essential. If possible to avoid it a war ought not to find us unprovided. It is conceived to be adviseable to endeavour to introduce from abroad at least one distinguished Engineer and one distingished Officer of Artillery.[5] They may be sought for preferably in the Austrian and next in the Prussian armies. The grade of Colonels with adequate pecuniary compensations may attract officers of a rank inferior to that grade in those armies, who will be of distinguished abilities and merit. But in this, as we know from past experience, nothing is more easy than to be imposed upon—nothing more difficult than to avoid imposition—and that therefore it is requisite to commit the business of procuring such characters to some very judicious hand—under every caution that can put him upon his guard.

5. In the margin H wrote: "Colonel & adequate."

If there shall be occasion for the actual employment of military force, a corps of riflemen will be for several purposes extremely useful. The eligible proportion of riflemen to infantry of the line may be taken at a twentieth. Hence in the apportionment of any army of fifty thousand men, in my letter of this date,[6] two thousand riflemen are included and in the estimate of arms to be provided two thousand rifles. There is a kind of rifle commonly called *Fergusons*[7] which will deserve particular attention. It is understood that it has in different European armies supplanted the old rifle, as being more quickly loaded and more easily kept clean. If the shot of it be equally or nearly equally sure those advantages entitle it to a preference. It is very desireable that this point and its comparitive merit in other respects be ascertained by careful examination & experiment.

Perhaps generally, but more certainly when the troops shall serve in Southern Climates, flannel shirts will be most conducive to health. Will it not be adviseable to make provision for retaining a discretion in such cases either to allow a less number of flannel shirts equivalent to the present allowance of linnen, or if this cannot be, to furnish the soldiery with the requisite number, deducting the difference of cost out of their pay?

The only provision for the appointment of a quarter Master General is to be found in the act of the 28th of May;[8] authorising the President to raise a provisional army, which limits his rank and emoluments to that of Lt Colonel. This provision is conceived to be

6. See H's draft of Washington to McHenry, first letter of December 13, 1798.

7. See Washington to H, November 12, 1798, note 15.

8. Section 7 of "An Act authorizing the President of the United States to raise a Provisional Army" provided "That in case the President shall judge the employment of a quartermaster general, physician-general and paymaster-general or either of them essential to the public interest, he is hereby authorized, by and with the advice and consent of the Senate, to appoint the same accordingly, who shall be entitled to the rank, pay and emoluments which follow viz.: quartermaster-general, the rank, pay and emoluments of a lieutenant-colonel; physician-general and paymaster-general each the pay and emoluments of a lieutenant-colonel. *Provided*, that in case the President shall judge it expedient to appoint a commander of the army, an inspector-general, adjutant-general, quartermaster-general, physician-general and paymaster-general, or either of them, in the recess of the Senate, he is hereby authorized to make any or all of said appointments and grant commissions thereon, which shall expire at the end of the next session of the Senate thereafter" (1 *Stat.* 559 [May 28, 1798]).

entirely inadequate. The military duties of the office are of a nature to render it of the first importance in an army; demanding great abilities and a character every way worthy of trust. Accordingly it is the general practice, founded upon very substantial reasons, to confide it to an officer of high Military rank. The probability is that without a similar arrangement on our part we shall not be able to command a fit character; and in taking one of inferior pretensions we shall subject the service to disadvantages out of all proportion to any objections which may be supposed to militate against the conferring of such rank. It is feared, that an appointment under the existing provision will only create embarrassment should there be real necessity for military exertions; and that the alternate must be either to leave the army destitute of so necessary an organ or to give it one likely in the progress of things to prove unequal to the task.

It was much desired for preventing future controversy to fix in the first instance the relative grades of the regimental officers. That of the field officers has been rendered impossible, without injustice and the hazard of much dissatisfaction, by the impossibility of completing the arrangement in Connecticut and the three most Southern States.[9] But upon close examination many obstacles opposed a definitive establishment of the relative rank even of the officers of companies in the regiments which have been organised. Numerous circumstances which ought to influence the decision are unknown; and without this knowlege a final arrangement might lead to very awkward and perplexing results. In consideration of this difficulty, no more than a temporary one, liable to future revision, has been adopted. It will be necessary to attend to this in the appointments, & to signify to the persons that they are to obey according to the order of nomination, but that the President reserves to himself the right, *where cogent reasons for it* shall appear to change the relative rank which that order may seem to recognise. He will judge whether in making the nomination to the senate a like reserve is necessary.

I am well aware that several of the matters suggested in this letter will require legislative provision. If the whole or any of them shall be approved by the Executive, no time ought to be lost in recom-

9. See H's draft of Washington to McHenry, first letter of December 13, 1798.

mending them to the consideration of Congress. As to some of them it is very desireable that the necessary provision by law should precede the inlistment of the men to avoid the obstacle to a change which may result from contract.[10]

With great respect & esteem   I have the honor to be Sir   Your Obed serv

10. In the George Washington Papers, Library of Congress, there is a brief outline in H's handwriting of a portion of this letter entitled "Organization."

From Benjamin Wells [1]

Connells Ville [Pennsylvania] December the 15th 1798

Sir

The hard treatment I have recieved from the government of the united States Since the western insurrection is the Cause of my apealing to you, in the Spring of 94—after the many insults and abuses I had recieved I purposed to you that I would resign you incouraged me by an asshurance that government would never let me Suffer. I have petitioned Congress for relief but to no purpose.[2] Now Sir if my former Services have met you aprobation pray dwo Something for me.

I am with respect yours   Benja Wells

ALS, Hamilton Papers, Library of Congress.
1. For background to this letter, see H to George Washington, August 5, September 2, 1794; H's draft of Edmund Randolph to Thomas Mifflin, August 7, 1794.
2. On November 22, 1797, "A Petition of Benjamin Wells, Collector of the Revenue in the fourth survey of the District of Pennsylvania, was presented to the House and read, praying compensation for losses and injuries which he sustained in his person and property, from certain persons in the Western counties of Pennsylvania, opposed to the execution of the laws laying duties on stills, and on spirits distilled within the United States" (*Journal of the House*, III, 82–83). On November 24, 1797, this petition was referred to the Committee of Claims (*Journal of the House*, III, 87). The committee report, dated May 2, 1798, stated that "the prayer of this Petition ought not to be granted" (copy, in Wells's handwriting, Hamilton Papers, Library of Congress; *Journal of the House*, III, 282). The copy in the Hamilton Papers, Library of Congress, was enclosed in Wells to H, March 1, 1800. On March 1, 1800, the House ordered "That the petition of Benjamin Wells, presented the twenty-second of November, one thousand seven hundred and ninety-seven, together

with a report of the Committee of Claims thereon, be referred to the Secretary of the Treasury, with instruction to examine the matter thereof, and report his opinion thereupon to the House" (*Journal of the House*, III, 610). On March 24 the House sent to Oliver Wolcott, Jr., "a petition of sundry inhabitants of Fayette County, in the State of Pennsylvania . . . stating certain reasons against granting the petition of Benjamin Wells . . ." (*Journal of the House*, III, 638). In his report, dated April 2, 1800, Wolcott recommended that Wells should not be responsible for paying back the money granted him by the act of February 27, 1795, and that he should be fully compensated for his losses in 1794, but that no discrimination should be made in his favor (*ASP, Claims*, 235–36; *Journal of the House*, III, 649). The Committee of Claims reported on April 21, and Wells's petition was deferred (*Journal of the House*, III, 673). The House deferred Wells's petition for a third time on February 1, 1803, but on November 30, 1803, the Committee of Claims reported favorably on Wells's petition (*Journal of the House*, IV, 258, 463). As a result, on December 13, 1803, the House passed "An Act for the relief of the officers of Government, and other citizens, who suffered in their property by the insurgents in the Western counties of Pennsylvania" (*Journal of the House*, IV, 486). On January 19, 1804, the Senate postponed consideration of this bill (*Journal of the House*, IV, 542). The Senate did not pass the bill.

To James Gunn [1]

N York Decr: 16th. 1798

Dr Sir.

I regretted that my excessive avocations did not permit me, as I intended to call upon you before I left Philadelphia. In addition to the pleasure of doing it I was desirous of knowing the state of your mind with regard to military service. It was not that there was any thing worth your acceptance, upon the disposal of which at the time I could have had any influence, but I wished to understand what would be agreeable to you, with a view to the progress of affairs. If we are to be seriously engaged in military operations, 'tis not a compliment to you to say, that you are one of those men who must be in the field. With such an enemy we shall want men who will not *barely do their duty*, but will do it with an energy equal to all dangers.

with very great regard   I am dear Sir   Your obed Servant

A Hamilton

General Gunn

Copy, in the handwriting of Philip Church, Hamilton Papers, Library of Congress.

1. Gunn was a member of the United States Senate from Georgia from 1789 to 1801. A veteran of the American Revolution, he was a brigadier general in the Georgia militia at the time this letter was written.

To James McHenry

Private   New York Decr. 16. 1798

Dr. Sir

I regretted that I was detained to the last moment of being in time for the stage, to which my baggage had been previously sent, and thereby prevented from calling upon you before my final departure from Philadelphia.

If the recruiting service is to be confided to me, I ought as soon as possible to be definitively apprised of it, and in the mean time, I shall be glad to have the instructions heretofore prepared for that purpose,[1] that I may endeavour to obtain for your final decision new lights from officers who have had experience in this branch of the service. My own was very limited, and it is of great importance to proceed upon a right plan.

You recollect that shortly after my first appointment, I was desired to turn my attention to a system of regulations for the tactics and discipline of the army.[2] From that moment I have devoted much of my time to the preliminary investigations—and I shall devote a much larger proportion, if I am to consider myself as now in service and intitled to the emoluments of the station. For to be frank with you, it is utterly out of my power to apply my time to the public service, without the compensations, scanty enough, which the law annexes to the office. If I were to receive them from the day of the appoint[ment] I should be at least a thousand pounds the worse for my acceptance. From the time it was first known that I had reengaged in military life, the uncertainty of my being able to render services for which I might be retained drove away more than half my professional practice, which I may moderately estimate at four thousand pounds a year. My pecuniary sacrifices already to the public ought to produce the reverse of a disposition every where to compel me to greater than the law imposes. This remark, I am well aware, is not necessary for you personally.

Again: If I am to discharge with effect the duties of my present office, I must make frequent journeys from one part of the army to another. Every body knows that the expences of such journeys would quickly eat out the narrow allowances of a Major General. It will be disagreeable to be exposed to the dilemma of compromitting my reputation and that of the Government by not producing the results to be expected from the department, or of ruining myself once more in performing services for which there is no adequate compensation. The precedent of last war is a full comment on the propriety of an extra allowance to the Inspector General. It is indeed indispensable if he is to be useful.

It is always disagreeable to speak of compensations for one's self but a man past 40 with a wife and six Children, and a very *small* property beforehand, is compelled to wave the scruples which his nicety would otherwise dictate.

With great esteem & regard   I remain Dr. Sir   Yr Obed servant
A Hamilton

P.S. I imagine it may be serviceable to communicate to *Wolcott* the *two* letters received from the Commander in Chief,[3] containing the results of our deliberations.

James Mc.Henry Esqr

ALS, James McHenry Papers, Library of Congress; copy, in Philip Church's handwriting, Hamilton Papers, Library of Congress.

1. This is a reference to the 1798 edition of the War Department printed pamphlet *Rules and Regulations Respecting the Recruiting Service.* See H to Jonathan Dayton, August 6, 1798, note 6.
2. See McHenry to H, July 20, 1798; H to McHenry, July 30, 1798.
3. See H's drafts of the first and third letters from George Washington to McHenry, December 13, 1798.

From Caleb Gibbs

Boston, December 17, 1798. ". . . Since my return to Boston I have been Inspecting and mustering the troops at Castle Island. . . . This Inspection and muster induces me to write this Letter, to give you my Ideas respecting recruiting. This company has upwards of fifty men Including Non Commissioned Officers and musick and I can assure you some of them are as likely men as I ever saw and a great proportion of them are young men from twenty to twenty five years of age. . . . The troops here are in great want of many necessaries. They want to be systemized. There is no regular commissary nor *no* Quarter Master. The Officers know not where to apply for any thing but to the butcher who very often supplies them with articles totally out of his line; and you may rest assured that it could be made to appear, that the United States will pay fifty pr. Cent more for the supplies of the troops in this quarter and what will be here (in all probability) for the want of some *responsible* person to act in the different capacities necessarily required. . . ."

ALS, Hamilton Papers, Library of Congress.

To James McHenry

Private   New York Decr. 17. 1798

Dear Sir

You will observe among the propositions lately communicated by the Commander in Chief, that of the addition of two troops to complete the Regiment of Cavalry to ten troops.[1] The idea was that these two troops should be *Hussars*.[2] It is much to be wished that Congress would agree to a present addition of two troops to be carried to the *actual* number of the others. In the distribution of New York into company districts, it will be well to allot to Capt Church [3] *Rensselaer* County and its Vicinity. *There* his Lieutenant [4] resides and there he has numerous and influential friends.

With true esteem & regard   Yr. Obed servant   A Hamilton

James Mc.Henry Esqr

ALS, The Sol Feinstone Collection, Library of the American Philosophical Society, Philadelphia; ALS (photostat), James McHenry Papers, Library of Congress.

1. See H's draft of the third letter from George Washington to McHenry, December 13, 1798.

2. In his report to John Adams, dated December 24, 1798, McHenry wrote:

"The two companies, which it is proposed to add to the actual number of the cavalry, it is desirable should be raised immediately. If this is agreed to, they might receive the denomination of Hussar companies—a description of cavalry extremely serviceable in an army" (*ASP, Military Affairs*, I, 125).

3. Philip Church.
4. Philip S. Schuyler.

Account with the Trustees of the American Iron Company [1]

[December 18, 1798]

Alexander Hamilton Esqr.   To the Trustees of the American
                                         Iron Company   Dr

To the last installment on lands in Crosby's Patent £605.13.5
Interest from 4 Decr. 1795 to April 1797 is 1 Year
4 Months   56.10.7
   do   do 4 April 1797 to 20 Decr 1798 is 1 Year 8 M.
16 Days   72.10.10
                                   £734.14.10 [2]

D, Miscellaneous Chancery Papers, American Iron Company, Clerk of the Court of Appeals, Albany, on deposit at Queens College, New York City.

1. For an explanation of the contents of this document, see the introductory note to Philip Schuyler to H, August 31, 1795. See also H to Phineas Bond, September 1, 1795; H to Robert Morris, September 1, 1795; H to Barent Bleecker, March 20, 1796, April 5, 1797; Peter Goelet to H, June 25, 27, 1796; "Receipt from Peter Goelet," October 4, 1796; "Deed from Peter Goelet, Robert Morris, and William Popham," April 4, 1797; Goelet and Morris to H, December 12, 1798.

2. This document is endorsed: "Calculation of Alexr Hamiltons Last payment & note to him Decr. 18, 1798."

To William Heth

[*New York, December 18, 1798.* On January 14, 1799, Heth wrote to Hamilton: "It is some days since I was made happy by the receipt of your kind favor of the 18th. Ulto." *Letter not found.*]

To John Jay

New York, December 18, 1798. "You may remember that I have heretofore recommended to you Mr.   [1] Inglis,[2] who studied the law with me, for the Office of Notary. He entertains an idea that a vacancy for such an appointment now exists, and has reminded me of my promise to be useful to him—I with pleasure reiterate my recommendation. . . ."

ALS, Columbia University Libraries.
  1. Space left blank in MS.
  2. James Inglis, Jr. See H to John Jay, September 17, 1798.

From James McHenry

Philad 18 Decr. 1798

My dear Sir

I have received this moment your two letters of the 16 & 17th instant, and have read them over cursorily tho' not without fully understanding them.

I intend that the recruiting service shall be wholly confided to you and shall send you the printed instructions [1] and a copy of the English system on which they are founded.[2] It cannot however be entered upon immediately or until our cloathing is in more forwardness.

It is certain, that you must have been a looser in the way you mention, by accepting the office you now hold, and as certain, that justice requires that none of the pay or emoluments annexed to it should be refused. I shall as early as possible obtain a proper decision.

I am preparing a report to the President, who has seen the two letters and all other papers & letters communicated to me by General Washington.[3] I shall add some matters to the subjects for congressional provisions they embrace when it will be transferred to Congress by message.[4]

The idea of two companies of Hussars is judicious.

Yours affecty.   James McHenry

Gen Hamilton Esq

ALS, Hamilton Papers, Library of Congress.

1. This is a reference to the 1798 edition of the War Department printed pamphlet *Rules and Regulations Respecting the Recruiting Service*. See H to Jonathan Dayton, August 6, 1798, note 6.

2. *Regulations and Instructions for carrying on the Recruiting Service for His Majesty's Forces stationed abroad* (London: War Office, printed and sold by J. Walter, 1796).

3. See H's drafts of the first and third letters George Washington wrote to McHenry on December 13, 1798.

4. See H's draft of the first letter from Washington to McHenry, December 13, 1798, note 1.

From Ebenezer Stevens [1]

New york 18th Decemr: 1798

Dear General

I have seen Mr. Furman, and we calculate that what is unpaid by him, and myself, for account of Gun Carriages, shot, Blacksmiths Work, and Laboratory expences, for the state, will amount to about Fourteen thousand Dollars [2]

I wish you to recommend me, to be the Agent for laying out the Money that is appropriated by this State for our defence.[3] I have always had the labouring part, and if any other person is appointed, or I am not allowed a salary, I must quit. I can obtain any security that may be required

You must be sensible that my time is altogether taken up with military business, and that I have been essentially useful to this State; but I have a large family to provide for, and must say, I wish to know the Compensation I am to receive.

I am Dear General   Yours sincerely   Eben Stevens.

Major Genl Hamilton

ALS, Hamilton Papers, Library of Congress.

1. For background to this document, see the introductory note to H to James McHenry, June 1, 1798.

2. See Stevens to H, November 17, 23, 29, 1798; H to Stevens, November 19, 1798.

3. On November 5, 1798, John Jay wrote to Matthew Clarkson: "I hope it will not be inconvenient to you to keep settle and pay all the accounts of the expenditures that shall be made of the monies appropriated by the State for fortifying the Port of New York" (ALS, New York Society Library, New York City). See Jay to H, November 5, 1798, note 1.

From James Gunn

[Philadelphia, December 19, 1798]

Dr Sir

I have received your very friendly and Obliging favor of the 16th. Inst. I was very Solicitous to Converse with you on the Subject of our military establishment, But it appeared to me that during your Stay in this City your Whole time was occupied with public business, and I was unwilling to interupt you. The only moment I had the pleasure of your conversation I certainly understood it to be your intention to return to this City in the course of a very few weeks. Indeed it appears to me indispensable.

You are not accustomed to engage in Objects of much moment without consideration, and Sir, I am persuaded it can be no part of your plan merely to Execute the feeble arrangements of other men. The President has no Talent for war, and Mc.Henry is an infant in *detail*, and if I am Correct, Genl. Washington is not to take the field, but in the event of the provisional army being called into Service. You are, of course, not only Charged With the Command of the army; But, in a great degree, the direction of the war department, and Sir, you will permit me to add that the Legislative aid necessary for the Support of that department must be arranged by yourself. I therefore Conclude that it is yet your intention to visit Phila. Which precludes the necessity of my going into detail. Trained up in the honorable pursuit of a Military life, I frankly Confess my regard for you as a Commander, and my passion for military Service; But my Worthy Sir, I have seen Such dishonorable means employed to wound the feellings of men, of unblemished integrity and have witnessed so many efforts to render the profession of Arms disreputable, that, I am disgusted with every thing connected with publick life. Situated in a Country, in the event of war, which, most probly will be the Scene of action, I have no wish, or expectation, that, it will be my lot to keep out of the field. But Sir, I am Sincere when I assure you, that, it is my fixed determination not to be Commanded by *Some men* now in Commission—by this declaration I wish it to be understood that my Objection doth not extend beyond ⟨White and Sevier⟩ [1] in the provisional army, and the *field officers* in Wilkinsons army. In any event I entreat you to believe it will give me infinite pleasure to do you all the service in my power.

Have the goodness to communicate your wishes with regard to the invigoration of the measures of defence.

With very great regard   I am   Dr. Sir,   Your Obt. Set.

James Gunn

Philadelphia, Decr. 19th. 1798

Genl. Hamilton

ALS, Hamilton Papers, Library of Congress.
    1. See James McHenry to H, July 25, 1798, notes 9, 10, and 11.

From Rufus King

Lond. Dec. 19 1798

Dear sir

The same uncertainty continues to perplex us concerning the Recommencement of the war. One day we are told that Naples has really begun & that Austria is on the way to support her; the next, that Naples is kept back by Austria to whom the Directory have made the most Advantageous offers. It is certain that france feels the change that has within the last six months taken place in Europe and is extremely anxious to defeat the projected Coalition.[1] Prussia observed & seems inclined to adhere to the same cautious policy that for some time has governed her administration.

Poor Spain is compleatly under the influence of the Directory, and however strange it may Seem the King who most cordially hates England shed tears and was inconsolable on the news of Nelsons victory. Portugal is threatened with a war with Spain unless she concludes a Peace on the Terms of the Directory.

There is great discontents in many of the french Departments, but still the Levy of the New Requisition proceeds. The Insurrection of Brabant extends itself,[2] but tho it will give the Directory some trouble, cannot prove successful unless the war soon recommences. Mr. Grenville an Elder Brother of the Minister, has gone on a special mission to Berlin.[3] He is said to be very clever, and has heretofore refused to go into the diplomatic course. Unless favorable circumstances of success exist, one wd. scarcely believe that the Minister would just now have employed his Brother. The french will lose all their Islands trade & influence in the mediterranean. Minorca has been taken by the English,[4] Malta must fall. Corsica will probably expel the french, tho England will not again accept of their capricious allegiance. Zante, Cerigo & Cephalonia, & probably Corfu have fallen into the Hands of the Turks & Russians.[5]

A Report from Constantinople states that Buonaparte has been assassinated; tho probable, it wants Confirmation.[6] Mr Pitt will be supported in the tax of 10. per C. on the income of the Nation; [7] indeed the People appear firm & resolved to support the Govt. & the prosperity of their manufactures & Trade enable them to do so.

Adieu   Yrs.   R K

P. S. I make you my hearty congratulations on the Settlement of the Question of Rank.[8]

Genl. Hamilton

ALS, Hamilton Papers, Library of Congress.
    1. This is a reference to the steps leading to the formation of the Second Coalition against France. On December 24, 1798, Russia and Great Britain formed an alliance to which Austria, Naples, Portugal, and the Ottoman Empire adhered.
    2. On November 10, 1798, The [London] Times reported: "Private letters from Holland mention, that very serious disturbances have taken place in the Low Countries, in consequence of the Agents of the French Directory having attempted to enforce the last requisition in the Provinces in Brabant. In several places the French troops sent to enforce the requisition have been murdered. At Antwerp in particular, the Tree of Liberty has been cut down, and much blood has been spilt there. The people at Mechlin have shown the same opposition, and both towns have been declared in a state of siege. The greatest discontent prevails in Brabant and Flanders, the people being universally tired of the French Government."
    3. On December 6, 1798, The [London] Times announced the selection of Thomas Grenville for "an important mission to Berlin," and on December 17 the same paper reported his departure for Berlin.
    4. For the reports of the British capture of Minorca, see The [London] Times, December 6, 10, 1798.
    5. On December 10, 1798, The [London] Times reported: "The following appears to be the general result of the intelligence received by the German and French papers:

"The Russian and Turkish fleets have taken the small Islands of *Cerigo*, or *Cytherea*, and also the Island of *Zante*. . . . Another division of these combined fleets went against *Provera*, which was taken after a short resistance, and the French garrison made prisoners.

"The above squadrons are understood to be about to form an attack on the Islands of *Corfu* and *Cephalonia*."

This report was incorrect, for it was not until May 1799, that a Russian-Turkish fleet was able to conquer the Ionian Islands from the French.

6. On December 15, 1798, *The* [London] *Times* reported: "These letters [from Constantinople] state that General Buonaparte having been made acquainted with the intentions of the Arab Chief, Mourad Bay, who was marching towards *Cairo*, with a very considerable force to attack him, summoned a Council of War, to which some of the leading men among the natives, who professed friendship to his views, as well as all the superior of his own army were invited to attend. . . .

"Buonaparte having opened the business of the meeting, a Gentleman from Tripoli, who was present, drew a pistol and shot Buonaparte dead on the spot. The native officers followed the example of the Tripolitan Gentleman, by falling on the other French officers, all of whom were put to death."

7. On December 4, 1798, *The* [London] *Times* reported: "Yesterday afternoon Mr. Pitt brought forward in the House of Commons, his new Plan of Finance, which . . . is to be a Tax upon Income, instead of upon Expenditures. The Assessed Taxes are to be altogether abolished; and in lieu of them, every Person is to contribute to the burthens of the State, according to his actual means and property. The parsimonious man will have to contribute in common with the man of more liberal principles and expenditure. The scale of contribution is to be similar to that which was last year adopted for the Assessed Taxes. The man enjoying 60 £ a year is to pay the 1-20th part of his income; and this proportion will rise gradually to an income of 200 £ when the contribution will be 1-10th part." On December 12 the same paper stated: "We are led to believe that there will not be any serious opposition to the new Tax Bill on Income." See King to H, November 9, 1798, note 7.

8. See the introductory note to George Washington to H, July 14, 1798.

To James McHenry [1]

Private   New York Decr. 19. 1798

Dear Sir

You are informed that Mr. *Hill* is in possession of drafts of surveys made during the last war of our harbour and bay.[2] It is very interesting that the Government should acquire these drafts. You will I presume think that they ought to be deposited in your department as an item in the general mass of information necessary towards plans of general defence. If so you will purchase them, if it be not already done; and in this case I will thank for the immediate loan of them; having been charged by the Governor of this state under the sanction of the President with the trust of preparing a plan for the fortification of our port[3]—which plan when digested will be sent to you. Should you decline the purchase, be so good as to say so to General Mc.Pherson,[4] who will be requested to procure the drafts for the use of this state.

With great esteem & regard   I remain Dr Sir   Yr. very Obed serv

A Hamilton

James McHenry Esq

ALS, Mr. Martin Weiner, Paterson, New Jersey; ALS (photostat), James McHenry Papers, Library of Congress; copy, in the handwriting of Philip Church, Hamilton Papers, Library of Congress.

1. For background to this document, see the introductory note to H to McHenry, June 1, 1798.
2. See McHenry to H, June 6, 1798.
3. See John Adams to H, October 17, 1798; H to Adams, October 29, 1798.
4. William Macpherson.

To James McHenry

Private   New York Decr. 20. 1798

Dear Sir

I have been reflecting on the subject of an arrangement for the command of the 2d. Regiment of Artillery and for the Inspectorship of Artillery. I believe on the whole you can do nothing better than appoint *Tousard*,[1] who I understand is next in rank after Burbeck,[2] to the command of the Regiment and Major Hoops[3] to the Inspectorship. Confidence, by *halves* is seldom wise. *Toussard* is in the service—delicate service has been and must be entrusted to him—his fidelity will be best secured by giving him a fair and equal chance, and shewing him that he is not suspected.[4] I shall be much mistaken, if he does not prove to merit confidence.

Hoops is very *intelligent* industrious and persevering—he also has a good deal of information. Perhaps he may have displeased by being sometimes importunate; but that ingredient in the character which may have led to this, as an indication of zeal and perseverance, ought to be no objection to him.

Yrs. truly   A Hamilton

J Mc.Henry Esq

ALS, Columbia University Libraries; ALS (photostat), James McHenry Papers, Library of Congress; copy, in the handwriting of Phillip Church, Hamilton Papers, Library of Congress.

1. Tousard, a former captain of artillery in the French army, was an aide to Lafayette in the American Revolution and a lieutenant colonel in the Continental Army. After the war he served with the French forces in Santo Domingo until 1792 and then returned to France, where he was imprisoned. In 1793 he returned to the United States, and in 1795 he became a major in the United States Army. Between 1795 and 1800 he planned and supervised the building of the fortifications of Fort Mifflin in Pennsylvania, of West Point in New York, and at Newport, Rhode Island. On August 7, 1798, Tousard wrote to H and applied for the position of inspector of artillery (letter listed in the appendix to this volume).

2. Henry Burbeck of Massachusetts was a veteran of the American Revolution who remained in service after the war. He was a lieutenant colonel in the Corps of Artillerists and Engineers.

3. In the seventeen-nineties, Hoops, a veteran of the American Revolution, surveyed the Genessee country in New York for Robert Morris. On June 1, 1798, he had been appointed a major in the Corps of Artillerists and Engineers (*Executive Journal*, I, 277, 279).

4. See John Adams to H, September 4, 1798, in which Adams expressed apprehension about appointing Tousard because Tousard's native country was France (letter listed in the appendix to this volume).

To James McHenry

Private   New York Decr. 20 1798

Dear Sir

I do not know what is the practice in nominations, as to annexing Counties to names; but I do know that to annex them to the military nominations about to be made will be likely to lead to error. In several cases it was somewhat uncertain what County was the place of residence, and if I recollect rightly there is certainly a mistake in this respect in at least one instance in the state of New York. I discover that *Andrew White* [1] is of Dutchess County. I think a different one is annexed to his name. [2] With true esteem & regard.

Yr. Obed servant   A Hamilton

James Mc.Henry Esqr.

ALS, Columbia University Libraries; ALS (photostat), James McHenry Papers, Library of Congress; copy, in the handwriting of Philip Church, Hamilton Papers, Library of Congress.

1. White, a veteran of the American Revolution, was appointed a captain in the Twelfth Regiment of Infantry on January 8, 1799 (*Executive Journal*, I, 299, 303).

2. White is listed as a resident of Schoharie County in the list entitled "Company Arrangement *New York*" (George Washington Papers, Library of Congress). See H's draft of George Washington to McHenry, second letter of December 13, 1798, note 2.

To James McHenry

Private   New York Dec. 20, 1798

Dear Sir

I am this moment favoured with your letter of the 18th. instant and thank you for the ideas personal to me.

Mr. Laurance,[1] somewhat abruptly, regrets that I promoted his son's nomination,[2] as it was his desire that he should continue to pursue his profession. As I could not divine this desire of his, he certainly had no cause of displeasure with me.

In case Laurance's name is witheld at the request of his father, I should be glad to see Young Harrison[3] (the son of our district Attorney[4] and a clever young man—about 20 already admitted to the bar) in his place. I do not mean as high up on the list.

Yrs. truly   A Hamilton

James McHenry Esq.

ALS, anonymous donor; ALS (photostat), James McHenry Papers, Library of Congress; copy, Hamilton Papers, Library of Congress.

1. John Laurance, a New York City lawyer, was a United States judge of the District of New York from 1794 to 1796 and a member of the United States Senate from 1796 to 1800. He and H were close friends and political associates.
2. John McDougal Laurance.
3. George F. Harison.
4. Richard Harison.

To Oliver Wolcott, Junior

[*New York, December 20, 1798.* On December 21, 1798, Wolcott wrote to Hamilton: "I have recd. your favour of the 20th." *Letter not found.*]

From Harrison Gray Otis

Phila Decr 21. 1798

Sir

I was very solicitous while you was in this city for the indulgence of an interview with you that would have enabled me to learn your opinion in relation to such defensive measures as ought now to be adopted by Congress, and I called upon you once with that view, but being then disappointed and perceiving afterwards the pressing nature of your immediate avocations, I chose rather to forego the advantage of your sentiments than invade the little leisure which you appeared able to command. Being since appointed Chairman of a committee to consider the policy of extending our *internal* means of defence,[1] the great confidence which I feel in the correctness of your political opinions, and your permission on a former occasion to avail myself of them induce me to request that I may be honored with your general ideas upon this subject, if you can without inconvenience devote an hour to my instruction. In particular; Is it advisable to augment the present permanent army under all circumstances; if not, would it be eligible to reduce the number of men in each regiment with a view to economy and to an application of the money saved to the extension of the naval armament; or are there any prominent defects in the military establishment which demand a reform. Will there be any utility in reviving the section of the act which establishes the provisional army,[2] or the act providing for the draft of eighty thousand militia.[3] Does good policy require very liberal grants of money for fortifications? Is it expedient to continue the act prohibiting intercourse with France and her *acknowledged* dominions.[4] If so, as the act now stands, may commerce be carried on between the United States, and any part of the French Dominions that shall withdraw from its allegiance to the Parent Country; or if this be doubtful, would it be politic to grant an express permission to the President to open the trade with any part of the French Dominions when in his opinion the public good would admit or require it.

Shall the President be authorized to attack, capture & hold all or any of the French West India Islands as an indemnity for the spoliations committed on our trade?

If upon these or any other subjects, you see fit to gratify me with your opinions, they will be cherished & respected by me, without a disclosure of the source from which they are derived; and if on the other hand you think this liberty is not warranted by the duration or intimacy of my personal acquaintance, you will I hope excuse and impute it to an habitual and profound respect for your character & talents.

I am Sir   yr most obedt Servt.   H. G. Otis

ALS, Hamilton Papers, Library of Congress.

1. On December 14, 1798, the House of Representatives, after resolving "itself into a Committee of the Whole House," agreed to four resolutions. The second of these resolutions reads: "Resolved, as the opinion of this committee, That so much of the speech of the President of the United States to both Houses of Congress, at the commencement of the present session, as relates to the 'policy of extending and invigorating the measures of defence heretofore adopted by the Government of the United States,' be referred to a committee." The House then "Ordered That Mr. Otis, Mr. [John] Rutledge [of South Carolina], Mr. [Chauncy] Goodrich [of Connecticut], Mr. Samuel Smith [of Maryland], Mr. [Christopher G.] Champlin [of Rhode Island], Mr. [Richard Dobbs] Spaight [of North Carolina], and Mr. [George] Dent [of Maryland], be appointed a committee pursuant to the second resolution" (*Journal of the House,* III, 410).

2. "An Act authorizing the President of the United States to raise a Provisional Army" (1 *Stat.* 558–61 [May 28, 1798]). This act authorized an army of ten thousand men.

3. "An Act authorizing a detachment from the Militia of the United States" (1 *Stat.* 522 [June 24, 1797]).

4. "An Act to suspend the commercial intercourse between the United States and France, and the dependencies thereof" (1 *Stat.* 565–66 [June 13, 1798]).

From Oliver Wolcott, Junior

Phila. Decr. 21. 1798

Dear Sir

I have recd. your favour of the 20th.[1] with Twenty Dollars. The sum I lent you was Thirty Dollars. Yesterday I sent you [2] a small bill which you forgot to pay. No Consul can be recd. at present.[3]

The result of all the enquiries which I have been able to make is, that a small sum, might be raised by the gradual sale of 7½ ℔ Cent Stock at par but that there can be no certainty, that a Loan would immediately be filled, for the sum we want under 8 ℔ Cent.[4]

If among your acquaintances you discover any circumstances to vary this opinion be pleased to inform me *soon.*

I am respectfully yrs   Oliv Wolcott.

A Hamilton Esqr

ALS, Hamilton Papers, Library of Congress; copy, Connecticut Historical Society, Hartford.
1. Letter not found.
2. Letter not found.
3. On the back of this letter is written: "William Kellock Mercht. Cork requests the appointment of American Consul for that port. He is a respectable Mercht. and resided some years in the United states where he was admitted a citizen."
4. "An Act to enable the President of the United States to borrow money for the public service" (1 *Stat.* 607–08 [July 16, 1798]) provided: "That the President of the United States shall be, and hereby is authorized to borrow, on behalf of the United States, from the Bank of the United States, which is hereby authorized to lend the same, or from any other body or bodies politic or corporate, or from any person or persons and upon such terms and conditions as he shall judge most advantageous for the United States, a sum not exceeding five millions of dollars, in addition to the monies to be received into the treasury of the United States, from taxes, for making up any deficiency in any appropriation heretofore made by law, or to be made during the present session of Congress; and defraying the expenses which may be incurred, by calling into actual service, any part of the militia of the United States, or by raising, equipping and calling into actual service any regular troops, or volunteers, pursuant to authorities vested or to be vested in the President of the United States, by law." The loan was to be reimbursable after fifteen years, and the surplus of duties on imports and tonnage was pledged for the repayment of principal and interest.
Under the provisions of this act the Government raised five million dollars by subscription and issued an equal amount of stock bearing eight percent interest yearly (Raphael A. Bayley, *The National Loans of the United States from July 4, 1776, to June 30, 1880* [Washington, 1882], 44).
In 1801 a House committee reported that this loan was "negotiated upon the best terms that could be procured, and with a laudable view to the public interest" (*ASP, Finance,* I, 692).

To James Gunn

[New York, December 22, 1798]

Introductory Note

This letter concerns proposals for reorganizing the Army. This is a complicated subject, for it involves a series of bewildering statutes en-

Copy, in the handwriting of Philip Church, James McHenry Papers, Library of Congress; copy, in the handwriting of Philip Church, Hamilton Papers, Library of Congress.

acted by Congress concerning the Regular Army, Additional Army, Provisional Army, and Eventual Army.

When the Constitution went into effect in 1789, the new government inherited an army which had served under the Continental Congress and which was the nucleus of the Regular Army of the United States.[1] To this force, which originally consisted of one regiment of infantry and one battalion of artillery,[2] a second regiment of infantry was added in 1791,[3] and in March, 1792, additional legislation provided for an army of four regiments of infantry, one battalion of artillery, and a squadron of light dragoons.[4] In an effort to achieve coordination among the three branches of the Army established by Congress, Major General Anthony Wayne on September 4, 1792, issued general orders transforming the Regular Army into the Legion of the United States.[5] The Legion, in turn, was divided into four sublegions, each of which consisted of one company of artillery, one regiment of infantry, and one troop of light dragoons.[6] During the next four years the only change in the Regular Army occurred in 1794 when the battalion of engineers was enlarged to a corps.[7] Throughout the period when the Army was divided into sublegions, officers held their appointments as infantrymen, artillerists, or dragoons in one of the four sublegions.

In 1796 Congress abolished the division of the armed forces into sublegions and enacted legislation providing for four regiments of infantry, a corps of artillerists and engineers, and two companies of light dragoons.[8] Two years later a regiment of artillerists and engineers was added to this force,[9] and in 1799 the Corps of Artillerists and Engineers

1. "An Act to recognize and adapt to the Constitution of the United States the establishment of the Troops raised under the Resolves of the United States in Congress assembled, and for other purposes therein mentioned" (1 *Stat.* 95–96 [September 29, 1789]). In 1789 this force consisted of 672 enlisted men (Henry Knox's report to George Washington, August 8, 1789 [*ASP, Military Affairs*, I, 5–6]).

2. See *JCC*, XXVII, 530–31; XXXI, 892–93; XXXIII, 603.

3. "An Act for raising and adding another Regiment to the Military Establishment of the United States, and for making farther provision for the protection of the frontiers" (1 *Stat.* 222–24 [March 3, 1791]). The authorized strength of this new regiment was 912 men and 57 commissioned officers (Heitman, *United States Army*, II, 561).

4. "An Act for making farther and more effectual Provision for the Protection of the Frontiers of the United States' (1 *Stat.* 241–43 [March 5, 1792]).

5. Heitman, *United States Army*, I, 139. The Legion was composed of 5,414 enlisted men and officers (Heitman, *United States Army*, II, 562).

6. Heitman, *United States Army*, I, 50, 79, 81.

7. "An Act providing for raising and organizing a Corp of Artillerists and Engineers" (1 *Stat.* 366–67 [May 9, 1794]). The Corps included 764 new noncommissioned officers, privates, and artificers, and the existing battalion of artillery.

8. "An Act to ascertain and fix the Military Establishment of the United States" (1 *Stat.* 483–86 [May 30, 1796]). This statute reduced the military force to 3,359 men.

9. "An Act to provide an additional regiment of Artillerists and Engineers" (1 *Stat.* 552–53 [April 27, 1798]).

was transformed into a regiment. By 1799, then, the Regular Army consisted of four regiments of infantry of eight companies each, two regiments of artillerists and engineers, and one regiment of light dragoons. Hamilton and his contemporaries usually referred to the Regular Army as the "old regiments" or the "old army."

Throughout the period when Hamilton served as inspector general, most of the Regular Army (with the exception of the Additional Army mentioned below) was stationed in the West. One regiment of infantry and two companies of cavalry were assigned to the frontiers of Georgia and Tennessee. The three other regiments of infantry were distributed along the Canadian border and at posts on the Miami, Ohio, Mississippi, and Tombigbee rivers. The members of a battalion of artillerists and engineers also served on the northern and western frontiers. The remainder of the artillerists and engineers, except for those in the field, manned the nation's coastal defenses.[10] Hamilton was in command of those troops on the western frontier and in the Middle Atlantic and New England states; Charles Cotesworth Pinckney commanded the cavalry and the troops in the southern states.

The Additional Army was created on July 16, 1798, with the passage by Congress of "An Act to augment the Army of the United States, and for other purposes." [11] This act increased the authorized strength of the Army from 4,173 to 14,421 officers and men [12] and authorized the President "to raise, in addition to the present military establishment, twelve regiments of infantry, and six troops of light dragoons to be enlisted for and during the continuance of the existing differences between the United States and the French Republic, unless sooner discharged. . . ." Although the twelve regiments provided for by this act were part of the Regular Army, they were a separate and distinct part and were treated as such, and the War Department handled the recruitment and officering of these regiments separately from those of the Regular Army.[13] Moreover, Hamilton held his commissions as major general and inspector general under the act of July 16, 1798, and during the last months of 1798 and all of 1799 he devoted a large part of his time and attention to raising the twelve additional regiments authorized by Congress.

Each of the infantry regiments in the Additional Army consisted of ten companies. These regiments were numbered from five to sixteen, and each was assigned a state or states from which it could draw its recruits. The Fifth Regiment was to enlist soldiers in South Carolina, Georgia, and Kentucky; the Sixth Regiment in North Carolina and Tennessee; the Seventh and Eighth regiments in Virginia; the Ninth

10. See James McHenry's report to John Adams, January 5, 1800 (*ASP, Military Affairs*, I, 139).

11. 1 *Stat.* 604-05. This act was somewhat modified by "An Act for the better organizing of the Troops of the United States; and for other purposes" (1 *Stat.* 749-55 [March 3, 1799]).

12. Heitman, *United States Army*, II, 566.

13. See McHenry to Washington, November 10, 1798, enclosed in Washington to H, November 12, 1798. See also H's draft of Washington to McHenry, first letter of December 13, 1798.

Regiment in Maryland; the Tenth Regiment in Pennsylvania; the Eleventh Regiment in Pennsylvania, New Jersey, and Delaware; the Twelfth Regiment in New York; the Thirteenth Regiment in Connecticut; the Fourteenth Regiment in Massachusetts; the Fifteenth Regiment in Massachusetts and the District of Maine; and the Sixteenth Regiment in New Hampshire, Rhode Island, and Vermont. Enlistees for the cavalry in the Additional Army were to be drawn from Pennsylvania, New Jersey, Virginia, Maryland, and South Carolina.[14] Hamilton was in command of those regiments of the Additional Army north of Virginia, and Pinckney commanded the cavalry and the infantry regiments in Virginia and the other southern states.[15]

The beginning of the end of the Additional Army was signalized on February 20, 1800, with the passage of "An Act to suspend in part, an act, intituled 'An act to augment the Army of the United States; and for other purposes,'" which provided: "That all further enlistments under the second section of an act, intituled 'An act to augment the army of the United States, and for other purposes' shall be suspended until the further order of Congress, unless in the recess of Congress, and during the continuance of the existing differences between the United States and the French Republic, war shall break out between the United States and the French Republic, or imminent danger of invasion of their territory by the said Republic, shall in the opinion of the President of the United States, be discovered to exist."[16] Then on May 14, 1800, Congress passed an act providing for the disbandment of most of the Additional Army.[17] Under this act it was "lawful for the President of the United States to suspend any further military appointments" to the Additional Army. In addition, this act provided: "That the President of the United States shall be, and hereby is authorized and empowered to discharge, on or before the fifteenth day of June next, all such officers, non-commissioned, or raised, under and by virtue of the said acts, or either of them, except the engineers, inspector of artillery, and inspector of fortifications. *Provided always*, that nothing in this act contained shall be construed to authorize any reduction of the first four regiments of infantry, the two regiments of artillerists and engineers, the two troops of light dragoons, or of the general and other staff, authorized by the several laws for the establishing and organizing of the aforesaid corps."

14. See Godfrey, "Provisional Army," 129–32.

15. According to McHenry, the following numbers of non-commissioned officers, privates, and musicians were actually in service: 116 in the two companies of cavalry, 1,501 in the two regiments of artillerists and engineers, 1,812 in the first four regiments of infantry, and 3,399 in the twelve additional infantry regiments (McHenry to Harrison Gray Otis of the Committee of Defence of the House of Representatives, January 2, 1800; McHenry's report to Adams, January 5, 1800 [*ASP, Military Affairs*, I, 132, 141]).

16. 2 *Stat.* 7.

17. "An Act supplementary to the act to suspend part of an act, intituled 'An act to augment the Army of the United States; and for other purposes'" (2 *Stat.* 85–86). This act fixed the size of the military establishment at 4,436 men and officers (Heitman, *United States Army*, II, 568).

The Provisional Army [18] was a paper organization which not only never took the field but was not even raised. On May 28, 1798, Congress passed an act authorizing the "President of the United States . . . in the event of a declaration of war against the United States, or of actual invasion of their territory, by a foreign power, or of imminent danger of such invasion discovered in his opinion to exist, before the next session of Congress, to cause to be enlisted, and to call into actual service, a number of troops, not exceeding ten thousand non-commissioned officers, musicians and privates, to be enlisted for a term not exceeding three years. . . ." [19] Congress reconvened on December 3, 1798, and on that date, in accordance with the terms of the act of May 28, 1798, the President lost his authority to raise a Provisional Army. In the interval between the passage of the act and the reconvening of Congress, Adams had made no effort to recruit anyone for the Provisional Army, but he did nominate—and the Senate approved—seven men to be officers in that army.[20] The commissions held by these officers did not, however, automatically lapse on December 3, 1798, for Section 9 of the act of May 28, 1798, provided that "the commander of the army . . . and the general, field and commissioned officers who may be appointed by virtue of this act, shall respectively continue in commission during such term only as the President shall judge requisite for the public service." [21] The point, however, is academic, for these officers had no troops to command either before or after December 3, 1798. Finally, to add still further to the confusion, no record has been found that either the President or the War Department ever informed these men that they were no longer officers in the Provisional Army.

To fill the statutory void created by the demise of the Provisional Army, Congress gave the President the authority to raise the Eventual Army. On March 2, 1799, Congress passed "An Act giving eventual authority to the President of the United States to augment the Army." [22] This act provided: "That it shall be lawful for the President of the United States, in case war shall break out between the United States and a foreign European power, or in case imminent danger of invasion of their territory by any such power shall, in his opinion, be discovered to exist, to organize and cause to be raised in addition to the other military force of the United States, twenty-four regiments of infantry, a regiment and a battalion of riflemen, a battalion of artillerists and engineers, and three regiments of cavalry, or such part thereof as he shall

18. The Provisional Army has frequently been confused with the Additional Army. See Washington to H, July 14, 1798, note 2.

19. "An Act authorizing the President of the United States to raise a Provisional Army" (1 *Stat.* 558–61).

20. The seven were George Washington as lieutenant general (*Executive Journal*, I, 284 [July 2, 3, 1798]), Henry Lee and Edward Hand as major generals, and Ebenezer Huntington, Anthony Walton White, William R. Davie, and John Sevier as brigadier generals (*Executive Journal*, I, 292, 293 [July 17, 1798]).

21. 1 *Stat.* 559–60.

22. 1 *Stat.* 725–27.

judge necessary; the non-commissioned officers and privates of which to be enlisted for a term not exceeding three years. . . ." The final section of this act stated that the President's power to raise such an army "shall cease at the expiration of the session of Congress next ensuing the present, unless . . . [it] shall be, by some future law, continued in force for a longer time." During the period that this law was in effect (that is, until May 14, 1800), Adams submitted to the Senate no nominations for officers in the Eventual Army. On the other hand, on March 11, 1799, James McHenry wrote to William Macpherson of Pennsylvania that he had been appointed a brigadier general in the Eventual Army and that he would command the troops sent to suppress Fries's Rebellion.[23] Macpherson thus had the distinction, if indeed it was a distinction, of being the only officer in the Eventual Army.

The bulk of the troops under Macpherson's command were from the Corps of Volunteers which was originally authorized on May 28, 1798, by Section 3 of "An Act authorizing the President of the United States to raise a Provisional Army." [24] Private citizens who organized themselves into volunteer companies and who provided their own arms and equipment could be accepted into the service of the United States by the President ". . . at any time within three years after the passing of this act, if in his opinion the public interest shall require," and they ". . . shall be liable to be called upon to do military duty at any time the President shall judge proper, within two years after he shall accept the same." An act of June 22, 1798, gave the President the authority to issue rules for the training and discipline of the volunteers,[25] and the conditions of service under which the volunteers would serve were later changed by an act of March 2, 1799.[26] Although many such companies were formed, the only ones which saw active duty were those commanded by Macpherson.

New York Decr. 22nd. 1798

My dear Sir

The post of yesterday brought me your favor of the 19th instant. The sentiments in it personal to me are extremely gratifying—and I am very glad to ascertain the military ground upon which you are not unwilling to stand. If things progress, I trust there will be no obstacle to your occupying it.

As to further military arrangements my ideas are these. Considering how little has been done towards raising the force already voted,[27] that an important tax is yet in the first stage of an Essay [28]—

23. Copy, James McHenry Papers, Library of Congress.
24. 1 *Stat.* 558–61.
25. "An Act supplementary to, and to amend the act, intituled 'An act authorizing the President of the United States to raise a provisional army'" (1 *Stat.* 569–70).
26. 1 *Stat.* 725–27.
27. The Additional Army.
28. See "An Act to lay and collect a direct tax within the United States" (1 *Stat.* 597–604 [July 14, 1798]).

that a prospect of peace is again presented by the temporizing conduct of France—that serious discontents exist [29] in parts of the country with regard to particular laws—it appears to me adviseable to postpone any actual augmentation of the army beyond the provisions of the existing laws; except as to the Regiment of Cavalry, which I should be glad to see increased, by the addition of two troops, and by the allowing it to be recruited to the complement which has been proposed by the commander in Chief as that of the war-establishment.[30] What this is will probably be communicated by the Secretary at War.[31]

But a considerable addition ought certainly to be made to our military supplies. The communications of the commander in Chief will also afford a standard for the increase in this respect, as far as concerns the force to be employed in the field. There are however some other objects of supply equally essential which were not within the view of those communications. Heavy Cannon for our fortifications and mortars for the case of a siege. Of the former, including those already procured and procuring, there ought not to be fewer than one thousand from eighteen to thirty two pounders, chiefly of twenty four—of the latter including those on hand, there ought to be fifty of ten inch Caliber. This you perceive looks to offensive operations. If we are to engage in war our game will be to attack where we can. France is not to be considered as separate from her ally.[32] Tempting objects will be within our Grasp.[33]

Will it not likewise be proper to renew and extend the idea of a Provisional Army? [34] The force which has been contemplated as sufficient in every event is 40,000 Infantry of the line, 2,000 Riflemen, 4,000 Cavalry, and 4,000 Artillery, making in the whole an army of fifty thousand. Why should not the *provisional* army go to the extent of the difference between that number and the actual

29. This is a reference to opposition to the Alien and Sedition Acts.
30. See H's draft of Washington to McHenry, first letter of December 13, 1798.
31. This is a reference to a report which McHenry submitted to President Adams on December 24, 1798, and which Adams submitted to Congress on December 31, 1798. This report is printed in *ASP, Military Affairs*, I, 124–29. See also McHenry to H, December 18, 1798, note 2.
32. Spain.
33. For an explanation of the contents of this sentence, see Francisco de Miranda to H, February 7, April 6–June 7, October 10–November 10, 1798; H to Miranda, August 22, 1798; H to Rufus King, August 22, 1798.
34. See the introductory note to this letter.

army? I think this ought to be the case, and that the President ought to be authorized immediately to nominate the Officers—to remain without pay till called into service. The arrangement can then be made with sufficient leisure for the best possible selection; and the persons designated will be employed in acquiring instructions.

It will likewise well deserve consideration whether provision ought to be made for classing all persons from eighteen to forty five inclusively, and for drafting out of them by lot *in case of Invasion* the number necessary to complete the entire army of fifty thousand. In the case of Invasion the expedient of drafting must be resorted to, and it will greatly expedite it, if there be a previous classing with a view to such an event.[35] The measure too will place the Country in a very imposing attitude and will add to the motives of caution on the part of our enemies.

These measures are all that appear to be adviseable with regard to our military establishment under present appearances. A loan as an auxiliary will of course be annexed.

With greatest esteem   I remain dear Sir   Your very obed Servant

General Gunn

This is communicated *in confidence*. I send [it] as well because I think it proper to do so & as because I wish you to see the train of my *ideas*.[36]

35. See Harrison Gray Otis to H, December 21, 1798.
36. The postscript is in H's handwriting. It does not appear on the copy in the Hamilton Papers, Library of Congress.

To John Laurance [1]

New York December 26. 1798

Dear Sir

Mr. Lenox [2] has just informed me that our joint bond for six thousand Dollars in his hands became due the middle of this month & that as yet no arrangement has been made for satisfying it, intimating at the same time that he was willing to take negotiable notes at short periods for the amount. He added that in a letter to him you spoke of my having to pay a part of the sum.

On this last point there is a misconception with one of us. If my calculation be right I have already advanced beyond my proportion of the land. My mind has been long since made up not to extend my share beyond what was originally intended. The operation is one very unpromising, and, as it turns out, very inconvenient to me. I have never made other speculations to compensate me for the badness of this one; of course I am not disposed to go further in it than was strictly my original concern. And I think when you reflect on my situation altogether, you will not expect that I shall voluntarily engage for more. I regret any embarrassment which may attend you but your resources are far greater than mine and you can more easily than me meet the demand.

I must accordingly entreat you my good friend to lose no time in taking up the bond. I shall be extremely pained if my credit suffers in a case in which I am only nominal.

If you can satisfy me by a statement of our mutual advances that on the ground of my interest in the premisses, I ought to pay a further sum I will exert myself to do it.

With great esteem & regard   I am Dr Sir   Yr. very obed serv

A Hamilton

PS. Pray attend carefully to this business

John Laurance Esq

ALS, New-York Historical Society, New York City.
1. For an explanation of the contents of this letter, see Jacob Mark and Company to John B. Church, H, and Laurance, May 30, 1797; Laurance to H, June 3, December 10, 1797.
2. Robert Lenox, a native of Scotland, immigrated to New York City, where he became a prominent merchant and an investor in city real estate. He remained in New York City during part of the American Revolution and served the British as a clerk in the office of commissary of naval prisoners. In 1797 he was also a New York City alderman and a director of the New York branch of the Bank of the United States. See "Certificate on Robert Lenox," January 11, 1796; Laurance to H, December 10, 1797, note 2.

From Herman LeRoy, William Bayard, and James McEvers

[*New York*] *December 26, 1798.* ". . . enclose him a Memorandum of payments made during the present year."

AL, in LeRoy's handwriting, Hamilton Papers, Library of Congress.

To Herman LeRoy and William Bayard

[*New York, December 26, 1798.* The dealer's catalogue description reads: "On money matters." *Letter not found.*]

Sold by G. Michelmore and Company, Catalogue No. 13.

To James McHenry

Private   New York Decr. 26. 1798

Dr Sir

As it may possibly not have come to you through any other channel, I think it well to inform you that General Huntington [1] has been displeased at not having received official notice of his appointment with his Commission. This, if not already so, ought to be remedied.

I hear nothing of nominations. What malignant influence hangs upon our military affairs?

With great esteem & regard   Yr. Obed servt   A Hamilton

P.S. I left with General Pinckney a project of a Military School, which he was to have sent me? Has he quitted Philadelphia? If so have you heared any thing of this paper? I want it.[2]

James McHenry Esqr.

ALS, James McHenry Papers, Library of Congress; copy, in the handwriting of Philip Church, Hamilton Papers, Library of Congress.
1. Ebenezer Huntington.
2. For the "project of a Military School," see H to Louis Le Bègue Du Portail, July 23, 1798; Du Portail to H, December 9, 1798.

To William Macpherson [1]

New York Decr. 26. 1798

Dear Sir

A Capt *Hill*, formerly of the British service, now in Philadelphia, is in possession of drafts of surveys, which were made during our war, of the Port & Harbour of New York. If the Secretary at War, of whom you will please to inquire, has not procured them for the United States, you will oblige me by purchasing them for the use of this State. The money which you may pay will be reimbursed upon Notice of the amount. If separable, I wish for those only from the *Narrows* downwards to the *Hook*. But if an entire draft, it must be purchased together.

Yrs very truly   A Hamilton

General Macpherson

ALS, Hamilton Papers, Library of Congress.
1. For background to this letter, see the introductory note to H to James McHenry, June 1, 1798; H to McHenry, December 19, 1798.

To Harrison Gray Otis

New York Decr: 27th 1798

Dr Sir

I did not receive 'till yesterday your letter dated 21st instant. No apology was necessary for so gratifying a mark of your good opinion, upon which I set the high value it so justly deserves.

In the inclosed extract of a letter [1] to another of the Government, you will find my ideas generally on the subject of your letter. I adopt this method of communication as equally effectual and best adapted to the multiplicity of my avocations. Some additional remarks in direct reference to your particular questions may perhaps be requisite to fulfil your object.

Any reduction of the actual force appears to me inexpedient. It will argue to our enemy that we are either very narrow in our resources or that our jealousy of his designs are abated. Besides that with a view to the possibility of internal disorders alone, the force authorised is not too considerable. The efficacy of Militia for suppressing such disorders is not too much to be relied upon. The experience of the Western expedition ought not to be .[2] That was a very uphill business. There were more than once appearances to excite alarm as to the perseverance of the troops and it is not easy to foresee what might have been the result had there been serious resistance. The repetition of similar exertions may be found very difficult—insomuch as to render it extremely [3] in these precarious times to have the Government armed with the whole of the force which has been voted.

There are several defects in the military establishment which demand reform as well for œconomy as efficiency. On these there has been an ample communication from the commander in Chief to the department of War. I cannot conceive why nothing has yet gone to Congress—certainly this cannot be much longer delayed.[4] Will it be amiss informally to interrogate the Minister? If the silence is persisted in, you shall know from me the objects.

The extract answers your question as to the Provisional army. I think the act respecting the 80,000 Milita ought likewise to be revived.[5] The effect abroad will be good, and it will likewise be so at home as the evidence of a reliance of the Government on the Militia.

Good policy does not appear to me to require extensive appropriations for fortifications at the *present juncture*. Money can be more usefully employed in other ways. A good deal of previous examination ought to lead to a plan for fortifying three or four *cardinal* points. More than this will be a misapplication of money. Secure position for Arsenals and Dock Yards are in this view a primary object.

Your last question respecting the West India Islands I shall reserve for a future communication.

With great esteem & regard   I am Dr Sir   Your very obed serv

A Hamilton

Copy, in the handwriting of Philip Church, Hamilton Papers, Library of Congress.

1. The enclosure may have been a copy of H to James Gunn, December 22, 1798.
2. Space left blank in MS.
3. Space left blank in MS.
4. See H's drafts of George Washington to James McHenry, first and third letters of December 13, 1798. McHenry's report to John Adams was sent on December 24, 1798. Adams in turn sent it to Congress on December 31, 1798 (*ASP, Military Affairs*, I, 124–29). See also McHenry to H, December 18, 1798.
5. See Otis to H, December 21, 1798.

From John Laurance [1]

Philadelphia
Dec 28 1798

Dear Sir

I have received your favor of the 26th Instant. The enclosed, which I had prepared to shew you, before your departure from this place, if correct, states the purchase, and payments, on account of it. You will perceive I have made my Interest one fourth of the whole, being the Interest you supposed I originally intended to have. The loss on the Bills I have not brought into account. My proportion of that loss I shall have to settle. I informed Mr Lennox I should have to pay, the greater part of the Obligation, and as this was the only Sum due, it was reasonable we should have a Release from Mr. Gilchrist, who held the Mortgage, of the parts we had, supposing the one fourth of Mr Marks', and the other Lands, Mortgaged by him, were sufficient Security, that this Security would increase, by our being able to improve the property, which, at present, we were not; owing to the Mortgage on it. I have applied to know what Ballance is due from Mr Mark, who ought to have paid the Instalments, as ours became due, but have not received it. You must remember that our paper was partly negotiable, and partly not, and the reasons for the latter were, that we should have credit on the Mortgage, and not be pressed to pay. I should be very sorry if your Credit should suffer, or mine either, by not paying this Obligation, with as much punctuality as a Note at Bank. I presume, considering the payments made, on this purchase, to Mr. Mark, and the ballance due from him on the Mortgage, affecting our property, if the Obligation had remained with him, neither your Credit, nor mine would suffer for not immediately discharging it; and why it should have this Effect, because it is in the possession of Mr. Lennox I cannot determine, but, I assure you, because it is in his hands I shall make exertions to pay it, which I should not have done had it remained with Mr Mark, after his Assurance to us, when we wished the last negotiable note to be placed to the Credit of the Mortgage, that he should be ready to pay, as the Instalments became due.

I am sorry the purchase has been an unprofitable one to you. It has been more so to myself; but I hope the result will be otherwise, when these times, which neither you nor myself could divine, would have happened, have passed away, and a state of things Exists, very different from the present. It has been my wish to divide this property, and to effect it, I wrote, last Summer, to Mr Wright,[2] who divided the Towns into Lots requesting he would class the Lots in each Town and divide them into four parts, excepting as many Lots from the Division, as were necessary, for the compact Settlements intended in No 21, and inclose the Information to Mr Church, that we might ballot for our respective Shares, you and Mr Church for two quarter parts, and Mr Mark and myself each a quarter. I have requested Col Troup to ask Mr Church whether he has received the Information; but as yet I am not informed on the Subject. If he has not received it I shall, when I am in New York, which I hope will be, in the course of next week, execute a Deed to Mr Church and yourself for an undivided Moiety holding Mr Marks quarter, subject to the Incumbrance on it, so that each person may dispose of his property as he deems best.

I am Dear Sir   respectfully & sincerely   Your obedient servant

John Laurance

Major Genl Hamilton

P.S. I beg you to be carefu⟨l of⟩ the Statement.

ALS, Yale University Library.
1. For background to this letter, see Jacob Mark and Company to John B. Church, H, and Laurance, May 30, 1797; Laurance to H, June 3, December 10, 1797; H to Laurance, December 26, 1798.
2. In November, 1794, Benjamin Wright surveyed Scriba's patent and divided it into towns (David E. E. Mix, ed., *Catalogue: Maps and Surveys, in the*

Offices of the Secretary of State, State Engineer and Surveyor, and Comptroller, and the New York State Library [Albany, 1859], 19).

From James McHenry

private   Philad. 28 Decr. 1798

Dear Sir

I have this moment received two letters from you under dates of the 20th & one dated the 26th.

The President desired the list of nominations to be submitted to the heads of Departments for their observations; [1] and I have not yet been favoured with these observations. I mean from all of these gentlemen. I expect them to day, and that the nominations will be made on monday.[2] Col Smith's [3] name will stand—several names will be omitted, some of whom would not accept if appointed others found to be disqualified. These places will not be filled up till time can be given for consideration & information.

Gen Pinckney has left Town & left no project of a military school with me.[4]

On the 24th Inst I finished my report to the President which will be laid before congress on the subject of our military affairs.[5] It embraces all the points noticed in Gen. Washingtons letters [6] with additional matter with which I hope you will be satisfied. I have in the report availed myself of his name. I conceived this course preferable as it respected the head of the department, than a submission in any form of his letters to Congress.

There would be no end to complainings and heartburning were a foreigner to be placed at the head of the 2d regt of artillery.[7] Hoops would be less exceptionable, and in a little time more scientific. I am not at all displeased with him. He will mend of the failing you mention, I have no doubt, as soon as he perceives it likely to stand in the way of his promotion.

I inclose you a copy of the recruiting instructions [8] & the bases upon which they have been formed.[9]

Your sincere friend   James McHenry

Majr Gen Alexr Hamilton E

ALS, Hamilton Papers, Library of Congress; ADf, James McHenry Papers, Library of Congress.

1. A copy of this list was enclosed in McHenry to Timothy Pickering, December 18, 1798 (LS, RG 59, Miscellaneous Letters, 1789–1825, National Archives).

2. McHenry submitted the list of officers selected by George Washington, H, and Charles Cotesworth Pinckney at their meetings in Philadelphia during November and December, 1798, to John Adams on December 29, 1798 (ADfS, James McHenry Papers, Library of Congress; LS, James McHenry Papers, Library of Congress).

On Monday, December 31, 1798, Adams sent to the Senate his list of nominations for officers to the Additional Army (*Executive Journal* I, 298–302). The Senate considered and acted on these nominations on January 8, 10, 14, 15, and 18 (*Executive Journal*, I, 303–07). Copies of this list are in the George Washington Papers, Library of Congress, and in the James McHenry Papers, Library of Congress, and are enclosed in McHenry to Pickering, December 18, 1798 (LS, RG 59, Miscellaneous Letters, 1798–1825, National Archives).

For H's lists of candidates for Army appointments, see the enclosure to H to McHenry, August 21, 1798; "Candidates for Army Appointments from Massachusetts," December 9–28, 1798; "Candidates for Army Appointments from Connecticut," November–December, 1798; "Candidates for Army Appointments from Delaware," November–December, 1798; "Candidates for Army Appointments from Kentucky," November–December, 1798; "Candidates for Army Appointments from Maryland," November–December, 1798; "Candidates for Army Appointments from Tennessee," November–December, 1798.

3. William S. Smith. See H's draft of Washington to McHenry, second letter of December 13, 1798, note 3.

4. See H to Louis Le Bègue Du Portail, July 23, 1798; Du Portail to H, December 9, 1798; H to McHenry, December 26, 1798.

5. Adams submitted McHenry's report of December 24, 1798, to Congress on December 31, 1798 (*Annals of Congress*, IX, 3614–27).

6. See H's drafts of three letters from Washington to McHenry, December 13, 1798.

7. See H to McHenry, first letter of December 20, 1798.

8. This is a reference to the 1798 edition of the War Department printed pamphlet *Rules and Regulations Respecting the Recruiting Service*. See H to Jonathan Dayton, August 6, 1798, note 6.

9. See McHenry to H, December 18, 1798, note 2.

To Oliver Wolcott, Junior

New York Decr: 28. 1798

Dear Sir,

I have embraced every opportunity since the receipt of yours of the 21st to obtain light on the subject of the loan. But my research has been essentially fruitless. Opinions are as various as they are vague. You must therefore conjecture, and you ought to act on the sure side for selling the loan.

For my part, I retain the opinion that the loan ought to be upon eight per Cent Interest, the Capital to be fixed for ten years, and then to become redeemable at pleasure; One per Cent to be appropriated cotemporarily as a purchasing fund for sinking the principal. And the loan to be open for competition, for the entire or any less sum time enough to let in European bidders. The true principle is to get as good terms as possible for the United States, exclusive of local considerations; which can only have a temporary and illusory operation. The Stock will find its way to its proper market wherever it may be first sold.

Yrs very truly   A Hamilton

Inclosed the sum necessary per your balance & the Hair dressers bill Account deducting two dollars which I paid him myself.

O Wolcott Esqr.

Copy, in the handwriting of Philip Church, Hamilton Papers, Library of Congress.

Report of the Committee of the Corporation and the Military Committee to the Common Council of the City of New York [1]

[New York, December 31, 1798]

The adjoining account [2] shews the expenditures & Nearly all the responsibilities of the Fortifying Committee. In addition to the fifty thousand Dollars already advanced by the Corporation, Ten thousand Dollars more is requisite to pay off the pressing demands for unsettled accounts; they therefore solicit the Corporation to advance them this further Sum, not doubting but the Legislature will in the present Session make provision for reimbursing the Sums. [3] They further observe that they have only compleated the objects, which it was originally calculated would not exceed the fifty thousand Dollars.

New York 31 Decr. 1798

Alexander Hamilton
Ebenr Stevens.

Jno. B. Coles
Gabriel Furman
John Bogert

DS, Municipal Archives and Records Center, New York City.

1. For background to this document, see the introductory note to H to James McHenry, June 1, 1798.

The Committee of the Corporation for the defense of New York City consisted of John B. Coles, Gabriel Furman, and John Bogert. See the introductory note to H to McHenry, June 1, 1798. The Military Committee consisted of H, Ebenezer Stevens, and Aaron Burr. See "Call for a Meeting," June 4, 1798, note 2.

2. D, Municipal Archives and Records Center, New York City. This account is entitled "An Account of Expenditures under the directions of the Committee of the Corporation and the Military Committee. For building Four Batteries, Mounting Artillery and providing Military Stores for them. For building Arsenals, And for Surveying the Harbour of New York. since 29th June 1798." The account shows total expenditures of $57,242.65.

3. On December 31, 1798, the Common Council also "Resolved that Aldn Gabriel Furman be authorized on behalf of this Board to draw from the Bank of New York such further Sums as may be necessary for the above purpose not exceedg 10,000 Dollars" (*Minutes of the Common Council*, II, 491).

To Elizabeth Hamilton

[*1798*]. "I am almost ready to abandon every thing & fly to you— But I am so entangled with war & law that it is impossible."

Copy, Columbia University Libraries.

To Martin S. Wilkins

[*1798*]. Acknowledges receipt of Wilkins's "notice as to the Trial between Gouverneur and Kemble and Gomez Lopez & Rivera."

ADf, Miscellaneous Papers in Chancery, Court of Appeals, Albany.

1. H wrote this letter as attorney for Louis Le Guen in his suit against Isaac Gouverneur and Peter Kemble. As the letter calendared above indicates, Gouverneur and Kemble were in turn the plaintiffs in a suit against Isaac Gomez, Jr., Moses Lopez, and Abraham R. Rivera. For these and related cases, see Goebel, *Law Practice*, II, 48–164.

Martin, a New York City lawyer, was counsel for Gouverneur and Kemble in their suit against Gomez, Lopez, and Rivera.

2. At the bottom of this letter is the draft of an affidavit signed by H and Brockholst Livingston stating that they had received notice of this trial.

Livingston was the attorney for the defendants in *Le Guen* v *Gouverneur and Kemble*.

1799

From Joseph Ward [1]

Boston, January 1, 1799. ". . . your sentiments if now communicated to energettic members of Congress might at this time do much good by preventing a lasting dishonor to the Government. The long injured creditors who hold the New Emission Bills, now lodged in the Treasury, have their petition [2] before the Senate, where a decision may be expected soon. But from past experience of disregard to the sacred pledge of national faith, to pay the Int. on this debt, the creditors have prepared an *Appeal* to Congress, to be published before the close of this session, in case no provision shall be made, & therein state the parts which prove that they are deprived of their right & property *in direct violation* of the pledged faith of the United States, & defrauded in opposition to every thing sacred in law, & the constitution. . . . The creditors wished to communicate these sentiments, & their intentions, to you, that your wisdom & patriotism might be employed to correct this error in govt. before the knowledge of it is made known to the world. . . ."

ALS, Hamilton Papers, Library of Congress.

1. Ward was a Boston stockbroker and real estate dealer. For earlier correspondence on the subject of the letter printed above, see H to Ward, May 26, 1791, May 6, 1793; Ward to H, February 18, 1793.

2. In 1795, 1796, and 1798, Ward and several others petitioned Congress for payment to holders of new emission bills. In each instance Congress refused to act on the petitions. For these petitions and their reception in Congress, see *Journal of the House*, II, 388, 629; III, 202, 221–23; *Annals of Congress*, VII, 517, 522; IX, 3659–61. For the act authorizing the new emission bills, see *JCC*, XVI, 263–66. See also Charles Pettit to H, April 30, 1791, note 3; "Report on a Plan for the Further Support of Public Credit," January 16, 1795.

From William Macpherson [1]

Philadelphia Jany. 3, 1799

Dear Sir

The Secretary at War not having in his possession the Drafts you wish to obtain, I applied to Captain Hill—who after taking some

Days to deliberate offers to furnish a Plan—with the condition that a Copy shall not be taken of it—for 600 Dollars. As this Sum is infinitely beyond what I supposed he would demand—I must beg to hear from you again before I say any thing more to him. "Its to be understood, that this Draft is to commence at Sandy Hook—comprehend Amboy, Staten Island, the North River as far as Greenwich—from thence to Blackwels Island, with part of Long Island—the works erected—as well as those contemplated by the British during the War, Soundings etc."

I shall at all times be happy to receive your commands and pray you to believe me

Most sincerely yours.   *W Macpherson*

ALS, Hamilton Papers, Library of Congress.
    1. This letter was written in reply to H to Macpherson, December 26, 1798. For background to this letter, see the introductory note to H to James McHenry, June 1, 1798.

From Thomas Cooper [1]

[*New York*] *January 5, 1799.* "Inclosed I send you the Dr. of a Deed, already executed by myself & Mr & Mrs Livingston to a Mr John Brown of Providence, Rhode Island.[2] Mr Bogart,[3] Mr Brown's Counsel has perused the original and approves it but as you have been associated as Counsel with him for Mr Brown, he is desirous that you should also peruse the Deed. . . ." [4]

ALS, Hamilton Papers, Library of Congress.
    1. Thomas Cooper was a New York City lawyer.
    2. The indenture, dated December 29, 1798, was "Between Thomas Cooper, Master in Chancery for the State of new york of the first Part, Philip Livingston of the City of new york in the State aforesaid, Esquire and Cornelia his wife of the second Part and John Brown of Providence in the State of Rhode Island Merchant of the third Part" (AD, Hamilton Papers, Library of Congress). According to this indenture, James Greenleaf in 1795 mortgaged property in New York City to Philip Livingston, who in turn mortgaged it to John Brown and others. When the money was not paid six months after the due date of June 4, 1798, Cooper put the mortgaged premises at public auction. At this time Brown bought the property for thirty-three thousand dollars.
    3. Cornelius Bogert.
    4. In Hamilton's Cash Book, 1795–1804, between the dates of March 21 and

March 29, 1799, there is the following entry: "received of Brown for opinion $40" (AD, Hamilton Papers, Library of Congress).

From James McHenry

private.   Philad 5 Jany 1799

Dear Sir

Inclosed is a copy of my report.[1] To give facility to the committee I think it would be proper that you should forthwith throw the 17 propositions it contains into the form of a bill, and send me the same as soon as possible.[2]

I shall write you on Monday if possible relative to preparatory steps for commencing early the recruiting service. I expect daily a report from Mr Francis[3] shewing the precise periods at which we may calculate upon certain quantities of cloathing.[4]

Yours sincerely   James McHenry

Majr Gen Alex. Hamilton

ALS, Hamilton Papers, Library of Congress; ADfS, James McHenry Papers, Library of Congress.

1. For this report, which is dated December 24, 1798, and which John Adams submitted to Congress on December 31, 1798, see *ASP, Military Affairs,* I, 124–29. See also H's drafts of George Washington to McHenry, first and third letters of December 13, 1798.

2. In the draft this paragraph contains the following additional sentence: "The session is you know limited and will not be extended."

3. On February 24, 1795, George Washington nominated Tench Francis as Purveyor of Public Supplies, and on February 25, 1795, the Senate approved the nomination (*Executive Journal,* I, 173, 174).

4. On January 8, 1799, Philip Church wrote to McHenry: "General Hamilton not being very well has desired me to inform you that he received by yesterday's post your letter with the enclosed report, and that he will immediately attend to it" (copy, in Philip Church's handwriting, Hamilton Papers, Library of Congress).

On January 12, 1799, Church wrote to McHenry: "General Hamilton has continued, since I last had the honor of writing to you, so indisposed as to have been frequently confined to his bed and consequently not able to attend to the report you sent him, but he is now much better and has desired me to inform you that he will forward by monday's post his ideas on the subject" (copy, in Philip Church's handwriting, Hamilton Papers, Library of Congress).

To Marquis de Lafayette

New York January 6. 1799 [1]

I have been made happy my dear friend by the receipt of your letter of the 12th of August last. No explanation of your political principles was necessary to satisfy me of the perfect consistency and purity of your conduct. The interpretation may always be left to my attachment for you. Whatever difference of opinion may on any occasion exist between us can never lessen my conviction of the goodness both of your head and heart. I expect from you a return of this sentiment so far as concerns the heart. Tis needless to detail to you my political tenets. I shall only say that I hold with *Montesquieu* that a government must be fitted to a nation as much as a Coat to the Individual,[2] and consequently that what may be good at Philadelphia may be bad at Paris and ridiculous at Petersburgh.

I join with you in regretting the misunderstanding between our two countries. You will have seen by the Presidents speech that a door is again opened for terminating them amicably.[3] And you may be assured that we are sincere, and that it is in the power of France by reparation to our merchants for past injury and the stipulation of justice in future to put an end to the controversy.

But I do not like much the idea of your being any way implicated in the affair, lest you should be compromitted in the opinion of one or the other of the parties. It is my opinion that it is best for you to stand aloof. Neither have I abandonned the idea that 'tis most adviseable for you to remain in Europe 'till the difference is adjusted. It would be very difficult for you here to steer a course which would not place you in a party and remove you from the broad ground which you now occupy in the hearts of all.[4] It is a favorite point with me that you shall find in the universal regard of this country all the consolations which the loss of your own (for so I consider it) may render requisite.

Mrs Church [5] and Mrs Hamilton unite in assurance of their affectionate remembrance. Believe me always

Your very cordial & faithful friend   A H

Marquis de la Fayette

Copy, in the handwriting of Philip Church, Hamilton Papers, Library of Congress.

1. In *JCHW*, VI, 504, this letter is incorrectly dated "1801."

2. This is a reference to the following statement: "Law in general is human reason, inasmuch as it governs all the inhabitants of the earth; the political and civil laws of each nation ought to be only the particular cases in which this human reason is applied.

"They should be adapted in such a manner to the people for whom they are made, as to render it very unlikely for those of one nation to be proper for another.

"They should be relative to the nature and principle of the actual, or intended government; whether they form it, as in the case of political laws, or whether they support it, as may be said of civil institutions.

"They should be relative to the climate of each country, to the quality of the soil, to its situation and extent, to the manner of living of the natives, whether husbandmen, huntsmen, or shepherds: they should have a relation to the degree of liberty which the constitution will bear; to the religion of the inhabitants, to their inclinations, riches, number, commerce, manners, and customs. In fine, they have relations amongst themselves, as also to their origin, to the intent of the legislator, and to the order of things on which they are established; in all which different lights they ought to be considered." (Charles Louis de Secondat, Baron de La Brède et de Montesquieu, *The Spirit of Laws*, trans. Mr. Nugent [3d ed.; 2 vols.; London: Printed for J. Nourse and P. Vaillant in the Strand, 1758], Book I, Ch. 3, 8–9.)

3. The President's speech on December 8, 1798, to both the Senate and the House of Representatives reads in part: ". . . You will, at the same time, perceive that the French Government appears solicitous to impress the opinion that it is averse to the rupture of this country, and that it has, in a qualified manner, declared itself willing to receive a Minister from the United States, for the purpose of restoring a good understanding. . . . It is peace that we have uniformly and perseveringly cultivated, and harmony between us and France may be restored at her option" (*Annals of Congress*, IX, 2420–24).

4. On June 17, 1799, Robert Liston, British Envoy Extraordinary and Minister Plenipotentiary to the United States, wrote to Lord Grenville, British Secretary of State for Foreign Affairs, concerning the rumor that France might send Lafayette as an ambassador or envoy extraordinary to the United States. Liston then wrote: "That this plan has actually been in contemplation, seems probable from a letter lately written by M. de La Fayette to General Hamilton (formerly Secretary of the Treasury) consulting him as an old friend, with regard to the probability of his accepting of it. General Hamilton informs me that if his advice is complied with, the project will not take place, for that he has represented the task as extremely arduous, if not impracticable in the present moment, and has told M. de La Fayette that he would in all probability *commit* himself with both countries, without effecting the object in view" (ALS, PRO: F.O. [Great Britain] 5/25a). For Lafayette's refusal to serve as French Minister to the United States, see Brand Whitlock, *La Fayette*, II (New York, 1929), 115.

5. Angelica Church was the wife of John B. Church and the sister of Elizabeth Hamilton.

To James McHenry [1]

New York Janry. 7th. 1799

Sir,

The unascertained situation, in which I have been, since my acceptance of the Military appointment, I now hold, has been not a little embarrassing to me. I had no sooner heard of the law creating the Office [2] than I was told by members of the Congress that I was generally considered as the person designated by circumstances to fill that office and that the expectation of those who most actively promoted the passing of the law was that the Inspector General would be brought into immediate activity, particularly to superintend the raising and organising of the Troops. This is mentioned as a mere item in the incidents which influenced my calculations and arrangements.

Very soon after, if not at the time, you communicated to me my appointment, you intimated though not officially your desire that I might occupy myself in preparing for the consideration of the Executive a system of Tactics and discipline. [3] And not long after you expressed to me your intention to commit to me the supervision of the recruiting service. [4]

In October, I received your summons to attend at the seat of Government with the Commander in Chief. [5] I obeyed and devoted to the purposes of this summons about a Month and a half.

I received in due course, a letter from your department stating the expectation of the President that the Generals would think it proper to wave the emoluments of their stations till called into service [6] In my reply I acquiesced. [7]

But presuming that I would speedily be officially charged with the execution of duties, which would draw along with them the compensations attached by the law to the station, [8] I have acted on that presumption. I have discontinued my practice as Attorney and Solictor, from which I had derived a considerable part of my professional profits; and I have applied no small portion of my time to preliminary investigations in order to the collection of the best lights for forming a system of Tactics and discipline as perfect as exists any where else.

The very circumstance of my having accepted a military appointment, from the moment it was known, withdrew from me a large proportion of my professional business. This it will be perceived, was a natural effect of the uncertainty of my being able in the progress of suits to render the services for which I might be engaged at the customary previous expence to the parties.

The result has been that the emoluments of my profession have been diminished more than one half and are still diminishing—and I remain in perfect uncertainty whether or when I am to derive from the scanty compensations of the office even a partial retribution for so serious a loss.

Were I rich I should be proud to be silent on such a subject. I should acquiesce without an observation—as long as any one might think the minutest public interest required an accumulation of sacrifices on my part. But after having to so advanced a period of my life devoted all my prospects of fortune to the service of the Country —and dependant as I am for the maintenance of a wife and six children on my professional exertions, now so seriously abridged—it is essential for me to forego the scruples of delicacy and to ask of you to define my situation; that I may determine whether to continue or to change my present plan.

It will easily be imagined that I should not accept compensations withheld from any other in a similar situation. If actual employment is to be the criterion in any other instance it must be so in mine; but then it is material to me to understand whether in the contemplation of the Executive, I now am, or immediately am to be employed or not. In the negative of this, my honor will compel submission to the consequent sacrifice, so far as it is unavoidable; but my arrangements will be different from what they are at present and will aim at making the sacrifice as small as possible.

An early answer to this inquiry will particularly oblige me. With great respect & regard

I have the honor to be   Sir   Your obed Servant   A Hamilton

The Secretary at War

Copy, in the handwriting of Philip Church, Hamilton Papers, Library of Congress.

1. For background to this letter, see George Washington to H, July 14, 1798.
2. See "An Act to augment the Army of the United States, and for other purposes" (1 *Stat.* 604–05 [July 16, 1798]).
3. See McHenry to H, July 20, 1798; H to McHenry, July 30, 1798.
4. H to McHenry, July 30, 1798; McHenry to H, August 10, 1798.
5. McHenry to H, October 15, 1798.
6. McHenry to H, July 25, 1798.
7. H to McHenry, July 28, 1798.
8. See H to McHenry, July 30, December 16, 1798.

From James McHenry

War department January 9. 1799

Sir

I have received your letter dated the 7th. instant.

The President has directed me to signify to you that he considers you in service from the first day of November 1798 in consequence of your being summoned by letter bearing date the 15 October to attend at Philadelphia or Trenton as soon as possible and in all events by the 10 November. Your pay and emoluments will therefore take date from the first day of November 1798.

I am Sir   with great respect   Your obed servant

James McHenry

Major Genl. Hamilton

LS, Hamilton Papers, Library of Congress.

From James McHenry [1]

[Philadelphia] 9 Jany 1799

Dear Hamilton.

The official letter of this date fixes the commencement of your pay and emoluments. I shall as soon as possible define your duties and command. In the mean while I should be glad to have your own ideas on the subject. You will proceed on your report for a system of tactics & discipline. You will also endeavour to ascertain the best positions for your recruiting parties and general rendzvouses within the several grand subdivisions—and will not forget the bill conformably to my report.[2] Church's nomination concurred in.[3] Several of those nominated for inferior grades postponed by the Senate for further information.[4]

yours sincerely   James McHenry

Gen Hamilton

ALS, Hamilton Papers, Library of Congress; ADf, James McHenry Papers, Library of Congress.
  1. This letter was written in reply to H to McHenry, January 7, 1799.
  2. See McHenry to H, January 5, 1799.
  3. On January 8, 1799, Philip Church was appointed a captain in the Twelfth Regiment of Infantry (*Executive Journal*, I, 299, 303).
  4. See *Executive Journal*, I, 302–03.

From James McHenry

War Department 10 Jany 1799

Dear Sir

I wrote you on the   [1] to request you to prepare a bill conformably to the propositions contained in my report of the 24th of Decr. ulto to the President. This morning Gen. Gun of the Committee of the Senate to whom this report has been committed [2] waited upon me with a request from the Committee that I should prepare and furnish them with a draught of two bills, one comprising whatever in the report relates to new provisions for the regular peace and war establishment; the other all new matters appertaining to the provisional army. He added, if I thought it proper, I might comprehend in these bills all the existing provisons relative to the provisional and regular army. I think the idea judicious; and request you to be so kind as to turn to the existing laws [3] and incorporate into the two bills all that *ought to be retained of them.*[4]

Yours sincerely & affly   James McHenry

Majr. Gen. Alexr. Hamilton

ALS, Hamilton Papers, Library of Congress; ADf, James McHenry Papers, Library of Congress.

1. Space left blank in MS. McHenry is referring to his letter of January 5, 1799.

2. On January 9, 1799, it was ordered in the Senate "That the report of the Secretary for the Department of War, communicated with the Message of the President of the United States of the 31st ultimo, be referred to the committee appointed the 18th of December last, on that part of the President's Speech respecting the extension and invigoration of the measures of defence, other than those which relate to a naval armament, to consider and report thereon to the Senate" (*Annals of Congress*, VIII, 2200–01). In addition to James Gunn, the other members of the committee appointed on December 18 were John E. Howard of Maryland and James Ross of Pennsylvania (*Annals of Congress*, VIII, 2196).

3. For the laws to which McHenry is referring, see the introductory note to H to Gunn, December 22, 1798.

4. On the back of this letter H wrote: "Pay of Officers whose ranks are changed."

From James McHenry

War Depart. 11 Jany 1799

Dear Sir

Permit me in addition to what I said yesterday to request, that laying aside other business you will occupy yourself on the two military bills only. The session is short, and but little of it to come. If possible let me have the bills by mondays mail or at furthest tuesdays.

I have not been able to ascertain what part some of our friends in the house mean to take respecting the appropriations necessary for the new army. Upon an examination of the laws I was obliged to relinqish the opinion, that they had provided for other expenditures on account of the new army than what might be incurred before the end of the next session of Congress—that is the present. See the act passed the 16 July 1798.[1] You know the causes and obstructions which prevented me from doing any thing to carry the law for raising the army into effect during the last year.[2]

Yours affectionately　　　　　　　　　　　　　　　　　James McHenry

If you want money let me know that I may send your pay.

Majr Gen Alexr Hamilton

ALS, Hamilton Papers, Library of Congress; ADf, James McHenry Papers, Library of Congress.

1. This is a reference to "An Act to enable the President of the United States to borrow money for public service." Section 1 of this act provided: "That the President of the United States shall be, and hereby is authorized to borrow, on behalf of the United States, from the Bank of the United States, which is hereby authorized to lend the same, or from any other body or bodies politic or corporate, or from any person or persons and upon such terms and conditions as he shall judge most advantageous for the United States, a sum not exceeding five millions of dollars, in addition to the monies to be received into the treasury of the United States, from taxes, for making up any deficiency in any appropriation heretofore made by law, or to be made during the present session of Congress; and defraying the expenses which may be incurred, by calling into actual service, any part of the militia of the United States, or by raising, equipping and calling into actual service any regular troops, or volunteers, pursuant to authorities vested or to be vested in the President of the United States, by law . . ." (1 *Stat.* 607 [July 16, 1798]). Section 3 of the same act provided: "That the sums to be borrowed, pursuant to this act, shall be paid into the treasury of the United States; and there separately accounted for; and that the same shall be, and hereby are appropriated in manner following: First, to make up any deficiency in any appropriations heretofore made by law, or to be made, during the present session of Congress; and secondly, to defray the expenses which may be incurred before the end of the next session of Congress, by calling into actual service, any part of the militia of the United States, or by raising, equipping and calling into actual service, any regular troops or volunteers, pursuant to authorities vested or to be vested in the President of the United States, by law" (1 *Stat.* 608).

2. This is a reference to "An Act to augment the Army of the United States, and for other purposes" (1 *Stat.* 604–05 [July 16, 1798]). There were two major reasons why McHenry could not implement this law. First, the question of who would serve directly under George Washington was not settled until October, 1798. See the introductory note to Washington to H, July 14, 1798. Second, John Adams did not submit to the Senate the names of all the other officers for the Additional Army until December 31, 1798, and the Senate did not act on any of these nominations until January 8, 1799 (*Executive Journal*, I, 299, 303).

From Joseph Mangin [1]

New York, January 11, 1799. States that he was originally hired to supervise the construction of the batteries for the defense of New York City, that he was subsequently hired to fortify Governors Island, and that he is now city surveyor. Complains that he is not adequately paid. Describes his qualifications as an engineer and asks Hamilton for a military rank.[2]

ALS, Hamilton Papers, Library of Congress.

1. For background to this letter, see Mangin to H, August 7, 1798; Ebenezer

Stevens to H, November 29, 1798. See also the introductory note to H to James McHenry, June 1, 1798.

2. This letter is in French.

From Stephen Van Rensselaer

[*January 11, 1799.* On January 27, 1799, Hamilton wrote to Van Rensselaer, "I ought to beg your pardon for not having before answered your letters of the 12th of Novem and 11th instant." *Letter of January 11, 1799, not found.*]

To Philip Church

[*New York, January 12, 1799.* ". . . In virtue of the privilege and authority to me given by law [1] I do hereby appoint you to be my Aide de Camp [2] to have and to hold all the compensations rights and authorities to the said Office annexed or appertaining so long as you shall continue therein. And I do hereby require all persons whom it may concern to obey and respect accordingly." [3] *Letter not found.*]

ADS, sold by Stan V. Henkels, Jr., May 15, 1931, Lot 21.

1. See "An Act to augment the Army of the United States, and for other purposes" (1 *Stat.* 604–05 [July 16, 1798]).

2. For the background to this appointment, see H to John Adams, August 24, October 20, 1798; Adams to H, September 3, October 29, 1798. In Godfrey, "Provisional Army," 164, the date of Church's appointment as H's aide-de-camp is incorrectly given as May 1, 1799.

3. Extract taken from dealer's catalogue.

From William Duer

[*New York, January 13, 1799.* The summary of this letter reads: "Thanks for Hamilton's interposition with Wolcott." [1] *Letter not found.*]

Letter listed in "Calendar Summary of Philip Church and Alexander Hamilton Papers," Personal Miscellaneous, Box 6, Schuyler, MS Division, New York Public Library.

1. See H to Oliver Wolcott, Jr., August 22, December 28, 1798; Wolcott to H, September 19, 1798.

From William Heth

Petersburg [Virginia] 14th. Jany 1799

Dear Sir

It is some days since I was made happy by the receipt of your kind favor of the 18th. Ulto.[1] A man of your lively feelings, can easily guess what my sensations were, on receiving this letter, when I tell you, that I had actually concluded you had forgotten me: and not so much on account of your not acknowledging the rect of my *pamphlet* of June last [2] as having two, if not three, other confidential letters,[3]—unanswerd—(for I know well your avocations, and consequently, know how to make allowances.) One of those letters enclosed a news paper, containing a piece that I was desirous you should see, and I have been much concerned, under an apprehension, that it miscarried [4]—for, it was sent by Water.

I thank you, my dear Sir, for the very flattering manner in which you are pleased to think of me, in case of a call *to Arms!* [5] Having spent some days lately, with my old friend, brother soldier, and fellow prisoner General Pinkney,[6] I understand from him, that you are as well acquainted as he is, with the confidential correspondence which I have had with our beloved chief, respecting the station which I should be proud to take in case of such a call.[7] When I presumed thus to suggest my wishes, I conceived that the *present* commander in chief would be indulged, if he wished an higher rank than is already provided by Law, for any particular character to serve near his person. Is it proper, do you think, to encourage such an Idea? It arose, not only from the consideration, that there was little reason to expect that rank in the line (Should my services be wanting), to which, I might suppose myself entitled from former service and experience; [8] but, from what I still consider, as a well founded opinion that one aid at least, to a Commander in chief, ought to hold an higher rank than a Colonel.[9] A consideration of this nature, affects, as you know, our friend Carrington. (we are in habits, as you may suppose, of the closest intimacy & confidence) for it never can be expected of him to take the Station, marked out for him, & which he is so peculiarly qualified to fill, under the rank at present attach'd to it.[10]

Should I be calld upon in the way I wish, or in any other way, there are considerations, which equally apply to Carrington and myself, and on which, he has no doubt, some time since written to the Commander in Chief. Viz.—After having experienced *much* labor, & anxiety of mind, for *little* compensation in bringing our Offices [11] to that reputation which they now hold, ought we to be deprived of them, just as they promise something handsome during life, or good behaviour—on being calld upon to fill other public stations, which may prove to be, but of Short duration? You will greatly oblige me, by your opinion on this subject.

You heard no doubt that I was deprived in September last without a moments notice scarce, of both my Clerks, by the Yellow fever. What my labor and application has been since, you, can easily guess. But, I am now happy to find, that in two or three months more, I shall be better supported than ever. A young gentleman of about five or six and Twenty—of very liberal education & fine talents; of uncommon Steadiness & application, of the most respectable connextions, and most unblemished character; has, after spending a quarter with me, engaged for the current year. This gentleman, in case of my being calld upon, could with great propriety discharge the duties of the Office in my name; or—if it would be better that he should be actually appointed to the Office, I could rely upon his resigning in my favor, in case I should be fortunate enough to *weather* another conflict, in defence of my injured, & insulted Country. Your sentiments on this question, would be highly gratifying. I could make my arrangements accordingly.

Persuaded that it will give you much pleasure to find how our friend Pinkney was recd at this place,[12] hitherto considered as highly Democratic—you have enclosed an *history* of our doings—which I hope you will think, at least worth the postage it will cost you.

The toasts you will say, are too long. True—but they are what I wished them to be, *pointed, unequivocal, & animated* and I do not think that such things can be made too public—for really, the faction appears to me, to be fast sinking—and, in my opinion, it requires only some great, energetic measure, like *open war*, to bring those *deluded* and *imposed* upon, of our fellow citizens, to a just sense of their weakness & folly. We now appear to have a most favorable oppy. to give a decided blow to French ambition & cruelty. WAR, *even brings* PEACE. I need not say more to a man of your quickness of comprehension, to convey what I mean.

You ask, "What do the faction in your State really aim at?" I answer—Nothing short of DISUNION, and the heads of JOHN ADAMS, and ALEXANDER HAMILTON; & some few others perhaps. So—take care of yourself.

I should appear more like an Irishman than I really am, were I to offer as an apology for the verbosity of this, my having been oblig'd to write in great hurry, & under much interruption: but, in truth, if I had time to correct and copy; or if I could have taken time to have *Marshal'd* my Ideas, I should certainly have been much more concise. However, if you will excuse this, and will be kind enough to drop me a few lines in answer, for I shall be impatient to hear from you—I promise not to trouble you with such a long letter again, unless I shall have more important things to communicate. Adieu— and believe me to be most affectionately and

Truly yours   W Heth

ALS, Hamilton Papers, Library of Congress.

1. Letter not found.
2. William Heth, *An Infallible Cure for Political Blindness, if Administered to Patients Possessing Sound Minds, Honest Hearts, and Independent Circumstances* (Richmond, 1798).
3. Heth to H, January 11, October 14, 1796.
4. Heth to H, January 11, 1796.
5. See H to George Washington, August 20, 1798.
6. Both Heth and Charles Cotesworth Pinckney had been taken prisoner by the British at Charleston in May, 1780.
7. See Washington to H, August 9, 1798, note 8.
8. Heth had served throughout the American Revolution until February, 1781, when he retired with the rank of colonel.
9. Section 5 of "An Act authorizing the President of the United States to raise a Provisional Army" provided that the commander of the Army had the "authority to appoint, from time to time, such number of aides not exceeding four . . . as he may judge proper, each to have the rank of lieutenant colonel" (1 *Stat.* 558–59 [May 28, 1798]).
10. See Washington to H, July 14, 1798, note 66.
11. Carrington was supervisor of the revenue for the District of Virginia, while Heth was collector of customs at Bermuda Hundred in Virginia.
12. A newspaper report from Petersburg, Virginia, dated January 11, 1799, reads: "It having been understood by mere accident on Friday, by the citizens

of this place, that Major-General Pinckney, one of the late envoys extraordinary to the French republic, was on his way from Richmond to this town; the mayor and a considerable number of respectable citizens, determined immediately to give him a public dinner, as a small testimony of their exalted opinion of his distinguished character and abilities.

"About eleven o'clock in the afternoon of Saturday, he arrived, and was saluted by a discharge of cannon. He was highly pleased with the martial and soldierly appearance of this excellent and well disciplined company.

"The citizens met about half after four o'clock, consisting of upwards of seventy respectable inhabitants of the town. An address to be presented to the general was submitted to them, and unanimously approved." ([Charleston] *City Gazette*, January 26, 1799.)

To James McHenry

New York Jany 14. 1799

Dr. Sir

I received on Saturday two letters from you [1] desiring that your different propositions might be thrown into two Bills & suggesting the idea of an Incorporation of the several existing laws into one system. This idea is a good one, but to accomplish it with sufficient correctness would require several days to examine carefully and prepare with accuracy. Besides this, I incline to the opinion that it will be best in the first instance to present the alterations and additions proposed independently—that the progress of them may not be embarrassed by the consideration of an entire system; and I had even thought of a distribution into more than two divisions to secure at all events the passage of some things. The organisation on my plan would form one bill comprehending the sections in the inclosed draft [2] No. 1 to   [3] inclusively. The Hospital department would form another Bill.[4] The provisional army & volunteers a third.[5] The miscellaneous points a fourth. The plan however of two Bills is now pursued, except that I shall prepare the sections for the Hospital establishment separately; which with the provisional army Bill will go by tomorrows Post.

I do not exactly seize your idea about the Inspector of Fortifications [6] and therefore have prepared nothing on that point. Is it essential to have a distinct Officer of th⟨is⟩ character? Or may not the objects of it be fulfilled by some one of the Engineers of the establishment? I will endeavour to embrace your plan on this head and if I do I will throw it into the form of a Section of a Bill.

I do not lose sight of the idea of an Incorporation of the whole Military system into one law; but I believe you will on more reflection judge it adviseable to make this a subsequent Operation of greater leisure and care.

I remain with great esteem & regard   Dr. Sir   Yr Obed serv

A Hamilton

Js Mc.Henry Esq.

ALS (photostat), James McHenry Papers, Library of Congress.
   1. McHenry to H, January 10, 11, 1799.
   2. H's draft, which has not been found, was the basis of "An Act for the better organizing of the Troops of the United States, and for other purposes" (1 Stat. 749–55 [March 3, 1799]).
   3. Space left blank in MS. H is referring to the list of seventeen recommendations in McHenry's report to John Adams of December 24, 1798 (ASP, Military Affairs, I, 124–29). The act of March 3, 1799, included all but four (Nos. 7, 14, 15, and 17) of McHenry's recommendations.
   4. See "An Act to regulate the Medical Establishment" (1 Stat. 721–23 [March 2, 1799]).
   5. H is referring to the Eventual Army. See the introductory note to H to James Gunn, December 22, 1798.
   6. This is a reference to recommendation No. 9 in McHenry's report to Adams, December 24, 1798. This recommendation reads: "To provide for the appointment of an inspector of fortifications" (ASP, Military Affairs, I, 127).

To Robert Liston

[*New York, January 15, 1799.* On January 20, 1799, Liston wrote to Hamilton: "Mr. Brunel [1] delivered to me yesterday your letter of the 15th of this month." *Letter not found.*]

   1. Marc Isambard Brunel was a French engineer who had lived in New York City since at least 1797.

To James McHenry

[New York, January 15, 1799]

Dr. Sir

I find I cannot have ready for this days post the bill for the Provisional army.[1] Inclosed are some additional clauses relating to organisation consequently to be inserted in the Bill sent by yesterdays post. You will easily determine their proper position there. They are necessary to systematic propriety. General provisions of this kind will prevent continual repetitions in every new law respecting the military force.

With esteem & regard   Yr. Obed servt.   A H

NYork Jany. 15. 1799

Js Mc.Henry Esq

ALS, Montague Collection, MS Division, New York Public Library; ALS (photostat), James McHenry Papers, Library of Congress; copy, in the handwriting of Philip Church, Hamilton Papers, Library of Congress.
    1. See H to McHenry, January 14, 1799, note 5.

From Silas Talbot [1]

New York, January 15, 1799. "The relative Rank of several persons who have been honored with an appointment as Captains in the Navy of the United States not having as yet been seetled by the Honorable the Executive,[2] and as some of those Officers claim of right the same rank, it follows of course, that, the good of the service requires this difference of opinion to be settled. It being the wish of the Executive to do perfect justice to all, they mean, as I have been well informed, to avail themselves of your opinion in this matter as a previous step to forming their own judgement. . . . The subject on which I understand Mr Stoddert means to request your opinion Regards the rank of Captain Thomas Truxton Captain Richard Dale and myself. On this subject Sir, I shall premise that so far as concerns myself, the Objections in my mind to being placed on the list of Captains in the Navy subject to the command of Captain Truxton do not arise from the smallest disrespect for his Character in any view it may be placed. They arise from a quite different source. It is because I consider the laws and usage of rank in service place me above both of those Gentlemen, And, for which I conceive it just and laudable in me to contend. It is well known to you that in the year 1794 Congress passed a Law providing that six ships of war should be built, for the protection of our commerce, and that six Captains were appointed to command those Ships . . . that myself was placed as the third Captain Dale as the fifth and Captain Truxton as the sixth. . . . When Captain Truxton accepted of his appointment under myself and Captain Dale it must be presumed that he did not think himself dishonored, for otherwise he would have declined an acceptance and have given his reasons for so doing. What have Captain Dale or myself done since that time that ought to injure us in our relative rank in the service or that would justify Capt. Truxtons being put above us. . . . I presume he founds his claim upon the suspension for a time the building of three of our Ships of war and the pay of those who were to command them, among whom myself was one, and that when Captains Barry, Nicholson and Truxtons commissions were made out the last mentioned got his commission market No: 3, and upon this ground he presumes that he is entitled to take rank over Captain Dale and myself, who have again been called into pay and service. . . . Sir the Law of Congress [3] and the usage of this Country during the war with Great Britain, and, which by the by is nearly all the service in the Navy known to this Country, has been that when an Officer of the Navy was out of command his pay and not his rank ceased, that when he was again called into service his pay commenced and his former rank was in no case disputed. . . ."

ALS, Hamilton Papers, Library of Congress.
   1. This letter concerns the relative rank of captains in the Navy who were originally appointed in accordance with "An Act to provide a Naval Armament" (1 *Stat.* 350–51 [March 27, 1794]). This act authorized the President to provide six frigates and to appoint a captain for each of these vessels. It also stated that if peace was concluded between the United States and Algiers, there should be "no further proceeding under this act." On June 3, 1794, George Washington nominated as captains "John Barry, Samuel Nicholson, Silas Talbot, Joshua Barney, Richard Dale, and Thomas Truxton," with the understanding that each was to be assigned to supervise the construction and outfitting of one of the six frigates provided for in "An Act to provide a Naval Armament" (*Executive Journal*, I, 160–61). On the following day the Senate approved the nominations in the order in which they had been presented (*Executive Journal*, I, 161). After Barney had refused his commission (Henry Knox to Barney, June 5, 1794 [LC, RG 45, Naval Records Collection of the Office of Naval Records and Library, Correspondence on Naval Affairs when the Navy was under the War Department, 1790–1798, National Archives]), he was replaced when Congress was not in session by James Sever (Knox to Sever, July 18, 1794 [LC, RG 45, Naval Records Collection of the Naval Records Office and Library, Correspondence on Naval Affairs when the Navy was under the War Department, 1790–1798, National Archives]). With Sever's

appointment the relative rank of the six captains was as follows: Barry, Nicholson, Talbot, Dale, Truxton, and Sever.

With the signing of a peace treaty with Algiers on September 5, 1795, and its ratification by the United States on March 7, 1796 (Hunter Miller, ed., *Treaties and Other International Acts of the United States of America* [Washington, 1931], II, 275–317), the statutory authorization for the captains' commissions and for the construction of the frigates lapsed. Washington, however, stated to the Senate and House on March 15, 1796, that he did not wish to drop the program until Congress had had an opportunity to act (*Annals of Congress*, V, 52–53). On April 20, 1796, Congress passed on "An Act supplementary to an act entitled 'An act to provide a Naval Armament,'" which authorized the President to continue the "construction and equipment" of three of the six frigates (1 *Stat.* 453). As a result of this act, construction was halted on the vessels commanded by Talbot, Dale, and Sever, who then either lost their commissions or were placed on the inactive list, while the status of Barry, Nicholson, and Truxton remained unchanged (James McHenry to Sever, June 4, 1796, January 18, 1797 [LC, RG 45, Naval Records Collection of the Office of Naval Records and Library, Correspondence on Naval Affairs when the Navy was under the War Department, 1790–1798, National Archives]; McHenry to Talbot, June 4, 1796 [copy, enclosed in Talbot to John Adams, July 9, 1799 (ALS, Adams Family Papers, deposited in the Massachusetts Historical Society, Boston)]).

Because of the threat of war with France, Congress provided by "An Act providing a Naval Armament" (1 *Stat.* 523–25 [July 1, 1797]) and "An Act for an additional appropriation to provide and support a Naval Armament" (1 *Stat.* 549 [March 27, 1798]) for resumption of the work on the three frigates whose construction had been halted by the act of April 20, 1796. On May 10, 1798, Adams nominated Talbot, Sever, and Dale in that order to be "Captains in the Navy of the United States," and on the following day the Senate approved the nominations (*Executive Journal*, I, 274, 275). With these nominations the ranking of the six officers in question was as follows: Barry, Nicholson, Truxton, Talbot, Sever, and Dale. The result was that Truxton, who had appeared sixth on the original list of nominees in 1794, now outranked Talbot and Dale. In addition, Adams placed Sever ahead of Dale, who thus had a double grievance.

2. By the autumn of 1798, Secretary of the Navy Benjamin Stoddert was aware of the difficulties posed by the ranking of the six captains appointed to the Navy, and he urged President Adams to make some arrangement that would be equitable to all concerned (Stoddert to Dale, October 9, 1798 [*Naval Documents, Quasi-War, February 1797–October, 1798*, 510]; Stoddert to Adams, October 10, 1798 [ALS, Adams Family Papers, deposited in the Massachusetts Historical Society, Boston]). Although on October 17, 1798, Adams replied to Stoddert: "Your letter . . . [concerning the relative rank of the Navy captains] is of much importance and deserves consideration" (LC, Adams Family Papers, deposited in the Massachusetts Historical Society, Boston), it was not until July 23, 1799, that he took any action in this matter, and then he ordered the Secretary of the Navy to restore Talbot to third place and return Truxton to fifth place on the list of Navy captains (LC, Adams Family Papers, deposited in the Massachusetts Historical Society, Boston).

3. This is a reference to a resolution of January 25, 1780, which reads: "That the pay of all officers of the navy, not in actual service, cease from this day: that such officers retain their rank, depositing their commissions in the respective navy boards, until they shall be called into actual service" (*JCC*, XVI, 85–86).

To James McHenry

New York Jany 16. 1799

Dr. Sir,

You will receive herewith the Draft of a Bill for a provisional army.[1] It includes only those things of the former Bill[2] which are appropriate to this object—the other parts of that Bill being now in full force. The operation of the Bill which has been already sent[3] you renders the repetition of several clauses in the present un[ne]cessary. The aim indeed ought to be to have a *fundamental arrangement* which will attack of course upon all subsequent provisions of force so that the law for every augmentation need only define the number to be raised and the duration of service and the mode of raising.

An eye has been had to this in the draught of the first Bill and of the two additional clauses now sent for the same Bill has the same view. This will be more deliberately & correctly attended to in the plan of a Bill which I shall begin to work upon from this time but which cannot be ready for a considerable time. A Bill for the Hospital establishment will follow in two or three days.

Yrs. truly   A H

PS. The considerable mutilation of the nominations proposed by the Commander in Chief as it appears in the result naturally excites curiosity. It ought to be presumed, and yet the mind involuntarily disputes the presumption, that there are good reasons for it and that the service will be finally benefitted. But I confess it would be a relief to me to know a little in detail what has influenced the departure—how the unfitness of those who have been declined has appeared and what means are in train to do better.[4] Pray be particular and confidential. You will not consider any letter of mine beginning with "Dear Sir" as Official.

ALS, Montague Collection, MS Division, New York Public Library; ALS (photostat), James McHenry Papers, Library of Congress; copy, in the handwriting of Philip Church, Hamilton Papers, Library of Congress.

1. H's draft has not been found, but see "An Act giving eventual authority to the President of the United States to augment the Army" (1 *Stat.* 725–27

[March 2, 1799]). See also the introductory note to H to James Gunn, December 22, 1798. This draft was requested in McHenry to H, January 10, 11, 1799.

2. See "An Act authorizing the President of the United States to raise a Provisional Army" 1 *Stat.* 558–61 [May 28, 1798]). Although President Adams's authority to raise a Provisional Army had lapsed on December 2, Sections 3, 5, 8, 9, 11, 12, 13, and 14 of the 1798 act were still in effect.

3. See H to McHenry, January 14, 1799, note 2.

4. This is a reference to Adams's Army nominations of December 31, 1798 (*Executive Journal*, I, 298–305). The Senate confirmed the appointments on January 8, 1799, and the list appeared on January 10, 1799, in the *Gazette of the United States, and Philadelphia Daily Advertiser.*

From William Duer

[*New York, January 17, 1799.* The summary of this letter reads: "On Duer's wretched condition." [1] *Letter not found.*]

Letter listed in "Calendar Summary of Philip Church and Alexander Hamilton Papers," Personal Miscellaneous, Box 6, Schuyler, MS Division, New York Public Library.

1. See H to Oliver Wolcott, Jr., August 22, December 28, 1798; Wolcott to H, September 19, 1798.

From Charles Cotesworth Pinckney

[*January 17, 1799.* On March 7, 1799, Hamilton wrote to Pinckney: "I duly received. . . Your letter of the 17th of January." *Letter not found.*]

From William Heth

Petersburg [Virginia] 18th. Jany 1799

Dear Sir

When I wrote you a long letter the other day,[1] I as little expected to intrude upon you again so soon, as that, our domestic tranquility would so *soon*, be seriously threatened.

Leave has been given within a few days past, in our Legislature, to bring in a bill, authorising persons taken up under the sedition Law,[2] to be removed to State Courts, or to be *released*, should our Judges see cause.[3] At least—this I understand to be the object of the bill. Judge Iredell,[4] who will hand you this, will be able to inform you more particularly, as he will receive full information, on passing thro' Richmond. As certainly, as such a bill shall be brought in, as certainly will it pass: And the next moment, some of those of the opposition, who are panting to become Martyrs in the *holy cause,* will throw themselves in the way of the Marshal,[5] or of some officer of the government whom they may suppose bound by oath & duty, to notice seditions, or treasonable expressions. And thus, the signal of Civil War will be given. I hope the Marshal may prove himself to be a Man of firmness & intrepidity.

Early in the present session, I understand, a resolution passed, to suspend the building of our Penitentiary House, & to apply a large Sum in the Treasury appropriated therefor, to the purchase of Arms.[6]

Under this alarming, & distressing prospect of public affairs, it is proper, that every *Man Should be known:* and persuaded that I shall be among the first in this quarter, whom the desperate faction will aim at, in case of open convulsion, I would wish to be among the first to be calld upon, to support the standard of the U. States. Presuming therefore, that Genl. Lee [7] will be immediately ordered to hold himself in readiness, to head part of the provisional army [8]—I should be glad, if propriety should not forbid it—to be also held in requisition, in *any way;* but, if such rank, as the Commander in chief & yourself, may think I merit, could be obtained for *one* of his aids de Camp,[9] and he could now, without any scruple or reluctance, appoint me to that station, my utmost wishes would be gratified, to serve with Lee in case of necessity, til otherwise calld upon. I would pledge myself not to draw pay, or other emoluments, except when in actual service. I have now written, My Dear sir, in the utmost confidence to you. If the Ideas which I have now suggested, are improper, I shall rely upon their going no further.

Burn this—and believe me to be as always Yrs sincerely & Affectionately   W Heth

The activity & zeal which I have late manifested in honor of my friend Pinkney,[10] as well as similar conduct last summer on Marshals arrival [11]—has occasiond me to be markd by the Democrats. In order to stimulate the Citizens of this Town to the measures in honor of Pinkney the other day, I rode down from Richmond the Morning the General left it to this place in 2 hours & 53 Minutes—25 Miles—a proof that I dont yet feel old age.

ALS, Hamilton Papers, Library of Congress.

1. Heth to H, January 14, 1799.

2. This is a reference to "An Act in addition to the act, entitled 'An act for the punishment of certain crimes against the United States'" (1 *Stat.* 596–97 [July 14, 1798]).

3. Although it cannot be stated with certainty, Heth was presumably referring to the fact that in the Virginia House of Delegates on January 11, 1799, it was ordered: "That leave be given to bring in a bill, 'to amend the act, directing the mode of sueing out and prosecuting writs of habeas corpus' and that Mr. John Taylor, Mr. [Samuel] Tyler, Mr. [Nicholas] Cabell, Mr. [Wilson Cary] Nicolas, and Mr. [William] Daniel, do prepare and bring in the same" (*Journal of the House of Delegates of Virginia, 1798*, 70).

4. James Iredell, a North Carolina Federalist, was an associate justice of the Supreme Court of the United States.

5. David Meade Randolph.

6. No such resolution was adopted by either branch of the Virginia legislature during its 1798–1799 session. For a refutation of this and similar charges by Heth to the effect that the Virginia legislature was preparing for forcible resistance to the authority of the Federal Government, see Philip G. Davidson, "Virginia and the Alien and Sedition Laws," *American Historical Review*, XXXVI (January, 1931), 336–42.

7. Henry Lee was appointed major general in the Provisional Army on July 18, 1798 (*Executive Journal*, I, 292, 293). He did not, however, serve, for no steps were ever taken to establish the Provisional Army. See the introductory note to H to James Gunn, December 22, 1798.

8. See "An Act authorizing the President of the United States to raise a Provisional Army" (1 *Stat.* 558–61 [May 28, 1798]).

9. See Heth to H, January 14, 1799.

10. See Heth to H, January 14, 1799, note 12.

11. Following his mission to France, John Marshall arrived in Richmond on August 8, 1798. For an account of his reception on his arrival in Richmond, see the *Gazette of the United States, and Philadelphia Daily Advertiser*, August 17, 1798.

From Susan Kean [1]

[*Elizabethtown, New Jersey, January 18, 1799.* On January 23, 1799, Hamilton wrote to Susan Kean and referred to her "letter of the 18th instant." *Letter not found.*]

1. Susan Kean, the daughter of Peter Van Brugh Livingston, was the widow of John Kean. Kean, a member of Congress from South Carolina from 1785

to 1787, had been cashier of the Bank of the United States from its founding in 1791 until his death in 1795.

From Rufus King

[*London, January 19, 1799.*[1] *Letter not found.*]

1. Letter listed in "Memorandum of Private Letters, &c., dates & persons, from 1796 to Augt 1802," owned by Mr. James G. King, New York City.

From Robert Liston

Philadelphia, January 20, 1799. "Mr Brunel[1] delivered to me yesterday your Letter of the 15th of this month;[2] and I have furnished him with the passport he wanted for England. . . ."

ALS, Hamilton Papers, Library of Congress.
1. H placed an asterisk after Brunel's name and at the bottom of the page wrote: "who went to England to obtain a Patent for a Copying Machine."
2. Letter not found.

From Rufus King

Lond. Jan 21. 1799.

Dear sir

We have the new york Papers to the 15. ult. These contain the Speech[1] as well as the answers of the two Houses.[2] All seems intended for the best, but it gives an ill Idea abroad of our Zeal, to find that our Army decreed so many months since remained to be raised. The difficulty and time necessary to find suitable Officers, reminds one of the like impediments which preceded the appointment of Monro to Paris.[3] I hope the Results will differ.

I am entirely disposed, indeed resolved, to treat the subject as the good Principles of all concerned merit; but I can't conceal from you my very great apprehension that too much is left to the chance & influence of Intrigue & diplomatic Skill. In the Light in wh. alone I can see the views of france, there seems to be no secure alternative; and the sooner we so say, and act, the less will be our Danger.

For gods sake attend to the very interesting Subject treated of in my ciphered Dispatches to the Sec. of State of the 10. 18. & 19. instant.[4] Connect it as it shd. be, with the main object, the time to accomplish wh. has arrived. Without superstition, Providence seems to have prepared the way and to have pointed out the instruments of its will. Our children will reproach us if we neglect our Duty; and Humanity will escape many Scourges if we act with wisdom & Decision. I am more confirmed than before that an efficient Force will be confederated to act agt: France. The Combination is *not yet, compleated,*[5] but as I have reason to believe, will soon be.

That will be the moment for us to settle upon immutable Foundations the extensive System of the american Station. Who can hinder us? One nation alone has the power; and She will cooperate in the accomplishment in So. Amer.[6] of what has been so well done in North.

Adieu! Yrs ever   R K

P.S. Mr. Church [7] knows very well Col. Maitland!! [8]

AL[S], Hamilton Papers, Library of Congress.

1. For John Adams's speech to Congress on December 8, 1798, see *Annals of Congress*, IX, 2420–24.

2. The Senate replied to Adams's speech on December 11, 1798 (*Annals of Congress*, VIII, 2192–93), and the House replied on December 13, 1798 (*Annals of Congress*, IX, 2438–39).

3. James Monroe had been appointed Minister Plenipotentiary to France on May 28, 1794 (*Executive Journal*, I, 157), but he was not George Washington's first choice for this position. See "List of Names From Whence to Take a Minister for France," May 19, 1794, note 1.

4. In this sentence King confused the dates and numbers of his dispatches to Timothy Pickering. He meant to refer to Dispatch No. 17 (dated January 10, 1799), Dispatch No. 18 (January 14, 1799), and Dispatch No. 19 (January 16, 1799).

Dispatches Nos. 17 and 19 concern United States relations with Santo Domingo, while Dispatch No. 18 discusses a new French decree that would affect American commerce adversely (copies, RG 59, Despatches from United States Ministers to Great Britain, 1791–1906, Vol. 8, January 3, 1799–December 18, 1800, National Archives). In reference to Santo Domingo, King reported that he was conferring with Lord Grenville on the possibility of a joint Anglo-American approach both to trade with the island and to the steps to be taken to prevent its slave insurrection from spreading to other countries. For Adams's reaction to King's proposals, see Adams to Pickering, April 17, 1799 (LC, Adams Family Papers, deposited in the Massachusetts Historical Society, Boston).

5. This is a reference to the first steps in the formation of the Second Coalition against France. On December 23, 1798, Turkey and Russia concluded a defensive and offensive alliance, and on January 2, 1799, Great Britain joined this alliance. The other important member of the coalition was Austria. France declared war on Austria on March 12, 1799.

6. This is a reference to Francisco de Miranda's plans for the liberation of the Spanish colonies in the western hemisphere. See Miranda to H, April 1, 1797, February 7, April 6–June 7, August 17, October 19–November 10, 1798; H to Miranda, August 22, 1798; King to H, May 12, July 31, October 20, 1798; H to King, August 22, 1798; Pickering to H, August 21–22, 1798.

7. John B. Church, Elizabeth Hamilton's brother-in-law.

8. In Dispatch No. 19 King had written to Pickering: ". . . they [the British] have concluded immediately to send Colo. Maitland on a frigate to New-York with full power to Mr. Liston. Col. Maitland who made the Convention with Toussaint, to settle the business between us and them and then to proceed with an agent on our part to St. Domingo in order to conclude it there."

Thomas Maitland had had firsthand experience with Santo Domingo, for he had served there under John Graves Simcoe, the former lieutenant governor of Upper Canada. Simcoe had been sent to Santo Domingo in 1796 to take command of the British part of the island. He was replaced in 1798, and in the interval between his departure and the arrival of his successor, Maitland arranged with François Dominique Toussaint L'Ouverture, the *de facto* ruler of Haiti and its former slaves, for the gradual evacuation of the British troops to Jamaica. On August 31, 1798, Maitland signed a secret treaty with Toussaint in which England agreed not to interfere with French Santo Domingo and Toussaint agreed not to interfere with Jamaica. Maitland returned to England, and in early 1799 he was sent to the United States, where he arrived on April 2, 1799, with Lord Grenville's instructions for a proposed Anglo-American agreement concerning trade with Santo Domingo.

From James McHenry

War Department, January 21, 1799. Encloses the "Proceedings of two Military Courts, held on Governeurs Island, one a General Court Martial on the 5th of September,[1] the other a Garrison Court Martial on the 25. of the same month" and discusses "certain irregularities. . . of the said Proceedings." Asks "Two Questions affecting the Legality of the General Court Martial. . . . 1st Can the Commandant of a Port or Garrison, where, there are a sufficient number of officers, to form a General Court Martial, *as such,* order a General Court Martial? 2d Do, or do not, the Rules, and Articles of War,[2] make the Judge Advocate, his Deputy, or some Person properly appointed, to act as Judge Advocate or Recorder, essential to a Court Martial; and as the Proceedings of the aforesaid Court, exhibit no Person, to have acted as Judge Advocate, was the Court properly constituted, and are the proceedings duly authenticated, by the signature of the President of the Court only?"

LS, Hamilton Papers, Library of Congress; LS, letterpress copy, James McHenry Papers, Library of Congress.

1. "Details of the proceedings of a General Court Martial on Goveneur's Island, on Wednesday the fifth day of September 1798—by order of Captain Fred. Frye (commanding officer) bearing date the second Inst." (DS, Hamilton Papers, Library of Congress).

2. See H to Jonathan Dayton, August 6, 1798, note 11.

From James McHenry

War Department 21 Jany. 1799

Dear Sir.

The Inclosed Schedule shews 1st Certain names contained in the list made out by the Generals, not sent to the Senate. 2d The names of those postponed by the Senate & 3d One name negatived by the Senate.[1]

I have not had an opportunity of learning from the Senators their reasons for putting a negative on the nomination of Nathaniel White.[2]

Bradbury Cilly declined. Caleb Gibb's was seriously objected to by Mr Goodhue, Mr Otis, Mr Sewell Mr Dwt. Foster & Mr Isaac Parker.[3] 1 As deficient in capacity for command of a Regiment. 2 As being of Boston, from which town or its vicinity it was inexpedient to take both Commandants.[4] 3 Because there were men who would accept, in other parts of the State, better qualified to command a Regiment, more respectable in Society, and whose influence would be more extensively felt in the recruiting service and upon the community.

John Hobby Marshal of Maine. Represented by the Secretary of the Treasury suspected of misconduct in Office—that an investigation of the subject is in train—and that he has either neglected to collect judgements on revenue bonds, or ha⟨s⟩ collected & detained or misapplied public mon⟨ies.⟩ [5]

John Chipman would not accep⟨t⟩ of a majority nor James

Sawyer of a Captaincy. They are said to be well qualified for higher grades.

George Woodward Wm. Switzer & Marmaduke Wait would not serve in the rank respectively assigned them.

Richard Motley would not accept an Ensigncy.

The observation of some on the Massachusetts arrangement is: that too great a number are selected from Boston, and that the residue are not well proportioned to different parts of the State—That most of the officers arranged for the district of Maine are from Mr Parkers part of the Country which it is said does not contain one fifth of the population.

Hermanus P Schuyler was withdrawn upon his own letter.

John McDougal Laurence not sent in at the instance of his father.

Wm. B. Peters postponed by the Senate for further information.[6]

George Taylor would not accept.

Thomas Swearingen Thos. Ralston Elisha P. Barrows & Edward Nichlas represented as antifederal.

Peter Jacquet represented as nobody.

Wm. S. Dallam opposed to the Government and of French principles.

D. C. Heath of Delaware. Saml. Davis not of sound principle.

Wm. K. Blue was an associate of Zacharia Coxe's.

George Hite—anti-governmental and of French principles.

Thomas Opie dead. Gerrard Roberts[7] postponed by the Senate for information.

I have just received your letter of the 19th respecting the rank of Lieutenant Brindley[8] of Rhode Island.

This gentleman, on the original schedule, made out by the general officers, stands the 4th Lieutenant. Francis Gardner of New Hampshire the 1st Lieutenant and Robert Overing of Rhode Island the 2d. I have informed him, resting upon your representation, that he should take the place of Overing, who I understand is a young man without experience and of inferior pretensions, and if on inquiry he could with propriety be placed first it should be done, with which he was satisfied.

The list as it appears in the news papers settled nothing, and it was so expressed in a note at the bottom of the appointments, which I suppose you did not see.[9] I intend to be guided by the relative rank, as established in the schedule unless cogent reasons, which the General Officers were unacquainted with, shall render deviations proper & necessary.

Yours sincerely   James McHenry

Majr. Gen. Alex Hamilton

[ENCLOSURE][10]

†	Nathaniel White	Lt: Colonel	New Hampshire.
O	Bradbury Cilley	Major	ditto.
O	Caleb Gibbs	Lt. Colonel	Massachusetts.
O	John Hobby	Major	ditto.
O	John Chipman	ditto	Vermont.
O	James Sawyer	Captain	ditto.
O	George Woodward	Lieut:	ditto.
O	William Switzer	ditto	ditto.
O	Marmaduke Wait	Ensign	ditto.
O	Richard Motley	ditto	Massachusetts [11]
withdrawn.	Hermanus p. Schuyler	Captain	New York.
O	John Mc.Dugal Laurence	Lieut:	ditto.
P	William B. peters	ditto	ditto.
O	Clement Woods	ditto	New Jersey.
O	George Taylor	Captain	pennsylvania.
O	Thomas Swearingen	ditto	ditto.
O	James Ralston	ditto	ditto.
O	Elisha p. Barrows	Lieut.	ditto.
O	Edward Nicholas	ditto	ditto.
O	Peter Jacquett	ditto	Delaware.
O	William S. Dallum	Captain	Maryland.
O	Daniel C. Heath	Lieut:	ditto.
O	Samuel Davis	Ensign	ditto.
O	William K. Blue	Captain	Virginia.
O	George Hite	ditto	ditto.
Dead.	O Thomas Opie	Lieut:	ditto.
P	Gerard Roberts	Ensign	ditto.

      † negatived by the Senate.
      O not sent in.
      P postponed.

ALS, Hamilton Papers, Library of Congress; ADf, James McHenry Papers, Library of Congress; ALS, letterpress copy, George Washington Papers, Library of Congress.

    1. For the list which George Washington, H, and Charles Cotesworth Pinckney prepared at meetings in Philadelphia during November and December, 1798, and for the nominations which John Adams sent to the Senate, see McHenry to H, December 28, 1798, notes 1 and 2.

    2. The Senate refused to confirm White's appointment on January 10, 1799 (*Executive Journal*, I, 305).

3. Benjamin Goodhue was United States Senator from Massachusetts, while Harrison Gray Otis, Samuel Sewall, Dwight Foster, and Isaac Parker were members of the House of Representatives from the same state.

4. Simon Elliot.

5. See Goodhue to H, December 8, 1798, note 3.

6. On January 15, 1799, the Senate refused to confirm Peter's appointment (*Executive Journal*, I, 307).

7. *Executive Journal*, I, 301, 305, 306.

8. Thomas Brindley had been appointed a lieutenant in the Additional Army on January 8, 1799 (*Executive Journal*, I, 300, 303). H's letter to McHenry of January 19, 1799, is listed in the appendix to this volume.

9. The list of appointments of January 8, 1799, appeared in the *Gazette of the United States, and Philadelphia Daily Advertiser* on January 10, 1799. The note referred to reads: "We understand that the above order is not to determine the relative rank of officers of the same grade."

10. D, Hamilton Papers, Library of Congress. Although this document is printed as an enclosure to this letter, McHenry forgot to enclose this schedule on January 21 and sent it as an enclosure to McHenry to H, January 22, 1799.

11. This word is in H's handwriting.

To James McHenry

[New York, January 21, 1799]

Dr. Sir

I send you the draft of a Bill for regulating the *Medical Establishment* [1] (I avoid purposely the term *department* which I would reserve for the great branches of Administration).[2] You will see that nothing but an organisation with a general outline of duty is provided for. Detail-regulations will properly come from the President and the Departments, and the less these are legislated upon, in such cases, the better. When fixed by law, they cannot be varied as experience advises.

This particular establishment, however, is one to the right fashioning of which I feel myself more than ordinarily incompetent.

You mention in one of your letters that by the law of the 16 of July the appropriation for the augmented army ceases at the end of the present session.[3] This is one construction of that law. A different might perhaps be maintained. But be this as it may, you find by a subsequent act of the same date intitled "An Act making certain appropriations &c" [4] that 900000 Dollars are there appropriated for the same object without any qualification—and I take it for granted that whatever money should have been *issued* from the Treasury for the use of the War Department, previous to the end of the session, upon the first of those acts might be expended afterwards by this department without any question about its regularity.

Yrs. truly   A Hamilton

New York Jany 21. 1799

James Mc.Henry Esq

ALS, National Library of Medicine, Bethesda, Maryland; ALS (photostat), James McHenry Papers, Library of Congress; ALS (photostat), Princeton University Library; copy, in the handwriting of Philip Church, Hamilton Papers, Library of Congress.

1. ADf, Hamilton Papers, Library of Congress. H's draft is similar to the first three sections of "An Act to regulate the Medical Establishment" (1 *Stat.* 721–23 [March 2, 1799]).

2. See McHenry to H, January 5, 1799. In a report to John Adams dated December 24, 1798, McHenry mentioned the need for a medical establishment and wrote: "As military hospitals are indispensable to an army, especially in time of war, it is respectively suggested, that provisions on the subject ought to be made by law . . ." (*ASP, Military Affairs,* I, 125).

3. See McHenry to H, January 11, 1799.

4. See "An Act making certain appropriations; and to authorize the President to obtain a Loan on the credit of the direct tax" (1 *Stat.* 609–10 [July 16, 1798]).

From James McHenry

War Department 22 Jany 1799

Dear Sir

I omitted to inclose to you yesterday the annexed schedule [1] upon which my letter was a commentary.

The General in Chief has mentioned to me in explicit terms that it is a part of his plan to decline the occupations of the office unless, and until his presence in the field should be required for actual operations or other imperious circumstances should require his assistance. That persevering in this plan he cannot undertake to assume a direct agency incompatible therewith and that a half way acting might be more inconvenient than totally declining it.[2] He then advises, in conformity with my opinion given to him in Philadelphia, a division of the military command between the existing general officers.[3] I mention this that you may experience no embarrassment in giving me your ideas upon the distribution most proper to be adopted.

I have this moment received your note of the 21. and the sketch of the Hospital Bill, and am ever you affectionate friend

James McHenry

You will see Francis [4] in New York who will inform you what progress he has made in preparing cloathing for the army &c.

ALS, Hamilton Papers, Library of Congress; ADf, James McHenry Papers, Library of Congress.

1. See the enclosure to McHenry to H, second letter of January 21, 1799, note 1.

2. The preceding two sentences are a paraphrase of a portion of a letter which George Washington wrote to McHenry on December 16, 1798 (copy, Hamilton Papers, Library of Congress; copy, George Washington Papers, Library of Congress).

3. In his letter to McHenry on December 16, 1798, Washington wrote in part: "Let the charge and direction of our military affairs in the three most Southern States, be entrusted to General Pinckney. If, indeed, it will not derange him too much, to take immediately, a more northerly position—and more convenient for the purpose, let Virginia be added, and his position be in it; leaving South Carolina and Georgia to the care of Brigadier General Washington, subject to the orders of the former, through whom all the military concerns of those States should pass to the War Office. General Hamilton may be charged with superintending, under your direction, all the Troops and Posts which shall not be confided to General Pinckney; including the Army under General Wilkinson. His proximity to the Seat of Government will render this not inconvenient. The Official Letters of the Commander of the Western Army may pass open through your hands, to enable you to give immediately Orders in cases which may be too urgent to wait for the Agency of General Hamilton. The Companies to be recruited, according to the plan laid before me, in the States of Kentuckey and Tennessee, should be subjected to the direction of Major General Pinckney; because they compose a part of the Regiments which are to be raised in the three Southern States; but the present force in Tennessee must be excluded therefrom, otherwise an interference with the Command of Brigadier General Wilkinson, and the mode of his communication with the department of War, would follow, and confusion result from it.

"It will be useful that the whole of the recruiting service should be under one direction, and this properly appertains to the Office of Inspector General. He will, of course, be authorized to call to his aid the other General Officers."

4. Tench Francis was purveyor of public supplies.

From James Gunn

[Philadelphia, January 23, 1799]

Dr. General

In haste I inclose you, by the days mail, a printed Copy of the Military Bill Reported to the Senate.[1] The Bill was handed me by

McHenry,[2] and he is engaged in drawing a Bill for Regulating the hospital department.[3] Have the goodness to Return the Bill With Such amendments as you think proper to make. I do not see the utility of a *full* Col. to a Regiment. If your other engagements are not too pressing you will greatly oblige me by enclosing a plan for the provisional army.[4] It is my opinion that every State ought to officer one regiment at least, and that the President be authorized to Commission *all* the officers Immediately. The policy of the thing will not be doubted. Our friends in the House of Representatives permit the enemy to gain time by long Speeches.[5]

With very great Regard   I am   Dr. Sir   Your Obdt ser.

James Gunn [6]

Philada. Jany. 23d. 1799.

General Hamilton.

ALS, Hamilton Papers, Library of Congress.
   1. "A Bill for the better organizing of the Troops of the United States, and for other purposes" (copy, Hamilton Papers, Library of Congress). The last line of the document reads: "January 21—Read and passed to second reading." For the final form of the act, see "An Act for the better organizing of the Troops of the United States; and for other purposes" (1 *Stat.* 749-55 [March 3, 1799]).
   2. H had drafted this bill for McHenry. See McHenry to H, January 5, 9, 10, 11, 1799; H to McHenry, January 14, 15, 16, 1799.
   3. H had drafted this bill for McHenry. See H to McHenry, January 21, 1799, note 1. See also H to McHenry, January 14, 16, 1799; McHenry to H, January 22, 1799.
   4. Gunn is referring to what became the Eventual (not Provisional) Army. See the introductory note to H to Gunn, December 22, 1798.
   5. This is a reference to the debates over the so-called "Logan Act" (*Annals of Congress*, IX, 2583-2648, 2677-2721). For the final form of this act, see "An Act for the punishment of certain Crimes therein specified" (1 *Stat.* 613 [January 30, 1799]).
   6. H endorsed this letter: "answered 24." Letter not found.

To Susan Kean

New York Jany 23. 1799

HONORED MADAM

How do you like, My dear friend, this mode of beginning my letter? Just as well, I presume, as I did the counterpart of it in your letter of the 18th instant,[1] which reached me only yesterday. Are you now to be told that the more familiarly you treat me, the more you will gratify my friendship and regard for you?

You consult me on a subject about which I have less skill than you suppose & much less than many others. But whatever my advice may be worth it is at your command whenever you imagine it can be of use to you. You appear desirous of promptly knowing my opinion. According to my present lights, you will do well to invest the money you have, partly in the purchase of the Stock of the New York Insurance Company [2] and partly in the proposed loan.[3] I like different investments because it divides whatever of risk may be. Either of these objects will give you good interest for your money. The chance is that both will rise rather than fall in price. Both are in my apprehension safe.

Loans on real security give too little income with great trouble in the collection. And in times of great national calamity, which alone can endanger other securities, that of real property, we have seen, is not without its hazards. By watching the course of things, it is possible to anticipate dangers and to slip out of them. You ladies know better than anybody else how to make a good retreat from slippery and perilous ground.

Eliza and Angelica [4] reciprocate the tender of affection. My friend Peter [5] must take care by becoming a very clever fellow to deserve success & 'tis many to one that he will then command it.

Adieu My Dear Madam   A Hamilton

ALS, Mrs. John Kean, Union, New Jersey.
1. Letter not found.
2. On April 2, 1798, the New York legislature passed "An Act to incorporate the stock-holders of the New-York Insurance Company." The corporation was authorized to insure maritime ventures, houses, goods, and lives (*New York Laws*, 21st Sess., Ch. LXXI).
3. This is a reference to the loan of five million dollars authorized by "An Act making certain appropriations; and to authorize the President to obtain a Loan on the credit of the direct tax" (1 *Stat.* 609–10 [July 16, 1798]).
4. Elizabeth Hamilton and Angelica Church.
5. Peter Philip James Kean, who was ten years old, was the son of Susan Kean.

To James Gunn

[*New York, January 24, 1799.* Hamilton endorsed Gunn's letter of January 23, 1799: "answered 24." *Letter not found.*]

To James McHenry

New York January 24 1799

Dear Sir

You ask my opinion as to proper arrangements for the command of the Military Force, on the ground that the Commander in Chief declines at present an active part.[1] This is a delicate subject for me— yet, in the shape in which it presents itself, I shall wave the scruples which are natural on the occasion.

If I rightly understood the Commander in Chief, his wish was that all the Military points and Military force every where should be put under the direction of the two Major Generals, who alone should be the organs of the Department of War. The objects of this plan are to disburthen the head of that department of infinite details which must unavoidably clog his general arrangements, and to establish a vigilant military superintendence over all the military points. There is no difficulty in this plan except as to the Western army. It will be a very natural disposition to give to the Inspector General the command of all the troops and posts North of Maryland and to General Pinckney the command of all the Troops and posts South of the district assigned to the Inspector General. How will this plan, as to the Western Army answer? Let all the troops upon the Lakes, including those on the Miami which communicates with Lake Erie, be united under the command of one Officer to be stationed at   .[2] Let all the troops in Tennessee be united under the command of one Officer to be stationed at   .[3] Let them consider themselves as under the orders of the General who commands the Western army [4]—and let the whole be placed under the superintendence of the Inspector General. The Officers commanding on the Lakes and in Tennessee to be permitted to correspond immediately with the Inspector General and receive orders from him. All the communication as well of these Officers as of the General of the Western army to be sent open under cover to the Secretary at War—who in urgent cases if the Inspector General be not on the spot will himself give orders which he will communicate for his future government to the Inspector General—and in cases not urgent will leave matters to the Agency of the Inspector General according to the instructions which he shall receive from the Department of War.

It is easy to perceive that there are objections to this plan. I am not sure that it ought to be adopted. The *pour* and the *contre* will readily occur to you—and you will take or reject as shall appear to you proper; assured always that personally I shall be content with any arrangement you may think adviseable

Affecty & truly yrs.   A Hamilton

The Secy at War

ALS, the Library of The Phillips Exeter Academy, Exeter, New Hampshire; copy, in the handwriting of Philip Church, Hamilton Papers, Library of Congress.
1. See McHenry to H, January 22, 1799.
2. Space left blank in MS.
3. Space left blank in MS.
4. James Wilkinson.

From John F. Hamtramck [1]

Fort Wayne [*Territory Northwest of the River Ohio*] *January 25, 1799.* "It Gives me a singular pleasure to have an opportunity of Congratulating you on the choice that the President and Senate have made in the appointment of the Inspector General of the Army. America will see once more those Military talents which formerly were confined in their execution to too small a Compass; now Diffuse themselves into every Department of the Profession, and Display themselves on a much larger scale—and the Pupil under your tuition will rejoice in having an opportunity of making himself perfect in the Art of War. I hope my Dear General that you will not give a wrong interpretation to my pen it is not flattery, *it is the real sentiments* I have always entertained of your abilities since I had the honor of serving under your immediate Command, and on the occasions I have proclaimed them to the Western Army. Long and long have I wished to introduce those principles you taught me, and much do I wish to see Duty done *à la Hamilton.* it is but a few Days ago since I returned from the army on the Mississippi: General Wilkinson having been an eye witness to the Decline of my Health, has permitted me to Return to this place, and has Recommended to the secretary of war to Give me the General Command of the Post on the lakes what will be done about it I know not. But it is absolutely necessary for the good of Service that Such a Commission Should exist with Some person. . . ."

ALS, Hamilton Papers, Library of Congress.
1. Hamtramck, who held the rank of captain during the American Revolution, had served in the Second New York Regiment under Major Nicholas Fish, who in turn was under the command of H. After the war Hamtramck remained in the Army, and at the time this letter was written he was lieutenant colonel commandant of the First Regiment of Infantry.

From John Jay [1]

Albany 25 Jany. 1799

Dear Sir

I have hitherto postponed making any Communications to our Legislature on the Subject of fortifying the Port of New York, in Expectation of receiving the Result of your proceedings relative to that object. Be pleased to inform me when I may expect it. Since your letter to me of the 19th. of November last, & which I answered on the 26th. of that month, none from you on the Subject in question have reached me. It being possible that the answer alluded to may have miscarried, I subjoin a copy [2] of it.

With great Respect & Esteem I am Dr. Sir your most obt. Servt
John Jay

P.S. I do not recollect that any subsequent Letter from you, mentions your having recd. mine of the 24 Octr. and 5 Novr. last.

Major General Hamilton

ALS, Hamilton Papers, Library of Congress; copy, Dr. Frank Monaghan, Washington, D.C.
1. For background to this letter, see the introductory note to H to James McHenry, June 1, 1798.

2. Jay wrote the copy of his letter of November 26, 1798, at the bottom of the letter printed above. Jay mistakenly dated the copy 1799 rather than 1798.

To Theodore Sedgwick

New York Jany 25 1799

My Dear Sir

The cold which I had when you were here increased after you left me & has a great part of the time confined me to bed. This is the chief cause that you have not heard from me in reply to your letter.[1] I have perused the answer in Chancery [2] & incline at present to the Opinion that we can at the ensuing term obtain a dissolution of the Injunction. I will shortly reperuse it & if I change my mind I will immediately inform you. If not I will make the application for the dissolution.

Yrs. truly   A H

Circumstances intervened which made me dispair of ⟨e⟩ffecting what I intimated.

Yrs.   A H

⟨Theodore Sedgwick⟩ Esq

ALS, Lloyd W. Smith Collection, Morristown National Historical Park, Morristown, New Jersey.

1. This letter, which has not been found, was enclosed in Samuel Mackay to H, January 23, 1799, which is listed in the appendix to this volume. Mackay, a retired British officer, wrote to H concerning his appointment to the Army.

2. This is a reference to the case of *Thomas Morris and James Wadsworth* v *William Bacon*. See Sedgwick to H, February 4, 1798.

To John Jay [1]

[New York, January 26–30, 1799]

Dr. Sir

I have received your Letter of the 25th. Various circumstances have prevented my being ready to make the Report you desire. The

Survey of the Port made while I was at Philadelphia was but partial; not extending beyond the Narrows. A survey of the lower part of the Bay, which presents some objects worthy of Consideration, was effected by some of the Commanders of the British Army—And is in the hands of a Mr. Hill, who holds it up at a higher price than I was willing to give.[2] But what is of more importance, I have not yet been able to obtain the engineering assistance which I deem essential.[3] On the whole Sir I must observe that this is a business of great intrinsic Difficulty requiring much more investigation and thought than there has yet been opportunity for, or than can be bestowed in time for offering any Specific plan to the Legislature.

Copy (incomplete), Dr. Frank Monaghan, Washington, D.C.
    1. For background to this letter, see the introductory note to H to James McHenry, June 1, 1798.
    2. See William Macpherson to H, January 3, 1799.
    3. See H to Jay, November 19, 1798.

To Harrison Gray Otis

New York January 26th 1799

Dear Sir

You will recollect that I reserved for a future answer part of a letter which I had the pleasure of receiving from you some time since.[1] These are my ideas on that Subject.

I should be glad to see, before the close of the Session, a law impowering the President, at his discretion, in case a negotiation between the United States and France should not be on foot by the first of August next, or being on foot should terminate without an adjustment of differences, to declare that a state of war exists between the two Countries, and thereupon to employ the Land and Naval forces of the United States in such manner as shall appear to him most effectual for annoying the Enemy and for preventing and frustrating hostile designs of France, either directly or *indirectly through any of her Allies.*

This course of proceeding, by postponing the event, and giving time for the intervention of negotiation, would be a further proof of moderation in the Government and would tend to reconcile our

Citizens to the last extremity, if it shall ensue; gradually accustoming their minds to look forward to it.

If France be really desirious of accommodation, this plan will accelerate her measures to bring it about. If she have not that desire, it is best to anticipate her final vengeance, and to throw whatever weight we have into the Scale opposed to her. This conduct may contribute to disable her to do the mischief, which she may meditate.

As it is every moment possible, that the project of taking possession of the Floridas and Louisiana, long since attributed to France, may be attempted to be put in execution, it is very important that the Executive should be cloathed with power to meet and defeat so dangerous an enterprise. Indeed if it is the policy of France to leave us in a state of semi-hostility 'tis preferable to terminate it; and by taking possession of those countries for ourselves, to obviate the mischief of their falling into the hands of an Active foreign power, and at the same time to secure to the United States the advantage of keeping the key of the Western Country. I have been long in the habit of considering the acquisition of those countries as essential to the permanency of the Union, which I consider as very important to the welfare of the whole.

If universal empire is still to be the pursuit of France, what can tend to defeat the purpose better than to detach South America from Spain [2] which is only the Channel, though which the riches of *Mexico* and *Peru* are conveyed to France? The Executive ought to be put in a situation to embrace favorable conjunctures for effecting that separation. Tis to be regretted that the preparation of an adequate Military force does not advance more rapidly. There is some sad nonsense on this Subject in some good heads. The reveries of some of the friends of the Government are more injurious to it than the attacks of its declared enemies. When will men learn to profit by experience?

Yrs with great esteem and regard   A Hamilton

Mr Otis

Copy, in the handwriting of Philip Church, Hamilton Papers, Library of Congress.

1. See Otis to H, December 21, 1798; H to Otis, December 27, 1798.

2. This is a reference to Francisco de Miranda's plans for the liberation of the Spanish colonies in the Western Hemisphere. See Miranda to H, April 1,

1797, February 7, April 6–June 7, August 17, October 19–November 10, 1798; H to Miranda, August 22, 1798; Rufus King, to H, May 12, July 31, October 20, 1798, January 21, 1799; H to King, August 22, 1798; Timothy Pickering to H, August 21–22, 1798.

From Rufus King

[*London, January 27, 1799.*[1] *Letter not found.*]

1. Letter listed in "Memorandum of Private Letters, &c., dates & persons, from 1796 to Augt 1802," owned by Mr. James G. King, New York City.

To Stephen Van Rensselaer

New York Jany 27. 1799

Dear Sir

I ought to beg your pardon for not having before answered your letters of the 12th. of Novemr and 11th instant.[1] You know the multitude of my engagements. Added to them, my health for a considerable time past has been very indifferent. Be indulgent.

I left a memorandum with the Secy at War respecting Mr. Tisdale.[2]

As to an Insolvent law,[3] these are my ideas. There is a serious doubt whether any such law, passed by a Legislature subsequent to the adoption of the Constitution of the UStates, will not be an infringement of that article, which forbids a state to pass "any law impairing the *obligation* of Contracts." I think it the better opinion that it will. What way so effectual to impair the obligation of a Contract as to defeat the means which the established laws allow for its enforcement? In the eye of a *human forum*, the essence of the obligation of a Contract consists in the sanctions by which it is carried into execution; by which, as between Debtor & Creditor, the former can obtain a satisfaction, whether by exertion of the *person* or *property* of the Debtor.

This difficulty out of the Way I should feel no great objection to a law like the following—

Providing that after a Debtor shall have been imprisonned by his Creditor upon execution for a term of *five* years, it shall be *in the discretion* of Commissioners to examine into the circumstances of the case, and to liberate the Debtor from imprisonment, upon the condition however of a surrender of all the property he has & leaving all he may acquire afterwards to be subject to the demands of his Creditors—in order to which the Debtor to account every *five* years on oath before the Commissioners for whatever surplus he may have acquired, they to direct what dividend shall be made among the Creditors and to permit him to retain from time to time so much as they may think expedient for carrying on whatever business he may be engaged in having regard to the interest of his Creditors. His Liberty also so long as he shall be called to account to be exempt from execution, the same as before his Insolvency.

The Commissioners to be selected and designated by the Council of Appointment with competent allowances. These may arise from fees.

As to the pretended decision of the Commissioners on the 6th article of the British Treaty [4] all I can say is, that it must be from the nature of things, matter of *conjecture* not of *knowlege* how far any principle they may have adopted will go in swelling the sum to be paid—that I have not heared of any decision likely to occasion it to amount to any thing near the sum which you state—that if the Commissioners by misconstruction exceed *their authority*, the UStates may & will dispute the validity of their decisions & probably by negotiation will rectify them.

It is true indeed that the Commissoners have shewn some disposition to stretch points—but any thing improper will be steadily resisted and it may be hoped with success. All this however is tender ground and must be trodden upon with caution. Eliza joins in love to Mrs. Rensselaer. [5] Adieu.

I remain   Yr sincere & ob ser   Alex Hamilton

Lt G Rensselaer

ALS, from the original in the New York State Library, Albany.

1. Neither letter has been found.

2. Thomas Trisdale. See the first enclosure to H to James McHenry, August 21, 1798. H's memorandum has not been found.

3. In August, 1798, the New York Assembly began to debate the bill that eventually became "An Act to amend the Act for the relief of Debtors with respect to the Imprisonment of their Persons" (*New York Laws*, 22nd Sess., Ch. LXXXV [April 2, 1799]). For the earlier statute, see "An Act for the

relief of debtors with respect to the imprisonment of their persons" (*New York Laws*, 12th Sess., Ch. XXIII [February 13, 1789]). For the debate in the Assembly, see *Journal of the Assembly of the State of New-York, 22nd Sess.,* 17, 20, 31–32, 34, 279.

4. This is a reference to the mixed commission authorized by Article 6 of the Jay Treaty. For the text of Article 6, see "Remarks on the Treaty . . . between the United States and Great Britain," July 9–11, 1795, note 13. See also the introductory note to H to George Washington, March 7, 1796; Oliver Wolcott, Jr., to H, August 9, 1798.

5. Margaret (Margarita) Schuyler Van Rensselaer was Elizabeth Hamilton's sister.

From Samuel Lewis [1]

War Department, January 28, 1799. Encloses a "Draft for four hundred and ninety six dollars and seventy Cents, on the Branch Bank at New York—the balance (forty dollars) I have paid into the hands of the Secy of War—the whole amounting to five hundred and thirty six dollars and seventy Cents, agreeably to a Warrant issued from the War Department on account of your Pay Subsistence and Forage for November and December 1798. . . ." [2]

ALS, Hamilton Papers, Library of Congress.

1. Lewis was a clerk in the War Department.

2. H endorsed this letter: "Jany 31 Answered & Rect. sent." H's letter and receipt to Lewis have not been found.

On January 29, 1799, H made the following entry in his Cash Book, 1795–1804: "Cash Dr to Military Service compensation for November & Decr. 536.70" (AD, Hamilton Papers, Library of Congress).

From James McHenry

War Department, January 29, 1799. "Until your instructions can be made out defining the extent of your Command you will be pleased to require the proper reports to be made to you by the Garrisons at New York and West point and to exercise such superintendance over the same as may consert with military rules and usage and to make from time to time the necessary communications to this department. . . ." [1]

LS, Hamilton Papers, Library of Congress.

1. On verso H wrote: "Acknowlege Receipt. I shall immediately proceed in

the execution of the duty which it assigns me. . . ." Letter not found. H also endorsed this letter: "Inclosed are papers respecting Doct [Samuel] Osborne." Osborne was a surgeon's mate in the Corps of Artillerists and Engineers.

Circular to the Commanding Officers at New York and West Point

New York January 30. 1799

Sir

A letter from the Secretary at War, of yesterday, places under my superintendence the Posts and troops under your immediate command. All future communications therefore respecting them, including reports and returns, are to be addressed to me; not as heretofore to the Secretary at War.

It is my wish as soon as possible to receive a full and particular communication of the state of things within your command—embracing the number and condition of the works and buildings—the quantities and kinds of Artillery arms and stores—the number of troops and their situation as to discipline equipment and supply; and that you will in future keep me regularly advised of whatever may be material for the successful discharge of your trust or the advancement of the service.

I cannot let this first opportunity pass, without calling your attention in an especial manner to the discipline of the troops. The cursory observation which I have been hitherto able to make, has been sufficient to satisfy me that there exists in this respect too general a relaxation; an evil which must at all events be corrected by the union of care prudence and energy. No argument is necessary to prove how essential is discipline to the respectability and success of the service, and consequently to the honor interest and individual importance of every officer of the army. To the exertions for maintaining it, my firm support at all times may be absolutely counted upon; as it will be my steady aim, on the one hand, to promote, to every reasonable extent, the comfort of the troops, on the other, to secure a strict observance of their duty.

With great consideration I am   Sir   Yr Obed serv

ADf, to George Ingersoll, Hamilton Papers, Library of Congress.

To Samuel Lewis

[*New York, January 31, 1799*. On the back of the letter Hamilton received from Lewis, dated January 28, 1799, Hamilton wrote: "Jany 31 Answered & Rect. sent." *Letter and receipt not found.*]

From Philip Schuyler

[Albany, January 31, 1799]

Introductory Note

The opening paragraph of the letter printed below contains the first reference in Hamilton's extant correspondence to a series of events that led to the chartering of the Manhattan Company.[1] This company, which eventually was to supply New York City with an inadequate water system and a major bank, owed its creation primarily to the ingenuity of Aaron Burr, who at the time the charter was granted was a member of the New York Assembly.[2] Although it is—and was—generally believed that Burr wished to create a bank that would be responsive and favorable to the Republican interests in the city, it is highly unlikely that he would have succeeded in obtaining a charter for the company without the support of Hamilton. Nor was this all, for Burr was assisted by other prominent Federalists, and one of the company's original directors was John B. Church, Hamilton's close friend and associate and his wife's brother-in-law.[3]

ALS, New-York Historical Society, New York City.
   1. For a full account of the founding of the Manhattan Company, see Beatrice G. Reubens, "Burr, Hamilton and the Manhattan Company. Part I: Gaining the Charter," *Political Science Quarterly*, LXXII (December, 1957), 578–607. The same author has written "Burr, Hamilton and the Manhattan Company. Part II: Launching a Bank," *Political Science Quarterly*, LXXIII (March, 1958), 100–25. See also Joseph Stancliffe Davis, *Essays in the Earlier History of American Corporations* ("Harvard Economic Studies," XVI [Cambridge, 1917]), II, 100–01, 252, 319; Sidney I. Pomerantz, *New York: An American City, 1783–1803* (Reprinted: Port Washington, New York, 1965), 187–92, 278–85.
   2. For a partisan (that is, Federalist) view of Burr's role in obtaining the charter for the Manhattan Company, see "To the Citizens of New York" by "A Citizen" (*The New-York Gazette and General Advertiser*, May 1, 1799). This article also appeared as a broadside (New-York Historical Society, New York City). See also the broadside entitled *A Yearly Tax of 140,000 Dollars!*, April 30, 1799 (New-York Historical Society, New York City).
   3. *New York Laws*, 22nd Sess., Ch. LXXXIV (April 2, 1799).

In 1799 politicians assumed that banks, like most other institutions, were dominated by one or the other of the major parties, and New York's Republicans charged that the city's two banks—the Bank of New York and the local branch of the Bank of the United States—discriminated against Republicans and used their influence to secure the election of Federalist candidates.[4] At the same time it was generally recognized that steps should be taken to improve the city's water supply. It remained for Burr to perceive a connection between these two apparently unrelated situations by developing a plan to establish a bank with a charter that created a company ostensibly for furnishing the city with water.

In February, 1796, the New York City Common Council appointed a special committee "on the subject of supplying this City with fresh Water." [5] Although the committee received numerous proposals from various individuals during the next three years,[6] it took no effective action until the yellow fever epidemic of 1798 convinced New Yorkers that the spread of the disease could be attributed in part to the impurity of the city's drinking water.[7] Among those presenting plans to the Common Council for an improved water supply was Dr. Joseph Browne, Burr's brother-in-law. In December, 1796, and again in July, 1798, Browne proposed to the Council that it should urge the state legislature to charter a private company to supply the city with water from the Bronx River.[8] On December 17, 1798, the Council approved the "Plan suggested by Doctor Joseph Brown for conveying the Waters of . . . [the Bronx] River . . . with some few variations. . . ." [9] At the same time it rejected Browne's plan for a private company, for it ordered that a bill be prepared and submitted to the legislature authorizing the city to establish and operate a municipal system.[10]

Any bill providing for a public water system posed an obvious threat to Burr's plan to use a law chartering a private water company as a device for the establishment of a new bank. But Burr proved more than equal to the situation. After February 16, 1799, when the Assembly "*Ordered,* That Mr. Burr have leave of absence for ten days," [11] he left Albany for New York, where he formed a committee of six, of which both he and Hamilton were members and which consisted of three Federalists and three Republicans. According to the minutes

---

4. For a detailed discussion of the points mentioned in this paragraph, see Reubens, "Burr, Hamilton and the Manhattan Company. Part I: Gaining the Charter," *Political Science Quarterly,* LXXII (December, 1957), 578–83.

5. *Minutes of the Common Council,* II, 212.

6. *Minutes of the Common Council,* II, 225, 307, 314, 320, 347, 420, 466, 467–68, 478, 480, 481, 483, 484, 486–90.

7. *Minutes of the Common Council,* II, 466, 467–68, 478, 480, 481, 494–509.

8. *Minutes of the Common Council,* II, 314; *Proceedings of the Corporation of New-York, on Supplying the City with Pure and Wholesome Water; With a Memoir of Joseph Browne* (New York: Printed by John Furman, 1799).

9. *Minutes of the Common Council,* II, 486.

10. *Minutes of the Common Council,* II, 486–87.

11. *Journal of the Assembly of the State of New-York; 22nd Sess., 2nd Meeting,* 123.

of the Common Council for February 25, 1799, "The Mayor [12] informed the Board That on Friday last Mr Burr one of the Members from this City in the Assembly of the State together with John Murray Esqr as the President of the Chamber of Commerce, Gulian Verplanck Esqr as the President of the Office of Discount and Deposit of the Bank of the United States in this City,[13] Peter H. Wendover as the President of the Mechanic Society together with Major General Hamilton and John Broome Esqr,[14] according to an Appointment by Mr Burr, called on him and stated to him in the Presence of the Recorder,[15] who was also requested to attend for the purpose, that great difficulties had arisen in the minds of the Members of the Legislature touching the Powers requested to be vested in this Board, by the Bill for supplying this City with Water and the Bill for investing this Board with adequate Powers in relation to certain objects of importance to the Health of the City: that it was Problematical whether those Bills would pass in the form Proposed and He therefore submitted the Propriety of this Board requesting the Legislature *that if those Bills respectively* should not be deemed Proper in the form proposed by the Board, the Legislature should make such Provisions on the several Subjects thereof as to them should appear most eligible.

"That after some Conversation with Mr Burr and the other Gentlemen accompanying him the Recorder and himself requested that their Propositions might be stated in Writing to be communicated to the Board as on this day. And Mr Recorder now laid before the Board a Paper without Signature which he stated to the Board he had received from Major General Hamilton [16] as the Propositions for their consideration this day, which being read

"Resolved, That before the Board proceed upon the said Propositions they ought to be sanctioned by the Signature of the parties recommending the same; And that the Nature and Circumstances of the Difficulties which have attended the several applications made on the behalf of this Board to the Legislature should also be stated.

"Resolved further that the above Resolution be communicated to Mr Burr and Major General Hamilton without delay; And as the objects above alluded to are of great importance to the welfare of the City, the Mayor be requested to call a special Meeting of this Board as soon

12. Richard Varick.

13. This is a mistake, for Verplanck was president of the Bank of New York. Murray and Verplanck were Federalists.

14. Broome was a New York City merchant and Republican politician. He had been a member of the New York Committee of One Hundred in 1775, the Provincial Congress of New York in 1776 and 1777, and the committee which drew up the New York Constitution of 1777. In the interval between 1799 and his death in 1810, he was a member of the state Senate, Assembly, and Council of Appointment, and when he died he was lieutenant governor of New York.

15. Richard Harison.

16. This "Paper" has not been found, but it is likely that it is the same as the enclosure to H to Varick, February 26, 1799.

as he shall receive the Proper communications in consequence of the above Resolution." [17]

In compliance with the request for a signed statement from the committee, Hamilton wrote to Mayor Richard Varick on February 26 and enclosed a memorandum containing the arguments for a private company. On February 28 the Council resolved that ". . . they will be perfectly satisfied if the objects in View are pursued in any Way that the Legislature may think proper by which their fellow Citizens may be benefitted in the most easy, safe and effectual method, and the Charter rights of the City remain inviolate." [18] But Hamilton was still not finished, for he then prepared a "memorial" to the legislature calling for a "Company . . . with a Capital not exceeding one Million of Dollars to be formed by voluntary subscriptions of fifty dollars to a share. . . ." [19]

"An act for supplying the city of New-York with pure and wholesome water," which was passed by the Assembly on March 28, 1799,[20] and by the Senate on March 30,[21] became law on April 2.[22] The provision which enabled the Manhattan Company to establish a bank was inserted toward the end of the measure and reads in its entirety: "*And be it further enacted,* That it shall and may be lawful for the said company to employ all such surplus capital as may belong or accrue to the said company in the purchase of public or other stock, or in any other monied transactions or operations not inconsistent with the constitution and laws of this state or of the United States, for the sole benefit of the said company." In 1799 the Manhattan Company established both a water system and a bank. The water system was inadequate from the outset and stopped operations in 1840. The bank survived, prospered, and exists today as the Chase Manhattan Bank.

Hamilton lived to regret the part that he had played in the chartering of the Manhattan Company. In the course of a letter to James A. Bayard on January 16, 1801, stating his opposition to Burr as President, Hamilton wrote: "I have been present when he has contended against Banking Systems with earnestness . . ." and then added: "Yet he has lately by a trick established a *Bank,* a perfect monster in its principle; but a very convenient instrument of *profit* & *influence.*"

Albany Jany. 31st 1799

My Dear Sir

This will be delivered to you by Mr Weston,[23] who has been requested by the Corporation of your city to a conference on the

17. *Minutes of the Common Council,* II, 514–15.
18. *Minutes of the Common Council,* II, 520.
19. H to the Legislature of the State of New York, February–March, 1799.
20. *Journal of the Assembly of the State of New-York; 22nd Sess., 2nd Meeting,* 263.
21. *Journal of the Senate of the State of New-York; 22nd Sess., 2nd Meeting,* 118.
22. *New York Laws,* 22nd Sess., Ch. LXXXIV.
23. Weston was an English engineer who from 1795 to 1799 was supervisor of construction for the Western and Northern Inland Lock Navigation com-

Subject of supplying the city with water.[24] Permit me to entreat your Attention to him.

Mrs. Church [25] writes me that you Suffer from want of exercise, that this and unremitted Attention to business injures your health. I believe It is difficult for an Active mind to moderate an application to business but My Dear Sir you must make some sacrifice to that health which is so precious to all who are dear to you, and to that country which revers and Esteems you. Let me then entreat you to use more bodily exercise, and less of that of the mind.[26]

---

panies in New York State. Schuyler was a leading proponent of canals in New York State and served as president of the Inland Lock companies.

24. On December 17, 1798, the Common Council adopted a report which, after approving Doctor Joseph Browne's proposal for supplying New York with water from the Bronx River, recommended "that Mr Weston who has been the Engineer for the Canal Companies in this State and whose abilities are well known, be requested to examine that River with the situation of the Grounds to be employed in the Aqueduct and such other Matters incident to the supply of the City with pure & wholesome Water from that or any other Source as he may think proper and that he be requested to report his Opinion to the Corporation with the requisite Plans & Estimates as soon as may be practicable" (Minutes of the Common Council, II, 486).

The Mayor submitted Weston's report to the Common Council on March 16, 1799 (Minutes of the Common Council, II, 527). For Weston's report, see Report of William Weston, Esquire, on the Practicability of Introducing the Water of the River Bronx into the City of New-York (New York: Printed by John Furman, 1799).

25. Angelica Schuyler Church, sister of Elizabeth Hamilton.

26. Whether the following letter illustrates mental or bodily activity may be difficult to determine, but it does indicate that H did not spend all his time working. In any event, on February 14, 1799, Peter A. Jay, the son of John Jay, wrote the following letter to his sister Anna about a party H attended on February 7, 1799, at John B. Church's house: "Mr. Ph[ilip]. Church being some time ago at Newark in Company with Mr. [Julian Ursyn] Nimscowich [Niemcewicz] a Polish Gentleman, formerly a Companion of Genl [Tadeusz] Koskiusco [Kościuszko], the latter asserted that he possessed a magical Secret imparted to him by that Genl. wh. enable[d] him [to] raise the Spirits of the Dead. . . . Mr. Church returning to town related to his Father & Genl. Hamilton this extraordinary Occurrence & their Curiosity being raised by his relation, it was agreed to invite Mr. Nimscowich to town & request him to exhibit a Specimen of his Art. He accordingly came & dined with Mr. Church on Friday last & in the evening proceeded to gratify their request. Gen Hamilton retired to a Room by himself & Mr. Church who remained with the Conjuror wrote on a card without the Knowledge of the Gen. the name of [Antoine Charles du Houx] Baron de Viominil [Vioménil]. This being given to Mr. Nimscowich, the latter proceeded to make incantations &c until Genl. H returned & declared that the Baron had appeared to him exactly in the Dress which he formerly wore & that a Conversation had passed between them wh. he was not at liberty to disclose. This is the substance of the Account given by Mr. Church & his Sons, which was afterwd. greatly embellished & spread thro the City with so much Rapidity that the Poet ought not to be accused of

By a Mistake of mine my Nephew Ph: Schuyler's name is not Corre[c]t. It should have been Philip Cortland Schuyler instead of Philip Stephen Schuyler,[27] there being another of the latter name. My Nephew has written on this Subject to the Secretary at War. Will you be so good as to interpose on the Occasion.

All here are well and Unite in love to you My Eliza & the Children.

I am My dear Sir Ever most Affectlly Yours Ph: Schuyler

Hone M: Genl Hamilton

Hyperbole who attributed to [John] Fenno only an hundred tongues. . . . It was not till a Day or too ago that Genl Hamilton explained the Mystery & declared [the] whole to be a contrivance between himself Ph. Church & the Pole to frighten the family for amusement, & that it was never intended to be made public. It seems that part of the Conjuration consisted in striking on a Bell when the card was given to the Wizard he gave as many strokes as were equal to the Number at which each letter of the Name stood in the Alphabet— 21 for V. 9 for J. &c & thus communicated to his Confederate in the other room the Name of the Person he was to pretend to have seen . . ." (ALS, Columbia University Libraries).

Niemcewicz, a Polish patriot, was a writer and poet. Kościuszko, who had fought in the American Revolution, had been captured by the Russians during the Polish uprising of 1794. Viomenil had served as second in command to Jean Baptiste Donatien de Vimeur, comte de Rochambeau, from 1780 to 1781. John B. Church had only one son, Philip, born in 1778.

27. On January 8, 1799, Philip Stephen Schuyler was appointed a lieutenant of the Twelfth Regiment of Infantry (*Executive Journal*, I, 300, 303).

From Daniel C. Brent

City of Washington, February 2, 1799. "The following is nearly a correct copy of a letter which I wrote to you on the 16th of July 1798. . . ."

ALS, Hamilton Papers, Library of Congress.

From John F. Hamtramck

Fort Wayne [*Territory Northwest of the River Ohio*] *February 2, 1799.* "It will no Doubt be Surprising to you to See an officer of my Rank, and of twenty one years service—make an application so incompatible with the profession of arms; But Sir the Military Establishment of the united States is So unsettled and so changeable, that a promotion frequently proves more injurious than advantageous to a man who Makes the art of war his profession. To be promoted for a few Days, and be discharged would be a fatal Stroke to me. . . . let me entreat you to guard against an appointment which might be the means of throwing me out of Service; *that is* if it Can be done with honor to my Self. . . ."

ALS, Hamilton Papers, Library of Congress.

To Theodore Sedgwick

New York Feby 2. 1799

What, My Dear Sir, are you going to do with Virginia? This is a very serious business, which will call for all the wisdom and firmness of the Government. The following are the ideas which occur to me on the occasion.

The first thing in all great operations of such a Government as ours is to secure the opinion of the people. To this end, the proceedings of Virginia and Kentucke [1] with the two laws complained of should be referred to a special Committee. That Committee should make a report exhibiting with great luminousness and particularity the reasons which support the constitutionality and expediency of those laws—the tendency of the doctrines advanced by Virginia and Kentucke to destroy the Constitution of the UStates [2]—and, with calm dignity united with pathos, the full evidence which they afford of a regular conspiracy to overturn the government. And the Report should likewise dwell upon the inevitable effect and probably the intention of these proceedings to encourage a hostile foreign power to decline accommodation and proceed in hostility. The Government must ⟨no⟩t merely ⟨de⟩fend itself ⟨bu⟩t must attack and arraign its enemies. But in all this, there should be great care to distinguish the people of Virginia from the legislature and even the greater part of those who may have concurred in the legislature from the Chiefs; manifesting indeed a strong confidence in the good sense and patriotism of the people, that they will not be the dupes of an insidious

plan to disunite the people of America to break down their constitution & expose them to the enterprises of a foreign power.

This Report should conclude with a declaration that there is
no cause for a Repeal of the laws. If however on examination any
modifications consistent with the general design of the laws, but in-
stituting better guards, can be devised it may [be] well to propose
them as a bridge for those who may incline to retreat over. Con-
cessions of this kind adroitly made have a good rather than a bad
effect. On a recent though hasty revision of the Alien law it seems
to me deficient in precautions against abuse and for the security of
Citizens. This should not be.

No pains or expence should be spared to desseminate this Report.
A little pamphlet containing it should find its way into every house
in Virginia.

This should be left to work and nothing to court a shock should
be adopted.

In the mean time the measures for raising the Military force should
proceed with activity.[3] Tis much to be lamented that so much
delay has attended the execution of this measure. In times like the
present not a moment ought to have been lost to secure the Government so powerful an auxiliary. Whenever the experiment shall be
made to subdue a *refractory* & powerful *state* by Militia, the event
will shame the advocates of their sufficiency. In the expedition
against the Western Insurgents I trembled every moment lest a great
part of the Militia should take it into their heads to return home
rather than go forward.

When a clever force has been collected let them be drawn towards
Virginia for which there is an obvious pretext—& then let measures
be taken to act upon the laws & put Virginia to the Test of resistance.

This plan will give time for the fervour of the moment to sub-
side, for reason to resume the reins, and by dividing its enemies will
enable the Government to triumph with ease.

As an auxiliary measure, it is very desireable that the Provisional
Army Bill[4] should pass & that the Executive should proceed to the
appointment of the Officers. The tendency of this needs no comment.

Yrs. affecy   A Hamilton

T. Sedgwick Es

ALS, Massachusetts Historical Society, Boston.

1. This is a reference to the Kentucky and Virginia resolutions protesting the Alien and Sedition Acts. For the Alien Acts, see H to Timothy Pickering, June 7, 1798, note 6. For the Sedition Act, see William Heth to H, January 18, 1799, note 2. The Virginia resolutions, which were written by James Madison and approved by the state legislature on December 24, 1798, are printed under the date of December 21, 1798, in the *Journal of the House of Delegates of Virginia, 1798*, 31. For the Kentucky resolutions, which were written by Thomas Jefferson and approved by the state legislature on November 16, 1798, see Paul Leicester Ford, ed., *The Writings of Thomas Jefferson* (New York, 1892–1899), VII, 289–309. The Kentucky legislature passed a second set of resolutions, also written by Jefferson, on November 22, 1799. For the text of these resolutions, see Jonathan Elliot, ed., *Debates in the Several State Conventions on the Adoption of the Federal Constitution* (2nd ed., Philadelphia, 1861), IV, 544–45.

2. In MS, "U stand."

3. See "An Act to augment the Army of the United States, and for other purposes" (1 *Stat.* 604–05 [July 16, 1798]).

4. This is a reference to what subsequently became "An Act giving eventual authority to the President of the United States to augment the Army" (1 *Stat.* 725–27 [March 2, 1799]). H is referring to the Eventual (rather than Provisional) Army. See the introductory note to H to James Gunn, December 22, 1798.

From Benjamin Walker [1]

Utica [New York] February 3, 1799. States: "Judge Cooper has written me that you are about setling the matter respecting his claim on the black river Land and he wishes me to give you my ideas on the business. . . ." Gives his version of this land dispute which involved Walker, Cooper, and others.

ALS, Hamilton Papers, Library of Congress.

1. For background to this letter, see H to Walker, William Inman, and William Cooper, September 9, 1798; Cooper to H, November 26, 1798.

From James McHenry [1]

War Department,
February 4th: 1799.[2]

Sir,

Lieutenant General Washington having declined agreeably to the condition upon which he accepted of his appointment, any Command whatever of the Army of the United States u⟨ntil⟩ such time as his presence in the Field shall be required for actu⟨al ope⟩rations, or his Services demanded by peculiar and urgent circum-⟨stances⟩ [3] it is therefore proper to make such arrangements respecting the distribution of the existing military authority, as shall most conduce to the go⟨od⟩ of the Service, is best adapted to our present situation, and to the objects to which our force may eventually be applied.[4]

Before entering into particulars upon the principal subject ⟨at⟩ present contemplated, it will be useful to enumerate the Stations of the Troops of the United States, and the course taken to communicate with them.

1. There are on the Lakes, viz: On Lake Ontario, the Garrisons of Oswego and Niagara: On Lake Erie and Lake St. Clair, the Garrisons of presqu'isle and Detroit: On Lake Huron at the entrance of the Straight leading to Lake Michigan, the Garrison of *Michilimachinac:* On the Miami River Fort Wayne: On the Ohio, Fort Franklin, Fort Washington and Fort Massac.

2. There are on the Mississippi, Garrisons at the Chickasaw Bluffs, Walnut Hills, and Natchez or Loftus' Heights.

3. There are several posts on the Creek frontier of the State of

LS, Hamilton Papers, Library of Congress; copy, George Washington Papers, Library of Congress; copy, James McHenry Papers, Library of Congress.

1. In the Hamilton Papers, Library of Congress, there is an undated document in H's handwriting entitled "Agenda." This document contains in outline form most of the points discussed by McHenry in the letter printed above.

2. McHenry did not send this letter to H until February 8, 1799, and H did not receive it until February 11. See McHenry to H, two letters of February 8, 1799; H to McHenry, February 11, 1799.

3. See McHenry to H, January 22, 1799.

4. See H to McHenry, January 24, 1799.

Georgia. 4. There are several posts on the Indian frontier of the State of Tennessee.

5. There are several Garrisons on the Sea-board from Maine to Georgia inclusive.

The first enumerated posts (except Oswego and Niagara) while General Wilkinson was at certain Stations in the North Western Territory,[5] have communicated through him with the Department of War. The Second do now communicate, through General Wilkinson, who is on the Mississippi. The third, through Lieutenant Colonel Butler.[6] The fourth, through Lieut: Colonel Gaither.[7] The fifth, through the medium of the Commandants of the several Garrisons.

I have said, that the first described Garrisons communicated through General Wilkinson while at certain Stations. For example when the General was stationary at pittsburg or Fort Washington on the Ohio, the whole of these Garrisons above and below him, except Oswego and Niagara, communicated directly with the General, and the General with the Secretary of War. Again. When the General held a position at Detroit all the Garrisons between him and the Seat of Government, though within his sphere of Command, communicated directly with the Secretary of War. Lastly, since the General entered into the Mississippi, all the Garrisons above him communicated directly with the Secretary of War.

Oswego and Niagara being in all the aforesaid positions of the General, too distant to enable him to give quick information respecting them, were always allowed to hold direct communications with the Department of War.

A slight view of the Map of the Country, over which troops are stationed, the distance between the Garrisons, the Routes by which it is practicable for them to communicate with each other and with the Seat of Government, added to a consideration of the serious inconveniencies that might have resulted during the unsettled state of things which has existed for some time past generally on the

5. Brigadier General James Wilkinson was commander of the Western Army.

6. Thomas Butler of Pennsylvania was a veteran of the American Revolution. He rejoined the Army in 1791 and at the time this letter was written was lieutenant colonel commandant of the Fourth Regiment of Infantry.

7. Henry Gaither of Maryland was a veteran of the American Revolution. He rejoined the Army in 1791 and at the time this letter was written was lieutenant colonel commandant of the Third Regiment of Infantry.

frontiers, rendered an adherence to the rule of making no communications to any of them, unless through the Commanding General, whatever might have been his position, dilatory beyond measure and too dangerous for practice during such a period

It has been deemed equally inconsistent with situation and dangerous to tranquillity, to make the General who is now at Loftis's Heights on the Mississippi the organ by which the Department of War should communicate with the Garrisons and troops on the sea-board, the frontiers of Georgia and Tennessee.

The state of things common to an Indian frontier, such as that of Georgia and Tennessee, has rendered it indispensible to the success of the measures of Government to obtain the earliest information of every circumstance that might lead to war in those quarters, or to serious embarrassments, if not early counteracted. That a rapid communication might at all times take place, the frontiers of Georgia and Tennessee have been formed into two districts, and the Commandant of the military force within each made the organ of communication for his respective district.

Few of the fortifications on the Sea-board, having been garrisoned before the law passed for raising a second Regiment or Corps of Artillerists and Engineers,[8] the whole of these Garrisons have been permitted to correspond directly with the Secretary of War.

You will see in the project of regulations, which I sketched some time since and which was put into your hands by General Washington[9] that I contemplated to arrange in separate Districts, the force and posts on the Seaboard, as well as on the Western frontiers and to combine as many of them as could be so done, with convenience to the Service under the Superintendance of the then General in Chief. This part of the regulation had for its basis the French ordinances relative to the same subject, was intended to introduce more order and system into our military affairs, and abridge as far as consistent with the general interest the epistolary

8. "An Act to provide an additional regiment of Artillerists and Engineers" (1 Stat. 552–53 [April 27, 1798]).

9. McHenry is mistaken, for H maintained that he did not have "the project of regulations." See H to McHenry, March 5, 1799; McHenry to H, March 21, 1799. In the James McHenry Papers, Library of Congress, however, there is an undated draft in McHenry's handwriting which outlines the organization and regulation of the Army. This document corresponds to McHenry's description of "the project of regulations."

labours of the Department. The execution of this project met with some obstruction and has been procrastinated by causes which it is deemed unnecessary to relate.

While the ideas presented to you exhibit the difficulties, that would attend the imposing upon any General Officer, the entire correspondence with the Army, unless indeed he was to be abstrac⟨ted⟩ wholly from the troops and to reside constantly at the seat of ⟨go⟩vernment, they point nevertheless to the practicability of divid⟨ing⟩ the Army into subordinate commands and of placing a certain number of such commands under the controul and superintendance of distinct Officers.

The president of the United States has accordingly directed me to make such an arrangement for our military force as may correspond with our situation, and to assign to the Major Generals who are to command it, the superintendance of such portions thereof, as may best tend to promote military discipline, the general interests of the Service, and the objects of the military establishment.

You will therefore be pleased, until otherwise instructed, to consider yourself invested with the entire command of all the troops in Garrison on the Northern Lakes in the North Western Territory, including both Banks of the Ohio, and on the Mississippi. You will, as an organ of communication between you and the Garrisons on the Lakes in the Northwestern Territory and occasionally those on the Mississippi, direct, if you judge it proper, Brigadier General Wilkinson to establish his Head Quarters at pittsburg or such other position as you may deem best calculated to facilitate his communications to you and also with the Garrisons you may place under his Superintendance. You will if you find it can be arranged to advantage, establish subordinate districts within his command, with each a Commandant who shall alone communicate with General Wilkinson and receive your orders through him relative to the Garrisons under their Superintendance respectively. You will make similar dispositions on the Mississippi for the Superintendance of the Garrisons within that District.[10]

In deciding upon these arrangements you will be particularly

10. The orders given in this paragraph are based on George Washington to McHenry, December 16, 1798 (Df, in the handwriting of Tobias Lear, George Washington Papers, Library of Congress).

careful, that they do not occasion inconvenient delays in the transmission of information to the Seat of Government, or throw obstructions in the way of immediate succours being given to the most remote Garrisons in cases of urgency; and will direct your corresponding Officers in the Northwestern Territory and on the Mississippi to pass all letters which they address to you open and through the Secretary of War, at least so long as your position shall be such as to afford to the Secretary an opportunity to know their contents, sooner than if they were to be received by you, in the first instance. By this arrangement it will be at all times in the power of the Secretary of War to give orders in emergencies which can afterwards be communicated to you for your future government.

Besides the command of the troops and Garrisons in the tract of Country before described, you will assume that of all the troops and posts which are or may be within the State of Maryland and all the States to the Northward and Eastward thereof.

Major General pinckney will be instructed [11] to take the Command of all the troops and posts, that are or may be within the States of Virginia, North Carolina, South Carolina, Georgia, Kentucky and Tennessee.

It is expected, and you will give orders accordingly, that the Garrisons and troops within your Command and Superintendance make *Returns and observe the enclosed Regulations.*[12]

The Recruiting Service is an object of primary importance; it is conceived to be particularly connected with the duties of the Inspector General, the sole direction of it is therefore, with a view to order and efficiency, confided to you alone.

It is to be lamented that circumstances have prevented the obtaining an early supply of necessary Clothing for the troops directed to be raised by the Act passed the 16th: of July 1798,[13] and that the

11. McHenry to Charles Cotesworth Pinckney, February 11, 1799 (Df, letterpress copy, James McHenry Papers, Library of Congress).

12. McHenry did not enclose regulations on the compilation and submission of returns because they had not yet been compiled. See McHenry to H, March 21, 1799. These regulations were finally issued in March, 1800. See "General Orders," March 28, 1800.

In the margin opposite the italicized words H placed an asterisk and wrote "None."

13. "An Act to augment the Army of the United States, and for other purposes" (1 *Stat.* 604–05).

progress made since it was practicable to enter upon the business, does not justify our immediately commencing the Recruiting service. Enclosed is a report by the purveyor of the public Supplies [14] which shews the quantities of the different articles of Clothing which he thinks may be relied on, and the times at which he presumes it will be ready for delivery.

Altho' however the impraticability of obtaining a proper supply of Clothing may impose the necessity of some delay in the actual commencement of the recruiting service, nevertheless certain preparatory arrangements, it is thought, may greatly facilitate the same. You are invited therefore to lose no time in dividing at least, the States, from which Officers have lately been appointed, into as many districts as there are Companies to be raised in them and forwarding to the Officers to be employed respectively in each district, through the Commandant their Recruiting Instructions, with orders, either to hold himself prepared to enter upon the Service the moment he receives your ulterior directions, or to engage provisionally as many recruits as are willing to enrole themselves on his list, and who may be promised pay from the day of their being enrolled and sworn with their bounty upon the Officer receiving his final Instructions, or, (which perhaps is safer,) upon their arrival at the general Rendezvous.

The instructions advert to the qualifications of Recruits in General terms.[15] It may be proper to be more particular than the Instructions are, respecting inlistments for the Cavalry.

The important Services to which the Cavalry are destined (the event of actions sometimes depending solely upon their valour and impression) renders it indispensible that such Corps be composed of the best materials, and in proportion to the small number assigned to the Army and the effects expected to be produced by them, that the utmost care be observed in their selection.

Let the Regulations then upon this point, restrict the recruiting Officers to engage none except Natives for this Corps, and of these

14. McHenry did not send this enclosure. See H to McHenry, March 5, 1799.

15. This is a reference to the 1798 edition of the War Department pamphlet entitled *Rules and Regulations Respecting the Recruiting Service*. See H to Jonathan Dayton, August 6, 1798, note 6. Article II reads: "No individual is to be enlisted healthy, robust, and without unsound or sore legs, scurvy, scald head, or other infirmity that may render him unfit for service."

such only as from their known character and fidelity may be trusted to the extent of their powers.[16]

The size of the Cavalry Recruit deserves a degree of attention. Warnery observes very justly, in his remarks on Cavalry, "that in every Specie of Cavalry, *the man ought to be proportioned to the size of his Horse,* and the arms with which he is to serve, adapted and proportioned to them both, and the nature of Service to be performed; consequently the Cuirassier should be larger, and his arms heavier than the Dragoon; and these more so than the Light Horse or Hussars; a small man has great difficulty to mount a large horse, particularly with a Cuirasse; they should all however be muscular and robust, but not heavy; the prussian Dragoons are too heavy for their Horses; and it is ridiculous to see a large Man upon a small horse, which by being strained with too much weight is very soon ruined, and the Trooper dismounted; a man who is more than *five feet, eight inches* ought not to be received into the Cavalry." [17]

It will be proper that Major General pinckney should attend to the recruiting Service in the division of Country assigned to his command and that he should receive from you all the necessary Instructions upon the subject.

You will report monthly to the Secretary of War an abstract of the number of Men recruited, the Clothing which may be wanted, and the necessary monies to be remitted for the Service.

Enclosed is a Schedule of the Officers [18] who have accepted their appointments with their respective places of residence annexed. Enclosed is also a list of the Officers at present employed in the Recruiting Service,[19] and their places of Rendezvous.

Should you think the existing Instructions to Recruiting Officers require revision or that additional Articles are necessary for the extensive field we are entering upon, to give more system to the business, you will report the alterations or additions, that they may

16. Article III reads: "Negroes mulottoes or indians are not to be enlisted. Natives of fair conduct and character are to be preferred; but foreigners of good reputation for sobriety and honesty may also be enlisted. . . ."

17. This is a quotation from Charles Emmanuel De Warnery, *Remarks on Cavalry . . . translated from the original by G. F. Kochler* (London, 1798), 30. For the original edition, see *Remarques sur la cavalrié, par M. de W.* (Lublin, 1781).

18. This enclosure was not sent. See H to McHenry, March 5, 1799.

19. This enclosure was not sent. See H to McHenry, March 5, 10, 1799.

be submitted to the president for his decision, incorporating therein those which respect the Cavalry.

You will also indicate to me as soon as possible the several Stations where Rations must be provided, that measures may be taken accordingly.

Connected with this subject is another of considerable importance; I mean, the permanent disposition of the Troops after they shall have been raised.

Having taken the opinion of General Washington on this point,[20] it is thought adviseable that it should be adopted, until a change of circumstances shall render a different disposition proper.

The General observed, that though it might now be premature to fix a permanent disposition of the troops, it might nevertheless be useful to indicate certain Stations where they may be assembled provisionally, and may probably be suffered to continue while matters remain in the present posture. The Stations eligible in this view may be found for two Regiments in the vicinity of providence River near *Uxbridge;* for two other Regiments in the vicinity of Brunswick in New Jersey; for two other Regiments in the vicinity of potowmac near Harper's Ferry; for two other Regiments in the vicinity of Augusta, but above the Falls of the Savannah. This disposition the General observed will unite considerations relative to the discipline and health of the Troops, and to the œconomical supply of their wants. It will also have sound military aspects; in the first instance towards the security of Boston and New Port; in the second towards that of New York and Philadelphia; in the third and fourth, towards that of Baltimore, Charlestown, Savannah and the Southern States generally; and in the third particularly towards the re-inforcement of the Western Army in certain events. But he subjoined, the military motives have only a qualified influence; since it is not doubted, that in the prospect of a serious attack upon this Country, the disposition of the Army ought to look emphatically to the Southern Region, as that which is by far most likely to be the scene of action.

It was also the Generals opinion, which is concurred in, that the Companies directed to be added to the Regiments of the old Establishment, ought as soon as is convenient, to re-inforce the Western

20. See the first letter which H drafted for George Washington to McHenry, December 13, 1798.

Army, and that their destination in the first instance may be pittsburg.

His opinion is also in general to be adopted relative to the disposition of the Artillery. He proposed to assign a complete Battalion to the Western Army; to the fortifications at Boston one Company, to those at New York two Companies, to those at New Port, two Companies, to those at West Point one; to those at Mud Island two; to those at Baltimore one; to those at Norfolk two; to those on Cape Fear River one; to those at Charlestown two; to those at Savannah one; to those at the mouth of St. Mary's one. It is thought there may be some other fortified place on the Sea-board that will require attention, which is left to you to decide upon, after you have taken a deliberate view of the subject. He is further of opinion that the remaining two Battalions had better be reserved for the Army in the field, and that during the winter they may retain the Stations they now occupy; but that as soon as they can conveniently go into Tents it will be adviseable to assemble them at some central or nearly central point, there to be put in a course of regular instruction, together with successive detachments of the Officers and Non commissioned officers of the Sea-board Garrisons until their Services shall be actually required.

You will therefore give effect to the aforesaid disposition, and so arrange the Companies of Artillery that those belonging to the same Regiment or Corps may form contiguous garrisons.

You will also make such an arrangement of the Subalterns to the Captains of Artillerists and Engineers as in your opinion will produce the greatest harmony among the Officers and good to the Service. Enclosed is a list of the names of all the officers in the Army classed according to their respective Regiments or Corps, with the date of their Commissions.[21]

A system of Regulations being wanted for the Government and discipline of the Volunteer Companies,[22] you will as soon as convenient report one for the consideration of the president.

Enclosed is the copy of a letter to Brigadier General Wilkinson

21. This list was not sent to H. See H to McHenry, March 5, 1799.
22. This is a reference to the Volunteer Corps originally authorized by "An Act authorizing the President of the United States to raise a Provisional Army" (1 *Stat.* 558–61 [May 28, 1798]). See the introductory note to H to James Gunn, December 22, 1798.

dated the 31st of January 1799,[23] by which you will perceive that he is instructed to wait your Orders.

Considering with what view the posts which our troops occupy on the Lakes were originally erected, it may be useful to employ a judicious Engineer to survey them, and the adjacent Country on the Lakes, in order that it may be ascertained, in the various relations of trade and defence, whether they are susceptible of any beneficial changes. You will for this purpose select from the Corps of Artillerists and Engineers, at a convenient time, a qualified Officer to make the necessary survey and report the result relative to these objects.

It is required that you report as soon as it can be done with convenience a system of regulations for the government of the Inspector General and the Assistant Inspector of every description, expressive of their duties and functions, and comprizing the duties of those officers to whom their functions are applicable.

I need not urge it upon you, to exercise the most vigilant superintendance over every branch of the Service within the sphere of your Command. I cannot avoid however calling your particular attention to the discovery of the causes which may induce irregularity in the police of the Armies, in the field, and in our posts or Garrisons upon the different frontiers of the United States, and enjoin that every legal and proper step to be instantly resorted to, which the laws or the usages of Armies authorize on such occasions, to punish the Offenders and produce a salutary result. It is expected that you will neglect no means of obliging, at the stated periods, the proper Officers to make all Returns requisite, to exhibit the number and state of the troops in every position, to forward their muster and pay Rolls, Returns of the quantity of Clothing delivered, on hand, or due to the Soldiers, of the distribution generally of the public property, of the quantity and situation of every article in store, of the supplies which are or may be wanted and every other exhibit and return necessary to the information of the Secretary of War, and indispensible to the accounting Officers of the War Department.

You know precisely how much the regularity and perfection of such returns depend on the disposition of Officers to execute their Orders; and that savings to the public or a judicious and well regu-

23. Two copies, Hamilton Papers, Library of Congress.

lated œconomy is rather more to be expected from the integrity, vigilance & knowledge of those who are intrusted or have a controul over the Army expenditures and property, than from the wisest general regulations or instructions that can possibly be devised. Whenever there is found a deficiency of secure deposits for, or a want of requisite qualities in the Officer charged with the care and management of the public property, it is expected that you will remedy the evil, if within your lawful powers or point to the circumstance, that it may be considered by the authority competent to the remedy.

Finally, I cannot conclude these instructions without expressing my most unlimitted confidence in your talents to execute the high trusts which the president reposes in you, and my own most perfect reliance upon your co-operation and assistance in every thing that concerns the Army establishment and the means to remedy whatever defects may be found to exist therein; and that I shall at all times recognize in the execution of the orders which you may receive, the most perfect evidences of your Candour and Friendship.

I have the honor to be,   with great regard and esteem,   Sir, your obedt. humble servant,   James McHenry

Major General Alexander Hamilton.

To Rufus King

New York Feby 6. 1799

Dr. Sir

This will be delivered to you by Mr. Isambard Brunell [1] French by birth, but *Anti-Jacobin* by principle, and by necessity an Inventor of Ingenious Machines. He goes to England to endeavour to obtain a patent for one, which he has contrived for the purpose of copying. He has a passport from Mr. Liston and I believe our Secretary of State. This letter is to ask for him such patronage as in your situation and in his may be proper.

You will have seen the *Kentucke & Virginia* resolutions. [2] If well managed this affair will turn to good account. In my apprehension it is only disagreeable not formidable. The general progress of things continues in a right direction.

Yrs. truly & Affecly   A Hamilton

R King Esq

ALS, New-York Historical Society, New York City.
1. See H to Robert Liston, January 15, 1799; Liston to H, January 20, 1799.
2. See H to Theodore Sedgwick, February 2, 1799, note 1.

To James McHenry

New York, February 6, 1799. ". . . I perceive that it will be useful for me in the progress of the trusts, which I am and shall be charged to execute, to have an accurate statement of the Officers of the corps of Artillerists and Engineers, and the distribution of them which has been heretofore made among the different portions of this Corps. . . ."

Copy, in the handwriting of Philip Church, Hamilton Papers, Library of Congress.

To James McHenry

New York Feby. 6. 1799

Dr. Sir

In one of your letters you desire me to think of the Distribution of the States into recruiting districts.[1] I have accordingly turned my attention to the subject. But the result is that it will be best to assign to each Regiment its district and to charge its commanding Officer with the arrangement into subdivisions. If you approve this idea you had better write me an official letter, briefly telling me that the Recruiting service is to be put under my direction & desiring me to make a preliminary arrangement for the distribution of the States into Recruiting Districts and rendezvouses; upon which I will send the proper instructions to the several Commanders of Regiments.

I have not yet observed that the places of the Officers omitted in the arrangement reported by the General Officers has been supplied.[2] I hope the Recruiting service will begin with complete not with mutilated or defective corps.

I regretted that *Gibbs* was not appointed.[3] There is good reason to believe that he would command a Regiment well, probably better than the person whom the Objectors to him would approve. Their rule of judging of military qualification is most likely no very accurate one.

I regret also that the objection against Antifœderalism has been carried so far as to exclude several of the characters proposed by us.[4] We were very attentive to the importance of appointing friends of the Governt. to Military stations—but we thought it well to relax the rule in favour of particular merit in a few instances and especially in reference to the inferior grades. It does not seem adviseable to exclude all hope & to give to appointments too absolute a party feature. Military situations, on young minds particularly, are of all others best calculated to inspire a zeal for the service and the cause in which the Incumbants are employed. When the President thinks of his son in law [5] he should be moderate in this respect.

The inclosed letter from Col Fairlie [6] relates to the *second* son of our late Chief Justice.[7] His father you know was Antifœderal. This young man has as yet no fixed political creed. They tell me there is nothing personally to his disadvantage. I am clear therefore that it will be expedient to give him an appointment.

Adieu My Dr friend   Yrs. truly   A H

J McHenry Esq

ALS, Historical Society of Pennsylvania, Philadelphia; copy, in the handwriting of Philip Church, Hamilton Papers, Library of Congress.
1. McHenry to H, January 9, February 4, 1799.
2. See McHenry to H, second letter of January 21, 1799.
3. See McHenry to H, second letter of January 21, 1799. On January 21, 1799, Caleb Gibbs wrote to H asking for his assistance in securing a commission in the Army (listed in the appendix to this volume).
4. See McHenry to H, second letter of January 21, 1799.
5. William S. Smith was John Adams's son-in-law. On July 19, 1798, the Senate rejected his nomination as adjutant general with the rank of brigadier general (*Executive Journal*, I, 292, 293; Timothy Pickering to H, July 18, 1798).
On January 8, 1799, he was appointed lieutenant colonel of the Twelfth Regiment of Infantry (*Executive Journal*, I, 299, 303).

6. A resident of Albany, James Fairlie served as a major and aide-de-camp to Baron von Steuben during the American Revolution. After the war he became a clerk in the Circuit Court of Oyer and Terminer, and in the seventeen-nineties he was clerk of the New York Supreme Court.

Fairlie's letter has not been found.

7. William Yates was the son of Robert Yates, chief justice of the New York Supreme Court from 1790 to 1798. Robert Yates was Fairlie's brother-in-law. On February 22, 1799, William Yates was appointed lieutenant in the First Regiment of Artillerists and Engineers (*Executive Journal*, I, 313, 317).

From Benjamin Stoddert [1]

Navy Depart. 6 Feby 1799

Sir

I have the honor to enclose a paper [2] containing the circumstances, & all the circumstances, connected in the relative rank of Captains Truxton, Talbot & Dale.

It appears to me, that Talbot & Dale, cannot now be placed above Truxton, but by dismissing the latter from the Service.

Dale who has permission to make an East India Voyage,[3] is reconciled to what He conceives unavoidable, to rank after Truxton. Entertaining a very high opinion of Talbot—I am anxious that he should also acquiesce. From conversation with him, I Judge it is in your power alone, to satisfy him.

The error was in not selecting the three Senior Captains, for the Three Frigates continued in Service. The President, I conceive had no power to continue more Captains, than Frigates.

If Talbot will continue, only Barry Nicholson & Truxton, will be above him. Nicholson cannot be long in his way. Barry is old & infirm, & not satisfied that he is not made an admiral. It is more than probable, Truxton & Talbot may not be on the same service.

I wrote you some Days ago [4] respecting Mr. Hy Seaton.[5] I ought to have waited long enough for an answer—but his appointment was so much pressed—He was so well recommended—I was so well satisfied, a Story which I had heard, was without foundation—and a Lieut. being instantly wanted—He is appointed. I wish he may turn out well. I am anxious too, that Daubeny [6] should continue to deserve your good opinion. They are both ordered on immediate Service.

I have the honor to be with great respect & esteem Sir Yr most
obed Servt   Ben Stoddert

ALS, Hamilton Papers, Library of Congress; LC, RG 45, Naval Records Collection of the Office of Naval Records and Library, Miscellaneous Letters Sent
by the Secretary of the Navy, 1790–1798, National Archives.
1. For background to this letter, see Silas Talbot to H, January 15, 1799.
2. This enclosure has neither a title nor a date (D, Hamilton Papers, Library
of Congress). The information in the document is similar to that in Talbot
to H, January 15, 1799, note 1.
3. See Stoddert to Richard Dale, February 1, 1799 (*Naval Documents, Quasi-
War, November, 1798–March, 1799*, 300).
4. Stoddert to H, February 1, 1799 (listed in the appendix to this volume).
5. Henry Seton, the son of the late William Seton, first cashier of the Bank
of New York, was appointed a lieutenant in the Navy on February 5, 1799
(*Executive Journal*, I, 309–10).
6. Lloyd S. Daubeny of New York had been appointed a lieutenant in the
Navy when the Senate was not in session in 1798. On February 5, 1799, the
Senate approved his nomination (*Executive Journal*, I, 308, 310).

From Theodore Sedgwick

Philadelphia 7th. Feby. 1799

I had the pleasure, my dear sir, the day before yesterday to receive
your favor of the 2nd.

With regard to the conduct of Virginia & Kentucky—The moment I came into town I applied to the *apparent* leaders in the house
of Representatives, & stated to them my opinion of the measures
which to me seemed expedient to be adopted—That it was necessary to preoccupy the ground—that, for this purpose it would be
expedient to appoint an able committee, to refer the addresses on
the subject, with an inten⟨tion⟩ of making a report, which should
have all the properties of an address. I had two reasons for proposing this being done by the house—because we had before the senate
no address on the subject and because, for obvious reasons, the conduct of the house would excite more attention and make a deeper
impression.[1] I spoke to no gentlem⟨an⟩ who did not explicitly concur with me in opinion but Nothing has been done, because, as I
understand, the gentlemen cannot agree on the precise mode in
which it is to be done. They still say, and I have this day had con-

versation with them on the subject, that the business will yet be done. Had it not been beleived that the house would have, before this time, executed this important object, it would have been, long since, in progress in the Senate. It is not yet, perhaps, too late, tho' I regret as much as any one can the delay.

You have seen, I presume, the address of the minority of the house of Representatives of Virga to their constituents.[2] It is said to have been drawn by Marshall. It is able, & elegant, and eloquent, but the eloquence is of a kind not to make a deep impression on the gross materials to which it is addressed. It shews that its authors beleive their situation critical & the danger iminent. It was, perhaps incompatible with the relation of the addressers, as a minority, to employ the instrument of denunciation, and yet, I am persuaded, no procedure of this kind can be effectual without it.

Under the present circumstances is it expedient that this subject should be undertaken by the Senate?

The delays in the military department are as unaccountable as they are injurious.[3] Immediately after receiving your letter I called on the Secy. at war. He told me that the delay had originated principally from a disappointment in obtaining clothing—that the contracts had failed. I replied that if such was the case by an immediate employment of all the tailors in the great towns cloths might be procured faster than they would be wanted by the recruits—that this was the season to inlist—that it would soon be passed and that if this opportunity was neglected, no one could foresee the evil consequences which might result. It would give encouragement to those who had already erected the Standard of opposition; it would dishearten the friends of the government and render the government itself unpopular. He said that the business of inlistment would be put under your immediate direction—that the orders for that purpose were in forwardness and would that day be compleated and submited to the President for his approbation and that the next day they would be forwarded to you by the mail.[4] Before this time, therefore, you have them, but if they are not impracticable I shall be agreeably disappointed. Is there no remedy for this evil? Will it be possible to get on in a state of war or insurrection?

I need not say that I write to you in the most perfect confidence. I last evening called to pay my respects to the President—he was alone, and, as I hoped, soon introduced the subject of our military. I gave him my view of the subject & some what at large. He replied nearly in the following words. "As to the Virginians, sir, it is weakness to apprehend any thing from them, but if you must have an army I will give it to you, but remember it will make the government more unpopular than all their other acts. They have submited with more patience than any people ever did to the burden of taxes which has been *liberally laid on,* but their patience will not last always." This was the text on which he dilated extensively. I cannot say that I was astonished. Astonishment is a sentiment which he has, for some time, lost the power to excite. During the time that I was with him the bill before the Senate for the new organization of the army was mentioned.[5] He asked me what additional authority it was proposed to give the commander in chief. I answered none—that all that was proposed was giving him a new title that of "General." [6] "What," said he "are you going to appoint him general over the President?" "I have not been so blind but I have seen a combined effort, among those who call themselves the friends of government to annihilate the essential powers given by the president. This sir (raising his voice) "my understanding has perceived and my heart felt." After an expression of supprise and a declaration of belief that he was mistaken, with *all humility* I prayed him to mention the facts from which he had made this inference. He answered that if I had not seen *it,* it was improper for him to go into the detail.

This shews that we are afflicted with an evil for which certainly no compleat remedy can be applied, but it might be paliated perhaps by bringing into the administration a man of talents ⟨and⟩ of that peculiar kind which gives an ascendency ⟨with⟩out its being perceived. This never was in any ⟨co⟩untry more important. Nor if the right character could be found is it an object unattainable. With all his good qualities, however, our friend C——n [7] is not the man. In official details and execution he has, perhaps, no superior, but in the other and more essential characteristic to my mind he is wholly deficient. But can a vacancy be made? While I have been continuing writing amidst the chit-chat of senatorial debate the mail is closed. Will you permit me to close this without revision? I have written I know not what, but I hope it is inteligible. This I do know that I am yours sincerely   T. S.

ALS, Hamilton Papers, Library of Congress.

1. Petitions presented to the House of Representatives in January and February, 1799, calling for the repeal of the Alien and Sedition Acts were referred to the Committee of the Whole (*Journal of the House*, II, 445, 452, 456, 457, 458, 461).

2. This is a reference to John Marshall's defense on January 22, 1799, of the constitutionality of the Alien and Sedition Acts. See *Journal of the House of Delegates of Virginia, 1798*, 90–95. On February 5, 1799, at the request of "Alpha," the *Gazette of the United States, and Philadelphia Daily Advertiser* published Marshall's address. It was also published as an untitled pamphlet (Richmond: Printed by Thomas Nicholson, n.d.).

3. See H to Sedgwick, February 2, 1799, note 3.

4. See James McHenry to H, February 4, 1799.

5. This is a reference to "A bill for the better organizing the troops of the United States, and for other purposes," which was introduced in the Senate on January 21, 1799 (*Annals of Congress*, VIII, 2204).

6. Section 9 of "An Act for the better organizing of the Troops of the United States; and for other purposes," which became law on March 3, 1799, provided "That a commander of the army of the United States shall be appointed and commissioned by the style of 'General of the Armies of the United States,' and the present office and title of Lieutenant-General shall thereafter be abolished" (1 *Stat.* 752).

7. Edward Carrington.

From James McHenry

Philad. 8 Febry 1799.

private & had better be
destroyed

Dear Hamilton

I have received your public letter of the 6 and another (private) dated also on the 6th. The latter this morning.

Your instructions are and have been some days with the President.[1] The moment he is pleased to decide so as to enable me to proceed you shall have them. I spoke to him yesterday, on the subject: he had not considered them, and seemed to insinuate the affair need not be hurried. I urged the necessity which existed to put you in possession of my orders, as soon as possible, for that no preparatory arrangements could be made respecting the recruiting service till then, &c &c &c.

The list you suggest makes one of several references annexed to the instructions.[2]

I have taken care in all my lists presented to the President for nominations, not to destroy hope, nor to exclude meritorious young men who had not acted like old unclaimable offenders.

⟨Gibbs⟩ [3] I think would have made a good officer but it is a fact, that his character is very low in Boston, that he is looked upon as a triffler, and has no weight whatever in that quarter of the union.

I shall endeavour to fill up the vacancies in the New Regiments as soon as possible.

Yours sincerely   James McHenry

ALS, Hamilton Papers, Library of Congress; ADf, James McHenry Papers, Library of Congress.
   1. For these "instructions," see McHenry to H, February 4, 1799. See also McHenry to H, second letter of February 8, 1799.
   2. See H to McHenry, first letter of February 6, 1799; McHenry to H, February 4, 1799, note 20.
   3. This word has been taken from the draft.

From James McHenry

War Department, February 8, 1799. "I have the honor to inclose your instructions [1] and shall send you the schedules and regulations referred to in them as soon as the same can be made out."

LS, Hamilton Papers, Library of Congress.
   1. For these "instructions," see McHenry to H, February 4, 1799, which was enclosed in the letter printed above. On March 30, 1799, McHenry wrote to George Washington: "Such has been the pressure of business upon the Clerks, that they have only been able to make out a copy of my instructions to General Hamilton dated the 4th of Feby ulto, which is inclosed. From these you will be at no loss to conceive of General Pinckney's, which will be sent to you as soon as they can be got copied" (ALS, George Washington Papers, Library of Congress).

From Timothy Pickering [1]

(confidential)   Philadelphia Feby. 9. 1799.

Dear Sir,

The law prohibiting intercourse with the French Dominions is renewed, and extended to the 3d of March 1800.[2] The material variation from the former law [3] consists in the authority given to the

President to open the intercourse with any part of those dominions when the safety and interest of the U. States will admit of it. This authority is comprised in the 4th section, a copy of which I inclose.[4]

I suppose every body understands the main object of this provision is to open the commercial intercourse with St. Domingo. Toussaint's agent, Mr. Bunel,[5] and our Consul, Mr. Meyer [6] who accompanied him at Toussant's request, will now speedily return to the Cape, where Toussaint is impatient to receive them, with information of the views and determination of our government.[7]

The President sees the immense advantages of the commerce of that Island, and will undoubtedly give to the act as liberal a construction as will be politically expedient. Toussaint, if certain of our commerce, will, Meyer assures me, declare the whole island of St. Domingo independent; confident in his power to defend it, provided *we* will allow of a free commercial intercourse, by which the islanders may exchange their productions for the supplies our vessels will carry to them. This act of independence I fully expect; & I persuade myself that Great Britain will consent to share in it; and that Genl. Maitland has made some arrangement with Toussaint for that purpose.[8]

Under these circumstances, my great anxiety is, That Toussaint & his Chief [9] may fix on a practicable & efficient plan for administering the government of the Island, and *settling the right of succession to the Chief command* (it cannot be a republic)—and *establishing a simple plan of* FINANCE that shall insure to him the means of supporting an army, & the government. If you can turn your attention to this subject & favour me with your ideas of the most eligible schemes, I shall be very much obliged. To what we advise, Toussaint would listen.

Adieu! T. Pickering.

ALS, Hamilton Papers, Library of Congress; ALS, letterpress copy, Massachusetts Historical Society, Boston.

1. For background to this letter, see Rufus King to H, January 21, 1799, notes 5 and 7.

2. "An Act further to suspend the Commercial Intercourse between the United States and France, and the dependencies thereof" (1 *Stat.* 613–16 [February 9, 1799]).

3. "An Act to suspend the commercial intercourse between the United States and France, and the dependencies thereof" (1 *Stat.* 565–66 [June 13, 1798]).

4. Copy, Hamilton Papers, Library of Congress.

5. Joseph Bunel had arrived in Philadelphia on December 19, 1798 ([Philadelphia] *Aurora. General Advertiser*, December 28, 1798).

6. George Washington had nominated "Jacob Mayer, a native citizen of Pennsylvania, to be Consul of the United States at the port of Cape François and its dependencies in the Island of St. Domingo" on May 30, 1796, and the Senate had confirmed the nomination the next day (*Executive Journal*, I, 213).

7. François Dominique Toussaint L'Ouverture hoped to secure some modification of the act of June 13, 1798. See note 3. As Pickering indicates in the first paragraph of the letter printed above, Toussaint was partially successful in attaining this objective. For Toussaint's proposals for the resumption of trade between Santo Domingo and the United States, see Toussaint to John Adams, November 6, 1798 (LC, RG 59, Consular Letters, Cape Haytien, Vol. I, National Archives).

8. This is a reference to Thomas Maitland's secret treaty with Toussaint. See King to H, January 21, 1799, note 7.

9. This is a reference to Benoit Joseph Rigaud.

To Timothy Pickering

New York Feby. 9, 1799

Dr. Sir

I am this moment favoured with your letter of the 9th instant. I shall immediately reflect on the most important point & tomorrow give you the result.

The provision in the law is ample. But in this My Dear Sir, as in every thing else we must unite caution with decision. The UStates must not be committed on the Independence of St Domingo—no guarantee no formal treaty—nothing that can rise up in Judgment. It will be enough to let *Toussaint* be assured verbally but explicitly that upon his declaration of independence a Commercial intercourse will be opened & continue while he maintains it & gives due protection to our vessels & property. I incline to think the Declaration of Independence ought to precede.

Yrs truly   AH

ALS, Massachusetts Historical Society, Boston.

To James McHenry

New York, February 11, 1799. "I have this moment received your letter of the 4th instant to the contents of which I shall pay particular attention."

Copy, in the handwriting of Philip Church, Hamilton Papers, Library of Congress.

To John Jay [1]

New York Feby. 12. 1799

Dear Sir

The survey of this port to the narrows inclusively has been executed and the expence defrayed out of the funds of the Corporation. But it is interesting to the question of the defence of our port to have a survey of the bay below the narrows to Sandy Hook. There are sand banks critically situated which merit consideration as proper sites for fortification. Such a survey was made under the direction of the British Commanders and a Mr. *Hill* possesses a draft of that part of the Bay.[2] He will not take less for it than 800 Dollars. I am told the survey of the upper part cost 600 Dollars. In proportion, that of the part below will be moderate at 800. I inquired of General Clarkeson as to the provision of funds for this object.[3] He answered that he had no more than 500 Dollars at command. If you agree in opinion with me that it will be well to obtain the draft in question for the price demanded, you will be so obliging as to give orders for the payment.

With great respect & esteem   Dr Sir. Yr. Obed serv   A Hamilton

Governor Jay

ALS, Columbia University Libraries; copy, Dr. Frank Monaghan, Washington, D.C.

1. For background to this letter, see the introductory note to H to James McHenry, June 1, 1798.
2. See William Macpherson to H, January 3, 1799.
3. See Jay to H, November 5, 1798; Ebenezer Stevens to H, December 18, 1798, note 3.

To John Jay [1]

New York Feby 12. 1799

Dear Sir

After a plan for fortifying our port shall have been settled, the execution of it with energy & dispatch will demand a very great portion of the time and attention of a competent character as Super-intendant. This task I cannot undertake consistently with my other occupations. Col Burr will be very equal to it and will I believe undertake it, if an *adequate compensation* be annexed. He would likewise be useful in the formation of a plan. I know not what collateral objections may have arisen from recent conduct of that Gentleman; [2] but independent of these I should favour his agency in the business. Clarkeson can still disburse the money which is all he will engage for.[3]

Respectfully & with true regard   Dr Sir   Yr obed ser

A Hamilton

Governor Jay.

ALS, C. P. Greenough Fuller Collection, Princeton University Library; copy (incomplete), Dr. Frank Monaghan, Washington, D.C.

1. For background to this letter, see the introductory note to H to James McHenry, June 1, 1798.

2. In 1797 Aaron Burr was elected to the New York Assembly, and he served from January 2, 1798, to April 3, 1799. On February 9, 1799, Burr had John Swartwout of New York City introduce a resolution in the New York Assembly calling for changes in the method of electing state senators and in the method of selecting Presidential electors. On the motion of Jedediah Peck of Otsego this resolution was divided into two resolutions, amended, and the separate resolutions were then approved. The second resolution called for a bill to allow the election of Presidential electors by the people rather than by the legislature (*Journal of the Assembly of the State of New-York; 22nd Sess., 2nd Meeting*, 106). By this resolution the Democratic-Republicans hoped to secure some of New York's electoral votes, for they anticipated a Federalist-controlled legislature in 1800. "An Act providing for the election of electors of a President and Vice President of the United States" was reported out of committee on March 7, 1799, and passed on March 22, 1799 (*Journal of the Assembly of the State of New-York; 22nd Sess., 2nd Meeting*, 179, 217, 239, 240–41). The bill was defeated in the New York Senate on April 1, 1799 (*Journal of the Senate of the State of New-York; 22nd Sess., 2nd Meeting*, 92–93, 96, 120–21).

3. See Jay to H, November 5, 1798; Ebenezer Stevens to H, December 18, 1798, note 3.

To James Wilkinson [1]

New York February 12. 1799

Sir

The interesting incidents, which have latterly occurred in our political situation, having rendered it expedient to enlarge the Sphere of our military arrangements, it has, in consequence become necessary to regulate the Superintendence of our military force, in its various and detached positions, in such a manner, as while it will serve to disburthen the Department of War of details incompatible with its more general and more important occupations, will likewise conduce to Uniformity and System in the different branches of the service.

The Commander in Chief, having for the present declined actual command, it has been determined in pursuance of the above views to place the military force every where under the Superintendence of Major General Pinckney and Myself.[2] In the allotment for this purpose, my agency is extended to the garrisons on the Northern Lakes and to all the Troops in the North Western Territory including both banks of the Ohio, and upon the Mississippi; in short to all the Western Army except the parts which may be in the States of Tennessee and Kentuke. Of this you will have been informed by the Secretary at War.

From the relation, which is thus constituted between us, I allow myself to anticipate great mutual Satisfaction. Every disposition on my part will certainly facilitate it, and tend to promote the discharge of your trust in the manner best adapted to your honor and to the advancement of the Service.

It was the united opinion of the Commander in Chief, General Pinckney and myself, when lately convened at Philadelphia, that your speedy presence in this quarter was necessary [3] towards a full discussion of the affairs of the Scene in which you have so long had the direction, in their various relations, and towards the formation, with the aid [of] your lights, of a more perfect plan for present and eventual arrangements. Much may be examined in a personal interview, which at so great a distance can not be effected by writing. The actual and probable Situation of our public affairs in reference to foreign powers renders this step indispensable. You will therefore be pleased, with all practicable expedition, to repair to Philadelphia; upon your arrival there giving me immediate advice of it. If this can be most conveniently accomplished by way of New Orleans, you are at liberty to take that route. On this point you are the best judge and will no doubt act with circumspection.

It must rest with you to dispose of the command of the troops at the different stations *during your absence*, and to give the proper instructions in conformity with those which have been received from the Secretary at War. On this head only one remark will be made. The confidence in your judgment has probably ⟨led to⟩ the reposing in you discretionary powers, too delicate to be intrusted to an Officer less tried; capable perhaps of being So used as to commit prematurely the peace of the United States. Discretions of this tendency ought not to be transferred, beyond what may be indispensable for defensive security. Care must be taken that the Nation be not embroiled, but in consequence of a deliberate policy in the Government.

Official Letters from you to me, as you have been apprised by the Secretary at War, are to be forwarded thro' him. They must be open and under cover. The design of this is, that he may have an opportunity, in case of great urgency which could not conveniently wait for my direction, to interpose with the requisite measures. In your *absence*, it will be proper that the Officer or Officers, you may substitute in the command, should communicate with you; also transmitting their letters open under cover to the Secretary at War. This will preserve unbroken the chain of your command.

With great consideration and esteem   I am Sir   Your Obedt Servt.   Alex Hamilton

Brigadier General Wilkinson

LS, University of Chicago Library; ADf, Hamilton Papers, Library of Congress.
   1. This letter was enclosed in H to James McHenry, February 13, 1799, which is listed in the appendix to this volume.
   2. See McHenry to H, February 4, 1799.
   3. See H's draft of George Washington to McHenry, first letter of December 13, 1798.

Circular to the Commanding Officers in Northern and Western United States [1]

New York, February 15, 1799. "A Letter from the Sec of War [2] places under my Superintendance the Posts and Troops under your immediate Command. All further Communications therefore respecting them, including Reports and Returns, are to be addressed to me, not as heretofore to the Sec. of War. . . ."

Copy, Chicago Historical Society.
    1. This letter is the same as "Circular to the Commanding Officers at New York and West Point," January 30, 1799.
    2. James McHenry to H, February 4, 1799.

From Samuel L. Mitchell [1]

New York Feby. 15. [–16] 1799

Sir

In estimating the requisites for a Course of Chemistry, regard should be had not merely to *the Time employed* by the Professor in giving his *public Instruction* to an audience, but also to the employment of Time in preparing, arranging and *conducting experiments*. Many of these require much Care and vigilance day after day to manage them properly & make them conduce to the desired end.

In forming an estimate of the good to be done in such a Course, it is not unworthy the attention of the Committee, to contemplate the *Expence of Money*. Chemical Experiments are attended with Cost, and some of them are consderable drawbacks upon the moderate Salary of a Professor. It can scarcely be expected, he will exhibit so many, or do them so well, when each of them is a draft upon his Pocket. It is desirable that a fund of fifty or sixty Dollars yearly should be provided for the purpose of procuring fuel & Materials for Experiments. Experiments are equally convincing to five hundred as to five Witnesses. It is economical then both in respect to *Time* and *Money* to collect all the Pupils, and oblige them to attend together. The annual Course of Chemistry now continues at the rate of five and sometimes six lessons a week from the beginning of November to the beginning of March. This must restrain the Season of Tuition on account of accomodating the *Students of Physick*. A Considerable Number of Persons who are not *attached to the College at all*, occasionally frequent these lectures, and can be best accomodated during the Winter. The undergraduate Class of the Students under the *Faculty of Arts*, might, I think, by an easy arrangement, be enabled to attend at the same hour with the rest.

There will be another advantage in thus collecting the whole Number at once. It will be thus known that the Science of Chemistry is fashionable. The applicants will keep each other in Countenance. There will exist a much more considerable Degree of Emulation.

Within the time mentioned, there can be delivered a Course which shall exhibit the great Principles of the Science, and their Application to a variety of Detail in Agriculture, Medicine, Economics, &c.

A Good Laboratory, and a fund for replacing spoiled or broken Apparatus, and for purchasing Specimens of Mineralogy, &c, are great Desiderata in the arrangement of the Chemical Department in the College. I am yours with great admiration and respect

Saml L Mitchell

Genl. Hamilton

P S. It may not be improper to add one or two more considerations to shew that the Professor of Chemistry is not unemployed, at the Times when he is not employed in lecturing; he is called upon from time to time to give Opinions on public questions of importance: he has, for instance been heretofore applied to by the President of the Chamber of Commerce [2] for an Opinion concerning the *Pot-ash of this Market*, by the Committee of the Corporation for an opinion on the Qualities of the *Brunx River Water*,[3] by various Classes of his fellow Citizens on the *Nature & Extinguishment of Pestilence*,[4] &c, & hardly a week passes, without a specimen of natural *minerological* Productions being offered for a Judgement of its Composition. For these Services he receives no Compensation. And yet the Assay or Analysis frequently involves considerable Time & Expence. Many of these Things are among the most useful the Professor can perform, and in a liberal Establishment of the Professorship, numberless occurrences of these kinds should be estimated as a part of the Duties thereof, and provided for accordingly. For it may be relied on as a fact, if Utility is contemplated, the Professor's *extra-collegiate* Services, are no less important, than those performed within the Walls.

Feb. 16. S. L. M.

ALS, Hamilton Papers, Library of Congress.

1. This letter was apparently addressed to H in his capacity as a trustee of Columbia College. H had been appointed one of twenty-nine trustees of the

college in 1787. See "An Act to institute an University within this State, and for other Purposes therein mentioned" (*New York Laws*, 10th Sess., Ch. LXXXII [April 13, 1787]). See also "Report of a Committee of the Trustees of Columbia College," December 6, 1787; March 2, 13, 1788. H remained a trustee until his death.

Mitchell received his medical degree from the University of Edinburgh and subsequently studied law. In 1791 he was a member of the New York Assembly from Queens County, and in 1792 he was appointed professor of chemistry, natural history, and philosophy at Columbia College.

2. John Murray.

3. Mitchell's opinion has not been found, but this committee was composed of John B. Coles, Gabriel Furman, John Bogert, and Jacob De la Montagnie. The committee's report was made on December 17, 1798 (*Minutes of the Common Council*, II, 486–87). See also the introductory note to Philip Schuyler to H, January 31, 1799.

4. This is a reference to two reports made by two joint committees. The joint committees were composed of members of the New York Common Council, the Chamber of Commerce, the Medical Society, and the Commissioners of the Health Office. Mitchell signed both reports as a member of the Medical Society. The first report on the causes of "Pestilential Disease" was made on January 21, 1799, and the second on "the best means to prevent its return" was made on January 28, 1799 (*Minutes of the Common Council*, II, 494–99, 500–08).

To George Washington [1]

New York February 15. 1799

Sir

The Secretary at War has communicated to me the following disposition with regard to the superintendence of our Military forces and Posts.[2] All those in States South of Maryland in Tennessee and Kentucke are placed under the Direction of Major General Pinckney: those every where else under my direction—to which he has added the general care of the Recruiting service.

The commencement of the business of recruiting, however, is still postponed: for the reason, as assigned by the Secretary, that a supply of cloathing is not yet ready.[3]

In conformity with your ideas, I have directed General Wilkinson to repair to the seat of government,[4] in order to a more full examination of the affairs of the Western scene [5] and to the concerting of ulterior arrangements.

On this, and on every other subject of our military concerns, I shall be happy to receive from time to time such suggestions and instructions as you may be pleased to communicate.

I shall regularly advise you of the progress of things and especially of every material occurrence. With perfect respect

I have the honor to be   Sir   Your very Obed Ser   A Hamilton

Lieutenant General Washington

ALS, George Washington Papers, Library of Congress; two copies, one in the handwriting of Philip Church, Hamilton Papers, Library of Congress.
  1. This letter was enclosed in H to Washington, February 16, 1799.
  2. James McHenry to H, February 4, 1799.
  3. See McHenry to H, February 4, 1799.
  4. See H to James Wilkinson, February 12, 1799.
  5. In MS, "scence."

To George Washington

Private

New York February 16. 1799

Dear Sir

Different reasons have conspired to prevent my writing to you since my return to New York [1]—the multiplicity of my avocations, an imperfect state of health [2] and the want of something material to communicate.

The official letter herewith transmitted [3] will inform you of the disposition of our military affairs which has been recently adopted by the Department of War. There shall be no want of exertion on my part to promote the branches of the service confided to my care.

But I more and more discover cause to apprehend that obstacles of a very peculiar kind stand in the way of an efficient and successful management of our military concerns. These it would be unsafe at present to explain.

It may be useful that I should be able to write to you hereafter some confidential matters relating to our Administration without the mention of names. When this happens, I shall designate the President by X, the Secretary of State by V of the Treasury by I and of the Department of War by C.

Every thing in the Northern Quarter, as far as I can learn, continues favourable to the Government.

Very Affectly & truly I remain   My Dear Sir   Your Obed servt

A Hamilton

General Washington

ALS, Hamilton Papers, Library of Congress; copy, in the handwriting of
Philip Church, Hamilton Papers, Library of Congress.

1. H had been in Philadelphia from November 10 until December 15, 1798,
to discuss military affairs with Washington, Charles Cotesworth Pinckney, and
members of the Adams Administration.

2. See H to Theodore Sedgwick, January 25, 1799; H to Stephen Van Rensselaer, January 27, 1799; Philip Schuyler to H, January 31, 1799.

3. H to Washington, February 15, 1799.

Circular on Recruiting Service [1]

Circular   [New York, February 18–19, 1799]

Sir

The recruiting service, as connected with the duties of Inspector
General, has been committed by the Department of War to my
superintendence.[2] It is expected that it will shortly commence for
the additional troops which are intended to be raised.[3] [Two Regiments of Infantry are] [4] assigned to Massachusettes. It is conceived to be expedient that for the purpose of recruiting them the
state shall be divided into [four] districts, and these four into
[twenty] sub districts or company rendezvousses within each of
which a Company is to be raised.

You will be pleased, [taking to your aid such of the field officers
heretofore appointed for the two regiments as you can convene without loss of time and consulting with General Brooks] [5] whose
opinion you will specially transmit to devise a plan for the distribution of the state into the necessary number of districts & sub districts
and you will without delay report the result to me. Dispatch is
essential; & I doubt not that upon this and upon every other occasion
you will display zeal and activity.

With great consideration I am   Sir   Your obed servant

New York   A   "One Regiment of Infantry is"
                  B   Two
                  C   ten

Connecticut	A	"One Regiment of Infantry"
	B	Two
	C	ten
Maryland	same	
Ne⟨w⟩ Hampshire	A	"Four Companies"
	B	One
	C	four
Rhode Island	A	Three Companies
	B	One
	C	three
Vermont	A	Three Companies
	B	One
	C	three
New Jersey	A	six companies
	B	Two
	C	six
Pensylvania	A	Thirteen Companies
	B	Three
	C	Thirteen
Virginia	~~A~~	~~four~~ [6]
	B	four
	C	Twenty
Massachusettes		
N Carolina	A	Nine Companies
	B	Two
	C	Nine
	D	consulting with Brigadier General Davy [7]
		if it can be done without material delay,

ADf, dated February 18, 1799, to Simon Elliot, Hamilton Papers, Library of Congress; ALS, dated February 18, 1799, to Ray Greene, sold at Goodspeed's Book Shop, Boston, March, 1941; ALS, dated February 18, 1799, to Ebenezer Huntington, sold at Parke-Bernet Galleries, Inc., May 14–15, 1945; LS, dated February 18, 1799, sold at Parke-Bernet Galleries, Inc., October 30–31, 1944; Df, dated February 19, 1799, to Daniel Morgan, in the handwriting of Philip Church with insertions by H, Hamilton Papers, Library of Congress; ALS, dated February 19, 1799, to Theodore Sedgwick, Massachusetts Historical Society, Boston; Df, dated February 19, 1799, to Theodore Sedgwick, in the handwriting of Philip Church with insertions by H, Hamilton Papers, Library of Congress.

1. H endorsed the draft of this letter: "To Lt Col Comrs. Circular Recruiting service." He also sought the opinion of prominent Federalists, for the letters listed above to Daniel Morgan, Ray Greene, and Theodore Sedgwick are simi-

lar in content to the draft though they differ in wording. See also H to Henry Lee, February 18, 1799, and Samuel Livermore to H, February 22, 1799 (listed in the appendix to this volume), in which Livermore divided New Hampshire into recruiting districts.

2. See James McHenry to H, February 4, 1799.

3. See "An Act to augment the Army of the United States, and for other purposes" (1 *Stat.* 604–05 [July 16, 1798]).

4. The material within brackets differs according to the recruiting requirements of the state in which the recipient of this circular lived. H marked the spaces where he put the brackets "A," "B," "C," and "D." These spaces were to be filled in from the material on the list he wrote at the bottom of the draft.

5. John Brooks was one of the brigadier generals nominated by John Adams to the Additional Army on July 18, 1799, and approved by the Senate on the following day (*Executive Journal*, I, 292, 293). He declined the appointment (Godfrey, "Provisional Army," 133).

6. In the letter sent to Daniel Morgan the number of regiments to be raised is "Two." Morgan, a veteran of the American Revolution, had been appointed a brigadier general on April 11, 1792 (*Executive Journal*, I, 117, 119).

7. William R. Davie.

From William Duer

[*New York, February 18, 1799*. The summary of this letter reads: "Hamilton's sympathy buoys him somewhat." [1] *Letter not found.*]

Letter listed in "Calendar Summary of Philip Church and Alexander Hamilton Papers," Personal Miscellaneous, Box 6, Schuyler, MS Division, New York Public Library.

1. See H to Oliver Wolcott, Jr., August 22, December 28, 1798; Wolcott to H, September 19, 1798.

To Henry Lee [1]

New York February 18. 1799

Dear Sir

The inclosed letter to Colonel Parker [2] will explain to you the plan upon which it is deemed expedient to pursue the recruiting service within the State of Virginia. It would be very pleasing to me, if you could yourself make it convenient to digest the arrangement which is referred to the Colonel. In this case, the letter need not be sent to him, unless you think his cooperation may be useful and it can be expeditiously had. For as it is expected the recruiting service will not speedily begin, it is desirable that this preliminary measure be completed without delay. Should you conclude for any reason to forward the letter to Col Parker, you may do it by express, the expence of which will be reimbursed.

With great esteem & regard   I am Dr. Sir   Your obed ser

Major General Lee

ADf, Hamilton Papers, Library of Congress.
    1. This letter was enclosed in H to George Washington, February 18, 1799.
    2. "Circular on Recruiting Service," February 18–19, 1799.
    Thomas Parker, a veteran of the American Revolution, was appointed lieutenant colonel on January 8, 1799 (*Executive Journal*, I, 299, 303). He was the commanding officer of the Eighth Regiment of Infantry, which was assigned to Virginia.

To George Washington

New York Feby. 18. 1799

My Dear Sir

Unwilling to take the liberty to ask you to give yourself any particular trouble on the subject I have written the enclosed letters.[1] I beg you to dispose of them as you suppose will best answer the end in view—that is to obtain a speedy distribution of the State into Districts and sub-districts.

With the truest attachment   I have the honor to be My Dear Sir Your obed servant   A Hamilton

Lt General Washington

ALS, George Washington Papers, Library of Congress; LS, Hamilton Papers, Library of Congress; copy, in the handwriting of Philip Church, Hamilton Papers, Library of Congress.
    1. For these enclosures, see H to Henry Lee, February 18, 1799.

From Theodore Sedgwick

Philadelphia 19th. Feby. 1799

My dear sir

The President yesterday, sent the Senate a nomination of Mr Murray[1] to be appointed Minister plenipy. to the french republic, accompanied by a letter, from Talleyrand to the Secy. of the french legation at Amsterdam.[2] By this letter it appears, that for some time, communications have been made to Mr. Murray, of the friendly dispositions of the french Govt. towards this Country, & it contains assurances that *any* minister from America will be received & treated with the respect due to the Representative of a *great powerful & independent nation*. I have neither time nor inclination to detail all the false & insidious declarations it contains. This measure, important & mischievous as it is, was the result of presidential *wisdom* without the knowledge of, or any intimation to, any one of the administration. Had the foulest heart & the ablest head in the world, been permitted to select the most embarrassing and ruinous measure, perhaps, it would have been precisely, the one, which has been adopted. In the dilemma to which we are reduced, whether we approve or reject the nomination, evils only, certain, great, but in extent incalculable, present themselves. This would be true was Mr. Murray the ablest negotiator in christendom—but with all his virtues he is feeble and guarded, credulous & unimpressive. I have not yet decided ultimately what I shall do. At present the nomination must be postponed.[3]

I am much obliged to you for the copy you sent me of the report [4] —it is excellent. I have made the best use of it in my power. I am with sincerity your friend   Theodore Sedgwick

Genl Hamilton

LS, Hamilton Papers, Library of Congress.

1. William Vans Murray, a Maryland lawyer and Federalist politician, was a member of the House of Representatives from 1791 to 1797. In March, 1797, he was appointed "Minister resident of the United States of America, to the United Netherlands" (*Executive Journal*, I, 228).

In his message to the Senate nominating Murray to be Minister Plenipotentiary to France, John Adams stated: "If the Senate shall advise and consent to his appointment, effectual care shall be taken, in his instructions, that he shall not go to France without direct and unequivocal assurances, from the French government, signified by their Minister of Foreign Relations [Charles Maurice de Talleyrand-Périgord], that he shall be received in character; shall enjoy the privileges attached to his character by the law of nations; and that a Minister of equal rank, title, and powers, shall be appointed to treat with him, to discuss and conclude all controversies between the two Republics by a new treaty" (*Executive Journal*, I, 313).

2. Talleyrand's letter, which is dated September 28, 1798, and is addressed to "Citizen [Louis André] Pichon, Secretary of Legation of the French Republic near the Batavian Republic," reads: "I have received successively, Citizen, your letters of the 22d and 27th Fructidor (8th and 13th of September). They afford

me more and more reason to be pleased with the measure you have adopted, to detail to me your conversations with Mr. Murray. These conversations, at first merely friendly, have acquired consistency, by the sanction I have given to them by my letter of the 11th Fructidor [August 28]. I do not regret that you have trusted to Mr. Murray's honor a copy of my letter: it was intended for you only, and contains nothing but what is conformable to the intentions of government. I am thoroughly convinced that should explanations take place, with confidence between the two Cabinets, irritation would cease; a crowd of misunderstandings would disappear; and the ties of friendship would be the more strongly united, as each party would discover the hand which sought to disunite them.

"But I will not conceal from you that your letters of the 2d and 3d Vendemiaire [September 23 and 24], just received, surprise me much. What Mr. Murray is still dubious of, has been very explicitly declared, even before the President's message to Congress, of the 3d Messidor [June 21] last, was known in France. I had written it to Mr. [Elbridge] Gerry, namely, on the 24th Messidor [July 12] and 4th Thermidor [July 22]; I did repeat it to him before he sat out. A whole paragraph of my letter to you, of the 11th Fructidor, of which Mr. Murray has a copy, is devoted to develop still more the fixed determination of the French government. According to these bases, you were right to assert, that, whatever Plenipotentiary the government of the United States might send to France to put an end to the existing differences between the two countries, would be undoubtedly received with the respect due to the representative of a free, independent, and powerful nation.

"I cannot persuade myself, Citizen, that the American government need any further declarations from us, to induce them, in order to renew the negotiations, to adopt such measures as would be suggested to them by their desire to bring the differences to a peaceable end. If misunderstandings on both sides have prevented former explanations from reaching that end, it is presumable that those misunderstandings being done away, nothing henceforth will bring obstacles to the reciprocal dispositions. The President's instructions to his Envoys at Paris, which I have only known by the copy given you by Mr. Murray, and received by me the 21st Messidor, (9th July) announce, if they contain the whole of the American government's intentions, dispositions which could only have added to those which the Directory has always entertained; and, notwithstanding the posterior acts of that government—notwithstanding the irritating and almost hostile measures they have adopted—the Directory has manifested its perseverance in the sentiments which are deposited both in my correspondence with Mr. Gerry, and in my letter to you of the 11th Fructidor; and which I have herein-before repeated in the most explicit manner. Carry, therefore, Citizen, to Mr. Murray the most positive expressions, in order to convince him of our sincerity, and prevail upon him to transmit them to his government. . . ." (*Executive Journal*, I, 313–14.)

A copy in French and a translation of Talleyrand's letter were enclosed in Murray to Adams, October 7, 1798 (ALS, Adams Family Papers, deposited in the Massachusetts Historical Society, Boston).

3. In describing the reaction to Murray's nomination, Robert Liston, the British Minister to the United States, wrote to Lord Grenville, British Secretary of State for Foreign Affairs, on February 22, 1799: "The federal party were thunderstruck with this step which to say the least of it appears to have been at the same time precipitate and unseasonable. It was taken by Mr Adams without the advice, indeed without the knowlege, of the Secretary of State or the other members of the Administration, and without consultation with any of his own political friends. It was not only of a nature to be generally obnoxious to the support of government, and calculated to damp the ardour of the nation, which he himself had contributed so much to raise, but it had a

particular tendency to check those measures of energy which were at the moment under the consideration of the House of Representatives, and to prevent that assembly from placing the Country in the respectable state of waiting preparation which would have been highly expedient even if a pacifick negotiation had been previously resolved on.

"This unfavourable effect was indeed felt in the Lower House. A Bill was under debate for the encouragement of the armed Ships of the United States by granting a premium on every gun taken from the French. An opposition Member of the Senate the moment the message of the President communicating his nomination of a Minister to France was received hastened to the House of Representatives, and imparted the intelligence to his friends. The consequence was that a man of some weight (Mr Josiah Parker of Virginia) who is an adherent to the popular party but is not accustomed in certain leading questions to support the Administration, rose and stated that although he had been all along an advocate for measures of that nature, and for the one before the House in particular, he would now oppose it, since the news he had just heard convinced him it was no longer necessary. The question was accordingly lost.

"The first idea among the federal members of the Senate was to refuse their sanction to the nomination of Mr Murray. The appearance however of a scission among the branches of the executive power was afflicting to the more moderate and patriotick members; and after a long consultation upon the subject in a general meeting of the friends of government it was resolved to avoid an immediate decision, to refer the consideration of the measure to a select committee (which, as the members are chosen by ballot, would of course consist of federal men) and by the delay of a few days to give the President time to reflect on what he had done, and to listen to the remonstrances of his friends—in hopes that he may finally be brought to withdraw the nomination—or so to modify the appointment as to render the measure less obnoxious and less mortifying to the feelings of those who have a regard for the honour of the Country." (PRO: F.O. [Great Britain] 5/25A/93–94.)

4. This report, which has not been found, concerned the case of *Thomas Morris and James Wadsworth* v *William Bacon.* See Sedgwick to H, February 4, 1798; H to Sedgwick, January 25, 1799.

From William Willcocks [1]

[New York, February 19, 1799]

Sir,

Messrs Ten Eyck [2] and Williams [3] are to meet at my house half past ten. If you will be so good as to have the thing signed by Troup [4] and Mr. Church [5] he will endeavor to get some other subscribers by Saturday. Mr. Pendleton [6] will subscribe if you send it to him. He attended at the meetings and recommended this mode &c &c.

Yours &c   Wm Willcocks

Feby. 19. 1799.

Genl. Hamilton

Would not Mr. Harrison [7] subscribe if your clerk carried it to him. Williams says he can commence with twenty five or thirty subscriptions.

ALS, Hamilton Papers, Library of Congress.
1. Willcocks, a veteran of the American Revolution, was a New York City lawyer. In 1794 he served as a Federalist member of the state Assembly.
2. John Ten Eyck was a New York City merchant.
3. William Williams was a New York City businessman.
4. Robert Troup.
5. John B. Church, the brother-in-law of Elizabeth Hamilton.
6. Nathaniel Pendleton.
7. Richard Harison, a New York City lawyer, was recorder of that city from 1798 to 1801.

From Timothy Pickering

Philadelphia Feby. 20. 1799

Dear Sir,

Since I wrote you on the 9th (which you acknowledge in a short letter,[1] promising further communications) Dr. Stevens has been appointed Consul General of St. Domingo,[2] and will probably embark before the close of next week. If you have written further to me in answer to my letter of the 9th the letter has miscarried, for I have recd. nothing. I must frame Dr. Stevens's instructions in a few days,[3] and wish to furnish him with your ideas on the points I stated.[4] This cannot be done *officially*—but he will know how to use it.

I am very respectfully   & sincerely yours   T Pickering

Genl Hamilton

ALS, Hamilton Papers, Library of Congress.
1. H to Pickering, February 9, 1799.
2. Edward Stevens was one of H's oldest and closest friends. The two men had known each other as young boys (H to Stevens, November 11, 1796). Stevens subsequently practiced medicine in Philadelphia, where he was H's and Elizabeth Hamilton's doctor when they had yellow fever (H to the College of Physicians, September 11, 1793). On February 16, 1799, John Adams nominated Stevens "to be Consul General of the United States, in the island of St. Domingo," and the Senate approved the nomination on February 21, 1799 (*Executive Journal*, I, 312, 316).
3. Pickering's instructions to Stevens are dated April 22, 1799 (copy, en-

closed in Pickering to Adams, April 23, 1799 [ALS, Adams Family Papers, deposited in the Massachusetts Historical Society, Boston]).

4. See Pickering to H, February 9, 1799.

To Timothy Pickering

New York Feby 21. 1799

My Dear Sir

The multiplicity of my avocations joined to imperfect health [1] has delayed the communication you desired respecting St Domingo.[2] And what is worse it has prevented my bestowing sufficient thought to offer at present any thing worth having.

No regular system of Liberty will at present suit St Domingo. The Government if independent must be military—partaking of the feodal system.

A hereditary Chief would be best but this I fear is impracticable.

Let there be then—

A single Executive to hold his place for life.

The person to succeed on a vacancy to be either the Officer *next in command in the Island at the time of the Death* of the Predecessor, or the person who by plurality of Voices of the Commandants of Regiments shall be designated within a certain time. In the mean time the Principal Military officers to administer.

All the males within certain ages to be arranged in Military Corps and to be compellable to Military service. This may be connected with the Tenure of Lands.

Let the supreme Judiciary authority be vested in twelve Judges to be chosen for life by the *Generals* or Chief Military Officers.

Trial by Jury in all Criminal causes not Military to be established. The mode of appointing them must be regulated with reference to the general spirit of the establishment.

Every law inflicting capital or other Corporal punishment or levying a tax or contribution in any shape to be proposed by the Executive to an Assemb[l]y composed of the Generals & commandants of Regiments for their sanction or rejection.

All other laws to be enacted by the sole authority of the Executive.

The Powers of War & Treaty to be in the Executive.

The Executive to be obliged to have three Ministers—of Finance war & foreign affairs—whom he shall nominate to the Generals for their approbation or rejection.

The Colonels & Generals when once appointed to hold their Offices during good behaviour removea⟨ble⟩ only by Conviction of an infamous crime in due course of law or the sentence of a Court Martial cashiering them.

Court Martials for Trial of Officers & Capital Offence to be not less than 12 & well guarded as to mode of appointment.

Duties of import & export, taxes on lands & buildings to constitute the Chief branches of Revenue.

These thoughts are very crude but perhaps they may afford some hints.

How is the sending an Agent to Toussaint to encourage the Independence of St Domingo & a Minister to France [3] to negotiate an accommodation reconciliable to consistency or good faith?

Yrs. truly   A H

ALS, Massachusetts Historical Society, Boston.
   1. See H to George Washington, February 16, 1799, note 2.
   2. See Pickering to H, February 9, 20, 1799.
   3. See Theodore Sedgwick to H, February 19, 1799, note 1.

To Theodore Sedgwick

New York Feby 21. 179[9] [1]

The step announced in your letter [2] just received in all its circumstances would astonish, if any thing from that quarter could astonish.

But as it has happened, my present impression is that the measure must go into effect with the additional idea of a Commission of three. The mode must be accommodated with the President. *Murray* is certainly not strong enough for so immensely important a mission.

Yrs. truly   A H

I will write tomorrow if my impression varies.

T Sedgwick Es

ALS, Massachusetts Historical Society, Boston.
1. H mistakenly dated this letter "1798."
2. Sedgwick to H, February 19, 1799.

From Theodore Sedgwick

Philadelphia 22. feby. 1799.

Dear sir

In answer to yours of the 19th.[1]—The gentlemen from Massa. have been together, I mean such as I requested, & have agreed on the following as the most eligible division of that state for the purpose of recruiting in your plan. Maine a district—four places of Rendezvous, Portland, Wiscasset, Augusta & custine. The Counties of Essex, Suffolk, Bristol, Dukes county, & Nantucket Barnstable & Plimouth a district—seven placaes of rendezvous—Haverhill, Newbury port, Salem, Boston, Plimouth, Taunton and Bridgewater. Middlesex, Norfolk & Worcester a district—five places of rendezvous—Groton, Watertown, Petersham, Worcester & Dedham. Hampshire & Berkshire a district—four places of rendezvous— Pittsfield, Worthington, Northampton & Springfield. I have presumed that it was not intended to mark the exact limits of each subdistrict, as this could not be done without an enumeration of all the towns in the State and, if expedient to be done at all, may be safely confided to the field officers.

I have seen as far as they are in the office of the Secy. of State Mr. Murray's communications relative to the intercourse between him and Pichon.[2] Part of his letters have been imediately addressed to the President. As far as I have seen there is more evidence of integrity than of wisdom. The details I have not time to write nor you to read.

It is one of the misfortunes to which we are subjected by the wild & irregular starts of a vain, jealous, and half frantic mind that we are obliged to practice an infraction of correct principle—a direct communication between the Prest. & Senate. I am this morning to wait on him & sollicit an interview between him & the committee [3] upon his nomination. The objects are to induce him to alter it, as it

respects the person & *instead* of an individual to propose a commission as it respects the principles on which the negotiation shall commence, and as it respects the scene within which it shall be *carried*
on. On all these points I am told & from good authority he has
formed strong opinions. If they are unalterable, I believe, I must vote
against the appointment, but at present I think that is not the inclination of a majority. A circumstance confirmatory of the Prests. total
ignorance of human nature is that he has frequently declared that
he believed the message would add to the federal energies of the
legislature.

I am most sincerely yours   Theodore Sedgwick

LS, Hamilton Papers, Library of Congress.
    1. "Circular on Recruiting Service," February 18–19, 1799.
    2. See Sedgwick to H, February 19, 1799; H to Sedgwick, February 21, 1799.
    3. On February 20, 1799, the Senate considered the nomination of William
Vans Murray as Minister Plenipotentiary to France and ordered that the nomination be referred to a committee consisting of Sedgwick, William Bingham
of Pennsylvania, Jacob Read of South Carolina, James Ross of Pennsylvania,
and Richard Stockton of New Jersey (*Executive Journal*, I, 315-16).

To James McHenry

New York February 23 1799

Sir

I have maturely considered the questions raised by your letter of
the 21 of January with the aid of such lights, as memory or inquiry
could furnish with regard to usage.

The truth is that the articles are so obscurely worded as to preclude a very clear construction.

The second article of the 18th section [1] of the original code seems
to me to be repealed by the first resolution of the 31 of May 1796 [2]
in the Appendix; [3] for it comes expressly within the description of
"an article relating to the holding of Courts Martial and the confirmation of the sentences thereof." I therefore pass it by in the
examination.

The 2d Article [4] of the appendix (title Administration of Justice)
provides that General Courts Martial shall be ordered by "*the*
General or officer commanding *the troops*" which standing alone

would seem to confine the Power to the Officer who should command the *whole army* of the UStates. "The troops" without any additional words of description would naturally comprehend "All the Troops of the UStates" and the terms *"the General"* look to a similar conclusion.

But the 23 Article [5] admits that the Commanding Officer of a Department may appoint a General Court Martial, & by *implication* that the Commanding Officer of a *Post* or *detachment* may do it.

And if a Judge Advocate is appropriate to a General Court Martial only, the 6th Article,[6] also by implication admits that the commanding Officer of a detachment or garrison may constitute such Court.

It is therefore admissible to adopt a broader construction & to say that other officers besides the Commander of all the Troops of the UStates may appoint a General Court-Martial.

There are two other kinds of Courts Martial contemplated by the Articles one Regimental—the other Garrison.

The special authority given by the 3d article [7] to the Commander of a Regiment or corps (by which I understand some single corps or integer of the army) to constitute Regimental Courts Martial, and to the commanding officer of any Garrison, Fort, barrack, or other place, to constitute a garrison Court Martial, each of which Courts is limited to three officers, excludes by implication the power to appoint a General Court Martial.

The Construction, which I incline to infer from the whole is, *affirmatively* that every General of a Department or of a distinct army, every General commanding troops at a Post or on a command so detached from the army as that its ordinary police is and must be distinct, and every Officer, who as a substitute for a General commanding an army, or such other Corps as being the proper command of a General officer is also in the situation last described, may appoint a General Court Martial—and *negatively*—that no other officer, especially no officer commanding only a Regiment or other corps (whether entire or consisting of detachments), which forms a command not superior to that of a Regiment, can appoint a General Court Martial; Consequently that no Officer commanding either of the Garrisons on the sea Board has power to constitute such a Court. In other words, none but a *General* or his *representative* can do it.

The application of this rule is not always obvious, but in most cases it will be so, & in all a satisfactory line may be drawn by the exercise of a sound discernment. It would however be well that there should be some more correct definitions by law.

According to my information the above construction is agreeable to Military usage.

As to the question how far a judge advocate or person acting in that capacity is essential to a Court Martial, I am of opinion that such an officer is essential to every General Court Martial and a Recorder to every Court of Inquiry, but neither of them to any other Court.

I infer this, first from what I understand to be military usage—

Secondly from several clauses in the articles of war.

The sixth article of the appendix directs that the Judge Advocate or his representative shall administer to each member of *a Court* certain oaths concluding thus "which oaths shall *also* be taken by all members of Regimental and Garrisons Courts Martial." If the office of Judge Advocate extended to these last Courts, the previous words were sufficient, & this clause is redundant, if not incorrect.

Again, that part of the 24 Article [8] which requires the Judge Advocate to transmit the proceedings and sentences of Courts Martial to the Secy at War is expressly confined to those which are General. This is a *circumstance* to imply that his agency is limited to such Courts.

The expediency of having a Judge Advocate or Recorder seems relative to cases of importance, and to those which are only preparatory to some ulterior arrangement. It may be inconvenient to carry it further.

Inclosed are the sentences which you transmitted to me, that you may finally direct what is to be done.

With great respect   I have the honor to be Sir   Yr. Obed serv

ADf, Hamilton Papers, Library of Congress.

1. Article 2 of Section XVIII of the articles of war adopted by the Continental Congress on September 20, 1776 (*JCC*, V, 788–807), reads: "The general, or commander in chief for the time being, shall have full power of pardoning or mitigating any of the punishments ordered to be inflicted, for any of the offences mentioned in the foregoing articles; and every offender convicted as aforesaid, by any regimental court-martial, may be pardoned, or have his punishment mitigated by the colonel, or officer commanding the regiment" (*JCC*, V, 806). This article was repealed and replaced by a resolution of April 14, 1777 (*JCC*, VII, 266).

2. H mistakenly wrote "1796"; the date should be 1786. The first resolution of May 31, 1786, reads: "*Resolved,* That the fourteenth section of the rules and Articles for the better government of the troops of the United States, and such other Articles as relate to the holding of Courts-Martial, and the confirmation of the sentences thereof, be, and they are hereby repealed" (*JCC,* XXX, 316). Section XIV contained twenty-two sections describing the structure and procedures of courts-martial (*JCC,* V, 800–04).

3. For the appendix to the articles of war, entitled "Administration of Justice," see *JCC,* XXX, 316–22. See also H to Jonathan Dayton, August 6, 1798, note 11.

4. *JCC,* XXX, 317.

5. *JCC,* XXX, 320.

6. *JCC,* XXX, 317–18.

7. *JCC,* XXX, 317.

8. *JCC,* XXX, 320–21.

From Ebenezer Stevens [1]

New York 23rd February 1799

Dear General

I promised you to commit to writing what I think ought to be done, for the compleating the Defence of this City, and the neighbouring Islands; with some other observations incident thereon—and submit them herein, for your government.

First.   To compleat Fort Jay & build, another Barrack in that Fort. the ensuing Summer.

second. For Government to purchase Ellis's Island, and this state to cede the jurisdiction of it, and also of Bedlows and Governors Island, to the United States.

Third.   For you to write the secretary of War, to claim from this State, the One thousand stands of small arms with Cartridge Boxes, which were loaned.

Fourth. To have the Arsenal, built here last summer, put in suitable order; to unpack, and place on Racks, provided for that purpose, the Three thousand stands of arms, now in my Store, belonging to the state, together with the Cartridge Boxes. I am certain, those articles are receiving damage, by being in boxes, and kept from the air.

Fifth.   To press the secretary of War, to name my compensation; for I am tired of working, without knowing, what I am to receive for my services. And as there is much Writing, and full employment, for a Clerk under me, as agent for the department of War, I would suggest, your recommending that One be allowed me; which would enable me, to devote more of my time to the inspection; and seeing the various objects in my department, properly executed; under my immediate view.

Sixth.   To recommend the secretary of War, to authorize me to establish a Laboratory on Governors Island, which might supply, both the Garrisons, and Navy with Ammunition, and Military Stores. and would be a School for our Commissioned Officers, to learn how to fix those matters, and materially concerns them to be acquainted with. It could be begun on a Small scale, and I would give some part of my time to this object.

I submit the above for your consideration, and respectfully remain Dear General   Yours affectionately   Ebenr Stevens.

P.S. I would earnestly recommend, your making application to His Excellency Governor Jay, for money to pay off the Balances due to sundry persons for the Erection of the fortifications and mounting of Cannon &c. &c—for the defence of this Island last summer, under the immediate direction of the military Committee,[2] which alderman Furman[3] cannot settle, for want of the means—and then, that all those accompts be audited by the military Committee.

Major Genl. Hamilton.

ALS, Hamilton Papers, Library of Congress; copy, New-York Historical Society, New York City.

1. For background to this letter, see the introductory note to H to James McHenry, June 1, 1798. See also Stevens to H, November 17, 23, 29, December 18, 1798; H to Stevens, November 19, 1798; and "Report of the Committee of the Corporation and the Military Committee to the Common Council of New York," December 31, 1798.

2. The Military Committee consisted of Aaron Burr, H, and Ebenezer Stevens. See "Call for a Meeting," June 4, 1798, note 2.

3. Gabriel Furman.

From Timothy Pickering

(confidential)

Philaa. Feby. 25. 1799.

My dear sir,

This morning I have recd. your favour of the 21st.

We have all been shocked and grieved at the nomination of a minister to negociate with France. There is but one sentiment on the subject among the friends of their country and the real supporters of the President's administration. Pains have been taken to ameliorate the measure by throwing it into a Commission: [1] but the President is fixed: the Senate must *approve* or *negative* the nomination: in the latter event, perhaps he will name Commissioners. I beg you to be assured that it is wholly *his own act*, without any participation or communication with any of us. It is utterly inconsistent with his late nomination of Mr. King to negociate a commercial treaty with Russia,[2] & of Mr. Smith to negociate a like treaty with the Porte: [3] both these objects will now be defeated. It was by the *proffered* aid of Russia & Great Britain that we were induced to propose to negociate with the Porte.[4] With respect to St. Domingo, the President will certainly do no act to encourage Touissaint to declare the island independent: but he will doubtless open the commercial intercourse when Dr. Stevens [5] (Consul General) shall certify that privateering is at an end, so that agreeably to the 4th section of the act,[6] the President may consider it safe & for the interests of the U. States to do it.

The foundation of this fatal nomination of Mr. Murray was laid in the President's speech at the opening of Congress.[7] He peremptorily determined (against our unanimous opinions) to leave open the door for the degrading and mischievous measure of sending another minister to France, even without waiting for *direct* overtures from her.

I am very truly & respectfully   yours   T. Pickering

Alexander Hamilton Esq

ALS, Hamilton Papers, Library of Congress; ALS, letterpress copy, Massachusetts Historical Society, Boston.

1. See Theodore Sedgwick to H, February 19, 22, 1799.

2. On February 6, 1799, John Adams nominated Rufus King, United States Minister Plenipotentiary to Great Britain, "to be a Minister Plenipotentiary, for the special purpose of negotiating . . . a treaty of amity and commerce between the United States and the emperor of all the Russias." The Senate approved the nomination on February 7, 1799 (*Executive Journal*, I, 310).

King had been approached by Simon Woronzow, the Russian Minister to Great Britain, on November 9, 1798. On November 10, 1798, King wrote to Pickering: "The Russian envoy of his own accord yesterday observed to me that we have considerable trade in the Baltic and it appeared some what singular that no direct intercourse or correspondence had ever subsisted between our two governments. . . .

"I answered that I could perceive considerable advantage in a commercial treaty with Russia. . . . He then proposed that we should take an early opportunity of resuming this conversation and concluded by saying that by writing to our respective governments if the measure should be found adviseable they might authorise the treaty to be negociated here. I have thought it best to report this conversation, tho' the subject is referred to another interview. Count Woronzow is a man of good principles and of great honor. I know not whether this intimation proceeds from himself or has been ordered by his court. I shall not fail to send you the result of our next conference." (copy [deciphered], RG 59, Despatches from United States Ministers to Great Britain, 1792–1906, Vol. 7, January 9–December 22, 1798, National Archives.)

3. On February 8, 1799, Adams nominated William Loughton Smith "Minister Plenipotentiary to the Court of Portugal, to be Envoy Extraordinary Minister Plenipotentiary to the Sublime Ottoman Porte, with full power to negotiate a treaty of amity and commerce between the United States of America and the dominions and dependencies of the Sublime Porte." The Senate approved the nomination on February 11, 1799 (*Executive Journal*, I, 311, 312).

4. King was interested in securing a treaty of amity and commerce with the Ottoman Empire. He wished to open the territories of the empire to American commerce, and he also hoped that the United States would be able to secure the assistance of the Porte in making treaties with the Barbary states of North Africa which were theoretically subject to the authority of the Porte. As early as January 24, 1797, King wrote to Pickering: "In one or two conversations with the Turkish ambassador [Yusuf Agah Effendi] at this Court relative to a treaty of commerce, I should infer if reliance can be placed on his opinion, that there would not be much difficulty in our concluding a valuable treaty with that power" (ALS [deciphered], RG 59, Despatches from United States Ministers to Great Britain, 1792–1906, Vol. 5, August 10, 1796–December 28, 1798, National Archives). King elaborated on his meetings with the Turkish Minister in a letter to Smith on March 26, 1799: "Previously to the return to Constantinople of the Turkish Ambassador, whom I found here on my arrival, and who was a quiet good old man, I had several conversations with him upon the Subject of a commercial Treaty, and on his going, gave him a short memoir, drawn up chiefly with a view of shewing the advantages which such a Treaty would give to Turkey.

"Upon the coming of the present ambassador [Ismail Ferruh Effendi], who is a more intelligent man, who *showed his exact knowledge* by saying, when I was first presented to him, that he was glad to see a man who came from the Country of Diamonds and of Gold!!! I took an early occasion to renew the conversation with him, but with more caution, as I was unable to discover his Sentiments." (LC, New-York Historical Society, New York City.)

On November 10, 1798, after the defeat of the French fleet by the English at Aboukir Bay and the entry of Turkey on September 2, 1798, into the war against France as Britain's ally, King wrote to Pickering: ". . . I cannot but think the present a favorable moment, not only for the extension of our trade in the Mediterranean but for the conclusion of a commercial treaty with the Porte. Speaking upon this subject to Lord Grenville he assured me that we might with confidence rely upon their good offices and influence at Constantinople in any arrangements we may be inclined to make there.

"The Russian envoy of his own accord yesterday observed to me . . . that they stood well at this moment with the porte with whom we might have an interest in making a commercial treaty and that he had no reason to doubt that the Emperor would be inclined not only to form a commercial treaty with us but moreover to afford us his influence in concluding one with the Porte.

"I answered that I could perceive considerable advantage in a commercial treaty with Russia and that it would undoubtedly be an object of importance to extend and establish our trade in the Levant." (copy [deciphered], RG 59, Despatches from United States Ministers to Great Britain, 1792–1906, Vol. 7, January 9–December 22, 1798, National Archives.)

5. See Pickering to H, February 20, 1799.

6. "An Act further to suspend the Commercial Intercourse between the United States and France, and the dependencies thereof" (1 *Stat.* 613–16 [February 9, 1799]).

7. This is a reference to Adams's Second Annual Address, which he delivered to Congress on December 8, 1798 (*Annals of Congress*, IX, 2420–24).

H, George Washington, Tobias Lear, and Charles Cotesworth Pinckney "entered the Hall, and took their places on the right of the Speaker's Chair" to hear Adams's speech (*Annals of Congress*, IX, 2420).

The relevant sections of Adams's address read: "The course of the transactions in relation to the United States and France, which have come to my knowledge during your recess, will be made the subject of a future communication. That communication will confirm the ultimate failure of the measures which have been taken by the Government of the United States towards an amicable adjustment of differences with that Power. You will, at the same time, perceive that the French Government appears solicitous to impress the opinion that it is averse to the rupture with this country, and that it has, in a qualified manner, declared itself willing to receive a Minister from the United States, for the purpose of restoring a good understanding. It is unfortunate for professions of this kind that they should be expressed in terms which may countenance the inadmissible pretension of a right to prescribe the qualifications which a Minister of the United States should possess. . . .

"Hitherto, therefore, nothing is discoverable in the conduct of France which ought to change or relax our measures of defence; on the contrary, to extend and invigorate them, is our true policy. We have no reason to regret that these measures have been thus far adopted and pursued; and, in proportion as we enlarge our view of the portentous and incalculable situation of Europe, we shall discover new and cogent motives for the full development of our energies and resources.

"But, in demonstrating by our conduct that we do not fear war, in the necessary protection of our rights and honor, we shall give no room to infer that we abandon the desire of peace. An efficient preparation for war can alone insure peace. It is peace that we have uniformly and perseveringly cultivated, and harmony between us and France may be restored at her option. But to send another Minister, without more determinate assurances that he would be received, would be an act of humiliation to which the United States ought not to submit. It must, therefore, be left to France, if she is indeed desirous of accomodation, to take the requisite steps. The United States will steadily observe the maxims by which they have hitherto been governed. They will respect the sacred rights of embassy. And with a sincere disposition on the part of France to desist from hostility, to make reparation for the injuries heretofore inflicted on our commerce, and to do justice in future, there will be no obstacle to the restoration of a friendly intercourse. . . ." (*Annals of Congress,* IX, 2421-22.)

From Theodore Sedgwick [1]

Phila. 25. feby. 1799

Dear sir

The comee. to whom was refered the Prests. message, nominating Mr. Murray, had a free conversation with him on saturday evening, under the protestation that it should not be mentioned in the report nor considered as a precedent.[2] During the conversation he declared, repeatedly, that to defend the executive against Oligarchic influence, it was indispensable, that he should insist, on a decision on the nomination; and he added, "I have on mature reflection made up my mind, & I will neither withdraw, nor modify the nomination." He was, however, pleased to Let us know, that, if Murray was negatived, he would then propose a commission, two of the members of which should be Gentlemen within the U.S. That the commission should be joint; but, that by instructions, any two should be authorised to act—and that in no case should the Gentlemen be permitted to leave the country, untill the positive assurances mentioned in his message of the 21st. of June shall have been given.[3] In consequence of these declarations at a meeting of the federal members, it was agreed to reject the nomination. I had already formed a report & was ready to make it when I was privately informed, that he wished I would postpone the report, as he was preparing a message on the subject. *That* is this moment delivered—is on the principles he had mentioned & the persons named are the Ch. Justice, Patrick Henry & Mr. Murray.[4] This is every thing which, under the circumstances, could be done.[5] I have written the above during debate. I hope it is intelligible. I am sincerely yours   Theodore Sedgwick

Pray is any thing done in my suit against Morris & Wadsworth? Let me know.[6]

ALS, Hamilton Papers, Library of Congress.

1. For background to this letter, see Sedgwick to H, February 19, 22, 1799; Timothy Pickering to H, February 25, 1799.

2. There is little agreement on what actually occurred at the conference. For Adams's version of the meeting, which he wrote in 1809, see Adams, *Works of John Adams*, IX, 248–50. For a quite different recollection of what took place, see Richard Stockton to Pickering, January 1, 1822 (ALS, Massachusetts Historical Society, Boston).

3. Sedgwick is referring to the following statement Adams made to Congress on June 21, 1798: "I will never send another Minister to France, without assurances that he will be received, respected, and honored as the representative of a great, free, powerful, and independent nation" (*Annals of Congress*, VIII, 2029).

4. On February 25, 1799, Adams sent the following message to the Senate: "The proposition of a fresh negotiation with France, in consequence of advances made by the French government, has excited so general an attention, and so much conversation, as to have given occasion to many manifestations of the public opinion, from which it appears to me, that a new modification of the embassy will give more general satisfaction to the legislature, and to the nation, and perhaps better answer the purposes we have in view.

"It is upon this supposition, and with this expectation, that I now nominate,

"Oliver Ellsworth, Esq. Chief Justice of the United States;

"Patrick Henry, Esq. late Governor of Virginia;

"and William Vans Murray, Esq. our Minister resident at the Hague, to be Envoys Extraordinary and Ministers Plenipotentiary to the French Republic, with full powers to discuss and settle, by a treaty, all controversies between the United States and France.

"It is not intended that the two former of these gentlemen shall embark for Europe, until they shall have received from the Executive Directory, assurances, signified by their Secretary of Foreign Relations, that they shall be received in character; that they shall enjoy all the prerogatives attached to that character by the law of nations; and that a Minister or Ministers, of equal powers, shall be appointed and commissioned to treat with them." (*Executive Journal*, I, 317.)

On February 27, 1799, the Senate approved the nominations of Ellsworth, Henry, and Murray (*Executive Journal*, I, 319). Henry, however, declined the appointment because of his "advanced age & encreasing debility" (Henry to Pickering, April 16, 1799 [ALS, Adams Family Papers, deposited in the Massachusetts Historical Society, Boston]). In May, 1799, Adams decided to nominate William R. Davie, Federalist governor of North Carolina, to replace Henry (Adams to Pickering, May 8, 1799 [LC, Adams Family Papers, deposited in the Massachusetts Historical Society, Boston]), and on June 1, 1799, Pickering sent Davie his commission (ALS, letterpress copy, Massachusetts Historical Society, Boston). Because the Senate was not in session when Davie was appointed, it did not approve his appointment until December 10, 1799 (*Executive Journal*, I, 326, 327).

5. On March 1, 1799, Robert Liston described these events to Lord Grenville as follows: "The President of the United States, after an interval of a few days and before the Select Committee of the Senate had come to any resolution respecting the nomination of Mr Murray as Minister Plenipotentiary to France, was prevailed upon by the advice and intreaties of his friends to send a second message to the Senate proposing a modification of the obnoxious step, which seems calculated in some degree to obviate the bad consequences that were apprehended from it.

"It was represented to Mr Adams that admitting the measure in itself to be wise and seasonable still the choice made of a negociator was liable to objections. That Mr Murray though a Gentleman of good parts and education and of amiable manners did not possess all that experience, firmness and dexterity, which appeared to be requisite for the conduct of such an important business at a distance which rendered it impossible to receive new instructions from home on the occurrence of any difficulty. The President has joined with him in a new nomination Mr Oliver Ellsworth, Chief Justice of the United States, and Mr Patrick Henry, late Governor of Virginia, Gentlemen of great respectability and distinguished talents.

"In the message first communicating the nomination of Mr Murray to the Senate, Mr Adams had mentioned that that Gentleman was not to leave the Hague until he (Mr Murray) did receive from the Executive Directory of France assurances that a Minister of equal rank had been appointed and empowered to treat with him—and from the professions made by M. de Talleyrand's letter to the French Chargé d'affaires at the Hague and communicated to Mr Murray, there was little doubt that this condition would immediately be complied with at Paris. On nominating Mr Elsworth and Mr Henry the President said that they shall not embark for Europe until formal ministerial assurances shall be received *here* that they shall meet with a proper reception—a circumstance which will necessarily occasion considerable delay.

"It is also uncertain that either of the Gentlemen now designated will accept the Commission. By the time that a refusal from thence can be received, the Session of Congress (which ends on the 4th of this month) will be closed. And it is expected that after what has passed, Mr Adams may decline availing himself of his constitutional power to make a new appointment during the recess.

"The object of the friends of government, which is to defeat the measure altogether, may thus possibly be in effect obtained." (PRO: F.O. [Great Britain] 5/25A/96–97.)

6. See Sedgwick to H, February 4, 1798.

From Richard Varick

[*New York, February 25, 1799.* On February 26, 1799, Hamilton wrote to Varick: "I last night received your letter dated Yesterday." *Letter not found.*]

From George Washington

Mount Vernon, Feby 25th. 1799

Sir,

I have been duly favoured with your letter of the 15th instant.

When the disposition was contemplated for assigning to Major General Pinckney and to yourself your respective districts of superintendence, I was of opinion (as you will see by the enclosed copy of a letter which I wrote to the Secretary of War [1] on my way from Philadelphia to this place) that the *whole* of General Wilkinson's Brigade should be considered as under your immediate direction; because, if a part of it which is, or may be stationed within States of Kentucky and Tennessee, should be under the Superintendence of General Pinckney, and the other part under your's, it might occasion great inconvenience, and perhaps confusion, for General Wilkinson to have to communicate sometimes with one of the Major Generals and sometimes with the other. This, I conceive, will still be the case, if the disposition, which [you] mention to have been communicated by the Secretary of War,[2] should continue. I am therefore yet decidedly of opinion, that the *whole* of General Wilkinson's Brigade should be under your superintendence.

If it be determined to pursue the recruiting business at all, I regret extremely that there should have been so much delay in it; for the favourable season is passing off every day, and when the Spring opens great numbers of those who would readily inlist now, will be then engaged in other avocations, and we shall lose the precious moment.

I shall hope to be regularly advised of every occurrence which takes place in your military Arrangements that you may think essential to communicate.

With very great regard, I am Sir, Your most obedt. Servt.

Go: Washington

Major General Hamilton

P. S. I enclose herewith returns of Troops, Stores &c at Niagara, which have been forwarded to me by Major Rivardi [3]—and shall, in acknowledging the receipt of them, desire that the Returns in future may pass through you to the War Office.

LS, Hamilton Papers, Library of Congress.
　1. Washington to James McHenry, December 16, 1798. See McHenry to H, January 22, 1799, note 3.
　2. McHenry to H, February 4, 1799.
　3. John J. U. Rivardi, a native of Switzerland, had been appointed in 1794 ". . . an engineer, for the purpose of fortifying the ports and harbors . . . [of] Baltimore, in the State of Maryland, Alexandria and Norfolk, in the State of Virginia" (Henry Knox to Rivardi, March 28, 1794 [*ASP, Military Affairs*, I, 87–88]). On February 26, 1795, he was commissioned a major in the Corps of Artillerists and Engineers (*Executive Journal*, I, 173, 174).

From George Washington

Private   Mount Vernon 25th. Feby. 1799.

My dear Sir

Your private letter of the 16th. instant came duly to hand, & safe: and I wish you at all times, and upon all occasions, to communicate interesting occurrences with your opinion thereon (in the manner you have designated) with the utmost unreservedness, to me.

If the augmented force was not intended as an interroram measure, the delay in Recruiting it, is unaccountable; and baffles all conjecture on reasonable grounds. The zeal and enthusiasm which were excited by the Publication of the Dispatches from our Commissioners at Paris (which gave birth to the Law authorising the raising of twelve Regiments &c) [1] are evaporated. It is now no more—and if this dull season, when men are idle from want of employment, and from that cause might be induced to enlist, is suffered to pass away also, we shall, by and by, when the business of Agriculture and other avocations call for the labour of them, set out as a forlorn hope to execute this business.

Had the formation of the Army followed closely the passage of this Act; and Recruiting Orders had tread on the heels of that, the Men which might have been raised at that time, would in point of numbers have been equal to any in the world; inasmuch as the most reputable yeomanry of the Country were ready to have stepped forward with alacrity.

Now, the measure is not only viewed with indifference, but deemed unnecessary by that class of People, whose attentions being turned to other matters, the Officers who in August & September could, with ease, have enlisted whole Companies of them, will find it difficult to Recruit any; and if this idle & dissipated Season is spent in inactivity, none but the riff-raff of the Country, & the Scape gallowses of the large Cities will be to be had.

Far removed from the Scene, I might ascribe these delays to wrong causes, and therefore will hazard no opinion respecting them; but I have no hesitation in pronouncing that, unless a material change takes place, our Military Theatre affords but a gloomy prospect to those who are to perform the principal parts in the Drama. Sincerely and Affectionately

I am always Yours   Go: Washington

Majr. Genl. Hamilton

ALS, Hamilton Papers, Library of Congress; ALS, letterpress copy, George Washington Papers, Library of Congress.

1. "An Act to augment the army of the United States, and for other purposes" (1 *Stat.* 604–05 [July 16, 1798]).

To Richard Varick [1]

New York Feby 26. 1799

Dr Sir

I last night received your Letter dated Yesterday.[2]

The Resolutions of the Common Council [3] discover a Mistake as to the Characters under which the Gentlemen named in them made their communication to yourself and the Recorder. They did not pretend to appear in an official Capacity, but intended to be considered merely as private individuals.

As such they gave information which they thought might be useful to the City. Specific Propositions in Writing were requested from not proposed by them—these were sent in an informal shape, because it was not meant to attach formality to their interposition. Having been digested by me as the Sum of a Previous conversation among ourselves, I have no objection to authenticate them by my Signature—and I freely add that the changes in the Plan of the Corporation which they suggest have the full concurrence of my opinion.

With respect and esteem I am   Dr Sir   Your Obed Servant

A. Hamilton

Richard Varick Esqr

Minutes of the Common Council, II, 517.

1. For background to this document, see the introductory note to Philip Schuyler to H, January 31, 1799.

2. Letter not found.

3. These resolutions are dated February 25, 1799, and are printed in the introductory note to Schuyler to H, January 31, 1799.

[ENCLOSURE]⁴

Among the objects on all hands agreed to be necessary towards preserving the City from Pestilential diseases are the following

1　The conveyance of Water in pipes through every Part of the City as well for the more convenient Washing and cleansing of the Streets, Alleys and Lanes as for the supply of the Inhabitants.

2　The filling up, lowering and draining of such Grounds within the City as may require it including the Lots adjacent to Hudsons River and the Sound as far into the Water as may be deemed expedient and causing proper bulkheads to be made adjoining or opposite to those Lots

3　The filling up, altering and amending of public Slips.

4　The filling up, altering and amending of Sinks and privies.

5　The establishment of Common Sewers or subterraneous drains and the altering and amending of such as may now exist.

As to the first Point, the Plan Proposed by the Corporation is that the Business shall be executed by the Corporation for their own benefit, and that towards enabling them to do this, the Legislature shall grant to them for a term of Years the Revenue arising from Sales at Auction.⁵ No other fund is indicated by the Bill. Probably it is contemplated that Loans may be obtained on the foundation of the revenue to arise from the supply of the Water and the Deficiency, if any, may be made up by taxes on the City.

The Success of this Plan is Problematical. It is doubtful whether the Legislature, diminished as are some of the resources of revenue, on which it has for sometime relied, will be willing to grant the fund arising from Auctions, for the *profit* of the Corporation, for such a term as will make it go far towards accomplishing the object. Computing it's annual Amount at 30,000 Dollars, if granted for twenty Years, which is as much as can be hoped, it would be equal only to a Capital of 344097 Dollars and 60 Cents, interest at 6 ⅌ Cent.,

4. *Minutes of the Common Council*, II, 517–20.
5. "An Act for the Regulation of Sales by public Auction" was passed on February 20, 1784. This act laid a duty of two and one-half percent on certain goods sold at auction (*New York Laws*, 7th Sess., Ch. IV). See also "An Act to amend an act entitled, 'An act for the regulation of sales by Public Auction'" (*New York Laws*, 14th Sess., Ch. XXVII [March 8, 1791]) and "An Act to prevent the pernicious Practice of Stock-Jobbing, and for regulating Sales at Public Auction" (*New York Laws*, 15th Sess., Ch. LXII [April 10, 1792]).

But it is hardly to be expected that money can be borrowed at so low a rate—How far short will this be of the Sum probably requisite! This cannot safely be estimated at less than a Milion of Dollars, if the business be done on a Scale sufficiently extensive. The Amount of the revenue to result from the supply of the Water must be for some time uncertain and under this uncertainty extensive loans on this basis ought not to be counted upon. To raise what may be wanted by taxes to carry on the enterprise with vigour might be found so burthensome on the Citizens as to occasion the operation to languish.

It is not to be doubted, that it will Promote the Convenience of the Citizens and secure the final Success of the object to let in the aid of a Capital to be created by the voluntary contributions of individuals.

This may be obtained on a Plan like the following:

Let a Company be incorporated of all those who shall subscribe to a fund with a Capital not exceeding a Milion of Dollars to be composed of Shares of fifty Dollars each, the affairs of which to be managed by seven directors annually chosen by the Subscribers, except that the Recorder of the City for the time being shall always be one.

Of this Capital a privilege to be reserved to the Corporation of the City to subscribe for any Number of Shares not exceeding a third; to enable them to do which a Grant of the Auction duties to continue to be solicited, and a power to be asked to raise on the City an annual revenue equal to the interest and gradual reimbursement of the Principal of such additional Loans as may be found necessary.

The Company to have Powers similar to those which the draft of the Bill contemplates to be given to the Corporation. Further details need not be specified.

By this expedient the success will become certain and the enterprise can be carried on with energy and dispatch.

As to the remaining points, they may be considered together.

The powers to be conferred by the Legislature will have reference first to the accomplishment of what is contemplated to be done in the first instance—secondly to the future execution of similar measures in cases hereafter to arise and the Preservation of things in the State in which they shall be placed.

In respect to the latter the Powers must be vested in a permanent body and the Corporation very naturally offers itself as that body. The Successive execution of the system in future may be reconciled with the attention which the Corporation is obliged to pay to its ordinary concerns.

But it is the opinion of many that the Prompt and vigorous execution of what is to be done, in the first instance, will be better effected by Commissioners to be appointed for the special Purpose, than by a body whose attention must necessarily be engrossed and distracted by a great multiplicity of other avocations.

It is by those who entertain this Opinion, desired that the powers for this primary operation may be vested in Commissioners not exceeding in Number seven. Their authority may be limitted to two Years and the like powers, to be exercised after that period, vested in the Corporation. All other powers contemplated to be obtained may remain as proposed in the Bill which has been prepared on behalf of the Corporation.

It will be seen that the only points of difference between this plan and that which has been adopted by the Corporation consist in the calling in the aid of private Capital for the Conveyance of Water to the City—and the vesting of the powers respecting the enumerated Points in the first instance in Commissioners instead of the Corporation.

It is believed, that the main object will be promoted, if the Corporation will signify to the Legislature, either directly by memorial, or indirectly, by a Communication to the members of this City, that alterations in their plan corresponding with the changes here suggested, if more agreeable to the Legislature, will not be unacceptable to them.   Alexander Hamilton.

From George Washington

Mount Vernon, February 26, 1799. "I received your letter of the 18th. instant yesterday. You refer me to enclosed letters for information on the subject therein mentioned. One letter only came, and that under a Seal to General Lee, which I shall forward, unopened, tomorrow by my Nephew Mr. Bushrod Washington, who is a neighbour of his. . . ."

ALS, Hamilton Papers, Library of Congress; ALS, letterpress copy, George Washington Papers, Library of Congress.

From Christopher Gore [1]

London 27. February 1799.

My dear Sir

The present crisis in the Affairs of the United States cannot fail to engage the attention of all, who are interested either in their Fate, or that of civil Society in any quarter of the Globe. Feeling in common with my fellow citizens the importance of our present conduct, and not seeing in the publications which have yet reach'd us, a display, according to my comprehension, of the true cause of our danger, of a remedy for the evils we now suffer or competent, under our circumstances, to avert those which all Europe teaches us to apprehend, I have been induc'd to commit my thoughts on this subject to paper, with the view of publishing them in America, in order to incite abler & more inform'd minds there to a serious consideration of our present state, and on the best mode of avoiding evil, & insuring future tranquility and prosperity to America.[2]

Though I entertain the most clear, & absolute conviction of our future lot in remaining in the present undecided state, and of the means of deriving immediate security, and future glory, as described in those remarks, I did not hold myself justified at this distance, necessarily ignorant of the plans & motives of the Government, to obtrude them on the Public, without the inspection, & approbation of some, whose judgment I should, on all occasions prefer to my own, & whose situation affords them much better means of deciding on the propriety of diffusing such sentiments abroad.

They are at your disposal, either to publish or not, as you may think conducive to the general interest, and in such manner, & place as you may judge expedient. If you shoud deem it most adviseable, that they shoud be printed in Boston, you will have the goodness to send them to our friend Cabot at Brooklyn [3] to whom, and to whom only I shall write on this subject.

I make but one restriction, of which you will see the propriety viz, that the writer shoud remain unknown. His name woud add no weight to the remarks, and his local situation might detract from their influence if they are entitled to any.

For altho' neither my personal nor official intercourse here has render'd me so partial to England, as to blind me to the interests of my own country, neither have I been able to discern any thing, that shoud lead the U. States to apprehend danger from a more intimate connection with G. Britain, for certain definite, & distinct objects, or from uniting so far as a common enemy renders necessary to the safety of both.

With sincere regards, & esteem   I am, my Dear Sir, your friend, & obedt. servt   C. Gore

This is a duplicate, the original went by Bristol. If both copies of the Remarks shoud arrive, you will have the goodness to send one to Mr Cabot, tho' you think it adviseable not to have them printed.

ALS, Hamilton Papers, Library of Congress.
1. Gore, a Massachusetts Federalist, had been a member of that state's House of Representatives in 1788 and 1789. He was United States attorney for the District of Massachusetts from 1789 to 1796, and on May 4, 1796, the Senate confirmed his nomination to the mixed commission appointed under Article 7 of the Jay Treaty to settle United States claims for spoliations (*Executive Journal*, I, 204, 205).
2. Copy, Hamilton Papers, Library of Congress. There is no title page to this document, but the manuscript is divided into eight chapters with a title for each. The title of Chapter I, for example, is "The Present State of the United States, and the Consequences of not adopting vigorous, and decisive measures of War against France." As this title suggests, Gore argued throughout this essay that the United States could best defend its rights by declaring war on France and, as a consequence, on Spain.
3. George Cabot of Brookline, Massachusetts.

From Ebenezer Stevens [1]

New York 28th February 1799

Dear Sir

On my being appointed by the secretary of War, agent for the War department in this City, he directed me to appoint an Engineer, to act in conjunction with messrs. Hills and Flemming, to view Bedlow, Oyster, and Governor's Island, and to form plans, Estimates

&c &c.[2] I forthwith appointed Mr Mangin to that Office under date of the 18th June last, and they compleated their business by the 10th august following; their different plans being all sent to the secretary of War, for his decision which to adopt—at this period, Mr. Hills and major Flemming retired, to their respective places of abode.

The Secretary of War, under date of the 25th August,[3] wrote me, and this is an Extract from his letter.

"I have received and examined the plans, and estimates, for the different defences of the City and Harbour of New York. The military Committee of New York being on the Spot and composed of Gentlemen of competent judgment, I have determined to submit, to their decision, the choice of a plan for the parapet for the work on Governors Island. They will, therefore, decide between the plans offered by Mr Mangin, and those of Mr Fleming & Hills."

The business, being thus left to the military Committee; it rested with them to designate which should be put into execution; and on my receiving this decision, I judged it requisite, and did appoint Mr. Mangin, under date of the 11th September, to carry the Works intended on Governors Island, into execution.

But it appears to me, from the Tenor of the inclosed Letter, and Extracts from the secretary of War's Letter to me, relative to Mangin's pay;[4] that he does not consider, the necessity of an Engineer (after the functions of Hills Fleming & Mangin in conjuction, had ceased), to mark out the Ground for the Foundations; and see that not only the Works on Governor's Island were begun, and carried on, in confor⟨mity⟩ to the plans chosen by the Military Committee —but also, that ⟨an⟩ Engineer was necessary, to draught a plan of the Barracks and Hospital, which were afterward concluded to be built, and have been since compleated—Nor in fact, the propriety of an Engineer, to see such part of the measures of Defence, yet to be erected, put into execution—and therefore, he supposes Mr Mangin's Services at an End, when Hills and Fleming went home.

I think, *you* will see otherways, and will obviate this difficulty with the secretary of War—and as One of the military Committee, represent the necessity of keeping Mangin employed; for as *you* gave the preference to his plans; it seems clear, that he was the fittest person to execute his own designs. I have paid him money on account, having viewed him from the 11th Septembr, as Engineer at the rate of Four Dollars per Day, while in employ for the United

States—which is the rate he was paid by Genl Knox, who chose him for the purpose of fortifying this port when it was first undertaken. My sole object in appointing him, was to expedite the Works; but as the Business has taken so unfavourable a turn, I will thank you to convince the secretary of War, that I acted from pure motives, and not from any disrespect towards him, or his Offices.

I remain Dear Sir   Your most obedt. Servt.   Eben Stevens.

Alexander Hamilton Esqr.

LS, Hamilton Papers, Library of Congress.
1. For background to this letter, see the introductory note to H to James McHenry, June 1, 1798.
2. On January 12, 1799, McHenry wrote to Stevens: "In my letter to you of the 16th June last you was directed to employ an Engineer, to assist Mr. [George] Fleming and Mr. [John] Hill[s], to examine and report upon the most eligible seites for new works, and to prepare the necessary plans and estimates for these, and the work required to be done on the fortifications on Governor's, Bedlow's, and Oyster Islands, and to put them in a condition to be defended, and to annoy an Enemy; and as Mr. [Joseph] Mangin was in consequence engaged by you, to assist in the aforesaid business, he is to be paid at the rate of Two dollars per diem, while so employed" (extract, Hamilton Papers, Library of Congress). See also McHenry to H, June 6, 1798, note 4; Mangin to the Military Committee of New York City, June 18, 1798; Mangin to H, August 7, 1798, January 11, 1799; Stevens to H, November 29, 1798.
3. Stevens was mistaken, for McHenry's letter to him is dated August 21, 1798 (copy, Hamilton Papers, Library of Congress). This letter was enclosed in McHenry to H, October 22, 1798.
4. This letter (McHenry to Stevens, February 26, 1799) reads in part: "The inclosed extract of a letter to you dated the 12 January ultimo will sufficiently explain to you the compensation to which I think Mr. Mangin intitled. You will settle with him accordingly.
"It may be proper to mention that Mr. Mangin is not to be paid for any services other than those rendered in pursuance and in the execution of instructions which you have received from this department." (LS, Hamilton Papers, Library of Congress.)

To the Legislature of the State of New York [1]

[New York, February–March,. 1799]

To the Honorable The Legislature of the State of New York

The Memorial of the Subscribers
Citizens of New York

Respectfully sheweth

That your Memorialists have become alarmed lest a difference of Opinion about the best mode of providing the means of conveying

water in pipes throughout this City (a measure which your Memorialists deem of essential consequence) should prevent any law being
passed on the subject.

That without desiring to interfere with the plan which under the
patronage of the Corporation of this City they understand has been
presented to Your Consideration, they have thought it may not be
improper to suggest an alternative in case that plan should not be
improved.

It is that a Company may be incorporated with a Capital not exceeding one Million of Dollars to be formed by voluntary subscriptions of fifty dollars to a share and with the necessary powers to
enable them to Act.

Of this Capital it may be expedient to reserve to the Corporation
at its option a number of shares not exceeding One-third—And it
may be provided that the Recorder shall be *ex officio* a Director of
the Company

It will likewise conduce materially to the success of the plan if
the Legislature will apply to this object the duties arising from the
sales by Auction.[2] It may be a fund for raising a correspondent principal to be invested in stock of the Company from which a superior
revenue may be eventually derived.

Your Memorialists deeming it unnecessary to enter into further
details pray leave to bring in a Bill for the above mentioned purpose.

ADf, Hamilton Papers, Library of Congress.
  1. For background to this document, see the introductory note to Philip
Schuyler to H, January 31, 1799.
  2. See H to Richard Varick, February 26, 1799.

To William J. Vredenburgh

[New York, February, 1799]

Willliam J. Vredenburgh Esq.[1]
            To Alexander Hamilton Dr

For my services as Counsel at Albany ⎫ Dollars
℔ account heretofore rendered   ⎬ 75
                                     ⎭ ——

Mr. Hamilton presents his comliments to Mr. Vredenburgh & requests the payment of the above. ⟨He will recall that⟩ Mr. Hamilton with Mr. Pendleton, argued his cause at Albany. The argument was successful. The amount was considerable. The points were nice. The above charge is certainly moderate. Under these circumstances Mr. Hamilton is not a little disappointed that so much delay has attended the satisfaction of his demand. He takes it for granted that Mr. V will feel the propriety of now satisfying it.

AL, Mr. Sedgwick Smith, The Cove, Skaneateles, New York.
    1. Vredenburgh was a New York City merchant.
    The bill that H submitted was for his services as counsel in the case of *Vredenburgh* v *Hallett and Browne* in the New York Supreme Court. For this case, see Goebel, *Law Practice*, II, 436, note 8. See also entries in H's Cash Book, 1795–1804, under the dates of February 21, October 16, 1797, and February 12, 1799 (AD, Hamilton Papers, Library of Congress).

To John J. U. Rivardi

New York March 1 1799

Sir

The inclosed letter [1] will inform you, that the Post you command has been placed under my superintendence by the Department of War. In consequence of this arrangement, the returns for December last, which you forwarded to the Commander in Chief, have been by him transmitted to me.

As my superintendence extends to all the Posts in the Northern & North Western quarters, I am desirous of revising the reasons upon which they have been established, in order to be enabled to judge whether the present disposition ought to be continued or altered.[2] To this end I am to request, that you will as early as may be visit the several Posts of Michilimacnac Detroit Fort Defiance on the Miami & Presque Isle together with such intervening & proximate positions as may present eligible Military Points; paying particular attention to the streight, which connects Lakes St. Clair & Erie & to the South Western extremity of the latter Lake: after doing which you will repair to New York to report to me the result of your observations and to confer on the subject at large. In this examination you will have an eye to the various considerations of Defence Settlement and Trade, with reference both to our British neighbours & to the Indians. I deem it unnecessary to enter into detail on these heads. The account I have received of your knowlege and discernment assures me that you will execute the commission with accurate observation and with comprehensive views. At the same time you will bear in mind that it particularly suits the state & temper of this Country to effect as much as possible with the least possible expence.

    With great consideration   I am Sir   Your Obed serv

Major Rivardi
Niagara

ADf, Hamilton Papers, Library of Congress.
  1. "Circular to the Commanding Officers in Northern and Western United States," February 15, 1799.
  2. See James McHenry to H, February 4, 1799.

From Rufus King

London Mar 4. 1799.

    Our opinions do not differ upon a very important subject,[1] that has more than once been mentioned in our correspondence: I am intirely ignorant of the Sentiments of the Pr. tho' I have again and again treated of it, and sometimes with earnestness, in my Dispatches This silence gives me some inquietude. Mr. G. will send you the Reflections [2] that have occurred to him, and will also explain the motives for putting them into your Hands. I cannot at this distance decide upon the Expediency of publishing these Reflections, but I am much inclined to recommend it, as all our Conjectures explained & confirmed by every thing we see, injoin upon us to look for Safety only in our own courage & upon our own Continent.

    With perfect regards and attachment   I am my Dear sir   Yr ob Ser
                                                      K.

A. Hamilton Esqr.

ALS, Hamilton Papers, Library of Congress; copy, New-York Historical Society, New York City.

1. This is a reference to Francisco de Miranda's plans for the liberation of Spanish America. See Miranda to H, April 1, 1797, February 7, April 6–June 7, August 17, October 19–November 10, 1798; H to Miranda, August 22, 1798; King to H, May 12, July 31, October 20, 1798, January 21, 1799; H to King, August 22, 1798; Timothy Pickering to H, August 21–22, 1798.

2. See Christopher Gore to H, February 27, 1799.

From George Washington

[*Mount Vernon, March 4, 1799.*[1] *Letter not found.*]

1. "List of Letters from G—— Washington to General Hamilton," Columbia University Libraries.

To James McHenry

New York, March 5, 1799. "I recur to your letters of the 31st of January[1] 4th 15[2] 21.[3] 22[4] 23 & 27[5] of February, for the purpose of doing whatever may remain to be done in relation to their contents.

". . . the complete formation of the several corps and their subdivisions which includes the appointment of the full complement of Officers is so essential to order that delay in this respect is very prejudicial to the service. I must therefore beg leave to urge that whatever remains to be done by the Executive towards this end may be completed, & that I may without delay be furnished with the necessary lights towards executing the part which has been assigned to me. . . . It is especially essential that no time be lost in giving to the different regiments the proper commanding Officers, in all the cases in which this has not been already done. . . .

"There are several points in your letter of the 4th of February upon which I cannot act with due information until I receive the documents promised by that letter. These are

"1 The Regulations which are intended by this paragraph of that letter 'It is expected &c that you will give orders that the Garrisons &c make Returns and observe the *enclosed regulations*'

"2 The Report of the Purveyor of supplies shewing the quantities of the different articles of cloathing &c.

"3 The schedule of the Officers who have accepted their appointments with the places of their residence.

"4 The list of Officers at present employed in the recruiting service and their places of rendezvous.

"5 The list of the names of all the Officers of the army classed according to their respective Regiments or Corps with the dates of their Commissions.

"Besides these documents it is necessary for me to be informed what are the returns and reports of different kinds which have heretofore been accustommed to be made to the War Department. . . .

"I ought also to know correctly the various channels of supply and the persons who administer them; and to understand generally the cases in which an application for any of them through the Secretary at War is necessary to the execution of the general system, as contradistinguished from those in which a call of the commanding General upon the Officer who is to furnish may be proper. . . .

"I have presumed that you have ready a competent number of printed pamphlets containing recruiting instructions [6] to be distributed among the Officers who shall be employed on that service. If so, I request that they may be forwarded to me. . . .

"You speak of a project of regulations which was communicated to me by the Commander in Chief.[7] I recollect to have seen a manuscript of this kind, but it was not left with me, and the circumstance of the conjuncture did not permit me to examine it. If now in your possession, will you oblige me by forwarding it? . . .

ADf, Hamilton Papers, Library of Congress.

1. McHenry to H, January 31, 1799 (listed in the appendix to this volume), enclosed Captain James Stille to John Caldwell, January 24, 1799, in which Stille requested that Lieutenant George Washington Carmichael be transferred.

2. McHenry to H, February 15, 1799 (listed in the appendix to this volume), enclosed a letter of January 15, 1799, from Captain James Bruff in which Bruff made charges against Major John J. U. Rivardi; a letter from Captain Frederick Frye of February 2, 1799, complaining of the quantity of provisions at Fort Jay; a letter from Rivardi of February 21, 1799, defending himself against Bruff's charges; and a letter from Amos Stoddard, January 27, 1799, complaining of the barracks at Portland, District of Maine. In his covering letter to H, McHenry requested that H speak with Ebenezer Stevens about the contract for supplying West Point with provisions.

3. McHenry to H, February 21, 1799 (listed in the appendix to this volume), enclosed Major Lewis Tousard to McHenry, February 10, 1799, in which Tousard asked to be given command of the battalion at those posts where he was employed as an engineer.

4. There are two letters of February 22, 1799, from McHenry to H listed in

the appendix to this volume. One enclosed Captain Lemuel Gates to McHenry, February 13, 1799, in which Gates complained of a deficiency of clothing and blankets, and the second enclosed letters concerning the arrest of Captain Samuel Vance.

5. McHenry to H, February 27, 1799 (listed in the appendix to this volume), concerned the discharge of an indentured servant from the Army.

6. This is a reference to the 1798 edition of a War Department pamphlet entitled *Rules and Regulations Respecting the Recruiting Service.* See H to Jonathan Dayton, August 6, 1798, note 6. For evidence that H had already received a copy, see McHenry to H, December 28, 1798.

7. See McHenry to H, February 4, 1798.

To Charles Cotesworth Pinckney

New York March 7. 1799

I duly received My Dear Sir Your letter of the 17th of January.[1] Accept my thanks for the remarks it contains on the plan for a Military School.[2]

We were extremely alarmed yesterday by the intelligence coming from Philadelphia of an accident to you at a Review. But an arrival here has greatly relieved us.[3] We earnestly desire a contradiction. Affectly & truly yrs.   A H

General Pinckney

ALS, Pinckney Family Papers, Library of Congress.
    1. Letter not found.
    2. For this plan, see H to Louis Le Bègue Du Portail, July 23, 1798; Du Portail to H, December 9, 1798; H to James McHenry, December 26, 1798, note 2; McHenry to H, December 28, 1798, note 4.
    3. This is a reference to the following item which appeared in *The New-York Gazette and General Advertiser*, March 7, 1799: "We have been at some pains to come at the source of the report of Gen. Pinckney's being shot at Charleston—but cannot. We believe it to be a fabrication."

To Charles Cotesworth Pinckney

New York March 7 1799

Sir

The Secretary at War has informed you that the General Superintendence of the Recruiting service is confided to me, as an incident to the Inspectorship.[1]

As a preliminary to this, it is requisite to distribute the States respectively into Districts and subdistricts the latter to correspond with the number of Companies to be raised in each State assigning one company to each subdistrict & the former to be proportioned [by] the number of field officers.

I request the favour of you as speedily as may be to make the distribution for the States of Georgia & the two Carolinas & to communicate to me the result.

I have been told that the commencement of the recruiting service depended on the completion of an adequate supply of Cloathing,[2] and I ought to calculate that this is nearly ready.

Perhaps it may promote expedition to transmit me successively the arrangement for each state as it shall be completed.

With great respect & esteem   I have the honor to be   Sir   Your Obed serv

Major General Pinckney

ADf, Hamilton Papers, Library of Congress.
    1. James McHenry to Pinckney, February 11, 1799 (Df, letterpress copy, James McHenry Papers, Library of Congress). See also McHenry to H, February 4, 1799.
    2. See McHenry to H, February 4, 1799.

From James McHenry

War Department
March 8th. 1799

Sir,

Certain inconveniences hitherto experienced relative to the pay of the troops induced me to recommend a Section to be adopted in the Bill for the organization of the Army which having passed into a law is now transmitted.[1]

As the greatest part of the Army will be on or near the Sea-board I can perceive considerable advantages of a public nature which would result from the Pay Master General being fixed at the seat of Government, in respect to the transmission of money for the pay of the troops to his Deputies and Regimental paymasters; to the

Officers who may be responsible for the disbursement of money for the recruiting Service; to the prompt execution of all orders originating in this department or from the General of the Armies, and the prompt settlement of his accounts at the proper and fixed periods. If you see the subject in this light, you will be pleased to instruct him accordingly.

Mr. Swan [2] who is the paymaster General is now at Cincinnati on the Ohio. You will necessarily direct him to appoint a deputy or deputies for the North Western and Mississippi Army and to take the securities required by law; to leave with them such orders as may be proper and conformable to his powers under the law and his Instructions, and having so done to hasten with all his Books and papers &c. to the Seat of Government, where he is to open his Office.

The Quarter Master General, Lieut: Colonel Wilkins,[3] is about establishing an Office in this City where he will receive either in person or by his deputy, your orders relative to the transport Service, and all matters of which he is to be the executive organ. Enclosed is copy of the 12th: Section of the Act [4] for the organization of the Army which respects this Officer.

I have the honor to be with great respect, Sir, Your obedt. servant   James McHenry

Major General
Alexander Hamilton.

LS, Hamilton Papers, Library of Congress; LS, letterpress copy, James McHenry Papers, Library of Congress; extract, in the handwriting of Philip Church, George Washington Papers, Library of Congress; extract, Hamilton Papers, Library of Congress.
1. The enclosure is a copy of Section 15 of "An Act for the better organizing of the Troops of the United States; and for other purposes" (1 *Stat.* 749–55 [March 3, 1799]). This section reads: "*And be it further enacted,* That the Paymaster general of the Armies of the United States, shall always Quarter at or near the head quarters of the main Army, or at such place as the Commander in chief shall deem proper; And that to the Army on the western frontiers, and to detachments from the main army intended to Act separately for a time, he shall appoint deputy pay-masters, who shall account to him for the money Advanced to them, and shall each give a Bond in the sum of fifteen thousand Dollars, with sufficient sureties for the faithful discharge of their duties respectively, and take an Oath faithfully to execute the duties of their offices; And the several Regimental pay masters shall also give Bond in the sum of five thousand Dollars, with one or more sufficient sureties, and take an Oath as aforesaid for the faithful discharge of the duties of their Offices re-

spectively, and that the pay-master-general shall receive eighty Dollars per Month with the rations and forage of a Major in full compensation for his services and travelling expences; and the deputy in addition to his pay and other emoluments thirty dollars per month in full compensation for his extra services and travelling expences" (copy, Hamilton Papers, Library of Congress; copy, George Washington Papers, Library of Congress).

2. Caleb Swan of Massachusetts was a veteran of the American Revolution. He had been paymaster of the United States Army since May 8, 1792 (*Executive Journal*, I, 124).

3. John Wilkins, Jr., a Pittsburgh businessman, had been a surgeon's mate during the American Revolution. On June 1, 1796, he was appointed quartermaster general of the Army (*Executive Journal*, I, 214).

4. Section 12 of "An Act for the better organizing of the Troops of the United States; and for other purposes" (1 *Stat.* 752) reads: "*And be it further enacted*, That to any Army of the United States, other than that in which the Quarter-master General shall serve, there shall be a deputy Quarter-master General, who shall be a field officer, and who, in addition to his other emoluments, shall be entitled to fifty dollars per month, which shall be in full compensation for his extra services and travelling expences, but the provisions of this Act are not to effect the present Quartermaster General of the Army of the United States, who, in case a Quarter-master General shall be appointed by virtue of this act, is to act as deputy Quarter-master General and shall hereafter have the rank of Lieutenant Colonel: And that to every Division of the Army, there shall be a Division quarter-master, who, in addition to his Other emoluments shall be entitled to thirty dollars pr month, which shall be in full compensation for his extra services and travelling expenses; and that to every Brigade there shall be a Brigade Quarter-master, who in addition to his other emoluments shall be entitled to twenty four dollars per month, which shall be in full compensation for his extra services and travelling expences; each of which Officers shall be chosen by the Quarter-master General from among the Regimental Officers" (copy, Hamilton Papers, Library of Congress).

From Chevalier de Colbert

[*New York*] *March 9* [*1799*]. Discusses at length his love for Catherine Church [2] and his desire to marry her. Asks Hamilton to serve as his counsel in his efforts to secure the lands granted by Georgia to Comte d'Estaing.[3]

ALS, Hamilton Papers, Library of Congress.
1. This letter is written in French.
Colbert served with the French navy during the American Revolution. Soon after the outbreak of the French Revolution, which he opposed, he went to England. He participated in the landing at Quiberon in June, 1795, and in the insurrection of Vendémaire in October of the same year. He then returned to England and in the winter of 1796–1797 came to the United States, where he remained until the end of the century. In 1800 he returned to Europe, where he traveled until 1802. He then settled in France.
2. Catherine Church was the daughter of John B. and Angelica Church.

3. In 1784 the Georgia legislature granted to Charles Henri Hector, comte d'Estaing, four tracts of land of five thousand acres each in Franklin County for his services during the American Revolution (S. G. McLendon, *History of the Public Domain of Georgia* [Atlanta, 1924], 45).

Estaing, who was guillotined in Paris in 1794, died without children. Colbert's claim to the land in question was based on the fact that he was Estaing's first cousin (see Robert Morris to William Constable, March 14, 1795 [LC, Robert Morris Papers, Library of Congress]; Colbert to George Washington, January, 1797 [ALS, George Washington Papers, Library of Congress]).

An entry in H's Cash Book, 1795–1804, under the date of May, 1799, reads: "To the Chevalier Colbert for *advance* toward expences incident to his land in Georgia   100" (AD, Hamilton Papers, Library of Congress).

From Rufus King [1]

London March 9. 1799

Dear sir,

By Mr. Erskine [2] whom I have introduced to you, I send you a Copy of the famous Map of So. america that Fayden has lately engraved: [3] it is a fac simile of the Spanish Map so carefully concealed at Madrid.

Fayden is employed in another Map upon the same scale of the Spanish Territories north of the Isthmus; it will be less accurate and authentic; but such as it is it will supply a desideratum. I am from many considerations restrained from saying what ought to be said, and must not be delayed, respecting this important Country. I am entirely convinced if it and its resources are not for us that they will speedily be against us.

Spain and Portugal are completely in check,[4] and the game may be terminated with them at the pleasure of France: the next step is plain and will be by and by unavoidable. What do we expect what without infatuation can we expect of France? Why then any further Reserves?

Yours Truly   R.K.

LC, New-York Historical Society, New York City.
   1. This letter concerns Francisco de Miranda's plans for the liberation of Spanish America. See Miranda to H, April 1, 1797, February 7, April 6–June 7, August 17, October 19–November 10, 1798; H to Miranda, August 22, 1798; King to H, May 12, July 31, October 20 1798, January 21, March 4, 1799; H to King, August 22, 1798; Timothy Pickering to H August 21–22, 1798.

1. David Montague Erskine was the son of Thomas Erskine, the first Baron Erskine, who was an English lawyer. In 1799 he married Frances Cadwalader, the daughter of General John Cadwalader of Philadelphia.

3. William Faden. For King's correspondence with Miranda concerning this map, see King to H, October 20, 1798, note 4.

4. By the Treaty of San Ildefonso, August 19, 1796, Spain became an ally of France (Georg Friedrich von Martens, *Recûeil des principaux Traités d'Alliance, de Paix, de Trêve, de Neutralité, de Commerce, de Limites, d'Echange etc. conclus par les puissances de l'Europe tant entre elles qu'avec les puissances et états dans d'autres parties du monde depuis 1761 jusqu'à présent*, 2nd edition [Göttingen, 1829], VI, 255–62). Portugal, an ally of England, was at war with France.

To James McHenry

private   New York March 10. 1799

Dr Sir

Ought it not to be a rule to forward from your department to the *Major* Generals, as they are passed, copies of all laws respecting the military establishment? At any rate you will oblige me by sending those of the session just finished.

I observe in the 5 § of the Recruiting Instructions,[1] filled up in Manuscript, the term of inlistment is *five* years. The law for augmenting the army [2] § 2 directs the inlistment to be "for and during the continuance of the existing differences between the Ustates & the French Republic." If there be any thing varying this, it has escaped me. Will you inform me? This inquiry is suggested by a new revision of the recruiting instructions.

As it may yet take time to prepare for me a complete list of the Officers of the army,[3] I should be glad to have one of the field Officers only, with a note of the stations or destinations to which they have been assigned. I want much to place them over the detached posts & to concenter the direction.

I observe the XIII § of the Recruiting Instructions [4] authorises the appointment of certain Courts Martial. Where is the power for this Regulation?

Sometime since I requested you to send me the organisation of the Officers as reported by the Commander in Chief.[5] You replied that no such document had come to you.[6] I imagine that I must not have expressed myself clearly for I well remember that the document, which I mean, was made out in Mr Lear's hand writing [7] for the purpose of being sent by you. It was an arrangement or distribution of the Officers who were nominated into Regiments batalions and Companies, assigning to each company, by their names, its proper complement of Officers.

It appears to me very important that the Regimental Pay Masters & Quarter Masters should be designated without delay. They are the proper organs through which all issues of monies & supplies ought to pass. If I remember rightly, in the late war, the Qr. Master & Adjutant were appointed by the Commander of the Regiment [8]— the Paymaster was designated by the Officers of each Regiment.[9] What has been the practice lately? Whatever be the mode I wish very much to be instructed to have the thing done.

Will it not be adviseable speedily to direct the field Officers of each Regiment to report for the consideration of the President an arrangement of the relative rank of their Officers in the Regiment? This will not work any inconvenience as to the corps, of which the Officers have not yet been appointed. And its being done will facilitate future operations.

Yrs. very truly   A Hamilton

Js. McHenry Esq

ALS, Columbia University Libraries; ALS (photostat), James McHenry Papers, Library of Congress; copy, in the handwriting of Philip Church, Hamilton Papers, Library of Congress.

    1. This is a reference to the 1798 edition of a War Department pamphlet entitled *Rules and Regulations Respecting the Recruiting Service.* See H to Jonathan Dayton, August 6, 1798, note 6. Article V reads: "Each recruit is to be enlisted for the term of   and to receive the bounty   but no part of the bounty to which a recruit is entitled, before joining his company or corps, is to be advanced until he shall have been sworn before a magistrate according to the form herein prescribed. The recruiting officer will be cautious to regulate the proportions of such advance, agreeably to law."

    In the 1798 edition in the George Washington Papers, Library of Congress, the first blank space is filled with the words "five years."

    2. This is a reference to "An Act to augment the Army of the United States, and for other purposes" (1 *Stat.* 604–05 [July 16, 1798]).

    3. See McHenry to H, February 4, 1799; H to McHenry, March 5, 1799.

    4. See H to Dayton, August 6, 1798, note 12.

    5. H to McHenry, February 16, 1799 (listed in the appendix to this volume).

    6. McHenry to H, February 19, 1799 (listed in the appendix to this volume).

    7. The lists in the handwriting of Tobias Lear are in the George Washington Papers, Library of Congress.

    8. H did not "remember rightly." In the general reorganization of the Army

which Congress enacted on May 27, 1778, it was provided: "That the adjutant and quarter master of a regiment be nominated by the field officers out of the subalterns, and presented to the Commander in Chief, or the commander in a separate department, for approbation; and that being approved of, they shall receive from him a warrant agreeable to such nomination" (JCC, XI, 542).

9. On June 25, 1776, the Continental Congress resolved "That a regimental pay master, who is not to be an officer of the army, be appointed by the said colonies to each of the said batallions . . ." (JCC, V, 479). On July 16, 1776, it was resolved "That a pay master be appointed to each regiment in the army of the United States . . ." (JCC, V, 564). The 1778 general reorganization of the Army provided: "That the pay master of a regiment be chosen by the officers of the regiment, out of the captains or subalterns, and appointed by warrant . . . : the officers are to risque their pay in his hands: the pay masters to have the charge of the cloathing, and to distribute the same" (JCC, XI, 542).

From Lewis Tousard

Newport [Rhode Island] March 10, 1799. Encloses a copy of his instructions from the Secretary of War.[1]

ALS, Hamilton Papers, Library of Congress.
1. James McHenry to Tousard, January 16, 1799 (LS, letterpress copy, James McHenry Papers, Library of Congress; copy, Hamilton Papers, Library of Congress).

McHenry's instructions to Tousard read in part: "1st. You will examine with all possible attention, the Points and Islands upon which Works have been erected, for the annoyance of Shipping and the defence of the harbour, and approach by water, to the Town of New Port.

"2d. You will weigh maturely, and state precisely, their several defects and advantages, and propose such works only to be undertaken, as shall appear indispensible. . . .

"3d. You will calculate the lines and angles of the plans, profiles &c. in order to the formation of a just opinion of the solidity, thickness &c. of the parts of each work, and of the whole, and exhibit a detailed statement of the quantity and price of the different materials, and the cost of workmanship, and labour of every kind, with every item of expence necessary to their completion. . . .

"4th. You will review Tamany hill in particular and the Island of New Port in general, so as to enable you to determine whether any real advantage can be derived from the erection of a Fort on the said hill. . . .

"5th. You will state the number of Men, and Cannon, necessary to the defence of each work.

"6th. It will be proper, that you should take the first opportunity to visit Marblehead. . . .

"7th. Portland is also to be visited, the works examined, their defects reported, and such alterations proposed for the further security of that harbour, as may appear indispensible.

"8th. It being important to place the fortifications for the defence of the harbour of Boston, in a respectable state, you will make a survey of the existing works, and report such repairs or additions to them, as may be thought necessary and indispensible to the security. You will give plans and estimates of the additions.

"It is foreseen, that to execute this trust will keep you in Towns where you must immediately incur a greater expence than if you was in Garrison, or on field duty with your Regiment; that it necessarily requires journeys to be made, and by removing you from the Command of a Post deprives you of the double rations you would there be entitled to receive. It is proper, I should not overlook the circumstances mentioned and that an Officer should not be compelled to waste his own means, while employed in extra service of so important a kind. You will therefore be allowed for yourself and servant, at the rate of two dollars and twenty five cents per diem while employed on this service, and remaining at Rhode Island, Marblehead, Portland, or Boston, and at the rate for travelling expences . . . of two dollars, for every forty miles when the distance does not exceed two hundred, and at the same rate for every thirty miles for all above two hundred, and not exceeding three hundred and fifty."

From Chevalier de Colbert

[*New York, March 11, 1799.*] Encloses documents to support his claim to lands granted Comte d'Estaing in Georgia.

ALS, Hamilton Papers, Library of Congress.
  1. This letter is written in French.
For background to this letter, see Colbert to H, March 9, 1799.

From William Armstrong [1]

New York, March 13, 1799. ". . . May I presume to request your good Offices in recommending my Brother in Law Mr Charles Ramsay" [2] as American consul "at the Havannah."

ALS, Hamilton Papers, Library of Congress.
  1. Armstrong was a New York City merchant.
  2. Ramsay, an American merchant who lived in Havana, was not appointed consul. On June 29, 1799, during the recess of the Senate, John Morton of New York received the appointment, which the Senate confirmed on December 6, 1799 (*Executive Journal*, I, 326).

From James McHenry

War Department 13 March 1799

private
Dear Sir
  I received your private letter of the 10th inst. last night.
  The mode in which the laws are published prevents me from re-

ceiving any of them sometimes for six weeks or two months after their being inacted, unless I take copies of them from the originals lodged with the Secry. of State and get them printed. This is what I have done with the organization [1] and eventual army acts,[2] and shall as soon as they are printed send you some copies.

The 5 Sect. of the recruiting instruction was filled up for inlistments in the 4 old Regiments and artillery corps.[3] For inlistments in the 12 Regiments of Infantry & 6 troops of Light Dragoons, it will be filled up "for and during the continuance of the existing differences between the U.S. and French Republic" [4] according to your conception.

The 13 sect. of the recruiting instructions [5] is founded on the 3 article of the articles of war under the head administration of justice, art. 3, p 32 & 33.[6] It is supposed that the officer commanding in each district will be a field officer.

I expect to be able to send you in a few days the list of officers conformably to the schedule A formed & reported by Gen Washington [7] with the exception of the alterations and directions of which you have been informed and that have originated in non-acceptances.[8]

In your letter of Febry the 16th [9] it is said "It is very material to me to have without delay the distribution of the additional 12 Regts & troops of horse &c &c" It is certain I understood this request to apply to the distribution of the 4 Regts. of Infantry and the cavalry, stations for eight of the 12 Regiments of Infantry only having been fixed on by the Commander in Chief. Where did the Commander in Chief contemplate to station these 4 regts. and the cavalry? I shall subjoin to the list aforesaid the officers appointed from Connecticut, arranged into companies by Mr Tracy [10] agreeably to the principle of contiguity or local convenience.

Quarter Masters, adjutants & Pay-Masters to Regiments by the late organization act must be *Lieutenants* and *as such* appointed by the Presidemt. Whether the law admits of the choice of Pay master from among the Lieutenants under the new organization being made by the officers, I cannot answer at this moment, my copy of the act being with the Printer. The pay master by the act, must give bond & security for the faithful discharge of his duties at least it was so intended.[11]

When you receive a copy of the schedule A you will determine whether to take the Captains and their subalterns as there arranged or to refer to their respective colonels for a new and different distribution.

I recvd. your letter dated the 5th inst on the 11th. I shall attend as soon as possible to its contents.

We have got an insurrection in Northampton County and adjoining parts,[12] which will require the presence of some of the military force to aid the Marshall to secure offenders. A proclamation will issue to day declaring its existence &c. It is contemplated to employ on this occasion the volunteers only,[13] a late law having authorised the President to use these in all cases in which he is authorised to employ Militia.[14]

Yours sincerely   James McHenry

Majr Gen Hamilton

ALS, Hamilton Papers, Library of Congress; ADfS, James McHenry Papers, Library of Congress.

1. "An Act for the better organizing of the Troops of the United States; and for other purposes" (1 Stat. 749–55 [March 3, 1799]).

2. "An Act giving eventual authority to the President of the United States to augment the Army" (1 Stat. 725–27 [March 2, 1799]).

3. For Article V of the 1798 edition of a War Department pamphlet entitled Rules and Regulations Respecting the Recruiting Service, see H to McHenry, March 10, 1799, note 1.

4. This quotation is taken from Section 2 of "An Act to augment the Army of the United States, and for other purposes" (1 Stat. 604 [July 16, 1798]).

5. For Article XIII of the 1798 edition of a War Department pamphlet entitled Rules and Regulations Respecting the Recruiting Service, see H to Jonathan Dayton, August 6, 1798, note 12.

6. McHenry is referring to Section III of Article 14 of the articles of war, which was called "Administration of Justice" in the 1794 edition of Rules and Articles for the Better Government of the Troops. See H to Dayton, August 6, 1798, note 11. Section III reads: "Every Officer commanding a regiment or Corps, may appoint of his own regiment or corps, Courts-Martial, to consist of three Commissioned Officers, for the trial of offences, not Capital, and the inflicting Corporeal punishments, and decide upon their sentences. For the same purpose, all Officers commanding any of the garrisons, forts, barracks, or other place where the troops consist of different Corps, may assemble Courts-Martial, to consist of three commissioned officers, and decide upon their sentences" (JCC, XXX, 317).

7. For the table exhibiting the proportion of officers and men in each state, see McHenry to George Washington, November 10, 1798, printed as an enclosure to Washington to H, November 12, 1798. See also H's draft of Washington to McHenry, first letter of December 13, 1798.

8. See McHenry to H, February 4, 1799.

9. This letter is listed in the appendix to this volume.

10. This document is entitled "Schedule B" and is divided into two parts.

The first, called "Connecticut Appointments," is signed by Uriah Tracy and dated March 12, 1799. The second part of the document is entitled "Appointments for the Army" (copy, Hamilton Papers, Library of Congress).

11. For the legislation concerning the points raised in this paragraph, see "An Act for the better organizing of the Troops of the United States, and for other purposes" (1 Stat. 749-55).

12. This is a reference to Fries's Rebellion, the term used to describe the resistance in Bucks, Northampton, and Montgomery counties in Pennsylvania to a Federal property tax imposed by two acts of Congress. The acts in question were "An Act to provide for the valuation of Lands and Dwelling-Houses, and the enumeration of Slaves within the United States" (1 Stat. 580-91 [July 9, 1798]) and "An Act to lay and collect a direct tax within the United States" (1 Stat. 597-604 [July 14, 1799]). John Fries, an itinerant auctioneer and a captain of a militia company in both the American Revolution and the Whiskey Insurrection, is generally considered to have been the leader of those opposed to the collection of the tax.

After threats of violence and armed opposition had made it impossible for the responsible officials in the three counties to carry out the provision of the law, President Adams on March 12, 1799, issued a proclamation calling out the Army to suppress "combinations too powerful to be suppressed by the ordinary course of judicial proceedings" (*Gazette of the United States, and Philadelphia Daily Advertiser*, March 12, 1799). Fries, who with other leaders of the opposition was quickly captured, was twice tried for treason and sentenced to be hanged (Francis Wharton, *State Trials of the United States During the Administrations of Washington and Adams* [Philadelphia, 1849], 458-648). In a letter dated May, 1800, he petitioned Adams for a pardon, and on May 23, 1800, the President issued a proclamation granting a "full, free, and absolute pardon, to all and every person or persons concerned in the said insurrection . . ." (Wharton, *State Trials*, 641-42).

13. This is a reference to the Volunteer Corps originally authorized by "An Act authorizing the President of the United States to raise a Provisional Army" (1 Stat. 558-61 [May 28, 1798]). See the introductory note to H to James Gunn, December 22, 1798.

14. This is a reference to Section 7 of "An Act giving eventual authority to the President of the United States to augment the Army" (1 Stat. 726 [March 2, 1799]), which authorized the President to use the volunteers ". . . in all cases, and to effect all the purposes for which he is authorized to call forth the militia by the act, entitled 'An act to provide for calling forth the militia, to execute the laws of the Union, suppress insurrections, and repel invasions, and to repeal the act now in force for these purposes.' "

From William S. Smith

New York, March 13, 1799. "I take the liberty of suggesting for your consideration, whether it would not be conducive to the good of the service, to authorize the officers to engage persons in the capacity of Servants particularly attached to their persons, with the pay and rations of a Soldier, exclusive of the established Rank & file of the Regiment, so that under no consideration the Battalion

Soldiers should be taken from the line, to fill those menial Stations. . . ."

ALS, Hamilton Papers, Library of Congress.

To Oliver Wolcott, Junior

New York March 13. 1799

Dear Sir

It is natural for people where their interest is concerned to die hard. Mr. Juhel,[1] the bearer of this, goes to Philadelphia to lay before you some supplementary evidence with regard to the Ship Germania, which he hopes may vary your determination.[2] At his request I give him this line to you merely to say—that he is a Merchant of this City of Reputation, and so far as his conduct has fallen under my observation of candour and probity. I wish him success as far as personal considerations alone are concerned & no general rule of policy is contravened.

But having occasion to write you on a subject connected with the law prohibiting intercourse with the French Territories—I ought not to withhold from you an opinion which I deliberately entertain. It is that whatever may have been the intention of the legislature in framing this law,[3] it is in fact so worded, that it will be a very violent thing in a Court of Justice to pronounce that the prohibition of the 3d. Section extends to any but a *French Bottom*.

The leading and prominent feature of the Prohibition as to the subject, is a *"French Ship or Vessel."* There are subsequent words which by implication look to vessels of other descriptions but they may be understood consistently with this *main & preliminary feature*.

Thus the provision excepts Ships or Vessels "bona fide the *property of*, or hired or employed by Citizens of the UStates." A french bottom, by her built & registry, may be the property of Citizens of the UStates. Again these words will be satisfied by supposing that they intend Ships & Vessels which were French immediately before the Voyage in question but were purchased for the Voyage by Citizens of the UStates.

And this construction will better consist with the principles which govern the interpretation of penal laws than to extend the prohibition which is to constitute the penalty beyond the letter by implication & force of a proviso which is introduced to make an *exception* to the general terms.

I am well aware of the Course which in such a case policy will dictate to the Executive—but if this view of the law be correct it may afford an argument for a mitigated course where no actual intention to evade appears.

Yrs. truly   A H

O Wolcott Esq

ALS, Connecticut Historical Society, Hartford.

1. John Juhel was a French merchant who lived in New York City and specialized in importing wine.

2. This is a reference to the petition of Juhel to the United States District Court for New York on February 21, 1799. As the agent for the firm of Rendtorff and Moller of Hamburg and consignee of the ship's cargo, Juhel asked the court to allow the ship *Germania*, which arrived on February 14, 1799, to enter the port of New York. He contended that the ship should be exempted from the law prohibiting trade with French territories because it was owned solely by Danish subjects and its cargo was the property of Rendtorff and Moller. He also maintained that the cargo of wines, brandies, and liquors, shipped from Bordeaux to New York, belonged to Rendtorff and Moller until it was sold in New York by their agents, John Juhel and Company. The court ordered that the facts and papers collected at the inquiry be sent to the Secretary of the Treasury for a decision (RG 21, Minutes of the United States District Court for the Southern District of New York, 1789–1801, National Archives).

On March 7, 1799, Wolcott stated that the "arrival of the said Ship Germania within the limits of the United States subsequent to the first Day of December last, was not occasioned by distress of weather or want of provision, and moreover that the said Ship and her Cargo are wholly owned by persons not resident within the United States and not Citizens thereof." He concluded that "said Ship Germania be required to depart with her Cargo out of the limits of the United States avoiding all unnecessary delay" (RG 21, Minutes of the United States District Court for the Southern District of New York, 1789–1801, National Archives).

Under the date of February 6, 1799, H made the following entry in his Cash Book, 1795–1804: "John Juhel Dr Costs for Opinion concerning . . . intercourse Bill & Petition &c to Court 20" (AD, Hamilton Papers, Library of Congress).

3. This is a reference to Section 3 of "An Act to suspend the commercial intercourse between the United States and France, and the dependencies thereof" (1 *Stat.* 565–66 [June 13, 1798]). This section reads: "*And be it further enacted,* That from and after due notice of the passing of this act, no French ship or vessel, armed or unarmed, commissioned by or for, or under the authority of the French Republic, or owned, fitted, hired or employed by any person resident within the territory of that republic, or any of the dependen-

cies thereof, or sailing or coming therefrom, excepting any vessel to which the President of the United States shall grant a passport, which he is hereby authorized to grant in all cases where it shall be requisite for the purposes of political or national intercourse, shall be allowed an entry, or to remain within the territory of the United States, unless driven there by distress of weather, or in want of provisions. And if contrary to the intent hereof any such ship or vessel shall be found within the jurisdictional limits of the United States, not being liable to seizure for any other cause, the company having charge thereof shall be required to depart and carry away the same, avoiding all unnecessary delay; and if they shall, notwithstanding, remain, it shall be the duty of the collector of the district, wherein, or nearest to which, such ship or vessel shall be, to seize and detain the same, at the expense of the United States: Provided, that ships or vessels which shall be *bona fide* the property of, or hired or employed by citizens of the United States, shall be excepted from this prohibition until the first day of December next, and no longer: And provided that in the case of vessels hereby prohibited, which shall be driven by distress of weather, or the want of provisions into any port or place of the United States, they may be suffered to remain under the custody of the collector there, or nearest thereto, until suitable repairs or supplies can be obtained, and as soon as may be thereafter shall be required and suffered to depart: but no part of the lading of such vessel shall be taken out or disposed of, unless by the special permit of such collector, or to defray the unavoidable expense of such repairs or supplies."

See also "An Act further to suspend the Commercial Intercourse between the United States and France, and the dependencies thereof" (1 *Stat.* 613–16 [February 9, 1799]).

To Henry Knox

New York March 14. 1799

My Dear Sir

The inclosed letters, as I conclude from others which accompanied them, have been a long time getting to hand. There was a moment, when their object seemed to present itself as one not intirely chimerical—but the probability has diminished. Tis however a thing on which the mind may still speculate as in the Chapter of extraordinary events which characterise the present wonderful epoch.

My judgment tells me, I ought to be silent on a certain subject— but my heart advises otherwise and my heart has always been the Master of my Judgment. Believe me, I have felt much pain at the idea that any circumstance personal to me should have deprived the public of your services or occasioned to you the smallest dissatisfaction.[1] Be persuaded also that the views of others, not my own, have given shape to what has taken place—and that there has been a serious struggle between my respect and attachment for you and the impression of duty. This sounds, I know, like affectation, but it is nevertheless the truth. In a case, in which such great public interests were concerned, it seemed to me the dictate of reason and propriety, not to exercise an opinion of my own, but to leave that of others, who could influence the issue, to take a free course. In saying this much my only motive is to preserve, if I may, a claim on your friendly disposition towards me, and to give you some evidence that my regard for you is unabated.

Adieu My Dear Sir   Very much Yrs.   A Hamilton

General Knox

ALS, Massachusetts Historical Society, Boston.
1. This is a reference to the relative rank of H and Knox in the Additional Army. See the introductory note to George Washington to H, July 14, 1798.

To James McHenry [1]

Private   New York March 14. 1799

Dear Sir

It is a construction of the law warranted by usage that the President shall appoint the requisite number of Lieutenants & leave three of them to be designated for Quarter Master & Pay Master in the manner practiced in the late army. But if this is supposed not to be a good construction the end may be produced by making it a rule that recommendations shall come through the described Channels to the President & that unless for some extraordinary reason he will as of course nominate or appoint.

But whatever be the mode pray let it be adopted at once & put in a train of execution that these essential officers may be appointed.

Yrs. truly   A H

P.S. Since writing the above, it has occurred to me as worthy of consideration whether it will not be expedient to inlist indiscriminately for all the corps and to insert an alternative in the oath as to the term of service thus—"for and during the continuance &c. or for the term of five years at the option of the UStates." As there are soldiers of both descriptions to be inlisted I incline to think the laws will bear out the alternative in point of executive propriety—& the option would be evidently valuable. The principal question is whether soldiers would not more readily inlist for the casual duration of *existing differences* than for the known term of five years.[2]

James McHenry Esq

ALS, The Sol Feinstone Collection, Library of the American Philosophical Society, Philadelphia; ALS (photostat), James McHenry Papers, Library of Congress; copy, Hamilton Papers, Library of Congress.
   1. For background to this letter, see H to McHenry, March 10, 1799; McHenry to H, March 13, 1799.
   2. See the introductory note to H to James Gunn, December 22, 1798, for an explanation of the various terms of service.

From Ebenezer Stevens

New York 14th March 1799

Dear General

I am often troubling you, but certain that you are my best friend, believe you will pardon the freedom I take with you. The secretary of War has written me on the Subject of Compensation for my Services, and that I might have a salary or be paid by a Commission on the amount of my Disbursemts but I am at a loss to act, in choosing the method of Compensation because it involves much consideration and places me in a delicate situation to decide. I inclose you the Extract of my Letter of the 15th January last [1] in answer to the above proposal from him and will leave it with you to advise me, which will be best. You must be sensible, that my time has been taken up wholly in attending to public matters. One of my Clerks was employed in keeping the accounts and making payments, almost constantly, while I was employed out of doors. The secretary of War does not know what service I have rendered, nor will he ever have a proper idea of it, unless you are so obliging to Explain to him. I wish to know of a certainty what I am to receive, that I may judge, whether it will be most for my interest to hold the appointment, or to resign it.

The amount of my disbursements is from 55 to 60000 Dollars and a Commission pr. Centum of what I might justly expect, would be considered high, without the peculiar services were explained—but this I have been particular in describing, in the inclosed Extract, and I will rely on your friendship to get the Compensation fixed.

Will you permit my first Clerk, who was with me throughout the whole operation, to explain this business to you, he has no Interest in it, whether I get much or little; and can give a faithful detail of my services—and perhaps, his description may be of use in respect to fixing your opinion of what I ought to have.

I am with sentiments of esteem   Dear Genl.   Your obliged friend & hble Servt.   Ebenezer Stevens

Alexr. Hamilton Esqr.

ALS, Hamilton Papers, Library of Congress; copy, New-York Historical Society, New York City.
1. Extract, in Stevens's handwriting, Hamilton Papers, Library of Congress.

To George Washington

New York March 14. 1799

Sir

I have the honor to send you the extract of a letter of the 8th instant (received two days since) from the Secretary of War, together with the Section of the Act to which it relates.

I am entirely of opinion with him, as to the expediency of causing the Pay Master General to reside at the seat of Government. But as the measure is of importance, and especially as the act expressly refers the point to the "Commander in Chief"—I did not think my self at liberty to act without your previous decision.

I request instruction on the point, as soon as shall be convenient, unless you shall think it proper to give yourself the necessary orders to the Pay Master General.

With perfect respect & attachment   I have the honor to be   Sir Your obed servt   A Hamilton

Lt General Washington

ALS, George Washington Papers, Library of Congress; two copies, in the handwriting of Philip Church, Hamilton Papers, Library of Congress; copy, Hamilton Papers, Library of Congress.

To George Washington

[*New York, March 14, 1799.*[1] *Second letter of March 14 not found.*]

1. In the "List of Letters from General Hamilton to General Washington," Columbia University Libraries, two letters from H are listed for March 14, 1799.

From James McHenry

War Department
15th. March 1799

Sir,

A Proclamation of the President of the United States, a Copy of which I enclose, will inform you that a combination to defeat the execution of the Laws, for the valuation of lands, and Dwelling houses, have existed, in the Counties of Northampton Montgomery, and Bucks in the State of Pennsylvania,[1] and proceeded in a manner subversive of the just authority of the Government, and that certain Persons in the County of Northampton exceeding one hundred in number, have been hardy enough to perpetrate certain acts, which he is advised amount to Treason, being overt acts of levying war against the United States; of the Presidents determination to call forth military force, to suppress the combinations, and cause the Laws aforesaid to be executed; and of his Command to all per⟨sons⟩ being insurgents as aforesaid and all others whom it may concern, on or before Monday next; being the 18th instant, to disperse and retire peaceably to their respective abodes.

The President has thought it most advisable upon the present occasion, to employ the Volunteer Companies[2] accepted by him in pursuance of the authority vested in him by the 7th Section of the

"Act giving eventual authority to the President of the United States to augment the Army," passed the 2d. March instant,[3] for the most active duties.

Among the reasons, which have induced to this determination, are the following—1st The Law just cited, of the 2d. instant. 2d. An Opinion, grounded upon information of the existing state of things, in the Counties, in insurrection, that a portion of the Volunteers, which may be drawn from the City of Philadelphia, will be competent to the object intended. 3d The utility and propriety of permitting (if possible) the militia to remain on their farms, at a time, when husbandry might suffer, by their absence.

Orders have accordingly been issued, to Brigadier General Macpherson, of the Provisional army,[4] to hold in readiness to march,[5] at the shortest notice, all the Companies of Volunteers, within the State of Pennsylvania, except a Company at Pittsburgh, with the intention however, unless circumstances change, of employing only a certain part of them.

It has occurred, that it would render a less number of volunteers necessary, and that their operations, would be facilitated, and made more certain, by the presence of a body of regulars, whose positions, might be such, as to act forcibly upon the fears of the insurgents, and cover the movements of the volunteers. I have therefore ordered Captain Shoemaker [6] of the Infantry, who is at Frederick Town Maryland, with a company of recruits, and Captain Irvine [7] who is at Carlisle, with a Company of artillerists and engineers to march forthwith, and rendezvous at Reading. I shall also put in motion a company of the Artillerists, from Fort Mifflin to rendezvous at the same place.[8] You will be pleased to direct two companies, say one from West Point to march by the nearest route, to Eastern Northampton County Pennsylvania, and one from New York, and Lieutenant Boote [9] with his recruits at Brunswick, to march by the nearest route, and rendezvous at Newtown Bucks County in the State of Pennsylvania—to wait at their destinations for orders from General Macpherson, the artillerists will march with muskets only, as the requisite pieces, will be sent from this City.

I shall instruct immediately, the Quarter Master General,[10] to authorize Colonel Stevens,[11] of New York, to cause to be provided, the means of transportation, and quarters on their route for the two companies, and the detachment under Lt Boote—and also quarters at the places of rendezvous.

Inclosed is a letter to the Contractor at New York,[12] directing him to appoint fit persons, to proceed with the Detachments, to provide for them rations, on the route, as well as at the places of rendezvous.

Time being now too pressing, to allow of instructing the Quarter Master General, and writing to the Contractor as just mentioned, you will effect both purposes, by your orders.

Perhaps you will think it proper, to order Mahlon Ford [13] Major of the Artillerists, at present in the Jersey near Morris Town, and unemployed, to join the Detachment, as there will be a Majors command of regular troops, should circumstances, render an union of the whole, at Bethlehem or any other place necessary.

You will direct the commanders of the different parties, to write me from every Post town advising of their progress—and also of their arrival at their destinations.

The Troops to take with them, Tents and other necessary equipage.

I am Sir   with great respect   your obedt. hble servant

James McHenry

If I have omitted any thing proper to be done or ordered you will be pleased to supply the omission.[14]

Alexander Hamilton
Major General of
the Armies of the United States

LS, Hamilton Papers, Library of Congress.

1. For Fries's Rebellion and John Adams's proclamation, see McHenry to H, March 13, 1799, note 12.

2. See McHenry to H, March 13, 1799, note 13.

3. 1 Stat. 725-27. See McHenry to H, March 13, 1799, note 14.

4. For William Macpherson's appointment, see the introductory note to H to James Gunn, December 22, 1798.

5. McHenry to Macpherson, March 14, 1799 (copy, James McHenry Papers, Library of Congress).

6. See McHenry to Peter Shoemaker, March 14, 1799 (LS, letterpress copy, James McHenry Papers, Library of Congress).

7. See McHenry to Callender Irvine, March 14, 1799 (LS, letterpress copy, James McHenry Papers, Library of Congress).

8. See McHenry to Joseph Elliott, March 14, 1799 (LS, letterpress copy, James McHenry Papers, Library of Congress).

9. William R. Boote was a second lieutenant in the Third Regiment of Infantry.

10. John Wilkins, Jr.

11. Ebenezer Stevens.

12. See McHenry to William Colfax, March 15, 1799 (LS, Hamilton Papers, Library of Congress).

13. John Adams recommended on February 20, 1799, that Ford be promoted to major in the First Regiment of Artillerists and Engineers, and the Senate approved the appointment on February 22 (*Executive Journal*, I, 315, 317).

14. This sentence is in McHenry's handwriting.

To James McHenry

New York March 15. 1799

Sir

I have digested some alterations in and additions to the Recruiting Instructions [1] which I now send for consideration and decision. The nature of each will announce its motive so as to render little comment necessary.

A few remarks will be seen in the margin of some of the clauses.

I shall be glad of a determination as soon as may be in order to the transmission of the instructions that they may be considered and understood—so that the officers may be ready to act the moment orders shall be given to recruit.

With great respect & esteem I have the honor to be Sir Yr. Obedt servant

P.S. I agree entirely in the opinion expressed in your letter of the 8th. instant (which was delayed in its transmission) respecting the residence of the Pay Master General. But as the act expressly requires the intervention of the "Commander in Chief" I have thought it right to ask the orders of General Washington.[2] I hope this will appear to you in the same light.

The Secretary of War.

ADf, Hamilton Papers, Library of Congress.

1. This is a reference to the 1798 edition of a War Department pamphlet entitled *Rules and Regulations Respecting the Recruiting Service*. See H to Jonathan Dayton, August 6, 1798, note 6.

McHenry had asked H to revise this pamphlet. See McHenry to H, February 4, 1799.

2. H to George Washington, March 14, 1798.

[E N C L O S U R E]

Alterations & Additions to the Recruiting Instructions [3]

To Section III   No foreigner by birth shall be enlisted unless he
                        shall have become a citizen of the UStates and
                        shall have resided at least one year in the County
                        where he shall be enlisted.[4]

To Section VI   These attestations must always be taken in the
                        presence of and certified by a Commissioned offi-
                        cer and must be forwarded to the Inspector
                        General (through the Commanding Officer of
                        the Regimental circle where there is one) and
                        must be sent by the Inspector General to the
                        Department of War. The terms of any engage-
                        ment which may be subscribed by recruits must
                        conform to the tenor of these attestations.[5]

To Section VII   Provided that the form of the Oath must be as
                        above directed.[6]

3. AD, Hamilton Papers, Library of Congress.
4. For Article III of the 1798 edition of *Rules and Regulations Respecting
the Recruiting Service*, see McHenry to H, February 4, 1799, note 16.
5. Article VI of the 1798 edition of *Rules and Regulations Respecting the
Recruiting Service* reads: "Every recruit, at the time of his enlisting, or within
six days afterwards, is to be brought before the next justice of the peace, or
the chief magistrate of any county or corporation, not being an officer of the
army, or where recourse cannot be had to the civil magistrate before the judge
advocate, to be sworn. In their attestations the day of enlistment as well as the
day and place of attesting, must be distinctly specified according to the form
annexed (No. 1). The utmost care is to be taken in filling them up correctly
and legibly. No recruit is to be sent to his regiment, corps, or general rendezvous on any pretence whatsoever, whose enlistment and attestation have not
been completely and finally executed conformably to the above directions, and
all the attestations of recruits raised in every two weeks, unless otherwise
ordered, are to be invariably transmitted to the officer commanding in the
district."
    In the margin opposite this paragraph H wrote: "It will be seen how it is
proposed to fill up the blanks in the Oaths. The chief point is to inlist 'for
the infantry the cavalry or the Artillery of the UStates' without restriction to a
particular corps which may embarrass."
6. For Article VII of the 1798 edition of *Rules and Regulations Respecting
the Recruiting Service*, see H to Dayton, August 6, 1798, note 11. The "form of
the Oath" to which H is referring reads:
                        "(No. 1.)

To Section VIII Each District will be divided into subdistricts or quarters corresponding with the number of Companies to be raised therein. And for the present the districts will be united into Regimental circles each circle to be under the superintendence of the Commandant of the Regiment.[7]

To Section IX At the foot of each return which shall bear the the name of any foreigner or foreigners by birth there shall be a note or notes specifying how when and where each such foreigner became a citizen. The returns shall be forwarded to the Inspector General to be by him sent to the Department of War. While the districts are united in circles, they shall be transmitted through the respective commandants of circles & shall be open to their Inspection.[8]

"I born in aged feet hair, having been enlisted on the day of do hereby agree to accept the present bounty and pay conformably to the act of Congress and such ration as is or shall be established by law. And I do solemnly (swear or affirm as the case may be) to bear true allegiance to the United States of America, and to serve them honestly and faithfully in the for and during the unless sooner discharged, against their Enemies or opposers whomever, and to observe and obey the orders of the President of the United States, and the orders of the Officers appointed over me according to the Rules and Articles of War."

7. Article VIII of the 1798 edition of *Rules and Regulations Respecting the Recruiting Service* reads: "The recruiting parties will be distributed in districts, and a field officer, when one can be so employed without injury to the service, stationed in each district.

"The field or other officer appointed to this duty will have the command of all recruiting parties in his district. He will give a conditional approval of the recruits whom he may judge fit for service, except in cases where regiments are so quartered, as to render it in point of distance, equally convenient for the recruits to be sent to their respective head-quarters."

In the margin opposite this paragraph H wrote: "While the Commandant of Regiments are in a situation to attend their agency will not only be natural but extremely useful."

8. Article IX of the 1798 edition of *Rules and Regulations Respecting the Recruiting Service* reads: "The senior officer in each quarter shall report weekly to the officer of the district, the number and strength of the parties therein, specifying the names of the commissioned officers belonging to them, and whether they have been absent during the week, the number of recruits under his command, with the names of those enlisted since the last return, and a description of their persons, the bounty advanced, the arms, accoutrements and clothing delivered to them, and the incidents that have taken place during the week; the whole to be drawn up according to the form annexed, No. 2; and all letters, containing the returns, shall be addressed to the Secretary of War, and to the care of the officer of the district."

To Section XIII [9]

To Section XIV   There being now an Inspector General the orders will pass through him. They will be sent by him to the Commandants of Circles, where there are such, and the returns and reports must also in this case pass through them.[10]

To Section XVI   The provision respecting *Serjeant Major* is to take effect only where there is not a Serjeant Major of the Regiment present to perform the Duty.[11]

To Section XIX   These certificates must be transmitted to the Inspector General to be by him sent to the Secretary of War.[12]

To Section XXX   A like receipt must be taken and transmitted for all arms accoutrements and cloaths which shall be issued to the Recruits. Every receipt taken must be in the presence of a commissioned Officer & certified by him.[13]

9. For Article XIII of the 1798 edition of *Rules and Regulations Respecting the Recruiting Service,* see H to Dayton, August 6, 1798, note 12. For H's comments on Section XIII, see H to McHenry, March 10, 1799.

10. Article XIV of the 1798 edition of *Rules and Regulations Respecting the Recruiting Service* reads: "The officers commanding districts will receive orders from the Secretary of War 'till an inspector general shall be appointed, specifying the returns (other than those mentioned) they are to send and to whom. All returns and reports are to come from the officers commanding districts, and nothing direct from the recruiting officers."

11. The relevant part of Article XVI of the 1798 edition of *Rules and Regulations Respecting the Recruiting Service* reads: "The officer commanding a district will be allowed to appoint a subaltern officer (not employed on the recruiting service) to do the duty of adjutant in the district with an allowance of   a day in addition to his pay and returns, and two sergeants one to act as sergeant-major and the other as clerk to the district, these sergeants to receive an allowance of   a day each. . . ."

12. Article XIX of the 1798 edition of *Rules and Regulations Respecting the Recruiting Service* reads: "When recruits abscond or refuse to go before a magistrate to be attested within the time prescribed, an attested certificate of the fact is to be immediately sent to the officer commanding in the district, in order to its being transmitted to the Inspector-General or Secretary of War, and also to the Head-Quarters of the regiment or corps, as no allowance will be made to the recruiting officer for recruits so absconding or refusing to go before a magistrate, and afterwards returned as deserters, although they should be sent under an escort to their regiments, corps, or general rendezvous, unless such certificate shall have been previously received."

13. Article XXX of the 1798 edition of *Rules and Regulations Respecting the Recruiting Service* reads: "Each recruiting officer shall transmit monthly to the officer of the district a duplicate receipt, signed by each recruit, for the

To Section XXI [14]   The monies will be furnished to the Commanding officers of Districts by the respective regimental Paymasters according to directions from
the commanding Officers of the Regiments.
When there is a Pay Master present in any circle
the settlements will be made with him. In every
case they will be only provisional & subject to
revision by the Department of War.[15]

To Section XXIII   The Commander of the District will immediately
report the same to the Commander of the Circle
and he to the Inspector General at his quarters
and to the Commanders of all the circles who
shall be nearer to his post than the Quarters of
the Inspector General to the end that measures
every where may be taken for the apprehension
of deserters & the prevention of impositions by
them [16]

---

bounty he shall have received within that period. This regulation is to be
strictly observed 'till the recruits have joined their respective corps, after
which it is not allowable for the officer to make them any payment on account
of their bounty. It is to be understood also, that no credit will be allowed to a
recruiting officer in the settlement of his accounts, which is not substantiated
by such receipts, thus transmitted, and that whatever part of the bounty remains due to a recruit on his union with his corps or company shall not be
paid by the recruiting officer, but be stated in the first pay-roll after his arrival,
and paid to him at the same time as his pay."

14. H is mistaken, for he is referring to Article XXXI rather than Article
XXI of the 1798 edition of *Rules and Regulations Respecting the Recruiting
Service.* Article XXXI reads: "The officer commanding each district will receive and be charged in the first instance, with all the monies which shall be
required within his district for the recruiting service. He will, using a sound
discretion, distribute such portions of the same, from time to time, to the
officers of the respective recruiting parties, as the service shall demand, exact-
ing from such recruiting officers a punctual settlement on correct vouchers at
the proper periods."

15. In the margin opposite this paragraph H wrote: "It is in my judgment a
very material point of order to make the Regimental Pay Master the organ of
all Disbursements."

16. H is referring to Article XXXIII rather than Article XXIII of the 1798
edition of *Rules and Regulations Respecting the Recruiting Service.* Article
XXXIII reads: "The commanding officer at each rendezvous will sign returns
for the issues of all rations and other necessary supplies for the troops, and on
the Saturday of each week, the returns made in the week are to be taken up,
and one general return made out and signed for the rations received in the
course of the week, noticing the daily issues.

"On the desertion of a recruit, besides the usual exertions and means to be
employed on such occasions, the recruiting officer will transmit, as soon as pos-

sible, a description of the deserter to the field officer of the district, and will cause all descriptions of deserters that may be sent to him, to be entered in a book kept for that purpose, and will use his endeavors to discover and apprehend all deserters."

To William S. Smith

New York, March 15, 1799. "I have received your letter of the 13th instant and thank you for the suggestions contained therein. . . ."

Df, in the handwriting of Philip Church, Library of Congress.

From Stephen Van Rensselaer

Albany, March 15, 1799. ". . . The Assembly have a Bill for electing Electors of Presdt & Vice President [1]—it will pass—are you of opinion that it would be proper for the Senate to concur? Unless NYork gives us a different representation the federalist are lost.[2] Whether we have any object now since the late conduct of the President [3]—you are a better judge than We if it is however necessary that we should still perservere pray let me hear from you. our friends are extremely pressing that I should write to you on this subject. . . ."

ALS, Hamilton Papers, Library of Congress.
1. See H to John Jay, February 12, 1799, note 1.
2. Before the 1798 election the majority of members of the House of Representatives from New York had been Federalists. In the 1798 election six Republicans and four Federalists were chosen to represent New York.
3. This is a reference to President Adams's peace mission to France. See Theodore Sedgwick to H, February 19, 1799, note 1, February 22, 25, 1799; Timothy Pickering to H, February 25, 1799.

From George Washington

[*Mount Vernon, March 15, 1799.*[1] *Letter not found.*]

1. "List of Letters from G—— Washington to General Hamilton," Columbia University Libraries.

To William R. Boote [1]

New York, March 16, 1799. "In consequence of orders from the Secretary of War, I am to desire, that you proceed with the party under your command to New Town in Bucks County—for which purpose you will join and accompany a detachment which will leave this quarter on Monday the 18th. instant, taking the orders of the commanding Officer of this detachment. . . . Let no time be lost."

LS, The Sol Feinstone Collection, Library of the American Philosophical Society, Philadelphia; ADf, Hamilton Papers, Library of Congress.
   1. For background to this letter, see James McHenry to H, March 13, 15, 1799.

To Adam Hoops [1]

New York March 16. 1799

Sir

You will be pleased to cause the two companies, which have been put under marching orders, to proceed on Monday next to New Town in Bucks County Pennsylvania, where they will receive further orders either from the Secretary of War or from General Mc.Pherson. The Contractor is directed to provide a boat to convey them to Amboy—whence they will march to Brunswick and thence by the most convenient route to New Town. The Commanding Officer must from every Post Town advise the Secretary of War of his progress—as he must also do of his arrival at the place of destination. From Brunswick, he must inform him of his intended route to New Town. There he will be joined by Lieutenant Boote with a party of Infantry. Col Stevens will appoint a person to accompany the detachment in capacity of Quarter Master. A competent number of tents, if they are to be had, must be sent with the party. No avoidable delay must be permitted to occur.

It is believed though not known that there is a contractor for the supply of provisions in New Jersey. This may be ascertained at

Brunswick and arrangements taken accordingly. If not, the person to be sent by Col Stevens will be authorized to supply the deficiency.

You will give instructions to the Commanding Officer in conformity with this letter.

With consideration & esteem   I am Sir   Your Obed ser

ADf, Hamilton Papers, Library of Congress.
1. For an explanation of the contents of this letter, see James McHenry to H, March 15, 1799. See also McHenry to H, March 13, 1799; H to William R. Boote, March 16, 1799; H to Ebenezer Stevens, March 16, 1799.

To James McHenry [1]

New York, March 16, 1799. "Though I have not as yet complete materials for arranging all the States into Districts and subdistricts— I now submit to you an arrangement as to some of them, in order that the recruiting service may begin in these, when you deem other things sufficiently mature to commence it. There occurs no important reason why it should not be successively undertaken. On the contrary, so far as I have the means of judging, I should conclude that it would be expedient to begin partially and extend as the provision of supplies extends. An arrangement will now be submitted for the States of Connecticut New York New Jersey & Pensylvania & Delaware. But if necessary, I am prepared to offer what may answer the end for the other States except the three most Southern and Kentucke & Tenessee. A plan for the two Carolinas & Georgia has been asked of General Pinckney,[2] but there has not been time to obtain his reply. If the business were otherwise prepared, there could be no inconvenience in referring it to him to make the distribution definitively. The arrangement for Tennessee & Kentucke may also be confided to persons on the spot. . . . As it is possible that in practice, it may be found convenient to alter some of the Districts & subdistricts—I request a general power for this purpose. . . ."

ADf, Hamilton Papers, Library of Congress.
1. For background to this letter, see McHenry to H, February 4, 8, 1799; H to McHenry, February 6, 11, March 5, 1799; "Circular on Recruiting Service," February 18–19, 1799; H to Henry Lee, February 18, 1799; Theodore Sedgwick

to H, February 22, 1799; H to Charles Cotesworth Pinckney, second letter of March 7, 1799. The following letters, all of which are listed in the appendix to this volume, were written in answer to the "Circular on Recruiting Service," February 18–19, 1799: Samuel Livermore to H, February 22, 1799; Ray Greene to H, February 23, 1799; Aaron Ogden to H, February 23, 1799; Thomas Lloyd Moore to H, February 25, 1799; Simon Elliott to H, February 28, 1799; Ebenezer Huntington to H, February 28, 1799; William S. Smith to H, February 28, March 11, 1799.

2. H to Pinckney, second letter of March 7, 1799.

To Ebenezer Stevens [1]

New York, March 16, 1799. "You have been requested to provide a competent person to attend in quality of Quarter Master, the detachment of Troops which is to proceed from Fort Jay on Monday next. . . ." [2]

LS, New-York Historical Society, New York City; ADf, Hamilton Papers, Library of Congress.

1. For background to this letter, see James McHenry to H, March 15, 1799; H to William R. Boote, March 16, 1799; H to Adam Hoops, March 16, 1799.
2. Stevens endorsed this letter: "Ansd 16." Letter not found.

From Ebenezer Stevens

[*March 16, 1799.* Stevens endorsed the envelope of Hamilton's letter of March 16, 1799: "Ansd 16." *Letter not found.*]

To Jonathan Dayton [1]

Private   New York March 18th. 1799

Dr Sir

The enclosed letter to Major Ford [2] directs him to take the command of some detachments of Artillerists which have been ordered to march as auxiliaries to the Volunteers under Mc:Pherson destined against the Northampton Insurgents.

Be so good as to have it forwarded by an expeditious and certain conveyance by express if none other equally prompt and certain offers.

Do me the favor also to inform me confidentially what is Ford's character as an Officer and as to political principle.

Yrs truly   A Hamilton

Copy, in the handwriting of Philip Church, Hamilton Papers, Library of Congress.
   1. For an explanation of the contents of this letter, see James McHenry to H, March 15, 1799.
   2. H to Mahlon Ford, March 18, 1799.

To Mahlon Ford [1]

New York March 18. 1799

Sir

Two companies of Artillerists have just been detached from this Quarter under the command of Capt Henry [2] of the 2 Regiment for New Town in Bucks County Pensylvania by the way of Amboy & Brunswick. At Brunswick they will be joined by Lt Boote with a party of Infantry. And Capt Shoemaker with a company of Infantry from Frederick Town Maryland and Capt Irvine with a Company of Artillerists from Carlisle Pensylvania and another company of Artillerists from Fort Mifflin have been ordered to rendezvous at Reading. It is contemplated that these corps may be united under one command, to act in support of the Pensylvania volunteers against the Insurgents of Northampton.

You are designated to this command and accordingly you will forthwith proceed to Brunswick & thence until you fall in with the Detachment first mentioned & you will take the command of the same & you will open a correspondence that the other companies which are ordered to Reading.

But as to the Union of the whole Corps and as to every ulterior movement you will take the orders of the Secy of War & of Brigadier General Mc.Pherson with whom you will for this purpose open a correspondence.

Capt Henry will communicate to you his instructions which will also serve as your guide.

I am Sir   Your Obed ser

Immediately on receipt of this letter you will please to acknowlege
it.

Major Ford
near Morris Town

ADf, Hamilton Papers, Library of Congress.
    1. For background to this letter, see James McHenry to H, March 13, 15,
1799. See also H to William R. Boote, March 16, 1799; H to Adam Hoops,
March 16, 1799; H to Ebenezer Stevens, March 16, 1799; H to Jonathan
Dayton, March 18, 1799.
    2. John Henry was a captain in the Second Regiment of Artillerists and
Engineers.

From James McHenry

War department, March 18. 1799

Sir,
    I have received your letter of the 15 instant with alterations and
additions proposed to be made to the recruiting instructions. These
have been considered, generally adopted, and with some further
alterations will be put into the hands of a printer to day, and a
sufficient number of Copies sent you as soon as they shall be printed.
    With great respect   I am Sir   Your obedient servant
                                                        James McHenry

Major General Hamilton

LS, Hamilton Papers, Library of Congress.

To James McHenry [1]

Private   New York March 18. 1799

    Beware, my Dear Sir, of magnifying a riot into an insurrection, by
employing in the first instance an inadequate force. Tis better far to
err on the other side. Whenever the Government appears in arms
it ought to appear like a *Hercules*, and inspire respect by the display

of strength. The consideration of expence is of no moment compared with the advantages of energy. Tis true this is always a relative question—but tis always important to make no mistake. I only offer a *principle* and a *caution.*

A large corps of auxiliary cavalry may be had in Jersey New York Delaware Maryland without interfering with farming pursuits.

Will it be inexpedient to put under marching Orders a large force provisionally, as in eventual support of the corps to be employed—to awe the disaffected?

Let all be well considered.

Yrs. truly   A Hamilton

James Mc.Henry Esq

ALS, Hamilton Papers, Library of Congress; copy, in the handwriting of Philip Church, Hamilton Papers, Library of Congress.
1. For background to this letter, see McHenry to H, March 13, 15, 1799.

To James McHenry [1]

New York March 18th. 1799.

Sir

In compliance with the object of your letter of the 15. instant, I have put in motion two companies of Artillerists from Fort Jay (Henrys and Cochrans) [2] who are to embark at ten this morning for Amboy and to proceed from thence by way of Brunswick to New Town in Bucks County. There (at Brunswick) Lt: Boote with his party is instructed to join them. The two companies as they march will exceed together seventy men, and will go provided with all necessaries except that the number of tents will be incomplete. If we had known the wants of Lt: Bootes party, they could not have been supplied from this place. Inclosed are the directions to him. Tomorrow you will be advised of the exact number of men and tents.

I trust you will excuse the deviation from your order as best calculated to fulfil its object. The march from West Point would have been attended with great difficulties and much delay. The River will speedily open and if necessary, the substitute can then be brought from West Point to Fort Jay. In the mean time no inconvenience is likely to ensue.

A person will go by concert between Coll. Stevens and the Contractor in the double capacity of Quarter Master and Commissary. He can easily do both duties. Perhaps indeed the expence of such a person might have been saved, had there been a sufficient number of Officers with the companies. But it has been impracticable to send more than one Captain and two Lieutenants.

I defer till tomorrow to give any order to Major Ford.[3] Were it not that the presence of Major Hoops was requisite here at a Court Martial which is to trye Captain Frye[4] and Doctor Osborne,[5] it would perhaps be more in order to send him with the major part of his Command. But this point is reserved

With great respect & esteem   I am   Sir   Your obed servt.

A Hamilton

Secy. at War

Copy, in the handwriting of Philip Church, Montague Collection, MS Division, New York Public Library; copy (photostat), in the handwriting of Philip Church, James McHenry Papers, Library of Congress; copy, Hamilton Papers, Library of Congress.

  1. For an explanation of the contents of this letter, see McHenry to H, March 13, 15, 1799. See also H to William R. Boote, March 16, 1799; H to Adam Hoops, March 16, 1799; H to Ebenezer Stevens, March 16, 1799; H to Jonathan Dayton, March 18, 1799.

  2. Walter L. Cochran, like John Henry, was a captain in the Second Regiment of Artillerists and Engineers. Cochran, a resident of New York, was a son of Elizabeth Hamilton's aunt Gertrude Schuyler Cochran, the wife of Dr. John Cochran.

  3. See H to Mahlon Ford, March 18, 1799.

  4. Captain Frederick Frye had been charged with "Irregular and disorderly conduct" (Adam Hoops to H, March 9, 1799, listed in the appendix to this volume).

  5. Doctor Samuel Osborne, a surgeon's mate, had been charged with disobeying his commanding officer (Osborne to McHenry, January 29, 1799, enclosed in McHenry to H, January 30, 1799, listed in the appendix to this volume).

From James McHenry

Philadelphia, March 19, 1799. Encloses "copies of two Letters from General Wilkinson, one dated Novr. 6,[1] the other Decr. 6, 1798. . . ."[2]

LS, Hamilton Papers, Library of Congress.

1. In this letter James Wilkinson wrote in part: "It is impossible for me to ascertain the Fact, but I have cause to believe that Governor [Manuel] Gayoso [de Lemos], notwithstanding his professions . . . has held connivance with [Zachariah] Cox, & entered into some population project with Him. . . . I observe that much discontent & disgust, prevail among the People. . . . Three things appear to me Essential to the repose & prosperity of this Territory —The presence of the Judges—The Settlement of the right of Soil & Jurisdiction—and the Establishment of some principle, by which to ascertain & fix Individual rights to Land, granted within the Territory . . ." (ALS, Hamilton Papers, Library of Congress; copy, Hamilton Papers, Library of Congress).

2. In this letter Wilkinson wrote to McHenry concerning the condition of the troops at Natchez, the escape of Zachariah Cox from Governor Winthrop Sargent's custody, and relations with the Indians (copy, Hamilton Papers, Library of Congress). Sargent was appointed governor of the Northwest Territory on May 7, 1798 (*Executive Journal*, I, 272, 274).

To James McHenry

Private   New York March 19. 1799

Dear Sir

I understand, that the Officers for Connecticut have been appointed & their names published,[1] but I have seen no paper containing them. If so, be so good as to send me the list, and if there have been other appointments since the lists transmitted me, pray let them be added.

Pursuant to your very proper idea of having at the seat of Government of the Chiefs of Different Departments [2]—it seems to me adviseable that you should have some *Agent* for the Commissariate or *provision-branch*, to whom applications may be addressed & from whom orders may issue to the different Contractors or sub Agents.

Did those provisions of the "Act for organising &c." which declares that the Adjutant General shall be *ex Officio* Depy. *Inspector General* [3] & which allow the Inspector General a Secretary continue in the Bill when passed? [4]

Is there any arrangement which prevents me calling for the assistance of the Adjutant General when I deem it necessary?

Yrs. truly   A Hamilton

The Secy at War.

ALS (photostat), James McHenry Papers, Library of Congress; copy, Hamilton Papers, Library of Congress.

1. The Connecticut officers were appointed on February 13, 1799 (*Executive Journal*, I, 311–12). On February 14, 1799, a list of the Connecticut appointments appeared in the *Gazette of the United States, and Philadelphia Daily Advertiser.*

2. See McHenry to H, March 8, 1799.

3. See Section 14 of "An Act for the better organizing of the Troops of the United States; and for other purposes" (1 *Stat.* 749–55 [March 3, 1799]).

4. Section 26 of "An Act for the better organizing of the Troops of the United States; and for other purposes" reads: "*And be it further enacted*, That there shall be allowed to the inspector-general, in addition to his allowance as major-general, and in full compensation for extra services and expenses in the execution of his office, the sum of fifty dollars per month, and that he shall be allowed a secretary to be appointed by himself, with the pay and emoluments of a captain" (1 *Stat.* 755).

To James McHenry

New York March 19. 1799

Sir

Yesterday about two oClock, the detachment proceeded on its destination.

It consisted of one Captain (Henry) Two Leutenants, Two Musicians, Ninety two Non Commissioned Officers & Privates. They had seventeen Tents with them.[1]

I send you a plan for dividing Connecticut, New York, New Jersey, Pensylvania and Delaware into Districts and subdistricts.[2]

It appears to me desireable that the recruiting service should begin in these states without delay, and adviseable that bounty money, cloathing and other articles should be furnished in the proportion of one half the whole number of men to be enlisted. According to this ratio, there will be required for each of the four regiments of Infantry, Four Thousand two hundred & twenty four Dollars making in the whole 16896 Dollars. For one Troop of Horse to be raised in New Jersey. Three hundred & Eighty four Dollars together with the cloathing and other articles mentioned in the inclosed return.[3]

I wait your sanction to put the business in motion in these states. But previously I am anxious that the Regimental Staff be appointed or at least that persons to act in these capacities be selected with the prospect of being appointed. I request your authority for this purpose.

Has any plan been determined upon for providing the requisite number of horses.

With great respect I have the honor to be &c &ca   your Obedient Servant

To The Secretary of War

P.S. It is requisite for me to know where contracts exist for the supply of provisions & Quarter Master Stores & the names of the Contractors.

Df, in the handwriting of Philip Church, Hamilton Papers, Library of Congress.
   1. For an explanation of this and the preceding paragraph, see McHenry to H, March 13, 15, 1799; H to McHenry, March 18, 1799. See also H to William R. Boote, March 16, 1799; H to Adam Hoops, March 16, 1799; H to Ebenezer Stevens, March 16, 1799; H to Jonathan Dayton, March 18, 1799; H to Mahlon Ford, March 18, 1799.
   2. Enclosure not found, but see H to McHenry, March 16, 1799.
   3. This enclosure is dated March 20, 1799, and is entitled "Return of Articles requisite for four Regiments of Infantry to be recruited on the proportion of one half the whole number of the non Commissioned Officers & Privates of the respective Corps" (ADS, Hamilton Papers, Library of Congress).

From Samuel H. Stackhouse and John Shute

New York, March 19, 1799. "We beg Leave in Behalf of ourselves and sixty more young men to offer our services & to Engage to repair without Delay to the Seat of Insurrection in Northampton County Pensylvania. . . ." [1]

ALS, Hamilton Papers, Library of Congress.
   1. See James McHenry to H, March 13, 15, 1799.

From John De Barth Walbach [1]

Wilmington [Delaware] March 19, 1799. "Ayant appris par les papiers publics, Que le Gouvernement Se preparoit a faire marcher des troupes, contre les insurgés, du Canton de Northampton; [2] et le Régiment, au quel j'ai l'honneur d'appartenir, n'etant pas encore levé; je prend la liberté, Général, de vous addresser la presente, pour offrir mes Services comme volontaire, Si vous le juger apropos. . . ." [3]

ALS, Hamilton Papers, Library of Congress.
  1. Walbach, a native of Germany, had been commissioned a lieutenant in the light dragoons on January 8, 1799 (*Executive Journal*, I, 298, 303).
  2. See James McHenry to H, March 13, 15, 1799.
  3. On the envelope H wrote: "The offer declined—desired to come to New York."

From Jonathan Dayton

Elizabeth town [New Jersey] March 20th. 1799

Dr. Sir,

Your favor dated the 18th. was received this morning. The letter accompanying it for Majr. Ford [1] was immediately sent to the Post office at Newark, from whence a Mail goes this afternoon to Morris.

In answer to your enquiry respecting the Major's character, I can assure you that he has ever been considered a good officer, and that I know him to be perfectly sound, correct & firm in his political principles. His family have been long looked up to as the head of the Federalists in Morris county, and have uniformly opposed themselves to the torrent of Jacobinism, more prevalent there than in any quarter of our State. He was a Subaltern in my father's Regiment [2] during the Revolutionary war, & acquitted himself always well.

I presume that neither the Secy. of War nor yourself are ignorant, that that portion of the people of N. Jersey which are most contiguous to the scene of insurrection [3] are that most uninformed, & consequently not the best disposed to support the Government & Administration. Some, more than common, precautions should therefore be taken in the selection of their Militia, or of their officers more particularly, if any draft should be made upon them for this service. As a certain number will doubtless be ordered to hold themselves in readiness to support Mc.Pherson, if required, it may be well for you to give a cautionary hint to our Governor [4] by letter.

I am Dr. General Yours very sincerely   Jona: Dayton

Majr. General Hamilton

ALS, Hamilton Papers, Library of Congress.
    1. H to Mahlon Ford, March 18, 1799.
    2. Elias Dayton of Elizabethtown, New Jersey, served throughout the Amer-
ican Revolution and in 1783 was promoted to the rank of brigadier general.
See "Continental Congress. Report on the Promotion of Colonels," January 7,
1783. Dayton was a member of the Continental Congress in 1787 and 1788 and
of the New Jersey Assembly in 1791 and 1792 and from 1794 to 1796.
    3. See James McHenry to H, March 13, 15, 1799.
    4. Richard Howell.

From John Henry [1]

Princeton [New Jersey]
March 21st. 1799

Sir

Presuming that it will be satisfactory to you to know the progress
I have made with the detachment under my command, I have the
honor to inform You that I arrived at Princeton late last evening.

The fatigue that necessarily results from marching in unfavourable weather, thro roads as deep and bad as can well be concieved,
renders several of the detachment unable to continue with the main
body so that for the sake of making some necessary arrangements
and to bring the party to the general Rendezvous in as complete
order as possible, I am induced to halt the whole of this day which
is very inclement. Should tomorrow prove more favourable I propose marching to Newton Bucks County; if otherwise I shall remain
at Trenton tomorrow evening, and proceed early the following
morning.

I foresaw that the soldiers would wear out the shoes they brought
from Fort Jay in a very short time; and the necessity of providing
against deficiences of this Kind suggested to me the propriety of
ordering Lieut. Boote to deliver to the Quarter master a quantity of
extra clothing which his detachment had no occasion for. I hope I
was not incorrect in issuing such an order to Mr. Boote, being only
authorized by the necessity of the case.

The officers and soldiers are in high spirits, and should they come
into real service, I am sure my expectation that they will acquire
reputation is well founded.

The detachment including the party under the command of Lieut. Boote consists of one hundred and thirty effective men.

I have the honor to be with the most profound respect & Consideration   your obedient Serv   John Henry
                                                                Capt 2d Regt. commg

Major General Hamilton

ALS, Hamilton Papers, Library of Congress.
    1. For background to this letter, see James McHenry to H, March 13, 15, 1799; H to McHenry, March 18, 19, 1799. See also H to William R. Boote, March 16, 1799; H to Adam Hoops, March 16, 1799; H to Ebenezer Stevens, March 16, 1799; H to Mahlon Ford, March 18, 1799.

From James McHenry

War department 21. March 1799.

Sir

I received your letter dated the 5. March on the 11. instant and would have replied sooner to its contents had it been possible to have furnished you with the necessary information & documents required.

The enclosed schedule A [1] exhibits the appointments which have been made conformably to the list of names presented by the General Officers with the exceptions noticed in my letter of the 21 of January Ultimo, and also the names of the persons appointed to fill the vacanies of those who were omitted or had declined accepting their appointments.

I have preserved in this schedule the numeri[c]al order and same classifications of Company Officers which is observed in the original list alluded to with an exception or two which is noticed and which it may be proper should take place.

This Schedule distinguishes that Gentlemen who have accepted of their appointments, those who have declined and those *who have not been heard from.*

Df, Hamilton Papers, Library of Congress; Df, letterpress copy, James McHenry Papers, Library of Congress.
    1. "Schedule A," which is undated, lists the appointments to the Army arranged by regiments (D, Hamilton Papers, Library of Congress).

Schedule B[2] exhibits the appointments made in Connecticut for One regiment, resolved into Companies by the Honble Uriah Tracy.

You will now have before you a complete list of Officers for ten regiments and three companies of Infantry and six companies of Cavalry excepting the Surgeons and Surgeons Mates and three additional Lieutenants annexed to each Regiment by the law of the 3d. March Ultimo.[3]

It was not possible to make the latter appointments after the law passed and before the departure of the President for Quincy. I have written to him however on the 16 instant,[4] to be authorized to select fit persons for those Offices—and to signify to them their appointments.

Want of time and other good reasons render it necessary, that I should leave it with you, in every case, in which an association of Company Officers or Majors different from the Schedule, may appear to be more conducive to harmony and promotive of the public service, to make the same definitively or provisionally as you may determine.

I leave it also to you to fix the *number* each regiment of Infantry is to be known by, beginning with number 5. and ending with Number 16. The old establishment has Number 1. 2 3. and 4. You will also be pleased to exercise the same discretion in fixing the relative rank of the *Company Officers* in each regiment, but it will be proper to leave the subject of the relative rank of the Lieutenant Colonels and Majors to future arrangements or till after the appointments for the whole establishment shall be completed.

You will of course communicate to me what changes you may make and the determinations you may adopt relative to the objects submitted.

The aforesaid documents will enable you to put the last hand to our arrangements for commencing the recruiting service.

It will be necessary for me to be informed 1st. Of the *stations* of your recruiting rendezvouses, or the stations in each State where it will be proper to provide *rations* and to *send the* Cloathing—2d.

2. See McHenry to H, March 13, 1799, note 10.

3. See Section 1 of "An Act for the better organizing of the Troops of the United States; and for other purposes" (1 *Stat.* 749–55 [March 3, 1799]).

4. ALS, Adams Family Papers, deposited in the Massachusetts Historical Society, Boston.

The *quantity of Cloathing to be sent to each rendezvous.* 3d. The Officers you may approve of who are to act as regimental Paymasters to the regimental Circles or districts and the Quantum of recruiting money proper to be remitted to each. 4th. The *numbers of* the regiments for which Cloathing is required in order that the buttons of the Clothing sent may correspond therewith. The Buttons are numbered from one to sixteen and the Cloathing made up regimentally.

I have reflected upon the idea whether it might not be expedient to *inlist indiscriminately* [5] for all the Corps. There are serious objections to such a measure. 1. As the recruit expects his Cloathing immediately upon his being inlisted, and as the Artillery regimental differs from the Infantry, and the Cavalry from both, it would be wholly an affair of Chance, whether upon a final distribution of the men, they would not have to change coats with each other. 2. Admitting the destination to be made by each recruiting Officer, such an arrangement would induce the necessity of having a deposit of the three kinds of regimentals at each recruiting place of rendezvous. 3d. It might obstruct the recruiting service inasmuch as men inlist with less reluctance or more willingness, when they know the Company Officers they are to serve under.

Upon the whole it may be attended with fewest present inconveniencies to follow the old practice.

With respect to the points upon which you require further information.

1. The regulations which are intended by this paragraph of my letter of the 4. of February "It is expected &c. that you will give orders that the Garrisons &c. make returns and observe the inclosed regulations." Until you can be charged with the regulations intended by this paragraph which I have not yet had time to make out no more will be necessary than to require the Garrisons to furnish their usual returns agreably to usage and existing regulations on that subject; those for the War department to the *proper* Officers of that department, and those to the *commanding* General to yourself or other proper Officer.

2. The report of the Purveyor of Supplies showing the quantities of the different articles of Cloathing &c.

5. See H to McHenry, March 14, 1799.

This report was forwarded on the 15. instant.[6]

3. The Schedule of the Officers who have accepted their appointment with the places of their residence.[7]

4. The list of Officers at present employed on the recruiting service and their places of rendezvous.[8]

5. The list of the names of all the Officers of the Army (old establishment) classed according to their respective regiments or Corps with the dates of their Commissions.[9]

These were transmitted on the 8. of March in a blank Cover.

The *Returns* &c. accustomed to be made to the War Department:

1. Returns of Ordnance Cloathing and military Stores to the Superintendant of Military Stores, Mr. Hodgdon.

2. Returns of Quarter Master Stores to the Quarter Master General. The Quarter Master General will stand charged for all supplies for his department by the Superintendant of Military Stores.

3. Returns by the Quarter Master General to the Superintendant of Military Stores exhibiting the stores distributed by him & persons chargeable with the same.

4. Return of Troops monthly.

5. Return of Troops on the first of October in every Year, noting the number whose terms will expire in every month.

I do not recollect at this moment *other returns* than what I have just enumerated.

It will be necessary in examining this subject and revising the returns accustomed to be made to provide for such other returns as will exhibit at *what* period each soldier receives his Clothing that

6. If McHenry enclosed this report in a letter dated March 15, 1799, the letter has not been found. For the "report of the Purveyor of Supplies," see Tench Francis to McHenry, March 12, 1799 (copy, Hamilton Papers, Library of Congress).

7. In the Hamilton Papers, Library of Congress, is an undated document listing the officers of the infantry and cavalry of the Additional Army who were appointed in December, 1798, and January, 1799, arranged by rank.

8. "Return of the several recruiting rendezvous in the United States, and the Names of the Officers recruiting" (D, with additions in H's handwriting, Hamilton Papers, Library of Congress).

9. In the Hamilton Papers, Library of Congress, is an undated list of the officers of the old Army. It includes all the officers of the infantry, artillery, and cavalry and is endorsed in H's handwriting: "Return of Officers in the cavalry Artillery and 4. Regiments previous to the late promotions. List of new promotions within."

frauds may be obviated and should any neglect in the Soldier render it necessary to furnish him with any additional article of dress, that a proper deduction may be made out of his pay for the same.

The channels of supply and the persons who administer them. All quarter Masters supplies in the hands of the Quarter Master General or his deputies are considered as subject to the orders of the Commander of the Army or Commandant of any division of the Army. The distribution of certain Stores and the quantity allowed for the consumption of Companies &c is fixed by regulations.

Quarter Masters supplies for recruiting parties where there is no Deputy or Quarter Master are obtained from the Contractor to the rendezvous and distributed according to fixed regulations.

When Agents of the Department of War may be called upon to furnish any post or posts with Quarter Masters or other articles it is by special instructions from the Secretary of War.

Where Contracts for supplying the Army or any parts thereof exist copies of the Contract are furnished the commanding General to whose troops or posts they have relation. These Contracts enable the commanding General to call for certain deposits of provisions &c. according to the nature of the service.

It is the duty of the Commander in Chief or Commander of a separate Army &c. to cause to be forwarded estimates of Military Stores—Cloathing, Quarter Masters Stores, Medicines &c. so as to enable order to be taken for their seasonable purchase and transportation to the Army posts or recruiting rendezvouses.

I send you by this days mail Ninety copies of the recruiting instructions revised and amended,[10] and request you will return to me those (now obsolete) that were lately sent to you.[11] You will see that I have adopted most of your alterations and additions [12] and where I have departed from them or added others, the reasons will be evident to you without the necessity of comment.

You are authorized to fill up the blank in Section 2d. in the fol-

10. McHenry is referring to the March, 1799, edition of a War Department pamphlet entitled *Rules and Regulations Respecting the Recruiting Service.* See H to Jonathan Dayton, August 6, 1798, note 6.

11. See McHenry to H, December 18, 28, 1798; H to McHenry, March 5, 10, 1799.

12. See H to McHenry, March 10, 15, 1799. H's revisions of *Rules and Regulations Respecting the Recruiting Service,* except for his criticism of Article III, were incorporated in the new edition of this pamphlet.

lowing words. "Musicians excepted, for the Infantry who is not five feet five inches in height; for the Cavalry who is less than five feet four inches, or more than five feet ten inches in height. Each recruit must be not less than eighteen nor more than forty years old, unless he shall have served before in the Army of the United States, nor of those who have served before shall there be more than eight admitted into a Company or troop who shall exceed forty six Years. Each Recruit must also be."

In filling up the Blank in article the 5 and the Oath you will preserve the distinctions of the law.[13]

I have also forwarded a number of copies of regulations to be observed in the delivery and distribution of fuel and straw to the Garrisons on the Sea Coast and recruiting parties,[14] and regulations respecting salutes.[15]

General Washington informed me that he put the project of regulations mentioned in my letter of the 4. of February into your hands. Possibly it may be among your papers, or possibly the General may have packed it up with his own.

Inclosed are copies of the act for the better organizing[16] of the Troops of the United States and for other purposes passed the 3d. of March 1799,[17] and an act giving eventual authority to the President of the United States to augment the Army" passed the 2d. March 1799.[18] being all the late military laws I have been able to get printed.

By the fourteenth section of the former act it is provided that "the adjutant General of the Army shall be ex officio Assistant Inspector General." If you conceive this Officer necessary to the due performance of your present duties you will be pleased to inform me, that he may be ordered into service.[19]

13. See H to McHenry, March 10, 1799; McHenry to H, March 13, 1799.
14. *Regulations to be Observed in the Delivery and Distribution of Fuel and Straw to the Garrisons on the Sea Coast. Given at the War Office of the United States in Philadelphia, This Twenty-Sixth Day of December, A. D. 1797. By Order of the President* (Philadelphia: Printed by William Ross, 1797).
15. McHenry issued the "regulations respecting salutes" from the "War office of the United States" on January 14, 1797 (copy, James McHenry Papers, Library of Congress).
16. In MS, "orgazining."
17. 1 *Stat.* 749–55.
18. 1 *Stat.* 725–27.
19. See H to McHenry, March 19, 1799. William North had been appointed to this position on July 19, 1798 (*Executive Journal*, I, 292).

As I have written this letter under a pressure of important business it is very possible I may not have fulfilled in my answers the Objects of your inquiries. Of this you will judge and return them upon me wherever I have been deficient, or may not be clearly understood.

I have the honor   to be with great respect   Your obedient servant

Major General Alexander Hamilton

From John J. U. Rivardi

Niagara [New York] March 21st. 1799.

Sir,

I was honored yesterday Night with your letters of the 15th.[1] Ult. & 1st. Inst. The Post Setting of again this Morning & my being Tormented with the fever will I hope Serve as an Apology for my laconism & for any incoherence which may Slip in my Answer.

Permit me first, Sir, To express my happiness at Seeing myself under the imediate orders of an Officer whom I have allways revered for his abilities & patriotism. I rejoice Sincerely at the Idea that in future My communications will not remain as they have been hither To unnoticed for it really appeared to me a Kind of conflict who Should Sooner be tired; myself of writing, Sending returns &ca or the Person who received them not to answer.

By Next Mail I Shall forward To you all the reports concerning this Garrison also a correct Plan of Detroit unless my health Should absolutely prevent me. The Annexed plan of Niagara [2] with the remarks accompanying it has twice been Sent by me To the board of War. As To The discipline of the troops under my comand I have done my utmost for Supporting it & met in consequence with a liberal Share of abuse in Beache's democratic paper.[3] In the present

ALS, Hamilton Papers, Library of Congress.

1. See "Circular to the Commanding Officers in Northern and Western United States," February 15, 1799.

2. An undated drawing of Fort Niagara may be found in the Hamilton Papers, Library of Congress.

3. This is apparently a reference to the [Philadelphia] Aurora. General Advertiser, which had been founded by Benjamin Franklin Bache in 1794. Al-

Situation of this Post garrisoned as it is by thirty nine Men Officers, Artificers, Extradutymen included—little can be done. A launce Corporal & three Men is our Guard detail & even that could not be Kept up without difficulty a few days ago the greatest part of that Small aggregate being without any clothing although they had been in that Situation for almost a whole year. A great cause of disorder in the Posts which I have Seen is the irregular payment of the troops —who being Seven or Eight months & Sometimes more without pay cannot procure Number of Small articles essential To Their cleanliness and comfort. They get discouraged—& when they receive at once a large Sum, it is Squandred away in riot without the least advantage but on the contrary with infinite detriment to Them—had every Corps a Military Chest with one or Two Months in advance —Payments might be made even as in Prussia weekly—& there would be a possibility of defraying expenses in case of desertion. Now the Officers are obliged To Take that money from their own Purse. Another inconvenient under which we labour is that the Soldier whose time expires is forced either to go To the Board of war for his Money or To take a certificate of pay due, which he negotiates at considerable loss—these circumstances & the want of funds for recruiting have made us lose a great number of valuable men who would have reinlisted had they had a prospect of being paid & clad regularly. As To the Quarter Master's department nothing being allowed To The Officer entrusted with it—a refusal of undertaking the trouble & responsibility ensues of course. I have by dint of entreaties & persuasion got the Surgeons mate [4] To act in that capacity *pro amore Dei* but he is horribly Tired of it, as he never received any funds To pay the men employed in that department & the bills incurred with Brittish Merchants for Necessaries indispensable To The garrison—Such as Stationary, Tools &ca. &ca. the want of which has been represented these eighteen months past. All these Evils are doubly felt as we are within Six hundred yards & in habits of friendship with a Garrison of three hundred men com-

---

though Bache had died on September 10, 1798, the paper, with some interruptions, continued publication and was frequently referred to as "Bache's paper."

4. Dr. John G. Coffin of Massachusetts was appointed a surgeon's mate in the Corps of Artillerists and Engineers on May 31, 1794 (*Executive Journal*, I, 159, 160). The *Executive Journal* incorrectly prints Coffin's first name as "Nathaniel."

pletely equiped & regularly paid.[5] The Situation of Oswego was Still
more deplorable when I received the last information—being all in
rags there was no more any parade & the Officer comanding [6] wrote
to me that he was in a Situation degrading To a Gentleman.

I Shall take the liberty of making one More observation with regard To The Artillery. This is the only Service in the World perhaps except the Brittish were the men are incumbered with long
coats. In france where they had them they were always left with
the arms when Stacked & vest with Sleeves put on previous To a
detachment entering the battery. Coats like those of the Infantry
with yellow tapes would in my opinion perfectly answer the purpose. I mention yellow tapes because Such triffling ornaments being
denied To The Artillery have within my Knowledge induced numbers To inlist in preference in the Infantry. I Should also recomend
for the Artillery long flat bayonets Sharp on both Sides & Short
pieces—these bayonets having an astonishing advantage as they answer as Sabres. I am informed that the old English dragrope exercise
(which they have abandoned themselves) is resumed by us instead
of the French mode of manœuvering with Slings, I can only Say
that I am very Sorry for it.

Now Sir, I Shall Take the liberty of Answering your letter of the
first of March with the frankness of a Soldier when he knows that
he writes To a Man of honor.

I feel with Sincere gratitude the mark of confidence which you
are pleased To give me by entrusting To me the care of visiting
the different Posts mentioned in your letter—please To excuse the
prolixity of what I have To observe on this Subject.

When I was honored with my comission—I was much elated with
the trust—hastened To my Regiment where unfortunately I Soon
found my Ideas of Service totally overturned—first by the mode of
life & Spirit of liberty of the Officers and men—Secondly by the
Strange insurrection against Coll. R.[7] then considered as an honest

5. This is a reference to Fort George, the British post, which was located
near Newark (later Niagara, Ontario) and was directly across the Niagara
River from Fort Niagara.

6. Lieutenant Nanning J. Visscher was the commanding officer at Fort
Oswego.

7. This is a reference to Stephen Rochefontaine who was appointed lieutenant colonel commandant of the Corps of Artillerists and Engineers on
February 25, 1795 (*Executive Journal*, I, 173-74), and who was exceedingly

man even by his enemies. I remained his only friend & Should have been So had the causes of complaint been greater because discipline is blind & because that affair was conducted in my opinion with as Much indecency as impropriety.[8] My Conduct in that business was followed by a Coolness on the Side of the Officers even of my own battalion. Major Burbeck [9] at that time Strongly urged To be relieved—it would have been Major Touzard's [10] tour—but I was ordered To Mackinac, as that Officer's affairs call'd him To The West Indies. I chearfully obeyed & was at considerable expense To move my family—Mrs. R—— having presented me with a Son three Months before. I arrived after a dangerous Journey at Detroit & was preparing To proceed To my destination when Genl. Wilkinson on an application of Major Burbeck To be continued at Mackinac granted the request & thus after much trouble & expense I was left at Fort Lernoult (an appendage of Detroit) at the head of a few Artillerymen transferred To That corps from the disbanded Dragoons &ca. After remaining ten Months during which with all possibile œconomy I Spent double my pay every thing being extravagantly dear & Not enjoying the advantages of Comanding Officers—I asked To be Sent to Niagara as the year's Comand of Captn. Bruff [11] was elapsed (a Term fixed by the then General orders) [12]

---

unpopular with his subordinate officers (Rochefontaine to Timothy Pickering, February 19, 1796 [ALS, Massachusetts Historical Society, Boston]). In 1796 he became involved in a duel with a fellow officer and was brought before a court of inquiry but was exonerated. See Rochefontaine to H, April 23, May 10, 1796.

8. At this point Rivardi is not altogether frank. Although he had supported Rochefontaine against the charges made by his fellow officers, on at least one occasion he complained to Pickering concerning Rochefontaine's behavior (Rivardi to Pickering, August 6, 1796 [ALS, Massachusetts Historical Society, Boston]).

9. Henry Burbeck, commanding officer at Michilimackinac in 1797, had been appointed a major in the Artillerists and Engineers in 1791.

10. Lewis Tousard.

11. James Bruff of Maryland had been appointed a captain in the Corps of Artillerists and Engineers on June 2, 1794 (*Executive Journal*, I, 159, 160). This is a reference to Section 21 of a general order which Brigadier General James Wilkinson had issued on May 22, 1797. This order provided in part that "Commanding Officers of posts under the grade of a Field Officer, are to be relieved annually . . ." (LC, RG 94, Adjutant General's Office, General Orders, General James Wilkinson, 1797–1808, National Archives).

12. On August 3, 1797, Wilkinson issued a general order which provided in part: ". . . Major Rivardi will avail himself of the first opportunity to repair to Niagara, there to take command. He is to be governed by the orders here-

it was granted with reluctance & the letter which I had To deliver
To The officer commanding was in Such Terms by what I have
learnt Since that I might truly call it Bellerophontic—it exas-
perated Captn. Bruff who was in it told that he could not resist to
my importunities &ca. &ca. however the Captn. like a true democrat
Knew how To dissemble—he watched every opportunity To rouse
my feelings—finally finding himself deserted by the other Officers—
he obtained leave of absence & the first Step he took in Philadelphia
was To lodge at the Secretary's of war charges as absurd as mali-
cious.[13] Just at a time when the Secretary in his report had in mass
thrown an aspersion on the foreigners in Service by observing that
experience had taught how difficult it was To avoid imposition [14]—

tofore given to Captain Bruff, by the minister of War and the commander in
chief . . ." (LC, RG 94, Adjutant General's Office, General Orders, General
James Wilkinson, 1797–1808, National Archives).

13. On January 15, 1799, Bruff wrote to James McHenry: ". . . That Rivardi
. . . when commanding the garrison at Niagara did agrieve me and injure the
service, by interfering with & taking upon himself the internal police of the
Soldiers then under my immediate command—thereby rendered them independent of their proper police officer, to the prejudice of discipline, & contrary
to the practice of armies.

"1st—By excusing soldiers under my command from duty and attendance in
parade who were included in the details.

"2d By detailing soldiers under my command for extra duty out of their
turn & without my knowledge.

"3d By making vexatious transfers from the Infantry to the Artillerists without authority, or the consent of their officers.

"4 By depriving me of my orderly Serjeant.

"5 By exempting a soldiers wife (who drew rations) from the proportion
of washing assigned her by her officer, conformable to General orders & the
practice of the army.

"6 By hearing & determining disputes & controversies between soldiers in
the first resort.

"I also, represent that he has wasted & injured the public property intrusted
to his care—

"1th By having the floors of most of the soldiers barracks torn up dis-
mantled of their doors & windows—put in a state of ruin & rendered useless: to
furnish seasoned materials for unnecessary additions & repairs to his quarters—
& for furniture.

"2d By imploying the Artificers about trifling & unnecessary accomodations for himself—while the works & buildings were neglected & going to ruin.

"3d By ordering rations to Women not imployed in washing for the soldiers
out of proportion to the men—contrary to general orders, & not included in
the Company returns." (Two copies, in Bruff's handwriting, Hamilton Papers,
Library of Congress.)

Bruff's letter was enclosed in McHenry to H, February 15, 1799, which is
listed in the appendix to this volume.

14. This is a reference to the following statement in McHenry's report of
December 24, 1798, which John Adams sent to Congress on December 31,

That ungenerous expression Which I read before I received Captain Bruffs impertinent Notice [15] wounded My feelings To The quick. I have friends in Europe who perhaps think me the only foreigner in the Artillery & who certainly never Shall be informed of Colonel Rochefontaine's transaction concerning the horses [16]—it is natural for them to conclude that I am alluded To & whatever value I may Set on my comission—My honor is Still dearer To me. Impressed with that Idea I wrote imediately To The Secretary of War, & To Coll. Pickering whom I know To be My friend. [17] I in general used To receive of Mr. McHenry a mere acknowledgement of My letters without any answer—but this time I had not even that to boast of. I Served in the Most despotic of all Armies but I never Saw yet the complaints of an Officer when his honor is attacked & when he represents it in respectfull terms remain unoticed. I transmitted by the Next mail the Original which Captn. Bruff Sent me of the charges exhibited against me, with a pressing request to have the affair investigated & a Notice that I had myself charges [18] To bring against my Accuser after he would have made an attempt to Substantiate his against me—but two Months have elapsed and I remain in Statu quo. If the Captain's charges are deemed frivolous & mali-

1798: ". . . it is conceived to be adviseable to endeavor to introduce from abroad, at least one distinguished engineer, and one distinguished officer of artillery. . . . But in this, as we know from past experience, nothing is more easy than to be imposed upon; nothing more difficult than to avoid imposition, and that therefore, should the measure be sanctioned by a law, it will be requisite to commit the business of procuring such characters to some very judicious hand, under every precaution that can put him upon his guard" (*ASP, Military Affairs*, I, 125).

15. Bruff to Rivardi, January 15, 1799 (copy, Hamilton Papers, Library of Congress). This letter enclosed a copy of the charges against Rivardi which Bruff had sent to McHenry.

16. In 1798 Rochefontaine was dismissed from the service for fraudulent use of horses belonging to the United States Government and for receiving public funds for the maintenance of these horses (Rochefontaine to Pickering, April 27, 30, May 16, 1798 [all ALS, Massachusetts Historical Society, Boston]; Pickering to Rochefontaine, May 30, 1798 [ALS, letterpress copy, Massachusetts Historical Society Boston]; Pickering's undated, untitled opinion on the court of inquiry [AD, Massachusetts Historical Society, Boston]).

17. Rivardi to Pickering, February 8, 1799 (ALS, Massachusetts Historical Society, Boston).

18. Rivardi to McHenry, February 21, 1799 (copy, enclosed in Rivardi to Tobias Lear, February 21, 1799 [ALS, Hamilton Papers, Library of Congress], enclosed in Lear to H, March 30, 1799 [listed in the appendix to this volume]). See also Rivardi to Pickering, February 21, 1799 (ALS, Massachusetts Historical Society, Boston).

cious a reprimand in orders will Satisfy me—if not I wish a board of Inquiry at this Post where all the evidences in my favor are collected. I was hesitating previous To this last Affair whether I Should not resign as I find it impossible To Support an increasing family on my pay. The prospect of a War particularly against a Nation Still reeking with the blood of the Swiss [19] & my partiality for the Army as well as for a Country which is become my own were my Motives for not doing it—but now the Most powerfull incitement is that Resignation would be construed into guilt. In these circumstances, Sir, I hope you will not insist on my performing the Journey mentioned in your letter—as other reasons for my begging To decline it I Shall add, that my health which I began To recover when I had the honor of first being introduced to you at my friend Thornton, is again Much impaired by the rambling life which in public Service either as an Engineer or an Officer I have been obliged to Submit to. I nearly died in Virginia of the dysentery comon to the climate & had a yearly relapse ever Since. The Lake fevers have after that much reduced me & having been nearly three years in this Country I had determined To request to be Stationed in the U. Ss. when those charges came which of Course fix me at this Post untill they are examined. An other impediment is my family. I am the only Officer in the army whose wife has no relations in America. I can not possibly except in Actual War Separate myself from her & my Children—particularly as her health is delicate & as She is deprived of the Comforts She has been used To enjoy. An other objection again is that of my fortune which Since the fate of Swisserland is probably annihilated. I have reduced My pecuniary means in an allarming degree by Journey's the expenses of which were only partialy defrayed—for Instance I was detained with my family twenty days at Fort Erie I charged only the hiring of quarters, but the Article was Struck out of my Account although I charged only twenty dollrs. where I had To pay for my Subsistance &ca. Eighty. Was I in easy circumstances this would not weigh with me but it is not every body who although they may have the will possess also like General Hamilton the power of making large Sacrifices To Their Country.

19. This is a reference to the establishment of the Helvetic Republic under French protection in June, 1798.

With regard To The Posts which you mention—I Shall as my health permits give you all the Information I have with regard To Detroit, Niagara & Oswego. General Wilkinson Took all the measures To obtain information To Mackinac where he repaired himself with Officers, Masons &ca. &ca.—he was at Fort Defiance & Should the Documents Not be Sufficient it would be easy To obtain Authentic ones from a Mr. MacNiff [20] formerly Assistant Engineer of the Brittish & Now a Magistrate under our Government at Detroit— he is poor & would for a Small consideration perform the tour again if it was necessary.

Before I conclude I Shall observe that the greatest uneasiness prevails among our Brittish Neighbours on account of the hostile intentions of the Northern & Northwestern Indians.[21] Sir John Johnson [22] is arrived at New Ark on that business which Seems To have originated from Captain Brent's Selling lands To which he had no claims.[23] A Body of Militia is ordered To prepare for encampment.

20. Patrick MacNiff had been a deputy surveyor for the British in Upper Canada but had been dismissed as incompetent. On September 29, 1796, he was appointed both justice of the peace in Wayne County, Northwest Territory, and surveyor. His commission as surveyor was revoked on August 20, 1798 (Carter, *Territorial Papers*, III, 454, 455).

21. On March 4, 1799, Rivardi wrote to McHenry: "I had from the best Authority . . . that the upper nations of Indians are very active in making preparations for War Should the French or Spaniards attempt any thing on Canada. In the present Situation of France I do not apprehend any determination of that Kind but I rather Suppose that the ferment existing among the Indians is a consequence of the intrigues of the French emissaries who were with them a year ago . . ." (ALS, Hamilton Papers, Library of Congress).

The "French emissaries" to whom Rivardi is referring were members of an expedition headed by Georges Henri Collot from March to December, 1796, to survey the Ohio and Mississippi rivers as the first step in France's plan to reconquer Louisiana. Collot, a French major general and former governor of Guadeloupe, had surrendered his command to the British in 1794 and had been paroled to Philadelphia.

22. Johnson, the son of Sir William Johnson of New York, was Superintendent General and Inspector General of Indian Affairs in British North America.

23. This is a reference to lands bordering the Grand River, which the British ceded on October 25, 1784, to the Mohawk Indians, led by Joseph Brant. This cession was designed to replace the lands in New York which the Mohawks had lost as a result of the tribe's support of the British during the American Revolution (Charles M. Johnston, *The Valley of the Six Nations: A Collection of Documents on the Indian Lands of the Grand River* [Toronto: The Champlain Society, 1964], 50–51). The patent granting these lands, dated January 14, 1793, provided that the Indians could not transfer these lands by sale, lease, or gift (Johnston, *Valley of Six Nations*, 73–74). Brant refused to accept the patent and proceeded to sell some of the lands in question.

They are mounting their Cannon at Fort George &ca.—these preparations make me look with encreased Anguish at my thirty odd men placed in a fort which would require three thousand if the outworks were to be Manned. I find that my apology for laconism was perfectly Needless—however necessary for inaccuracies. Permit me to assure you that it is with heartfelt regret that I am induced by unavoidable Necessity To beg To decline the comission entrusted To me in your Second letter. I have been used To obey implicitly without even considering the consequences—however the peculiarity of my Situation will I hope Serve me as an apology. With the Most respectful consideration I have the honor to be

Sir Your Most Obedient & very Humble Servant

J J U Rivardi
Majr. 1st. Regt. A & E

Peter Russell, who was the administrator of Upper Canada from 1796 to 1799, in the absence of Lieutenant Governor John Graves Simcoe, agreed in 1797 to confirm all past sales and leases of these lands and to arrange for future sales. Brant, however, remained dissatisfied with these arrangements.

To Oliver Wolcott, Junior

New York March 21. 1799

I hope you will have understood that I did not mean by any thing in my late letter [1] to blame the plan pursued with regard to vessels arriving contrary to the *Non-Intercourse* laws. I mean only to give you testimony of the character of an Individual & to place before you my professional ideas of the defective wording of the law as a kind of caution in the execution. I agree with you that the Executive must adopt in the Construction what was doubtless intended by the Legislature & is essential to the policy of the act.

It is a good principle for the Government of the UStates to employ directly its own means—only do not let this be carried so far as to confine it to the use of inadequate means or to embarrass the auxiliary means which circumstances may require.

The idea of the late Presidents administration of considering the Governor of each State as the first General of the Militia & its im-

mediate organ in acting upon the Militia [2] was well considered & in
my opinion wisely adopted—and well to be adhered to. In its general operation it will obviate many difficulties & collisions & by en-
hancing their importance tend to draw the State executives to the
General Government.

Take good care, that in the present instance the force employed
be not inadequate.

Some underwriters here have represented to me as a hardship that
having resolved to alter the forms of their policies they are not permitted to *exchange* the *blanks* for *others*. If there be not some very
cogent & unperceived objection will it not be well to allow the exchange in such cases—to avoid the appearance of greediness & rigor
in the Government?

You recommended to me Young *Wharton* [3] as Secretary. I believe
a late law [4] permits the Inspector General to have one & he wants an
aid of this description. But the person ought to be a person of mind
he ought to be able to conceive well & compose correctly. Does this
description suit Young Wharton? Is he still desirous of the employment?

Yrs. truly   A H

O Wolcot Esqr

ALS, Connecticut Historical Society, Hartford.
  1. H to Wolcott, March 13, 1799.
  2. See H to Henry Lee, August 25, 1794; Lee to H, January 5, 1795.
  3. See Wolcott to H, August 9, 1798 (listed in the appendix to this volume).
  4. See Section 26 of "An Act for the better organizing of the Troops of
the United States; and for other purposes" (1 *Stat.* 755 [March 3, 1799]),
quoted in H to James McHenry, first letter of March 19, 1799, note 4.

From Jonathan Dayton [1]

Elizabethtown [*New Jersey*] *March 22, 1799.* "Your letter addressed to Major Ford [2] reached the Post office in Newark a few
minutes after the mail for Morris was sent off. . . . I was compelled
to hire an express for 3 & ½ Dollars who delivered the letter to the
Major this morng & brought back from him the enclosed to you." [3]

ALS, Hamilton Papers, Library of Congress.
1. For background to this letter, see H to Dayton, March 18, 1799; Dayton to H, March 20, 1799.
2. H to Mahlon Ford, March 18, 1799.
3. Ford to H, March 22, 1799 (listed in the appendix to this volume). In this letter Ford acknowledged H's order to proceed to New Brunswick, New Jersey.
H's endorsement of the letter printed above reads: "Express Hire to be paid."

From Rufus King

London Mar 22 1799[1]

Dear sir

War is again declared by france agt. the temporising cabinet of vienna,[2] and this has been the signal for Prussia to resume her former System of insecure neutrality.

We may every hour expect the Result of a Battle between Jourdan & the arch duke who according to our last accounts were respectively advancing upon each other[3]—the first Blow has been unfortunate for the allies, the whole of the austrian Corps (5000) at coire in the country of the Grisons having fallen into the Hands of the french commanded by Massena.[4] I wish that I felt more confident that this first success would not be followed by more important victories. The 25000 Russians who were some time in the neighbourhood of vienna are on their march for Italy where tomorrow an old Russian Officer is to command the combined armies.[5]

If Prussia with the north of Germany which together have an army of more than 300 000 Men, had joined heartily and honestly in the League agt. france, the Directory might have been shaken, but my Hopes are weaker than my fears with Regard to the partial and ill-joined Confederacy with which it is at present engaged. The Publication of ⟨the⟩ [6] Treaty of Campo formio,[7] so disgraceful ⟨to⟩ the court of Vienna, will prove ⟨useful⟩ to the Directory, by confirming the Jeal⟨ousy⟩ of Prussia, and exciting Distrust of the Emperor [8] throughout Germany, the interest & Safety of wh. was sacrificed by that Treaty.

Yrs &c   R K

ALS, Hamilton Papers, Library of Congress; copy, New-York Historical Society, New York City.

1. This letter is incorrectly dated May 22, 1799, in *JCHW*, VI, 407; King, *The Life and Correspondence of Rufus King*, III, 18; and the copy in the New-York Historical Society, New York.

2. On March 12, 1799, France declared war on Austria. This news was reported in *The* [London] *Times*, March 19, 1799.

3. On March 22, 1799, *The* [London] *Times* reported: "Letters from Paris of the 16th, mention, that a very few days would probably determine in a great measure the fate of the campaign. General [Jean Baptiste] Jourdan's object was to attack the Archduke's army without delay. . . ." The anticipated battle occurred on March 25, 1799, at Stockach, and the Archduke Charles's army repulsed the forces under Jourdan's command.

4. On March 19, 1799, *The* [London] *Times* printed the following quotation from a French newspaper: "We joyfully announce a happy prelude of success on the part of our armies. A Courier just arrived from Switzerland brings intelligence that the troops under command of [André] Massena . . . have taken four thousand five hundred Austrians, together with the Commandant of *Coire* (Chur) the capital of the Grison Country; and all the Staff of that Army." On March 22, 1799, *The Times* reported: "The loss of the Austrians was 5000 men. . . . There is no reason to doubt the truth of this statement."

5. This is a reference to Aleksanor Vasilyevich Suvarov. On March 22, 1799, *The* [London] *Times* reported: "It is confirmed that General Suwarrow is to command the Austrian forces in Italy. He left Petersburgh on the 27th ult. for that purpose."

6. The words within broken brackets have been taken from the copy.

7. The reference is to the Treaty of Campo Formio, October 17, 1797, which contained both secret and public articles. On March 22, 1799, *The* [London] *Times* reported: "At length the Treaty of *Campo Formio* between the Emperor and the French Republic is made known. . . . In this treaty the Emperor has betrayed the German Empire, and exposed it to all the aggressions and devastations which the war just commenced will not fail to bring with it." See King to H, August 6–10, 1797, note 2.

8. Francis II of Austria, the Holy Roman Emperor.

From James McHenry

Private   War Department 22 March 1799

Dear Sir

You will have seen by the News-papers that governor Mifflin has been required to hold in readiness to march certain companies of Cavalry, to assist in quelling the insurrection existing in the State of Pennsylvania. Govr. Howell has also been called upon to hold 8 companies of Cavalry in readiness to March for the same purpose.[1]

Would it interfere with your arrangements or be throwing the troops at *Windsor* in the State of Vermont too far from their ultimate place of destination, to order them to Easton or Bethlehem? It may be proper to keep a certain force in one or other of the rebellious counties for a time. Capn. *Leonard* has above or about 100 recruits.[2] If you think they ought to be so disposed of, you will give orders for their immediate March to Easton or Bethlehem and direct the appropriate artillery officers to join him.

Yours affectionately & truly   James McHenry

Alex. Hamilton Esq
Major General &c

ALS, Hamilton Papers, Library of Congress; ADfS, James McHenry Papers, Library of Congress.
    1. For McHenry's letter to Governor Thomas Mifflin of Pennsylvania, dated March 20, 1799, see the *Gazette of the United States, and Philadelphia Daily Advertiser,* March 21, 1799. A similar letter was sent on the same date to Governor Richard Howell of New Jersey (*Gazette of the United States, and Philadelphia Daily Advertiser,* March 26, 1799).
    For the "insurrection . . . in . . . Pennsylvania," see McHenry to H, March 13, 15, 1799.
    2. Nathaniel Leonard, the recruiting officer at Windsor, Vermont, was a lieutenant in the Second Regiment of Artillerists and Engineers.

From James McHenry

War Department, March 22, 1799. "I transmit for your information copies of several letters, viz, one from Captain Wm Littlefield dated Fort Wolcott 2nd Feby 1799 [1] and one from General Hamtramck dated Fort Wayne 21st Jany 1799,[2] together with a letter from Edward Livingston Esq. dated New York 9th March, one from John Dover dated Novr. 24th. 1798 directed to Mr Livingston [3] and one from the accountant [4] of the Department, dated 1 Feby 1799. . . ."

LS, Hamilton Papers, Library of Congress.
    1. Littlefield, the commanding officer at Fort Wolcott, wrote to McHenry concerning two deserters (copy, Hamilton Papers, Library of Congress).
    2. John F. Hamtramck wrote to McHenry: "As you are no doubt well acquainted with the disposition of the people of the states of Kentucky and Tenessee; I shall only confine myself to one General observation—that is, that they execrate the Federal Government and its officers. In almost every company I have been in, I have been more or less insulted—they think nothing of condemning the measures of Congress, damning our beloved President. . . .
    "Mr. Zachariah Coxe who made his escape from the Natchez, and who went

to New Orleans has returned to Nash-Ville. He came across through the Chocktaw Nation, where one Mr. [Samuel] Mitchell who is there one of our agents, had directions from Governor [Winthrop] Sargent that if Mr. Coxe should pass that Country, for him, Mitchell, to take him up and send him to the Natchez. How it has happened that Mitchell did not comply with the Governor's directions I Know not. I am informed that Mitchell is concerned with Coxe in the speculation of the Muscle Shoals—if so, Mr. Mitchell's conduct can be easily accounted for. . . .

"General Wilkinson has ordered a house to be built for the *Turtle* and another for the *Toad*, a Miami Chief, I find that the two carpenters at this place are not more than sufficient to Keep the works and barracks in repair. If these houses are to be built, more Carpenters will be wanted. Soldiers employed in that Kind of labor will no doubt expect payment. I will be obliged to you to give me the necessary directions. . . .

"Lieut. [Rezin] Webster of the second regiment was, last summer, ordered into Kentucky by Genl. Wilkinson to recruit—and I think, if I recollect right, the General told me he was to be stationed about Lexington. I am informed that he has long ago been at the Rapids of the Ohio, and is there still; I mention this circumstance to you because I think that place is no way calculated for recruiting, and that I have reason to believe that he has taken that position for personal accomodation. . . ." (ALS and copy, Hamilton Papers, Library of Congress.)

H endorsed Hamtramck's letter to McHenry: "Answered April 29 1799."

3. Livingston enclosed a letter from John Dover and asked McHenry to comply with Dover's request (ALS, Hamilton Papers, Library of Congress). Dover had written to Livingston asking for his help in having Dover's son discharged from the Army. Dover wrote: "he has now been better than Eight years in the Service . . . he is Listed under the Name of John Thompson Soldier in Capt [Andrew] McClarys Company 2nd U S Regiment Detroit" (ALS, Hamilton Papers, Library of Congress).

4. William Simmons wrote to Livingston, February 1, 1799: "I . . . find . . . his [John Thompson's] last inlistment expired on the 12th . . . of January 1798 at which time he . . . reinlisted . . . for five years. If Mr Dover wishes him discharged application must be made to the Commanding Officer at Detroit who will judge of the propriety of granting it . . ." (ALS, Hamilton Papers, Library of Congress).

To William Macpherson [1]

New York, March 22, 1799. ". . . It will be satisfactory to me, as far as may be convenient, to receive from you, from time to time, statements of the situation & progress of the Insurrection in Pennsylvania. . . ."

ALS, Columbia University Libraries.

1. For background to this letter, see James McHenry to H, March 13, 15, 1799; H to McHenry, March 18, 19, 1799.

Circular to the Commandants of Regiments

Circular   New York March 23, 1799

Sir

As it is expected that the recruiting service will speedily commence, it is desireable that the Regimental staff should be ready to enter upon their functions.

The laws have not declared how these Officers are to be appointed under the new system of organisation, and it is a question whether the direct sanction of the President be not necessary. At the same time it is thought adviseable, that these officers should be designated in the modes heretofore practiced. To conciliate the different considerations, I request—

That you will, without delay, nominate fit characters among the Lieutenants for Quarter Master & Adjutant.

That You will also without delay convene as many of your Officers as can expeditiously be assembled, & that these by plurality of Voices nominate from among the Lieutenants a fit character for Pay Master. It is proper to inform you, that when confirmed he must give bond to the United States of America in five thousand Dollars, with one or more sufficient sureties; & that the nominations now required are to be considered only as recommendations.[1]

Inclosed is a List of the officers who are to compose your Regiment distributed into Companies.[2] They will rank for the present as they are numbered. But in order to a definitive regulation of this point, you will be pleased, in concert with your Majors, to suggest for consideration such alterations as from circumstances may be deemed expedient, with the reasons for those alterations.[3] Many things requisite to a just judgment could not be known when the appointments were made. To prevent future discontent it may be best that silence should be observed respecting the alterations which shall be proposed.

With great consideration I have the honor to be   Sir   Yr Obed serv [4]

ADf Hamilton Papers, Library of Congress; LS, to Aaron Ogden, with corrections in H's handwriting, Lloyd W. Smith Collection, Morristown National
Historical Park, Morristown, New Jersey.

1. For the selection of these regimental staff officers, see H to James Mc-
Henry, March 10, 14, 19, 1799; McHenry to H, March 13, 21, 1799.

2. See McHenry to H, March 21, 1799.

3. See H to McHenry, March 10, 1799; McHenry to H, March 13, 21, 1799.

4. At the end of the draft H wrote: "Post Script to N Carolina." The postscript, which is not in H's handwriting, reads: "P.S. It is mentioned above, this
letter being a circular, that the Officers are distributed into Companies. This
however has not been done and I think it best to leave this matter also with
you, in consultation with your majors."

To James McHenry

New York March 23, 1799

Sir

Your letter of the 21st instant came to hand by the post of to day.

There are some points in it respecting the recruiting service which
demand immediate attention.

"1. The *Stations* of the recruiting rendezvouses or the stations in
each state where it will be proper to provide rations and send the
Cloathing."

My letter of the 19th designated these stations in the five States,
in which it is proposed immediately to commence the recruiting service. The particular Town indicated as the *rendezvous* of each subdistrict is intended for the station in that subdistrict. But the Cloathing for a Regiment will best be sent together to one point, where
it can be received by the Quarter M⟨aster⟩ of the Regiment and
thence forwarded by him to the several subdistricts. This course is
very material to order.

"2. The Quantity of Cloathing to be sent to each rendezvous."
The same letter is accompanied by a return for the purpose, con-
templating the abovementioned Agency of the Regimental Quarter
Master for the distribution among the several rendezvouses.

"3. The officers for Regimental Pay Masters." I shall immediately
write to the respective commandants of Regiments to cause nominations to be made in the mode practiced during the Revolution War,
which is likely to be the most satisfactory; observing to them however, that these nominations will only be considered as recommen-

dations. I shall at the same time desire them to designate also by way of recommendation Quarter Masters & Adjutants.[1]

4. The numbers of the Regiments.

In settling these, which I extend to the whole sixteen, I have been governed by geographical idea—according to the order which was adopted last war, when the army faced the sea board. I thought this rule as good as any other, an⟨d⟩ lit⟨tle⟩ liable to criticism.

The result is that the two Regiments to be raised in Georgia, the Carolinas, Tenessee & Kentucke will be numbered 5 & 6. And it is now proposed that the following Regiments be thus numbered, having reference to the arrangement proposed by the General officers and exhibited in schedule A transmitted with your letter. (viz)

That of which William Bently is Lt Col commandant to be No. 7 That of which Thomas Parker is Lt. Co. Commandant No. 8 That of which Josias C. Hall is Lieutenant Col Commandant No. 9 That which Thomas L Moore is Lt. Col Commandant No 10—That of which Aaron Ogden is Lt Col Commandt No. 11 That of which William S Smith is Lt Col Commandant No. 12 That of which Timothy Taylor (Connecticut) is Lt Col Commandant No. 13 That of which N Rice is Lt Col Comt. No. 14—That of which Richard Hunnewell is Lt Col Commandant No. 15 That which is to comprehend the Companies to be raised in N Hampshire Vermont & Rhode Island No. 16. If this arrangement is adopted by you, it is desireable that I should be speedily enabled to apprise the respective Commandants of it.

You have not rightly apprehended the suggestion of an indiscriminate inlistment for the army at large. It was intended that *in fact* & practice the troops inlisted by the Officers of each Corps should constitute that Corps; which avoids all the objections you mention: But that the legal tenor of the engagement, as expressed in the oath or otherwise, should be to serve in the *Infantry* or in the *Artillery* or in the Cavalry of the UStates; thereby to leave no question that the men may be transfered from one Regiment to another, that fragments of different regiments may be incorporated into one—&c. &c.; which in the course of service are frequently necessary, and of the right to do which, there may be doubt if the inlistment is more specific in its terms.

I think it adviseable that the Adjutant General[2] should be called into service. The duties to be fulfilled by him cannot be executed by the Commanding General without too much complication and of course delay and disorder. And in an army commanded by the Inspector General it is doubtful whether his place can be supplied by a Deputy Inspector General. But at any rate it is best for him to begin to exercise himself in the duties of his station. The additional expence would be compensated by the additional advantage.[3]

With great respect   I have the honor to be Sir   Your Obed Ser

The Secretary of War

ADf, Hamilton Papers, Library of Congress.
 1. See "Circular to the Commandants of Regiments," March 23, 1799.
 2. William North.
 3. Under the provisions of "An Act to augment the Army of the United States, and for other purposes" (1 *Stat.* 604–05 [July 16, 1798]), the adjutant general received the rank, pay, and emoluments of a brigadier general. His pay commenced when he was called into actual service.

From Henry Lee

Stratford Virga March 24th [1799]

dear Sir

I never received yr letr. on the subject of the recruiting service enclosing one to Colo Parker till the last evening.[1]

I woud with much pleasure contribute any aid in my power towards the successful execution of yr object for I really believe the best plan & the best execution will still be very slow in fruit among us.

A consultation with the officers to be employed in the conduct of the business might probably be useful. This not being directed & requiring time, must I suppose be dispensed with. Yet I beleive such a preliminary Step judicious.

The weight which has ever been thrown in this state agst the govt. operates constantly & applys its effect to all objects which concern the govt. It would be peculiarly pleasing to a certain set to see the recruiting service frowned on by our people; this they predict will be the case & this end they will latently conspire to produce.

Exclusive of this artificial obstruction which that business will have to encounter, there are natural clogs arising from the turn of our people, the facility with which the poor live, & the high price of labour.

If the law had allowed yr. use of popular characters as recruiting officers to be paid pr head for recruits I believe essential good would be derived in this state from such instrumentality. I know not whether there be such a provision.

I will reflect on what is best to be done & if by myself or thro Col. Parker or unitedly any assistance can be afforded on my part it shall be given. I wish I could hear in reply before I did begin. The law having expired under which I was nominated, I consider that nomination at an end; [2] nevertheless I shall always be happy in advancing yr. objects in this country.

With great regard   I am yr friend & obt   Henry Lee

ALS, Hamilton Papers, Library of Congress.
    1. See H to Lee, February 18, 1799.
    2. Lee was mistaken. "An Act authorizing the President of the United States to raise a Provisional Army" (1 *Stat.* 558–61 [May 28, 1798]) had expired on December 3, 1798. The officers already holding commissions under this act were never called up and therefore never served. See the introductory note to H to James Gunn, December 22, 1798.

From William Macpherson

Philadelphia March 25 1799

Dear sir

I have the pleasure to acknowledge the receipt of your Letter of the 22d on the subject of the insurrection in this State and should have replied immediately, but knowing that I was to receive my Instructions from the War Office on this day, I thought it best to wait. The fact is, Sir, that in the Counties of Northampton, Berks, Montgomery and part of Bucks, the people have manifested the strongest determination to oppose the Laws, by openly, & with a military Force, rescuing from the Marshall a number of prisoners. I say military Force for they were headed by Officers who are commissioned under the State, and were completely armed and equipped; it is also certain that in addition to this party that effected the Rescue, several detachments were on their march to accomplish the same purpose, when hearing that the Business was done they retired. In short the people of the before-mentioned Counties seem ripe for anything, and I am sorry to add, very strong indications of a similar disposition have appeared in the County of Northumberland, and although it is not likely that they have as yet any systematic mode of Operation it however appears to be a very dangerous combination, and that the most energetic Conduct on the part of administration is absolutely indispensable. How far the Executive accord with my Sentiments you will judge when I have this day received orders to march as soon as the Force can be collected with 240 Horse (to use the secretarys expression) to the Theatre of insurrection. My supporting Parties are the Detachments under Capt Henry [1] who has arrived at Newton in the County of Bucks, and two Companies of Artillerists who are ordered to rendezvous at Reading in the County of Berks; the two most opposite points the Secretary could have hit on, and which I cannot correct unless I oblige the party at Reading to take a very circuitous Route or march them through the heart of the disaffected Country which I should not from the smallness of their numbers be justified in doing. I have therefore determined to leave them at that point, and shall tomorrow send orders to Capt Henry to move across the County of Bucks by a Course I shall point out which will be perfectly safe, untill he comes in contact with my Route when I shall take post somewhere in the neighbourhood of Bethlem and use my best endeavours to accomplish the purpose of my Command.

I confess I could have wished a different mode of operation had been adopted and which I am convinced would have made a more serious and lasting impression, than my scampering through the Country with a few Horse. My plan would have been to march the volunteer Infantry of this City who, with Capt Henrys Detachment, would have given me a sufficient Force to take any post in the disaffected Country, from which I could make excursions with my Horse in every proper direction. But the Secretary thinks otherwise and I shall obey.

I shall from time to time give you information of my progress and of every important occurrence.

I am with great Regard   most truly Yours.   W. Macpherson

Major General Hamilton

LS, Hamilton Papers, Library of Congress.
1. See John Henry to H, March 21, 1799.

From Lewis Tousard

Newport [Rhode Island] March 25, 1799. ". . . Auprès d'une ville, la Garnison reste souvent sand officers; on se croit à son devoir, parceque le fort n'est pas éloigné, et peutêtre au moment d'un évenement le fort seroit attaqué, avant qu'on eut pu avertir un seul d'entre les officiers. . . . il seroit essentiel que le General en chef commandant dans le departement Ordonnat . . . que dans les circonstances présentes ou nous pouvons certes nous regarder comme en état de guerre; J'eusse à tenir la main à ceque sous aucun pretexte, le fort ne restat jamais sans un officier. . . ."

ALS, Hamilton Papers, Library of Congress.

From George Washington

Mount Vernon 25th Mar: 1799

Dear Sir

Your letter of the 14th. instant, with its enclosures, came to hand by the last Post.

In the present State of the Army (or more properly the Embryo of one, for I do not perceive from any thing that has come to my knowledge that we are likely to move beyond this) and until the Augmented force shall have been Recruited, Assembled and in the Field, the residence of the Paymaster Genl (I did not know there was one until your letter announced it) will be found most eligable at the seat of the General Government; and you will please to give such Orders respecting it, as you shall think proper, for I am unwilling to issue any.

Under this Cover, you will find a letter which I have just received from Colo. Hamtramck,[1] with a short acknowledgement of its receipt;[2] which you will be so good as to forward with your dispatches for the Western Army.

With very great esteem & regd. I am Dr Sir Yr. Most Obedt. Servt.   Go: Washington

Majr. Genl. Hamilton

ALS, Hamilton Papers, Library of Congress; ALS, letterpress copy, George Washington Papers, Library of Congress.

1. John F. Hamtramck wrote to Washington on January 28, 1799, and congratulated him on "having once more taken up the sword" (ALS, Hamilton Papers, Library of Congress).

2. Washington to Hamtramck, March 25, 1799 (ALS, letterpress copy, George Washington Papers, Library of Congress).

From James McHenry

War department 26. March 1799

Sir

I have received this morning your letter of the 23d inst.

I shall write to day or to morrow to a Mr. Timothy Phelps a Merchant in New Haven Connecticut to know whether he will undertake to store and deliver the Cloathing to the Quarter Master for the 1. and 2d. District formed in that State and if he will I shall send the apportioned quantity to him as soon as it comes into the public store.

I shall also send the required quantity of Cloathing for the station within the State of New York to Colonel Ebenezer Stevens. That for New Jersey Pennsylvania and Delaware, will be forwarded from Philadelphia by the Quarter Master General to the several Stations.

If you will advert to the Purveyor's letter to me of the 12. March [1] infr. a copy of which you have been furnished with it will be perceived that there are no *Woolen Overalls* stated in it.

The money for the bounties for the recruiting service will be forwarded to the provisional regimental paymasters as soon as possible after they shall have been designated.

Your idea respecting indiscriminate enlistment as I now understand it is conformable to the practice we have pursued. You will of course cause it to be adopted.

I shall direct the Adjutant General to enter upon his duties and transmit the letter to him perhaps by next post.[2]

With great respect   I am Sir   Your obed servant

James McHenry

General Hamilton

LS, Hamilton Papers, Library of Congress; LS, letterpress copy, James McHenry Papers, Library of Congress.

1. See McHenry to H, March 21, 1799, note 6.
2. William North.

Circular to the Commandants of Regiments

New York March 27th [–April 17] [1] 1799

Sir

I send you herewith thirteen Setts of Rules and Regulations for the Recruiting service,[2] one for each field Officer, and one for each Captain of a company. You will carefully fill the blanks according to the example in No 1.

The sooner you distribute these, the better, that the Officers may, by studying them, be prepared to enter upon the business of recruiting when the order shall be given for it which it is hoped will not be long delayed.

With great consideration   I am Sir   Your obed Servt:

A Hamilton

LS, to Aaron Ogden, Lloyd W. Smith Collection, Morristown National Historical Park, Morristown, New Jersey; ADf, to William S. Smith, Hamilton Papers, Library of Congress.

1. This letter was also sent to some commanding officers on April 17, 1799. See William Bentley to H, May 3, 1799; James Read to H, May 3, 1799 (both letters listed in the appendix to Volume XXIII).

2. See H to Jonathan Dayton, August 6, 1798, note 6; James McHenry to H, March 21, 1799.

From James McHenry

War Department,
March 27th: 1799.

Sir,

Inclosed is a letter to the Adjutant General [1] informing him that his presence and aid is considered essential to the due performance of the duties to be fulfilled by you, and placing him under your Orders.

On looking over your letter of the 23rd: and my reply,[2] I find I have omitted to approve formally, the numbers which you proposed to designate the new Regiments by. The arrangement of the Regiments and their numbers being approved of, you will give the necessary information to their respective Commandants.

I have the honor to be, with great respect, Sir, Your obedt: servant   James McHenry

Major General Alexander Hamilton.

LS, Hamilton Papers, Library of Congress.
  1. McHenry to William North, March 27, 1799 (LS, letterpress copy, James McHenry Papers, Library of Congress).
  2. McHenry to H, March 26, 1799.

To George Washington

Private   New York March 27. 1799.

Dr. Sir

At length we are on the point of commencing the recruiting service in five of the States, Connecticut, New York, New Jersey, Pensylvania & Delaware. It is hoped, that it will not be long in successively embracing the others, where officers have been appointed. But in our affairs 'till a thing is actually begun, there is no calculating the delays which may ensue. You have been informed that the recruiting service has been put under my direction, but for many matters of detail I must go to the Secretary for a sanction and it is not always that it is rapidly obtained. Things however are at last getting into such a state that this business may be expected to progress without interruption.

The letter some time since sent you for General Lee [1] was intended to be left open. It respected the division of Virginia into four districts and Twenty sub-districts or company rendezvouses, designating a place in each for the head Quarters of the rendezvous. I have as yet had no acknowlegement of it.

Before General Morgan [2] left Philadelphia, I got him to give me a plan. Inclosed is a copy.[3] If you think a better arrangement can be made, shall I ask the favour of you to have it done. For I cannot now rely on the success of my resort to General Lee in any reasonable time.

Very respectfully & Affecly   I have the honor to be   Sir   Your obed serv   A Hamilton

Will you have the goodness to put the letters [4] herewith in train to reach their destination with certainty. They are open that you may perceive their object.

General Washington

ALS, George Washington Papers, Library of Congress; copy, Hamilton Papers, Library of Congress.

1. See H to Washington, February 18, 1799.
2. Daniel Morgan.
3. See "Circular on Recruiting Service," February 18–19, 1799.
The enclosure, which is undated, is entitled "Virginia divided and subdivided into Districts, for recruiting" (copy, Hamilton Papers, Library of Congress).
4. Enclosures not found. They were, however, addressed to Thomas Parker and William C. Bentley, and they were copies of "Circular to the Commandants of Regiments," March 23, 1799.

From James McHenry

Private   Philada. 29 March 1799

Dear Sir

I have to acknowledge your private letters under date of the 14, 18 [1] & 19th inst.

All I intended by the observation in my public letter [2] relative to the regimental Paymasters &c. was, that as these were to be Lieutenants, and the 3 additional lieutenants described in the late law,[3] under these characters, had not been, it was proposed they should be appointed. I have no objection to the custom which has prevailed for selecting pay-masters from the body of Lieutenants.

You will see by the law that Regimental paymasters must give bond in the sum of 5000 Dollars, with one or more sufficient securities, for the faithful discharge of the duties of ⟨their⟩ office. You will of course take measures to have this done, and the bonds transmitted to me as soon as possible, that there may exist no reason for delaying the transmission to them of the recruiting money. The same operation must be performed by the pay-masters on the old establishment respecting which you will also take order.

I like the alternative suggested in the oath of Inlistment, as to the term of service viz. "for and during the continuance &c, or for the term of 5 years at the option of the U S." [4] and yet I foresee that such a measure might excite clamours, and be misunderstood.

It may be thought, that by this option, the Executive would actually raise 13,000 men for 5 years *certain*, whereas the law enables it to raise about 5000 only for this period.[5] That consequently this option would be an essential departure from law.

The saving to the public, in case of the new army being soon disbanded by filling up the old army to its compliment with the soldiers would be wholly overlooked.

Upon the whole it will be perhaps the safest course to follow the letter of the law in the articles of inlistment. It strikes me besides as it seems to have done you, that men will more readily inlist for the casual duration, than for the known term of five years.

You sent but one letter for General Wilkinson.[6] I have had advice of its arrival at Knoxville in Tenessee and of its having been sent forward by express.

I have never observed in Elliot any strong desire of Independence or disregard to orders. Perhaps his being of the Court Martial prevented him from answering your letter.[7]

I intended that you would put every thing in train for commencing the recruiting service the moment you received an account that a sufficiency of cloathing was ready for the purpose, and that, if you thought proper, you might direct inlistments in a certain way to be made in the mean while.

I have now noticed most if not all the points contained in your private letters and I believe most all your ideas in any public ones.

The regular troops ordered to the scene of Insurrection have all reached their first points of destination, except the company from this place which is to march when ordered by Gen. Macpherson.[8] The general received his instructions on Monday last and every thing dependent on me has been done which regards the expedition. It seems that the adjutant general from this State [9] has not yet been able to furnish him with certain necessary returns. Is it not remarkable that however slightly the present Governor of Pennsylvania comes in contact with insurrection that delay becomes unavoidable in quelling it.[10]

yours sincerely and affectionately   James McHenry

Majr Gen Alex Hamilton

ALS, Hamilton Papers, Library of Congress; ADf, James McHenry Papers, Library of Congress.

1. H's private letter to McHenry of March 18, 1799, is listed in the appendix to this volume. See notes 6 and 7.

2. McHenry to H, March 13, 1799. McHenry is mistaken in writing "public letter," as this letter is marked "private."

3. For the legislation discussed in this and the following paragraph, see "An Act for the better organizing of the Troops of the United States; and for other purposes" (1 *Stat.* 749–55 [March 3, 1799]).

4. See H to McHenry, March 14, 1799.

5. See the introductory note to H to James Gunn, December 22, 1798, for an explanation of the various terms of service.

6. H to James Wilkinson, February 12, 1799, which was enclosed in H to McHenry, February 13, 1799 (listed in the appendix to this volume). McHenry acknowledged the receipt of this letter on February 16, 1799 (listed in the appendix to this volume). In his private letter of March 18, 1799 (listed in the appendix to this volume), H asked McHenry if it was necessary to send three copies in order to ensure that Wilkinson would receive one of them.

7. This is an answer to a question asked by H in his private letter of March 18, 1799 (listed in the appendix to this volume), about the failure of Joseph Elliott to answer H's letter of March 5, 1799 (also listed in the appendix to this volume). Elliott was a member of the court-martial of Captain Samuel Vance. For documents relating to this court-martial, see McHenry to H, Febuary 22, 1799 (listed in the appendix to this volume).

8. This is a reference to the troops sent to suppress Fries's Rebellion. See McHenry to H, March 13, 15, 18, 1799. See also H to William R. Boote, March 16, 1799; H to Adam Hoops, March 16, 1799; H to Jonathan Dayton, March 18, 1799; H to Mahlon Ford, March 18, 1799; William Macpherson to H, March 25, 1799.

9. Peter Baynton.

10. See McHenry to H, March 22, 1799.

To James McHenry

New York March 29. 1799

Sir

I have the honor to acknowlege the receipt of your letter of the 19th instant with the copies of letters from General Wilkinson mentioned therein.

This communication reminds me that it will be necessary for me

to peruse at large all that part of the correspondence of General
Wilkinson, which relates to permanent or unfinished objects, in order that I may know how to direct in regard to the occurrences
which shall from time to time arise.

You will determine how far his letters can be without inconvenience forwarded to me to be returned after they shall have been
perused, together with copies of such leading communications from
your department as will put me in possession of the past train of
Affairs.

With the greatest respect   I have the honor to be   Sir   Your
obed ser

Js McHenry Esqr

ADf, Hamilton Papers, Library of Congress.

From James McHenry

War Department
March 30th: 1799

Sir,

I have directed two parcels of Cloathing nearly equal to your
requisition of the 19th. Instant, for the Connecticut and New York
Recruiting Districts, one addressed to Col. Stevens, the other to
Timothy Phelps Esq of New Haven, with directions that they shall
be delivered and forwarded agreeably to your Orders.[1]

Considering that April is a good month for Recruiting, and that
circumstances render it indispensable that no time should be lost
to put the recruiting business in motion, I believe it will be proper
that you should issue your Orders for this purpose without too
strict an adherence to the System. If therefore you will designate
the persons to whom I may send money it shall be immediately
transmitted to them.

Having withdrawn Captain Shoemaker [2] from Frederick Town in
Maryland (to the scene of Insurrection) [3] who has recruited a very
fine Company in that quarter, I would propose to you to have his
place forthwith supplied by Captain Valentine Brothers [4] who lives

in Frederick Town, is greatly respected by the Dutch and possesses a very extensive influence. Besides his being the fittest person to employ at Frederick Town, the measure will be attended with very good effects. He can quickly raise a Company there.

Captain Brothers is entitled, as far as my information extends, to stand first Captain in his Regiment, and should no contravening information be presented to you I wish it to be kept in mind in the final arrangement of relative rank.

Let, I pray you, all those who can be immediately employed in the Recruiting Service, commence their operations forthwith.

It is truly unfortunate that preparatory arrangements only can be made for enlisting in North Carolina. Upon the 16th: instant I received from Genl. pinckney, a list, (of which the enclosed is a copy)[5] of Officers proposed to be appointed from that State. On the same day I transmitted the list to the president as mentioned in my letter of the 21st: requesting authority to announce to the persons therein named, their appointments. I do not doubt but that I shall receive the authority desired. You will judge upon this ground how far it will be prudent to proceed. I am extremely anxious that every thing may be done upon our part respecting this Service, which can be attempted with propriety.

I have just received your letter of the 28th: The recruiting Districts presented to me in this, as well in your letter of the 16th: instant is approved of. It will not be necessary in future to transmit the Districts to me for any other purpose than to inform me of the different places of Rendezvous and where articles are to be procured or sent.

I have the honor to be with great respect, Sir, Your obedt: servant, James McHenry

Major General
Alexander Hamilton.

LS, Hamilton Papers, Library of Congress; LC, James McHenry Papers, Library of Congress.

1. See McHenry to H, March 26, 1799.

2. Peter Shoemaker was appointed a lieutenant in the Second Regiment of Infantry on March 3, 1799 (*Executive Journal*, I, 320, 323).

3. This is a reference to Fries's Rebellion. See McHenry to H, March 13, 1799, note 12.

4. Brothers was appointed a captain in the Ninth Regiment of Infantry on March 3, 1799 (*Executive Journal*, I, 322–23).

5. "Officers in North Carolina appointed in the twelve additional Regiments" (copy, Hamilton Papers, Library of Congress). H's endorsement of this document reads: "List of Officers recommended by General Pinckney for N. Carolina &c."

To James McHenry

New York March 30th 1799

Sir

I have been honored with your several letters of the 21. 22. 26. 27 and 28 instant. All necessary directions have been given towards the commencement of the business of Recruiting in the states of Connecticut New York New Jersey Pensylvania & Delaware the moment the necessary supplies of bounty money and cloathing shall have been furnished, and towards the preparation for it in the other States as far South as Virginia inclusively, when the necessary intermediate measures shall have been matured.[1]

I conclude from your silence [2] that you do not think your special *fiat* necessary as to the arrangement for the Distribution of the abovementioned five States into Districts and Subdistricts, and on this supposition I have ventured to proceed upon it as adopted. If you meditate alterations, these can be transmitted when known. Connecticut, New York New Jersey & Pensylvania will form each a Regimental Circle. Delaware, and three of the subdistricts of Pensylvania (to be excepted out of that Circle) will be annexed to the Circle of New Jersey. The circles will be numbered in correspondency with the Regiments.

But I observe that it is intended that the Cloathing for New Jersey Pensylvania & Delaware shall be forwarded from Philadelphia by the Quarter Master General to the *several Stations*. Allow me to observe that this will break in upon that plan of accountability for the supplies from time to time to be issued to the several Regiments which is in my opinion essential to regularity and safety. Wherever it is practicable the whole ought to be delivered to the proper officer of the Regimental Staff to be by him distributed among the companies.

On recollection, it occurs that in the practice of our Revolution Army as well as in that of the present, the Pay Master has acted as Regimental Clothier.[3] And differently from my first impression, I now think that this ought to be the plan. It will facilitate the deduction for *extra* Cloathing, when obliged to be furnished, out of the pay of the soldiery.

Pursuant to this idea, I have directed that the Pay Masters of the Regiments of Moore & Ogden [4] make direct application at Philadelphia for the Cloathing intended to be supplied for those Regiments.

The advanced state of the Spring renders it immaterial whether Woolen overalls can now be furnished for the Recruits. Those of Linnen will suffice.

I have not yet been informed of the names of the Contractors or Agents of the War Department in the respective States in order to direct the Commandants of Regiments where to resort for provisions and other supplies.

With very great respect I have the honor to be Sir Yr. Obed serv

The Secy. of War

ADf, Hamilton Papers, Library of Congress.
    1. See H to McHenry, March 16, 19, 1799; "Circular to the Commandants of Regiments," March 23, 31, 1799.
    2. See H to McHenry, March 16, 1799.
    3. See H to McHenry, March 10, 1799, note 9.
    4. Letters not found. Lieutenant Colonel Thomas Lloyd Moore was the commanding officer of the Tenth Regiment of Infantry in Pennsylvania, and Lieutenant Colonel Aaron Ogden was the commanding officer of the Eleventh Regiment of Infantry in New Jersey.

Circular to the Commandants of Regiments [1]

New York March 31 1799

Sir

[The State of   [2] is to form a Circle and to be divided into
    Districts and   sub-districts according to the plan in-

ADf, Hamilton Papers, Library of Congress; LS, to Aaron Ogden, Lloyd W. Smith Collection, Morristown National Historical Park, Morristown, New Jersey.
    1. For background to this letter, see James McHenry to H, March 21, 1799; H to McHenry, March 23, 30, 1799.
    2. This space and other spaces in the letter were left blank in MS.

closed.] [3] The recruiting service within this circle is to be for your Regiment and under your superintendence. You will assign each of the Majors of your Regiment to a district and each of your Captains to a subdistrict. He will take to his aid such of his Lieutenants as shall not have been appointed to other duties. The particular Town specified as the *rendezvous* of each subdistrict, you will understand to be the point to which the recruits for each company are to be sent as soon as possible, there to be cloathed and subsisted until they shall march for their Regimental rendezvous; which is to be   . Here will be your station and that of your Regimental staff.

The Pay Master will act as Regimental Clothier. He will distribute the bounty money among the Captains or Officers superintending the subdistricts according to the orders which you shall give—in which you will be regulated by the progress of the recruiting service in each. The same course must be pursued as to Cloathing.

The number by which your Regiment is to be distinguished is [five]. This has been determined by a Geographical rule. The same number will also distinguish the Circle under your direction.

When you have made the Nomination of your Pay Master in the mode pointed out let him immediately give bond to the UStates with two sureties whom you shall think sufficient and send it to me with your opinion to be submitted to the Secy at War.[4] The doing of this at once will accelerate the Recruiting service [*which for your Regiment only waits for the appointment of the Regimental Staff.* The nominations being made and forwarded, as soon as you shall be informed that money and cloathing are furnished; (*which it is expected will be immediately done,*) You will begin the recruiting for your Regiment without waiting for a further order.] [5]

With great consideration   I am Sir   Yr. Obed servant

Postscript   Connecticut
It is expected that the bounty money & Cloathing for your Regi-

3. The brackets in this letter were placed there by H to indicate material which varied according to whom the letter was addressed.
In the margin opposite this sentence H wrote: "Connecticut New York Maryland." He also wrote and crossed out "Massachusettes."
4. See "Circular to the Commandants of Regiments," March 23, 1799.
5. In the margin opposite this sentence H wrote: "Connecticut
New York
New Jersey   } 4
Pensylvania"

ment will be sent to Mr. Timothy Phelps [6] Merchant, New Haven to be delivered to your Pay Master upon your order.

Same NY except that Col E Stevens, NY, to be substituted.

N Jersey & Pensylvania

Let the Person designated as Pay Master immediately proceed to Philadelphia to receive the bounty money & Cloathing for your Regiment.

Commenandent Massachusettes

The State of Massachusettes is to form four Districts and Twenty Subdistricts according to the plan enclosed. The districts Numbered 1. 2 are to compose a circle; [7] and

3. 4

Same Virginia

N Hampshire &c

The States of New Hampshire Vermont & Rhode Island are to form one Circle and be divided into two Districts & twenty Subdistricts according to the inclosed Plan. [8]

N Jersey

The State of New Jersey is to form a Circle & to be divided into two Districts and six subdistricts according to the Plan inclosed to which is to be added the State of Delaware forming itself a district and having for the present no subdistrict. [9] The Recruiting service within this Circle is to be for your Regiment and under your superintendence which is likewise to embrace three of the subdistricts in Pensylvania to be indicated by Col Moore as those within which the captains for your Regiment can be employed in recruiting with most convenience to general arrangement for Pensylvania which is referred to him. These three subdistricts will be annexed by you to the superintendence of the Major who shall be assigned to the Western District of New Jersey. You will accordingly assign &c.

6. See McHenry to H, March 26, 1799.
7. In the margin opposite this paragraph H wrote: "Two letters one 1. 2 the other 3. 4."
8. "Plan for the Distribution of the 16th Circle into *Districts* and *Subdistricts*" (AD, Hamilton Papers, Library of Congress).
9. In the margin opposite this sentence H wrote: "Omit."

The state of Pensylvania is to form a Circle and to be divided into three districts and thirteen subdistricts according to the plan inclosed. The Recruiting service within this Circle is to be for your Regiment and under your superintendence with the exception of three of the subdistricts which you will assign to the three captains who are to form part of Col Ogdens Regiment, namely

The trouble of making this assignment to them falls to you, from its being a part of the general arrangement for Pensylvania.[10] You will therefore assign each of your Majors to a district and each of your Captains to a subdistrict—having regard to those local considerations which promise most success to particular Officers; and after doing this, you will, with an eye to the same considerations, assign the remaining three subdistricts to the three Captains above named, and you will forthwith communicate to me the result. These three subdistricts you will consider as excepted out of your Circle and annexed to that of Col Ogden.

The particular Town &c [11]

Added to the letter of Nathan Rice Esqr.[12]

P.S. I had hoped that before this letter was sent I should have been provided with the Definitive arrangement of the State into Districts and Subdistricts. I conclude to send this letter as it regards other objects. I am anxious as soon as possible to be possessed of the result of your deliberations on this point and of the names of your Regimental Staff.

Added to the letter of Josias C. Hall Esqr.[13]

P.S. I am much disappointed in not being inabled by your reply to communicate the arrangement as adopted for districts and Subdistricts. I much urge that it be speedily forwarded & the names of your Regimental Staff.

10. In the margin opposite this sentence H wrote: "Regimental Rendezvous Connecticut *New Haven* New York *West Chester* N. Jersey Brunswick Pensylvania Bristol."

11. The remainder of this letter is in the handwriting of Philip Church.

12. Rice was appointed a lieutenant colonel in the Additional Army on March 3, 1799 (*Executive Journal*, I, 322, 323).

13. Hall was appointed a lieutenant colonel in the Additional Army on January 8, 1799 (*Executive Journal*, I, 299, 303).

REGIMENTAL RENDEZVOUSSES

1–2	Massachusetts	Somerset
3–4	ditto	Berwick
	Maryland	Havre de Grace
1–2	Virginia	Richmond
3–4	ditto	Alexandria

Added to all the letters—If any considerations which do not occur should render the place named as your Regimental Rendezvous inconvenient, you will please to mention them.

APPENDIX

JULY, 1798

AUGUST, 1798

From Nathan Levy, August 1, 1798 (ALS, Hamilton Papers, Library of Congress).   II

From James De Haert, August 4, 1798 (ALS, Hamilton Papers, Library of Congress).   II

From Alexander Mowatt, August 4, 1798 (ALS, Hamilton Papers, Library of Congress). Acknowledges H's letter of August 3, 1798. *Letter not found.*   II

From Henry Van Schaack, August 4, 1798 (ALS, Hamilton Papers, Library of Congress).   I

From Henry Van Schaack, August 6, 1798 (ALS, Hamilton Papers, Library of Congress).   I

From Lewis Tousard, August 7, 1798 (ALS, Hamilton Papers, Library of Congress).   II

From Oliver Wolcott, Jr., August 9, 1798 (ALS, Hamilton Papers, Library of Congress).   I

From Samuel Hoffman, August 10, 1798 (ALS, Hamilton Papers, Library of Congress).   II

From Dowe Fondey, August 17, 1798 (ALS, Hamilton Papers, Library of Congress).   II

From Hunloke Woodruff, August 17, 1798 (ALS, Hamilton Papers, Library of Congress).   I

From Bezaleel Howe, August 19, 1798 (ALS, Hamilton Papers, Library of Congress).   II

From Abraham Russel and John Stephens, Sr., August 19, 1798 (LS, Hamilton Papers, Library of Congress).   I

To John Adams, August 22, 1798 (ALS, Adams Family Papers, deposited in the Massachusetts Historical Society, Boston).   I

From Josiah Hedden, August 28, 1798 (ALS, Hamilton Papers, Library of Congress).   II

SEPTEMBER, 1798

From Henry Livingston, September 1, 1798 (ALS, Hamilton Papers, Library of Congress).   I

From John Adams, September 4, 1798 (LS, Hamilton Papers, Library of Congress; LC, Adams Family Papers, deposited in the Massachusetts Historical Society, Boston).   I

From George Shepherd, September 19, 1798 (ALS, Hamilton Papers, Library of Congress).   II

From William North, September 25, 1798 (ALS, Hamilton Papers, Library of Congress).   I

OCTOBER, 1798

From Charles Carroll of Carrollton, October 9, 1798 (ALS, Hamilton Papers, Library of Congress), enclosing testimonial of Maurice, Prince de Salm Kyrbourg, January 10, 1794, and testimonial of Comte de Vioménil, February 13, 1794 (copies, in the handwriting of Carroll, Hamilton Papers, Library of Congress).   I

From Samuel A. Barker, October 17, 1798 (ALS, Hamilton Papers, Library of Congress). H's endorsement reads: "Answered. Will be attended to." *Letter not found.*   I

From Richard Bland Lee, October 20, 1798 (ALS, Hamilton Papers, Library of Congress). H's endorsement reads: "answered 31." On verso H wrote a draft of his reply. *Letter not found.*   III

NOVEMBER, 1798

From Charles Carroll of Carrollton, November 6, 1798 (ALS, Hamilton Papers, Library of Congress), enclosing Comte Charles de Moëlien to Carroll, November 4, 1798 (AL, Hamilton Papers, Library of Congress). Acknowledges undated letter from H which he received October 30, 1798. *Letter not found.*   I

From James F. Armstrong, November 16, 1798 (ALS, Hamilton Papers, Library of Congress).   I   II

From Lewis Tousard, November 19, 1798 (ALS, Hamilton Papers, Library of Congress).   II

DECEMBER, 1798

From Adam Hoops, December 10, 1798 (ALS, Hamilton Papers, Library of Congress), enclosing Hoops to George Washington, December 10, 1798 (ALS, Hamilton Papers, Library of Congress), and an accompanying statement prepared by Hoops (AD, Hamilton Papers, Library of Congress).   II

From William North, December 15, 1798 (ALS, Hamilton Papers, Library of Congress).   I

From Jacob Glen, December 20, 1798 (ALS, Hamilton Papers, Library of Congress).   II

From Gershem North, December 27, 1798 (ALS, Hamilton Papers, Library of Congress). II

From Job Smith [1798] (ALS, Hamilton Papers, Library of Congress). II

JANUARY, 1799

From Charles Carroll of Carrollton, January 1, 1799 (ALS, Hamilton Papers, Library of Congress). I

From Benjamin Stoddert, January 1, 1799 (ALS, Hamilton Papers, Library of Congress). H's endorsement reads: "Ansd." *Letter not found.* I

From John V. Glen, January 11, 1799 (ALS, Hamilton Papers, Library of Congress). II

To James McHenry, January 19, 1799 (ALS, Mr. Pierce Gaines, Fairfield, Connecticut; ALS [photostat], James McHenry Papers, Library of Congress). I

From Caleb Gibbs, January 21, 1799 (ALS, Hamilton Papers, Library of Congress). II

From Samuel Mackay, January 23, 1799 (ALS, Hamilton Papers, Library of Congress), enclosing letter from Theodore Sedgwick to H. *Letter not found.* II

From James Cochran, January 29, 1799 (ALS, Hamilton Papers, Library of Congress). I

From George W. Kirkland, January 29, 1799 (ALS, Hamilton Papers, Library of Congress). On verso H wrote a draft of his reply. *Letter not found.* V

From James McHenry, January 30, 1799 (ALS, Hamilton Papers, Library of Congress), enclosing Samuel Osborne to McHenry, January 29, 1799 (ALS, Hamilton Papers, Library of Congress). IV

To James Cochran, January 31, 1799 (LS, sold at Anderson Galleries, October 19, 1926, Lot No. 159). *Letter not found.* V

To George W. Kirkland, January 31, 1799 (LS, sold at Anderson Galleries, October 19, 1926, Lot No. 159). *Letter not found.* V

To John Lillie, January 31, 1799 (LS, in the handwriting of Philip Church, Princeton University Library). Acknowledges Lillie's letter of January 21, 1799. *Letter not found.* II

From James McHenry, January 31, 1799 (ALS, Hamilton Papers, Library of Congress), enclosing James Stille to John Caldwell, III

January 24, 1799 (ALS, Hamilton Papers, Library of Congress).

FEBRUARY, 1799

From Benjamin Stoddert, February 1, 1799 (LC, RG 45, Naval Records Collection of the Office of Naval Records and Library, Miscellaneous Letters Sent by the Secretary of the Navy, 1790–1798, National Archives).   I

To Samuel Osborne, February 6, 1799 (ALS, from the original in the New York State Library, Albany, courtesy of Mrs. Henry M. Sage; copy, Hamilton Papers, Library of Congress).   IV

From Adam Hoops, February 8, 1799 (ALS, Hamilton Papers, Library of Congress), enclosing "View of the names, number & State of the officers of the garrison at Fort Jay," February 8, 1799 (ADS, Hamilton Papers, Library of Congress).   VI

From Adam Hoops [February 11, 1799] (ALS, Hamilton Papers, Library of Congress), enclosing "Memorandum of Quarters at Fort Jay" (AD, Hamilton Papers, Library of Congress).   VI

From George Ingersoll, February 11, 1799 (ALS, Hamilton Papers, Library of Congress).   VI

From Samuel Osborne, February 11, 1799 (ALS, Hamilton Papers, Library of Congress; ADf, Papers of Samuel Osborne, Library of Congress).   IV

To James McHenry, February 13, 1799 (ADf, Hamilton Papers, Library of Congress).   IX

From James McHenry, February 15, 1799 (ALS, Hamilton Papers, Library of Congress), enclosing James Bruff to McHenry, January 15, 1799 (two copies, in Bruff's handwriting, Hamilton Papers, Library of Congress); Bruff to McHenry, January 15, 1799 (copy, Hamilton Papers, Library of Congress); Frederick Frye to McHenry, February 2, 1799 (copy, Hamilton Papers, Library of Congress); John J. U. Rivardi to McHenry [January] 21, 1799 (copy, Hamilton Papers, Library of Congress); Amos Stoddard to McHenry, January 27, 1799 (copy, Hamilton Papers, Library of Congress).   III VII

From James McHenry, February 16, 1799 (LS, Hamilton Papers, Library of Congress).   IX

To James McHenry, February 16, 1799 (LS, Montague Collection, MS Division, New York Public Library; LS [photostat], James McHenry Papers, Library of Congress; ADf, Hamilton Papers, Library of Congress).   V

From George Ingersoll, February 18, 1799 (ALS, Hamilton Papers, Library of Congress).   VII

From James McHenry, February 19, 1799 (ALS, Hamilton Papers, Library of Congress; ADfS, James McHenry Papers, Library of Congress).   V

To James McHenry, February 19, 1799 (copy, in the handwriting of Philip Church, Hamilton Papers, Library of Congress).   VII

From James McHenry, February 21, 1799 (LS, Hamilton Papers, Library of Congress), enclosing Lewis Tousard to McHenry, February 10, 1799 (copy, Hamilton Papers, Library of Congress).   VI

From Samuel Livermore, February 22, 1799 (ALS, Hamilton Papers, Library of Congress).   V

From James McHenry, first letter of February 22, 1799 (LS, Hamilton Papers, Library of Congress), enclosing Lemuel Gates to McHenry, February 13, 1799 (copy, Hamilton Papers, Library of Congress). On verso H wrote a draft of his reply. *Letter not found.*   III

From James McHenry, second letter of February 22, 1799 (LS, Hamilton Papers, Library of Congress; LS, letterpress copy, James McHenry Papers, Library of Congress), enclosing William Simmons to McHenry, February 20, 21, 1799 (copies, Hamilton Papers, Library of Congress); McHenry to Samuel Vance, February 20, 1799 (copy, Hamilton Papers, Library of Congress); Vance to McHenry, February 21, 1799 (copy, Hamilton Papers, Library of Congress); four statements by clerks in the accounting office of the War Department, February 20, 1799 (copies, Hamilton Papers, Library of Congress); statement by John Knight, February 21, 1799 (copy, Hamilton Papers, Library of Congress).   IV

From Staats Morris, February 22, 1799 (ALS, Hamilton Papers, Library of Congress).   V

From Ray Greene, February 23, 1799 (ALS, Hamilton Papers, Library of Congress), enclosing two undated plans entitled "Division of the State of Rhode Island &c into three districts" and "Division of said State into four districts" (AD, Hamilton Papers, Library of Congress).   V

From Aaron Ogden, February 23, 1799 (ALS, Hamilton Papers, Library of Congress).   V

From Dowe Fondey, February 25, 1799 (ALS, Hamilton Papers, Library of Congress). On verso H wrote a draft of his acknowledgment. *Letter not found.*   II

From Thomas Lloyd Moore, February 25, 1799 (ALS, Hamilton   V
Papers, Library of Congress), enclosing undated document en-
titled "Large Districts Pennsylvania" (AD, Hamilton Papers,
Library of Congress).

From Staats Morris, February 25, 1799 (ALS, Hamilton Papers,   IV
Library of Congress).   VII

From Moses Blackly, February 26, 1799 (ALS, Hamilton Papers,   II
Library of Congress).

From George Ingersoll, February 26, 1799 (ALS, Hamilton Pa-   III
pers, Library of Congress).

From Daniel Jackson, February 27, 1799 (ALS, Hamilton Papers,   V
Library of Congress).   VII

From James McHenry, February 27, 1799 (LS, Hamilton Papers,   III
Library of Congress).

To Thomas Lloyd Moore, February [27], 1799 (ADf, Hamilton   IV
Papers, Library of Congress).

To William S. Smith, February 27, 1799 (copy, Hamilton Papers, IV
Library of Congress).

To William Willcocks, February 27, 1799 (copy, Hamilton Pa-   IV
pers, Library of Congress).

From Simon Elliot, February 28, 1799 (ALS, Hamilton Papers,   III
Library of Congress).

From Adam Hoops, February 28, 1799 (ALS, Hamilton Papers,   VII
Library of Congress).

From Ebenezer Huntington, February 28, 1799 (ALS, Hamilton   V
Papers, Library of Congress), enclosing "The state of Connecticut divided into two districts & ten sub districts," February
28, 1799 (AD, Hamilton Papers, Library of Congress).

From William S. Smith, February 28, 1799 (ALS, Hamilton Pa-   V
pers, Library of Congress).

MARCH, 1799

From William Littlefield, March 2, 1799 (ALS, Hamilton Papers, IV
Library of Congress).

From Jacob Morris, March 2, 1799 (ALS, Hamilton Papers, Li-   I
brary of Congress), enclosing Elihu Phinney, Jacob Morris,
Richard Edwards, and Joseph Griffin to James McHenry, February 19, 1799 (LS, Hamilton Papers, Library of Congress).

From James Cochran, March 3, 1799 (ALS, Hamilton Papers,   IV
Library of Congress).

From Amos Stoddard, March 3, 1799 (ALS, Hamilton Papers,   VII
Library of Congress).

From Nehemiah Freeman, March 4, 1799 (ALS, Hamilton Papers,   III
Library of Congress).

To Adam Hoops, March [4], 1799 (ADf, Hamilton Papers, Li-   VII
brary of Congress).

From Thomas Lloyd Moore, March 4, 1799 (ALS, Hamilton Pa-   IV
pers, Library of Congress), enclosing undated document entitled "Officers of the Court Martial" (AD, Hamilton Papers,
Library of Congress).

To Ebenezer Stevens, March 4, 1799 (LS, in the handwriting of   VII
Philip Church, New-York Historical Society, New York City;
ADf, Hamilton Papers, Library of Congress).

To James Bruff, March 5, 1799 (ADf, Hamilton Papers, Library   IV
of Congress).

To Joseph Elliott, March 5, 1799 (ADf, Hamilton Papers, Li-   IV
brary of Congress).

To Charles W. Hare, March 5, 1799 (ADf, Hamilton Papers,   IV
Library of Congress).

To James McHenry, March 5, 1799 (ADf, Hamilton Papers, Li-   IV
brary of Congress).

To Thomas Lloyd Moore, March 5, 1799 (ADf, Hamilton Pa-   IV
pers, Library of Congress).

From Simon Elliot, March 6, 1799 (ALS, Hamilton Papers Li-   V
brary of Congress), enclosing John Brooks's proposals for the
division of Massachusetts into recruiting districts, March 5,
1799 (D, in the handwriting of John Brooks, Hamilton Papers,
Library of Congress).

To Samuel Vance, March 6, 1799 (Df, Hamilton Papers, Library   IV
of Congress).

From Thomas Church, March 7, 1799 (ALS, Hamilton Papers,   II
Library of Congress). On verso H wrote a draft of his reply.
Letter not found.

To Samuel Osborne, March 7, 1799 (ADf, Hamilton Papers, Li-   IV
brary of Congress).

To Lewis Tousard, March 7, 1799 (copy, in the handwriting of   III
Philip Church, Hamilton Papers, Library of Congress).

To George Ingersoll, March 8, 1799 (ADf, in the handwriting of   III
H and Philip Church, Hamilton Papers, Library of Congress).

From Adam Hoops, March 9, 1799 (ALS, Hamilton Papers, Library of Congress). IV

From John P. Boyd, March 10, 1799 (ALS, Hamilton Papers, Library of Congress), enclosing "letter of introduction from General [Benjamin] Lincoln." *Letter not found.* II

From Lewis Tousard, March 10, 1799 (ALS, Hamilton Papers, Library of Congress), enclosing John Rutledge, Jr., to Tousard, February 28, 1799 (ALS, Hamilton Papers, Library of Congress), and James McHenry to Tousard, January 16, 1799 (copy, Hamilton Papers, Library of Congress). II III VIII

From John A. Winans, March 10, 1799 (ALS, Hamilton Papers, Library of Congress). II

From John T. Gilman, March 11, 1799 (ALS, Hamilton Papers, Library of Congress). V

From Charles W. Hare, March 11, 1799 (ALS, Hamilton Papers, Library of Congress). IV

From William S. Smith, March 11, 1799 (ALS, Hamilton Papers, Library of Congress), enclosing the "General Return of the State of New York . . . with the Counties and towns divided into two Grand Divisions and Ten Sub divisions, Specifying the Beats of each Company recruiting for the New York Regt.," March 11, 1799 (DS, Hamilton Papers, Library of Congress). VII

From Thomas Brinley, March 12, 1799 (ALS, Hamilton Papers, Library of Congress). II

From Josias Carvel Hall, March 12, 1799 (ALS, Hamilton Papers, Library of Congress). V

From Charles W. Hare, March 12, 1799 (ALS, Hamilton Papers, Library of Congress), enclosing the "interrogatories to be put to the witnesses in Dr. Osborne's case" (ADS, Hamilton Papers, Library of Congress). On verso H wrote a draft of his reply. *Letter not found.* IV

To Aaron Ogden, March 12, 1799 (LS, Lloyd W. Smith Collection, Morristown National Historical Park, Morristown, New Jersey; ADf, Hamilton Papers, Library of Congress). IV

From James McHenry, March 13, 1799 (LS, Hamilton Papers, Library of Congress). VII

From James McHenry, March 14, 1799 (LS, Hamilton Papers, Library of Congress; LS, letterpress copy, James McHenry Papers, Library of Congress), enclosing Frederick Frye to Mc- IV

Henry, March 11, 1799 (copy, Hamilton Papers, Library of Congress), and "Exhibit of the charges and Specifications advanced against Captain Frederick Frye by Major Adam Hoops," March 8, 1799 (copy, Hamilton Papers, Library of Congress).

To Washington Morton, March 14, 1799 (copy, Hamilton Papers, Library of Congress). IV

From Aaron Ogden, March 14, 1799 (ALS, Hamilton Papers, Library of Congress). IV

To William S. Smith, March 14, 1799 (copy, in the handwriting of Philip Church, Hamilton Papers, Library of Congress). IV

From James McHenry, March 16, 1799 (LS, Hamilton Papers, Library of Congress), enclosing John McClallen to McHenry, March 11, 1799 (ALS, Hamilton Papers, Library of Congress). III

From Alexander MacWhorter, March 16, 1799 (ALS, Hamilton Papers, Library of Congress). I

To Ebenezer Stevens, March 16, 1799 (ALS, New-York Historical Society, New York City). Endorsed by Stevens: "Ansd 17." *Letter not found.* III

From Adam Hoops, March 17–18, 1799 (ALS, Hamilton Papers, Library of Congress). H's endorsement reads: "Consent given." *Letter not found.* III

From Daniel Jackson, March [17], 1799 (LS, Hamilton Papers, Library of Congress), enclosing "A Plan of the Works at Salem" and "a plan of the Brick Block House at Marblehead" (Hamilton Papers, Library of Congress). II

To James McHenry, March 18, 1799 (ALS, The Sol Feinstone Collection, Library of the American Philosophical Society, Philadelphia; ALS [photostat], James McHenry Papers, Library of Congress; copy, Hamilton Papers, Library of Congress). IV

To Aaron Ogden, March 18, 1799 (copy, in the handwriting of Philip Church, Hamilton Papers, Library of Congress). IV

To William S. Smith, March 18, 1799 (Df, Hamilton Papers, Library of Congress). IV

From Lewis Tousard, March 18, 1799 (LS, Hamilton Papers, Library of Congress). III

From George Washington Duncan, March 19, 1799 (ALS, Hamilton Papers, Library of Congress). II

To James McHenry, March 19, 1799 (ADf, Hamilton Papers, Library of Congress).   III

From Aaron Ogden, March 19, 1799 (ALS, Hamilton Papers, Library of Congress).   IV

From Horatio Dayton, March 20, 1799 (ALS, Hamilton Papers, Library of Congress).   III

To Horatio Dayton, March 20, 1799 (Df, Hamilton Papers, Library of Congress).   III

From Charles W. Hare, March 21, 1799 (ALS, Hamilton Papers, Library of Congress).   IV

From Mahlon Ford, March 22, 1799 (ALS, Hamilton Papers, Library of Congress).   III

From William W. Wands, March 23, 1799 (ALS, Hamilton Papers, Library of Congress).   IV

From George Ingersoll, March 24, 1799 (ALS, Hamilton Papers, Library of Congress). Acknowledges H's letter of March 14, 1799. *Letter not found.*   III

To Nathaniel Leonard, March 24, 1799 (ALS [facsimile], Clarence W. Bowen, *The History of Woodstock, Connecticut* [Norwood, Massachusetts, 1926–1943], I, 217; ADf, Hamilton Papers, Library of Congress).   VIII

From Lewis Tousard, March 25, 1799 (LS, Hamilton Papers, Library of Congress).   IV

To Charles W. Hare, March 27, 1799 (copy, in the handwriting of Philip Church, Hamilton Papers, Library of Congress).   IV

From James McHenry, March 28, 1799 (LS, Hamilton Papers, Library of Congress), enclosing James Steel to McHenry, March 5, 1799 (ALS, Hamilton Papers, Library of Congress).   III

To James McHenry, March 28, 1799 (copy, in the handwriting of Philip Church, Hamilton Papers, Library of Congress).   IV V VII

From Aaron Ogden, March 28, 1799 (ALS, Hamilton Papers, Library of Congress).   VI

From Jonathan Trumbull, March 28, 1799 (ADfS, Connecticut Historical Society, Hartford).   II

From Charles W. Hare, March [29], 1799 (ALS, Hamilton Papers, Library of Congress).   IV

To William Colfax, March 30, 1799 (ADf, Hamilton Papers, Library of Congress).   VII VIII

From Caleb Gibbs, March 30, 1799 (ALS, Hamilton Papers, Library of Congress). VI

From Tobias Lear, March 30, 1799 (ALS, George Washington Papers, Library of Congress), enclosing John J. U. Rivardi to Lear, February 21, 1799 (ALS, Hamilton Papers, Library of Congress), and Rivardi to James McHenry, February 21, 1799 (copy, Hamilton Papers, Library of Congress). IV

From James McHenry, March 30, 1799 (ALS, Hamilton Papers, Library of Congress). III

INDEX

COMPILED BY JEAN G. COOKE

William and Mary College, 213
Williams, Eleazar (Eliaza), 317, 328, 338
Williams, Elie, 307, 308
Williams, Henry A., 187
Williams, John, 92
Williams, Leonard, 118
Williams, Otho H., 304, 307
Williams, Samuel P., 272
Williams, Thomas U., 48
Williams, Timothy, 336
Williams, William (Mass.), 318, 332
Williams, William (N.Y.), 490-91
Williamson, Benjamin, 129, 130, 131
Williamson, Charles, 170
Williamson, Hugh, 311-12
Willing, Richard, 35-36, 140
Willing, Thomas, 35-36
Wilmer, John P., 303
Wilmer, Jonathan R., 295, 296, 304
Wilson, James, 260
Winans, John A.: *letter from,* 609
Winchester, James, 312
Winchester, William, 290-91, 307
Windsor, Vt., 577-78
Wingate, Paine, 112
Winn, Timothy, 283
Winslow, Isaac, 317, 335, 337
Winslow, Samuel, 324
Winstanley (Winstanly), William, 93
Wiscasset, District of Maine, 494
Wister, William, 140
Witherspoon, David, 284
Witner, Herman (Harman), 133
Witner, Thomas, 145
Witney, *see* Whitney
Wolcott, Elizabeth Stoughton (Mrs. Oliver, Jr.), 232
Wolcott, Oliver, Jr., 232, 235, 279, 326, 412, 428; and Hamilton, advice to, 197, cipher of, 483; *letters from,* 16, 64-66, 185-87, 196-98, 382-83, 575, 602; *letter from* John Adams, 16; *letters from* James McHenry, 16-17, 243; *letters to,* 58-59, 153-54, 158, 185, 380, 398-99, 533-35, 574-75; *letter to* John Adams, 10-14; *letter to* Thomas Hazard, 186-87; *letter to* Rufus King, 243; *letters to* James McHenry, 17, 248; on James

McHenry, 64-65; and U.S. Army, clothing for, 50, military supplies for, 243, money for, 243, 244, 248, 346, plans for and organization of, 148-49, 153, 247, 369, rank of major generals, 10-14, 16, 159, 179, 180, 185-86, 196-97, 202; on War Department, 65, 197; and Benjamin Wells, 367
Wood, Abiel (Obiel), 326, 332
Wood, Samson, 336
Wood, Silas, 102
Woodridge, Fleming, 285, 287
Woodruff, Abner, 126
Woodruff, Hunloke: *letter from,* 602
Woods, Clement, 430
Woodward, George, 118, 119, 429, 430
Woodward, William, 116, 119
Wooster, Thomas, 95
Worcester, Mass., 494
Worcester Co., Mass., 494
Woronzow, Simon, 501
Worrell, Benjamin, 132, 146
Worthington, Mass., 494
Wortman, Tunis, 91
Wright, Benjamin, 396-97
Wright, Nathan N., 290
Wyllys, Samuel, 278
Wynants, John G., 130
Wynkoop, Henry, 91

XYZ affair, 3-4, 217

Yancey, Robert, 311
Yates, Joseph C., 96
Yates, Robert, 467-68
Yates, William, 97, 467-68
Yazoo lands, 187
Yeats, Donaldson, 303
Yeisser (Yeyser), Englehard, 297, 302
Yellow fever, 414; in New York City, 186-87, 193-94, 197-98, 202, 253, 267, 447; in Philadelphia, 65-66, 68, 147, 491
Yerving, Solomon, 307
Yeyser, *see* Yeisser
Young, William, Jr., 279
Youngs, Samuel, 104, 108

Zante, 376, 377